TOGAF™ Version 9

About the TOGAF series

The TOGAF series contains the official publications on TOGAF on behalf of The Open Group.
The following publications are, or soon will be, available:
- TOGAF™ 2007 Edition (Incorporating 8.1.1)
- TOGAF™ Version 8.1.1 Enterprise Edition – Study Guide
- TOGAF™ Version 8.1.1 Enterprise Edition – A Pocket Guide
- TOGAF™ Version 9
- TOGAF™ Version 9 – A Pocket Guide

For the latest information on TOGAF, visit www.opengroup.org/togaf.

Other publications by Van Haren Publishing

Van Haren Publishing specializes in titles on Best Practices, methods and standards within IT and
business management.
These publications are grouped in the following series: ITSM Library, Best Practice and IT Management
Topics. Van Haren Publishing is also publisher on behalf of ITSMF, HDI, ASL Foundation, TSO/OGC,
PMI Nederland and Platform Outsourcing Nederland.

For the latest information on VHP publications, visit www.vanharen.net.

TOGAF™
Version 9

www.opengroup.org

Title:	**TOGAF™ Version 9**
A Publication of:	The Open Group
Publisher:	Van Haren Publishing, Zaltbommel, www.vanharen.net
ISBN	978 90 8753 230 7
Edition:	9th edition, 1st impression, January 2009
	9th edition, 2nd impression, May 2009
	9th edition, 3rd impression, December 2009
Layout and design:	The Open Group
Cover design:	CO2 Premedia, Amersfoort-NL
Print:	Wilco, Amersfoort-NL
Copyright:	2005-2009 The Open Group

Any comments relating to the material contained in this document may be submitted by email to: OGSpecs@opengroup.org

For any further enquiries about Van Haren Publishing, please send an email to: info@vanharen.net.

Contents

Contents

Contents

Contents

Contents

Contents

Contents

List of Figures

Contents

Contents

List of Tables

Preface

The Open Group Architecture Framework (TOGAF) — Version 9, Enterprise Edition — is an open, industry consensus framework and method for enterprise architecture.

This Document

There are seven main parts to the TOGAF document:

PART I   (Introduction) This part provides a high-level introduction to the key concepts of enterprise architecture and in particular the TOGAF approach. It contains the definitions of terms used throughout TOGAF and release notes detailing the changes between this version and the previous version of TOGAF.

PART II   (Architecture Development Method) This is the core of TOGAF. It describes the TOGAF Architecture Development Method (ADM) — a step-by-step approach to developing an enterprise architecture.

PART III   (ADM Guidelines & Techniques) This part contains a collection of guidelines and techniques available for use in applying TOGAF and the TOGAF ADM.

PART IV   (Architecture Content Framework) This part describes the TOGAF content framework, including a structured metamodel for architectural artifacts, the use of re-usable architecture building blocks, and an overview of typical architecture deliverables.

PART V   (Enterprise Continuum & Tools) This part discusses appropriate taxonomies and tools to categorize and store the outputs of architecture activity within an enterprise.

PART VI   (TOGAF Reference Models) This part provides a selection of architectural reference models, which includes the TOGAF Foundation Architecture, and the Integrated Information Infrastructure Reference Model (III-RM).

PART VII   (Architecture Capability Framework) This part discusses the organization, processes, skills, roles, and responsibilities required to establish and operate an architecture function within an enterprise.

Intended Audience

TOGAF is intended for enterprise architects, business architects, IT architects, data architects, systems architects, solutions architects, and anyone responsible for the architecture function within an organization.

Keywords

architecture, architecture framework, architecture development method, architect, architecting, enterprise architecture, enterprise architecture framework, enterprise architecture method, method, methods, open, group, technical reference model, standards, standards information base

About The Open Group

The Open Group

The Open Group is a vendor-neutral and technology-neutral consortium, whose vision of Boundaryless Information Flow™ will enable access to integrated information within and between enterprises based on open standards and global interoperability. The Open Group works with customers, suppliers, consortia, and other standards bodies. Its role is to capture, understand, and address current and emerging requirements, establish policies, and share best practices; to facilitate interoperability, develop consensus, and evolve and integrate specifications and Open Source technologies; to offer a comprehensive set of services to enhance the operational efficiency of consortia; and to operate the industry's premier certification service, including UNIX® certification.

Further information on The Open Group is available at www.opengroup.org.

The Open Group has over 15 years' experience in developing and operating certification programs and has extensive experience developing and facilitating industry adoption of test suites used to validate conformance to an open standard or specification.

More information is available at www.opengroup.org/certification.

The Open Group publishes a wide range of technical documentation, the main part of which is focused on development of Technical and Product Standards and Guides, but which also includes white papers, technical studies, branding and testing documentation, and business titles. Full details and a catalog are available at www.opengroup.org/bookstore.

As with all *live* documents, Technical Standards and Specifications require revision to align with new developments and associated international standards. To distinguish between revised specifications which are fully backwards-compatible and those which are not:

- A new *Version* indicates there is no change to the definitive information contained in the previous publication of that title, but additions/extensions are included. As such, it *replaces* the previous publication.

- A new *Issue* indicates there is substantive change to the definitive information contained in the previous publication of that title, and there may also be additions/extensions. As such, both previous and new documents are maintained as current publications.

Readers should note that Corrigenda may apply to any publication. Corrigenda information is published at www.opengroup.org/corrigenda.

Participants

This document was prepared by The Open Group Architecture Forum. When The Open Group approved this document on October 23, 2008, the membership of the Architecture Forum was as follows:

Chris Forde, American Express, Chair
Jane Varnus, Bank of Montreal, Vice-Chair
Len Fehskens, The Open Group, Forum Director
Andrew Josey, The Open Group, Director of Standards
Garry Doherty, The Open Group, TOGAF Product Manager
Cathy Fox, The Open Group, Technical Editor

Architecture Forum Technical Reviewers

Technical reviewers are those individuals who have submitted comments during the company review, or participated in a face-to-face issue resolution meeting.

Rob Aalders	Peter Hertel	Florian Quarre
Mick Adams	Paul Homan	Greg Reh
Chris Armstrong	Dave Hornford	Saverio Rinaldi
John T. Bell	Dave Jackson	Roberto Rivera
Gerhard Botha	Judith Jones	Matthew Rouse
Stuart Crawford	Andrew Josey	Eelco Rouw
Simon Dalziel	John Kerr	Richard Schaeren
Fatma Dandashi	Janine Kemmeren	Mrudul Shah
Marne de Vries	Frank Kroon	Vernon Smith
Caroline Dempsey	Louw Labuschagne	Mike Turner
Jorge Diaz	Mike Lambert	Harmen van den Berg
William Estrem	Jerry Larivee	Paul van der Merwe
Belinda Fivaz	Stuart Macgregor	Dave van Gelder
Chris Forde	Philip Mason	Peter van Hoof
Henry Franken	Ian McCall	Arnold van Overeem
Mats Gejnevall	Graham Meaden	Tom van Sante
Chris Greenslade	E.G. Nadhan	Jane Varnus
Roger Griessen	Tim O'Neill	Sarina Viljoen
Ken Hales	Thomas Obitz	Vish Viswanathan
Chris Harding	Peter Oldershaw	Robert Weisman
Ed Harrington	Timothy Persons	Gary Zeien
Juergen Heck	Ian Prinsloo	

Architecture Forum Members

The following organizations were members of the Architecture Forum at the time of approval.

Aalders Analysis & Design Pty Ltd.
ABIO BV
Accenture
ACORD Corporation
act! consulting GmbH
ADP, Inc.
AIPEX Pty Ltd.
alfabet AG
Allied Irish Bank
American Express
Analytix Holdings Ltd.
Applied Research Lab/The Pennsylvania State University
Applied Technology Solutions, Inc.
Architecting-the-Enterprise
ARISMORE
Armscor
Armstrong Process Group, Inc.
Austin Energy
Avolution
Bank of Montreal
BEA Systems, Inc.
BeAligned CVBA
BearingPoint, Inc.
BIZZdesign Holding
Bodø University College
Boehringer Ingelheim
BP International
British Telecom Plc
Build the Vision, Inc.
Business Connexion
C&C Technology Ltd.
CA, Inc.
Capgemini SA
Capita IT Services
Cardiff University
Casewise Systems Ltd.
CC and C Solutions
CEISAR
Celestial Consulting Ltd.
Centre for Open Systems
CGI Group, Inc.
Cisco Systems, Inc.
CLARS Limited
Cognizant, CTS
Companhia Vale do Rio Doce
Deccan Global Solutions LLC
Deloitte Consulting LLP
Detecon International GmbH
Devoteam Consulting
Digiterra (Pty) Ltd.
Discover Financial Services

DMTF
DWP Programme & Systems Delivery Group
EA Global Ltd.
EASD-CIOB (Treasury Board of Canada Secretariat)
EDS
Elegant Group
Eli Lilly & Company Ltd.
Elparazim
Energistics
Enterprise Architects
Equinox Limited
Eskom
Fannie Mae Corporation
FEAC Institute
Flashmap Systems, Inc.
Focus on the Family
France Telecom
Fujitsu Services
Future Tech Systems, Inc.
Getronics
Grant MacEwan College
Griffiths Waite
Heck Consulting
Hewlett-Packard
Hi-Q Systems Ltd.
Highmark, Inc.
Hornford Associates
Hotel Technology Next Generation
HSBC Bank plc
IBM
ICMG Private Limited
IDS Scheer AG
Infosys Technologies Ltd.
Infovide SA
Innenministerium NRW
Inspired
Integration Consortium
Intel Corporation
Intercall, Inc.
Investec Limited South Africa
ISES International BV
IT Advisor, Inc.
IT Frontier Corporation
Iwate Prefectural University
JISC
Johnson & Johnson
Kamehameha Schools
King's College London
Knotion Consulting
Kynetia Networks SL
Kyoto University

Participants

La Poste
Lawrence Technological University
Learning and Skills Council
Letsema Consulting
Liverpool John Moores University
Lockheed Martin Corporation
Mantix Limited
Marathon Oil Corporation
Marriott International
Massachusetts Institute of Technology, Lincoln Laboratory
Mega International
Metaplexity Associates
Metastorm
Mizuho Information and Research Institute, Inc.
Model Driven Solutions
Molimax Consulting Limited
N2 Services, Inc.
NASA SEWP (Sci. & Eng. Workstation Procurement)
National Computerization Agency
National IT and Telecom Agency, IT-Architecture Division
National University of Singapore
NEC Corporation
NEHTA
Nissan Motor Co., Ltd.
Nomura Research Institute, Ltd.
NTNU
NTT Data Corporation
NYS Office of Temporary & Disability Assistance
OMG
Online Business Systems
Open GIS Consortium, Inc.
Orbus Software
Oslo Software
Parity Training Limited
plenum Management Consulting
PricewaterhouseCoopers LLP
Procter & Gamble Company
Promis Solutions
Q-Tips BV
QR Systems, Inc.
QualiWare ApS
Raytheon
Real IRM Solutions (Pty) Ltd.
Research Environment for Global Information Society, ReGIS
Resilience Corporation
Resultex Limited
Rococo Co Ltd.
Roehampton University
Rolls-Royce plc
Royal Institute of Technology
SAP

SASOL
Satyam Computer Services, Limited
SCC (Specialist Computer Centres)
Schools Interoperability Framework Association
SDT
Serono International SA
Shenzhen Kingdee Middleware
Shift Technologies
SIOS Technology, Inc.
Smart421 Ltd.
SNA Technologies, Inc.
Sogeti SAS
Solvera Solutions
Sparx Systems
State Services Commission
Sun Microsystems
Swiss Federal Administration
Symantec Corp
Systems Flow, Inc.
t2b
Tata Consultancy Services
Teamcall Ltd.
Telelogic
TeleManagement Forum
Telephone & Data Systems, Inc.
Telkom SA Ltd.
TenFold, Inc.
The Boeing Company
The MITRE Corporation
The Salamander Organization Limited
The University of Reading
Tieturi OY
TONEX
Toyota InfoTechnology Center Co. Ltd.
triVector (Pty) Ltd.
Troux Technologies AS
Tshwane University of Technology
TSYS
UK MoD
Unisys
University of Cambridge
University of Colorado at Boulder
University of Denver
University of Johannesburg
University of Pretoria
University of South Africa
Veriserve Corporation
Wachovia Bank
White Knight Management
Wipro Technologies
Xantus Consulting

Trademarks

COBIT® is a registered trademark of the Information Systems Audit and Control Association and the IT Governance Institute.

CORBA®, MDA®, Model Driven Architecture®, Object Management®, OMG®, and UML® are registered trademarks and BPMN™, Business Process Modeling Notation™, and Unified Modeling Language™ are trademarks of the Object Management Group.

Energistics™ is a trademark of Energistics.

FICO® is a registered trademark of Fair Isaac Corporation.

IBM® and WebSphere® are registered trademarks of International Business Machines Corporation.

IEEE® is a registered trademark of the Institute of Electrical and Electronics Engineers, Inc.

ITIL® is a registered trademark of the Office of Government Commerce in the United Kingdom and other countries.

Java® is a registered trademark of Sun Microsystems, Inc.

Microsoft® is a registered trademark of Microsoft Corporation.

OAGIS® is a registered trademark of the Open Applications Group, Inc.

OpenGL® is a registered trademark of SGI.

PRINCE® is a registered trademark and PRINCE2™ is a trademark of the Office of Government Commerce in the United Kingdom and other countries.

SAP® is a registered trademark of SAP AG in Germany and in several other countries.

TOGAF™ and Boundaryless Information Flow™ are trademarks and UNIX® and The Open Group® are registered trademarks of The Open Group in the United States and other countries.

The following are registered trademarks of the Software Engineering Institute (SEI):

- CMMI® (Capability Maturity Model Integration)
- IPD-CMM® (Integrated Product Development Capability Maturity Model)
- P-CMM® (People Capability Maturity Model)
- SA-CMM® (Software Acquisition Capability Maturity Model)
- SCAMPI® (Standard CMMI Appraisal Method for Process Improvement)
- SE-CMM® (Systems Engineering Capability Maturity Model)
- SW-CMM® (Capability Maturity Model for Software)

The Open Group acknowledges that there may be other company names and products that might be covered by trademark protection and advises the reader to verify them independently.

Acknowledgements

The Open Group gratefully acknowledges The Open Group Architecture Forum for developing The Open Group Architecture Framework (TOGAF).

The Open Group gratefully acknowledges those past and present members of the Architecture Forum who have served as its officers (Chairs and Vice-Chairs) since its inception. In alphabetical order:

Christer Askerfjord, Sweden Post
Terence Blevins, The MITRE Corporation
Bill Estrem, Metaplexity Associates
Hugh Fisher, UK National Health Service
Chris Forde, American Express
Chris Greenslade, CLARS
Ed Harrington, Model Driven Solutions
David Jackson, Armstrong Process Group
Stuart Macgregor, Real IRM Solutions
Ian McCall, IBM Corporation
Barry Smith, The MITRE Corporation
Walter Stahlecker, Hewlett-Packard Company
Dave Van Gelder, Capgemini
Jane Varnus, Bank of Montreal
Vish Viswanathan, CC&C Solutions
Hal Wilson, Litton PRC

The Open Group gratefully acknowledges the following member organizations who have contributed materials in the development of this document:

Architecting-the-Enterprise
Capgemini
CGI
Metaplexity Associates
Real IRM Solutions
SAP

The Open Group gratefully acknowledges the following individuals who have made contributions in the development of this document:

Mick Adams, Capgemini
Christopher Blake, Architecting-the-Enterprise
Stuart Crawford, Capgemini
Bill Estrem, Metaplexity Associates
Judith Jones, Architecting-the-Enterprise
Andrew Macaulay, Capgemini
Mike Turner, Capgemini
Paul van der Merwe, Real IRM Solutions
Robert Weisman, Build the Vision

Referenced Documents

The following documents are referenced in the TOGAF specification:

- Analysis Patterns — Reusable Object Models, M. Fowler, ISBN: 0-201-89542-0, Addison-Wesley.

- A Pattern Language: Towns, Buildings, Construction, Christopher Alexander, ISBN: 0-19-501919-9, Oxford University Press, 1979.

- Books of Knowledge — Project Management and System Engineering, Project Management Institute (refer to www.pmi.org) and the International Council of Systems Engineers (refer to http://g2sebok.incose.org).

- Business Transformation Enablement Program (BTEP), Canadian Government; refer to www.tbs-sct.gc.ca/btep-pto/index_e.asp.

- Business Process Modeling Notation (BPMN) Specification, Object Management Group (OMG); refer to www.bpmn.org.

- Business Executive's Guide to IT Architecture White Paper, October 2004 (W043), published by The Open Group; refer to www.opengroup.org/bookstore/catalog/w043.htm.

- Common Object Request Broker Architecture (CORBA), Object Management Group (OMG); refer to www.corba.org.

- Control Objectives for Information and related Technology (COBIT), Version 4.0, IT Governance Institute, 2005.

- Corporate Governance, Ranami Naidoo, ISBN: 1-919-903-0086, Double Storey, 2002.

- Design Patterns: Elements of Reusable Object-Oriented Software, Erich Gamma, Richard Helm, Ralph Johnson, & John Vlissides, ISBN: 0-201-63361-2, Addison-Wesley, October 1994.

- Enterprise Architecture as Strategy, Jeanne Ross, Peter Weill, & David C. Robertson, ISBN: 1-59139-839-8, Harvard Business School Press, 2006.

- Enterprise Architecture Capability Maturity Model (ACMM), Version 1.2, United States Department of Commerce, December 2007.

- Enterprise Architecture Maturity Model, Version 1.3, National Association of State CIOs (NASCIO), December 2003.

- Enterprise Architecture Planning (EAP): Developing a Blueprint for Data, Applications, and Technology, Steven H. Spewak & Steven C. Hill, ISBN: 0-47-159985-9, John Wiley & Sons, 1993.

- Federal Enterprise Architecture Framework (FEAF), Version 1.1, US Federal Chief Information Officer (CIO) Council, September 1999; refer to www.cio.gov/documents/fedarch1.pdf.

- Headquarters Air Force Principles for Information Management, US Air Force, June 29, 1998.

- IEEE Std 1003.0-1995, Guide to the POSIX Open System Environment (OSE), identical to ISO/IEC TR 14252 (administratively withdrawn by IEEE).

- IEEE Std 1003.23-1998, Guide for Developing User Organization Open System Environment (OSE) Profiles (administratively withdrawn by IEEE).

- Implementing Enterprise Architecture — Putting Quality Information in the Hands of Oil and Gas Knowledge Workers (SPE 68794), G.A. Cox, R.M. Johnston, SPE, & R. M. Palermo, Aera Energy LLC, Copyright 2001, Society of Petroleum Engineers, Inc.

- Interoperable Enterprise Business Scenario Business Scenario, October 2002 (K022), published by The Open Group; refer to www.opengroup.org/bookstore/catalog/k022.htm.

- ISO 10303, Industrial Automation Systems and Integration — Product Data Representation and Exchange.

- ISO/IEC 10746-1: 1998, Information Technology — Open Distributed Processing — Reference Model: Overview.

- ISO/IEC 10746-4: 1998, Information Technology — Open Distributed Processing — Reference Model: Architectural Semantics.

- ISO/IEC TR 14252: 1996, Information Technology — Guide to the POSIX Open System Environment (OSE) (identical to IEEE Std 1003.0).

- ISO/IEC 17799: 2005, Information Technology — Security Techniques — Code of Practice for Information Security Management.

- ISO/IEC 20000: 2005, Information Technology — Service Management.

- ISO/IEC 42010: 2007, Systems and Software Engineering — Recommended Practice for Architectural Description of Software-Intensive Systems, Edition 1 (technically identical to ANSI/IEEE Std 1471-2000).

- IT Portfolio Management Facility (ITPMF) Specification, Object Management Group (OMG).

- Mapping of TOGAF 8.1 with COBIT 4.0 by the IT Governance Institute (ITGI) White Paper, July 2007 (W072), published by The Open Group; refer to www.opengroup.org/bookstore/catalog/w072.htm.

- Model Driven Architecture (MDA) Specification, Object Management (OMG); refer to www.omg.org/mda.

- OECD Principles of Corporate Governance, Organization for Economic Co-operation and Development, December 2001; refer to www.oecd.org.

- Pattern-Oriented Software Architecture: A System of Patterns, F. Buschmann, R. Meunier, H. Rohnert, P. Sommerlad, & M. Stal, ISBN: 0-471-95869-7, John Wiley & Sons, 1996.

- Patterns and Software: Essential Concepts and Terminology, Brad Appleton; refer to www.enteract.com/˜bradapp/docs/patterns-intro.html.

- Practical Guide to Federal Enterprise Architecture, Version 1.0, US Federal Chief Information Officer (CIO) Council, February 2001; a cooperative venture with the General Accounting Office (GAO) and the Office of Management and Budget (OMB).

- REA: A Semantic Model for Internet Supply Chain Collaboration, Robert Haugen and William E. McCarthy, January 2000; refer to www.jeffsutherland.org/oopsla2000/mccarthy/mccarthy.htm.

- Resource-Event-Agent (REA) Business Model, William E. McCarthy; refer to www.msu.edu/user/mccarth4.

- Service Component Architecture (SCA) Specification, Version 1.0, published by OSOA, March 2007.

- Service Data Objects (SDO) for C Specification, Version 2.1, published by OSOA, September 2007.

- Service Data Objects (SDO) for C++ Specification, Version 2.1, published by OSOA, December 2006.

- Service Data Objects (SDO) for COBOL Specification, Version 2.1, published by OSOA, September 2007.

- Service Data Objects (SDO) for Java Specification, Version 2.1, published by OSOA, November 2006.

- Software Processing Engineering Metamodel (SPEM) Specification, Version 2.0, Object Management Group (OMG), April 2008; refer to www.omg.org/spec/SPEM/2.0.

- STandard for the Exchange of Product model data (STEP); also ISO 10303, Industrial Automation Systems and Integration — Product Data Representation and Exchange.

- The Art of Systems Architecting, Eberhardt Rechtin & Mark W. Maier.

- The Command and Control System Target Architecture (C2STA), Electronic Systems Center (ESC), US Air Force, 2000.

- The Oregon Experiment, Christopher Alexander, ISBN: 0-19-501824-9, Oxford University Press, 1975.

- The Timeless Way of Building, Christopher Alexander, ISBN: 0-19-502402-8, Oxford University Press, 1979.

- UML Profile and Metamodel for Services (UPMS) RFP (OMG soa/2006-09-09), Object Management Group (OMG), June 2007.

- Unified Modeling Language (UML) Specification, Object Management Group (OMG); refer to www.uml.org.

- US Treasury Architecture Development Guidance (TADG), formerly known as the Treasury Information System Architecture Framework (TISAF).

- Volere Requirements Specification Template; refer to www.volere.co.uk/template.htm.

The following web sites provide useful reference material:

- IBM Patterns for e-business: www.ibm.com/framework/patterns

- IBM Patterns for e-business Resources (also known as the "Red Books"): www.ibm.com/developerworks/patterns/library

- The Information Technology Governance Institute: www.itgi.org

  This web site has many resources that can help with corporate assessment of both IT and governance in general.

- The Patterns Home Page: hillside.net/patterns

  This web site is hosted by The Hillside Group and provides information about patterns, links to online patterns, papers, and books dealing with patterns, and patterns-related mailing lists.

- The Patterns-Discussion FAQ: g.oswego.edu/dl/pd-FAQ/pd-FAQ.html

  This web site is maintained by Doug Lea and provides a thorough and highly readable FAQ about patterns.

The Open Group Architecture Framework (TOGAF)

Part I:

Introduction

The Open Group

Chapter 1: Introduction

The Open Group Architecture Framework (TOGAF) is a framework — a detailed method and a set of supporting tools — for developing an enterprise architecture. It may be used freely by any organization wishing to develop an enterprise architecture for use within that organization (see Section 4.5.1).

TOGAF is developed and maintained by members of The Open Group, working within the Architecture Forum (refer to www.opengroup.org/architecture). The original development of TOGAF Version 1 in 1995 was based on the Technical Architecture Framework for Information Management (TAFIM), developed by the US Department of Defense (DoD). The DoD gave The Open Group explicit permission and encouragement to create TOGAF by building on the TAFIM, which itself was the result of many years of development effort and many millions of dollars of US Government investment.

Starting from this sound foundation, the members of The Open Group Architecture Forum have developed successive versions of TOGAF and published each one on The Open Group public web site.

If you are new to the field of enterprise architecture and/or TOGAF, you are recommended to read the Executive Overview (refer to Section 1.2), where you will find answers to questions such as:

- What is enterprise architecture?

- Why do I need an enterprise architecture?

- Why do I need TOGAF as a framework for enterprise architecture?

1.1 Structure of the TOGAF Document

The structure of the TOGAF documentation reflects the structure and content of an architecture capability within an enterprise, as shown in Figure 1-1.

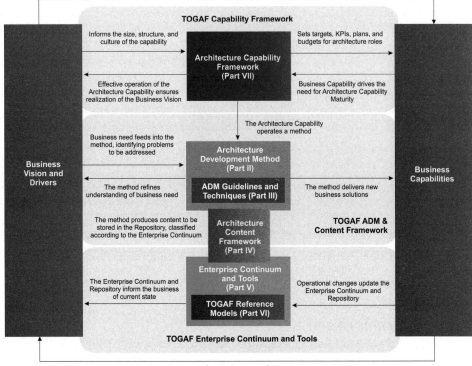

Figure 1-1 Structure of the TOGAF Document

There are seven main parts to the TOGAF document:

PART I   (Introduction) This part provides a high-level introduction to the key concepts of enterprise architecture and in particular the TOGAF approach. It contains the definitions of terms used throughout TOGAF and release notes detailing the changes between this version and the previous version of TOGAF.

PART II   (Architecture Development Method) This part is the core of TOGAF. It describes the TOGAF Architecture Development Method (ADM) — a step-by-step approach to developing an enterprise architecture.

PART III   (ADM Guidelines and Techniques) This part contains a collection of guidelines and techniques available for use in applying TOGAF and the TOGAF ADM.

PART IV   (Architecture Content Framework) This part describes the TOGAF content framework, including a structured metamodel for architectural artifacts, the use of re-usable architecture building blocks, and an overview of typical architecture deliverables.

PART V   (Enterprise Continuum & Tools) This part discusses appropriate taxonomies and tools to categorize and store the outputs of architecture activity within an enterprise.

PART VI   (TOGAF Reference Models) This part provides a selection of architectural reference models, which includes the TOGAF Foundation Architecture, and the Integrated Information Infrastructure Reference Model (III-RM).

PART VII   (Architecture Capability Framework) This part discusses the organization, processes, skills, roles, and responsibilities required to establish and operate an architecture function within an enterprise.

The intention of dividing the TOGAF specification into these independent parts is to allow for different areas of specialization to be considered in detail and potentially addressed in isolation. Although all parts work together as a whole, it is also feasible to select particular parts for adoption whilst excluding others. For example, an organization may wish to adopt the ADM process, but elect not to use any of the materials relating to architecture capability.

As an open framework, such use is encouraged, particularly in the following situations:

- Organizations that are new to TOGAF and wish to incrementally adopt TOGAF concepts are expected to focus on particular parts of the specification for initial adoption, with other areas tabled for later consideration.

- Organizations that have already deployed architecture frameworks may choose to merge these frameworks with aspects of the TOGAF specification.

1.2   Executive Overview

According to The Open Group Business Executive's Guide to IT Architecture:[1]

> "An effective enterprise architecture is critical to business survival and success and is the indispensable means to achieving competitive advantage through IT."

This section provides an executive overview of enterprise architecture, the basic concepts of what it is (not just another name for IT Architecture), and why it is needed. It provides a summary of the benefits of establishing an enterprise architecture and adopting TOGAF to achieve that.

What is an enterprise? What is enterprise architecture?

TOGAF defines "enterprise" as any collection of organizations that has a common set of goals. For example, an enterprise could be a government agency, a whole corporation, a division of a corporation, a single department, or a chain of geographically distant organizations linked together by common ownership.

The term "enterprise" in the context of "enterprise architecture" can be used to denote both an entire enterprise — encompassing all of its information and technology services, processes, and infrastructure — and a specific domain within the enterprise. In both cases, the architecture crosses multiple systems, and multiple functional groups within the enterprise.

---

1.   Available at: www.opengroup.org/bookstore/catalog/w043.htm.

Confusion often arises from the evolving nature of the term "enterprise". An extended enterprise nowadays frequently includes partners, suppliers, and customers. If the goal is to integrate an extended enterprise, then the enterprise comprises the partners, suppliers, and customers, as well as internal business units.

The business operating model concept is useful to determine the nature and scope of the enterprise architecture within an organization. Large corporations and government agencies may comprise multiple enterprises, and may develop and maintain a number of independent enterprise architectures to address each one. However, there is often much in common about the information systems in each enterprise, and there is usually great potential for gain in the use of a common architecture framework. For example, a common framework can provide a basis for the development of an Architecture Repository for the integration and re-use of models, designs, and baseline data.

Why do I need an enterprise architecture?

The purpose of enterprise architecture is to optimize across the enterprise the often fragmented legacy of processes (both manual and automated) into an integrated environment that is responsive to change and supportive of the delivery of the business strategy.

Today's CEOs know that the effective management and exploitation of information through IT is a key factor to business success, and an indispensable means to achieving competitive advantage. An enterprise architecture addresses this need, by providing a strategic context for the evolution of the IT system in response to the constantly changing needs of the business environment.

Furthermore, a good enterprise architecture enables you to achieve the right balance between IT efficiency and business innovation. It allows individual business units to innovate safely in their pursuit of competitive advantage. At the same time, it ensures the needs of the organization for an integrated IT strategy are met, permitting the closest possible synergy across the extended enterprise.

The advantages that result from a good enterprise architecture bring important business benefits, which are clearly visible in the net profit or loss of a company or organization:

- A more efficient IT operation:
    - Lower software development, support, and maintenance costs
    - Increased portability of applications
    - Improved interoperability and easier system and network management
    - Improved ability to address critical enterprise-wide issues like security
    - Easier upgrade and exchange of system components
- Better return on existing investment, reduced risk for future investment:
    - Reduced complexity in IT infrastructure
    - Maximum return on investment in existing IT infrastructure
    - The flexibility to make, buy, or out-source IT solutions
    - Reduced risk overall in new investment, and the costs of IT ownership

- Faster, simpler, and cheaper procurement:
    - Buying decisions are simpler, because the information governing procurement is readily available in a coherent plan.
    - The procurement process is faster — maximizing procurement speed and flexibility without sacrificing architectural coherence.
    - The ability to procure heterogeneous, multi-vendor open systems.

What specifically would prompt me to develop an enterprise architecture?

Typically, an enterprise architecture is developed because key people have concerns that need to be addressed by the IT systems within the organization. Such people are commonly referred to as the "stakeholders" in the system. The role of the architect is to address these concerns, by identifying and refining the requirements that the stakeholders have, developing views of the architecture that show how the concerns and the requirements are going to be addressed, and by showing the trade-offs that are going to be made in reconciling the potentially conflicting concerns of different stakeholders.

Without the enterprise architecture, it is highly unlikely that all the concerns and requirements will be considered and met.

What is an architecture framework?

An architecture framework is a foundational structure, or set of structures, which can be used for developing a broad range of different architectures. It should describe a method for designing a target state of the enterprise in terms of a set of building blocks, and for showing how the building blocks fit together. It should contain a set of tools and provide a common vocabulary. It should also include a list of recommended standards and compliant products that can be used to implement the building blocks.

Why do I need TOGAF as a framework for enterprise architecture?

TOGAF has been developed through the collaborative efforts of 300 Architecture Forum member companies from some of the world's leading IT customers and vendors and represents best practice in architecture development. Using TOGAF as the architecture framework will allow architectures to be developed that are consistent, reflect the needs of stakeholders, employ best practice, and give due consideration both to current requirements and to the likely future needs of the business.

Architecture design is a technically complex process, and the design of heterogeneous, multi-vendor architectures is particularly complex. TOGAF plays an important role in helping to "de-mystify" and de-risk the architecture development process. TOGAF provides a platform for adding value, and enables users to build genuinely open systems-based solutions to address their business issues and needs.

Who would benefit from using TOGAF?

Any organization undertaking, or planning to undertake, the design and implementation of an enterprise architecture for the support of mission-critical business applications will benefit from use of TOGAF.

Organizations seeking Boundaryless Information Flow can use TOGAF to define and implement the structures and processes to enable access to integrated information within and between enterprises.

Organizations that design and implement enterprise architectures using TOGAF are assured of a design and a procurement specification that can facilitate an open systems implementation, thus enabling the benefits of open systems with reduced risk.

Chapter 2: Core Concepts

For the purposes of TOGAF 9, the core concepts provided in this chapter apply.

2.1 What is TOGAF?

TOGAF is an architecture framework — The Open Group Architecture Framework. TOGAF provides the methods and tools for assisting in the acceptance, production, use, and maintenance of an enterprise architecture. It is based on an iterative process model supported by best practices and a re-usable set of existing architecture assets.

2.2 What is Architecture in the Context of TOGAF?

ISO/IEC 42010:2007 defines "architecture" as:

> "The fundamental organization of a system, embodied in its components, their relationships to each other and the environment, and the principles governing its design and evolution."

TOGAF embraces but does not strictly adhere to ISO/IEC 42010:2007 terminology. In TOGAF, "architecture" has two meanings depending upon the context:

1. A formal description of a system, or a detailed plan of the system at component level to guide its implementation

2. The structure of components, their inter-relationships, and the principles and guidelines governing their design and evolution over time

In TOGAF we endeavor to strike a balance between promoting the concepts and terminology of ISO/IEC 42010:2007 — ensuring that our usage of terms defined by ISO/IEC 42010:2007 is consistent with the standard — and retaining other commonly accepted terminology that is familiar to the majority of the TOGAF readership. For more on terminology, refer to Chapter 3 and Part IV, Chapter 35.

2.3   What Kind of Architecture Does TOGAF Deal With?

There are four architecture domains that are commonly accepted as subsets of an overall enterprise architecture, all of which TOGAF is designed to support:

- The **Business Architecture** defines the business strategy, governance, organization, and key business processes.

- The **Data Architecture** describes the structure of an organization's logical and physical data assets and data management resources.

- The **Application Architecture** provides a blueprint for the individual application systems to be deployed, their interactions, and their relationships to the core business processes of the organization.

- The **Technology Architecture** describes the logical software and hardware capabilities that are required to support the deployment of business, data, and application services. This includes IT infrastructure, middleware, networks, communications, processing, standards, etc.

2.4   Architecture Development Method

The TOGAF Architecture Development Method (ADM) provides a tested and repeatable process for developing architectures. The ADM includes establishing an architecture framework, developing architecture content, transitioning, and governing the realization of architectures.

All of these activities are carried out within an iterative cycle of continuous architecture definition and realization that allows organizations to transform their enterprises in a controlled manner in response to business goals and opportunities.

Phases within the ADM are as follows:

- The **Preliminary Phase** describes the preparation and initiation activities required to prepare to meet the business directive for a new enterprise architecture, including the definition of an Organization-Specific Architecture framework and the definition of principles.

- **Phase A: Architecture Vision** describes the initial phase of an architecture development cycle. It includes information about defining the scope, identifying the stakeholders, creating the Architecture Vision, and obtaining approvals.

- **Phase B: Business Architecture** describes the development of a Business Architecture to support an agreed Architecture Vision.

- **Phase C: Information Systems Architectures** describes the development of Information Systems Architectures for an architecture project, including the development of Data and Application Architectures.

- **Phase D: Technology Architecture** describes the development of the Technology Architecture for an architecture project.

- **Phase E: Opportunities & Solutions** conducts initial implementation planning and the identification of delivery vehicles for the architecture defined in the previous phases.

■ **Phase F: Migration Planning** addresses the formulation of a set of detailed sequence of transition architectures with a supporting Implementation and Migration Plan.

■ **Phase G: Implementation Governance** provides an architectural oversight of the implementation.

■ **Phase H: Architecture Change Management** establishes procedures for managing change to the new architecture.

■ **Requirements Management** examines the process of managing architecture requirements throughout the ADM.

2.5   Deliverables, Artifacts, and Building Blocks

Architects executing the ADM will produce a number of outputs as a result of their efforts, such as process flows, architectural requirements, project plans, project compliance assessments, etc. The TOGAF Architecture Content Framework (see Part IV, Chapter 33) provides a structural model for architectural content that allows major work products to be consistently defined, structured, and presented.

The Architecture Content Framework uses the following three categories to describe the type of architectural work product within the context of use:

■ A **deliverable** is a work product that is contractually specified and in turn formally reviewed, agreed, and signed off by the stakeholders. Deliverables represent the output of projects and those deliverables that are in documentation form will typically be archived at completion of a project, or transitioned into an Architecture Repository as a reference model, standard, or snapshot of the Architecture Landscape at a point in time.

■ An **artifact** is a more granular architectural work product that describes an architecture from a specific viewpoint. Examples include a network diagram, a server specification, a use-case specification, a list of architectural requirements, and a business interaction matrix. Artifacts are generally classified as catalogs (lists of things), matrices (showing relationships between things), and diagrams (pictures of things). An architectural deliverable may contain many artifacts and artifacts will form the content of the Architecture Repository.

■ A **building block** represents a (potentially re-usable) component of business, IT, or architectural capability that can be combined with other building blocks to deliver architectures and solutions.

Building blocks can be defined at various levels of detail, depending on what stage of architecture development has been reached. For instance, at an early stage, a building block can simply consist of a name or an outline description. Later on, a building block may be decomposed into multiple supporting building blocks and may be accompanied by a full specification. Building blocks can relate to "architectures" or "solutions".

— **Architecture Building Blocks (ABBs)** typically describe required capability and shape the specification of Solution Building Blocks (SBBs). For example, a customer services capability may be required within an enterprise, supported by many SBBs, such as processes, data, and application software.

— **Solution Building Blocks (SBBs)** represent components that will be used to implement the required capability. For example, a network is a building block that can be described through complementary artifacts and then put to use to realize solutions for the enterprise.

The relationships between deliverables, artifacts, and building blocks are shown in Figure 2-1.

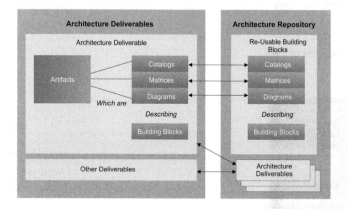

Figure 2-1 Relationships between Deliverables, Artifacts, and Building Blocks

For example, an Architecture Definition Document is a deliverable that documents an architecture description. This document will contain a number of complementary artifacts that are views of the building blocks relevant to the architecture. For example, a process flow diagram (an artifact) may be created to describe the target call handling process (a building block). This artifact may also describe other building blocks, such as the actors involved in the process (e.g., a Customer Services Representative). An example of the relationships between deliverables, artifacts, and building blocks is illustrated in Figure 33-2.

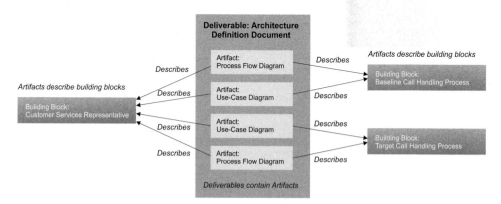

Figure 2-2 Example — Architecture Definition Document

2.6   Enterprise Continuum

TOGAF includes the concept of the Enterprise Continuum, which sets the broader context for an architect and explains how generic solutions can be leveraged and specialized in order to support the requirements of an individual organization. The Enterprise Continuum is a view of the Architecture Repository that provides methods for classifying architecture and solution artifacts as they evolve from generic Foundation Architectures to Organization-Specific Architectures. The Enterprise Continuum comprises two complementary concepts: the Architecture Continuum and the Solutions Continuum.

An overview of the structure and context for the Enterprise Continuum is shown in Figure 2-3.

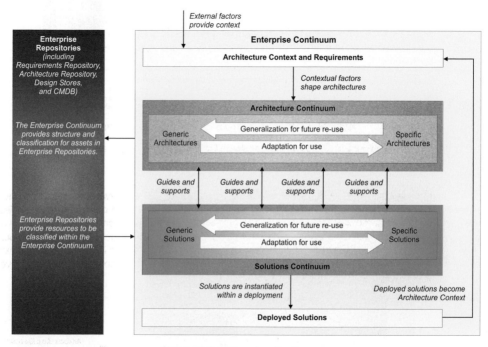

Figure 2-3 Enterprise Continuum

2.7   Architecture Repository

Supporting the Enterprise Continuum is the concept of an Architecture Repository which can be used to store different classes of architectural output at different levels of abstraction, created by the ADM. In this way, TOGAF facilitates understanding and co-operation between stakeholders and practitioners at different levels.

By means of the Enterprise Continuum and Architecture Repository, architects are encouraged to leverage all other relevant architectural resources and assets in developing an Organization-Specific Architecture.

In this context, the TOGAF ADM can be regarded as describing a process lifecycle that operates at multiple levels within the organization, operating within a holistic governance framework and producing aligned outputs that reside in an Architecture Repository. The Enterprise Continuum provides a valuable context for understanding architectural models: it shows building blocks and their relationships to each other, and the constraints and requirements on a cycle of architecture development.

The structure of the TOGAF Architecture Repository is shown in Figure 2-4.

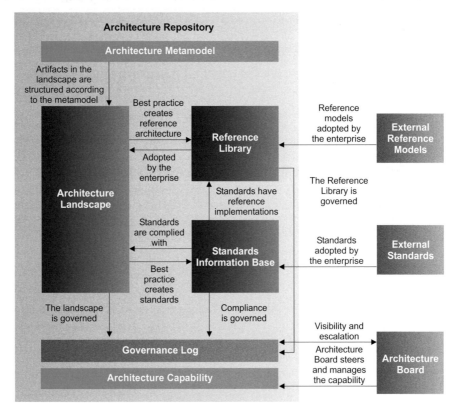

Figure 2-4 TOGAF Architecture Repository Structure

The major components within an Architecture Repository are as follows:

- The **Architecture Metamodel** describes the organizationally tailored application of an architecture framework, including a metamodel for architecture content.

- The **Architecture Capability** defines the parameters, structures, and processes that support governance of the Architecture Repository.

- The **Architecture Landscape** shows an architectural view of the building blocks that are in use within the organization today (e.g., a list of the live applications). The landscape is likely to exist at multiple levels of abstraction to suit different architecture objectives.

- The **Standards Information Base** (SIB) captures the standards with which new architectures must comply, which may include industry standards, selected products and services from suppliers, or shared services already deployed within the organization.

- The **Reference Library** provides guidelines, templates, patterns, and other forms of reference material that can be leveraged in order to accelerate the creation of new architectures for the enterprise.

- The **Governance Log** provides a record of governance activity across the enterprise.

2.8   Establishing and Maintaining an Enterprise Architecture Capability

In order to carry out architectural activity effectively within an enterprise, it is necessary to put in place an appropriate business capability for architecture, through organization structures, roles, responsibilities, skills, and processes. An overview of the TOGAF architecture capability is shown in Figure 2-5.

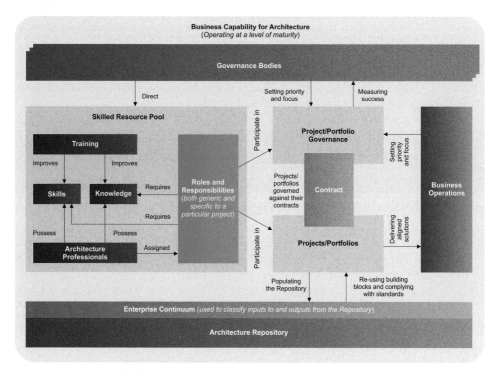

Figure 2-5 TOGAF Architecture Capability Overview

2.9   Establishing the Architecture Capability as an Operational Entity

Barring architecture capabilities set up to purely support change delivery programs, it is increasingly recognized that a successful enterprise architecture practice must sit on a firm operational footing. In effect, an enterprise architecture practice must be run like any other operational unit within a business; i.e., it should be treated like a business. To this end, and over and above the core processes defined within the ADM, an enterprise architecture practice should establish capabilities in the following areas:

- Financial Management (see Section 3.41)
- Performance Management (see Section 3.60)
- Service Management (see Section 3.73)
- Risk Management (see Section A.76)
- Resource Management (see Section 3.69)
- Communications and Stakeholder Management (see Section 3.33)
- Quality Management (see Section 3.65)
- Supplier Management (see Section A.83)
- Configuration Management (see Section A.15)
- Environment Management (see Section 3.40)

Central to the notion of operating an ongoing architecture is the execution of well-defined and effective governance, whereby all architecturally significant activity is controlled and aligned within a single framework.

As governance has become an increasingly visible requirement for organizational management, the inclusion of governance within TOGAF aligns the framework with current business best practice and also ensures a level of visibility, guidance, and control that will support all architecture stakeholder requirements and obligations.

The benefits of architecture governance include:

- Increased transparency of accountability, and informed delegation of authority
- Controlled risk management
- Protection of the existing asset base through maximizing re-use of existing architectural components
- Proactive control, monitoring, and management mechanisms
- Process, concept, and component re-use across all organizational business units
- Value creation through monitoring, measuring, evaluation, and feedback
- Increased visibility supporting internal processes and external parties' requirements; in particular, increased visibility of decision-making at lower levels ensures oversight at an appropriate level within the enterprise of decisions that may have far-reaching strategic consequences for the organization
- Greater shareholder value; in particular, enterprise architecture increasingly represents the core intellectual property of the enterprise — studies have demonstrated a correlation between increased shareholder value and well-governed enterprises

- Integrates with existing processes and methodologies and complements functionality by adding control capabilities

Further detail on establishing an enterprise architecture capability is given in Part VII, Chapter 45.

2.10   Using TOGAF with Other Frameworks

Two of the key elements of any enterprise architecture framework are:

- A definition of the deliverables that the architecting activity should produce
- A description of the method by which this should be done

With some exceptions, the majority of enterprise architecture frameworks focus on the first of these — the specific set of deliverables — and are relatively silent about the methods to be used to generate them (intentionally so, in some cases).

Because TOGAF is a generic framework and intended to be used in a wide variety of environments, it provides a flexible and extensible content framework that underpins a set of generic architecture deliverables.

As a result, TOGAF may be used either in its own right, with the generic deliverables that it describes; or else these deliverables may be replaced or extended by a more specific set, defined in any other framework that the architect considers relevant.

In all cases, it is expected that the architect will adapt and build on the TOGAF framework in order to define a tailored method that is integrated into the processes and organization structures of the enterprise. This architecture tailoring may include adopting elements from other architecture frameworks, or integrating TOGAF methods with other standard frameworks, such as ITIL, CMMI, COBIT, PRINCE2, PMBOK, and MSP. Guidelines for adapting the TOGAF ADM in such a way are given in Part II, Section 5.3.

As a generic framework and method for enterprise architecture, TOGAF also complements other frameworks that are aimed at specific vertical business domains, specific horizontal technology areas (such as security or manageability), or specific application areas (such as e-Commerce).

2.11   TOGAF Document Categorization Model

A TOGAF document categorization model exists to structure the release management of the TOGAF specification. It is not intended to serve as an implementation guide for practitioners.

Within the model, the content of the TOGAF document is categorized according to the following four categories:

- **TOGAF Core** consists of the fundamental concepts that form the essence of TOGAF.
- **TOGAF Mandated** consists of the normative parts of the TOGAF specification. These elements of TOGAF are central to its usage and without them the framework would not be recognizably TOGAF. Strong consideration must be given to these elements when applying TOGAF.

- **TOGAF Recommended** consists of a pool of resources that are specifically referenced in TOGAF as ways in which the TOGAF Core and Mandated processes can be accomplished (e.g., the SEI Architecture Trade-Off Analysis Method or business scenarios).

- **TOGAF Supporting** consists of additional resources that are not referenced in the other three TOGAF categories itself but provide valuable assistance.

The following table maps the content of this document to the four categories.

Section		Category	Comments
	Preface	TOGAF Mandated	
	Part I: Introduction		
1	Introduction		
1.1	Structure of the TOGAF Document	TOGAF Core	
1.2	Executive Overview	TOGAF Core	
2	Core Concepts	TOGAF Core	
3	Definitions	TOGAF Mandated	
4	Release Notes	TOGAF Supporting	
	Part II: Architecture Development Method		
5	Introduction		
5.1	ADM Overview		
5.1.1	The ADM, Enterprise Continuum, and Architecture Repository	TOGAF Mandated	
5.1.2	The ADM and the Foundation Architecture	TOGAF Recommended	
5.1.3	ADM and Supporting Guidelines & Techniques	TOGAF Supporting	
5.2	Architecture Development Cycle		
5.2.1	Key Points	TOGAF Core	
5.2.2	Basic Structure	TOGAF Core	
5.3	Adapting the ADM	TOGAF Mandated	
5.4	Architecture Governance	TOGAF Recommended	
5.5	Scoping the Architecture	TOGAF Core	Concepts of scoping are Core; specific ways are Recommended.
5.5.1	Enterprise Scope/Focus	TOGAF Recommended	
5.5.2	Architecture Domains	TOGAF Core	
5.5.3	Vertical Scope/Level of Detail	TOGAF Recommended	
5.5.4	Time Period	TOGAF Recommended	
5.6	Architecture Integration	TOGAF Recommended	
5.7	Summary	TOGAF Supporting	
6	Preliminary Phase		
6.1	Objectives	TOGAF Mandated	
6.2	Approach	TOGAF Recommended	
6.3	Inputs	TOGAF Mandated	
6.4	Steps	TOGAF Mandated	
6.5	Outputs	TOGAF Mandated	
7	Phase A: Architecture Vision		
7.1	Objectives	TOGAF Mandated	
7.2	Approach	TOGAF Recommended	

Section		Category	Comments
7.3	Inputs	TOGAF Mandated	
7.4	Steps	TOGAF Mandated	
7.5	Outputs	TOGAF Mandated	
8	Phase B: Business Architecture		
8.1	Objectives	TOGAF Mandated	
8.2	Approach	TOGAF Recommended	
8.3	Inputs	TOGAF Mandated	
8.4	Steps	TOGAF Mandated	
8.5	Outputs	TOGAF Mandated	
9	Phase C: Information Systems Architectures		
9.1	Objectives	TOGAF Mandated	
9.2	Approach	TOGAF Recommended	
9.3	Inputs	TOGAF Mandated	
9.4	Steps	TOGAF Mandated	
9.5	Outputs	TOGAF Mandated	
10	Phase C: Data Architecture		
10.1	Objectives	TOGAF Mandated	
10.2	Approach	TOGAF Recommended	
10.3	Inputs	TOGAF Mandated	
10.4	Steps	TOGAF Mandated	
10.5	Outputs	TOGAF Mandated	
11	Phase C: Application Architecture		
11.1	Objectives	TOGAF Mandated	
11.2	Approach	TOGAF Recommended	
11.3	Inputs	TOGAF Mandated	
11.4	Steps	TOGAF Mandated	
11.5	Outputs	TOGAF Mandated	
12	Phase D: Technology Architecture		
12.1	Objectives	TOGAF Mandated	
12.2	Approach	TOGAF Recommended	
12.3	Inputs	TOGAF Mandated	
12.4	Steps	TOGAF Mandated	
12.5	Outputs	TOGAF Mandated	
13	Phase E: Opportunities & Solutions		
13.1	Objectives	TOGAF Mandated	
13.2	Approach	TOGAF Recommended	
13.3	Inputs	TOGAF Mandated	
13.4	Steps	TOGAF Mandated	
13.5	Outputs	TOGAF Mandated	
14	Phase F: Migration Planning		
14.1	Objectives	TOGAF Mandated	
14.2	Approach	TOGAF Recommended	
14.3	Inputs	TOGAF Mandated	
14.4	Steps	TOGAF Mandated	
14.5	Outputs	TOGAF Mandated	

Section		Category	Comments
15	Phase G: Implementation Governance		
15.1	Objectives	TOGAF Mandated	
15.2	Approach	TOGAF Recommended	
15.3	Inputs	TOGAF Mandated	
15.4	Steps	TOGAF Mandated	
15.5	Outputs	TOGAF Mandated	
16	Phase H: Architecture Change Management		
16.1	Objectives	TOGAF Mandated	
16.2	Approach	TOGAF Recommended	
16.3	Inputs	TOGAF Mandated	
16.4	Steps	TOGAF Mandated	
16.5	Outputs	TOGAF Mandated	
17	ADM Architecture Requirements Management		
17.1	Objectives	TOGAF Mandated	
17.2	Approach	TOGAF Recommended	
17.3	Inputs	TOGAF Mandated	
17.4	Steps	TOGAF Mandated	
17.5	Outputs	TOGAF Mandated	
	Part III: ADM Guidelines & Techniques		
18	Introduction	TOGAF Supporting	
19	Applying Iteration to the ADM	TOGAF Core	Concept of iteration is Core; iteration cycles are Recommended.
20	Applying the ADM at Different Enterprise Levels	TOGAF Recommended	
21	Security Architecture and the ADM	TOGAF Recommended	
22	Using TOGAF to Define & Govern SOAs	TOGAF Supporting	
23	Architecture Principles	TOGAF Supporting	
23.1	Introduction		
23.2	Characteristics of Architecture Principles	TOGAF Recommended	
23.3	Components of Architecture Principles	TOGAF Recommended	
23.4	Developing Architecture Principles	TOGAF Recommended	
23.5	Applying Architecture Principles	TOGAF Recommended	
23.6	Example Set of Architecture Principles	TOGAF Recommended	
24	Stakeholder Management		
24.1	Introduction	TOGAF Mandated	
24.2	Approach to Stakeholder Management	TOGAF Mandated	
24.3	Steps in the Stakeholder Management Process	TOGAF Recommended	
24.4	Template Stakeholder Map	TOGAF Recommended	
25	Architecture Patterns	TOGAF Supporting	
26	Business Scenarios	TOGAF Recommended	
27	Gap Analysis	TOGAF Recommended	
28	Migration Planning Techniques	TOGAF Recommended	
29	Interoperability Requirements	TOGAF Recommended	
30	Business Transformation Readiness Assessment	TOGAF Recommended	

Section		Category	Comments
31	Risk Management	TOGAF Recommended	
32	Capability-Based Planning	TOGAF Recommended	
	Part IV: Architecture Content Framework		
33	Introduction	TOGAF Recommended	
34	Content Metamodel	TOGAF Recommended	
35	Architectural Artifacts	TOGAF Recommended	For the views, the content example is Supporting.
36	Architecture Deliverables	TOGAF Mandated	
37	Building Blocks		
37.1	Overview	TOGAF Core	
37.2	Introduction	TOGAF Core	
37.3	Building Blocks and the ADM	TOGAF Recommended	
37.4	Building Block Example	TOGAF Recommended	
	Part V: Enterprise Continuum & Tools		
38	Introduction	TOGAF Supporting	
39	Enterprise Continuum	TOGAF Mandated	
40	Architecture Partitioning	TOGAF Supporting	
41	Architecture Repository	TOGAF Supporting	
42	Tools for Architecture Development	TOGAF Recommended	Current contents are Supporting.
42.1	Overview	TOGAF Supporting	
42.2	Issues in Tool Standardization	TOGAF Supporting	
42.3	Evaluation Criteria and Guidelines	TOGAF Supporting	
	Part VI: TOGAF Reference Models		
43	Foundation Architecture: Technical Reference Model		
43.1	Concepts	TOGAF Mandated	
43.2	High-Level Breakdown	TOGAF Recommended	
43.3	TRM in Detail	TOGAF Recommended	
43.4	Application Platform — Taxonomy	TOGAF Recommended	
43.5	Detailed Platform Taxonomy	TOGAF Recommended	
44	Integrated Information Infrastructure Reference Model	TOGAF Recommended	
	Part VII: Architecture Capability Framework		
45	Introduction	TOGAF Supporting	
46	Establishing an Architecture Capability	TOGAF Recommended	
47	Architecture Board	TOGAF Recommended	
48	Architecture Compliance	TOGAF Recommended	
49	Architecture Contracts	TOGAF Recommended	
50	Architecture Governance	TOGAF Recommended	
51	Architecture Maturity Models	TOGAF Supporting	
52	Architecture Skills Framework	TOGAF Supporting	
A	Glossary of Supplementary Definitions	TOGAF Supporting	
B	Abbreviations	TOGAF Supporting	

Chapter 3: Definitions

For the purposes of TOGAF 9, the following terms and definitions apply. Appendix A should be referenced for supplementary definitions not defined in this chapter.

3.1 Abstraction

The technique of providing summarized or generalized descriptions of detailed and complex content.

Abstraction, as in "level of abstraction", can also mean providing a focus for analysis that is concerned with a consistent and common level of detail or abstraction. Abstraction in this sense is typically used in architecture to allow a consistent level of definition and understanding to be achieved in each area of the architecture in order to support effective communication and decision-making. It is especially useful when dealing with large and complex architectures as it allows relevant issues to be identified before further detail is attempted.

3.2 Activity

A task or collection of tasks that support the functions of an organization. For example, a user entering data into an IT system or traveling to visit customers.

3.3 Actor

A person, organization, or system that has a role that initiates or interacts with activities; for example, a sales representative who travels to visit customers. Actors may be internal or external to an organization. In the automotive industry, an original equipment manufacturer would be considered an actor by an automotive dealership that interacts with its supply chain activities.

3.4 Application

A deployed and operational IT system that supports business functions and services; for example, a payroll. Applications use data and are supported by multiple technology components but are distinct from the technology components that support the application.

3.5 Application Architecture

A description of the major logical grouping of capabilities that manage the data objects necessary to process the data and support the business.

Note: Application Architecture is described in Part II, Chapter 11.

3.6 Application Platform

The collection of technology components of hardware and software that provide the services used to support applications.

3.7 Application Platform Interface (API)

The interface, or set of functions, between application software and/or the application platform.

3.8 Architectural Style

The combination of distinctive features in which architecture is performed or expressed.

3.9 Architecture

1. A formal description of a system, or a detailed plan of the system at component level, to guide its implementation (source: ISO/IEC 42010:2007).

2. The structure of components, their inter-relationships, and the principles and guidelines governing their design and evolution over time.

3.10 Architecture Building Block (ABB)

A constituent of the architecture model that describes a single aspect of the overall model.

See also Section 3.24.

3.11   Architecture Continuum

A part of the Enterprise Continuum. A repository of architectural elements with increasing detail and specialization. This Continuum begins with foundational definitions like reference models, core strategies, and basic building blocks. From there it spans to Industry Architectures and all the way to an organization's specific architecture.

See also Section 3.39.

3.12   Architecture Development Method (ADM)

The core of TOGAF. A step-by-step approach to develop and use an enterprise architecture.

Note: The ADM is described in Part II: Architecture Development Method (ADM).

3.13   Architecture Domain

The architectural area being considered. There are four architecture domains within TOGAF: business, data, application, and technology.

3.14   Architecture Framework

A foundational structure, or set of structures, which can be used for developing a broad range of different architectures. It should contain a method for designing an information system in terms of a set of building blocks, and for showing how the building blocks fit together. It should contain a set of tools and provide a common vocabulary. It should also include a list of recommended standards and compliant products that can be used to implement the building blocks.

3.15   Architecture Governance

The practice and orientation by which enterprise architectures and other architectures are managed and controlled at an enterprise-wide level. It is concerned with change processes (design governance) and operation of product systems (operational governance).

See also Section 3.45.

3.16   Architecture Landscape

The architectural representation of assets deployed within the operating enterprise at a particular point in time. The views are segmented into strategic, segment, and capability levels of abstraction to meet diverse stakeholder needs.

3.17 Architecture Principles

A qualitative statement of intent that should be met by the architecture. Has at least a supporting rationale and a measure of importance.

Note: A sample set of architecture principles is defined in Part III, Chapter 23.

3.18 Architecture View

See Section 3.88.

3.19 Architecture Vision

1. A high-level, aspirational view of the Target Architecture.

2. A phase in the ADM which delivers understanding and definition of the Architecture Vision.

3. A specific deliverable describing the Architecture Vision.

Note: Phase A (Architecture Vision) is described in Part II, Chapter 7.

3.20 Artifact

An architectural work product that describes an architecture from a specific viewpoint. Examples include a network diagram, a server specification, a use-case specification, a list of architectural requirements, and a business interaction matrix. Artifacts are generally classified as catalogs (lists of things), matrices (showing relationships between things), and diagrams (pictures of things). An architectural deliverable may contain multiple artifacts and artifacts will form the content of the Architecture Repository.

See also Section 3.24.

3.21 Baseline

A specification that has been formally reviewed and agreed upon, that thereafter serves as the basis for further development or change and that can be changed only through formal change control procedures or a type of procedure such as configuration management.

3.22 Baseline Architecture

The existing defined system architecture before entering a cycle of architecture review and redesign.

3.23   Boundaryless Information Flow

1.   A trademark of The Open Group.

2.   A shorthand representation of "access to integrated information to support business process improvements" representing a desired state of an enterprise's infrastructure specific to the business needs of the organization.

An infrastructure that provides Boundaryless Information Flow has open standard components that provide services in a customer's extended enterprise that:

- Combine multiple sources of information

- Securely deliver the information whenever and wherever it is needed, in the right context for the people or systems using that information.

Note: The need for Boundaryless Information Flow is described in Part VI, Chapter 44.

3.24   Building Block

Represents a (potentially re-usable) component of business, IT, or architectural capability that can be combined with other building blocks to deliver architectures and solutions.

Building blocks can be defined at various levels of detail, depending on what stage of architecture development has been reached. For instance, at an early stage, a building block can simply consist of a name or an outline description. Later on, a building block may be decomposed into multiple supporting building blocks and may be accompanied by a full specification. Building blocks can relate to "architectures" or "solutions".

See also Section 3.20.

Note: Building blocks are described in Part IV, Chapter 37.

3.25   Business Architecture

The business strategy, governance, organization, and key business processes information, as well as the interaction between these concepts.

Note: Business Architecture is described in Part II, Chapter 8.

3.26   Business Domain

A grouping of coherent business functions and activities (in the context of a business sector) over which meaningful responsibility can be taken. For example, Finance, Human Resources (HR), Automobile Manufacturing, Retail, etc. The phrase is often used to identify specific business knowledge (a business domain expert).

3.27 Business Function

Delivers business capabilities closely aligned to an organization, but not necessarily explicitly governed by the organization.

3.28 Business Governance

Concerned with ensuring that the business processes and policies (and their operation) deliver the business outcomes and adhere to relevant business regulation.

3.29 Business Service

Supports business capabilities through an explicitly defined interface and is explicitly governed by an organization.

3.30 Capability

An ability that an organization, person, or system possesses. Capabilities are typically expressed in general and high-level terms and typically require a combination of organization, people, processes, and technology to achieve. For example, marketing, customer contact, or outbound telemarketing.

3.31 Capability Architecture

A highly detailed description of the architectural approach to realize a particular solution or solution aspect.

3.32 Capability Increment

The output from a business change initiative that delivers an increase in performance for a particular capability of the enterprise.

3.33 Communications and Stakeholder Management

The management of needs of stakeholders of the enterprise architecture practice. It also manages the execution of communication between the practice and the stakeholders and the practice and the consumers of its services.

Note: Architecture stakeholder management is described in Chapter 24.

3.34 Concerns

The key interests that are crucially important to the stakeholders in a system, and determine the acceptability of the system. Concerns may pertain to any aspect of the system's functioning, development, or operation, including considerations such as performance, reliability, security, distribution, and evolvability.

See also Section 3.80.

3.35 Constraint

An external factor that prevents an organization from pursuing particular approaches to meet its goals. For example, customer data is not harmonized within the organization, regionally or nationally, constraining the organization's ability to offer effective customer service.

3.36 Data Architecture

The structure of an organization's logical and physical data assets and data management resources.

Note: Data Architecture is described in Part II, Chapter 10.

3.37 Deliverable

An architectural work product that is contractually specified and in turn formally reviewed, agreed, and signed off by the stakeholders. Deliverables represent the output of projects and those deliverables that are in documentation form will typically be archived at completion of a project, or transitioned into an Architecture Repository as a reference model, standard, or snapshot of the Architecture Landscape at a point in time.

3.38 Enterprise

The highest level (typically) of description of an organization and typically covers all missions and functions. An enterprise will often span multiple organizations.

3.39   Enterprise Continuum

A categorization mechanism useful for classifying architecture and solution artifacts, both internal and external to the Architecture Repository, as they evolve from generic Foundation Architectures to Organization-Specific Architectures.

See also Section 3.11 and Section 3.79.

3.40   Environment Management

The provision and management of the environment required to support the operations of the enterprise architecture practice, including facilities, equipment, tools, and information systems.

3.41   Financial Management

The management of the financial aspects of the enterprise architecture practice; e.g., budgeting and forecasting.

3.42   Foundation Architecture

An architecture of generic services and functions that provides a foundation on which more specific architectures and architectural components can be built. The TOGAF Foundation Architecture includes a Technical Reference Model (TRM).

3.43   Framework

A structure for content or process that can be used as a tool to structure thinking, ensuring consistency and completeness.

3.44 Gap

A statement of difference between two states. Used in the context of gap analysis, where the difference between the Baseline and Target Architecture is identified.

Note: Gap analysis is described in Part III, Chapter 27.

3.45 Governance

The discipline of monitoring, managing, and steering a business (or IS/IT landscape) to deliver the business outcome required.

See also Section 3.15, Section 3.28, and Section A.60 in Appendix A.

3.46 Information

Any communication or representation of facts, data, or opinions, in any medium or form, including textual, numerical, graphic, cartographic, narrative, or audio-visual forms.

3.47 Information Technology (IT)

1. The lifecycle management of information and related technology used by an organization.

2. An umbrella term that includes all or some of the subject areas relating to the computer industry, such as Business Continuity, Business IT Interface, Business Process Modeling and Management, Communication, Compliance and Legislation, Computers, Content Management, Hardware, Information Management, Internet, Offshoring, Networking, Programming and Software, Professional Issues, Project Management, Security, Standards, Storage, Voice and Data Communications. Various countries and industries employ other umbrella terms to describe this same collection.

3. A term commonly assigned to a department within an organization tasked with provisioning some or all of the domains described in (2) above.

4. Alternate names commonly adopted include Information Services, Information Management, et al.

3.48 Interoperability

1. The ability to share information and services.

2. The ability of two or more systems or components to exchange and use information.

3. The ability of systems to provide and receive services from other systems and to use the services so interchanged to enable them to operate effectively together.

3.49 Knowledge

The awareness and understanding of facts, truths, or information gained in the form of experience or learning (*a posteriori*), or through introspection (*a priori*). Knowledge is an appreciation of the possession of interconnected details which, in isolation, are of lesser value.

3.50 Logical

An implementation-independent definition of the architecture, often grouping related physical entities according to their purpose and structure. For example, the products from multiple infrastructure software vendors can all be logically grouped as Java application server platforms.

3.51 Metadata

Data about data, of any sort in any media, that describes the characteristics of an entity.

3.52 Metamodel

A model that describes how and with what the architecture will be described in a structured way.

3.53 Method

A defined, repeatable approach to address a particular type of problem.

See also Section 3.54.

3.54   Methodology

A defined, repeatable series of steps to address a particular type of problem, which typically centers on a defined process, but may also include definition of content.

See also Section 3.53.

3.55   Model

A representation of a subject of interest. A model provides a smaller scale, simplified, and/or abstract representation of the subject matter. A model is constructed as a "means to an end". In the context of enterprise architecture, the subject matter is a whole or part of the enterprise and the end is the ability to construct "views" that address the concerns of particular stakeholders; i.e., their "viewpoints" in relation to the subject matter.

See also Section 3.80, Section 3.88, and Section 3.89.

3.56   Modeling

A technique through construction of models which enables a subject to be represented in a form that enables reasoning, insight, and clarity concerning the essence of the subject matter.

3.57   Objective

A time-bounded milestone for an organization used to demonstrate progress towards a goal; for example, "Increase Capacity Utilization by 30% by the end of 2009 to support the planned increase in market share".

3.58   Organization

A self-contained unit of resources with line management responsibility, goals, objectives, and measures. Organizations may include external parties and business partner organizations.

3.59 Patterns

A technique for putting building blocks into context; for example, to describe a re-usable solution to a problem. Building blocks are what you use: patterns can tell you how you use them, when, why, and what trade-offs you have to make in doing so.

See also Section 3.24.

3.60 Performance Management

The monitoring, control, and reporting of the enterprise architecture practice performance. Also concerned with continuous improvement.

3.61 Physical

A description of a real-world entity. Physical elements in an enterprise architecture may still be considerably abstracted from Solution Architecture, design, or implementation views.

3.62 Platform

A combination of technology infrastructure products and components that provides that pre-requisites to host application software.

3.63 Platform Services

A technical capability required to provide enabling infrastructure that supports the delivery of applications.

3.64 Principle

See Section 3.17.

3.65 Quality Management

The management of the quality aspects of the enterprise architecture practice; e.g., management plans, quality criteria, review processes.

3.66   Reference Model (RM)

A reference model is an abstract framework for understanding significant relationships among the entities of [an] environment, and for the development of consistent standards or specifications supporting that environment. A reference model is based on a small number of unifying concepts and may be used as a basis for education and explaining standards to a non-specialist. A reference model is not directly tied to any standards, technologies, or other concrete implementation details, but it does seek to provide common semantics that can be used unambiguously across and between different implementations.

Note: The source of this definition is OASIS; refer to www.oasis-open.org/committees/tc_home.php?wg_abbrev=soa-rm.

3.67   Repository

A system that manages all of the data of an enterprise, including data and process models and other enterprise information. Hence, the data in a repository is much more extensive than that in a data dictionary, which generally defines only the data making up a database.

3.68   Requirement

A quantitative statement of business need that must be met by a particular architecture or work package.

3.69   Resource Management

The acquisition, development, and management of human resources within the enterprise architecture practice in response to demand for enterprise architecture services and financial constraints.

Note: The Architecture Skills Framework is described in Part VII, Chapter 52.

3.70   Roadmap

An abstracted plan for business or technology change, typically operating across multiple disciplines over multiple years. Normally used in the phrases Technology Roadmap, Architecture Roadmap, etc.

3.71   Role

1. The usual or expected function of an actor, or the part somebody or something plays in a particular action or event. An Actor may have a number of roles.

2. The part an individual plays in an organization and the contribution they make through the application of their skills, knowledge, experience, and abilities.

See also Section 3.3.

3.72   Segment Architecture

A detailed, formal description of areas within an enterprise, used at the program or portfolio level to organize and align change activity.

See also Section 3.82.

3.73   Service Management

The management of the execution and performance of the enterprise architecture practice services. This includes managing the "pipeline" plus current service portfolio.

3.74   Service Orientation

A way of thinking in terms of services and service-based development and the outcomes of services.

See also Section 3.75.

3.75   Service Oriented Architecture (SOA)

An architectural style that supports service orientation. It has the following distinctive features:

- It is based on the design of the services — which mirror real-world business activities — comprising the enterprise (or inter-enterprise) business processes.

- Service representation utilizes business descriptions to provide context (i.e., business process, goal, rule, policy, service interface, and service component) and implements services using service orchestration.

- It places unique requirements on the infrastructure — it is recommended that implementations use open standards to realize interoperability and location transparency.

- Implementations are environment-specific — they are constrained or enabled by context and must be described within that context.

- It requires strong governance of service representation and implementation.
- It requires a "Litmus Test", which determines a "good service".

See also Section 3.8 and Section 3.74.

3.76   Skill

The ability to perform a job-related activity, which contributes to the effective performance of a task.

3.77   Solution Architecture

A description of a discrete and focused business operation or activity and how IS/IT supports that operation. A Solution Architecture typically applies to a single project or project release, assisting in the translation of requirements into a solution vision, high-level business and/or IT system specifications, and a portfolio of implementation tasks.

3.78   Solution Building Block (SBB)

A candidate physical solution for an Architecture Building Block (ABB); e.g., a Commercial Off-The-Shelf (COTS) package, that is a component of the Acquirer view of the architecture.

3.79   Solutions Continuum

A part of the Enterprise Continuum. A repository of re-usable solutions for future implementation efforts. It contains implementations of the corresponding definitions in the Architecture Continuum.

See also Section 3.39 and Section 3.11.

3.80   Stakeholder

An individual, team, or organization (or classes thereof) with interests in, or concerns relative to, the outcome of the architecture. Different stakeholders with different roles will have different concerns.

See also Section A.86 in Appendix A.

3.81   Standards Information Base (SIB)

A database of standards that can be used to define the particular services and other components of an Organization-Specific Architecture.

Note: The Standards Information Base is described in Part V, Section 41.4.

3.82   Strategic Architecture

A summary formal description of the enterprise, providing an organizing framework for operational and change activity, and an executive-level, long-term view for direction setting.

3.83   Target Architecture

The description of a future state of the architecture being developed for an organization. There may be several future states developed as a roadmap to show the evolution of the architecture to a target state.

3.84   Taxonomy of Architecture Views

The organized collection of all views pertinent to an architecture.

3.85   Technical Reference Model (TRM)

A structure which allows components of an information system to be described in a consistent manner (i.e., the way in which you describe the components).

See also Section 3.66.

3.86   Technology Architecture

The logical software and hardware capabilities that are required to support deployment of business, data, and application services. This includes IT infrastructure, middleware, networks, communications, processing, and standards.

Note: Technology Architecture is described in Part II, Chapter 12.

3.87   Transition Architecture

A formal description of the enterprise architecture showing periods of transition and development for particular parts of the enterprise. Transition Architectures are used to provide an overview of current and target capability and allow for individual work packages and projects to be grouped into managed portfolios and programs.

Note: Transition Architectures are described in Part IV, Section 36.2.22.

3.88   View

The representation of a related set of concerns. A view is what is seen from a viewpoint. An architecture view may be represented by a model to demonstrate to stakeholders their areas of interest in the architecture. A view does not have to be visual or graphical in nature.

See also Section 3.80 and Section 3.89.

3.89   Viewpoint

A definition of the perspective from which a view is taken. It is a specification of the conventions for constructing and using a view (often by means of an appropriate schema or template). A view is what you see; a viewpoint is where you are looking from — the vantage point or perspective that determines what you see.

See also Section A.56 in Appendix A.

3.90   Work Package

A set of actions identified to achieve one or more objectives for the business. A work package can be a part of a project, a complete project, or a program.

Chapter 4: Release Notes

For the purposes of TOGAF 9, the release notes provided in this chapter apply.

4.1 What's New in TOGAF 9?

This section provides an overview of the major new features within TOGAF 9.

Modular Structure

One focus of TOGAF 9 development has been to ensure that the specification content is structured in a modular way. The modular seven-part structure of TOGAF allows for the concepts in each part to be developed with limited impacts on other parts. Content that was contained within the TOGAF 8.1.1 Resource Base has been classified and moved into parts that have a defined purpose (as opposed to generic "resources").

The modular structure in TOGAF is intended to support greater usability, as each part has a defined purpose and can be read in isolation as a stand-alone set of guidelines. The modular structure is also expected to support incremental adoption of the TOGAF specification. Finally, the modular structure supports more sophisticated release management of the TOGAF specification. In future, individual parts may evolve at different speeds and the current specification structure is intended to allow changes in one area to take place with limited impacts across the specification.

Content Framework

A significant addition of new content to the TOGAF specification is the content framework. The TOGAF content framework provides a detailed model of architectural work products, including deliverables, artifacts within deliverables, and the architectural building blocks that artifacts represent. The intention of including a content framework within TOGAF is to drive greater consistency in the outputs that are created when following an Architecture Development Method (ADM).

The benefit of including a content framework applies at a number of levels. Firstly, within a single architecture development initiative the content framework provides a comprehensive checklist of architecture outputs that could be created and consequently reduce the risk of gaps within the final architecture deliverable set.

The second major benefit of inclusion of a content framework applies when attempting to integrate architectural work products across an enterprise. The content framework is intended to be adapted and then adopted by an enterprise in order to mandate standard architectural concepts, terms, and deliverables. If all architecture initiatives use the same models for content, their outputs can be combined much more easily than in situations where each architect uses a completely different approach.

Finally, a substantial benefit of the inclusion of a content framework within TOGAF is that it provides (for the first time) a detailed open standard for how architectures should be described. The existence of this standard allows tools vendors, product vendors, and service vendors to adopt consistent ways of working, which in turn will result in greater consistency between architecture tools, better tool interoperability, more consistent reference architectures, and better comparability between related reference architectures.

Extended Guidance on Adopting TOGAF within an Enterprise

Within larger organizations, the practice of enterprise architecture requires a number of individuals and teams that work together on many architectures. Although each architecture will address a specific problem, in an ideal situation architectures can be considered as a group in order to develop an overall integrated view of how the enterprise is changing.

This version of TOGAF features an extended set of concepts and guidelines to support the establishment of an integrated hierarchy of architectures being developed by teams that operate within an overarching architectural governance model. In particular, the following concepts are introduced:

- **Partitioning**: In order to develop architectures that have manageable levels of cost and complexity, it is necessary to partition the enterprise into specific architectures. TOGAF discusses the concept of partitioning and provides a variety of techniques and considerations on how to partition the various architectures within an enterprise.

- **Architecture Repository**: TOGAF provides a logical information model for an Architecture Repository, which can be used as an integrated store for all outputs created by executing the ADM.

- **Capability Framework**: This version of TOGAF provides a more structured definition of the organization, skills, roles, and responsibilities required to operate an effective enterprise architecture capability. The new TOGAF materials also provide guidance on a process that can be followed to identify and establish an appropriate architecture capability.

Explicit Consideration of Architectural Styles, Including SOA and Security Architecture

The new Part III: ADM Guidelines & Techniques brings together a set of supporting materials that show in more detail how the ADM can be applied to specific situations. The new guidelines discuss:

- The varying uses of iteration that are possible within the ADM and when each technique should be applied

- The linkages between the TOGAF ADM and Service Oriented Architecture (SOA)

- The specific considerations required to address security architecture within the ADM

- The various types of architecture development required within an enterprise and how these relate to one another

Additional ADM Detail

This version of the TOGAF specification includes more detailed information supporting the execution of the ADM. Particular areas of enhancement are:

- The Preliminary phase, which features extended guidance on establishing an enterprise architecture framework and planning for architecture development. The extended Preliminary phase also provides pointers to the definition of a governance model for architecture benefit realization and also discusses the linkage between TOGAF and other management frameworks.

- The Opportunities & Solutions phase and Migration Planning phase, which feature a more detailed and robust method for defining and planning enterprise transformation, based on the principles of capability-based planning.

4.2   The Benefits of TOGAF 9

TOGAF 9 provides a wide-ranging set of revisions to the TOGAF specification. When combined, these edits seek to achieve a set of objectives to improve the value of the TOGAF framework.

Greater Usability

A number of enhancements within TOGAF 9 support greater usability of the overall specification. Firstly, the modular structure of the specification makes it easier for an architect to consider a specific aspect of the architecture capability. In all areas, the specification seeks to add detail and clarity above and beyond previous TOGAF versions.

More Focus on Holistic Enterprise Change

TOGAF has a solid history in IT architecture, considering the ways in which IT can support enterprise change. However, as TOGAF has grown in depth and maturity it has become a framework for managing the entire spectrum of change required to transform an enterprise towards a target operating model. TOGAF 9 continues this evolution and incorporates a broader perspective of change that allows enterprise architecture to be used to specify transformation across the business, data, application, and technology domains.

More Consistency of Output

Previous versions of TOGAF focused on providing a consistent process for developing architectures. TOGAF 9 includes a greatly enhanced consideration of architectural work products to ensure that a consistent process is used to produce consistent outputs. The Architecture Content Framework provides a detailed model of the outputs to be created by the ADM. Additionally, the Enterprise Continuum, Architecture Partitioning, and Architecture Repository sections provide detailed guidance on how architectural deliverables can be scoped, governed, and integrated.

4.3   Mapping of the TOGAF 8.1.1 Structure to TOGAF 9

Listed below are the Parts of the TOGAF 8 specification. For each Part, a description is given to explain where the TOGAF 8 content can be found within the current specification.

Part I: Introduction

The Introduction part of the TOGAF 8.1.1 specification has been used as the basis for creation of Part I: Introduction in TOGAF 9. The introduction to TOGAF 9 reflects the content of TOGAF 9 rather than the content of TOGAF 8.1.1, and also features a number of enhancements to improve accessibility.

Part II: Architecture Development Method

The essence of the TOGAF 8.1.1 ADM has been retained in TOGAF 9. Part II: Architecture Development Method (ADM) within TOGAF 9 is structured along similar lines to Part II of the TOGAF 8.1.1 document. TOGAF ADM phase inputs and outputs (Chapter 16 of TOGAF 8.1.1) have been moved from the ADM section of TOGAF 8.1.1 to Part IV: Architecture Content Framework of TOGAF 9.

TOGAF 9 ADM features additional content in the majority of ADM phases, which in the most part adds further detail and clarification to the same approach that was described in TOGAF 8.1.1.

Part III: Enterprise Continuum

The TOGAF 8.1.1 Enterprise Continuum has seen a substantial degree of change. The Enterprise Continuum concept is retained within Part V: Enterprise Continuum & Tools. The TOGAF Technical Reference Model and Integrated Information Infrastructure Reference Model are extracted and placed within Part VI: TOGAF Reference Models in TOGAF 9.

TOGAF 9 adds new materials that describe an approach to architecture partitioning and also provides a structured model of an Architecture Repository. These concepts support and elaborate on the original intent of the Enterprise Continuum.

TOGAF 9 removes the Standards Information Base from the TOGAF specification. However, an example SIB remains at The Open Group web site (www.opengroup.org). The concept of a Standards Information Base is important within TOGAF, but the breadth and speed of change of relevant architectural standards mean that it is impractical to maintain a current and relevant collection of standards within a specification such as TOGAF.

Part IV: Resource Base

The Resource Base is not included in this version of TOGAF. Some elements of the Resource Base have been deprecated from the TOGAF specification, but will still be available in White Paper form. Other elements of the Resource Base have been moved to other areas of the specification.

The following table illustrates where TOGAF 8.1.1 Resource Base content can now be located.

TOGAF 8.1.1 Resource	Current Location
Architecture Board	Moved to Part VII: Architecture Capability Framework
Architecture Compliance	Moved to Part VII: Architecture Capability Framework
Architecture Contracts	Moved to Part VII: Architecture Capability Framework

TOGAF 8.1.1 Resource	Current Location
Architecture Governance	Moved to Part VII: Architecture Capability Framework
Architecture Maturity Models	Moved to Part VII: Architecture Capability Framework
Architecture Patterns	Moved to Part III: ADM Guidelines & Techniques
Architecture Principles	Moved to Part III: ADM Guidelines & Techniques
Architecture Skills Framework	Moved to Part VII: Architecture Capability Framework
Developing Architecture Views	Elements retained within Part IV: Architecture Content Framework
Building Blocks	Elements retained within Part IV: Architecture Content Framework
Business Process Domain Views	Elements retained within Part IV: Architecture Content Framework
Business Scenarios	Moved to Part III: ADM Guidelines & Techniques
Case Studies	Removed. Case Studies will be available on The Open Group web site.
Glossary	Moved to Part I: Introduction
Other Architectures & Frameworks	Removed. This material will be available on The Open Group web site as a White Paper.
Tools for Architecture Development	Moved to Part V: Enterprise Continuum & Tools
ADM and the Zachman Framework	Removed. This material will be available on The Open Group web site as a White Paper.

4.4   Mapping of TOGAF 9 Structure to TOGAF 8.1.1

The following table illustrates where TOGAF 9 chapters map to those of TOGAF 8.1.1:

	TOGAF 9 Chapter	Derivation from TOGAF 8.1.1
	Part I: Introduction	
1	Introduction	Material revised; based on Chapter 1
2	Core Concepts	New chapter
3	Definitions	Material derived from Chapter 36, reworked into formal definitions and abbreviations sections
4	Release Notes	New chapter
	Part II: Architecture Development Method	
5	Introduction	Material revised; based on Chapter 3
6	Preliminary Phase	Material revised; based on Chapter 4
7	Phase A: Architecture Vision	Material revised; based on Chapter 5
8	Phase B: Business Architecture	Material revised; based on Chapter 6
9	Phase C: Information Systems Architectures	Material revised; based on Chapter 7
10	Phase C: Data Architecture	Material revised; based on Chapter 8
11	Phase C: Application Architecture	Material revised; based on Chapter 9
12	Phase D: Technology Architecture	Material revised; based on Chapter 10
13	Phase E: Opportunities & Solutions	Material revised; based on Chapter 11

TOGAF 9 Chapter		Derivation from TOGAF 8.1.1
14	Phase F: Migration Planning	Material revised; based on Chapter 12
15	Phase G: Implementation Governance	Material revised; based on Chapter 13
16	Phase H: Architecture Change Management	Material revised; based on Chapter 14
17	ADM Architecture Requirements Management	No material change; maps to Chapter 15
Part III: ADM Guidelines & Techniques		
18	Introduction	New chapter
19	Applying Iteration to the ADM	New chapter
20	Applying the ADM at Different Enterprise Levels	New chapter
21	Security Architecture and the ADM	New chapter; derived from Security White Paper (W055)
22	Using TOGAF to Define & Govern SOAs	New chapter
23	Architecture Principles	No material change; maps to Chapter 29
24	Stakeholder Management	New chapter
25	Architecture Patterns	No material change; maps to Chapter 28
26	Business Scenarios	No material change; maps to Chapter 34
27	Gap Analysis	New chapter; derived from Gap Analysis
28	Migration Planning Techniques	New chapter
29	Interoperability Requirements	New chapter
30	Business Transformation Readiness Assessment	New chapter
31	Risk Management	New chapter
32	Capability-Based Planning	New chapter
Part IV: Architecture Content Framework		
33	Introduction	New chapter
34	Content Metamodel	New chapter
35	Architectural Artifacts	Derived from Chapter 31, plus new material
36	Architecture Deliverables	Revised; was Chapter 16
37	Building Blocks	Revised from Chapter 32
Part V: Enterprise Continuum & Tools		
38	Introduction	New chapter
39	Enterprise Continuum	Derived from Chapters 17 and 18 with substantial revisions
40	Architecture Partitioning	New chapter
41	Architecture Repository	New chapter
42	Tools for Architecture Development	No material change; maps to Chapter 38
Part VI: TOGAF Reference Models		
43	Foundation Architecture: Technical Reference Model	No material change; maps to Chapters 19 and 20
44	Integrated Information Infrastructure Reference Model	No material change; maps to Chapter 22
Part VII: Architecture Capability Framework		
45	Introduction	New chapter
46	Establishing an Architecture Capability	New chapter
47	Architecture Board	Minimal change; maps to Chapter 23
48	Architecture Compliance	Minimal change; maps to Chapter 24
49	Architecture Contracts	Minimal change; maps to Chapter 25

	TOGAF 9 Chapter	Derivation from TOGAF 8.1.1
50	Architecture Governance	Minimal change, maps to Chapter 26
51	Architecture Maturity Models	Minimal change; maps to Chapter 27
52	Architecture Skills Framework	Some cosmetic changes; maps to Chapter 30
A	Glossary of Supplementary Definitions	Derived from Chapter 36
B	Abbreviations	Derived from Chapter 36

4.5   Using TOGAF

4.5.1   Conditions of Use

The TOGAF documentation is freely available for viewing online without a license. Alternatively, the complete TOGAF documentation set may be downloaded and stored under license, as explained on the TOGAF information web site.

In either case, the TOGAF documentation may be used freely by any organization wishing to do so to develop an architecture for use within that organization. No part of it may be reproduced, stored in a retrieval system, or transmitted, in any form or by any means, electronic, mechanical, photocopying, recording, or otherwise, for any other purpose including, but not by way of limitation, any use for commercial gain, without the prior permission of the copyright owners.

4.5.2   How Much Does TOGAF Cost?

The Open Group operates as a not-for-profit consortium committed to delivering greater business efficiency by bringing together buyers and suppliers of information systems to lower the barriers of integrating new technology across the enterprise. Its goal is to realize the vision of Boundaryless Information Flow.

TOGAF is a key part of its strategy for achieving this goal, and The Open Group wants TOGAF to be taken up and used in practical architecture projects, and the experience from its use fed back to help improve it.

The Open Group therefore publishes TOGAF on its public web server, and allows and encourages its reproduction and use free-of-charge by any organization wishing to use it internally to develop an enterprise architecture. (There are restrictions on its commercial exploitation, however; see Section 4.5.1.)

4.5.3   Downloads

Downloads of the TOGAF documentation, including a printable PDF file, are available under license from the TOGAF information web site (refer to www.opengroup.org/architecture/togaf). The license is free to any organization wishing to use TOGAF entirely for internal purposes (for example, to develop an enterprise architecture for use within that organization).

4.6   Why Join The Open Group?

Organizations wishing to reduce the time, cost, and risk of implementing multi-vendor solutions that integrate within and between enterprises need The Open Group as their key partner.

The Open Group brings together the buyers and suppliers of information systems worldwide, and enables them to work together, both to ensure that IT solutions meet the needs of customers, and to make it easier to integrate IT across the enterprise.

TOGAF is a key enabler in this task.

Yes, TOGAF itself is freely available. But how much will you spend on developing or updating your enterprise architecture using TOGAF? And how much will you spend on procurements based on that architecture?

The price of membership of The Open Group is insignificant in comparison with these amounts.

In addition to the general benefits of membership, as a member of The Open Group you will be eligible to participate in The Open Group Architecture Forum, which is the development program within which TOGAF is evolved, and in which TOGAF users come together to exchange information and feedback.

Members of the Architecture Forum gain:

- Immediate access to the fruits of the current TOGAF work program (not publicly available until publication of the next edition of the TOGAF document) — in effect, the latest information on TOGAF

- Exchange of experience with other customer and vendor organizations involved in enterprise architecture in general, and networking with architects using TOGAF in significant architecture development projects around the world

- Peer review of specific architecture case study material

The Open Group Architecture Framework (TOGAF)

Part II:

Architecture Development Method (ADM)

The Open Group

Chapter 5: Introduction

This chapter describes the Architecture Development Method (ADM) cycle, adapting the ADM, architecture scope, and architecture integration.

5.1   ADM Overview

The TOGAF ADM is the result of continuous contributions from a large number of architecture practitioners. It describes a method for developing an enterprise architecture, and forms the core of TOGAF. It integrates elements of TOGAF described in this document as well as other available architectural assets, to meet the business and IT needs of an organization.

5.1.1   The ADM, Enterprise Continuum, and Architecture Repository

The Enterprise Continuum provides a framework and context to support the leverage of relevant architecture assets in executing the ADM. These assets may include architecture descriptions, models, and patterns taken from a variety of sources, as explained in Part V: Enterprise Continuum & Tools.

The Enterprise Continuum is thus a tool for categorizing architectural source material — both the contents of the organization's own Architecture Repository, and the set of relevant, available reference models in the industry.

The practical implementation of the Enterprise Continuum will typically take the form of an Architecture Repository (see Part V, Chapter 41) that includes reference architectures, models, and patterns that have been accepted for use within the enterprise, and actual architectural work done previously within the enterprise. The architect would seek to re-use as much as possible from the Architecture Repository that was relevant to the project at hand. (In addition to the collection of architecture source material, the repository would also contain architecture development work-in-progress.)

At relevant places throughout the ADM, there are reminders to consider which, if any, architecture assets from the Architecture Repository the architect should use. In some cases — for example, in the development of a Technology Architecture — this may be the TOGAF Foundation Architecture (see Part VI: TOGAF Reference Models). In other cases — for example, in the development of a Business Architecture — it may be a reference model for e-Commerce taken from the industry at large.

The criteria for including source materials in an organization's Architecture Repository will typically form part of the enterprise architecture governance process. These governance processes should consider available resources both within and outside the enterprise in order to determine when general resources can be adapted for specific enterprise needs and also to determine where specific solutions can be generalized to support wider re-use.

In executing the ADM, the architect is not only developing a snapshot of the enterprise at particular points in time, but is also populating the organization's own Architecture Repository, with all the architectural assets identified and leveraged along the way, including, but not limited to, the resultant enterprise-specific architecture.

Architecture development is a continuous, cyclical process, and in executing the ADM repeatedly over time, the architect gradually adds more and more content to the organization's Architecture Repository. Although the primary focus of the ADM is on the development of the enterprise-specific architecture, in this wider context the ADM can also be viewed as the process of populating the enterprise's own Architecture Repository with relevant re-usable building blocks taken from the "left", more generic side of the Enterprise Continuum.

In fact, the first execution of the ADM will often be the hardest, since the architecture assets available for re-use will be relatively scarce. Even at this stage of development, however, there will be architecture assets available from external sources such as TOGAF, as well as the IT industry at large, that could be leveraged in support of the effort.

Subsequent executions will be easier, as more and more architecture assets become identified, are used to populate the organization's Architecture Repository, and are thus available for future re-use.

5.1.2   The ADM and the Foundation Architecture

The ADM is also useful to populate the Foundation Architecture of an enterprise. Business requirements of an enterprise may be used to identify the necessary definitions and selections in the Foundation Architecture. This could be a set of re-usable common models, policy and governance definitions, or even as specific as overriding technology selections (e.g., if mandated by law). Population of the Foundation Architecture follows similar principles as for an enterprise architecture, with the difference that requirements for a whole enterprise are restricted to the overall concerns and thus less complete than for a specific enterprise.

It is important to recognize that existing models from these various sources, when integrated, may not necessarily result in a coherent enterprise architecture. "Integratability" of architecture descriptions is considered in Section 5.6.

5.1.3   ADM and Supporting Guidelines and Techniques

Part III: ADM Guidelines & Techniques is is a set of resources — guidelines, templates, checklists, and other detailed materials — that support application of the TOGAF ADM.

The individual guidelines and techniques are described separately in Part III: ADM Guidelines & Techniques so that they can be referenced from the relevant points in the ADM as necessary, rather than having the detailed text clutter the description of the ADM itself.

5.2   Architecture Development Cycle

5.2.1   Key Points

The following are the key points about the ADM:

- The ADM is iterative, over the whole process, between phases, and within phases (see Part III, Chapter 19). For each iteration of the ADM, a fresh decision must be taken as to:
  - The breadth of coverage of the enterprise to be defined
  - The level of detail to be defined
  - The extent of the time period aimed at, including the number and extent of any intermediate time periods
  - The architectural assets to be leveraged, including:
    - Assets created in previous iterations of the ADM cycle within the enterprise
    - Assets available elsewhere in the industry (other frameworks, systems models, vertical industry models, etc.)
- These decisions should be based on a practical assessment of resource and competence availability, and the value that can realistically be expected to accrue to the enterprise from the chosen scope of the architecture work.
- As a generic method, the ADM is intended to be used by enterprises in a wide variety of different geographies and applied in different vertical sectors/industry types. As such, it may be, but does not necessarily have to be, tailored to specific needs. For example, it may be used in conjunction with the set of deliverables of another framework, where these have been deemed to be more appropriate for a specific organization. (For example, many US federal agencies have developed individual frameworks that define the deliverables specific to their particular departmental needs.)

These issues are considered in detail in Section 5.3.

5.2.2   Basic Structure

The basic structure of the ADM is shown in Figure 5-1.

Throughout the ADM cycle, there needs to be frequent validation of results against the original expectations, both those for the whole ADM cycle, and those for the particular phase of the process.

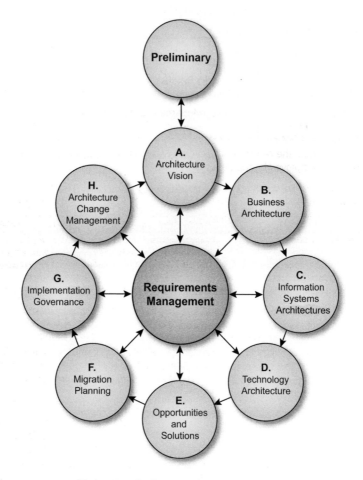

Figure 5-1 Architecture Development Cycle

The phases of the ADM cycle are further divided into steps; for example, the steps within the Technology Architecture phase are as follows:

- Select reference models, viewpoints, and tools
- Develop Baseline Technology Architecture Description
- Develop Target Technology Architecture Description
- Perform gap analysis
- Define roadmap components

- Resolve impacts across the Architecture Landscape
- Conduct formal stakeholder review
- Finalize the Technology Architecture
- Create Architecture Definition Document

The phases of the cycle are described in detail in the following chapters within Part II.

Note that output is generated throughout the process, and that the output in an early phase may be modified in a later phase. The versioning of output is managed through version numbers. In all cases, the ADM numbering scheme is provided as an example. It should be adapted by the architect to meet the requirements of the organization and to work with the architecture tools and repositories employed by the organization.

In particular, a version numbering convention is used within the ADM to illustrate the evolution of Baseline and Target Architecture Definitions. Table 5-1 describes how this convention is used.

Phase	Deliverable	Content	Version	Description
A: Architecture Vision	Architecture Vision	Business Architecture	0.1	Version 0.1 indicates that a high-level outline of the architecture is in place.
		Data Architecture	0.1	Version 0.1 indicates that a high-level outline of the architecture is in place.
		Application Architecture	0.1	Version 0.1 indicates that a high-level outline of the architecture is in place.
		Technology Architecture	0.1	Version 0.1 indicates that a high-level outline of the architecture is in place.
B: Business Architecture	Architecture Definition Document	Business Architecture	1.0	Version 1.0 indicates a formally reviewed, detailed architecture.
C: Information Systems Architecture	Architecture Definition Document	Data Architecture	1.0	Version 1.0 indicates a formally reviewed, detailed architecture.
		Application Architecture	1.0	Version 1.0 indicates a formally reviewed, detailed architecture.
D: Technology Architecture	Architecture Definition Document	Technology Architecture	1.0	Version 1.0 indicates a formally reviewed, detailed architecture.

Table 5-1 ADM Version Numbering Convention

5.3   Adapting the ADM

The ADM is a generic method for architecture development, which is designed to deal with most system and organizational requirements. However, it will often be necessary to modify or extend the ADM to suit specific needs. One of the tasks before applying the ADM is to review its components for applicability, and then tailor them as appropriate to the circumstances of the individual enterprise. This activity may well produce an "enterprise-specific" ADM.

One reason for wanting to adapt the ADM, which it is important to stress, is that the order of the phases in the ADM is to some extent dependent on the maturity of the architecture discipline within the enterprise. For example, if the business case for doing architecture at all is not well recognized, then creating an Architecture Vision is almost always essential; and a detailed Business Architecture often needs to come next, in order to underpin the Architecture Vision, detail the business case for remaining architecture work, and secure the active participation of key stakeholders in that work. In other cases a slightly different order may be preferred; for example, a detailed inventory of the baseline environment may be done before undertaking the Business Architecture.

The order of phases may also be defined by the business and architecture principles of an enterprise. For example, the business principles may dictate that the enterprise be prepared to adjust its business processes to meet the needs of a packaged solution, so that it can be implemented quickly to enable fast response to market changes. In such a case, the Business Architecture (or at least the completion of it) may well follow completion of the Information Systems Architecture or the Technology Architecture.

Another reason for wanting to adapt the ADM is if TOGAF is to be integrated with another enterprise framework (as explained in Part I, Section 2.10). For example, an enterprise may wish to use TOGAF and its generic ADM in conjunction with the well-known Zachman Framework,[2] or another enterprise architecture framework that has a defined set of deliverables specific to a particular vertical sector: Government, Defense, e-Business, Telecommunications, etc. The ADM has been specifically designed with this potential integration in mind.

Other possible reasons for wanting to adapt the ADM include:

- The ADM is one of the many corporate processes that make up the corporate governance model. It is complementary to, and supportive of, other standard program management processes, such as those for authorization, risk management, business planning and budgeting, development planning, systems development, and procurement.

- The ADM is to be used as a method for something other than enterprise architecture; for example, as a general program management method.

- The ADM is being mandated for use by a prime or lead contractor in an outsourcing situation, and needs to be tailored to achieve a suitable compromise between the contractor's existing practices and the contracting enterprise's requirements.

- The enterprise is a small-to-medium enterprise, and wishes to use a "cut-down" method more attuned to the reduced level of resources and system complexity typical of such an environment.

- The enterprise is very large and complex, comprising many separate but interlinked "enterprises" within an overall collaborative business framework, and the architecture method needs to be adapted to recognize this. Different approaches to planning and

---

2.   The Zachman Institute for Framework Advancement (ZIFA) is at: www.zifa.org.

integration may be used in such cases, including the following (possibly in combination):

— Top-down planning and development — designing the whole interconnected meta-enterprise as a single entity (an exercise that typically stretches the limits of practicality)

— Development of a "generic" or "reference" architecture, typical of the enterprises within the organization, but not representing any specific enterprise, which individual enterprises are then expected to adapt in order to produce an architecture "instance" suited to the particular enterprise concerned.

— Replication — developing a specific architecture for one enterprise, implementing it as a proof-of-concept, and then taking that as a "reference architecture" to be cloned in other enterprises.

- In a vendor or production environment, a generic architecture for a family of related products is often referred to as a "Product Line Architecture", and the analogous process to that outlined above is termed "(Architecture-based) Product Line Engineering". The ADM is targeted primarily at architects in IT user enterprises, but a vendor organization whose products are IT-based might well wish to adapt it as a generic method for a Product Line Architecture development.

5.4   Architecture Governance

The ADM, whether adapted by the organization or used as documented here, is a key process to be managed in the same manner as other architecture artifacts classified through the Enterprise Continuum and held in the Architecture Repository. The Architecture Board should be satisfied that the method is being applied correctly across all phases of an architecture development iteration. Compliance with the ADM is fundamental to the governance of the architecture, to ensure that all considerations are made and all required deliverables are produced.

The management of all architectural artifacts, governance, and related processes should be supported by a controlled environment. Typically this would be based on one or more repositories supporting versioned object and process control and status.

The major information areas managed by a governance repository should contain the following types of information:

- **Reference Data** (collateral from the organization's own repositories/Enterprise Continuum, including external data; e.g., COBIT, ITIL): Used for guidance and instruction during project implementation. This includes the details of information outlined above. The reference data includes a description of the governance procedures themselves.

- **Process Status**: All information regarding the state of any governance processes will be managed; examples of this include outstanding compliance requests, dispensation requests, and compliance assessments investigations.

- **Audit Information**: This will record all completed governance process actions and will be used to support:

  — Key decisions and responsible personnel for any architecture project that has been sanctioned by the governance process

— A reference for future architectural and supporting process developments, guidance, and precedence

The governance artifacts and process are themselves part of the contents of the Architecture Repository.

5.5   Scoping the Architecture

There are many reasons to constrain (or restrict) the scope of the architectural activity to be undertaken, most of which relate to limits in:

- The organizational authority of the team producing the architecture

- The objectives and stakeholder concerns to be addressed within the architecture

- The availability of people, finance, and other resources

The scope chosen for the architecture activity should ideally allow the work of all architects within the enterprise to be effectively governed and integrated. This requires a set of aligned "architecture partitions" that ensure architects are not working on duplicate or conflicting activities. It also requires the definition of re-use and compliance relationships between architecture partitions.

The division of the enterprise and its architecture-related activity is discussed in more detail in Chapter 40.

Four dimensions are typically used in order to define and limit the scope of an architecture:

- **Enterprise Scope or Focus**: What is the full extent of the enterprise, and how much of that extent should the architecting effort focus on?

  — Many enterprises are very large, effectively comprising a federation of organizational units that could validly be considered enterprises in their own right.

  — The modern enterprise increasingly extends beyond its traditional boundaries, to embrace a fuzzy combination of traditional business enterprise combined with suppliers, customers, and partners.

- **Architecture Domains**: A complete enterprise architecture description should contain all four architecture domains (business, data, application, technology), but the realities of resource and time constraints often mean there is not enough time, funding, or resources to build a top-down, all-inclusive architecture description encompassing all four architecture domains, even if the enterprise scope is chosen to be less than the full extent of the overall enterprise.

- **Vertical Scope or Level of Detail**: To what level of detail should the architecting effort go? How much architecture is "enough"? What is the appropriate demarcation between the architecture effort and other, related activities (system design, system engineering, system development)?

- **Time Period**: What is the time period that needs to be articulated for the Architecture Vision, and does it make sense (in terms of practicality and resources) for the same period to be covered in the detailed architecture description? If not, how many intermediate Target Architectures are to be defined, and what are their time periods?

Typically, the scope of an architecture is first expressed in terms of enterprise scope, time period, and level of detail. Once the organizational scope is understood, a suitable combination of architecture domains can be selected that are appropriate to the problem being addressed.

Figure 5-2 shows how architecture deliverables from different phases of the ADM may actually occupy different scope areas, with each phase progressively adding more specific detail.

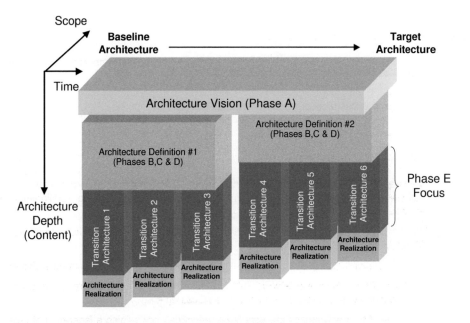

Figure 5-2 Progressive Architecture Development

This approach can be particularly effective when a long-term vision is needed, but the initial stages of implementation will only deliver a fraction of that vision. In these circumstances the more detailed architectures can initially be produced to address a much shorter time period, with additional architectures developed "just in time" for the next phase of implementation.

An alternative and complementary approach to segmenting the architecture in this respect is to use a full cycle of the ADM to address a particular area of scope. Subsequent ADM cycles can then be used to create more detailed architectures, as needed.

Techniques for using the ADM to develop a number of related architectures are discussed in Section 20.4.

The four dimensions of architecture scope are explored in detail below. In each case, particularly in largescale environments where architectures are necessarily developed in a federated manner, there is a danger of architects optimizing within their own scope of activity, instead of at the level of the overall enterprise. It is often necessary to sub-optimize in a particular area, in order to optimize at the enterprise level. The aim should always be to seek the highest level of commonality and focus on scalable and re-usable modules in order to maximize re-use at the enterprise level.

5.5.1   Enterprise Scope/Focus

One of the key decisions is the focus of the architecture effort, in terms of the breadth of overall enterprise activity to be covered (which specific business sectors, functions, organizations, geographical areas, etc.). *ZACHMAN (WHAT, HOW, WHERE, WHO, WHEN WHY)*

One important factor in this context is the increasing tendency for largescale architecture developments to be undertaken in the form of "federated architectures" — independently developed, maintained, and managed architectures that are subsequently integrated within a meta-architecture framework. Such a framework specifies the principles for interoperability, migration, and conformance. This allows specific business units to have architectures developed and governed as stand-alone architecture projects. More details and guidance on specifying the interoperability requirements for different solutions can be found in Chapter 29.

Complex architectures are extremely hard to manage, not only in terms of the architecture development process itself, but also in terms of getting buy-in from large numbers of stakeholders. This in turn requires a very disciplined approach to identifying common architectural components, and management of the commonalities between federated components — deciding how to integrate, what to integrate, etc.

There are two basic approaches to federated architecture development:

- The overall enterprise is divided up "vertically", into enterprise "segments", each representing an independent business sector within the overall enterprise, and each having its own enterprise architecture with potentially all four architecture domains (business, data, application, technology). These separate, multi-domain architectures can be developed with a view to subsequent integration, but they can also be implemented in their own right, possibly with interim target environments defined, and therefore represent value to the enterprise in their own right.

- The overall enterprise architecture is divided up "horizontally", into architectural "super-domains", in which each architecture domain (business, data, application, technology) covering the full extent of the overall enterprise is developed and approved as a major project independently of the others, possibly by different personnel. For example, a Business Architecture for the complete overall enterprise would form one independent architecture project, and the other domains would be developed and approved in separate projects, with a view to subsequent integration.

SEEMS THE BEST

The vertical segmentation approach discussed above is supported in TOGAF by the use of "partitioning" architectures into areas of discrete scope coverage. The approach to partitioning is discussed in Part V, Chapter 40.

Current experience does seem to indicate that, in order to cope with the increasingly broad focus and ubiquity of architectures, it is often necessary to have a number of different architectures existing across an enterprise, focused on particular timeframes, business functions, or business requirements; and this phenomenon would seem to call into question the feasibility of a single enterprise-wide architecture for every business function or purpose. In such cases, the paramount need is to manage and exploit the "federations" of architecture. A good starting point is to adopt a publish-and-subscribe model that allows architecture to be brought under a governance framework. In such a model, architecture developers and architecture consumers in projects (the supply and demand sides of architecture work) sign up to a mutually beneficial framework of governance that ensures that:

- Architectural material is of good quality, up-to-date, fit-for-purpose, and published (reviewed and agreed to be made public).

- Usage of architecture material can be monitored, and compliance with standards, models, and principles can be exhibited, via:

  — A Compliance Assessment process that describes what the user is subscribing to, and assesses their level of compliance

  — A dispensation process that may grant dispensations from adherence to architecture standards and guidelines in specific cases (usually with a strong business imperative)

Publish and subscribe techniques are being developed as part of general IT governance and specifically for the Defense sphere.

5.5.2   Architecture Domains

A complete enterprise architecture should address all four architecture domains (business, data, application, technology), but the realities of resource and time constraints often mean there is not enough time, funding, or resources to build a top-down, all-inclusive architecture description encompassing all four architecture domains.

Architecture descriptions will normally be built with a specific purpose in mind — a specific set of business drivers that drive the architecture development — and clarifying the specific issue(s) that the architecture description is intended to help explore, and the questions it is expected to help answer, is an important part of the initial phase of the ADM.

For example, if the purpose of a particular architecture effort is to define and examine technology options for achieving a particular capability, and the fundamental business processes are not open to modification, then a full Business Architecture may well not be warranted. However, because the Data, Application, and Technology Architectures build on the Business Architecture, the Business Architecture still needs to be thought through and understood.

While circumstances may sometimes dictate building an architecture description not containing all four architecture domains, it should be understood that such an architecture cannot, by definition, be a complete enterprise architecture. One of the risks is lack of consistency and therefore ability to integrate. Integration either needs to come later — with its own costs and risks — or the risks and trade-offs involved in not developing a complete and integrated architecture need to be articulated by the architect, and communicated to and understood by the enterprise management.

5.5.3   Vertical Scope/Level of Detail

Care should be taken to judge the appropriate level of detail to be captured, based on the intended use of the enterprise architecture and the decisions to be made based on it. It is important that a consistent and equal level of depth be completed in each architecture domain (business, data, application, technology) included in the architecture effort. If pertinent detail is omitted, the architecture may not be useful. If unnecessary detail is included, the architecture effort may exceed the time and resources available, and/or the resultant architecture may be confusing or cluttered. Developing architectures at different levels of detail within an enterprise is discussed in more detail in Chapter 20.

It is also important to predict the future uses of the architecture so that, within resource limitations, the architecture can be structured to accommodate future tailoring, extension, or re-use. The depth and detail of the enterprise architecture needs to be sufficient for its purpose, and no more.

However, it is not necessary to aim to complete a detailed architecture description at the first attempt. Future iterations of the ADM, in a further architecture development cycle, will build on the artifacts and the competencies created during the current iteration.

The bottom line is that there is a need to document all the models in an enterprise, to whatever level of detail is affordable, within an assessment of the likelihood of change and the concomitant risk, and bearing in mind the need to integrate the components of the different architecture domains (business, data, application, technology). The key is to understand the status of the enterprise's architecture work, and what can realistically be achieved with the resources and competencies available, and then focus on identifying and delivering the value that is achievable. Stakeholder value is a key focus: too broad a scope may deter some stakeholders (no return on investment).

5.5.4   Time Period

The ADM is described in terms of a single cycle of Architecture Vision, and a set of Target Architectures (Business, Data, Application, Technology) that enable the implementation of the vision.

However, when the enterprise scope is large, and/or the Target Architectures particularly complex, the development of Target Architecture Descriptions may encounter major difficulties, or indeed prove "mission impossible", especially if being undertaken for the first time.

In such cases, a wider view may be taken, whereby an enterprise is represented by several different architecture instances (for example, strategic, segment, capability), each representing the enterprise at a particular point in time. One architecture instance will represent the current enterprise state (the "as-is", or baseline). Another architecture instance, perhaps defined only partially, will represent the ultimate target end-state (the "vision"). In-between, intermediate or "Transition Architecture" instances may be defined, each comprising its own set of Target Architecture Descriptions. An example of how this might be achieved is given in Part III, Chapter 20.

By this approach, the Target Architecture work is split into two or more discrete stages:

1. First, develop Target Architecture Descriptions for the overall (largescale) system, demonstrating a response to stakeholder objectives and concerns for a relatively distant timeframe (for example, a six-year period).

2. Then develop one or more "Transition Architecture" descriptions, as increments or plateaus, each in line with and converging on the Target Architecture Descriptions, and describing the specifics of the increment concerned.

In such an approach, the Target Architectures are evolutionary in nature, and require periodic review and update according to evolving business requirements and developments in technology, whereas the Transition Architectures are (by design) incremental in nature, and in principle should not evolve during the implementation phase of the increment, in order to avoid the "moving target" syndrome. This, of course, is only possible if the implementation schedule is under tight control and relatively short (typically less than two years).

The Target Architectures remain relatively generic, and because of that are less vulnerable to obsolescence than the Transition Architectures. They embody only the key strategic architectural decisions, which should be blessed by the stakeholders from the outset, whereas the detailed architectural decisions in the Transition Architectures are deliberately postponed as far as possible (i.e., just before implementation) in order to improve responsiveness *vis a vis* new technologies and products.

The enterprise evolves by migrating to each of these Transition Architectures in turn. As each Transition Architecture is implemented, the enterprise achieves a consistent, operational state on the way to the ultimate vision. However, this vision itself is periodically updated to reflect changes in the business and technology environment, and in effect may never actually be achieved, as originally described. The whole process continues for as long as the enterprise exists and continues to change.

Such a breakdown of the architecture description into a family of related architecture products of course requires effective management of the set and their relationships.

5.6   Architecture Integration

There is a need to provide an integration framework that sits above the individual architectures. This can be an "enterprise framework" such as the Content Framework (see Part IV, Chapter 33) to position the various domains and artifacts, or it may be a meta-architecture framework (i.e., principles, models, and standards) to allow interoperability, migration, and conformance between federated architectures. The purpose of this meta-architecture framework is to:

- Allow the architect to understand how components fit into the framework

- Derive the architectural models that focus on enterprise-level capabilities

- Define the conformance standards that enable the integration of components for maximum leverage and re-use

There are varying degrees of architecture description "integratability". At the low end, integratability means that different architecture descriptions (whether prepared by one organizational unit or many) should have a "look-and-feel" that is sufficiently similar to enable critical relationships between the descriptions to be identified, thereby at least indicating the need for further investigation. At the high end, integratability ideally means that different descriptions should be capable of being combined into a single logical and physical representation.

Architectures that are created to address a subset of issues within an enterprise require a consistent frame of reference so that they can be considered as a group as well as point deliverables. The dimensions that are used to define the scope boundary of a single architecture (e.g., level of detail, architecture domain, etc.) are typically the same dimensions that must be addressed when considering the integration of many architectures. Figure 5-3 illustrates how different types of architecture need to co-exist.

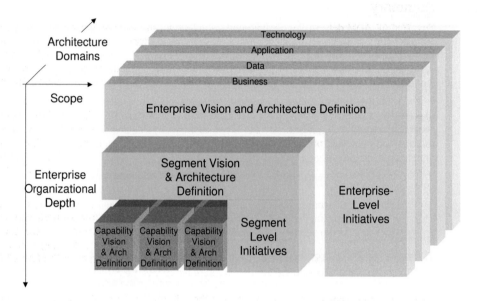

Figure 5-3 Integration of Architecture Artifacts

At the present time, the state of the art is such that architecture integration can be accomplished only at the lower end of the integratability spectrum. Key factors to consider are the granularity and level of detail in each artifact, and the maturity of standards for the interchange of architectural descriptions.

As organizations address common themes (such as Service Oriented Architecture (SOA), and integrated information infrastructure), and universal data models and standard data structures emerge, integration toward the high end of the spectrum will be facilitated. However, there will always be the need for effective standards governance to reduce the need for manual co-ordination and conflict resolution.

5.7 Summary

The TOGAF ADM defines a recommended sequence for the various phases and steps involved in developing an architecture, but it cannot recommend a scope — this has to be determined by the organization itself, bearing in mind that the recommended sequence of development in the ADM process is an iterative one, with the depth and breadth of scope and deliverables increasing with each iteration. Each iteration will add resources to the organization's Architecture Repository.

The choice of scope is critical to the success of the architecting effort. The key factor here is the sheer complexity of a complete, horizontally and vertically integrated enterprise architecture, as represented by a fully populated instantiation of the Zachman Framework. Very few enterprise architecture developments today actually undertake such an effort in a single development project, simply because it is widely recognized to be at the limits of the state of the art, a fact that John Zachman himself recognizes:

> "Some day, you are going to wish you had all these models ... However, I am not so altruistic to think that we have to have them all today ... or even that we understand how to build and manage them all today. But the very fact that we can identify conceptually where we want to get *some* day, makes us think more about what we are doing in the current timeframe that might prevent us from getting to where we want to go in the future." (Quote from email correspondence from John Zachman to George Brundage.)

John Zachman himself likes to point out the alternatives available to those who can't countenance the amount of work implied in developing all the models required in his framework. There are only three choices:

1. Trial and error ("knocking down the walls")

2. Starting from new

3. Reverse engineering the architecture from the existing systems

all of which are risky and/or hugely expensive. What is necessary due to the pace of change is to have a set of readily deployable artifacts and a process for assembling them swiftly.

While such a complete framework is useful (indeed, essential) to have in mind as the ultimate long-term goal, in practice there is a key decision to be made as to the scope of a specific enterprise architecture effort. This being the case, it is vital to understand the basis on which scoping decisions are being made, and to set expectations right for what is the goal of the effort.

The main guideline is to focus on what creates value to the enterprise, and to select horizontal and vertical scope, and time periods, accordingly. Whether or not this is the first time around, understand that this exercise will be repeated, and that future iterations will build on what is being created in the current effort, adding greater width and depth.

Chapter 6: Preliminary Phase

This chapter describes the preparation and initiation activities required to meet the business directive for a new enterprise architecture, including the definition of an Organization-Specific Architecture framework and the definition of principles.

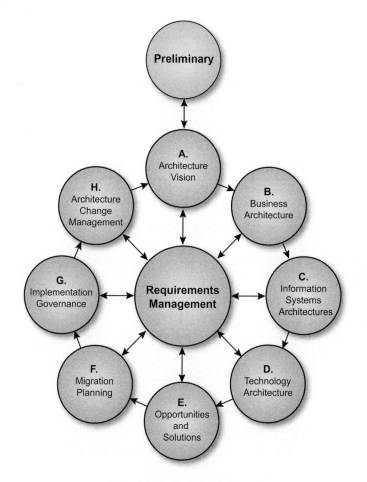

Figure 6-1 Preliminary Phase

6.1   Objectives

The objectives of the Preliminary phase are:

- To review the organizational context for conducting enterprise architecture
- To identify the sponsor stakeholder(s) and other major stakeholders impacted by the business directive to create an enterprise architecture and determine their requirements and priorities from the enterprise, their relationships with the enterprise, and required working behaviors with each other
- To ensure that everyone who will be involved in, or benefit from, this approach is committed to the success of the architectural process
- To enable the architecture sponsor to create requirements for work across the affected business areas
- To identify and scope the elements of the enterprise organizations affected by the business directive and define the constraints and assumptions (particularly in a federated architecture environment)
- To define the "architecture footprint" for the organization — the people responsible for performing architecture work, where they are located, and their responsibilities
- To define the framework and detailed methodologies that are going to be used to develop enterprise architectures in the organization concerned (typically, an adaptation of the generic ADM)
- To confirm a governance and support framework that will provide business process and resources for architecture governance through the ADM cycle; these will confirm the fitness-for-purpose of the Target Architecture and measure its ongoing effectiveness (normally includes a pilot project)
- To select and implement supporting tools and other infrastructure to support the architecture activity
- To define the architecture principles that will form part of the constraints on any architecture work

6.2   Approach

This Preliminary phase is about defining "where, what, why, who, and how we do architecture" in the enterprise concerned. The main aspects are as follows:

- Defining the enterprise
- Identifying key drivers and elements in the organizational context
- Defining the requirements for architecture work
- Defining the architecture principles that will inform any architecture work
- Defining the framework to be used
- Defining the relationships between management frameworks

- Evaluating the enterprise architecture maturity

The enterprise architecture provides a strategic, top-down view of an organization to enable executives, planners, architects, and engineers to coherently co-ordinate, integrate, and conduct their activities. The enterprise architecture framework provides the strategic context for this team to operate within.

The term enterprise architecture was first coined by John Zachman as a means of creating a coherent way of modeling an enterprise to enable the efficient and effective deployment of IT. It leveraged concepts from other management and engineering frameworks making it easier to integrate enterprise architecture into the overall corporate culture and governance.

Therefore, developing the enterprise architecture is not a solitary activity and the enterprise architects need to recognize the interoperability between their frameworks and the rest of the business.

Strategic, interim, and tactical business objectives and aspirations need to be met. Similarly, the enterprise architecture needs to reflect this requirement and allow for operation of architecture discipline at different levels within the organization.

Depending on the scale of the enterprise and the level of budgetary commitment to enterprise architecture discipline, a number of approaches may be adopted to sub-divide or partition architecture teams, processes, and deliverables. Approaches for architecture partitioning are discussed in Part V, Chapter 40. The Preliminary phase should be used to determine the desired approach to partitioning and to establish the groundwork for the selected approach to be put into practice.

When using an iterative process for architecture development, the activities within the Preliminary phase may be revisited a number of times, alongside related activities within the Architecture Vision phase, in order to ensure that the tailored framework is suitable to address a specific architecture problem.

6.2.1   Enterprise

One of the main challenges of enterprise architecture is that of enterprise scope. In many organizations enterprise architecture is part of the Chief Information Officer (CIO) responsibilities and accountabilities and is considered a strategic planning asset that is becoming increasingly an integral part of business management.

In other organizations, enterprise architecture has an even broader remit and more generally supports the management of strategic change across all aspects of the enterprise. In either case, the strategic perspective that enterprise architecture can bring is required from the outset.

Therefore, the scope will determine those stakeholders who will derive most benefit from the new or enhanced enterprise architecture. It is imperative that a sponsor is appointed at this stage to ensure that the resultant activity has resources to proceed and the clear support of the business management. The enterprise may encompass many organizations and the duties of the sponsors are to ensure that all stakeholders are included in some part in the resultant architecture work, definitions, and work products.

6.2.2   Organizational Context

In order to make effective and informed decisions about the framework for architecture to be used within a particular enterprise, it is necessary to understand the context surrounding the architecture framework. Specific areas to consider would include:

- The commercial models for enterprise architecture and budgetary plans for enterprise architecture activity. Where no such plans exist, the Preliminary phase should be used to develop a budget plan.

- The stakeholders for architecture in the enterprise; their key issues and concerns.

- The intentions and culture of the organization, as captured within board business directives, business imperatives, business strategies, business principles, business goals, and business drivers.

- Current processes that support execution of change and operation of IT, including the structure of the process and also the level of rigor and formality applied within the organization. Areas for focus should include:

  — Current methods for architecture description

  — Current project management frameworks and methods

  — Current systems management frameworks and methods

  — Current project portfolio management processes and methods

  — Current application portfolio management processes and methods

  — Current technology portfolio management processes and methods

  — Current information portfolio management processes and methods

  — Current systems design and development frameworks and methods

- The Baseline Architecture landscape, including the state of the enterprise and also how the landscape is currently represented in documentation form.

- The skills and capabilities of the enterprise and specific organizations that will be adopting the framework.

Review of the organizational context should provide valuable requirements on how to tailor the architecture framework in terms of:

- Level of formality and rigor to be applied

- Level of sophistication and expenditure required

- Touch-points with other organizations, processes, roles, and responsibilities

- Focus of content coverage

6.2.3 Requirements for Architecture Work

The business imperatives behind the enterprise architecture work drive the requirements and performance metrics for the architecture work. They should be sufficiently clear so that this phase may scope the business outcomes and resource requirements, and define the outline enterprise business information requirements and associated strategies of the enterprise architecture work to be done. For example, these may include:

- Business requirements
- Cultural aspirations
- Organization intents
- Strategic intent
- Forecast financial requirements

Just one or a combination of these need to be articulated so that the sponsor can identify all the key decision-makers and stakeholders involved and generate a Request for Architecture Work.

6.2.4 Principles

The Preliminary phase defines the architecture principles that will form part of the constraints on any architecture work undertaken in the enterprise. The issues involved in this are explained in Part III, Chapter 23.

The definition of architecture principles is fundamental to the development of an enterprise architecture. Architecture work is informed by business principles as well as architecture principles. The architecture principles themselves are also normally based in part on business principles. Defining business principles normally lies outside the scope of the architecture function. However, depending on how such principles are defined and promulgated within the enterprise, it may be possible for the set of architecture principles to also restate, or cross-refer to a set of business principles, business goals, and strategic business drivers defined elsewhere within the enterprise. Within an architecture project, the architect will normally need to ensure that the definitions of these business principles, goals, and strategic drivers are current, and to clarify any areas of ambiguity.

The issue of architecture governance is closely linked to that of architecture principles. The body responsible for governance will also normally be responsible for approving the architecture principles, and for resolving architecture issues. This will normally be one of the principles cited. The issues involved in governance are explained in Part VII, Chapter 50.

6.2.5 Management Frameworks

The TOGAF Architecture Development Method (ADM) is a generic method, intended to be used by enterprises in a wide variety of industry types and geographies. It is also designed for use with a wide variety of other enterprise architecture frameworks, if required (although it can be used perfectly well in its own right, without adaptation).

TOGAF has to co-exist with and enhance the operational capabilities of other management frameworks that are present within any organization either formally or informally. In addition to these frameworks, most organizations have a method for the development of solutions, most of which have an IT component. The significance of systems is that it brings together the various domains (also known as People, Processes, and Material/Technology) to deliver a business capability.

The main frameworks suggested to be co-ordinated with TOGAF are:

- **Business Capability Management** (Business Direction and Planning) that determines what business capabilities are required to deliver business value including the definition of return on investment and the requisite control/performance measures.

- **Portfolio/Project Management Methods** that determine how a company manages its change initiatives.

- **Operations Management Methods** that describe how a company runs its day-to-day operations, including IT.

- **Solution Development Methods** that formalize the way that business systems are delivered in accordance with the structures developed in the IT architecture.

As illustrated in Figure 6-2, these frameworks are not discrete and there are significant overlaps between them and the Business Capability Management. The latter includes the delivery of performance measured business value.

The overall significance is that the enterprise architect applying TOGAF cannot narrowly focus on the IT implementation, but must be aware of the impact that the architecture has on the entire enterprise.

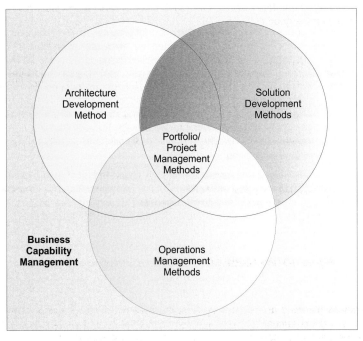

Figure 6-2 Management Frameworks to Co-ordinate with TOGAF

The Preliminary phase therefore involves doing any necessary work to adapt the ADM to define an organization-specific framework, using either the TOGAF deliverables or the deliverables of another framework. The issues involved in this are discussed in Section 5.3.

6.2.6   Relating the Management Frameworks

Figure 6-3 illustrates a more detailed set of dependencies between the various frameworks and business planning activity that incorporates the enterprise's strategic plan and direction. The enterprise architecture can be used to provide a structure for all of the corporate initiatives, the Portfolio Management Framework can be used to deliver the components of the architecture, and the Operations Management Framework supports incorporation of these new components within the corporate infrastructure.

The business planners are present throughout the process and are in a position to support and enforce the architecture by retaining approval for resources at the various stages of planning and development.

The solution development methodology is used within the Portfolio Management Framework to plan, create, and deliver the architectural components specified in the portfolio and project charters. These deliverables include, but are not exclusively, IT; for example, a new building, a new set of skills, production equipment, hiring, marketing, and so on. Enterprise architecture potentially provides the context for all enterprise activities.

The management frameworks are required to complement each other and work in close harmony for the good of the enterprise.

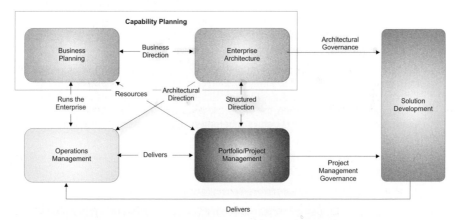

Figure 6-3 Interoperability and Relationships between Management Frameworks

Business planning at the strategy level provides the initial direction to enterprise architecture. Updates at the annual planning level provide a finer level of ongoing guidance. Capability-based Planning is one of many popular techniques for business planning.

Enterprise architecture structures the business planning into an integrated framework that regards the enterprise as a system or system of systems. This integrated approach will validate the business plan and can provide valuable feedback to the corporate planners. In some organizations, the enterprise architects have been moved to or work very closely with the strategic direction groups. TOGAF delivers a framework for enterprise architecture.

Portfolio/project management is the delivery framework that receives the structured, detailed direction that enables them to plan and build what is required, knowing that each assigned deliverable will be in context (i.e., the piece of the puzzle that they deliver will fit into the corporate puzzle that is the enterprise architecture). Often this framework is based upon the Project Management Institute or UK Office of Government Commerce (PRINCE2) project management methodologies. Project architectures and detailed out-of-context design are often based upon systems design methodologies.

Operations management receives the deliverables and then integrates and sustains them within the corporate infrastructure. Often the IT service management services are based upon ISO 20000 or BS15000 (ITIL).

6.2.7 Planning for Enterprise Architecture/Business Change Maturity Evaluation

Capability Maturity Models (CMMs — detailed in Part VII, Chapter 51) are useful ways of assessing selected factors. Once the factors have been determined, it is preferable that the capability models be customized for each factor and then used in workshops as a guide for evaluating how to best develop and implement the architecture. These workshops could serve as an excellent way of enlisting major stakeholder support within the organization.

The actual levels of maturity provide a strategic measure of the organization's ability to change, as well as a series of sequential steps to improve that ability. It is mainly a business as well as a technical assessment and gives executives (line of business as well as IT) an insight into how to pragmatically move forward.

It is important that the workshops include a representation from all of the stakeholders identified in the Preliminary phase and later.

A good enterprise architecture maturity model covers a wide range of enterprise characteristics, both business and technical, many of which can already be determined through an analysis of the derived Target Architecture. Organizations can determine their own factors and derive the appropriate maturity models, but it is recommended to take an existing "open" model and customize it if only to avoid delays inherent in getting organizational agreement on the factors and maturity models.

A good example of such a model is the NASCIO Enterprise Architecture Maturity Model[3] which has adopted the following criteria:

- **Administration**: Governance roles and responsibilities.
- **Planning**: Enterprise Architecture program roadmap and Implementation Plan.
- **Framework**: Processes and templates used for enterprise architecture.
- **Blueprint**: Collection of the actual standards and specifications.
- **Communication**: Education and distribution of enterprise architecture and blueprint detail.

---

3. National Association of State CIOs (NASCIO) Enterprise Architecture Maturity Model, Version 1.3, December 2003.

- **Compliance**: Adherence to published standards, processes, and other enterprise architecture elements, and the processes to document and track variances from those standards.

- **Integration**: Touch-points of management processes to the enterprise architecture.

- **Involvement**: Support of the enterprise architecture program throughout the organization.

Other examples include the US Federal Enterprise Architecture Maturity Model. Even though the models are originally from government, they are equally applicable to industry.

6.3 Inputs

This section defines the inputs to the Preliminary phase.

6.3.1 Reference Materials External to the Enterprise

- TOGAF

- Other architecture framework(s), if required

6.3.2 Non-Architectural Inputs

- Board strategies and board business plans, business strategy, business principles, business goals, and business drivers, when pre-existing

- Major frameworks operating in the business; e.g., portfolio/project management

- Governance and legal frameworks, including architecture governance strategy, when pre-existing

- Budget for scoping project

- Partnership and contract agreements

- IT strategy

6.3.3 Architectural Inputs

Pre-existing models for operating an enterprise architecture capability can be used as a baseline for the Preliminary phase. Inputs would include:

- Organizational Model for Enterprise Architecture (see Part IV, Section 36.2.16), including:
  - Scope of organizations impacted
  - Maturity assessment, gaps, and resolution approach
  - Roles and responsibilities for architecture team(s)
  - Budget requirements

- — Governance and support strategy
- ■ Existing Architecture Framework, if any, including:
  - — Architecture method
  - — Architecture content (deliverables and artifacts)
  - — Configured and deployed tools
- ■ Existing architecture principles, if any (see Part IV, Section 36.2.4)
- ■ Existing Architecture Repository (see Part IV, Section 36.2.5), if any (framework description, architectural descriptions, existing target descriptions, etc.)

6.4   Steps

The TOGAF ADM is a generic method, intended to be used by a wide variety of different enterprises, and in conjunction with a wide variety of other architecture frameworks, if required. The Preliminary phase therefore involves doing any necessary work to initiate and adapt the ADM to define an organization-specific framework. The issues involved with adapting the ADM to a specific organizational context are discussed in detail in Section 5.3.

The level of detail addressed in the Preliminary phase will depend on the scope and goals of the overall architecture effort.

The order of the steps in the Preliminary phase (see below) as well as the time at which they are formally started and completed should be adapted to the situation at hand in accordance with the established architecture governance.

The steps within the Preliminary phase are as follows:

- ■ Scope the enterprise organizations impacted (see Section 6.4.1)
- ■ Confirm governance and support frameworks (see Section 6.4.2)
- ■ Define and establish enterprise architecture team and organization (see Section 6.4.3)
- ■ Identify and establish architecture principles (see Section 6.4.4)
- ■ Select and tailor architecture framework(s) (see Section 6.4.5)
- ■ Implement architecture tools (see Section 6.4.6)

6.4.1   Scope the Enterprise Organizations Impacted

- ■ Identify core enterprise (units) — those who are most affected and achieve most value from the work
- ■ Identify soft enterprise (units) — those who will see change to their capability and work with core units but are otherwise not directly affected
- ■ Identify extended enterprise (units) — those units outside the scoped enterprise who will be affected in their own enterprise architecture

- Identify communities involved (enterprises) — those stakeholders who will be affected and who are in groups of communities
- Identify governance involved, including legal frameworks and geographies (enterprises)

6.4.2 Confirm Governance and Support Frameworks

The architecture framework will form the keystone to the flavor (centralized or federated, light or heavy, etc.) of architecture governance organization and guidelines that need to be developed. Part of the major output of this phase is a framework for architecture governance. We need to understand how architectural material (standards, guidelines, models, compliance reports, etc.) is brought under governance; i.e., what type of governance repository characteristics are going to be required, what relationships and status recording are necessary to ascertain which governance process (dispensation, compliance, take-on, retirement, etc.) has ownership of an architectural artifact.

It is likely that the existing governance and support models of an organization will need to change to support the newly adopted architecture framework.

To manage the organizational change required to adopt the new architectural framework, the current enterprise governance and support models will need to be assessed to understand their overall shape and content. Additionally, the sponsors and stakeholders for architecture will need to be consulted on potential impacts that could occur.

Upon completion of this step, the architecture touch-points and likely impacts should be understood and agreed by relevant stakeholders.

6.4.3 Define and Establish Enterprise Architecture Team and Organization

- Determine existing enterprise and business capability
- Conduct an enterprise architecture/business change maturity assessment, if required
- Identify gaps in existing work areas
- Allocate key roles and responsibilities for enterprise architecture capability management and governance
- Define requests for change to existing business programs and projects:
    - Inform existing enterprise architecture and IT architecture work of stakeholder requirements
    - Request assessment of impact on their plans and work
    - Identify common areas of interest
    - Identify any critical differences and conflicts of interest
    - Produce requests for change to stakeholder activities
- Scope new enterprise architecture work
- Determine constraints on enterprise architecture work

- Review and agree with sponsors and board
- Assess budget requirements

6.4.4 Identify and Establish Architecture Principles

Architecture principles (see Part III, Chapter 23) are based on business principles and are critical in setting the foundation for architectural governance. Once the organizational context is understood and a tailored framework is in place, it is important to define a set of architecture principles that is appropriate to the enterprise.

6.4.5 Select and Tailor Architecture Framework(s)

Assuming that TOGAF is the base framework to be adopted by the enterprise, in this step determine what, if any, tailoring is required. Consider the need for:

- **Terminology Tailoring**: As much as is possible, architecture practitioners should use terminology that is generally understood across the enterprise. Tailoring should produce an agreed terminology set for description of architectural content.

- **Process Tailoring**: The TOGAF ADM provides a generic process for carrying out architecture. Process tailoring provides the opportunity to remove tasks that are already carried out elsewhere in the organization, add organization-specific tasks (such as specific checkpoints) and to align the ADM processes to external process frameworks and touch-points. Key touch-points to be addressed would include:

  — Links to (project and service) portfolio management processes

  — Links to project lifecycle

  — Links to operations handover processes

  — Links to operational management processes (including configuration management, change management, and service management)

  — Links to procurement processes

- **Content Tailoring**: Using the TOGAF Architecture Content Framework and Enterprise Continuum as a basis, tailoring of content structure and classification approach allows adoption of third-party content frameworks and also allows for customization of the framework to support organization-specific requirements.

6.4.6 Implement Architecture Tools

The level of formality used to define and manage architecture content will be highly dependent on the scale, sophistication, and culture of the architecture function within the organization. With an understanding of the desired approach to architecture, it is possible to select appropriate architecture tools to underpin the architecture function.

The approach to tools may be based on relatively informal usage of standard office productivity applications, or may be based on a customized deployment of specialist architecture tools. Depending on the level of sophistication, the implementation of tools may range from a trivial task to a more involved system implementation activity.

Criteria for selection of architecture tools are discussed in Part V, Chapter 42.

6.5 Outputs

The outputs of the Preliminary phase are:

- Organizational Model for Enterprise Architecture (see Part IV, Section 36.2.16), including:
  - Scope of organizations impacted
  - Maturity assessment, gaps, and resolution approach
  - Roles and responsibilities for architecture team(s)
  - Constraints on architecture work
  - Re-use requirements
  - Budget requirements
  - Requests for change
  - Governance and support strategy
- Tailored Architecture Framework (see Part IV, Section 36.2.21), including:
  - Tailored architecture method
  - Tailored architecture content (deliverables and artifacts)
  - Architecture principles (see Part IV, Section 36.2.4)
  - Configured and deployed tools, including evaluation report if conducted
- Initial Architecture Repository (see Part IV, Section 36.2.5), populated with framework content
- Restatement of, or reference to, business principles, business goals, and business drivers (see Part IV, Section 36.2.9)
- Request for Architecture Work (see Part IV, Section 36.2.17)
- Governance Framework

Chapter 7: Phase A: Architecture Vision

This chapter describes the initial phase of the Architecture Development Method (ADM). It includes information about defining the scope, identifying the stakeholders, creating the Architecture Vision, and obtaining approvals.

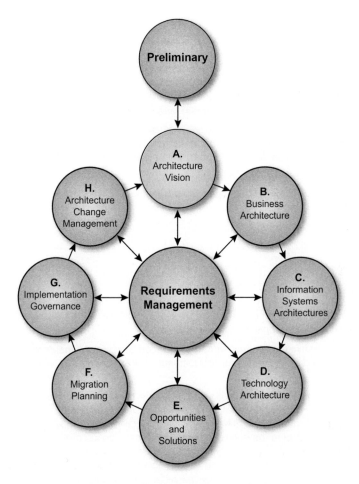

Figure 7-1 Phase A: Architecture Vision

7.1   Objectives

The objectives of Phase A are:

- To ensure that this evolution of the architecture development cycle has proper recognition and endorsement from the corporate management of the enterprise, and the support and commitment of the necessary line management

- To define and organize an architecture development cycle within the overall context of the architecture framework, as established in the Preliminary phase

- To validate the business principles, business goals, and strategic business drivers of the organization and the enterprise architecture Key Performance Indicators (KPIs)

- To define the scope of, and to identify and prioritize the components of, the Baseline Architecture effort

- To define the relevant stakeholders, and their concerns and objectives

- To define the key business requirements to be addressed in this architecture effort, and the constraints that must be dealt with

- To articulate an Architecture Vision and formalize the value proposition that demonstrates a response to those requirements and constraints

- To create a comprehensive plan that addresses scheduling, resourcing, financing, communication, risks, constraints, assumptions, and dependencies, in line with the project management frameworks adopted by the enterprise (such as PRINCE2 or PMBOK)

- To secure formal approval to proceed

- To understand the impact on, and of, other enterprise architecture development cycles ongoing in parallel

7.2   Approach

7.2.1   General

Phase A starts with receipt of a Request for Architecture Work from the sponsoring organization to the architecture organization.

The issues involved in ensuring proper recognition and endorsement from corporate management, and the support and commitment of line management, are discussed in Part VII, Section 50.1.4.

Phase A also defines what is in and what is outside the scope of the architecture effort and the constraints that must be dealt with. Scoping decisions need to be made on the basis of a practical assessment of resource and competence availability, and the value that can realistically be expected to accrue to the enterprise from the chosen scope of architecture work. The issues involved in this are discussed in Section 5.5. Scoping issues addressed in the Architecture Vision phase will be restricted to the specific objectives for this ADM cycle and will be constrained within the overall scope definition for architecture activity as established within the Preliminary phase and embodied within the architecture framework.

In situations where the architecture framework in place is not appropriate to achieve the desired

Architecture Vision, revisit the Preliminary phase and extend the overall architecture framework for the enterprise.

The constraints will normally be informed by the business principles and architecture principles, developed as part of the Preliminary phase (see Chapter 6).

Normally, the business principles, business goals, and strategic drivers of the organization are already defined elsewhere in the enterprise. If so, the activity in Phase A is involved with ensuring that existing definitions are current, and clarifying any areas of ambiguity. Otherwise, it involves defining these essential items for the first time.

Similarly, the architecture principles that form part of the constraints on architecture work will normally have been defined in the Preliminary phase (see Chapter 6). The activity in Phase A is concerned with ensuring that the existing principles definitions are current, and clarifying any areas of ambiguity. Otherwise, it entails defining the architecture principles for the first time, as explained in Part III, Chapter 23.

7.2.2   Creating the Architecture Vision

The Architecture Vision provides the sponsor with a key tool to sell the benefits of the proposed capability to stakeholders and decision-makers within the enterprise. Architecture Vision describes how the new capability will meet the business goals and strategic objectives and address the stakeholder concerns when implemented.

Clarifying and agreeing the purpose of the architecture effort is one of the key parts of this activity, and the purpose needs to be clearly reflected in the vision that is created. Architecture projects are often undertaken with a specific purpose in mind — a specific set of business drivers that represent the return on investment for the stakeholders in the architecture development. Clarifying that purpose, and demonstrating how it will be achieved by the proposed architecture development, is the whole point of the Architecture Vision.

Normally, key elements of the Architecture Vision — such as the enterprise mission, vision, strategy, and goals — have been documented as part of some wider business strategy or enterprise planning activity that has its own lifecycle within the enterprise. In such cases, the activity in Phase A is concerned with verifying and understanding the documented business strategy and goals, and possibly bridging between the enterprise strategy and goals on the one hand, and the strategy and goals implicit within the current architecture reality.

In other cases, little or no Business Architecture work may have been done to date. In such cases, there will be a need for the architecture team to research, verify, and gain buy-in to the key business objectives and processes that the architecture is to support. This may be done as a free-standing exercise, either preceding architecture development, or as part of the ADM initiation phase (Preliminary phase).

The Architecture Vision provides a first-cut, high-level description of the Baseline and Target Architectures, covering the business, data, application, and technology domains. These outline descriptions are developed in subsequent phases.

Business scenarios are an appropriate and useful technique to discover and document business requirements, and to articulate an Architecture Vision that responds to those requirements. Business scenarios are described in Part III, Chapter 26.

Once an Architecture Vision is defined and documented in the Statement of Architecture Work, it is critical to use it to build a consensus, as described in Part VII, Section 50.1.4. Without this consensus it is very unlikely that the final architecture will be accepted by the organization as a whole. The consensus is represented by the sponsoring organization signing the Statement of Architecture Work.

7.2.3   Business Scenarios

The ADM has its own method (a "method-within-a-method") for identifying and articulating the business requirements implied in new business capability to address key business drivers, and the implied architecture requirements. This process is known as "business scenarios", and is described in Part III, Chapter 26. The technique may be used iteratively, at different levels of detail in the hierarchical decomposition of the Business Architecture.

7.3   Inputs

This section defines the inputs to Phase A.

7.3.1   Reference Materials External to the Enterprise

- Architecture reference materials (see Part IV, Section 36.2.5)

7.3.2   Non-Architectural Inputs

- Request for Architecture Work (see Part IV, Section 36.2.17)
- Business principles, business goals, and business drivers (see Part IV, Section 36.2.9)

7.3.3   Architectural Inputs

- Organizational Model for Enterprise Architecture (see Part IV, Section 36.2.16), including:
  — Scope of organizations impacted
  — Maturity assessment, gaps, and resolution approach
  — Roles and responsibilities for architecture team(s)
  — Constraints on architecture work
  — Re-use requirements
  — Budget requirements
  — Requests for change
  — Governance and support strategy
- Tailored Architecture Framework (see Part IV, Section 36.2.21), including:
  — Tailored architecture method

— Tailored architecture content (deliverables and artifacts)

— Architecture principles (see Part IV, Section 36.2.4), including business principles, when pre-existing

— Configured and deployed tools

- Populated Architecture Repository (see Part IV, Section 36.2.5) — existing architectural documentation (framework description, architectural descriptions, baseline descriptions, ABBs, etc.)

7.4   Steps

The level of detail addressed in Phase A will depend on the scope and goals of the Request for Architecture Work, or the subset of scope and goals associated with this iteration of architecture development.

The order of the steps in Phase A (see below) as well as the time at which they are formally started and completed should be adapted to the situation at hand in accordance with the established architecture governance.

The steps in Phase A are as follows:

- Establish the architecture project (see Section 7.4.1)
- Identify stakeholders, concerns, and business requirements (see Section 7.4.2)
- Confirm and elaborate business goals, business drivers, and constraints (see Section 7.4.3)
- Evaluate business capabilities (see Section 7.4.4)
- Assess readiness for business transformation (see Section 7.4.5)
- Define scope (see Section 7.4.6)
- Confirm and elaborate architecture principles, including business principles (see Section 7.4.7)
- Develop Architecture Vision (see Section 7.4.8)
- Define the Target Architecture value propositions and KPIs (see Section 7.4.9)
- Identify the business transformation risks and mitigation activities (see Section 7.4.10)
- Develop enterprise architecture plans and Statement of Architecture Work; secure approval (see Section 7.4.11)

7.4.1   Establish the Architecture Project

Execution of ADM cycles should be conducted within the project management framework of the enterprise. In some cases, architecture projects will be stand-alone. In other cases, architectural activities will be a subset of the activities within a larger project. In either case, architecture activity should be planned and managed using accepted practices for the enterprise.

Conduct the necessary (enterprise-specific) procedures to secure enterprise-wide recognition of the project, the endorsement of corporate management, and the support and commitment of the necessary line management. Include references to other management frameworks in use within the enterprise, explaining how this project relates to those frameworks.

7.4.2   Identify Stakeholders, Concerns, and Business Requirements

Identify the key stakeholders and their concerns/objectives, and define the key business requirements to be addressed in the architecture engagement. Stakeholder engagement at this stage is intended to accomplish three objectives:

- To identify candidate vision components and requirements to be tested as the Architecture Vision is developed

- To identify candidate scope boundaries for the engagement to limit the extent of architectural investigation required

- To identify stakeholder concerns, issues, and cultural factors that will shape how the architecture is presented and communicated

The major product resulting from this step is a stakeholder map for the engagement, showing which stakeholders are involved with the engagement, their level of involvement, and their key concerns (see Part III, Section 24.3 and Section 24.4). The stakeholder map is used to support various outputs of the Architecture Vision phase, and to identify:

- The concerns and viewpoints that are relevant to this project; this is captured in the Architecture Vision (see Part IV, Section 36.2.8)

- The stakeholders that are involved with the project and as a result form the starting point for a Communications Plan (see Part IV, Section 36.2.12)

- The key roles and responsibilities within the project, which should be included within the Statement of Architecture Work (see Part VII, Section 36.2.20)

Another key task will be to consider which architecture views and viewpoints need to be developed to satisfy the various stakeholder requirements. As described in Part III, Chapter 24, understanding at this stage which stakeholders and which views need to be developed is important in setting the scope of the engagement.

7.4.3   Confirm and Elaborate Business Goals, Business Drivers, and Constraints

Identify the business goals and strategic drivers of the organization.

If these have already been defined elsewhere within the enterprise, ensure that the existing definitions are current, and clarify any areas of ambiguity. Otherwise, go back to the originators of the Statement of Architecture Work and work with them to define these essential items and secure their endorsement by corporate management.

Define the constraints that must be dealt with, including enterprise-wide constraints and project-specific constraints (time, schedule, resources, etc.). The enterprise-wide constraints may be informed by the business and architecture principles developed in the Preliminary phase or clarified as part of Phase A.

7.4.4   Evaluate Business Capabilities

A business capability assessment is used to define what capabilities an organization will need to fulfil its business goals and business drivers.

A business capability can be thought of as a synonym for a macro-level business function.

This step first seeks to understand the capabilities and desires of the business, then identifies options to realize those capabilities. For example, an organization may possess a finance capability and have a desire to reduce the cost of operating this capability. A suitable technique for reducing cost may be to adopt an outsourced service from a service provider. This would require the business to accept the functional limits of the packaged software, and adapt to these constraints. The business is constrained in its ability to differentiate itself in the marketplace in this functional area, should custom software be needed to support unique operations and business practices. Therefore, it is necessary for the organization to understand where it needs to differentiate itself and where a model of sufficiency at lowest cost is preferred.

Once the current and desired business capabilities are understood, their likely implications for the organization's technology capability can be assessed, creating an initial picture of new IT capability that will be required to support the Target Architecture Vision.

Showing the baseline and target capabilities within the context of the overall enterprise can be supported by creating Value Chain diagrams that show the linkage of related capabilities at the macro level, either within an individual enterprise, or across a network of related enterprises.

The results of the assessment are documented in a Capability Assessment (see Part IV, Section 36.2.10).

7.4.5   Assess Readiness for Business Transformation

A Business Transformation Readiness Assessment can be used to evaluate and quantify the organization's readiness to undergo a change. This assessment is based upon the determination and analysis/rating of a series of readiness factors, as described in Chapter 30.

The results of the readiness assessment should be added to the Capability Assessment (see Part IV, Section 36.2.10). These results are then used to shape the scope of the architecture, to identify activities required within the architecture project, and to identify risk areas to be addressed.

7.4.6   Define Scope

Define what is inside and what is outside the scope of the Baseline Architecture and Target Architecture efforts, understanding that the baseline and target need not be described at the same level of detail. In many cases, the Baseline is described at a higher level of abstraction, so more time is available to specify the Target in sufficient detail. The issues involved in this are discussed in Section 5.5. In particular, define:

- The breadth of coverage of the enterprise
- The level of detail required
- The partitioning characteristics of the architecture (see Part V, Chapter 40 for more details)
- The specific architecture domains to be covered (business, data, application, technology)
- The extent of the time period aimed at, plus the number and extent of any intermediate time period
- The architectural assets to be leveraged, or considered for use, from the organization's Enterprise Continuum:
  - Assets created in previous iterations of the ADM cycle within the enterprise
  - Assets available elsewhere in the industry (other frameworks, systems models, vertical industry models, etc.)

7.4.7   Confirm and Elaborate Architecture Principles, including Business Principles

Review the principles under which the architecture is to be developed. Architecture principles are normally based on the principles developed as part of the Preliminary phase. They are explained, and an example set given, in Part III, Chapter 23. Ensure that the existing definitions are current, and clarify any areas of ambiguity. Otherwise, go back to the body responsible for architecture governance and work with them to define these essential items for the first time and secure their endorsement by corporate management.

7.4.8   Develop Architecture Vision

Based on the stakeholder concerns, business capability requirements, scope, constraints, and principles, create a high-level view of the Baseline and Target Architectures. The Architecture Vision typically covers the breadth of scope identified for the project, at a high level. Informal techniques are often employed. A common practice is to draw a simple solution concept diagram that illustrates concisely the major components of the solution and how the solution will result in benefit for the enterprise.

Business scenarios are an appropriate and useful technique to discover and document business requirements, and to articulate an Architecture Vision that responds to those requirements. Business scenarios may also be used at more detailed levels of the architecture work (e.g., in Phase B) and are described in Part III, Chapter 26.

This step generates the first, very high-level definitions of the baseline and target environments, from a business, information systems, and technology perspective, as described in Section 7.5.

These initial versions of the architecture should be stored in the Architecture Repository, organized according to the standards and guidelines established in the architecture framework.

7.4.9 Define the Target Architecture Value Propositions and KPIs

- Develop the business case for the architectures and changes required

- Produce the value proposition for each of the stakeholder groupings

- Assess and define the procurement requirements

- Review and agree the value propositions with the sponsors and stakeholders concerned

- Define the performance metrics and measures to be built into the enterprise architecture to meet the business needs

- Assess the business risk (see Part III, Chapter 31)

The outputs from this activity should be incorporated within the Statement of Architecture Work to allow performance to be tracked accordingly.

7.4.10 Identify the Business Transformation Risks and Mitigation Activities

Identify the risks associated with the Architecture Vision and assess the initial level of risk (e.g., catastrophic, critical, marginal, or negligible) and the potential frequency associated with it. Assign a mitigation strategy for each risk. A risk management framework is described in Part III, Chapter 31.

There are two levels of risk that should be considered, namely:

- **Initial Level of Risk**: Risk categorization prior to determining and implementing mitigating actions.

- **Residual Level of Risk**: Risk categorization after implementation of mitigating actions (if any).

Risk mitigation activities should be considered for inclusion within the Statement of Architecture Work.

7.4.11 Develop Enterprise Architecture Plans and Statement of Architecture Work; Secure Approval

Assess the work products that are required to be produced (and by when) against the set of business performance requirements. This will involve ensuring that:

- Performance metrics are built into the work products.

- Specific performance-related work products are available.

Then, activities will include:

- Identify new work products that will need to be changed

- Provide direction on which existing work products, including building blocks, will need to be changed and ensure that all activities and dependencies on these are co-ordinated

- Identify the impact of change on other work products and dependence on their activities

- Based on the purpose, focus, scope, and constraints, determine which architecture domains should be developed, to what level of detail, and which architecture views should be built

- Assess the resource requirements and availability to perform the work in the timescale required; this will include adhering to the organization's planning methods and work products to produce the plans for performing a cycle of the ADM

- Estimate the resources needed, develop a roadmap and schedule for the proposed development, and document all these in the Statement of Architecture Work

- Define the performance metrics to be met during this cycle of the ADM by the enterprise architecture team

- Develop the specific enterprise architecture Communications Plan and show where, how, and when the enterprise architects will communicate with the stakeholders, including affinity groupings and communities, about the progress of the enterprise architecture developments

- Review and agree the plans with the sponsors, and secure formal approval of the Statement of Architecture Work under the appropriate governance procedures

- Gain sponsor's sign-off to proceed

7.5   Outputs

The outputs of Phase A are:

- Approved Statement of Architecture Work (see Part IV, Section 36.2.20), including in particular:
  - Scope and constraints
  - Plan for the architectural work
  - Roles and responsibilities
  - Risks and mitigating activity
  - Work product performance assessments
  - Business case and KPI metrics

- Refined statements of business principles, business goals, and business drivers (see Part IV, Section 36.2.9)

- Architecture principles (see Part IV, Chapter 23)

- Capability Assessment (see Part IV, Section 36.2.10)

- Tailored Architecture Framework (see Part IV, Section 36.2.21) (for the engagement), including:
  - Tailored architecture method
  - Tailored architecture content (deliverables and artifacts)
  - Configured and deployed tools

- Architecture Vision (see Part IV, Section 36.2.8), including:

- — Refined key high-level stakeholder requirements
- — Baseline Business Architecture, Version 0.1
- — Baseline Technology Architecture, Version 0.1
- — Baseline Data Architecture, Version 0.1
- — Baseline Application Architecture, Version 0.1
- — Target Business Architecture, Version 0.1
- — Target Technology Architecture, Version 0.1
- — Target Data Architecture, Version 0.1
- — Target Application Architecture, Version 0.1
- Communications Plan (see Part IV, Section 36.2.12)
- Additional content populating the Architecture Repository (see Part IV, Section 36.2.5)

Note: Multiple business scenarios may be used to generate a single Architecture Vision.

Chapter 8: Phase B: Business Architecture

This chapter describes the development of a Business Architecture to support an agreed Architecture Vision.

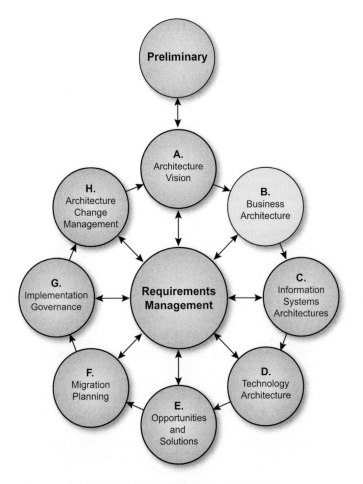

Figure 8-1 Phase B: Business Architecture

8.1   Objectives

The objectives of Phase B are:

- To describe the Baseline Business Architecture

- To develop a Target Business Architecture, describing the product and/or service strategy, and the organizational, functional, process, information, and geographic aspects of the business environment, based on the business principles, business goals, and strategic drivers

- To analyze the gaps between the Baseline and Target Business Architectures

- To select and develop the relevant architecture viewpoints that will enable the architect to demonstrate how the stakeholder concerns are addressed in the Business Architecture

- To select the relevant tools and techniques to be used in association with the selected viewpoints

8.2   Approach

8.2.1   General

A knowledge of the Business Architecture is a prerequisite for architecture work in any other domain (Data, Application, Technology), and is therefore the first architecture activity that needs to be undertaken, if not catered for already in other organizational processes (enterprise planning, strategic business planning, business process re-engineering, etc.).

In practical terms, the Business Architecture is also often necessary as a means of demonstrating the business value of subsequent architecture work to key stakeholders, and the return on investment to those stakeholders from supporting and participating in the subsequent work.

The scope of the work in Phase B will depend to a large extent on the enterprise environment. In some cases, key elements of the Business Architecture may be done in other activities; for example, the enterprise mission, vision, strategy, and goals may be documented as part of some wider business strategy or enterprise planning activity that has its own lifecycle within the enterprise.

In such cases, there may be a need to verify and update the currently documented business strategy and plans, and/or to bridge between high-level business drivers, business strategy, and goals on the one hand, and the specific business requirements that are relevant to this architecture development effort. The business strategy typically defines what to achieve — the goals and drivers, and the metrics for success — but not how to get there. That is role of the Business Architecture.

In other cases, little or no Business Architecture work may have been done to date. In such cases, there will be a need for the architecture team to research, verify, and gain buy-in to the key business objectives and processes that the architecture is to support. This may be done as a free-standing exercise, either preceding architecture development, or as part of Phase A.

In both of these cases, the business scenario technique (see Part III, Chapter 26) of the TOGAF ADM, or any other method that illuminates the key business requirements and indicates the implied technical requirements for IT architecture, may be used.

A key objective is to re-use existing material as much as possible. In architecturally more mature environments, there will be existing Architecture Definitions, which (hopefully) will have been maintained since the last architecture development cycle. Where architecture descriptions exist, these can be used as a starting point, and verified and updated if necessary; see Part V, Section 39.4.1.

Gather and analyze only that information that allows informed decisions to be made relevant to the scope of this architecture effort. If this effort is focused on the definition of (possibly new) business processes, then Phase B will necessarily involve a lot of detailed work. If the focus is more on the Target Architectures in other domains (data/information, application systems, infrastructure) to support an essentially existing Business Architecture, then it is important to build a complete picture in Phase B without going into unnecessary detail.

8.2.2 Developing the Baseline Description

If an enterprise has existing architecture descriptions, they should be used as the basis for the Baseline Description. This input may have been used already in Phase A in developing an Architecture Vision, and may even be sufficient in itself for the Baseline Description.

Where no such descriptions exist, information will have to be gathered in whatever format comes to hand.

The normal approach to Target Architecture development is top-down. In the Baseline Description, however, the analysis of the current state often has to be done bottom-up, particularly where little or no architecture assets exist. In such a case, the architect simply has to document the working assumptions about high-level architectures, and the process is one of gathering evidence to turn the working assumptions into fact, until the law of diminishing returns sets in.

Business processes that are not to be carried forward have no intrinsic value. However, when developing Baseline Descriptions in other architecture domains, architectural components (principles, models, standards, and current inventory) that are not to be carried forward may still have an intrinsic value, and an inventory may be needed in order to understand the residual value (if any) of those components.

Whatever the approach, the goal should be to re-use existing material as much as possible, and to gather and analyze only that information that allows informed decisions to be made regarding the Target Business Architecture. It is important to build a complete picture without going into unnecessary detail.

8.2.3 Business Modeling

Business models should be logical extensions of the business scenarios from the Architecture Vision, so that the architecture can be mapped from the high-level business requirements down to the more detailed ones.

A variety of modeling tools and techniques may be employed, if deemed appropriate (bearing in mind the above caution not to go into unnecessary detail). For example:

- **Activity Models** (also called **Business Process Models**) describe the functions associated with the enterprise's business activities, the data and/or information exchanged between activities (internal exchanges), and the data and/or information exchanged with other activities that are outside the scope of the model (external exchanges). Activity models are hierarchical in nature. They capture the activities performed in a business process, and the ICOMs (inputs, controls, outputs, and mechanisms/resources used) of those activities. Activity models can be annotated with explicit statements of business rules, which represent relationships among the ICOMs. For example, a business rule can specify who can do what under specified conditions, the combination of inputs and controls needed, and the resulting outputs. One technique for creating activity models is the IDEF (Integrated Computer Aided Manufacturing (ICAM) DEFinition) modeling technique.

The Object Management Group (OMG) has developed the Business Process Modeling Notation (BPMN), a standard for business process modeling that includes a language with which to specify business processes, their tasks/steps, and the documents produced.

- **Use-Case Models** can describe either business processes or systems functions, depending on the focus of the modeling effort. A use-case model describes the business processes of an enterprise in terms of use-cases and actors corresponding to business processes and organizational participants (people, organizations, etc.). The use-case model is described in use-case diagrams and use-case specifications.

- **Class Models** are similar to logical data models. A class model describes static information and relationships between information. A class model also describes informational behaviors. Like many of the other models, it can also be used to model various levels of granularity. Depending on the intent of the model, a class model can represent business domain entities or systems implementation classes. A business domain model represents key business information (domain classes), their characteristics (attributes), their behaviors (methods or operations), and relationships (often referred to as multiplicity, describing how many classes typically participate in the relationship), and cardinality (describes required or optional participation in the relationship). Specifications further elaborate and detail information that cannot be represented in the class diagram.

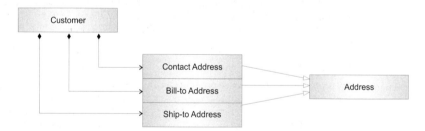

Figure 8-2 UML Business Class Diagram

All three types of model above can be represented in the Unified Modeling Language (UML), and a variety of tools exist for generating such models.

Certain industry sectors have modeling techniques specific to the sector concerned. For example, the Defense sector uses the following models. These models have to be used carefully, especially if the location and conduct of business processes will be altered in the visionary Business Architecture.

- The **Node Connectivity Diagram** describes the business locations (nodes), the "needlines" between them, and the characteristics of the information exchanged. Node connectivity can be described at three levels: conceptual, logical, and physical. Each needline indicates the need for some kind of information transfer between the two connected nodes. A node can represent a role (e.g., a CIO), an organizational unit, a business location or facility, and so on. An arrow indicating the direction of information flow is annotated to describe the characteristics of the data or information — for example, its content, media, security or classification level, timeliness, and requirements for information system interoperability.

- The **Information Exchange Matrix** documents the information exchange requirements for an enterprise architecture. Information exchange requirements express the relationships across three basic entities (activities, business nodes and their elements, and information flow), and focus on characteristics of the information exchange, such as performance and security. They identify who exchanges what information with whom, why the information is necessary, and in what manner.

Although originally developed for use in the Defense sector, these models are finding increasing use in other sectors of government, and may also be considered for use in non-government environments.

8.2.4   Architecture Repository

As part of Phase B, the architecture team will need to consider what relevant Business Architecture resources are available from the Architecture Repository (see Part V, Chapter 41), in particular:

- Generic business models relevant to the organization's industry sector. These are "Industry Architectures", in terms of the Enterprise Continuum. They are held in the Reference Library of the Architecture Repository (see Part V, Section 41.3). For example:

  - The Object Management Group (OMG) — www.omg.org — has a number of vertical Domain Task Forces developing business models relevant to specific vertical domains such as Healthcare, Transportation, Finance, etc.

  - The TeleManagement Forum (TMF) — www.tmforum.org — has developed detailed business models relevant to the Telecommunications industry.

  - Government departments and agencies in different countries have reference models and frameworks mandated for use, intended to promote cross-departmental integration and interoperability. An example is the Federal Enterprise Architecture Business Reference Model, which is a function-driven framework for describing the business operations of the Federal Government independent of the agencies that perform them.

- Business models relevant to common high-level business domains — such as electronic commerce, supply chain management, etc. — that are published within the IT industry. (These are "Common Systems Architectures", in terms of the Enterprise Continuum.) For example:

  - The Resource-Event-Agent (REA) business model was originally created by William E. McCarthy (refer to www.msu.edu/user/mccarth4) of Michigan State University, mainly for modeling of accounting systems. It has proved so useful for better understanding of business processes that it has become one of the major modeling frameworks for both traditional enterprises and e-Commerce systems. In particular, it has been extended by Robert Haugen and McCarthy for supply chain management (refer to www.jeffsutherland.org/oopsla2000/mccarthy/mccarthy.htm).

— The STEP Framework (STandard for the Exchange of Product model data) is concerned with product design and supply chain interworking. STEP is an ISO standard (ISO 10303). Implementation of the STEP standard has been led by some large aerospace manufacturers, and has also been taken up in other industries that have a need for complex graphic and process data, such as the construction industry.

— The Open Applications Group (OAG) — www.openapplications.org — is focused on defining a framework for allowing heterogeneous business applications to communicate together. Its OAGIS integration model and specification address the needs of traditional Enterprise Resource Planning (ERP) integration, as well as supply chain management and electronic commerce.

— RosettaNet — www.rosettanet.org — is a consortium created by leading companies in the computer, electronic component, and semiconductor manufacturing supply chains. Its mission is to develop a complete set of standard e-Business processes for these supply chains, and to promote and support their adoption and use.

■ Enterprise-specific building blocks (process components, business rules, job descriptions, etc.).

■ Applicable standards.

8.3   Inputs

This section defines the inputs to Phase B.

8.3.1   Reference Materials External to the Enterprise

■ Architecture reference materials (see Part IV, Section 36.2.5)

8.3.2   Non-Architectural Inputs

■ Request for Architecture Work (see Part IV, Section 36.2.17)

■ Business principles, business goals, and business drivers (see Part IV, Section 36.2.9)

■ Capability Assessment (see Part IV, Section 36.2.10)

■ Communications Plan (see Part IV, Section 36.2.12)

8.3.3   Architectural Inputs

■ Organizational Model for Enterprise Architecture (see Part IV, Section 36.2.16), including:

— Scope of organizations impacted

— Maturity assessment, gaps, and resolution approach

— Roles and responsibilities for architecture team(s)

- — Constraints on architecture work
- — Budget requirements
- — Governance and support strategy
- Tailored Architecture Framework (see Part IV, Section 36.2.21), including:
  - — Tailored architecture method
  - — Tailored architecture content (deliverables and artifacts)
  - — Configured and deployed tools
- Approved Statement of Architecture Work (see Part IV, Section 36.2.20)
- Architecture principles (see Part IV, Section 36.2.4), including business principles, when pre-existing
- Enterprise Continuum (see Part V, Chapter 39)
- Architecture Repository (see Part IV, Section 36.2.5), including:
  - — Re-usable building blocks
  - — Publicly available reference models
  - — Organization-specific reference models
  - — Organization standards
- Architecture Vision (see Part IV, Section 36.2.8), including:
  - — Refined key high-level stakeholder requirements
  - — Baseline Business Architecture, Version 0.1
  - — Baseline Technology Architecture, Version 0.1
  - — Baseline Data Architecture, Version 0.1
  - — Baseline Application Architecture, Version 0.1
  - — Target Business Architecture, Version 0.1
  - — Target Technology Architecture, Version 0.1
  - — Target Data Architecture, Version 0.1
  - — Target Application Architecture, Version 0.1

8.4   Steps

The level of detail addressed in Phase B will depend on the scope and goals of the overall architecture effort.

New business processes being introduced as part of this effort will need to be defined in detail during Phase B. Existing business processes to be carried over and supported in the target environment may already have been adequately defined in previous architectural work; but, if not, they too will need to be defined in Phase B.

The order of the steps in Phase B (see below) as well as the time at which they are formally started and completed should be adapted to the situation at hand, in accordance with the established architecture governance. In particular, determine whether in this situation it is appropriate to conduct Baseline or Target Architecture development first, as described in Part III, Chapter 19.

All activities that have been initiated in these steps must be closed during the Finalize the Business Architecture step (see Section 8.4.8). The documentation generated from these steps must be formally published in the Create Architecture Definition Document step (see Section 8.4.9).

The steps in Phase B are as follows:

- Select reference models, viewpoints, and tools (see Section 8.4.1)
- Develop Baseline Business Architecture Description (see Section 8.4.2)
- Develop Target Business Architecture Description (see Section 8.4.3)
- Perform gap analysis (see Section 8.4.4)
- Define roadmap components (see Section 8.4.5)
- Resolve impacts across the Architecture Landscape (see Section 8.4.6)
- Conduct formal stakeholder review (see Section 8.4.7)
- Finalize the Business Architecture (see Section 8.4.8)
- Create Architecture Definition Document (see Section 8.4.9)

8.4.1   Select Reference Models, Viewpoints, and Tools

Select relevant Business Architecture resources (reference models, patterns, etc.) from the Architecture Repository, on the basis of the business drivers, and the stakeholders and concerns.

Select relevant Business Architecture viewpoints (e.g., operations, management, financial); i.e., those that will enable the architect to demonstrate how the stakeholder concerns are being addressed in the Business Architecture.

Identify appropriate tools and techniques to be used for capture, modeling, and analysis, in association with the selected viewpoints. Depending on the degree of sophistication warranted, these may comprise simple documents or spreadsheets, or more sophisticated modeling tools and techniques, such as activity models, business process models, use-case models, etc.

8.4.1.1   Determine Overall Modeling Process

For each viewpoint, select the models needed to support the specific view required, using the selected tool or method.

Ensure that all stakeholder concerns are covered. If they are not, create new models to address concerns not covered, or augment existing models (see Section 8.2.3). Business scenarios are a useful technique to discover and document business requirements, and may be used iteratively, at different levels of detail in the hierarchical decomposition of the Business Architecture. Business scenarios are described in Part III, Chapter 26.

Activity models, use-case models, and class models are mentioned earlier as techniques to enable the definition of an organization's business architecture. In many cases, all three approaches can be utilized in sequence to progressively decompose a business.

- **Structured Analysis**: Identifies the key business functions within the scope of the architecture, and maps those functions onto the organizational units within the business.

- **Use-case Analysis**: The breakdown of business-level functions across actors and organizations allows the actors in a function to be identified and permits a breakdown into services supporting/delivering that functional capability.

- **Process Modeling**: The breakdown of a function or business service through process modeling allows the elements of the process to be identified, and permits the identification of lower-level business services or functions.

The level and rigor of decomposition needed varies from enterprise to enterprise, as well as within an enterprise, and the architect should consider the enterprise's goals, objectives, scope, and purpose of the enterprise architecture effort to determine the level of decomposition.

8.4.1.2   Identify Required Service Granularity Level, Boundaries, and Contracts

The TOGAF content framework differentiates between the functions of a business and the services of a business. Business services are specific functions that have explicit, defined boundaries that are explicitly governed. In order to allow the architect flexibility to define business services at a level of granularity that is appropriate for and manageable by the business, the functions are split as follows: micro-level functions will have explicit, defined boundaries, but may not be explicitly governed. Likewise, macro business functions may be explicitly governed, but may not have explicit, defined boundaries.

The Business Architecture phase therefore needs to identify which components of the architecture are functions and which are services. Services are distinguished from functions through the explicit definition of a service contract. When Baseline Architectures are being developed, it may be the case that explicit contracts do not exist and it would therefore be at the discretion of the architect to determine whether there is merit in developing such contracts before examining any Target Architectures.

A service contract covers the business/functional interface and also the technology/data interface. Business Architecture will define the service contract at the business/functional level, which will be expanded on in the Application and Technology Architecture phases.

The granularity of business services should be determined according to the business drivers, goals, objectives, and measures for this area of the business. Finer-grained services permit closer management and measurement (and can be combined to create coarser-grained services), but require greater effort to govern. Guidelines for identification of services and definition of their contracts can be found in Part III, Chapter 22.

8.4.1.3   Identify Required Catalogs of Business Building Blocks

Catalogs capture inventories of the core assets of the business. Catalogs are hierarchical in nature and capture the decomposition of a building block and also decompositions across related building blocks (e.g., organization/actor).

Catalogs form the raw material for development of matrices and views and also act as a key resource for portfolio managing business and IT capability.

The following catalogs should be considered for development within a Business Architecture:

- Organization/Actor catalog
- Driver/Goal/Objective catalog
- Role catalog
- Business Service/Function catalog
- Location catalog
- Process/Event/Control/Product catalog
- Contract/Measure catalog

The structure of catalogs is based on the attributes of metamodel entities, as defined in Part IV, Chapter 34.

8.4.1.4   Identify Required Matrices

Matrices show the core relationships between related model entities.

Matrices form the raw material for development of views and also act as a key resource for impact assessment, carried out as a part of gap analysis.

The following matrices should be considered for development within a Business Architecture:

- Business interaction matrix (showing dependency and communication between organizations and actors)
- Actor/role matrix (showing the roles undertaken by each actor)

The structure of matrices is based on the attributes of metamodel entities, as defined in Part IV, Chapter 34.

8.4.1.5   Identify Required Diagrams

Diagrams present the Business Architecture information from a set of different perspectives (viewpoints) according to the requirements of the stakeholders.

The following Diagrams should be considered for development within a Business Architecture:

- Business Footprint diagram
- Business Service/Information diagram
- Functional Decomposition diagram
- Goal/Objective/Service diagram

- Use-case diagram

- Organization Decomposition diagram

- Process Flow diagram

- Events diagram

The structure of diagrams is based on the attributes of metamodel entities, as defined in Part IV, Chapter 34.

8.4.1.6 *Identify Types of Requirement to be Collected*

Once the Business Architecture catalogs, matrices, and diagrams have been developed, architecture modeling is completed by formalizing the business-focused requirements for implementing the Target Architecture. These requirements may relate to the business domain, or may provide requirements input into the Data, Application, and Technology Architectures.

Within this step, the architect should identify types of requirement that must be met by the architecture implementation, including:

- Functional requirements

- Non-functional requirements

- Assumptions

- Constraints

- Domain-specific Business Architecture principles

- Policies

- Standards

- Guidelines

- Specifications

In many cases, the Architecture Definition will not be intended to give detailed or comprehensive requirements for a solution (as these can be better addressed through general requirements management discipline). The expected coverage of requirements content should be established during the Architecture Vision phase.

8.4.2 Develop Baseline Business Architecture Description

Develop a Baseline Description of the existing Business Architecture, to the extent necessary to support the Target Business Architecture. The scope and level of detail to be defined will depend on the extent to which existing business elements are likely to be carried over into the Target Business Architecture, and on whether architecture descriptions exist, as described in Section 8.2. To the extent possible, identify the relevant Business Architecture building blocks, drawing on the Architecture Repository (see Part V, Chapter 41).

Where new architecture models need to be developed to satisfy stakeholder concerns, use the models identified within Step 1 as a guideline for creating new architecture content to describe the Baseline Architecture.

8.4.3   Develop Target Business Architecture Description

Develop a Target Description for the Business Architecture, to the extent necessary to support the Architecture Vision. The scope and level of detail to be defined will depend on the relevance of the business elements to attaining the Target Architecture Vision, and on whether architectural descriptions exist. To the extent possible, identify the relevant Business Architecture building blocks, drawing on the Architecture Repository (see Part V, Chapter 41).

Where new architecture models need to be developed to satisfy stakeholder concerns, use the models identified within Step 1 as a guideline for creating new architecture content to describe the Target Architecture.

8.4.4   Perform Gap Analysis

First, verify the architecture models for internal consistency and accuracy:

- Perform trade-off analysis to resolve conflicts (if any) among the different views
- Validate that the models support the principles, objectives, and constraints
- Note changes to the viewpoint represented in the selected models from the Architecture Repository, and document
- Test architecture models for completeness against requirements
- Identify gaps between the baseline and target:
    — Create gap matrix, as described in Part III, Chapter 27
    — Identify building blocks to be carried over, classifying as either changed or unchanged
    — Identify eliminated building blocks
    — Identify new building blocks
    — Identify gaps and classify as those that should be developed and those that should be procured

8.4.5   Define Roadmap Components

Following creation of a Baseline Architecture, Target Architecture, and gap analysis results, a business roadmap is required to prioritize activities over the coming phases.

This initial Business Architecture roadmap will be used as raw material to support more detailed definition of a consolidated, cross-discipline roadmap within the Opportunities & Solutions phase.

8.4.6 Resolve Impacts Across the Architecture Landscape

Once the Business Architecture is finalized, it is necessary to understand any wider impacts or implications.

At this stage, other architecture artifacts in the Architecture Landscape should be examined to identify:

- Does this Business Architecture create an impact on any pre-existing architectures?
- Have recent changes been made that impact on the Business Architecture?
- Are there any opportunities to leverage work from this Business Architecture in other areas of the organization?
- Does this Business Architecture impact other projects (including those planned as well as those currently in progress)?
- Will this Business Architecture be impacted by other projects (including those planned as well as those currently in progress)?

8.4.7 Conduct Formal Stakeholder Review

Check the original motivation for the architecture project and the Statement of Architecture Work against the proposed Business Architecture, asking if it is fit for the purpose of supporting subsequent work in the other architecture domains. Refine the proposed Business Architecture only if necessary.

8.4.8 Finalize the Business Architecture

- Select standards for each of the building blocks, re-using as much as possible from the reference models selected from the Architecture Repository
- Fully document each building block
- Conduct final cross-check of overall architecture against business goals; document rationale for building block decisions in the architecture document
- Document final requirements traceability report
- Document final mapping of the architecture within the Architecture Repository; from the selected building blocks, identify those that might be re-used (working practices, roles, business relationships, job descriptions, etc.), and publish via the Architecture Repository
- Finalize all the work products, such as gap analysis results

8.4.9   Create Architecture Definition Document

- Document rationale for building block decisions in the Architecture Definition Document

- Prepare the business sections of the Architecture Definition Document, comprising some or all of:

  — A business footprint (a high-level description of the people and locations involved with key business functions)

  — A detailed description of business functions and their information needs

  — A management footprint (showing span of control and accountability)

  — Standards, rules, and guidelines showing working practices, legislation, financial measures, etc.

  — A skills matrix and set of job descriptions

  If appropriate, use reports and/or graphics generated by modeling tools to demonstrate key views of the architecture. Route the document for review by relevant stakeholders, and incorporate feedback.

8.5   Outputs

The outputs of Phase B are:

- Refined and updated versions of the Architecture Vision phase deliverables, where applicable, including:

  — Statement of Architecture Work (see Part IV, Section 36.2.20), updated if necessary

  — Validated business principles, business goals, and business drivers (see Part IV, Section 36.2.9), updated if necessary

  — Architecture principles (see Part IV, Section 36.2.4)

- Draft Architecture Definition Document (see Part IV, Section 36.2.3), including:

  — Baseline Business Architecture, Version 1.0 (detailed), if appropriate

  — Target Business Architecture, Version 1.0 (detailed), including:

    — Organization structure — identifying business locations and relating them to organizational units

    — Business goals and objectives — for the enterprise and each organizational unit

    — Business functions — a detailed, recursive step involving successive decomposition of major functional areas into sub-functions

    — Business services — the services that the enterprise and each enterprise unit provides to its customers, both internally and externally

    — Business processes, including measures and deliverables

     — Business roles, including development and modification of skills requirements

     — Business data model

     — Correlation of organization and functions — relate business functions to organizational units in the form of a matrix report

    — Views corresponding to the selected viewpoints addressing key stakeholder concerns

- Draft Architecture Requirements Specification (see Part IV, Section 36.2.6, on page 486), including such Business Architecture requirements as:

     — Gap analysis results

     — Technical requirements — identifying, categorizing, and prioritizing the implications for work in the remaining architecture domains; for example, by a dependency/priority matrix (for example, guiding trade-off between speed of transaction processing and security); list the specific models that are expected to be produced (for example, expressed as primitives of the Zachman Framework)

     — Updated business requirements

- Business Architecture components of an Architecture Roadmap (see Part IV, Section 36.2.7)

Chapter 9: Phase C: Information Systems Architectures

This chapter describes the Information Systems Architectures for an architecture project, including the development of Data and Application Architectures.

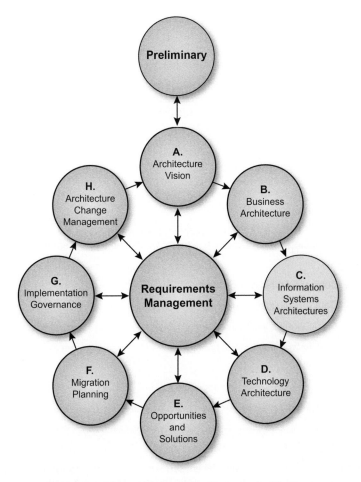

Figure 9-1 Phase C: Information Systems Architectures

9.1   Objectives

The objective of Phase C is to develop Target Architectures covering either or both (depending on project scope) of the data and application systems domains.

Information Systems Architecture focuses on identifying and defining the applications and data considerations that support an enterprise's Business Architecture; for example, by defining views that relate to information, knowledge, application services, etc.

9.2   Approach

9.2.1   Development

Phase C involves some combination of Data and Application Architecture, in either order. Advocates exist for both sequences. For example, Steven Spewak's Enterprise Architecture Planning (EAP) recommends a data-driven approach.

On the other hand, major applications systems — such as those for Enterprise Resource Planning (ERP), Customer Relationship Management (CRM), etc. — often provide a combination of technology infrastructure and business application logic, and some organizations take an application-driven approach, whereby they recognize certain key applications as forming the core underpinning of the mission-critical business processes, and take the implementation and integration of those core applications as the primary focus of architecture effort (the integration issues often constituting a major challenge).

9.2.2   Implementation

Implementation of these architectures may not necessarily follow the same order. For example, one common implementation approach is top-down design and bottom-up implementation:

- Design:
    - Business Architecture design
    - Data (or Application) Architecture design
    - Application (or Data) Architecture design
    - Technology Architecture design
- Implementation:
    - Technology Architecture implementation
    - Application (or Data) Architecture implementation
    - Data (or Application) Architecture implementation
    - Business Architecture implementation

An alternative approach is a data-driven sequence, whereby application systems that create data are implemented first, then applications that process the data, and finally applications that archive data.

9.3 Inputs

This section defines the inputs to Phase C.

9.3.1 Reference Materials External to the Enterprise

- Architecture reference materials (see Part IV, Section 36.2.5)

9.3.2 Non-Architectural Inputs

- Request for Architecture Work (see Part IV, Section 36.2.17)
- Capability Assessment (see Part IV, Section 36.2.10)
- Communications Plan (see Part IV, Section 36.2.12)

9.3.3 Architectural Inputs

- Organizational Model for Enterprise Architecture (see Part IV, Section 36.2.16), including:
  — Scope of organizations impacted
  — Maturity assessment, gaps, and resolution approach
  — Roles and responsibilities for architecture team(s)
  — Constraints on architecture work
  — Budget requirements
  — Governance and support strategy
- Tailored Architecture Framework (see Part IV, Section 36.2.21), including:
  — Tailored architecture method
  — Tailored architecture content (deliverables and artifacts)
  — Configured and deployed tools
- Application principles (see Part III, Section 23.6.3), if existing
- Data principles (see Part III, Section 23.6.2), if existing
- Statement of Architecture Work (see Part IV, Section 36.2.20)
- Architecture Vision (see Part IV, Section 36.2.8)
- Architecture Repository (see Part IV, Section 36.2.5), including:
  — Re-usable building blocks
  — Organization-specific reference models
  — Organization standards
- Draft Architecture Definition Document (see Part IV, Section 36.2.3), including:

- — Baseline Business Architecture, Version 1.0 (detailed), if appropriate
- — Target Business Architecture, Version 1.0 (detailed)
- — Baseline Data Architecture, Version 0.1
- — Target Data Architecture, Version 0.1
- — Baseline Application Architecture, Version 0.1
- — Target Application Architecture, Version 0.1
- Draft Architecture Requirements Specification (see Part IV, Section 36.2.6), including:
  - — Gap analysis results (from Business Architecture)
  - — Relevant technical requirements that will apply to Phase C
- Business Architecture components of an Architecture Roadmap (see Part IV, Section 36.2.7)

9.4   Steps

Detailed steps for Phase C are given separately for each architecture domain:

- Data Architecture (see Chapter 10)
- Application Architecture (see Chapter 11)

9.5   Outputs

The main outputs of Phase C are:

- Refined and updated versions of the Architecture Vision phase deliverables, where applicable, including:
  - — Statement of Architecture Work (see Part IV, Section 36.2.20), updated if necessary
- Draft Architecture Definition Document (see Part IV, Section 36.2.3), including:
  - — Baseline Data Architecture, Version 1.0
  - — Target Data Architecture, Version 1.0
  - — Baseline Application Architecture, Version 1.0
  - — Target Application Architecture, Version 1.0
  - — Data Architecture views corresponding to the selected viewpoints addressing key stakeholder concerns
  - — Application Architecture views corresponding to the selected viewpoints addressing key stakeholder concerns
- Draft Architecture Requirements Specification (see Part IV, Section 36.2.6), including such Information Systems Architecture requirements as:

- — Gap analysis results
- — Relevant technical requirements that will apply to this evolution of the architecture development cycle
- — Constraints on the Technology Architecture about to be designed
- — Updated business requirements, if appropriate
- ■ Information systems components of an Architecture Roadmap (see Part IV, Section 36.2.7)

Chapter 10: Phase C: Information Systems Architectures — Data Architecture

This chapter describes the Data Architecture part of Phase C.

10.1 Objectives

The objective here is to define the major types and sources of data necessary to support the business, in a way that is:

- Understandable by stakeholders
- Complete and consistent
- Stable

It is important to note that this effort is *not* concerned with database design. The goal is to define the data entities relevant to the enterprise, not to design logical or physical storage systems. (However, linkages to existing files and databases may be developed, and may demonstrate significant areas for improvement.)

10.2 Approach

10.2.1 Key Considerations for Data Architecture

10.2.1.1 Data Management

When an enterprise has chosen to undertake largescale architectural transformation, it is important to understand and address data management issues. A structured and comprehensive approach to data management enables the effective use of data to capitalize on its competitive advantages.

Considerations include:

- A clear definition of which application components in the landscape will serve as the system of record or reference for enterprise master data
- Will there be an enterprise-wide standard that all application components, including software packages, need to adopt (in the main packages can be prescriptive about the data models and may not be flexible)?
- Clearly understand how data entities are utilized by business functions, processes, and services

- Clearly understand how and where enterprise data entities are created, stored, transported, and reported

- What is the level and complexity of data transformations required to support the information exchange needs between applications?

- What will be the requirement for software in supporting data integration with the enterprise's customers and suppliers (e.g., use of ETL tools during the data migration, data profiling tools to evaluate data quality, etc.)?

10.2.1.2 Data Migration

When an existing application is replaced, there will be a critical need to migrate data (master, transactional, and reference) to the new application. The Data Architecture should identify data migration requirements and also provide indicators as to the level of transformation, weeding, and cleansing that will be required to present data in a format that meets the requirements and constraints of the target application. The objective being that the target application has quality data when it is populated. Another key consideration is to ensure that an enterprise-wide common data definition is established to support the transformation.

10.2.1.3 Data Governance

Data governance considerations ensure that the enterprise has the necessary dimensions in place to enable the transformation, as follows:

- **Structure**: This dimension pertains to whether the enterprise has the necessary organizational structure and the standards bodies to manage data entity aspects of the transformation.

- **Management System**: Here enterprises should have the necessary management system and data-related programs to manage the governance aspects of data entities throughout its lifecycle.

- **People**: This dimension addresses what data-related skills and roles the enterprise requires for the transformation. If the enterprise lacks such resources and skills, the enterprise should consider either acquiring those critical skills or training existing internal resources to meet the requirements through a well-defined learning program.

10.2.2 Architecture Repository

As part of this phase, the architecture team will need to consider what relevant Data Architecture resources are available in the organization's Architecture Repository (see Part V, Chapter 41), in particular, generic data models relevant to the organization's industry "vertical" sector. For example:

- ARTS has defined a data model for the Retail industry.

- Energistics has defined a data model for the Petrotechnical industry.

10.3   Inputs

This section defines the inputs to Phase C (Data Architecture).

10.3.1   Reference Materials External to the Enterprise

- Architecture reference materials (see Part IV, Section 36.2.5)

10.3.2   Non-Architectural Inputs

- Request for Architecture Work (see Part IV, Section 36.2.17)
- Capability Assessment (see Part IV, Section 36.2.10)
- Communications Plan (see Part IV, Section 36.2.12)

10.3.3   Architectural Inputs

- Organizational Model for Enterprise Architecture (see Part IV, Section 36.2.16), including:
  - Scope of organizations impacted
  - Maturity assessment, gaps, and resolution approach
  - Roles and responsibilities for architecture team(s)
  - Constraints on architecture work
  - Budget requirements
  - Governance and support strategy
- Tailored Architecture Framework (see Part IV, Section 36.2.21, on page 496), including:
  - Tailored architecture method
  - Tailored architecture content (deliverables and artifacts)
  - Configured and deployed tools
- Data principles (see Part III, Section 23.6.2), if existing
- Statement of Architecture Work (see Part IV, Section 36.2.20)
- Architecture Vision (see Part IV, Section 36.2.8)
- Architecture Repository (see Part IV, Section 36.2.5), including:
  - Re-usable building blocks (in particular, definitions of current data)
  - Publicly available reference models
  - Organization-specific reference models
  - Organization standards
- Draft Architecture Definition Document (see Part IV, Section 36.2.3), including:

— Baseline Business Architecture, Version 1.0 (detailed), if appropriate

— Target Business Architecture, Version 1.0 (detailed)

— Baseline Data Architecture, Version 0.1, if available

— Target Data Architecture, Version 0.1, if available

— Baseline Application Architecture, Version 1.0 (detailed) or Version 0.1 (Vision)

— Target Application Architecture, Version 1.0 (detailed) or Version 0.1 (Vision)

— Baseline Technology Architecture, Version 0.1 (Vision)

— Target Technology Architecture, Version 0.1 (Vision)

- Draft Architecture Requirements Specification (see Part IV, Section 36.2.6), including:

  — Gap analysis results (from Business Architecture)

  — Relevant technical requirements that will apply to this phase

- Business Architecture components of an Architecture Roadmap (see Part IV, Section 36.2.7)

10.4 Steps

The level of detail addressed in Phase C will depend on the scope and goals of the overall architecture effort.

New data building blocks being introduced as part of this effort will need to be defined in detail during Phase C. Existing data building blocks to be carried over and supported in the target environment may already have been adequately defined in previous architectural work; but, if not, they too will need to be defined in Phase C.

The order of the steps in this phase (see below) as well as the time at which they are formally started and completed should be adapted to the situation at hand in accordance with the established architecture governance. In particular, determine whether in this situation it is appropriate to conduct Baseline Description or Target Architecture development first, as described in Part III, Chapter 19.

All activities that have been initiated in these steps must be closed during the Finalize the Data Architecture step (see Section 10.4.8). The documentation generated from these steps must be formally published in the Create Architecture Definition Document step (see Section 10.4.9.

The steps in Phase C (Data Architecture) are as follows:

- Select reference models, viewpoints, and tools (see Section 10.4.1)

- Develop Baseline Data Architecture Description (see Section 10.4.2)

- Develop Target Data Architecture Description (see Section 10.4.3)

- Perform gap analysis (see Section 10.4.4)

- Define roadmap components (see Section 10.4.5)

- Resolve impacts across the Architecture Landscape (see Section 10.4.6)
- Conduct formal stakeholder review (see Section 10.4.7)
- Finalize the Data Architecture (see Section 10.4.8)
- Create Architecture Definition Document (see Section 10.4.9)

10.4.1 Select Reference Models, Viewpoints, and Tools

Review and validate (or generate, if necessary) the set of data principles. These will normally form part of an overarching set of architecture principles. Guidelines for developing and applying principles, and a sample set of data principles, are given in Part III, Chapter 23.

Select relevant Data Architecture resources (reference models, patterns, etc.) on the basis of the business drivers, stakeholders, concerns, and Business Architecture.

Select relevant Data Architecture viewpoints (for example, stakeholders of the data — regulatory bodies, users, generators, subjects, auditors, etc.; various time dimensions — real-time, reporting period, event-driven, etc.; locations; business processes); i.e., those that will enable the architect to demonstrate how the stakeholder concerns are being addressed in the Data Architecture.

Identify appropriate tools and techniques (including forms) to be used for data capture, modeling, and analysis, in association with the selected viewpoints. Depending on the degree of sophistication warranted, these may comprise simple documents or spreadsheets, or more sophisticated modeling tools and techniques such as data management models, data models, etc. Examples of data modeling techniques are:

- Entity-relationship diagram
- Class diagrams
- Object role modeling

10.4.1.1 *Determine Overall Modeling Process*

For each viewpoint, select the models needed to support the specific view required, using the selected tool or method.

Examples of data models include:

- The Department of Defense Architecture Framework (DoDAF) Logical Data Model
- ARTS Data Model for the Retail industry
- Energistics Data Model for the Petrotechnical industry

Ensure that all stakeholder concerns are covered. If they are not, create new models to address concerns not covered, or augment existing models (see above).

The recommended process for developing a Data Architecture is as follows:

- Collect data-related models from existing Business Architecture and Application Architecture materials

- Rationalize data requirements and align with any existing enterprise data catalogs and models; this allows the development of a data inventory and entity relationship

- Update and develop matrices across the architecture by relating data to business service, business function, access rights, and application

- Elaborate Data Architecture views by examining how data is created, distributed, migrated, secured, and archived

10.4.1.2   *Identify Required Catalogs of Data Building Blocks*

The organization's data inventory is captured as a catalog within the Architecture Repository. Catalogs are hierarchical in nature and capture a decomposition of a metamodel entity and also decompositions across related model entities (e.g., logical data component → physical data component → data entity).

Catalogs form the raw material for development of matrices and diagrams and also act as a key resource for portfolio managing business and IT capability.

During the Business Architecture phase, a Business Service/Information diagram was created showing the key data entities required by the main business services. This is a prerequisite to successful Data Architecture activities.

Using the traceability from application to business function to data entity inherent in the content framework, it is possible to create an inventory of the data needed to be in place to support the Architecture Vision.

Once the data requirements are consolidated in a single location, it is possible to refine the data inventory to achieve semantic consistency and to remove gaps and overlaps.

The following catalogs should be considered for development within a Data Architecture:

- Data Entity/Data Component catalog

The structure of catalogs is based on the attributes of metamodel entities, as defined in Part IV, Chapter 34.

10.4.1.3   *Identify Required Matrices*

Matrices show the core relationships between related model entities.

Matrices form the raw material for development of diagrams and also act as a key resource for impact assessment.

At this stage, an entity to application systems matrix could be produced to validate this mapping. How data is created, maintained, transformed, and passed to other applications, or used by other applications, will now start to be understood. Obvious gaps such as entities that never seem to be created by an application or data created but never used, need to be noted for later gap analysis.

The rationalized data inventory can be used to update and refine the architectural diagrams of how data relates to other aspects of the architecture.

Once these updates have been made, it may be appropriate to drop into a short iteration of Application Architecture to resolve the changes identified.

The following matrices should be considered for development within a Data Architecture:

- Data Entity/Business Function (showing which data supports which functions and which business function owns which data)
- Business Service/Information (developed during the Business Architecture phase)
- System/Data (developed across the Application Architecture and Data Architecture phases)

The structure of matrices is based on the attributes of metamodel entities, as defined in Part IV, Chapter 34.

10.4.1.4 Identify Required Diagrams

Diagrams present the Data Architecture information from a set of different perspectives (viewpoints) according to the requirements of the stakeholders.

Once the data entities have been refined, a diagram of the relationships between entities and their attributes can be produced.

It is important to note at this stage that information may be a mixture of enterprise-level data (from system service providers and package vendor information) and local-level data held in personal databases and spreadsheets.

The level of detail modeled needs to be carefully assessed. Some physical system data models will exist down to a very detailed level; others will only have core entities modeled. Not all data models will have been kept up-to-date as applications were modified and extended over time. It is important to achieve a balance in the level of detail provided (e.g., reproducing existing detailed system physical data schemas or presenting high-level process maps and data requirements, highlight the two extreme views).

The following diagrams should be considered for development within a Data Architecture:

- Class diagram
- Data Dissemination diagram
- Data Lifecycle diagram
- Data Security diagram
- Data Migration diagram
- Class Hierarchy diagram

10.4.1.5 Identify Types of Requirement to be Collected

Once the Data Architecture catalogs, matrices, and diagrams have been developed, architecture modeling is completed by formalizing the data-focused requirements for implementing the Target Architecture.

Within this step, the architecture engagement should identify types of requirement that must be met by the architecture implementation, including:

- Functional requirements
- Non-functional requirements

- Assumptions
- Constraints
- Domain-specific Data Architecture principles
- Policies
- Standards
- Guidelines
- Specifications

10.4.2 Develop Baseline Data Architecture Description

Develop a Baseline Description of the existing Data Architecture, to the extent necessary to support the Target Data Architecture. The scope and level of detail to be defined will depend on the extent to which existing data elements are likely to be carried over into the Target Data Architecture, and on whether architectural descriptions exist, as described in Section 10.2. To the extent possible, identify the relevant Data Architecture building blocks, drawing on the Architecture Repository (see Part V, Chapter 41).

Where new architecture models need to be developed to satisfy stakeholder concerns, use the models identified within Step 1 as a guideline for creating new architecture content to describe the Baseline Architecture.

10.4.3 Develop Target Data Architecture Description

Develop a Target Description for the Data Architecture, to the extent necessary to support the Architecture Vision and Target Business Architecture. The scope and level of detail to be defined will depend on the relevance of the data elements to attaining the Target Architecture, and on whether architectural descriptions exist. To the extent possible, identify the relevant Data Architecture building blocks, drawing on the Architecture Repository (see Part V, Chapter 41).

Where new architecture models need to be developed to satisfy stakeholder concerns, use the models identified within Step 1 as a guideline for creating new architecture content to describe the Target Architecture.

10.4.4 Perform Gap Analysis

First, verify the architecture models for internal consistency and accuracy.

Note changes to the viewpoint represented in the selected models from the Architecture Repository, and document.

Test architecture models for completeness against requirements.

Identify gaps between the baseline and target:

- Create gap matrix, as described in Part III, Chapter 27
- Identify building blocks to be carried over, classifying as either changed or unchanged

- Identify eliminated building blocks
- Identify new building blocks
- Identify gaps and classify as those that should be developed and those that should be procured

10.4.5 Define Roadmap Components

Following creation of a Baseline Architecture, Target Architecture, and gap analysis, a data roadmap is required to prioritize activities over the coming phases.

This initial Data Architecture roadmap will be used as raw material to support more detailed definition of a consolidated, cross-discipline roadmap within the Opportunities & Solutions phase.

10.4.6 Resolve Impacts Across the Architecture Landscape

Once the Data Architecture is finalized, it is necessary to understand any wider impacts or implications.

At this stage, other architecture artifacts in the Architecture Landscape should be examined to identify:

- Does this Data Architecture create an impact on any pre-existing architectures?
- Have recent changes been made that impact the Data Architecture?
- Are there any opportunities to leverage work from this Data Architecture in other areas of the organization?
- Does this Data Architecture impact other projects (including those planned as well as those currently in progress)?
- Will this Data Architecture be impacted by other projects (including those planned as well as those currently in progress)?

10.4.7 Conduct Formal Stakeholder Review

Check the original motivation for the architecture project and the Statement of Architecture Work against the proposed Data Architecture. Conduct an impact analysis to identify any areas where the Business and Application Architectures (e.g., business practices) may need to change to cater for changes in the Data Architecture (for example, changes to forms or procedures, application systems, or database systems).

If the impact is significant, this may warrant the Business and Application Architectures being revisited.

Identify any areas where the Application Architecture (if generated at this point) may need to change to cater for changes in the Data Architecture (or to identify constraints on the Application Architecture about to be designed).

If the impact is significant, it may be appropriate to drop into a short iteration of the Application Architecture at this point.

Identify any constraints on the Technology Architecture about to be designed, refining the proposed Data Architecture only if necessary.

10.4.8 Finalize the Data Architecture

- Select standards for each of the building blocks, re-using as much as possible from the reference models selected from the Architecture Repository

- Fully document each building block

- Conduct final cross-check of overall architecture against business requirements; document rationale for building block decisions in the architecture document

- Document final requirements traceability report

- Document final mapping of the architecture within the Architecture Repository; from the selected building blocks, identify those that might be re-used, and publish via the Architecture Repository

- Finalize all the work products, such as gap analysis

10.4.9 Create Architecture Definition Document

Document rationale for building block decisions in the Architecture Definition Document.

Prepare Data Architecture sections of the Architecture Definition Document, comprising some or all of:

- Business data model

- Logical data model

- Data management process model

- Data Entity/Business Function matrix

- Data interoperability requirements (e.g., XML schema, security policies)

- If appropriate, use reports and/or graphics generated by modeling tools to demonstrate key views of the architecture; route the document for review by relevant stakeholders, and incorporate feedback

10.5   Outputs

The outputs of Phase C (Data Architecture) include:

- Refined and updated versions of the Architecture Vision phase deliverables, where applicable:
  - — Statement of Architecture Work (see Part IV, Section 36.2.20), updated if necessary
  - — Validated data principles (see Part III, Section 23.6.2), or new data principles (if generated here)
- Draft Architecture Definition Document (see Part IV, Section 36.2.3), including:
  - — Baseline Data Architecture, Version 1.0, if appropriate
  - — Target Data Architecture, Version 1.0
    - — Business data model
    - — Logical data model
    - — Data management process models
    - — Data Entity/Business Function matrix
  - — Views corresponding to the selected viewpoints addressing key stakeholder concerns
- Draft Architecture Requirements Specification (see Part IV, Section 36.2.6), including such Data Architecture requirements as:
  - — Gap analysis results
  - — Data interoperability requirements
  - — Relevant technical requirements that will apply to this evolution of the architecture development cycle
  - — Constraints on the Technology Architecture about to be designed
  - — Updated business requirements, if appropriate
  - — Updated application requirements, if appropriate
- Data Architecture components of an Architecture Roadmap (see Part IV, Section 36.2.7)

Chapter 11: Phase C: Information Systems Architectures — Application Architecture

This chapter describes the Application Architecture part of Phase C.

11.1 Objectives

The objective here is to define the major kinds of application system necessary to process the data and support the business.

It is important to note that this effort is *not* concerned with applications systems design. The goal is to define what kinds of application systems are relevant to the enterprise, and what those applications need to do in order to manage data and to present information to the human and computer actors in the enterprise.

The applications are not described as computer systems, but as logical groups of capabilities that manage the data objects in the Data Architecture and support the business functions in the Business Architecture. The applications and their capabilities are defined without reference to particular technologies. The applications are stable and relatively unchanging over time, whereas the technology used to implement them will change over time, based on the technologies currently available and changing business needs.

11.2 Approach

11.2.1 Architecture Repository

As part of this phase, the architecture team will need to consider what relevant Application Architecture resources are available in the Architecture Repository (see Part V, Chapter 41).

In particular:

- Generic business models relevant to the organization's industry "vertical" sector; for example:
  - The TeleManagement Forum (TMF) — www.tmforum.org — has developed detailed applications models relevant to the Telecommunications industry.
  - The Object Management Group (OMG) — www.omg.org — has a number of vertical Domain Task Forces developing software models relevant to specific vertical domains such as Healthcare, Transportation, Finance, etc.

- Application models relevant to common high-level business functions, such as electronic commerce, supply chain management, etc.

The Open Group has a Reference Model for Integrated Information Infrastructure (III-RM) — see Part VI, Chapter 44 — that focuses on the application-level components and services necessary to provide an integrated information infrastructure.

In addition, the ebXML initiative — www.ebxml.org — aims to provide an open, XML-based infrastructure enabling global use of electronic business information in an interoperable, secure, and consistent manner. The Unified Modeling Language (UML) is used for modeling aspects and XML for syntax aspects. The initiative was formed as a joint venture by the UN/CEFACT community and the OASIS Consortium, with ANSI X.12 also fully participating.

11.3 Inputs

This section defines the inputs to Phase C (Application Architecture).

11.3.1 Reference Materials External to the Enterprise

- Architecture reference materials (see Part IV, Section 36.2.5)

11.3.2 Non-Architectural Inputs

- Request for Architecture Work (see Part IV, Section 36.2.17)
- Capability Assessment (see Part IV, Section 36.2.10)
- Communications Plan (see Part IV, Section 36.2.12)

11.3.3 Architectural Inputs

- Organizational Model for Enterprise Architecture (see Part IV, Section 36.2.16), including:
  — Scope of organizations impacted
  — Maturity assessment, gaps, and resolution approach
  — Roles and responsibilities for architecture team(s)
  — Constraints on architecture work
  — Budget requirements
  — Governance and support strategy
- Tailored Architecture Framework (see Part IV, Section 36.2.21), including:
  — Tailored architecture method
  — Tailored architecture content (deliverables and artifacts)

- — Configured and deployed tools
- ■ Application principles (see Part III, Section 23.6.3), if existing
- ■ Statement of Architecture Work (see Part IV, Section 36.2.20)
- ■ Architecture Vision (see Part IV, Section 36.2.8)
- ■ Architecture Repository (see Part IV, Section 36.2.5), including:
  - — Re-usable building blocks
  - — Publicly available reference models
  - — Organization-specific reference models
  - — Organization standards
- ■ Draft Architecture Definition Document (see Part IV, Section 36.2.3), including:
  - — Baseline Business Architecture, Version 1.0 (detailed), if appropriate
  - — Target Business Architecture, Version 1.0 (detailed)
  - — Baseline Data Architecture, Version 1.0 (detailed), or Version 0.1 (Vision)
  - — Target Data Architecture, Version 1.0 (detailed), or Version 0.1 (Vision)
  - — Baseline Application Architecture, Version 0.1, if appropriate and if available
  - — Target Application Architecture, Version 0.1, if available
  - — Baseline Technology Architecture, Version 0.1 (Vision)
  - — Target Technology Architecture, Version 0.1 (Vision)
- ■ Draft Architecture Requirements Specification (see Part IV, Section 36.2.6), including:
  - — Gap analysis results (from Business Architecture and Data Architecture, if available)
  - — Relevant technical requirements that will apply to this phase
- ■ Business and Data Architecture components of an Architecture Roadmap, if available (see Part IV, Section 36.2.7)

11.4   Steps

The level of detail addressed in Phase C will depend on the scope and goals of the overall architecture effort.

New application building blocks being introduced as part of this effort will need to be defined in detail during Phase C. Existing application building blocks to be carried over and supported in the target environment may already have been adequately defined in previous architectural work; but, if not, they too will need to be defined in Phase C.

The order of the steps in this phase (see below as well as the time at which they are formally started and completed should be adapted to the situation at hand in accordance with the established architecture governance. In particular, determine whether in this situation it is appropriate to conduct Baseline Description or Target Architecture development first, as described in Part III, Chapter 19.

All activities that have been initiated in these steps must be closed during the Finalize the Application Architecture step (see Section 11.4.8). The documentation generated from these steps must be formally published in the Create Architecture Definition Document step (see Section 11.4.9).

The steps in Phase C (Application Architecture) are as follows:

- Select reference models, viewpoints, and tools (see Section 11.4.1)

- Develop Baseline Application Architecture Description (see Section 11.4.2)

- Develop Target Application Architecture Description (see Section 11.4.3)

- Perform gap analysis (see Section 11.4.4)

- Define roadmap components (see Section 11.4.5)

- Resolve impacts across the Architecture Landscape (see Section 11.4.6)

- Conduct formal stakeholder review (see Section 11.4.7)

- Finalize the Application Architecture (see Section 11.4.8)

- Create Architecture Definition Document (see Section 11.4.9)

11.4.1 Select Reference Models, Viewpoints, and Tools

Review and validate (or generate, if necessary) the set of application principles. These will normally form part of an overarching set of architecture principles. Guidelines for developing and applying principles, and a sample set of application principles, are given in Part III, Chapter 23.

Select relevant Application Architecture resources (reference models, patterns, etc.) from the Architecture Repository, on the basis of the business drivers, the stakeholders, and their concerns.

Select relevant Application Architecture viewpoints (for example, stakeholders of the applications — viewpoints relevant to functional and individual users of applications, etc.); i.e., those that will enable the architect to demonstrate how the stakeholder concerns are being addressed in the Application Architecture.

Identify appropriate tools and techniques to be used for capture, modeling, and analysis, in association with the selected viewpoints. Depending on the degree of sophistication warranted, these may comprise simple documents or spreadsheets, or more sophisticated modeling tools and techniques.

Consider using platform-independent descriptions of business logic. For example, the OMG's Model Driven Architecture (MDA) offers an approach to modeling Application Architectures that preserves the business logic from changes to the underlying platform and implementation technology.

11.4.1.1 *Determine Overall Modeling Process*

For each viewpoint, select the models needed to support the specific view required, using the selected tool or method.

Examples of applications models are:

- The TeleManagement Forum (TMF) — www.tmforum.org — has developed detailed applications models relevant to the Telecommunications industry.

- The Object Management Group (OMG) — www.omg.org — has a number of vertical Domain Task Forces developing software models relevant to specific vertical domains such as Healthcare, Transportation, Finance, etc.

Ensure that all stakeholder concerns are covered. If they are not, create new models to address concerns not covered, or augment existing models (see above).

The recommended process for developing an Application Architecture is as follows:

- Understand the list of applications or application components that are required, based on the baseline Application Portfolio, what the requirements are, and the business architecture scope

- Identify logical applications and the most appropriate physical applications

- Develop matrices across the architecture by relating applications to business service, business function, data, process, etc.

- Elaborate a set of Application Architecture views by examining how the application will function, capturing integration, migration, development, and operational concerns

The level and rigor of decomposition needed varies from enterprise to enterprise, as well as within an enterprise, and the architect should consider the enterprise's goals, objectives, scope, and purpose of the enterprise architecture effort to determine the level of decomposition.

The level of granularity should be sufficient to enable identification of gaps and the scope of candidate work packages.

11.4.1.2 *Identify Required Catalogs of Application Building Blocks*

The organization's Application Portfolio is captured as a catalog within the Architecture Repository. Catalogs are hierarchical in nature and capture a decomposition of a metamodel entity and also decompositions across related model entities (e.g., logical application component → physical application component → information system service).

Catalogs form the raw material for development of matrices and diagrams and also act as a key resource for portfolio managing business and IT capability.

The structure of catalogs is based on the attributes of metamodel entities, as defined in Part IV, Chapter 34.

The following catalogs should be considered for development within an Application Architecture:

- Application Portfolio catalog
- Interface catalog

11.4.1.3 *Identify Required Matrices*

Matrices show the core relationships between related model entities.

Matrices form the raw material for development of diagrams and also act as a key resource for impact assessment.

Once the baseline Application Portfolio has been assembled, it is necessary to map the applications to their purpose in supporting the business. The initial mapping should focus on business services within the Business Architecture, as this is the level of granularity where architecturally significant decisions are most likely to be needed.

Once applications are mapped to business services, it will also be possible to make associations from applications to data, through the business-information diagrams developed during Business Architecture.

If readily available, baseline application data models may be used to validate the Business Architecture and also to identify which data is held locally and which is accessed remotely.

The Data Architecture phase will focus on these issues, so at this point it may be appropriate to drop into a short iteration of Data Architecture if it is deemed to be valuable to scope of the architecture engagement.

Using existing information in the baseline application catalog, the Application Architecture should identify user and organizational dependencies on applications. This activity will support future state planning by determining impacted user communities and also facilitating the grouping of application by user type or user location.

A key user community to be specifically considered is the operational support organization. This activity should examine application dependencies on shared operations capabilities and produce a diagram on how each application is effectively operated and managed.

Specifically considering the needs of the operational community may identify requirements for new or extended governance capabilities and applications.

The following matrices should be considered for development within an Application Architecture:

- System/Organization matrix
- Role/System matrix
- Application Interaction matrix
- System/Function matrix

The structure of matrices is based on the attributes of metamodel entities, as defined in Part IV, Chapter 34.

11.4.1.4 *Identify Required Diagrams*

Diagrams present the Application Architecture information from a set of different perspectives (viewpoints) according to the requirements of the stakeholders.

Once the desired functionality of an application is known, it is necessary to perform an internal assessment of how the application should be best structured to meet its requirements.

In the case of packaged applications, it is likely to be the case that the application supports a number of configuration options, add-on modules, or application services that may be applied to the solution. For custom developed applications, it is necessary to identify the high-level structure of the application in terms of modules or sub-systems as a foundation to organize design activity.

The following diagrams should be considered for development within an Application Architecture:

- Application Communication diagram
- Application and User Location diagram
- Enterprise Manageability diagram
- Process/System Realization diagram
- Application Migration diagram
- Software Distribution diagram
- Software Engineering diagram

The structure of diagrams is based on the attributes of metamodel entities, as defined in Part IV, Chapter 34.

11.4.1.5 Identify Types of Requirement to be Collected

Once the Application Architecture catalogs, matrices, and diagrams have been developed, architecture modeling is completed by formalizing the application-focused requirements for implementing the Target Architecture.

Within this step, the architecture engagement should identify types of requirement that must be met by the architecture implementation, including:

- Functional requirements
- Non-functional requirements
- Assumptions
- Constraints
- Domain-specific Application Architecture principles
- Policies
- Standards
- Guidelines
- Specifications

11.4.2   Develop Baseline Application Architecture Description

Develop a Baseline Description of the existing Application Architecture, to the extent necessary to support the Target Application Architecture. The scope and level of detail to be defined will depend on the extent to which existing applications are likely to be carried over into the Target Application Architecture, and on whether architecture descriptions exist, as described in Section 11.2. To the extent possible, identify the relevant Application Architecture building blocks, drawing on the Architecture Repository (see Part V, Chapter 41). If not already existing within the Architecture Repository, define each application in line with the Application Portfolio catalog (see Part IV, Chapter 34).

Where new architecture models need to be developed to satisfy stakeholder concerns, use the models identified within Step 1 as a guideline for creating new architecture content to describe the Baseline Architecture.

11.4.3 Develop Target Application Architecture Description

Develop a Target Description for the Application Architecture, to the extent necessary to support the Architecture Vision, Target Business Architecture, and Target Data Architecture. The scope and level of detail to be defined will depend on the relevance of the applications elements to attaining the Target Architecture Vision, and on whether architectural descriptions exist. To the extent possible, identify the relevant Application Architecture building blocks, drawing on the Architecture Repository (see Part V, Chapter 41).

Where new architecture models need to be developed to satisfy stakeholder concerns, use the models identified within Step 1 as a guideline for creating new architecture content to describe the Target Architecture.

11.4.4 Perform Gap Analysis

First, verify the architecture models for internal consistency and accuracy.

Note changes to the viewpoint represented in the selected models from the Architecture Repository, and document.

Test architecture models for completeness against requirements.

Identify gaps between the baseline and target:

- Create gap matrix, as described in Part III, Chapter 27
- Identify building blocks to be carried over, classifying as either changed or unchanged
- Identify eliminated building blocks
- Identify new building blocks
- Identify gaps and classify as those that should be developed and those that should be procured

11.4.5 Define Roadmap Components

Following creation of a Baseline Architecture, Target Architecture, and gap analysis, an application roadmap is required to prioritize activities over the coming phases.

This initial Application Architecture roadmap will be used as raw material to support more detailed definition of a consolidated, cross-discipline roadmap within the Opportunities & Solutions phase.

11.4.6 Resolve Impacts Across the Architecture Landscape

Once the Application Architecture is finalized, it is necessary to understand any wider impacts or implications.

At this stage, other architecture artifacts in the Architecture Landscape should be examined to identify:

- Does this Application Architecture create an impact on any pre-existing architectures?

- Have recent changes been made that impact the Application Architecture?

- Are there any opportunities to leverage work from this Application Architecture in other areas of the organization?

- Does this Application Architecture impact other projects (including those planned as well as those currently in progress)?

- Will this Application Architecture be impacted by other projects (including those planned as well as those currently in progress)?

11.4.7 Conduct Formal Stakeholder Review

Check the original motivation for the architecture project and the Statement of Architecture Work against the proposed Application Architecture. Conduct an impact analysis, to identify any areas where the Business and Data Architectures (e.g., business practices) may need to change to cater for changes in the Application Architecture (for example, changes to forms or procedures, application systems, or database systems). If the impact is significant, this may warrant the Business and Data Architectures being revisited.

Identify any constraints on the Technology Architecture (especially the infrastructure) about to be designed.

11.4.8 Finalize the Application Architecture

- Select standards for each of the building blocks, re-using as much as possible from the reference models selected from the Architecture Repository

- Fully document each building block

- Conduct final cross-check of overall architecture against business requirements; document rationale for building block decisions in the architecture document

- Document final requirements traceability report

- Document final mapping of the architecture within the Architecture Repository; from the selected building blocks, identify those that might be re-used, and publish via the Architecture Repository

- Finalize all the work products, such as gap analysis

11.4.9 Create Architecture Definition Document

- Document rationale for building block decisions in the Architecture Definition Document
- Prepare Application Architecture sections of the Architecture Definition Document; if appropriate, use reports and/or graphics generated by modeling tools to demonstrate key views of the architecture; route the document for review by relevant stakeholders, and incorporate feedback

11.5 Outputs

The outputs of Phase C (Application Architecture) include:

- Refined and updated versions of the Architecture Vision phase deliverables, where applicable:
  - Statement of Architecture Work (see Part IV, Section 36.2.20), updated if necessary
  - Validated application principles, or new application principles (if generated here)
- Draft Architecture Definition Document (see Part IV, Section 36.2.3), including:
  - Baseline Application Architecture, Version 1.0, if appropriate
  - Target Application Architecture, Version 1.0
    - Process systems model
    - Place systems model
    - Time systems model
    - People systems model
  - Views corresponding to the selected viewpoints, addressing key stakeholder concerns
- Draft Architecture Requirements Specification (see Part IV, Section 36.2.6), including such Application Architecture requirements as:
  - Gap analysis results
  - Applications interoperability requirements
  - Relevant technical requirements that will apply to this evolution of the architecture development cycle
  - Constraints on the Technology Architecture about to be designed
  - Updated business requirements, if appropriate
  - Updated data requirements, if appropriate
- Application Architecture components of an Architecture Roadmap (see Part IV, Section 36.2.7)

Chapter 12: Phase D: Technology Architecture

This chapter describes the development of a Technology Architecture for an architecture project.

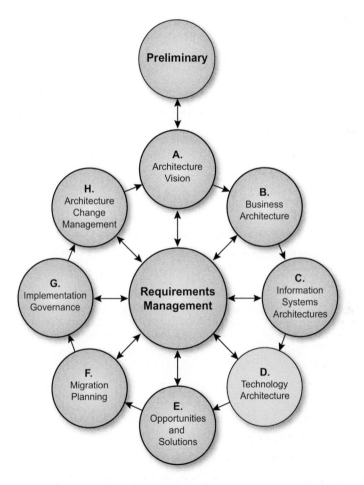

Figure 12-1 Phase D: Technology Architecture

12.1 Objectives

The Technology Architecture phase seeks to map application components defined in the Application Architecture phase into a set of technology components, which represent software and hardware components, available from the market or configured within the organization into technology platforms.

As Technology Architecture defines the physical realization of an architectural solution, it has strong links to implementation and migration planning.

Technology Architecture will define baseline (i.e., current) and target views of the technology portfolio, detailing the roadmap towards the Target Architecture, and to identify key work packages in the roadmap. Technology Architecture completes the set of architectural information and therefore supports cost assessment for particular migration scenarios.

12.2 Approach

12.2.1 Architecture Repository

As part of Phase D, the architecture team will need to consider what relevant Technology Architecture resources are available in the Architecture Repository (see Part V, Chapter 41).

In particular:

- Existing IT services as documented in the IT repository or IT service catalog
- TOGAF Technical Reference Model (TRM)
- Generic technology models relevant to the organization's industry "vertical" sector

  For example, the TeleManagement Forum (TMF) — www.tmforum.org — has developed detailed technology models relevant to the Telecommunications industry.

- Technology models relevant to Common Systems Architectures

  For example, The Open Group has a Reference Model for Integrated Information Infrastructure (III-RM) — see Part VI, Chapter 44 — that focuses on the application-level components and underlying services necessary to provide an integrated information infrastructure.

12.3   Inputs

This section defines the inputs to Phase D.

12.3.1   Reference Materials External to the Enterprise

- Architecture reference materials (see Part IV, Section 36.2.5)
- Product information on candidate products

12.3.2   Non-Architectural Inputs

- Request for Architecture Work (see Part IV, Section 36.2.17)
- Capability Assessment (see Part IV, Section 36.2.10)
- Communications Plan (see Part IV, Section 36.2.12)

12.3.3   Architectural Inputs

- Organizational Model for Enterprise Architecture (see Part IV, Section 36.2.16), including:
  - Scope of organizations impacted
  - Maturity assessment, gaps, and resolution approach
  - Roles and responsibilities for architecture team(s)
  - Constraints on architecture work
  - Budget requirements
  - Governance and support strategy
- Tailored Architecture Framework (see Part IV, Section 36.2.21), including:
  - Tailored architecture method
  - Tailored architecture content (deliverables and artifacts)
  - Configured and deployed tools
- Technology principles (see Part III, Section 23.6.4), if existing
- Statement of Architecture Work (see Part IV, Section 36.2.20)
- Architecture Vision (see Part IV, Section 36.2.8)
- Architecture Repository (see Part IV, Section 36.2.5), including:
  - Re-usable building blocks
  - Publicly available reference models
  - Organization-specific reference models
  - Organization standards

- Draft Architecture Definition Document (see Part IV, Section 36.2.3), including:
  - Baseline Business Architecture, Version 1.0 (detailed)
  - Target Business Architecture Version 1.0 (detailed)
  - Baseline Data Architecture, Version 1.0 (detailed)
  - Target Data Architecture, Version 1.0 (detailed)
  - Baseline Application Architecture, Version 1.0 (detailed)
  - Target Application Architecture, Version 1.0 (detailed)
  - Baseline Technology Architecture, Version 0.1 (vision)
  - Target Technology Architecture, Version 0.1 (vision)
- Draft Architecture Requirements Specification (see Part IV, Section 36.2.6), including:
  - Gap analysis results (from Business, Data, and Application Architectures)
  - Relevant technical requirements from previous phases
- Business, Data, and Application Architecture components of an Architecture Roadmap (see Part IV, Section 36.2.7)

12.4 Steps

The level of detail addressed in Phase D will depend on the scope and goals of the overall architecture effort.

New technology building blocks being introduced as part of this effort will need to be defined in detail during Phase D. Existing technology building blocks to be supported in the target environment may need to be redefined in Phase D to ensure interoperability and fit-for-purpose within this specific Technology Architecture.

The order of the steps in Phase D (see below) as well as the time at which they are formally started and completed should be adapted to the situation at hand in accordance with the established architecture governance. In particular, determine whether in this situation it is appropriate to conduct Baseline Description or Target Architecture development first, as described in Part III, Chapter 19.

All activities that have been initiated in these steps must be closed during the Finalize the Technology Architecture step (see Section 12.4.8). The documentation generated from these steps must be formally published in the Create Architecture Definition Document step (see Section 12.4.9).

The steps in Phase D are as follows:

- Select reference models, viewpoints, and tools (see Section 12.4.1)
- Develop Baseline Technology Architecture Description (see Section 12.4.2)
- Develop Target Technology Architecture Description (see Section 12.4.3)
- Perform gap analysis (see Section 12.4.4)

- Define roadmap components (see Section 12.4.5)
- Resolve impacts across the Architecture Landscape (see Section 12.4.6)
- Conduct formal stakeholder review (see Section 12.4.7)
- Finalize the Technology Architecture (see Section 12.4.8)
- Create Architecture Definition Document (see Section 12.4.9)

12.4.1 Select Reference Models, Viewpoints, and Tools

Review and validate the set of technology principles. These will normally form part of an overarching set of architecture principles. Guidelines for developing and applying principles, and a sample set of application principles, are given in Part III, Chapter 23.

Select relevant Technology Architecture resources (reference models, patterns, etc.) from the Architecture Repository (see Part V, Chapter 41, on page 559), on the basis of the business drivers, stakeholders, and their concerns.

Select relevant Technology Architecture viewpoints that will enable the architect to demonstrate how the stakeholder concerns are being addressed in the Technology Architecture.

Identify appropriate tools and techniques to be used for capture, modeling, and analysis, in association with the selected viewpoints. Depending on the degree of sophistication required, these may comprise simple documents and spreadsheets, or more sophisticated modeling tools and techniques.

12.4.1.1 *Determine Overall Modeling Process*

For each viewpoint, select the models needed to support the specific view required, using the selected tool or method. Ensure that all stakeholder concerns are covered. If they are not, create new models to address them, or augment existing models (see above).

The process to develop a Technology Architecture incorporates the following steps:

- Define a taxonomy of platform services and logical technology components (including standards)
- Identify relevant locations where technology is deployed
- Carry out a physical inventory of deployed technology and abstract up to fit into the taxonomy
- Look at application and business requirements for technology
- Is the technology in place fit-for-purpose to meet new requirements (i.e., does it meet functional and non-functional requirements)?
  — Refine the taxonomy
  — Product selection (including dependent products)
- Determine configuration of the selected technology
- Determine impact:

— Sizing and costing

— Capacity planning

— Installation/governance/migration impacts

In the earlier phases of the ADM, certain decisions made around service granularity and service boundaries will have implications on the technology component and the platform service. The areas where the Technology Architecture may be impacted will include the following:

- **Performance**: The granularity of the service will impact on platform service requirements. Coarse-grained services contain several units of functionality with potentially varying non-functional requirements, so platform performance should be considered. In addition, coarse-grained services can sometimes contain more information than actually required by the requesting system.

- **Maintainability**: If service granularity is too coarse, then introducing changes to that service becomes difficult and impacts the maintenance of the service and the platform on which it is delivered.

- **Location and Latency**: Services might interact with each other over remote links and inter-service communication will have in-built latency. Drawing service boundaries and setting the service granularity should consider platform/location impact of these inter-service communications.

- **Availability**: Service invocation is subject to network and/or service failure. So high communication availability is an important consideration during service decomposition and defining service granularity

Product selection processes may occur within the Technology Architecture phase where existing products are re-used, incremental capacity is being added, or product selection decisions are a constraint during project initiation.

Where product selection deviates from existing standards, involves significant effort, or has wide-ranging impact, this activity should be flagged as an opportunity and addressed through the Opportunities & Solutions phase.

12.4.1.2   *Identify Required Catalogs of Technology Building Blocks*

Catalogs are inventories of the core assets of the business. Catalogs are hierarchical in nature and capture a decomposition of a metamodel entity and also decompositions across related model entities (e.g., platform service → logical technology component → physical technology component).

Catalogs form the raw material for development of matrices and diagrams and also act as a key resource for portfolio managing business and IT capability.

The Technology Architecture should create technology catalogs as follows:

- Based on existing technology catalogs and analysis of applications carried out in the Application Architecture phase, collect a list of products in use.

- If the requirements identified in the Application Architecture are not met by existing products, extend the product list by examining products available on the market that provide the functionality and meet the required standards.

- Classify products against the TOGAF TRM if appropriate, extending the model as necessary to fit the classification of technology products in use.

- If technology standards are currently in place, apply these to the technology component catalog to gain a baseline view of compliance with technology standards.

The following catalogs should be considered for development within a Technology Architecture:

- Technology standards

- Technology portfolio

The structure of catalogs is based on the attributes of metamodel entities, as defined in Part IV, Chapter 34.

12.4.1.3 Identify Required Matrices

Matrices show the core relationships between related model entities.

Matrices form the raw material for development of diagrams and also act as a key resource for impact assessment.

The following matrix should be considered for development within a Technology Architecture:

- System/Technology matrix

12.4.1.4 Identify Required Diagrams

Diagrams present the Technology Architecture information from a set of different perspectives (viewpoints) according to the requirements of the stakeholders.

This activity provides a link between platform requirements and hosting requirements, as a single application may need to be physically located in several environments to support local access, development lifecycles, and hosting requirements.

For major baseline applications or application platforms (where multiple applications are hosted on the same infrastructure stack), produce a stack diagram showing how hardware, operating system, software infrastructure, and packaged applications combine.

If appropriate, extend the Application Architecture diagrams of software distribution to show how applications map onto the technology platform.

For each environment, produce a logical diagram of hardware and software infrastructure showing the contents of the environment and logical communications between components. Where available, collect capacity information on the deployed infrastructure.

For each environment, produce a physical diagram of communications infrastructure, such as routers, switches, firewalls, and network links. Where available, collect capacity information on the communications infrastructure.

The following diagrams should be considered for development within a Technology Architecture:

- Environments and Locations diagram

- Platform Decomposition diagram

- Processing diagram

- Networked Computing/Hardware diagram

- Communications Engineering diagram

The structure of diagrams is based on the attributes of metamodel entities, as defined in Part IV, Chapter 34.

12.4.1.5 Identify Types of Requirement to be Collected

Once the Technology Architecture catalogs, matrices, and diagrams have been developed, architecture modeling is completed by formalizing the data-focused requirements for implementing the Target Architecture.

Within this step, the architecture engagement should identify types of requirement that must be met by the architecture implementation, including:

- Functional requirements

- Non-functional requirements

- Assumptions

- Constraints

- Domain-specific Technology Architecture principles

- Policies

- Standards

- Guidelines

- Specifications

12.4.1.6 Select Services

The services portfolios are combinations of basic services from the service categories in the TOGAF TRM that do not conflict. The combination of services are again tested to ensure support for the applications. This is a pre-requisite to the later step of defining the architecture fully.

The previously identified requirements can provide more detailed information about:

- Requirements for organization-specific elements or pre-existing decisions (as applicable)

- Pre-existing and unchanging organizational elements (as applicable)

- Inherited external environment constraints

Where requirements demand definition of specialized services that are not identified in TOGAF, consideration should be given to how these might be replaced if standardized services become available in the future.

For each building block, build up a service description portfolio as a set of non-conflicting services. The set of services must be tested to ensure that the functionality provided meets application requirements.

12.4.2 Develop Baseline Technology Architecture Description

Develop a Baseline Description of the existing Technology Architecture, to support the Target Technology Architecture. The scope and level of detail to be defined will depend on the extent to which existing technology components are likely to be carried over into the Target Technology Architecture, and on whether architectural descriptions exist, as described in Section 12.2.

Identify the relevant Technology Architecture building blocks, drawing on any artifacts held in the Architecture Repository. If nothing exists within the Architecture Repository, define each application in line with the Technology Portfolio catalog (see Part IV, Chapter 34).

Begin by converting the description of the existing environment into the terms of the organization's Foundation Architecture (e.g., the TOGAF Foundation Architecture's TRM). This will allow the team developing the architecture to gain experience with the model and to understand its component parts. The team may be able to take advantage of a previous architectural definition, but it is assumed that some adaptation may be required to match the architectural definition techniques described as part of this process. Another important task is to set down a list of key questions which can be used later in the development process to measure the effectiveness of the new architecture.

Where new architecture models need to be developed to satisfy stakeholder concerns, use the models identified within Step 1 as a guideline for creating new architecture content to describe the Baseline Architecture.

12.4.3 Develop Target Technology Architecture Description

Develop a Target Description for the Technology Architecture, to the extent necessary to support the Architecture Vision, Target Business Architecture, and Target Information Systems Architecture. The scope and level of detail to be defined will depend on the relevance of the technology elements to attaining the Target Architecture, and on whether architectural descriptions exist. To the extent possible, identify the relevant Technology Architecture building blocks, drawing on the Architecture Repository (see Part V, Chapter 41).

A key process in the creation of a broad architectural model of the target system is the conceptualization of building blocks. Architecture Building Blocks (ABBs) describe the functionality and how they may be implemented without the detail introduced by configuration or detailed design. The method of defining building blocks, along with some general guidelines for their use in creating an architectural model, is described in Part IV, Section 37.3, and illustrated in detail in Section 37.4).

Where new architecture models need to be developed to satisfy stakeholder concerns, use the models identified within Step 1 as a guideline for creating new architecture content to describe the Target Architecture.

12.4.4 Perform Gap Analysis

First, verify the architecture models for internal consistency and accuracy.

Note changes to the viewpoint represented in the selected models from the Architecture Repository, and document.

Test architecture models for completeness against requirements.

Identify gaps between the baseline and target:

- Create gap matrix, as described in Part III, Chapter 27
- Identify building blocks to be carried over, classifying as either changed or unchanged
- Identify eliminated building blocks
- Identify new building blocks
- Identify gaps and classify as those that should be developed and those that should be procured

12.4.5 Define Roadmap Components

Following creation of a Baseline Architecture, Target Architecture, and gap analysis, a Technology Roadmap is required to prioritize activities over the coming phases.

This initial Technology Architecture roadmap will be used as raw material to support more detailed definition of a consolidated, cross-discipline roadmap within the Opportunities & Solutions phase.

12.4.6 Resolve Impacts Across the Architecture Landscape

Once the Technology Architecture is finalized, it is necessary to understand any wider impacts or implications.

At this stage, other architecture artifacts in the Architecture Landscape should be examined to identify:

- Does this Technology Architecture create an impact on any pre-existing architectures?
- Have recent changes been made that impact the Technology Architecture?
- Are there any opportunities to leverage work from this Technology Architecture in other areas of the organization?
- Does this Technology Architecture impact other projects (including those planned as well as those currently in progress)?
- Will this Technology Architecture be impacted by other projects (including those planned as well as those currently in progress)?

12.4.7 Conduct Formal Stakeholder Review

Check the original motivation for the architecture project and the Statement of Architecture Work against the proposed Technology Architecture, asking if it is fit for the purpose of supporting subsequent work in the other architecture domains. Refine the proposed Technology Architecture only if necessary.

12.4.8 Finalize the Technology Architecture

- Select standards for each of the building blocks, re-using as much as possible from the reference models selected from the Architecture Repository

- Fully document each building block

- Conduct final cross-check of overall architecture against business goals; document rationale for building block decisions in the architecture document

- Document final requirements traceability report

- Document final mapping of the architecture within the Architecture Repository; from the selected building blocks, identify those that might be re-used (working practices, roles, business relationships, job descriptions, etc.), and publish via the Architecture Repository

- Finalize all the work products, such as gap analysis

12.4.9 Create Architecture Definition Document

Document the rationale for building block decisions in the Architecture Definition Document.

Prepare the technology sections of the Architecture Definition Document, comprising some or all of:

- Fundamental functionality and attributes — semantic, unambiguous including security capability and manageability

- Dependent building blocks with required functionality and named interfaces

- Interfaces — chosen set, supplied (APIs, data formats, protocols, hardware interfaces, standards)

- Map to business/organizational entities and policies

If appropriate, use reports and/or graphics generated by modeling tools to demonstrate key views of the architecture. Route the document for review by relevant stakeholders, and incorporate feedback.

12.5   Outputs

The outputs of Phase D are:

- Refined and updated versions of the Architecture Vision phase deliverables, where applicable:
    - Statement of Architecture Work (see Part IV, Section 36.2.20), updated if necessary
    - Validated technology principles, or new technology principles (if generated here)
- Draft Architecture Definition Document (see Part IV, Section 36.2.3), including:
    - Target Technology Architecture, Version 1.0 (detailed), including:
        - Technology Components and their relationships to information systems
        - Technology platforms and their decomposition, showing the combinations of technology required to realize a particular technology "stack"
        - Environments and locations — a grouping of the required technology into computing environments (e.g., development, production)
        - Expected processing load and distribution of load across technology components
        - Physical (network) communications
        - Hardware and network specifications
    - Baseline Technology Architecture, Version 1.0 (detailed), if appropriate
    - Views corresponding to the selected viewpoints addressing key stakeholder concerns
- Draft Architecture Requirements Specification (see Part IV, Section 36.2.6), including such Technology Architecture requirements as:
    - Gap analysis results
    - Requirements output from Phases B and C
    - Updated technology requirements
- Technology Architecture components of an Architecture Roadmap (see Part IV, Section 36.2.7)

12.6   Postscript

Choosing the scope of an architecture development cycle carefully will accelerate the pay-back. In contrast, an excessively large scope is unlikely to lead to successful implementation.

Chapter 13: Phase E: Opportunities & Solutions

This chapter describes the process of identifying delivery vehicles (projects, programs, or portfolios) that effectively deliver the Target Architecture identified in previous phases.

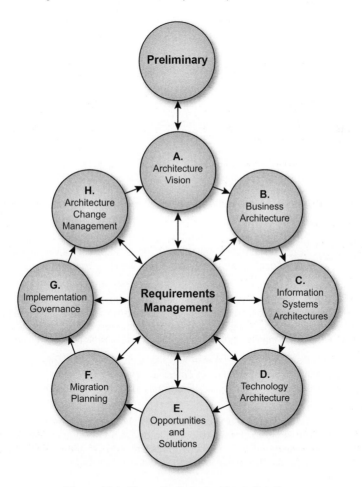

Figure 13-1 Phase E: Opportunities & Solutions

13.1   Objectives

The objectives of Phase E are:

- To review the target business objectives and capabilities, consolidate the gaps from Phases B to D, and then organize groups of building blocks to address these capabilities

- To review and confirm the enterprise's current parameters for and ability to absorb change

- To derive a series of Transition Architectures that deliver continuous business value (e.g., capability increments) through the exploitation of opportunities to realize the building blocks

- To generate and gain consensus on an outline Implementation and Migration Strategy

13.2   Approach

Phase E is the first phase which is directly concerned with the structure of how the Target Architecture will be implemented.

Phase E concentrates on how to deliver the architecture. It takes both a corporate business and technical perspective to rationalize the IT activities, and logically group them into project work packages within the IT portfolio and also within any other portfolios that are dependent upon IT. This is a collaborative effort with key enterprise stakeholders from business and IT (those who develop and implement/run the infrastructure) to assess the organization's business transformation readiness, identify opportunities and solutions, and identify all implementation constraints. Focus on business value, flexibility, co-ordination, and compromise will be keys to success.

When this phase is approached from an enterprise strategic change perspective, the identification of opportunities and solutions is done in a top-down fashion based on the architectural work to date, often with phased delivery working towards the Target Architecture.

However, in some circumstances the organizational environment does not allow for a top-down approach. In these circumstances this phase is approached in a tactical opportunistic way. Projects and factors outside the control of the corporate planners are influenced to achieve some of the planning objectives. In between these two extremes is a scenario where this phase is executed in a top-down fashion, but with a more limited timeframe and/or more focused scope.

The inputs into this phase are extensive and the architects and planners have to consolidate, integrate, and analyze the information to determine the best way ahead. Existing building blocks and case studies from the Architecture Repository can be useful when deciding how to move forward.

All of the previous architecture artifacts (especially the gap analysis results) are consolidated and their inter-dependencies closely assessed to derive an initial critical path. The overall intent is to simplify the transformation process by ruthlessly reducing the number of building blocks to be created as well as the administrative overhead associated with portfolio and project management.

Co-existence and interoperability issues (from a business, information, and technology perspective) are examined and clarified to provide precise development and implementation guidance. Implementation risks are identified, consolidated, and pragmatically accepted, transferred, and/or mitigated leaving residual risks that have to be documented and accepted.

A high-level Implementation and Migration Strategy (that will be part of the Implementation and Migration Plan) is created to illustrate the overall implementation approach based upon the outline critical path resulting from the dependencies analysis. At this point the work packages on the path are organized into portfolios, projects, or initiatives given a clear context (business value and fit) by the enterprise architecture. An impact analysis on the enterprise — especially the existing IT infrastructure — is conducted to assess further required activities (e.g., re-training of staff to handle new building blocks).

Finally, the architectures from Phases A to D are used to develop a series of Transition Architectures that show incremental progress from the Baseline Architecture to the Target. In smaller-scale change efforts, it may be possible to move directly from the Baseline to the Target, in which case, the Target Architecture is the only transition stage. When larger-scale change is being considered, several interim stages may be required, each described by a Transition Architecture.

Transition Architectures consist of a set of co-ordinated and well-defined building blocks grouped into work packages that define the scope of delivery vehicles (i.e., portfolios, projects, and initiatives). The Transition Architectures incrementally implement building blocks focusing on the delivery of a continuous flow of business value in support of corporate business objectives.

An advantage of using the phased Transition Architecture approach is that most organizations find that a change of architecture has too much impact on the organization to be undertaken in a single phase. Migration often requires consideration of a number of business and technical issues, not the least of which are those associated with the means of introducing change to operational systems.

The Transition Architecture delivers discrete business value based upon the overall enterprise capabilities that they are attempting to deliver, as well as the architecture dependencies discovered in the previous phase. Transition Architectures integrate and in turn support implementation governance and any follow-on design, or detailed architecture definition.

In many cases, simultaneous work will be conducted on several architectures at different levels of detail. It is perfectly possible for several Transition Architectures to be worked on simultaneously. While one Transition Architecture is being built, another is being designed, and another is being planned.

The success of the transformation is often dependent on factors and projects outside the control of the corporate planners. Enterprise business drivers and constraints provide guidance, constraints, and potential opportunities where existing portfolios, projects, and initiatives are creating associated change. The participation of key stakeholders — preferably those from corporate strategic planning — is highly recommended for the derivation of the potential Transition Architectures and the outline Implementation and Migration Plan.

13.3   Inputs

This section defines the inputs to Phase E.

13.3.1   Reference Materials External to the Enterprise

- Architecture reference materials (see Part IV, Section 36.2.5)
- Product information

13.3.2   Non-Architectural Inputs

- Request for Architecture Work (see Part IV, Section 36.2.17)
- Capability Assessment (see Part IV, Section 36.2.10)
- Communications Plan (see Part IV, Section 36.2.12)
- Planning methodologies

13.3.3   Architectural Inputs

- Organizational Model for Enterprise Architecture (see Part IV, Section 36.2.16), including:
  - Scope of organizations impacted
  - Maturity assessment, gaps, and resolution approach
  - Roles and responsibilities for architecture team(s)
  - Constraints on architecture work
  - Budget requirements
  - Governance and support strategy
- Governance models and frameworks:
  - Enterprise Architecture Management Framework
  - Capability Management Framework
  - Portfolio Management Framework
  - Project Management Framework
  - Operations Management Framework
- Tailored Architecture Framework (see Part IV, Section 36.2.21), including:
  - Tailored architecture method
  - Tailored architecture content (deliverables and artifacts)
  - Configured and deployed tools
- Statement of Architecture Work (see Part IV, Section 36.2.20)

- Architecture Vision (see Part IV, Section 36.2.8)
- Architecture Repository (see Part IV, Section 36.2.5), including:
  - Re-usable building blocks
  - Publicly available reference models
  - Organization-specific reference models
  - Organization standards
- Draft Architecture Definition Document (see Part IV, Section 36.2.3), including:
  - Baseline Business Architecture, Version 1.0 (detailed)
  - Target Business Architecture, Version 1.0 (detailed)
  - Baseline Data Architecture, Version 1.0 (detailed)
  - Target Data Architecture, Version 1.0 (detailed)
  - Baseline Application Architecture, Version 1.0 (detailed)
  - Target Application Architecture, Version 1.0 (detailed)
  - Baseline Technology Architecture, Version 1.0 (detailed)
  - Target Technology Architecture, Version 1.0 (detailed)
- Draft Architecture Requirements Specification (see Part IV, Section 36.2.6), including:
  - Gap analysis results (from Business, Data, Application, and Technology Architecture)
  - Architectural requirements
  - IT service management integration requirements
- Change Requests for existing business programs and projects (see Part IV, Section 36.2.11)

13.4   Steps

The level of detail addressed in Phase E will depend on the scope and goals of the overall architecture effort.

The order of the steps in Phase E (see below) as well as the time at which they are formally started and completed should be adapted to the situation at hand in accordance with the established architecture governance.

The steps in Phase E are as follows:

- Determine/confirm key corporate change attributes (see Section 13.4.1)
- Determine business constraints for implementation (see Section 13.4.2)
- Review and consolidate gap analysis results from Phases B to D (see Section 13.4.3)
- Review IT requirements from a functional perspective (see Section 13.4.4)

- Consolidate and reconcile interoperability requirements (see Section 13.4.5)

- Refine and validate dependencies (see Section 13.4.6)

- Confirm readiness and risk for business transformation (see Section 13.4.7)

- Formulate high-level Implementation and Migration Strategy (see Section 13.4.8)

- Identify and group major work packages (see Section 13.4.9)

- Identify Transition Architectures (see Section 13.4.10)

- Create portfolio and project charters and update the architectures (see Section 13.4.11)

13.4.1 Determine/Confirm Key Corporate Change Attributes

Determine how the enterprise architecture can be best implemented to take advantage of the organization's business culture. This should include the creation of an Implementation Factor Assessment and Deduction matrix (see Section 13.4.1.1) to serve as a repository for architecture implementation and migration decisions. It should also include an assessment of the organizations involved, their culture, and abilities.

For organizations where end-to-end enterprise architecture is well established, this step can be simple, but the matrix has to be established so that it can act as a repository of decisions.

13.4.1.1 *Create an Implementation Factor Assessment and Deduction Matrix*

The creation of an Implementation Factor Assessment and Deduction matrix ensures that relevant factors are considered and documented. It should become part of the Implementation and Migration Plan and document the rationale for key architecture decisions in this phase. These factors will help to identify solutions and opportunities and simplify the formulation of the Implementation and Migration Plan.

For a description of the Implementation Factor Assessment and Deduction matrix, see Part III, Section 28.1.

13.4.1.2 *Assess Transition Capabilities of Corporate and Partner Organizations*

Assess the capability to transition for the corporate organization and any partner organizations that are part of the corporate workflows (e.g., supply chain). The assessment should address at least the following factors:

- The organizational impact on shaping the Transition Architecture, such as how the business units or lines of business co-ordinate their activities; for example, the solution will be different for a company that is decentralized consisting of regional business units controlling all lines of business in their area *versus* a company that is organized along lines of business globally with strong central control

- The assignment of responsibilities within the organization for the implementation, so that the enterprise architecture becomes entrenched within the organization

- Corporate cultural influences for handling change; for example, a small to medium size organization in a rapidly evolving industrial sector with intense competitive pressures may change at a different rate than a large global company or government where there are more dependencies and the scale of the business transformation is more significant

These factors should be documented in the Implementation Factor Assessment and Deduction matrix.

13.4.1.3 *Assess Transition Capabilities of the Enterprise and IT Organization*

Conduct an assessment of the enterprise, and specifically the IT organization, to ensure that at least the following factors are addressed:

- The organization and culture of the enterprise and the IT organization; for example, a decentralized enterprise and/or IT culture organized regionally or along lines of business will be different to deal with than a centralized enterprise and/or IT organization delivering corporate shared services

- The enterprise personnel skill sets; these could be a major limitation to realizing a Target Architecture that needs a major shift in skill sets — this assessment can determine whether training and/or contracted assistance and/or outsourcing may be required in certain areas

- The gap analysis between the Baseline and Target Architectures; it can be useful to compare the Technical Reference Models produced for the Baseline and Target Architecture as a way to systematically assess services

These factors should be documented in the Implementation Factor Assessment and Deduction matrix.

13.4.2 **Determine Business Constraints for Implementation**

Identify any business drivers that would constrain the sequence of implementation. This should include a review of the corporate and line of business strategic and business plans and a review of the Enterprise Architecture Maturity Assessment.

13.4.2.1 *Review Corporate Strategic Plan*

Perform a review of the corporate strategic and business plans in order to validate the fundamental business drivers for the enterprise architecture so that the enterprise architecture can explicitly address each one. As these drivers may not be self-evident or even documented (e.g., the company is in merger discussions or in the process of either acquiring or being acquired) it is important to discover them as they could have a major impact on Transition Architectures and the associated Implementation and Migration Plan.

Each of the business drivers should be assessed with respect to implementation issues and documented in the Implementation Factor Assessment and Deduction matrix.

13.4.2.2 *Review the Enterprise Architecture Maturity Assessment*

Review the enterprise architecture maturity assessment that was conducted in the Preliminary phase and update the Implementation Factor Assessment and Deduction matrix with any actions, activities, initiatives, and projects that have to be undertaken.

13.4.2.3 Review Corporate Line-of-Business Strategic Plans

Perform a review of the line of business strategic and business plans in order to identify any initiatives, portfolios, projects, or activities that could be leveraged to accelerate the move to the Target Architecture.

This assessment will also determine whether there are any initiatives that could create problems for the enterprise architecture implementation. For the latter, the deductions should be in the form of mitigating efforts including changes to the enterprise architecture or to the line-of-business plan, or both.

Document all of the factors and deduced actions in the Implementation Factor Assessment and Deduction matrix.

13.4.3 Review and Consolidate Gap Analysis Results from Phases B to D

Consolidate and integrate the gap analysis results from the Business, Information Systems, and Technology Architectures (created in Phases B to D) and assess their implications with respect to potential solutions/opportunities and inter-dependencies.

13.4.3.1 Create a Consolidated Gaps, Solutions, and Dependencies Matrix

Create a Consolidated Gaps, Solutions, and Dependencies matrix, as described in Part III, Section 28.2. This enables identification of SBBs which could potentially address one or more gaps and their associated ABBs.

In the course of the activity, any additional "factors" should be added to the Implementation Factor Assessment and Deduction matrix.

13.4.3.2 Review the Phase B, C, and D Gap Analysis Results

The gap analysis results from each one of the architecture phases should be reviewed and consolidated in one long list that will become the basis for the work breakdown structure.

The gaps should be consolidated along with potential solutions to the gaps and dependencies. A recommended technique for determining the dependencies is to create a CRUD (Create, Read, Update, and Delete) to relate business functions to information.

In the course of the activity, any additional "factors" should be added to the Implementation Factor Assessment and Deduction matrix.

13.4.3.3 Rationalize the Consolidated Gaps, Solutions, and Dependencies Matrix

Once all of the gaps have been documented, re-organize the gap list and place like items together. When grouping the gaps, refer to the factor assessment table and review the implementation factors. This will lead into the next step when examining functional requirements.

In the course of the activity, any additional "factors" should be added to the Implementation Factor Assessment and Deduction matrix.

13.4.4 Review IT Requirements from a Functional Perspective

Assess the IT requirements, gaps, solutions, and factors to identify a minimal set of functional requirements whose integration into work packages would lead to a more efficient and effective implementation of the Target Architecture.

This functional perspective leads to the satisfaction of multiple requirements through the provision of shared solutions and services. The implications of this consolidation of requirements with respect to architectural components can be significant with respect to the provision of resources. For example, several requirements raised by several lines of business are resolved through the provision of a shared set of IT services within a work package/project. In many organizations the funding of these services by multiple lines of business is an issue that has to be addressed at the CxO level.

13.4.4.1 Assess the IT Requirements from a Functional Perspective

Review all of the information acquired so far to determine whether the solutions to the "gaps" can be functionally consolidated. The requirements so far collected should also be assessed in conjunction with the Target Architecture, the Consolidated Gaps, Solutions, and Dependencies matrix, and the Implementation Factor Assessment and Deduction matrix for verification and review.

This activity consolidates the requirements functionally and groups them together to act as the basis for work packages. A major benefit will be the reduction to an absolute minimum of projects that have to be managed, administered, and co-ordinated.

Once this is completed, then refine the Consolidated Gaps, Solutions, and Dependencies matrix, listing the new "gaps" that will form the basis for work packages.

13.4.4.2 Determine Issues Associated with Functional Integration

Often, requirements can be derived and funded in a siloed manner aligned with corporate business processes, leading to the same functionality being required (and possibly delivered) in many different places.

The Target Architecture offers an integrated solution with little or no redundancy, but the integration of requirements, and the associated funding often by lines of business, may be problematic. A useful heuristic is that it costs about twice as much to build a generic re-usable component or service *versus* a single-purpose component. An individual line of business may not wish to absorb the cost of building a shared service. An assessment of this issue may lead to a modification of the enterprise architecture to be less efficient, but still ensure that line of business funding is maintained.

These issues and outcomes should be documented in the Implementation Factor Assessment and Deduction matrix and, as required, included in the Consolidated Gaps, Solutions, and Dependencies matrix.

13.4.5 Consolidate and Reconcile Interoperability Requirements

Consolidate interoperability requirements identified in previous phases. Reconcile the consolidated requirements with potential solutions.

13.4.5.1 Consolidate Interoperability Requirements

During Phase A (Architecture Vision), the corporate operating model and interoperability levels should have been clearly defined and the latter refined in Phases B though D following the guidance described in Part III, Chapter 29.

The Architecture Vision and Target Architectures, as well as the Implementation Factor Assessment and Deduction matrix and Consolidated Gaps, Solutions, and Dependencies matrix, should now be consolidated and reviewed to look for any constraints on interoperability required by the potential set of solutions.

13.4.5.2 Reconcile Interoperability Requirements with Potential Solutions

The enterprise architect will have to ensure that there are no interoperability conflicts, especially if there is an intention to re-use existing SBBs and/or Commercial Off-The-Shelf (COTS) products, or third-party service providers.

The most significant issue to be addressed is business interoperability. Most SBBs, COTS, or third-party service providers will have their own business processes. Changes to embedded business processes will often require so much work that the advantages of re-using solutions will be lost. An alternative approach is to review business processes embedded within the Target Architecture and see whether they can be aligned with the SBB, COTS, or third-party service provider processes, and supporting Information Systems and Technology Architecture. The enterprise architect will have to ensure that any change to the Target Architecture or the SBB, COTS, or third-party service provider is signed off by the business architects and architecture sponsors in a revised Statement of Architecture Work.

13.4.6 Refine and Validate Dependencies

Refine the initial dependencies, ensuring that any constraints on the Implementation and Migration Plans are identified.

There are several key dependencies, described below, that have to be taken discretely into account, namely:

- Business dependencies
- Information dependencies
- Workflow dependencies
- IT dependencies
- Foundation dependencies

In assessing the dependencies, examine the projects and see whether logical increments of deliverables can be identified. The dependencies will also help to identify when the identified increment can be delivered.

Once finished, these dependencies should be grouped into a Dependency Analysis Report that becomes a governance artifact as part of the Transition Architecture, and serves as the basis for migration planning.

13.4.6.1 Assess Business Dependencies

Business dependencies are matters outside of the IT domain that impact the successful delivery of the IT service. These dependencies, when taken into a business capability-based planning perspective (see Part III, Chapter 32), could include matters such as:

- Professional development and training to implement, operate, and sustain the IT capability in both a business and technical context

- Infrastructure that is to provide the physical building to house the new business capability enhanced by IT (e.g., corporate data fusion center)

- Processes that enable the business use of the IT capability through the establishment of workflows, processes, and governance arrangements to ensure that the IT resources can be appropriately leveraged

- Policies, including government legislation, that guide the development of and use of the IT resources

13.4.6.2 Assess Information Dependencies

Information dependencies have to be assessed to ensure that IT resources and systems that create the data precede those that use the data. This can be achieved through the development of an information sequence for the projects, as described in the Phase C (Data Architecture).

It is recommended that the CRUD (Create, Read, Update, and Delete) matrix created in Section 13.4.3 be used to help sequence the projects such that projects that create information precede projects that read or update that information. Laying out the projects in that manner will be a valuable guide for the transformation planners.

13.4.6.3 Assess Workflow Dependencies

Business workflow dependencies include those that ensure that work processes are supported in a logical manner so that the workflows can be implemented in an incremental manner and as expeditiously as possible. This is closely linked to the information dependencies, but is more subtle as it relies on the support of workflow steps in a logical business-driven manner.

This could be sequential (e.g., Steps 1, 2, 3, and so on) or business-driven (e.g., Step 1, 5, 4, 6, and so on) depending upon the requirements. Sequential is straightforward to deal with, but the business-driven steps require a solid understanding of what the real business needs are.

Capability-based planning (refer to Part III, Chapter 32), for example, would see business sponsors and architects co-ordinating a series of projects and project increments to deliver business value on a continual basis. The fully implemented ideal workflow could well be preceded by an abbreviated one focusing on the critical and/or high return on investment processes.

13.4.6.4 Assess IT Dependencies

IT dependencies include those endeavors outside of the IT portfolio whereby IT resources/systems are critical to the achievement of their business capabilities. These could be triggered by business policy decisions. For example, the Business Re-engineering Group has deemed that a decrease in the corporate workforce could be compensated for through the introduction of new business processes enabled by IT. In this case, the delivery of certain key IT resources may be predicated by the wave of retirements in certain areas.

Some of the areas containing these dependencies are referred to in Part III, Chapter 32, specifically the capability dimensions.

13.4.6.5 Assess Foundation Dependencies and Interim Capabilities

Foundation dependencies include the assessment of the required resources, determining the optimal implementation path within the constraints of the enterprise's capacity for creating and absorbing change.

This "molding" to enable the continuous provision of business capabilities may necessitate the creation of interim or partial SBBs. For example, the creation of a partial information environment with information provider applications may be necessary for the first applications creating the information.

Avoid an "all or nothing" approach. For example, the management of client information does not require the presence of an entire information environment or a complete corporate data model. A minimal subset that will enable the initial applications to show business values will suffice and ensure that the funding envelope will be sustained for the fuller implementation of the Target Architecture.

Often, enterprise architecture involves top-down design and bottom-up implementation; however, the need to deliver business value in the short term will most likely necessitate implementation compromises and creates planned rework. The foundation dependencies will highlight the impact of decisions made and the extent of the rework that should be factored into the final resource bill.

13.4.6.6 Rationalize and Consolidate Dependencies

Dependency rationalization and consolidation includes the integration of the dependencies, many of which will have been repeated in the different areas. These dependencies should be included in a Dependency Analysis Report that will be part of the documentation of the Implementation and Migration Plan and will become a governance artifact.

13.4.7 Confirm Readiness and Risk for Business Transformation

Assess the readiness of the organization to undergo the business transformation changes necessary to leverage the enterprise architecture. Assess the ability of the organization to adapt to change and capture the associated risks. The actual Business Transformation Readiness Assessment or equivalent will have been conducted in Phase A as part of the Architecture Vision and the accompanying roadmap.

At this point, the architects should review the findings and determine the impact of the findings on the Transition Architecture.

There will always be risks associated with any transformation effort and it is important to identify, classify, and mitigate them before starting so that they can be tracked throughout any specific transformation effort. See Part III, Chapter 30 for a detailed description of the conduct of a Business Transformation Readiness Assessment, and Chapter 31 for a Risk Management Framework.

In enterprise architecture, the shortest distance between two points (the Baseline and Target Architectures) may not be a straight line, but rather a more indirect path that the organization can realistically negotiate. The determination of this path will be key in identifying what the Transition Architectures will be.

The outcome will help the enterprise architect to determine implementation approaches that will be culturally as well as technically feasible for both tactical and strategic success.

13.4.8 Formulate High-Level Implementation and Migration Strategy

Create an overall solutions strategy that will guide the Target Architecture implementation and structure the Transition Architectures.

The first activity is to determine an overall strategic approach to implementing the solutions and/or exploiting opportunities. The move to a new architecture paradigm (e.g., SOA) will require a different strategy to the upgrade of existing IT infrastructure. Formulation of an appropriate strategic approach will rely on the analysis of the previously identified risks.

Next, determine an approach to implement the overall strategic direction just selected, that will address and mitigate the risks identified in the Consolidated Gaps, Solutions, and Dependencies matrix.

In all cases, there is a need for high-level business and technical consensus as the implications of the approach could be significant. For example, a strategic investment could be highly profitable in the long term, but have a significant negative impact on stock price in the short term unless properly communicated.

13.4.8.1 Determine Overall Strategic Implementation Direction

Once the enterprise's capacity to create and absorb change is understood, it is important to determine what strategic approach will be taken to implement the Target Architecture. This critical step is often overlooked and the Target Architecture is decomposed into a series of projects that proceed independently with unfortunate results. Stakeholders need to know how the strategic goals are to be achieved.

Essentially there are three basic approaches as follows:

- **Greenfield**: start from the beginning
- **Revolutionary**: radical change (switch on, switch off); need for major surge resourcing (double/shadow system)
- **Evolutionary**: includes strategy of convergence; a phased approach is needed to introduce most capabilities

The greenfield and revolutionary approaches may be the most profitable strategically, but the intermediate costs must be taken into account, with the potential necessity to sustain two parallel environments. The costs are more than fiscal, but also include the impact of business transformation and a *de facto* reduction in management flexibility during the transition period. If either of these two approaches is adopted, then the impact on the Transition Architectures could be significant and, potentially, the Transition Architecture period could be significantly extended with in-service use being scheduled at a future point in time.

By far, the most common approach is the evolutionary one with ever-increasing levels of capability being introduced into the enterprise supported by a strategy of convergence to gradually integrate the existing corporate IT infrastructure.

It is recommended to collaborate with enterprise stakeholders to select a transformation approach and then to ensure that the resources will be provided to support its implementation.

13.4.8.2 Determine an Implementation Approach

The implementation approach addresses how the strategic implementation direction is to be executed to provide direction to both architects and portfolio/project managers alike.

The most common implementation methodology recommendations include:

- Quick win (snapshots)
- Achievable targets
- Value chain method (e.g., NASCIO methodology)

These approaches and the identified dependencies should become the rationale basis for the creation of the Transition Architectures.

This activity terminates with agreement on the Implementation and Migration Strategy for the enterprise.

13.4.9 Identify and Group Major Work Packages

Logically group the architectural activities into a coherent set of portfolios and projects, respecting the strategic implementation direction and approach.

Using the Consolidated Gaps, Solutions, and Dependencies matrix and Implementation Factor Assessment and Deduction matrix, logically group the various activities into work packages (where a work package is an inter-dependent set of activities and deliverables that deliver a discrete enterprise outcome). Although the outcome will be at the enterprise level, the work packages may not necessarily have a direct business outcome but might deliver a foundation artifact that will support other work packages that do. The architecture is a way to communicate the value of all work.

Then, analyze and refine these activities with respect to their business transformation issues and the agreed to strategic implementation approach.

Finally, group the work packages into portfolios and then projects within the portfolios taking into consideration the dependencies and the strategic implementation approach.

13.4.9.1 Identify Major Work Packages

Examine the Implementation Factor Assessment and Deduction matrix and Consolidated Gaps, Solutions, and Dependencies matrix. Add a column to the latter that recommends the proposed solution mechanism.

The best way to conduct this is to hold a working session with the domain architects and operations management personnel to determine what potentially the best solutions would be.

Indicate for every gap/activity whether the solution should be oriented towards:

- New development
- Based upon a existing product and/or solution that can be purchased

An existing system may resolve the requirement with minor enhancements.

For new development, this is a good point to determine whether the work is to be conducted in-house or through a contract, possibly requiring the involvement of procurement experts. Especially in government, significant lead times should be allowed, to perform the Request for Proposals/Quotes (RFP/RFQ) processes involved in awarding a contract.

Finally, group like solutions together as potential work packages.

By the end of this activity, there should be a re-grouped Consolidated Gaps, Solutions, and Dependencies matrix with an additional column addressing proposed solutions.

It might be useful to classify every current system as:

- **Mainstream Systems**: part of the future information system.
- **Contain Systems**: Expected to be replaced or modified in the planning horizon (next three years).
- **Replace Systems**: To be replaced in the planning horizon.

13.4.9.2 Analyze the Work Packages with Respect to Business Transformation

The enterprise architect should assess the business transformation-related activities and group them together as potential projects.

For example, as a result of the business transformation, a new line of business may be formed, so it may well be logical for activities pertaining to this new organization to be grouped together so that they can take ownership of the activities and mold them to their needs. In many organizations details are sometimes protected and the enterprise architecture team has to be sufficiently trusted to be perceived as key players and facilitators in the business transformation process.

The work packages should be re-grouped with respect to dependencies (including workflow) and this final analysis used as the basis for project identification. Slightly harder to identify are the projects required to update or replace existing functions which must be done differently in the new environment. One of the options to be considered here is leaving an existing system in place, retro-fitted to be able to co-exist with the new environment.

Once the projects are identified, then their project charter and scope statements should be clearly written and initial (i.e., order of magnitude) resource estimates completed. The benefits can also now be framed in the context in an enterprise-wide context using the enterprise architecture. High return on investment projects should be identified as potential pathfinders to show early success.

During this final step in the specification of building blocks it must be verified that the organization-specific requirements will be met. Key to this is checking against the original business scenario(s) driving the scope of the projects. It is important to note that the ensuing development process must include recognition of dependencies and boundaries for functions and should take account of what products are available in the marketplace. An example of how this might be expressed can be seen in the building blocks example (see Part IV, Chapter 37).

13.4.10 Identify Transition Architectures

Where the scope of change required to realize the Target Architecture requires an incremental approach, then the enterprise architects will need to develop a series of Transition Architectures as necessary.

Development of Transition Architectures must be based upon the preferred implementation approach, the Consolidated Gaps, Solutions, and Dependencies matrix, the listing of projects and portfolios, as well as the enterprise's capacity for creating and absorbing change. At this point, business capabilities and the supporting projects and portfolios will be broken down into realizable increments.

Transition Architectures provide an ability to continuously deliver business value. This must be measurable and either direct or indirect (i.e., supporting, foundational) business value. Transition Architectures do not have to be of uniform duration, but the timing of the Transition Architectures should not be considered at this point as it will be dealt with in the Migration Plan.

Finally, group the projects and portfolios into Transition Architectures.

13.4.10.1 Identify Transition Architecture and Capability Increments

Key stakeholders, planners, and the enterprise architect(s) will re-assess the missing business capabilities identified in the Architecture Vision and Target Architecture. They will decompose these targeted capabilities into capability increments each having clearly identified and measurable business value. The supporting top-level projects are in their turn decomposed into increments to deliver the capability increments.

It is useful to determine where the "hard" activities are. Unless there are compelling reasons, do not attack the hardest activities first. Rather, focus on activities that most easily deliver missing capability. Through the development of missing capability and any associated improvement to create and absorb change, perform hard activities, and manage associated risks, the enterprise's capacity will increase.

Most of the challenges in creating and absorbing change are challenges based upon an enterprise's maturity and are expressed in organization and cultural barriers to change.

If there is a business transformation organization within the enterprise, its staff should be involved in definition of capability increments, as they will often have to synchronize several enterprise portfolios delivering their part of the overall transformed set of capabilities. At this point, it may be desirable to assign capability managers whose job it will be to align all of the projects delivering their part of the capability increment.

This co-operation between the architects and business transformation office will help ensure co-ordination and at the same time facilitate the future approval (and release of resources) for the Implementation and Migration Plan.

The collaborative creation of capability increments should identify what activities and outcomes can be grouped together and roughly in what sequence they should be delivered.

13.4.10.2 Group Portfolios and Projects into Increments

This activity takes the sequence of activities and outcomes and groups the delivery vehicles (the portfolios and projects) into increments, specifying what should be delivered in each increment.

The projects should be broken down into increments based upon the deliverables required in each one of the Transition Architectures.

13.4.11 Create Portfolio and Project Charters and Update the Architectures

The approach is to complete the portfolio and major project charters with their deliverables being grouped into increments and scheduled for release within Transition Architecture increments. These architectures provide the enterprise context allowing projects to start their system development methodology initiation, planning, and requirements assessment phases.

Subsequently, the Architecture Vision, Architecture Definition Document, and Architecture Requirements Specification are updated with any additional relevant outcomes from this phase.

13.4.11.1 Create the Portfolio Charters

Review and consolidate the portfolio and potentially major project charters and ensure that their architectural outcomes are clearly defined. These architectural outcomes will give the portfolios enterprise context and determine the "fit" and "value" of the deliverables for governance.

13.4.11.2 Create the Project Charters

Review and consolidate the project charters and ensure that their architectural outcomes are clearly defined. These architectural outcomes will give the projects enterprise context and determine the "fit" and "value" of the deliverables for governance. These project charters will enable the projects to start with their system development method in particular initiation, planning, and requirements gathering.

13.4.11.3 Create the Transition Architectures

Create Transition Architectures that will form the basis for Migration Planning in Phase F. These Transition Architectures should have a clear set of outcomes and a specification of which delivery vehicle (portfolios/projects) will deliver them.

Generally speaking, each Transition Architecture will be expressed at a similar level of detail to the Architecture Definition Document developed in Phases B, C, and D. Where significant additional detail is required, the architect may elect to re-visit Phases B, C, and D for further elaboration. Alternatively, the architecture definition work could be deferred to a future work effort.

13.4.11.4 Conduct Overall Architecture Updates

Update the Architecture Vision with interoperability policy decisions and any other information that will remain relatively stable for the strategic duration and is largely technology-independent. The Architecture Vision also identifies all of the business capabilities that are to be implemented, and the subset of these capabilities that are to be implemented in the initial Architecture Definition Document.

The narrower scope of the Architecture Definition Document has to have a definitive list of targeted capabilities grouped into Transition Architectures that deliver capability increments through specific projects. The scope of each project is included within their charters that are outlined in the Architecture Definition Document.

13.5   Outputs

The outputs of Phase E are:

- Refined and updated versions of the Architecture Vision, Business Architecture, Information Systems Architecture, and Technology Architecture phase deliverables, where applicable:
    - Statement of Architecture Work (see Part IV, Section 36.2.20)
    - Architecture Vision (see Part IV, Section 36.2.8), including definition of types and degrees of interoperability
    - Draft Architecture Definition Document (see Part IV, Section 36.2.3), including:
        - Identification of increments
        - Interoperability and co-existence requirements
        - Inclusion of project list and project charters
    - Draft Architecture Requirements Specification (see Part IV, Section 36.2.6)
- Consolidated and validated Architecture Roadmap (see Part IV, Section 36.2.7)
- Capability Assessment (see Part IV, Section 36.2.10), including:
    - Enterprise Architecture Maturity Profile
    - Transformation Readiness Report
- Transition Architecture, Version 1.0 (see Part IV, Section 36.2.22), including:
    - Consolidated Gaps, Solutions, and Dependencies Assessment
    - Risk Register, Version 1.0
    - Impact analysis — project list
    - Dependency Analysis Report
    - Implementation Factor Assessment and Deduction Matrix
- Implementation and Migration Plan, Version 0.1 (see Part IV, Section 36.2.14) including the high-level Implementation and Migration Strategy

Chapter 14: Phase F: Migration Planning

This chapter addresses the formulation of an Implementation and Migration Plan that realizes some or all of the Transition Architectures identified in Phase E.

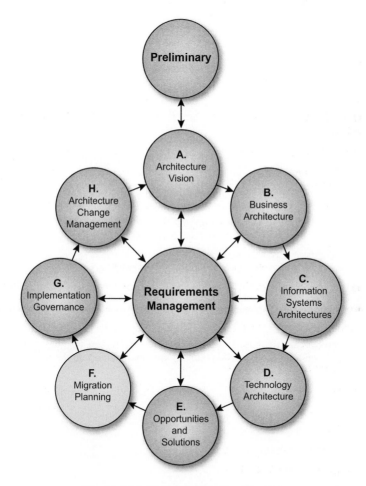

Figure 14-1 Phase F: Migration Planning

14.1   Objectives

The objectives of Phase F are to finalize a detailed Implementation and Migration Plan; specifically:

- To ensure that the Implementation and Migration Plan is co-ordinated with the various management frameworks in use within the enterprise

- To prioritize all work packages, projects, and building blocks by assigning business value to each and conducting a cost/business analysis

- To finalize the Architecture Vision and Architecture Definition Documents, in line with the agreed implementation approach

- To confirm the Transition Architectures defined in Phase E with relevant stakeholders

- To create, evolve, and monitor the detailed Implementation and Migration Plan providing necessary resources to enable the realization of the Transition Architectures, as defined in Phase E

14.2   Approach

The main focus of Phase F is the creation of a viable Implementation and Migration Plan in co-operation with the portfolio and project managers.

Phase F activities include assessing the dependencies, costs, and benefits of the various migration projects. The prioritized list of projects will form the basis of the detailed Implementation and Migration Plan that will supplement the architectures with portfolio and project-level detail assigning tasks to specific resources.

The Implementation and Migration Plan is part of a family of plans issued by enterprise management frameworks that have to be closely co-ordinated to ensure that business value is delivered and that the resources are made available to complete the necessary work. This phase ensures that all concerned agencies outside of the enterprise architecture world are aware of the scope and import of the Implementation and Migration Plan and its implications with respect to their activities.

Finally, the architecture evolution cycle should be established to ensure that the architecture stays relevant, and lessons learned should be documented to enable continuous process improvement.

14.3   Inputs

This section defines the inputs to Phase F.

14.3.1   Reference Materials External to the Enterprise

- Architecture reference materials (see Part IV, Section 36.2.5)

14.3.2   Non-Architectural Inputs

- Request for Architecture Work (see Part IV, Section 36.2.17)
- Capability Assessment (see Part IV, Section 36.2.10)
- Communications Plan (see Part IV, Section 36.2.12)

14.3.3   Architectural Inputs

- Organizational Model for Enterprise Architecture (see Part IV, Section 36.2.16), including:
  - Scope of organizations impacted
  - Maturity assessment, gaps, and resolution approach
  - Roles and responsibilities for architecture team(s)
  - Constraints on architecture work
  - Budget requirements
  - Governance and support strategy
- Governance models and frameworks:
  - Enterprise Architecture Management Framework
  - Capability Management Framework
  - Portfolio Management Framework
  - Project Management Framework
  - Operations Management Framework
- Tailored Architecture Framework (see Part IV, Section 36.2.21), including:
  - Tailored architecture method
  - Tailored architecture content (deliverables and artifacts)
  - Configured and deployed tools
- Statement of Architecture Work (see Part IV, Section 36.2.20)
- Architecture Vision (see Part IV, Section 36.2.8)
- Architecture Repository (see Part IV, Section 36.2.5), including:

- — Re-usable building blocks
- — Publicly available reference models
- — Organization-specific reference models
- — Organization standards

■ Draft Architecture Definition Document (see Part IV, Section 36.2.3), including:

- — Strategic Migration Plan
- — Baseline Business Architecture, Version 1.0 (detailed)
- — Target Business Architecture, Version 1.0 (detailed)
- — Baseline Data Architecture, Version 1.0 (detailed)
- — Target Data Architecture, Version 1.0 (detailed)
- — Baseline Application Architecture, Version 1.0 (detailed)
- — Target Application Architecture, Version 1.0 (detailed)
- — Baseline Technology Architecture, Version 1.0 (detailed)
- — Target Technology Architecture, Version 1.0 (detailed)
- — Impact analysis — project list and charters

■ Draft Architecture Requirements Specification (see Part IV, Section 36.2.6), including:

- — Architectural requirements
- — Gap analysis results (from Business, Data, Application, and Technology Architecture)
- — IT service management integration requirements

■ Change Requests for existing business programs and projects (see Part IV, Section 36.2.11)

■ Consolidated and validated Architecture Roadmap (see Part IV, Section 36.2.7)

■ Capability Assessment (see Part IV, Section 36.2.10), including:

- — Enterprise Architecture Maturity Profile
- — Transformation Readiness Report

■ Transition Architecture, Version 1.0 (see Part IV, Section 36.2.22), including:

- — Consolidated Gaps, Solutions, and Dependencies Assessment
- — Risk Register, Version 1.0
- — Impact analysis — project list
- — Dependency Analysis Report
- — Implementation Factor Assessment and Deduction Matrix

■ Implementation and Migration Plan, Version 0.1 (see Part IV, Section 36.2.14) including the high-level Implementation and Migration Strategy

14.4   Steps

The level of detail addressed in Phase F will depend on the scope and goals of the overall architecture effort.

The order of the steps in Phase F (see below) as well as the time at which they are formally started and completed should be adapted to the situation at hand in accordance with the established architecture governance.

The steps in Phase F are as follows:

- Confirm management framework interactions for Implementation and Migration Plan (see Section 14.4.1)

- Assign a business value to each project (see Section 14.4.2)

- Estimate resource requirements, project timings, and availability/delivery vehicle (see Section 14.4.3)

- Prioritize the migration projects through the conduct of a cost/benefit assessment and risk validation (see Section 14.4.4)

- Confirm Transition Architecture increments/phases and update Architecture Definition Document (see Section 14.4.5)

- Generate the Architecture Implementation Roadmap (Time-Lined) and Migration Plan (see Section 14.4.6)

- Establish the architecture evolution cycle and document lessons learned (see Section 14.4.7)

14.4.1   Confirm Management Framework Interactions for Implementation and Migration Plan

Establish what the Implementation and Migration Plan should include and ensure that it is co-ordinated with the other frameworks. There are four management frameworks that have to work closely together for the Migration Plan to succeed, namely:

- **Business Planning** that conceives, directs, and provides the resources for all of the activities required to achieve concrete business objectives/outcomes.

- **Enterprise Architecture** that structures and gives context to all enterprise activities delivering concrete business outcomes primarily but not exclusively in the IT domain; currently IT governance addresses many of these requirements.

- **Portfolio/Project Management** that co-ordinates, designs, and builds the business systems that deliver the concrete business outcomes.

- **Operations Management** that integrates, operates, and maintains the deliverables that deliver the concrete business outcomes.

If some of these areas are not managed, then the enterprise architect/CIO should at least create an *ad hoc* management framework capability with a plan to mature and formalize it over time.

The Implementation and Migration Plan will impact and consequently have to be reflected in each one of these frameworks. In the course of this step, understand the frameworks within the organization and ensure that these plans are co-ordinated and inserted (in a summary format) within the plans of each one of these frameworks.

The outcome of this step may well be that the Implementation and Migration Plan will not be discrete but part of a different plan produced by another one of the frameworks with enterprise architecture participation.

14.4.1.1 Align Implementation and Migration Plan with Business/Capability Planning

The Implementation and Migration Plan has to be aligned with the business strategy and plans for all aspects of the organization. The enterprise architect, with the Transition Architectures, will be able to view the strategic and in particular business plans from an architecture perspective to determine fitness-for-purpose. The assessment of business dependencies in Phase E will have ensured that there is a business fit.

The enterprise architect has to determine what can be leveraged from the strategic and business plans and conversely what has to be inserted as an addition to these plans in the upcoming release cycle. There will also be items that have to be repeated, or preferably referred to, in the Implementation and Migration Plan so that the corporate plan is synchronized. The key alignment target is the delivery of measurable, incremental business value at the end of each Transition Architecture.

14.4.1.2 Examine Business Transformation Aspects

Strategic business planning should address business transformation, as in virtually all cases of enterprise architecture implementation there is a significant business transformation element.

There are two main components, namely business transformation within and without the IT lines of service. The former is critical for the successful implementation of the IT resources and the strategic (vice-tactical/operational) planners should be made aware of and action this.

Changes within the IT operational infrastructure impact the Implementation and Migration Plan. Enterprise architecture enables a CIO/CTO to redirect the energies of his staff from maintaining a highly complex and less co-ordinated infrastructure to one where the staff can spend more time on contributing directly to business value. Where change results in downsizing an organization, a migration plan should include activities to reposition staff within the business and/or external placement.

Human capital is paramount in a knowledge-based economy and their acceptance of the changes cannot be taken for granted (in many case studies they have actually disabled or sabotaged the architectural innovations). New processes, union consultations, retraining, and appropriate severance are critical to the success of the enterprise architecture.

14.4.1.3 Assess the Synchronization of the Enterprise Architecture and Existing IT Planning Framework

The Implementation and Migration Plan is often a large subset of the corporate IT strategic and business plans. Their synchronization is essential and the need for them to proceed in alignment will be a major change in working approach for planners used to working without an enterprise architecture framework.

Enterprise architecture will provide the enterprise architecture planners with a context for their activities and provide the essential governance "fit" criteria. It will also allow for a systematic impact assessment of changes.

Ensure that the Implementation and Migration Plan is well-positioned within the IT business plan, in whatever level of detail required to ensure that resources will be provided to enable the execution of the plans. This may require a new business process to couple the planning and architecture functions.

14.4.1.4 *Align Implementation and Migration Plan with the Project Management Framework*

Every organization has a delivery methodology and most have some form of portfolio and project management framework at differing levels of maturity.

The Architecture Definition Document provides a Baseline Architecture, Target Architecture, gap analysis, and dependencies between building blocks. The Implementation and Migration Plan adds further detail on how the Target Architecture is to be realized through change activity.

The Implementation and Migration Plan may be part of the IT business plan (which may act as a high-level IT portfolio plan) or part of the plans managed by an IT portfolio management office. Regardless, the relationship between enterprise architecture and IT planning is symbiotic and must be leveraged.

The Implementation and Migration Plan has to be embedded within the appropriate and, more importantly, funded delivery vehicle. An important aspect to recall is that projects are transient delivery vehicles, whereas the enterprise architecture is permanent and manages the enterprise architecture artifacts delivered by the projects throughout their lifecycle.

Knowledge of the appropriate project delivery methodology (e.g., PRINCE2, PMBOK) should be used to frame the Implementation and Migration Plan. The enterprise architect and CIO will have to assess the best way for ensuring that the Implementation and Migration Plan is created and executed.

14.4.1.5 *Align Implementation and Migration Plan with the Operations Management Framework*

The linkage between implementation of the architecture and operations management has several dimensions that have to be directly addressed in the Implementation and Migration Plan.

The Operations Management function (if it exists) will have been closely involved in the establishment of the Baseline Architecture and have been solicited for recommendations for the Target Architectures.

The Operations Management function will be the recipient of the architecture artifacts which are the project deliverables (as indicated in the Implementation and Migration Plan and detailed by the systems development method) and it will take the ultimate decision as to whether they are to be implemented and when. This function runs the corporate infrastructure and the minute that an artifact is handed to them it comes under their configuration management and control, not the projects' nor the architects'.

The Implementation and Migration Plan has to cater for the hand-off to the operations management group and arrange for the co-ordination of the artifact configuration management. Operations management constantly execute "maintenance fixes" to the existing infrastructure. These could have significant architectural implications and complicate the integration of project deliverables unless properly co-ordinated. These "bottom-up" changes to the portfolios and architecture are very important as these Change Requests highlight either more efficient ways of implementing and/or deficiencies. Changes to the Solution Building Blocks (SBBs) are not a major issue as long as the interfaces and business rules are respected, and the SBB is made available across the organization. However, changes to the Architecture Building Blocks (ABBs) and interfaces will require architecture co-operation.

The intent should be to co-ordinate the service management functions and ideally create a combined configuration management database to hold the artifacts. Other services, such as release and change management, should be catered for in the Implementation and Migration Plan especially when lead times and processes have to be respected. Conversely, the Implementation and Migration Plan will give the operations management staff advanced consolidated insight into upcoming changes and allow for them to prepare as well as focus the expenditure of their limited funding. Conceptually the introduction of new building blocks should be treated as a Request for Change (RFC) and managed accordingly. Recommended processes will be discussed in some detail in Phase H (Architecture Change Management).

14.4.1.6 Establish Plans for Enterprise Architecture Management

The Implementation and Migration Plan sits at the intersection of numerous technical and management frameworks; indeed it may be part of an overall plan within another framework and be generated by the enterprise architecture team. The intent is to get the Implementation and Migration Plan executed and the actual vehicle used to present and resource it is actually moot.

The enterprise architecture framework (established in the Preliminary phase) should reflect the interactions, but may have to be modified to explicitly state how the architecture is to be implemented and migrated. Ensuring that the Implementation and Migration Plan (however presented) is followed is detailed in Phase G (Architecture Governance).

At this point, a Tailored Architecture Framework should be completed and a vehicle for the Implementation and Migration Plan established.

14.4.2 Assign a Business Value to Each Project

Establish and assign business values to all of the projects and project increments. The intent is to first establish what constitutes business value within the organization, how it can be measured, and then apply it to each one of the projects and project increments.

14.4.2.1 Confirm Organizational Business Value, Return on Investment, and Performance Measurement Parameters

This activity will ensure that the business value parameters are well-understood and serve as the basis for the creation and monitoring of the Implementation and Migration Plan. The intent is to enable the generation of continuous business value, even accepting that this might involve planned rework in subsequent sets of deliverables. There are several issues to address in this activity:

- **Performance Evaluation Criteria** are used by portfolio and capability managers to approve and monitor the progress of the architecture transformation.

- **Return on Investment Criteria** have to be detailed and signed off by the various executive stakeholders. Some of the IT contributions (e.g., business applications) to the realization of capabilities will be highly visible, while others (e.g., messaging services) might be critical but not visible. It is important that the CIO, as part of the corporate executive, establish return on investment criteria that ensure that the IT contribution is appropriately measured.

- **Business Value** has to be defined as well as techniques, such as the value chain (e.g., NASCIO), which are to be used to illustrate the IT role (as well as other business functions) in achieving tangible business outcomes. The business value will be used by portfolio and capability managers to allocate resources and, in cases where there are cutbacks, business value in conjunction with return on investment are the two prime factors used to determine whether an endeavor proceeds, is delayed, or canceled.

- **Critical Success Factors (CSF)** should be established to define success for a project and/or project increment. These will provide managers and implementers with a gauge as to what constitutes a successful implementation; it is also a form of contract between clients and developers/builders that will ensure a mutual understanding of business value.

- **Measures of Effectiveness (MOE)** are often performance criteria and many corporations include them in the CSFs. Where they are treated discretely, the enterprise architecture Transformation Plan should be clear as to how these criteria are to be grouped (e.g., in defense they include categories such as Persistence, Agility, Reach, Information, etc.).

- **Strategic Fit** based upon the overall enterprise architecture (all tiers) will be the critical factor for allowing the approval of any new endeavor (project/initiative or whatever) or determining the value of any deliverable. For example, the implementation of a new service will be assessed with respect to the enterprise architecture models; if it is to be delivered strategically fine; if it is *not* in the plan, then either the project is not approved or the architecture model can be changed to accommodate a good idea.

This activity should result in the establishment of a concrete set of criteria with which to assess the business value, return on investment, and measures to ascertain how the project is meeting their objectives.

14.4.2.2 Assign Risk to the Projects and Project Increments

The Consolidated Gaps, Solutions, and Dependencies Assessment (from Phase E) has a column of risks for each of the activities. The activities were logically grouped into portfolios, projects, and project increments in Phase E. The action is to aggregate the risks associated with each activity for the projects and their potential increments.

14.4.2.3 Assign Business Value to the Projects and Project Increments

Develop an estimated value to the business for each project. This should be completed with business management input with the enterprise architects ensuring that the value of the business enabling IT infrastructure is well understood (e.g., the single data environment that supports six other work packages).

14.4.2.4 Determine Continuous Business Value Assessment Technique

This assessment could be developed through the use of a matrix based on a value index dimension and a risk index dimension. An example is shown in Part III, Section 28.5.

This activity should be conducted by both business clients and the IT body. These measures will be used in portfolio management where the projects are often assessed with respect to this value-risk matrix with size and status (performance measurement) being graphically displayed. Value in this case should also be largely premised upon strategic fit that is directly attributed to the enterprise architecture.

Add project/SBB business value to the project list.

14.4.3 Estimate Resource Requirements, Project Timings, and Availability/Delivery Vehicles

Determine the required resources and times for each project and project increment and provide the initial cost estimates for the projects. The costs should be broken down into capital (to create the capability) and operations and maintenance (to run and sustain the capability). Note that operations and maintenance funding will have to commence as soon as the first increment is delivered to the operations management organization, so it has to be clear from the outset where both types of funding are coming from (and whether they are affordable). Excellent examples of the challenges are the cost of software maintenance and the costs associated with upgrading (including some of the custom software modifications that were made).

Costs should be inclusive of all capability expenses including business process development, interoperability requirements, training, new personnel, facilities, and so on, keeping in mind that the actual cost estimate will be refined by the project once it has been established.

Using dependencies, opportunities should be identified where the costs associated with delivering new and/or better capability can be offset by sun-setting existing systems whose maintenance that might absorb a disproportionate amount of resources. This should be clearly annotated.

Assign required resources to each activity and aggregate them at the project increment and project level.

14.4.3.1 Determine Personnel and Infrastructure (Capital) Costs

Against each SBB, determine what the costs will be in terms of personnel and infrastructure. For personnel, this estimate should also include the costs associated with training, moving, and severance. Each organization accounts differently for these costs and the architect should be aware of what comes from the project budget and what does not. Ensure that all infrastructure costs are captured, including office space, furniture, and so on, charging them against the activities or against the project. For IT infrastructure costs, include hardware and software that has to be acquired.

Aggregate the SBB costs to come up with a total for capital costs for the project and project increment and then add this project capital cost to the list of projects.

14.4.3.2 Determine Operations and Maintenance Costs

These costs are associated with the total cost of ownership for a SBB. These costs are triggered after the SBB has been handed over to operations management from the project delivery organization. When delivering increments, projects will have in-service building blocks while they are still creating others. However, the project will be well over before the lifecycle of the SBB expires. The operations and maintenance costs for the incremental building blocks in service during the life of the project have to be factored in by either the project or the operations management organization.

This cost estimate will ensure that there are sufficient resources available to service the SBB while in the field, so it should address the entire SBB lifecycle. The operations and maintenance costs should be added to the SBB construction cost to give a total cost of ownership. This total cost of ownership should now be added to the list of projects.

14.4.3.3 Determine Transition Architecture/Project Increment Timings

The determination of resources will enable an initial estimate of the time that the projects and project increments will take. This gross estimate should be included by every SBB being envisaged.

14.4.3.4 Assess Best Delivery Vehicle

The architect should use this estimate to look at the resources available within the organization and determine whether the delivery vehicle should be internal, by contract, or a combination thereof.

In many organizations, the implications of contracting are time-consuming, but the availability of an enterprise architecture and a series of well-defined building blocks should greatly facilitate the composition of the Statement of Architecture Work and result in well-focused bids that address the needs.

14.4.4 Prioritize the Migration Projects through the Conduct of a Cost/Benefit Assessment and Risk Validation

Prioritize the projects by ascertaining the business value of the artifacts delivered by the projects against the cost of delivering them. The approach is to first determine, as clearly as possible, the net benefit of all of the SBBs delivered by the projects, then verify that the risks have been effectively mitigated and factored in. Afterwards, the intent is to gain the requisite consensus (often at the enterprise level) to create a prioritized list of projects (based upon SBB net benefit and risk) that will provide the basis for resource allocation.

14.4.4.1 Derive Cost Benefit Analysis for the Migration Projects

Use the previously derived business drivers (Phase E) to initiate the cost/benefit analysis and drive the return on investment. The return on investment has to be clear and take into account the stakeholders for which it is being prepared. There are many ways of presenting a return on investment, not all of which involve the compilation of a complex report and a never-ending presentation.

Sensitivity to stakeholders' concerns is paramount. For example, if employee retention is a top priority, then the transferability of the skill sets being made redundant by a new system has to be taken into consideration and a retraining effort factored into the cost/benefit arrangement.

The important part of this step is to discover all costs, and ensure that executives deal with the net benefit (cost savings over time — cost of initiative over time). Surprises can impact the credibility of the entire architecture transformation and migration effort. Update the list of projects with the project net benefit supported by comments.

14.4.4.2 Validate the Risk Assessment

In this activity the architect reviews the risks documented in the Gaps, Solutions, and Dependencies Report and ensures that the risks for the project artifacts have been mitigated as much as possible. Update the project list with risk-related comments.

14.4.4.3 Prioritize the Projects

Using the previously calculated net benefits, and the Gaps, Solutions, and Dependencies Analysis, get consensus amongst the stakeholders to agree upon a prioritization of the projects and a validation/update of the corporate risk assessment based upon the prioritization.

Prioritization criteria will include the key business drivers identified in Phase E as well as those relating to individual stakeholders' agendas, such as:

- Reduction of costs
- Consolidation of services
- Ability to handle change
- A goal to have a minimum of "interim" solutions (they often become long-term/strategic!)

The outcome of this step is critical as the funding line will be clearly drawn somewhere down the list and projects below the line will have to wait or be canceled. The stakeholders creating the prioritization should be fully familiar with the risk assessment and have it (preferably an executive summary) close at hand when prioritizing the various projects/initiatives.

Make sure that foundation projects (i.e., those that were the result of the requirements analysis and consolidated common requirements into one project) are identified. The stakeholders should be able to agree to a funding line (projects above are funded and those below are not, unless extra funds become available) that will extend over the duration of the strategic plan (dependent upon the organization and its definition of strategic).

The list of projects should clearly highlight dependencies; often the line cannot be arbitrarily drawn as dependencies might dictate that either more or even less funding will be required. For example, there may be no point in only funding Projects A-D and not Project E because Project D needs Project E functionality to run. It is a business decision as to whether to:

- Fund Project E
- Cancel Project D
- Re-scope Project D to include the dependent functionality Project E was to deliver

From an IT perspective, it is essential that the foundation projects, that are often invisible to the end client but an essential intermediary, be understood and supported by senior management. The approach of top-down design and partial bottom-up implementation is easy to grasp but hard to implement as some of the business functionality may initially have to be given a lower implementation priority than some of the core IT work (e.g., implementing a portal or setting up the network).

Conversely, foundation projects have to be business success-aware and be able to support business outcomes as soon as possible. This means that the technical implementation roadmap may initially be less than technically optimal, but through the delivery of consistent business success, converge upon an ideally optimized (at least managed) solution. For example, the optimal way of implementing a full-service portal is to buy a complete solution and integrate it, but to get business results, creating an initial portal capability (using an *ad hoc* approach) to deliver a very narrow range of services might suffice in the short term. Strategically, a complete portal offering can be designed and planned for the future, incorporating implementation lessons learned. [Efficient, no; but effective (in business terms), yes.] Naturally the CIO has to ensure that corporate governance is aware of and takes ownership of this approach.

Finally, the stakeholders have to review the risk assessment and revise it as necessary ensuring that there is a full understanding of the residual risk associated with the prioritization and the projected funding line.

Update and reorder the list of projects with a "Priorities" column documenting the agreed priorities.

14.4.5 Confirm Transition Architecture Increments/Phases and Update Architecture Definition Document

An incremental implementation infers that concurrent activity may occur on multiple Transition Architectures that are defined to the necessary, but minimum, level of detail.

Confirm the proposed Transition Architecture increments and content. Review the work to date to assess what the Transition Architecture time-spans should be, taking into consideration the business value (or capability) increments to be delivered and all other factors. Once the Transition Architecture increments have been determined, consolidate the deliverables by project increment for each Transition Architecture. This will result in the initial Transition Architecture Roadmap.

14.4.5.1 Confirm Transition Architecture Time-Spans

The first activity is to agree to a time-span of an increment. This is challenging and has to take into account the area where the architecture has to be implemented and the results of the analysis of the enterprise list of events and timings (i.e., Zachman Column 5, Rows 1 and 2).

For example, in a government agency the tendering process may end up determining how long an increment will be; in other enterprises it could be the budgetary cycle and in another support of a corporate strategic objective. In most cases, a budgetary cycle will be the key factor influencing the delivery of an increment, with the rationale being that if a future increment's funding is delayed, at least there will be a solid delivery of business capability by the preceding increment. The phases mark natural checkpoints to re-evaluate and refocus portfolios and projects that are not delivering as expected.

Ultimately, it is the availability of funding that will determine whether increments move forward or not.

14.4.5.2 Confirm Business Value Delivered by the Increments

Once the length of an increment is clearly established, review gap analyses, dependencies, and prioritized portfolios/projects and validate that discrete business outcomes can be delivered in increments.

This should be completed at the portfolio level as entire projects may be re-scheduled to allow others to move forward more rapidly. A successful basic strategy is to focus on projects that will deliver short-term pay-offs and so create an impetus for proceeding with longer-term projects.

This again has to be conducted with business and IT staff contributing. Based upon the previously determined business value criteria and the consolidated list of dependencies, the business capability managers and the IT enterprise architects have to determine realistic "chunks" of business capability that the inter-dependent prioritized projects can realistically deliver in increments.

From an IT perspective, it is again important to align the architectures of the foundation projects to ensure that they flexibly, and potentially sub-optimally, deliver the requisite support to achieving the business outcomes. For example, the implementation of e-Government could start in the first increment with the issuance of "licenses" with each subsequent increment delivering ever-increasing levels of functionality.

14.4.5.3 Update Previously Created Architecture Deliverables

If the implementation approach has shifted as a result of confirming the implementation increments, update the Transition Architectures to reflect the revised direction. Update the Architecture Definition, assigning project objectives and aligning projects and their deliverables with the enterprise architecture increments. An example using a tabular form assigning projects their incremental deliverables is shown in Part III, Section 28.3.

The main feature is that the enterprise Architecture Definition is technology-aware but, as much as possible, technology-independent. The composition of the enterprise Architecture Definition Document is as described in Part IV, Chapter 36.

14.4.6 Generate the Architecture Implementation Roadmap (Time-Lined) and Migration Plan

This step generates the Implementation and Migration Plan sequence and details.

One of the main innovations of the tiered architecture is that it focuses on the continuous delivery of incremental business value and allows for the opportunistic exploitation of new technologies through the creation of just-in-time Transition Architectures.

The cost of this agility and flexibility is that there is significant concurrent activity that has to be closely co-ordinated. There are normally three to four Transition Architectures being managed concurrently, namely delivery, construction, design, and planning. There will be no one enterprise architecture and supporting plan with a myriad of detail, much of which will not stand the test of time; either from a business event or technology evolution perspective. Rather it will evolve over time towards a target state and be directed by a series of converging architecture states opportunistically moving towards a strategically defined Target Architecture. The enterprise architecture and Architecture Repository will also become ever-richer with enhanced content, re-usable resources and an ever-increasing amount of detail as the enterprise becomes self-documenting.

The main feature of architecture planning is that there will be a great deal of concurrent activity and the Implementation and Migration Plan will be the "glue" holding all of these artifacts together.

Much of the detail for the plan has already been gathered and this step brings it all together using accepted portfolio/project planning and management techniques.

14.4.6.1 Confirm Enterprise Architecture Evolution

There is a need to confirm the actual evolution of the architecture to co-ordinate the development of several concurrent instances of the various architectures. Resources have to be assigned to move the architectures ahead in a coherent manner, taking advantage of opportunities and innovations as well as coping with significant business events such as mergers, acquisitions, and the sell-off of certain lines of business.

This first part of the Implementation and Migration Plan shows the evolution of the architectures, that addresses the co-ordination of architectures created at different levels of granularity, and their various domain (business, data, application, and technology) components/building blocks. Detailed architectures are concerned with the state of the architecture at specific points in time, whereas more abstracted architectures are concerned with the state of the enterprise spanning a roadmap of many projects.

14.4.6.2 Enterprise Architecture State Evolution

This part of the Implementation and Migration Plan will show the proposed state of the architectures at various levels of detail depending upon how far in the future the snapshot is. This snapshot describes the functionality (in terms of implemented SBBs) delivered by the enterprise architecture at a particular point in time.

This can be effectively done through the use of the Foundation Architecture Technical Reference Model (TRM) and shows how the capabilities in each area evolve through the Transition Architectures.

14.4.6.3 Detailed Implementation and Migration Plan

The enterprise architect should complete this activity in conjunction with the portfolio management staff, whose primary responsibility will be to govern the implementation of the Target Architecture.

In Phase E and in previous steps within Phase F, most of the portfolio planning actions will have been completed and this step brings all the detail together into an overall plan.

Formally integrate all of the projects, project increments, and activities as well as dependencies into a project plan, preferably using a project scheduling and management tool that uses a standard methodology such as Critical Path Method or the like. The Transition Architecture states, with their defined business value, will act as portfolio milestones.

Ensure that all external dependencies are captured and included. For example, a delay in passing a certain piece of legislation may free up resources that can be used on another priority project.

Conduct resource leveling to ascertain the overall availability of resources with precedence being given to the priorities previously allocated. This exercise will clearly determine what can be done internally or externally with contract support. This will ensure that the architects allocate/reserve sufficient funds to projects with which to start their detailed planning. With the project architects already having participated in the specification of the Transition Architecture, these estimates should be fairly complete at this point in time.

14.4.6.4 Incorporate Project Schedules

Projects will take their assigned roles and ensure that their deliverables are thoroughly planned. Their project plans should be in part rolled up (in part or in their entirety) into the Implementation and Migration Plan. The enterprise architect might also find that the plan cannot accommodate their project concerns and must be updated.

The enterprise architect will then ensure that the plan is adjusted so that it has the best chance for success.

This activity results in the finalized Implementation and Migration Plan.

14.4.6.5 Plan the Migration Details

A building block is delivered when it becomes part of the corporate infrastructure and handed over to the operations management function.

The Migration Plan focuses on the actual handover of the constructed building blocks and their integration into the infrastructure.

The Migration Plan must cater for the ongoing operations and maintenance of the delivered building block and ensure that either the project and/or operations management have the resources to ensure that the building block is effectively sustained. As new project deliverables are often dependent upon those building blocks already in service, it is important that these deliverables are quickly but systematically placed into service.

14.4.7 Establish the Architecture Evolution Cycle and Document Lessons Learned

This treats the strategic enterprise Architecture Definition and Transition Architectures as configuration items that are managed in accordance with an accepted standard such as Information Technology Infrastructure Library (ITIL) that is now the basis for BS 15000 and ISO 20000.

Enterprise architectures must be kept up-to-date or they will slowly become irrelevant, superseded by portfolio and/or project architectures. The time required to translate a change from the strategic to the project architecture is significant and must be understood and catered for within the organization.

Furthermore, lessons learned are crucial within a learning organization and should be documented and assessed as part of the enterprise evolution process. The architecture evolution cycle will both impact and be governed by the enterprise's Architecture Change Management (Phase H).

14.4.7.1 Confirm the Enterprise Architecture Evolution Cycle

The set of architectures are dynamic and the transformation cycle will have to be subject to strict control in order to ensure that the architectures remain relevant and provide the critical guidance to the projects designing and delivering the SBBs.

There is also no point in creating a family of architecture artifacts that are not being maintained as they will become obsolete relatively quickly. In support of corporate business agility and to enable the incorporation of relevant emerging technology, there has to be a regular update mechanism built into the architecture transformation process.

Allocate sufficient time to execute this update cycle, considering the many activities to be co-ordinated. Specifically, there will be a "ripple" effect that will impact not only architectures, but portfolio and project plans. For example, a change in the enterprise Architecture Definition will probably impact two if not three Transition Architectures. This has to be taken into consideration when approving changes and formulating the update cycle.

There will also be a need to closely co-ordinate with the Enterprise Continuum and the ABBs and SBBs being actually deposited through the portfolio/project and Operations Management Frameworks. This will be part of the Architecture Governance phase.

14.4.7.2 *Confirm the Enterprise Architecture Management Processes*

Release management is particularly important so that everybody is able to contribute in a timely manner and that architects within the enterprise are using the authoritative architectures. Configuration management is also critical to ensure that the Enterprise Continuum and architectures are co-ordinated and that the architectures accurately reflect current and planned reality.

14.4.7.3 *Document Lessons Learned*

Lessons learned should be documented and treated as governance artifacts, reviewed and actioned, in the form of one or more change requests, or changes in processes, organizations, or whatever is needed to improve the development and implementation of enterprise architecture.

14.5 Outputs

The outputs of Phase F are:

- Implementation and Migration Plan, Version 1.0 (see Part IV, Section 36.2.14)
- Finalized Architecture Definition Document (see Part IV, Section 36.2.3)
- Finalized Architecture Requirements Specification (see Part IV, Section 36.2.6)
- Finalized Architecture Roadmap (see Part IV, Section 36.2.7)
- Finalized Transition Architecture (see Part IV, Section 36.2.22)
- Re-Usable Architecture Building Blocks (see Part IV, Section 36.2.1)
- Requests for Architecture Work (see Part IV, Section 36.2.17) for the architecture aspects of implementation projects (if any)
- Architecture Contracts (standard) (see Part VII, Chapter 49) for implementation projects
- Implementation Governance Model (see Part IV, Section 36.2.15)
- Change Requests arising from lessons learned

Chapter 15: Phase G: Implementation Governance

This chapter provides an architectural oversight of the implementation.

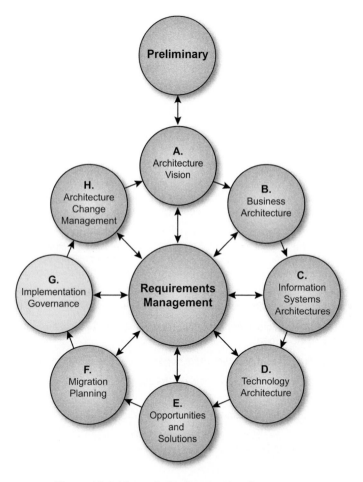

Figure 15-1 Phase G: Implementation Governance

15.1 Objectives

The objectives of Phase G are:

- To formulate recommendations for each implementation project
- To govern and manage an Architecture Contract covering the overall implementation and deployment process
- To perform appropriate governance functions while the solution is being implemented and deployed
- To ensure conformance with the defined architecture by implementation projects and other projects
- To ensure that the program of solutions is deployed successfully, as a planned program of work
- To ensure conformance of the deployed solution with the Target Architecture
- To mobilize supporting operations that will underpin the future working lifetime of the deployed solution

15.2 Approach

It is here that all the information for successful management of the various implementation projects is brought together. Note that, in parallel with Phase G, there is the execution of an organizational-specific development process, where the actual development happens.

To enable early realization of business value and benefits, and to minimize the risk in the transformation and migration program, the favored approach is to deploy the Target Architecture as a series of transitions. Each transition represents an incremental step towards the target, and each delivers business benefit in its own right. Therefore, the overall approach in Phase G is to:

- Establish an implementation program that will enable the delivery of the Transition Architectures agreed for implementation during the Migration Planning phase
- Adopt a phased deployment schedule that reflects the business priorities embodied in the Architecture Roadmap
- Follow the organization's standard for corporate, IT, and architecture governance
- Use the organization's established portfolio/program management approach, where this exists
- Define an operations framework to ensure the effective long life of the deployed solution

Phase G establishes the connection between architecture and implementation organization, through the Architecture Contract.

Project details are developed, including:

- Name, description, and objectives
- Scope, deliverables, and constraints

- Measures of effectiveness
- Acceptance criteria
- Risks and issues

Implementation governance is closely allied to overall architecture governance, which is discussed in Part VII, Chapter 50.

A key aspect of Phase G is ensuring compliance with the defined architecture(s), not only by the implementation projects, but also by other ongoing projects within the enterprise. The considerations involved with this are explained in detail in Part VII, Chapter 48.

15.3   Inputs

This section defines the inputs to Phase G.

15.3.1   Reference Materials External to the Enterprise

- Architecture reference materials (see Part IV, Section 36.2.5)

15.3.2   Non-Architectural Inputs

- Request for Architecture Work (see Part IV, Section 36.2.17)
- Capability Assessment (see Part IV, Section 36.2.10)

15.3.3   Architectural Inputs

- Organizational Model for Enterprise Architecture (see Part IV, Section 36.2.16), including:
  — Scope of organizations impacted
  — Maturity assessment, gaps, and resolution approach
  — Roles and responsibilities for architecture team(s)
  — Constraints on architecture work
  — Budget requirements
  — Governance and support strategy
- Tailored Architecture Framework (see Part IV, Section 36.2.21), including:
  — Tailored architecture method
  — Tailored architecture content (deliverables and artifacts)
  — Configured and deployed tools
- Statement of Architecture Work (see Part IV, Section 36.2.20)

- Architecture Vision (see Part IV, Section 36.2.8)
- Architecture Repository (see Part IV, Section 36.2.5), including:
  - Re-usable building blocks
  - Publicly available reference models
  - Organization-specific reference models
  - Organization standards
- Architecture Definition Document (see Part IV, Section 36.2.3)
- Architecture Requirements Specification (see Part IV, Section 36.2.6), including:
  - Architectural requirements
  - Gap analysis results (from Business, Data, Application, and Technology Architectures)
- Architecture Roadmap (see Part IV, Section 36.2.7)
- Transition Architecture (see Part IV, Section 36.2.22), including:
- Implementation Governance Model (see Part IV, Section 36.2.15)
- Architecture Contract (standard) (see Part VII, Chapter 49)
- Request for Architecture Work (see Part IV, Section 36.2.17) identified during Phases E and F
- Implementation and Migration Plan (see Part IV, Section 36.2.14)

15.4 Steps

The level of detail addressed in Phase G will depend on the scope and goals of the overall architecture effort.

The order of the steps in Phase G (see below) as well as the time at which they are formally started and completed should be adapted to the situation at hand in accordance with the established architecture governance.

The steps in Phase G are as follows:

- Confirm scope and priorities for deployment with development management (see Section 15.4.1)
- Identify deployment resources and skills (see Section 15.4.2)
- Guide development of solutions deployment (see Section 15.4.3)
- Perform enterprise architecture compliance reviews (see Section 15.4.4)
- Implement business and IT operations (see Section 15.4.5)
- Perform post-implementation review and close the implementation (see Section 15.4.6)

15.4.1 Confirm Scope and Priorities for Deployment with Development Management

- Review migration planning outputs and produce recommendations on deployment
- Identify enterprise architecture priorities for development teams
- Identify deployment issues and make recommendations
- Identify building blocks for replacement, update, etc.
- Perform gap analysis on enterprise architecture and solutions framework

  The gaps in the existing enterprise solutions framework need to be identified and the specific Solution Building Blocks (SBBs) required to fill these gaps will be the identified by the solutions architects. These SBBs may have a one-to-one or many-to-one relationship with the projects. The solutions architects need to define exactly how this will be done. There may be other projects working on these same capabilities and the solutions architects need to ensure that they can leverage best value from these investments.

- Produce a gap analysis report

15.4.2 Identify Deployment Resources and Skills

The project resources will include the development resources which will need to be educated in the overall enterprise architecture deliverables and expectations from the specific development and implementation projects.

The following considerations should be addressed in this step:

- Identify system development methods required for solutions development

  Note: There are a range of systems development methods and tools available to the project teams. The method should ideally be able to interoperate with the architecture outputs; for example, generate code from architecture artifacts delivered to date. This could be achieved through the use of modeling languages used for the enterprise architecture development that may be captured as inputs to the systems development tools and thereby reduce the cost of solutions development.

- Ensure that the systems development method enables feedback to the architecture team on designs

15.4.3 Guide Development of Solutions Deployment

- Formulate project recommendation

  For each separate implementation and deployment project, do the following:

  — Document scope of individual project in impact analysis

  — Document strategic requirements (from the architectural perspective) in impact analysis

  — Document change requests (such as support for a standard interface) in impact analysis

  — Document rules for conformance in impact analysis

  — Document timeline requirements from roadmap in impact analysis

- Document Architecture Contract

  — Obtain signature from all developing organizations and sponsoring organization

- Update Enterprise Continuum directory and repository for solutions

- Guide development of business & IT operating models for services

- Provide service requirements derived from enterprise architecture

- Guide definition of business & IT operational requirements

- Carry out gap analysis between the Solution Architecture and operations

- Produce Implementation Plan

15.4.4 Perform Enterprise Architecture Compliance Reviews

- Review ongoing implementation governance and architecture compliance for each building block

- Conduct post-development reviews

- Close development part of deployment projects

15.4.5 Implement Business and IT Operations

- Carry out the deployment projects including: IT services delivery implementation; business services delivery implementation; skills development & training implementation; communications documentation publication

- Publish new Baseline Architectures to the Architecture Repository and update other impacted repositories, such as operational configuration management stores

15.4.6 Perform Post-Implementation Review and Close the Implementation

- Conduct post-implementation reviews

- Publish reviews and close projects

Closure on Phase G will be when the solutions are fully deployed once.

15.5   Outputs

The outputs of Phase G are:

- Architecture Contract (signed) (see Part VII, Chapter 49), as recommended in the architecture-compliant implemented architectures
- Compliance Assessments (see Part IV, Section 36.2.13)
- Change Requests (see Part IV, Section 36.2.11)
- Architecture-compliant solutions deployed including:
  - The architecture-compliant implemented system

    Note: The implemented system is actually an output of the development process. However, given the importance of this output, it is stated here as an output of the ADM. The direct involvement of architecture staff in implementation will vary according to organizational policy, as described in Part VII, Chapter 50.

  - Populated Architecture Repository
  - Architecture compliance recommendations and dispensations
  - Recommendations on service delivery requirements
  - Recommendations on performance metrics
  - Service Level Agreements (SLAs)
  - Architecture Vision, updated post-implementation
  - Architecture Definition Document, updated post-implementation
  - Transition Architecture, updated post-implementation
  - Business and IT operating models for the implemented solution

Chapter 16: Phase H: Architecture Change Management

This chapter looks at establishing procedures for managing change to the new architecture.

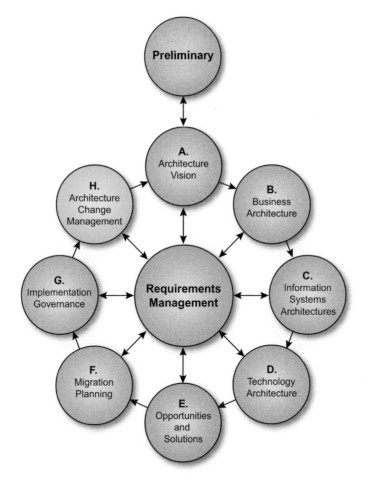

Figure 16-1 Phase H: Architecture Change Management

16.1 Objectives

The objectives of Phase H are:

- To ensure that baseline architectures continue to be fit-for-purpose
- To assess the performance of the architecture and make recommendations for change
- To assess changes to the framework and principles set up in previous phases
- To establish an architecture change management process for the new enterprise architecture baseline that is achieved with completion of Phase G
- To maximize the business value from the architecture and ongoing operations
- To operate the Governance Framework

16.2 Approach

The goal of an architecture change management process is to ensure that the architecture achieves its original target business value. This includes managing changes to the architecture in a cohesive and architected way.

This process will typically provide for the continual monitoring of such things as governance requests, new developments in technology, and changes in the business environment. When changes are identified, change management will determine whether to formally initiate a new architecture evolution cycle.

Additionally, the architecture change management process aims to establish and support the implemented enterprise architecture as a dynamic architecture; that is, one having the flexibility to evolve rapidly in response to changes in the technology and business environment.

Monitoring business growth and decline is a critical aspect of this phase. Usage of the enterprise architecture is the most important part of the architecture development cycle. All too often the business has been left with an enterprise architecture that works for the organization of yesterday but may not give back sufficient capability to meet the needs of the enterprise of today and tomorrow.

In many cases the architecture continues to fit, but the solutions underlying them may not, and some changes are required. The enterprise architect needs to be aware of these change requirements and considers this an essential part of constant renewal of the architecture.

Capacity measurement and recommendations for planning is a key aspect of this phase. While the architecture has been built to deliver a steady state Business Architecture with agreed capacity during the lifecycle of this enterprise architecture, the growth or decline in usage needs to be continually assessed to ensure that maximum business value is achieved.

For example, some Solution Architectures may not lend themselves to be scalable by a large factor — say 10 — or alternative solutions may be more economic when scaled up. While the architecture specifications may not change, the solutions or their operational context may change.

If the performance management and reporting has been built into the work products through previous phases, then this phase is about ensuring the effectiveness of these. If there needs to be additional monitoring or reporting, then this phase will handle the changes.

The value and change management process, once established, will determine:

- The circumstances under which the enterprise architecture, or parts of it, will be permitted to change after deployment, and the process by which that will happen

- The circumstances under which the architecture development cycle will be initiated again to develop a new architecture

The architecture change management process is very closely related to the architecture governance processes of the enterprise, and to the management of the Architecture Contract (see Part VII, Chapter 49) between the architecture function and the business users of the enterprise.

In Phase H it is critical that the governance body establish criteria to judge whether a Change Request warrants just an architecture update or whether it warrants starting a new cycle of the Architecture Development Method (ADM). It is especially important to avoid "creeping elegance", and the governance body must continue to look for changes that relate directly to business value.

An Architecture Compliance report should state whether the change is compliant to the current architecture. If it is non-compliant, an exemption may be granted with valid rationale. If the change has high impact on the architecture, then a strategy to manage its impact should be defined.

Guidelines for establishing these criteria are difficult to prescribe, as many companies accept risk differently, but as the ADM is exercised, the maturity level of the governance body will improve, and criteria will become clear for specific needs.

16.2.1 Drivers for Change

The main purpose for the development of the enterprise architecture so far has been strategic direction and top-down architecture and project generation to achieve corporate capabilities. However, enterprise architecture does not operate in a vacuum. There is usually an existing infrastructure and business which is already providing value.

There are also probably drivers for change which are often bottom-up, based upon modifying the existing infrastructure to enhance functionality. Enterprise architecture changes this paradigm by a strategic top-down approach to a degree, although the delivery of increments makes the equation more complex.

There are three ways to change the existing infrastructure that have to be integrated:

- Strategic, top-down directed change to enhance or create new capability (capital)

- Bottom-up changes to correct or enhance capability (operations and maintenance) for infrastructure under operations management

- Experiences with the previously delivered project increments in the care of operations management, but still being delivered by ongoing projects

Governance will have to handle the co-ordination of these Requests for Change, plus there needs to be a lessons learned process to allow for problems with the recently delivered increments to be resolved and changes made to the Target Architectures being designed and planned.

A lessons learned process ensures that mistakes are made once and not repeated. They can come from anywhere and anyone and cover any aspect of the enterprise architecture at any level (strategic, enterprise architecture definition, transition, or project). Often an enterprise architecture-related lesson may be an indirect outcome of a lesson learned elsewhere in the organization.

The Architecture Board (see Part VII, Chapter 47) assesses and approves Requests for Change (RFC). An RFC is typically in response to known problems but can also include improvements. A challenge for the Architecture Board when handling an RFC is to determine whether it should be approved or whether a project in a Transition Architecture will resolve the issue.

When assessing project or solution fit into the architecture, there may also be the case when an innovative solution or RFC drives a change in the architecture.

In addition, there are many technology-related drivers for architecture Change Requests. For example:

- New technology reports
- Asset management cost reductions
- Technology withdrawal
- Standards initiatives

This type of Change Request is normally manageable primarily through an enterprise's change management and architecture governance processes.

In addition, there are business drivers for architecture change, including:

- Business-as-usual developments
- Business exceptions
- Business innovations
- Business technology innovations
- Strategic change

This type of Change Request often results in a complete re-development of the architecture, or at least in an iteration of a part of the architecture development cycle, as explained below.

16.2.2 Enterprise Architecture Change Management Process

The enterprise architecture change management process needs to determine how changes are to be managed, what techniques are to be applied, and what methodologies used. The process also needs a filtering function that determines which phases of the architecture development process are impacted by requirements. For example, changes that affect only migration may be of no interest in the architecture development phases.

There are many valid approaches to change management, and various management techniques and methodologies that can be used to manage change; for example, project management methods such as PRINCE2, service management methods such as ITIL, management consultancy methods such as Catalyst, and many others. An enterprise that already has a change management process in place in a field other than architecture (for example, in systems development or project management) may well be able to adapt it for use in relation to architecture.

The following describes an approach to change management, aimed particularly at the support of a dynamic enterprise architecture, which may be considered for use if no similar process currently exists.

The approach is based on classifying required architectural changes into one of three categories:

- **Simplification change**: A simplification change can normally be handled via change management techniques.

- **Incremental change**: An incremental change may be capable of being handled via change management techniques, or it may require partial re-architecting, depending on the nature of the change (see Section 16.2.3 for guidelines).

- **Re-architecting change**: A re-architecting change requires putting the whole architecture through the architecture development cycle again.

Another way of looking at these three choices is to say that a simplification change to an architecture is often driven by a requirement to reduce investment; an incremental change is driven by a requirement to derive additional value from existing investment; and a re-architecting change is driven by a requirement to increase investment in order to create new value for exploitation.

To determine whether a change is simplification, incremental, or re-architecting, the following activities are undertaken:

1. Registration of all events that may impact the architecture

2. Resource allocation and management for architecture tasks

3. The process or role responsible for architecture resources has to make assessment of what should be done

4. Evaluation of impacts

16.2.3 Guidelines for Maintenance versus Architecture Redesign

A good rule-of-thumb is:

- If the change impacts two stakeholders or more, then it is likely to require an architecture redesign and re-entry to the ADM.

- If the change impacts only one stakeholder, then it is more likely to be a candidate for change management.

- If the change can be allowed under a dispensation, then it is more likely to be a candidate for change management.

For example:

- If the impact is significant for the business strategy, then there may be a need to redo the whole enterprise architecture — thus a re-architecting approach.

- If a new technology or standards emerge, then there may be a need to refresh the Technology Architecture, but not the whole enterprise architecture — thus an incremental change.

■ If the change is at an infrastructure level — for example, ten systems reduced or changed to one system — this may not change the architecture above the physical layer, but it will change the Baseline Description of the Technology Architecture. This would be a simplification change handled via change management techniques.

In particular, a refreshment cycle (partial or complete re-architecting) may be required if:

■ The Foundation Architecture needs to be re-aligned with the business strategy.

■ Substantial change is required to components and guidelines for use in deployment of the architecture.

■ Significant standards used in the product architecture are changed which have significant end-user impact; e.g., regulatory changes.

If there is a need for a refreshment cycle, then a new Request for Architecture Work must be issued (to move to another cycle).

16.3 Inputs

This section defines the inputs to Phase H.

16.3.1 Reference Materials External to the Enterprise

■ Architecture reference materials (see Part IV, Section 36.2.5)

16.3.2 Non-Architectural Inputs

■ Request for Architecture Work (see Part IV, Section 36.2.17) identified during Phases E and F

16.3.3 Architectural Inputs

■ Organizational Model for Enterprise Architecture (see Part IV, Section 36.2.16), including:

— Scope of organizations impacted

— Maturity assessment, gaps, and resolution approach

— Roles and responsibilities for architecture team(s)

— Constraints on architecture work

— Budget requirements

— Governance and support strategy

■ Tailored Architecture Framework (see Part IV, Section 36.2.21), including:

— Tailored architecture method

- Tailored architecture content (deliverables and artifacts)
- Configured and deployed tools
- Statement of Architecture Work (see Part IV, Section 36.2.20)
- Architecture Vision (see Part IV, Section 36.2.8)
- Architecture Repository (see Part IV, Section 36.2.5), including:
  - Re-usable building blocks
  - Publicly available reference models
  - Organization-specific reference models
  - Organization standards
- Architecture Definition Document (see Part IV, Section 36.2.3)
- Architecture Requirements Specification (see Part IV, Section 36.2.6), including:
  - Gap analysis results (from Business, Data, Application, and Technology Architectures)
  - Architectural requirements
- Architecture Roadmap (see Part IV, Section 36.2.7)
- Change Request (see Part IV, Section 36.2.11), — technology changes:
  - New technology reports
  - Asset management cost reduction initiatives
  - Technology withdrawal reports
  - Standards initiatives
- Change Request (see Part IV, Section 36.2.11), — business changes:
  - Business developments
  - Business exceptions
  - Business innovations
  - Business technology innovations
  - Strategic change developments
- Change Request (see Part IV, Section 36.2.11), — from lessons learned
- Transition Architecture (see Part IV, Section 36.2.22)
- Implementation Governance Model (see Part IV, Section 36.2.15)
- Architecture Contract (signed) (see Part VII, Chapter 49)
- Compliance Assessments (see Part IV, Section 36.2.13)
- Implementation and Migration Plan (see Part IV, Section 36.2.14)

16.4   Steps

The level of detail addressed in Phase H will depend on the scope and goals of the overall architecture effort.

The order of the steps in Phase H (see below) as well as the time at which they are formally started and completed should be adapted to the situation at hand in accordance with the established architecture governance.

The steps in Phase H are as follows:

- Establish value realization process (see Section 16.4.1)
- Deploy monitoring tools (see Section 16.4.2)
- Manage risks (see Section 16.4.3)
- Provide analysis for architecture change management (see Section 16.4.4)
- Develop change requirements to meet performance targets (see Section 16.4.5)
- Manage governance process (see Section 16.4.6)
- Activate the process to implement change (see Section 16.4.7)

16.4.1   Establish Value Realization Process

Influence business projects to exploit the enterprise architecture for value realization (outcomes).

16.4.2   Deploy Monitoring Tools

Ensure monitoring tools are deployed and applied to enable the following:

- Monitor technology changes which could impact the Baseline Architecture
- Monitor business changes which could impact the Baseline Architecture
- Business value tracking; e.g., investment appraisal method to determine value metrics for the business objectives
- Monitor enterprise architecture capability maturity
- Track and assess asset management programs
- Track the QoS performances and usage
- Determine and track business continuity requirements

16.4.3 Manage Risks

Manage enterprise architecture risks and provide recommendations for IT strategy.

16.4.4 Provide Analysis for Architecture Change Management

Provide analysis for architecture change management:

- Analyze performance
- Conduct enterprise architecture performance reviews with service management
- Assess Change Requests and reporting to ensure that the expected value realization and Service Level Agreement (SLA) expectations of the customers are met
- Undertake a gap analysis of the performance of the enterprise architecture
- Ensure change management requests adhere to the enterprise architecture governance and framework

16.4.5 Develop Change Requirements to Meet Performance Targets

Make recommendations on change requirements to meet performance targets and development of position to act.

16.4.6 Manage Governance Process

Manage governance process and framework for architecture:

- Arrange meeting of Architecture Board (or other Governing Council)
- Hold meeting of the Architecture Board with the aim of the meeting to decide on handling changes (technology and business and dispensations)

16.4.7 Activate the Process to Implement Change

Activate the architecture process to implement change:

- Produce a new Request for Architecture Work and request for investment
- Ensure any changes implemented in this phase are captured and documented in the Architecture Repository

16.5   Outputs

The outputs of Phase H are:

- Architecture updates (for maintenance changes)
- Changes to architecture framework and principles (for maintenance changes)
- New Request for Architecture Work (see Part IV, Section 36.2.17), to move to another cycle (for major changes)
- Statement of Architecture Work (see Part IV, Section 36.2.20), updated if necessary
- Architecture Contract (see Part IV, Chapter 49), updated if necessary
- Compliance Assessments (see Part IV, Section 36.2.13), updated if necessary

Chapter 17: ADM Architecture Requirements Management

This chapter looks at the process of managing architecture requirements throughout the ADM.

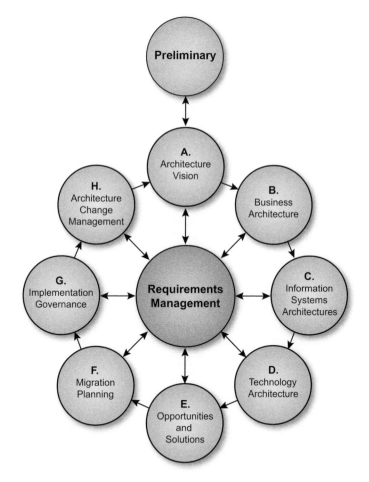

Figure 17-1 ADM Architecture Requirements Management

17.1   Objectives

The objectives of the Requirements Management phase are:

- To define a process whereby requirements for enterprise architecture are identified, stored, and fed into and out of the relevant ADM phases

17.2   Approach

17.2.1   General

As indicated by the "Requirements Management" circle at the center of the ADM graphic, the ADM is continuously driven by the requirements management process.

It is important to note that the Requirements Management circle denotes, not a static set of requirements, but a dynamic process whereby requirements for enterprise architecture and subsequent changes to those requirements are identified, stored, and fed into and out of the relevant ADM phases.

The ability to deal with changes in requirements is crucial. Architecture is an activity that by its very nature deals with uncertainty and change — the "grey area" between what stakeholders aspire to and what can be specified and engineered as a solution. Architecture requirements are therefore invariably subject to change in practice. Moreover, architecture often deals with drivers and constraints, many of which by their very nature are beyond the control of the enterprise (changing market conditions, new legislation, etc.), and which can produce changes in requirements in an unforeseen manner.

Note also that the requirements management process itself does not dispose of, address, or prioritize any requirements; this is done within the relevant phase of the ADM. It is merely the process for managing requirements throughout the overall ADM.

17.2.2   Resources

The world of requirements engineering is rich with emerging recommendations and processes for requirements management. TOGAF does not mandate or recommend any specific process or tool; it simply states what an effective requirements management process should achieve (i.e., the "requirements for requirements", if you like).

17.2.2.1   Business Scenarios

One effective technique that is described in TOGAF itself is business scenarios, which are an appropriate and useful technique to discover and document business requirements, and to articulate an Architecture Vision that responds to those requirements. Business scenarios are described in detail in Part III, Chapter 26.

17.2.2.2 Volere Requirements Specification Template

Architecture requirements is very much a niche area within the overall requirements field. One useful resource is the Volere Requirements Specification Template, available from Volere[4] (refer to www.volere.co.uk/template.htm). While not designed with architecture requirements in mind, this is a very useful requirements template, which is freely available and may be modified or copied (for internal use, provided the copyright is appropriately acknowledged).

One interesting item in this template is the "waiting room", which is a hold-all for requirements in waiting. There are often requirements identified which, as a result of the prioritization activity that forms part of the requirements management process (see below), are designated as beyond the planned scope, or the time available, for the current iteration of the architecture. The waiting room is a repository of future requirements. Having the ability to store such requirements helps avoid the perception that they are simply being discarded, while at the same time helping to manage expectations about what will be delivered.

17.2.2.3 Requirements Tools

There is a large, and increasing, number of Commercial Off-The-Shelf (COTS) tools available for the support of requirements management, albeit not necessarily designed for architecture requirements. The Volere web site has a very useful list of leading requirements tools (see www.volere.co.uk/tools.htm).

17.3 Inputs

Inputs to the Requirements Management phase are:

- A populated Architecture Repository (see Part IV, Section 36.2.5),
- Organizational Model for Enterprise Architecture (see Part IV, Section 36.2.16), including:
    - Scope of organizations impacted
    - Maturity assessment, gaps, and resolution approach
    - Roles and responsibilities for architecture team(s)
    - Constraints on architecture work
    - Budget requirements
    - Governance and support strategy
- Tailored Architecture Framework (see Part IV, Section 36.2.21), including:
    - Tailored architecture method
    - Tailored architecture content (deliverables and artifacts)
    - Configured and deployed tools
- Statement of Architecture Work (see Part IV, Section 36.2.20)

---

4.   The Volere web site is hosted by the Atlantic Systems Guild (see www.systemsguild.com).

- Architecture Vision (see Part IV, Section 36.2.8)

- Architecture requirements, populating an Architecture Requirements Specification (see Part IV, Section 36.2.6)

- Requirements Impact Assessment (see Part IV, Section 36.2.18)

The first high-level requirements are articulated as part of the Architecture Vision, generated by means of the business scenario or analogous technique.

Each architecture domain then generates detailed design requirements specific to that domain, and potentially to other domains (for example, areas where already designed architecture domains may need to change to cater for changes in this architecture domain; constraints on other architecture domains still to be designed.)

Deliverables in later ADM phases also contain mappings to the design requirements, and may also generate new types of requirements (for example, conformance requirements, time windows for implementation).

17.4   Steps

The steps in the Requirements Management phase are described in the table below:

	Requirements Management Steps	ADM Phase Steps
Step 1		Identify/document requirements — use business scenarios, or an analogous technique
Step 2	Baseline requirements: a. Determine priorities arising from current phase of ADM b. Confirm stakeholder buy-in to resultant priorities c. Record requirements priorities and place in requirements repository	
Step 3	Monitor baseline requirements	
Step 4		Identify changed requirements: a. Remove or re-assess priorities b. Add requirements and re-assess priorities c. Modify existing requirements

	Requirements Management Steps	ADM Phase Steps
Step 5	Identify changed requirements and record priorities: a. Identify changed requirements and ensure the requirements are prioritized by the architect(s) responsible for the current phase, and by the relevant stakeholders b. Record new priorities c. Ensure that any conflicts are identified and managed through the phases to a successful conclusion and prioritization d. Generate Requirements Impact Statement (see Section 36.2.18) for steering the architecture team **Notes** ■ Changed requirements can come in through any route. To ensure that the requirements are properly assessed and prioritized, this process needs to direct the ADM phases and record the decisions related to the requirements. ■ The Requirements Management phase needs to determine stakeholder satisfaction with the decisions. Where there is dissatisfaction, the phase remains accountable to ensure the resolution of the issues and determine next steps.	

	Requirements Management Steps	ADM Phase Steps
Step 6		a. Assess impact of changed requirements on current (active) phase b. Assess impact of changed requirements on previous phases c. Determine whether to implement change, or defer to later ADM cycle; if decision is to implement, assess timescale for change management implementation d. Issue Requirements Impact Statement, Version $n+1$
Step 7		Implement requirements arising from Phase H The architecture can be changed through its lifecycle by the Architecture Change Management phase (Phase H). The requirements management process ensures that new or changing requirements that are derived from Phase H are managed accordingly.
Step 8	Update the requirements repository with information relating to the changes requested, including stakeholder views affected	
Step 9		Implement change in the current phase

	Requirements Management Steps	ADM Phase Steps
Step 10		Assess and revise gap analysis for past phases
		The gap analysis in the ADM Phases B through D identifies the gaps between Baseline and Target Architectures. Certain types of gap can give rise to gap requirements.
		The ADM describes two kinds of gap:
		■ Something that is present in the baseline, but not in the target (i.e., eliminated — by accident or design)
		■ Something not in the baseline, but present in the target (i.e., new)
		A "gap requirement" is anything that has been eliminated by accident, and therefore requires a change to the Target Architecture.
		If the gap analysis generates gap requirements, then this step will ensure that they are addressed, documented, and recorded in the requirements repository, and that the Target Architecture is revised accordingly.

17.5 Outputs

The outputs of the requirements management process itself are:

- Requirements Impact Assessment (see Part IV, Section 36.2.18)
- Updated Architecture Requirements Specification (see Part IV, Section 36.2.6), if necessary

The requirements repository contains the current requirements for the Target Architecture. When new requirements arise, or existing ones are changed, a Requirements Impact Statement is generated, which identifies the phases of the ADM that need to be revisited to address the changes. The statement goes through various iterations until the final version, which includes the full implications of the requirements (e.g., costs, timescales, business metrics) on the architecture development.

The Open Group Architecture Framework (TOGAF)

Part III:

ADM Guidelines and Techniques

The Open Group

Chapter 18: Introduction

This chapter provides an overview of the contents of Part III.

18.1 Guidelines for Adapting the ADM Process

The Architecture Development Method (ADM) process can be adapted to deal with a number of different usage scenarios, including different process styles (e.g., the use of iteration) and also specific specialist architectures (such as security). Guidelines included within this part of TOGAF are as follows:

- Applying Iteration to the ADM (see Chapter 19) discusses the concept of iteration and shows potential strategies for applying iterative concepts to the ADM.

- Applying the ADM at Different Enterprise Levels (see Chapter 20) discusses the different types of architecture engagement that may occur at different levels of the enterprise. This section then also discusses how the ADM process can be focused to support different types of engagement.

- Security Architecture and the ADM (see Chapter 21) provides an overview of specific security considerations that should be considered during different phases of the ADM.

- Using TOGAF to Define & Govern SOAs (see Chapter 22) shows how SOA concepts can be supported by the TOGAF framework and the specific SOA considerations for different phases of the ADM.

18.2 Techniques for Architecture Development

The following techniques are described within Part III: ADM Guidelines & Techniques to support specific tasks within the ADM:

- Architecture Principles (see Chapter 23) — principles for the use and deployment of IT resources across the enterprise — describes how to develop the set of general rules and guidelines for the architecture being developed.

- Stakeholder Management (see Chapter 24) describes Stakeholder Management, an important discipline that successful architecture practitioners can use to win support for their projects.

- Architecture Patterns (see Chapter 25) provides guidance on using architectural patterns.

- Business Scenarios (see Chapter 26) describes the Business Scenarios technique, a method for deriving business requirements for architecture and the implied technical requirements.

- Gap Analysis (see Chapter 27) describes the technique known as gap analysis. It is widely used in the TOGAF ADM to validate an architecture that is being developed.

- Migration Planning Techniques (see Chapter 28) describes a number of techniques to support migration planning in Phases E and F.

- Interoperability Requirements (see Chapter 29) describes a technique for determining interoperability requirements.

- Business Transformation Readiness Assessment (see Chapter 30) describes a technique for identifying business transformation issues.

- Risk Management (see Chapter 31) describes a technique for managing risk during an architecture/business transformation project.

- Capability-Based Planning (see Chapter 32) describes the technique of capability-based planning.

Chapter 19: Applying Iteration to the ADM

19.1 Overview

The Architecture Development Method (ADM) is a flexible process that can be used to support the development of architecture as a stand-alone process, or as an extension to other solution development or project management methods.

Many organizational factors will influence the extent to which the ADM should be used in an iterative fashion. Particular factors for consideration would include:

- **The formality and nature of established process checkpoints within the organization**. Does the organization mandate that certain groups of activities are carried out between checkpoints? Does the organization mandate that certain activities must be finalized before other activities can be carried out?

- **The level of stakeholder involvement expected within the process**. Are stakeholders expecting to be closely involved within the development of a solution, or are they expecting to see a complete set of deliverables for review and approval?

- **The number of teams involved and the relationships between different teams**. Is the entire architecture being developed by a specific team, or is there a hierarchy of teams with governance relationships between them?

- **The maturity of the solution area and the expected amount of re-work and refinement required to arrive at an acceptable solution**. Can the solution be achieved in a single pass, or does it require extensive proof-of-concept and prototyping work to evolve a suitable outcome?

- **Attitude to risk**. Does the organizational culture react negatively to partially complete work products being circulated? Does the organizational culture require solutions to be proved in a trial environment before they can be implemented for mainstream application?

The ADM supports a number of concepts that could be characterized as iteration. It is expected that:

- Project teams will iterate through the entire ADM cycle, commencing new vision activity as a result of Architecture Change Management.

- Project teams may cycle between ADM phases, in planned cycles covering multiple phases (e.g., Business Architecture, Information Systems Architecture, Technology Architecture).

- Project teams may return to previous phases in order to circle back and update work products with new information.

■ Many project teams may operate their own ADM cycles concurrently, with relationships between different teams. For example, one architecture team may trigger a request for work for another architecture team.

All of these techniques are valid applications of the ADM and can be used to ensure that the approach to architecture development is sufficiently flexible to accommodate other methods and frameworks.

19.2   Iteration Cycles

When considering planned iteration cycles that span a number of ADM phases, the following guidelines can be used to effectively group related architectural activities to achieve a specific purpose.

These ADM iteration cycles are intended to span multiple phases of activity and allow formal review upon completion of each multi-phase iteration cycle (for example, an Architecture Definition should be reviewed with visibility of the Business, Data, Application, and Technology Architectures, rather than in isolation).

The suggested iteration cycles are shown in Figure 19-1.

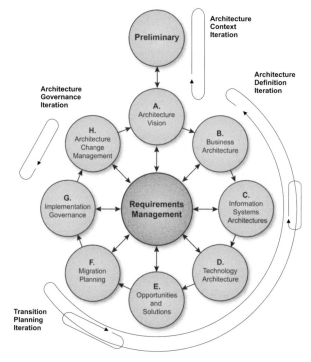

Figure 19-1 Iteration Cycles

- **Architecture Context** iterations allow initial mobilization of architecture activity by establishing the architecture approach, principles, scope, and vision.

- **Architecture Definition** iterations allow the creation of architecture content by cycling through Business, Information Systems, and Technology Architecture phases. These iterations also allow viability and feasibility tests to be carried out by looking at opportunities and migration planning.

- **Transition Planning** iterations support the creation of formal change roadmaps for a defined architecture.

- **Architecture Governance** iterations support governance of change activity progressing towards a defined Target Architecture.

Some iteration cycles can be executed once, whereas others have a natural minimum number of cycles. For some iteration cycles, each iteration follows the same process; where there is more than one iteration within a cycle, the process differs slightly for each of the iterations.

When considering the usage of iteration cycles, it is also necessary to consider where to place appropriate checkpoints within the process. If the expected level of stakeholder involvement is high, it may be sensible to carry out very frequent but informal checkpoints to ensure that the process is moving in the intended direction. If stakeholders are less closely involved, then checkpoints may be less frequent but more formal. Checkpoints at the completion of each iteration cycle, or at the end of several iteration cycles, are common.

19.3   Two Styles of Architecture Definition

Two process styles can be adopted within the ADM for the definition of architectures:

- **Baseline First**: In this style, an assessment of the baseline (i.e., current state) landscape is used to identify problem areas and improvement opportunities. This process is suitable when a target solution is not clearly understood and agreed upon.

- **Target First**: In this style, the target solution is elaborated in detail and then mapped back to the baseline, in order to identify change activity. This process is suitable when a target state is agreed at a high level and where the enterprise wishes to avoid proliferating current business practice into the target model.

The rationale for these two styles is that, in many cases, consideration of the target is deferred until conclusions have been made on the baseline. Premature consideration in these situations may be disruptive or politically sensitive (because the Target Architecture influences organization, roles, and responsibilities). Equally, initiatives that are examining Target Architectures run the risk of being constrained by the baseline or appearing to be constrained by the baseline if significant time is spent examining existing solutions.

In practical terms, an architecture team will always give informal consideration to the baseline when analyzing the target (and *vice versa*). In situations where baseline and target are expected to be considered in parallel by stakeholders, it is recommended that the architecture team focuses priority on one state within the internal structure of that engagement in order to maintain focus and consistency of execution.

19.4   Mapping TOGAF Phases to Iteration Cycles

Each iteration cycle crosses multiple TOGAF ADM phases. The following tables show at a high level which phases should be completed for which iteration cycle, showing activity that is core (i.e., the primary focus of the iteration), activity that is light (i.e., the secondary focus of the iteration), and activity that may be informally conducted (i.e., some activity may be carried out, but it is not explicitly mentioned in the ADM).

TOGAF Phase		Architecture Context — Initial Iteration	Architecture Definition — Iteration 1	Architecture Definition — Iteration 2	Architecture Definition — Iteration n	Transition Planning — Iteration 1	Transition Planning — Iteration n	Architecture Governance — Iteration 1	Architecture Governance — Iteration n
Preliminary		Core	Informal	Informal	Informal				Light
Architecture Vision		Core	Informal	Informal	Informal	Informal	Informal		Light
Business Architecture	Baseline	Informal	Core	Light	Core	Informal	Informal		Light
	Target	Informal	Informal	Core	Core	Informal	Informal		Light
Application Architecture	Baseline	Informal	Core	Light	Core	Informal	Informal		Light
	Target	Informal	Informal	Core	Core	Informal	Informal		Light
Data Architecture	Baseline	Informal	Core	Light	Core	Informal	Informal		Light
	Target	Informal	Informal	Core	Core	Informal	Informal		Light
Technology Architecture	Baseline	Informal	Core	Light	Core	Informal	Informal		Light
	Target	Informal	Informal	Core	Core	Informal	Informal		Light
Opportunities and Solutions		Informal	Light	Light	Light	Core	Core	Informal	Informal
Migration Planning		Informal	Light	Light	Light	Core	Core	Informal	Informal
Implementation Governance						Informal	Informal	Core	Core
Change Management			Informal	Informal	Informal	Informal	Informal	Core	Core

Core: primary focus activity for the iteration

Light: secondary focus activity for the iteration

Informal: potential activity for the iteration, not formally mentioned in the method

Figure 19-2 Activity by Iteration for Baseline First Architecture Definition

TOGAF Phase		Architecture Context		Architecture Definition			Transition Planning		Architecture Governance	
		Initial Iteration	Iteration 1	Iteration 2	Iteration *n*	Iteration 1	Iteration *n*	Iteration 1	Iteration *n*
Preliminary		Core	Informal	Informal	Informal				Light
Architecture Vision		Core	Informal	Informal	Informal	Informal	Informal		Light
Business Architecture	Baseline	Informal	Informal	Core	Core	Informal	Informal		Light
	Target	Informal	Core	Light	Core	Informal	Informal		Light
Application Architecture	Baseline	Informal	Informal	Core	Core	Informal	Informal		Light
	Target	Informal	Core	Light	Core	Informal	Informal		Light
Data Architecture	Baseline	Informal	Informal	Core	Core	Informal	Informal		Light
	Target	Informal	Core	Light	Core	Informal	Informal		Light
Technology Architecture	Baseline	Informal	Informal	Core	Core	Informal	Informal		Light
	Target	Informal	Core	Light	Core	Informal	Informal		Light
Opportunities and Solutions		Informal	Light	Light	Light	Core	Core	Informal	Informal
Migration Planning		Informal	Light	Light	Light	Core	Core	Informal	Informal
Implementation Governance						Informal	Informal	Core	Core
Change Management			Informal	Informal	Informal	Informal	Informal	Core	Core

☐ Core: primary focus activity for the iteration

☐ Light: secondary focus activity for the iteration

☐ Informal: potential activity for the iteration, not formally mentioned in the method

Figure 19-3 Activity by Iteration for Target First Architecture Definition

Iteration Cycle	Iteration	Purpose	Description
Architecture Context	Initial Iteration	Establish the approach, principles, scope, and vision for the engagement.	This iteration comprises a pass through the Preliminary and Architecture Vision phases of the ADM.
Architecture Definition (Baseline First)	Iteration 1	Define the Baseline Architecture.	This iteration comprises a pass through the Business Architecture, Information Systems Architecture, and Technology Architecture phases of the ADM, focusing on definition of the baseline. Opportunities, solutions, and migration plans are also considered to drive out the focus for change and test feasibility.

Iteration Cycle	Iteration	Purpose	Description
	Iteration 2	Define the Target Architecture and gaps.	This iteration comprises a pass through the Business Architecture, Information Systems Architecture, and Technology Architecture phases of the ADM, focusing on definition of the target and analyzing gaps against the baseline.
			Opportunities, solutions, and migration plans are also considered to test viability.
	Iteration *n*	Refine baseline, target, and gaps.	Subsequent Architecture Definitions attempt to correct and refine the target to achieve an outcome that is beneficial, feasible, and viable.
Architecture Definition (Target First)	Iteration 1	Define the Target Architecture.	This iteration comprises a pass through the Business Architecture, Information Systems Architecture, and Technology Architecture phases of the ADM, focusing on definition of the target.
			Opportunities, solutions, and migration plans are also considered to drive out the focus for change and test feasibility.
	Iteration 2	Define the Baseline Architecture and gaps.	This iteration comprises a pass through the Business Architecture, Information Systems Architecture, and Technology Architecture phases of the ADM, focusing on definition of the baseline and analyzing gaps against the target.
			Opportunities, solutions, and migration plans are also considered to test viability.
	Iteration *n*	Refine baseline, target, and gaps.	Subsequent Architecture Definitions attempt to correct and refine the target to achieve an outcome that is beneficial, feasible, and viable.
Transition Planning	Iteration 1	Define and agree a set of improvement opportunities, aligned against a provisional Transition Architecture.	The initial iteration of transition planning seeks to gain buy-in to a portfolio of solution opportunities in the Opportunities & Solutions phase of ADM.
			This iteration also delivers a provisional Migration Plan.

Iteration Cycle	Iteration	Purpose	Description
	Iteration *n*	Agree the Transition Architecture, refining the identified improvement opportunities to fit.	Subsequent iterations of Transition Planning seek to refine the migration plan, feeding back issues into the Opportunities & Solutions phase for refinement.
Architecture Governance	Iteration 1	Mobilize architecture governance and change management processes.	The initial Architecture Governance iteration establishes a process for governance of change and also puts in place the appropriate people, processes, and technology to support managed access to and change of the defined architecture.
	Iteration *n*	Carry out architecture governance and change control.	Subsequent iterations of the Architecture Governance cycle focus on period reviews of change initiatives to resolve issues and ensure compliance.

Chapter 20: Applying the ADM at Different Enterprise Levels

20.1   Overview

The TOGAF Architecture Development Method (ADM) is intended to be used as a model to support the definition and implementation of architecture at multiple levels within an enterprise. As discussed in Part V, Chapter 40, it is not possible to develop a single architecture that addresses all the needs of all stakeholders. Therefore, the enterprise must be partitioned into different areas, each of which can be supported by architectures. As discussed in Part V, enterprise architectures are typically partitioned according to Subject Matter, Time Period, and Level of Detail, as illustrated in Figure 20-1.

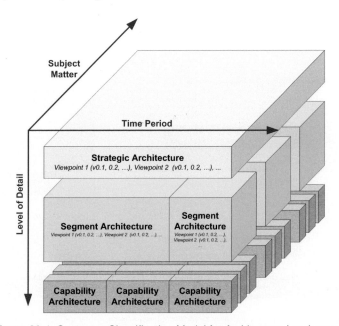

Figure 20-1 Summary Classification Model for Architecture Landscapes

This chapter discusses the types of engagement that architects may be required to perform and how the ADM can be used to co-ordinate the activities of various teams of architects, working at different levels of the enterprise.

20.2 Classes of Architecture Engagement

An architecture function or services organization may be called on to assist an enterprise in a number of different contexts, as architects range from summary to detail, broad to narrow coverage, and current state to future state. Typically, there are three areas of engagement for architects:

- **Identification of Required Change**: Outside the context of any change initiative, architecture can be used as a technique to provide visibility of the IT capability in order to support strategic decision-making and alignment of execution.

- **Definition of Change**: Where a need to change has been identified, architecture can be used as a technique to define the nature and extent of change in a structured fashion. Within largescale change initiatives, architectures can be developed to provide detailed Architecture Definition for change initiatives that are bounded by the scope of a program or portfolio.

- **Implementation of Change**: Architecture at all levels of the enterprise can be used as a technique to provide design governance to change initiatives by providing big-picture visibility, supplying structural constraints, and defining criteria on which to evaluate technical decisions.

Figure 20-2 and the following table show the classes of enterprise architecture engagement.

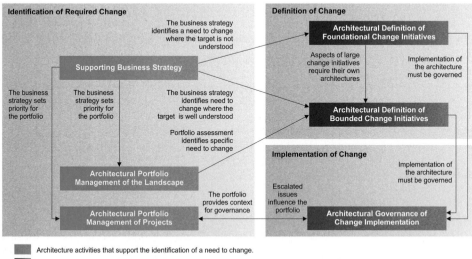

Figure 20-2 Classes of Enterprise Architecture Engagement

Each of these architecture engagement types is described in the table below.

Area of Engagement	Architecture Engagement	Description
Definition of Change	Architectural Definition of Foundational Change Initiatives	Foundational change initiatives are change efforts that have a known objective, but are not strictly scoped or bounded by a shared vision or requirements.
		In foundational change initiatives, the initial priority is to understand the nature of the problem and to bring structure to the definition of the problem.
		Once the problem is more effectively understood, it is possible to define appropriate solutions and to align stakeholders around a common vision and purpose.
	Architectural Definition of Bounded Change Initiatives	Bounded change initiatives are change efforts that typically arise as the outcome of a prior architectural strategy, evaluation, or vision.
		In bounded change initiatives, the desired outcome is already understood and agreed upon. The focus of architectural effort in this class of engagement is to effectively elaborate a baseline solution that addresses the identified requirements, issues, drivers, and constraints.
Implementation Change	Architectural Governance of Change Implementation	Once an architectural solution model has been defined, it provides a basis for design and implementation.
		In order to ensure that the objectives and value of the defined architecture are appropriately realized, it is necessary for continuing architecture governance of the implementation process to support design review, architecture refinement, and issue escalation.

Different classes of architecture engagement at different levels of the enterprise will require focus in specific areas, as shown below.

Engagement Type	Focus Iteration Cycles	Scope Focus
Supporting Business Strategy	Architecture Context Architecture Definition (Baseline First)	Broad, shallow consideration given to the Architecture Landscape in order to address a specific strategic question and define terms for more detailed architecture efforts to address strategy realization.
Architectural Portfolio Management of the Landscape	Architecture Context Architecture Definition (Baseline First)	Focus on physical assessment of baseline applications and technology infrastructure to identify improvement opportunities, typically within the constraints of maintaining business as usual.
Architectural Portfolio Management of Projects	Transition Planning Architecture Deployment	Focus on projects, project dependencies, and landscape impacts to align project sequencing in a way that is architecturally optimized.
Architectural Definition of Foundational Change Initiatives	Architecture Context Architecture Definition (Baseline First) Transition Planning	Focus on elaborating a vision through definition of baseline and identifying what needs to change to transition the baseline to the target.
Architectural Definition of Bounded Change Initiatives	Architecture Definition (Target First) Transition Planning	Focus on elaborating the target to meet a previously defined and agreed vision, scope, or set of constraints. Use the target as a basis for analysis to avoid perpetuation of baseline, sub-optimal architectures.
Architectural Governance of Change Implementation	Architecture Deployment	Use the Architecture Vision, constraints, principles, requirements, Target Architecture definition, and transition roadmap to ensure that projects realize their intended benefit, are aligned with each other, and are aligned with wider business need.

20.3   Developing Architectures at Different Levels

The previous sections have identified that different types of architecture are required to address different stakeholder needs at different levels of the organization. Each architecture typically does not exist in isolation and must therefore sit within a governance hierarchy. Broad, summary architectures set the direction for narrow and detailed architectures.

A number of techniques can be employed to use the ADM as a process that supports such hierarchies of architectures. Essentially there are two strategies that can be applied:

1. Architectures at different levels can be developed through iterations within a single cycle of the ADM process.

2. Architectures at different levels can be developed through a hierarchy of ADM processes, executed concurrently.

At the extreme ends of the scale, either of these two options can be fully adopted. In practice, an architect is likely to need to blend elements of each to fit the exact requirements of their Request for Architecture Work.

Each of these approaches is described in the sections below.

20.4   ADM Cycle Approaches

20.4.1   Using Iterations within a Single ADM Cycle

In situations where a single architecture team is tasked with defining architectures at many levels within the enterprise, it is possible to use iterations within a single ADM cycle to create all required architectures.

Using this approach, the Architecture Vision phase can be used to develop a strategic view of the architecture. Phases B, C, and D then provide a more detailed and formal architectural view of the landscape for different segments or time periods. Phases E and F then develop a detailed Migration Plan, which may include even more detailed and specific Capability Architectures.

A summary of the approach is shown in Figure 20-3.

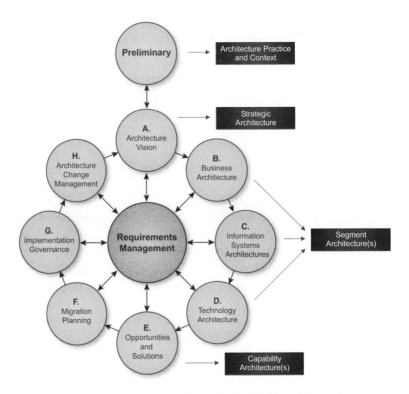

Figure 20-3 Iterations within a Single ADM Cycle Example

The key benefits of this approach are:

- It is lightweight, as multiple architectures can be developed against a single Request for Work, project plan, etc.
- It allows for very close integration of architectures at different levels in the organization.
- It works well when all architectures are being developed by a single team.

The key limitations of this approach are:

- It does not explicitly set out governance and change management relationships between the different architectures.
- It requires all architectures to be completed in sequence and potentially released at the same time. This may delay the release of strategic architectures or prevent specific Capability Architectures from being developed.
- Similar architectural activities are repeated within a number of phases within the ADM. It may become difficult to distinguish the differences between different phases.

Generally speaking, this approach should be used when a number of architectures are being developed within a similar time period by a single team.

20.4.2   Using a Hierarchy of ADM Processes

In cases where larger-scale architectures need to be developed by a number of different architecture teams, a more hierarchical application of the ADM may be used. This approach to the ADM uses the Migration Planning phase of one ADM cycle to initiate new projects, which will also develop architectures. This approach is illustrated in Figure 20-4.

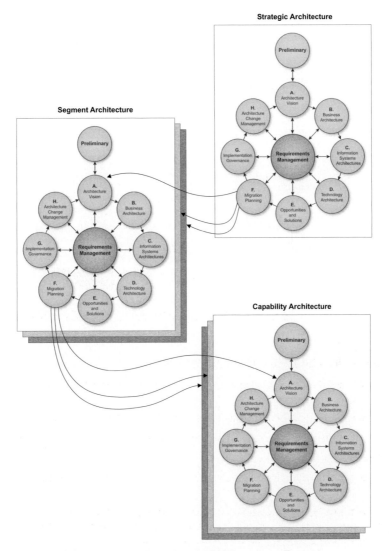

Figure 20-4 A Hierarchy of ADM Processes Example

The key benefits of this approach are:

- It is comprehensive. All ADM activities are carried out at all levels.
- It establishes explicit governance relationships between architectures.
- It allows for federated development of architectures at different levels in the organization.

The key limitations of this approach are:

- It requires the establishment of an enterprise-wide governance hierarchy to be effective.
- It does not work well when many architectures are being developed by the same team of architects.

Generally speaking, this approach should be used when architectures are being developed over different timelines by different teams.

Chapter 21: Security Architecture and the ADM

21.1 Overview

The goal of this chapter is to explain the security considerations that need to be addressed during application of the TOGAF Architecture Development Method (ADM).

21.2 Introduction

Architecture development using the ADM is iterative in nature, as many areas of concern are revisited but at a finer-grained level of examination. Through the several phases the reader might see topics repeated, or in an earlier phase a topic might be treated at a higher level than the reader might expect. Architecture development methods are also tools in the hands of the practitioner to be used as best fits the practitioner's experience. The guidance included here is intended to help practitioners avoid missing a critical security concern. It is expected that elements included by the authors in specific phases will be modified and shifted according to the practitioner's experience.

This chapter is not intended to be a security architecture development methodology. It is intended for the enterprise architect deploying the TOGAF ADM, to inform the enterprise architect of what the security architect will need to carry out their security architecture work. It is also intended as a guide to help the enterprise architect avoid missing a critical security concern.

Discussion of security architecture has the tension of being separate from the remainder of enterprise architecture development and at the same time needing to be fully integrated in it. The focus of the security architect is enforcement of security policies of the enterprise, which at times can be seen as inhibiting advancement of projects undertaken by the enterprise architect and application development team. Security architects spend a good deal of effort proving the negative.

Security architectures generally have the following characteristics:

- Security architecture has its own methods. These methods might be the basis for a discreet security methodology.

- Security architecture composes its own discrete view and viewpoints.

- Security architecture addresses non-normative flows through systems and among applications.

- Security architecture introduces its own normative flows through systems and among applications.

- Security architecture introduces unique, single-purpose components in the design.

- Security architecture calls for its own unique set of skill requirements in the IT architect.

21.3   Guidance on Security for the Architecture Domains

Pervasively throughout the architecture domains and in all phases of the architecture development, security concerns of the enterprise need to be accounted for. Security is called out separately because it is infrastructure that is rarely visible to the business function being added to the Target Architecture to derive value. Its fundamental purpose is to protect the value of the systems and information assets of the enterprise. The nature of security in the enterprise is that it is deemed successful if nothing happens that is visible to the user or other observer, and no damage or losses occur. That is, if the enterprise retains the use and value of its information assets, the goals of security in the enterprise have been met. These assets might be obvious — like the data in a customer records database — or intangible — like not having the company name appear in an article in the news saying that its data systems had been compromised.

While security architecture does have its own single-purpose components, security is experienced as a quality of systems in the architecture. The Enterprise Security view of the architecture calls out its own unique building blocks, collaborations, and interfaces. These security-unique elements must interface with the business systems in a balanced and cost-effective way, so as to maintain the security policies of the enterprise, but not interfere with system operations and functions. It is least costly and most effective to plan for and implement security-specific functions in the Target Architecture as early as possible in the development cycle to avoid costly retrofit or rework because required building blocks for security were not added or used during systems development and deployment. The approach of the IT architect operating in the security domain is also different from IT architects operating in other architecture domains. The security architect considers not only the normal flow of the application, but also the abnormal flows, failure modes, and ways the systems and applications can be interrupted. Put differently, the IT architect tends to focus mostly on how a system will work, while the security architect focuses primarily on how the system might fail.

All groups of stakeholders in the enterprise will have security concerns. These concerns might not be obvious as security-related concerns unless there is special awareness on the part of the IT architect. It is desirable to bring a security architect into the project as early as possible. Throughout the phases of the ADM, guidance will be offered on security-specific information which should be gathered, steps which should be taken, and artifacts which should be created. Architecture decisions related to security, like all others, should be traceable to business and policy decisions, which should derive from a risk analysis. The generally accepted areas of concern for the security architect are:

- **Authentication**: The substantiation of the identity of a person or entity related to the system in some way.

- **Authorization**: The definition and enforcement of permitted capabilities for a person or entity whose identity has been established.

- **Audit**: The ability to provide forensic data attesting that the system was used in accordance with stated security policies.

- **Assurance**: The ability to test and prove that the system has the security attributes required to uphold the stated security policies.

- **Availability**: The ability of the system to function without service interruption or depletion despite abnormal or malicious events.

- **Asset Protection**: The protection of information assets from loss or unintended disclosure, and resources from unauthorized and unintended use.

- **Administration**: The ability to add and change security policies, add or change how policies are implemented in the system, and add or change the persons or entities related to the system.

- **Risk Management**: The organization's attitude and tolerance for risk. (This risk management is different from the special definition found in financial markets and insurance institutions that have formal risk management departments.)

Typical security architecture artifacts would include:

- Business rules regarding handling of data/information assets
- Written and published security policy
- Codified data/information asset ownership and custody
- Risk analysis documentation
- Data classification policy documentation

21.4   ADM Architecture Requirements Management

The security policy and security standards become part of the enterprise requirements management process. Security policy is established at an executive level of the business, is long-lived, and resistant to whimsical change. Security policy is not tied to any specific technology. Once the security policies are established, they can be referred to as requirements for all architecture projects.

Security standards change more frequently and state technology preferences used to support security policies. New technologies that support the implementation of security policies in a better way can be adopted as needed. The improvements can be in reduced costs or increased benefits. Security standards will manifest themselves as security-related building blocks in the Enterprise Continuum. Security patterns for deploying these security-related building blocks are referred to in the Security Guidance to Phase E.

New security requirements arise from many sources:

1. A new statutory or regulatory mandate
2. A new threat realized or experienced
3. A new IT architecture initiative discovers new stakeholders and/or new requirements

In the case where 1. and 2. above occur, these new requirements would be drivers for input to the change management system discussed in Phase H. A new architecture initiative might be launched to examine the existing infrastructure and applications to determine the extent of changes required to meet the new demands. In the case of 3. above, a new security requirement will enter the requirements management system.

Is our security good?

This question inevitably comes from management to the security architect. No security measures are ever perfect, and the potential exists for the amount of money and effort expended to become very large for little additional return. Security assurance testing should be in place so that the security systems can be measured to ensure that they keep the security policies for which they were designed. Security policy audits should be held and might be mandatory by statute or regulation. These security audits and possible security policy changes are the exact reason why separation of policy enforcement from application code is so strongly emphasized.

Nothing useful can be said about a security measure outside the context of an application, or a system and its environment

The efficacy of a security measure is considered in relation to the risk it mitigates. An enterprise cannot determine how much it will be willing to spend on securing an asset until it understands the asset value. For example, the use of that asset in an application and the concomitant risk the asset is exposed to as a result, will determine the true requirements for security. Additionally, the organization's tolerance for risk is a factor. In other words, the question asked should not be: "Is it secure?" but rather: "Is it secure enough?" The latter is ultimately a question to be answered by risk analysis.

21.5 Preliminary Phase

Define and document applicable regulatory and security policy requirements

The framework and principles rarely change, and so the security implications called out in the objectives of this phase should be fairly straightforward. A written security policy for the organization must be in place, and there should be regular notification and education established for employees. ISO/IEC 17799:2005 is a good place to start the formation of a security policy, and can be used to assess the security readiness of an organization. Without a written and published security policy, enforcement is difficult. Security policies refer to many aspects of security for the organization — such as physical premises security — that are remotely related to security of systems and applications. The security policy should be examined to find relevant sections, and updated if necessary. Architecture constraints established in the security policy must be communicated to the other members of the architecture team.

In a similar fashion, there may be regulatory requirements that specify obligations the system must fulfil or actions that must be taken. Whether the system will be subject to regulation will depend upon the functionality of the system and the data collected or maintained. In addition, the jurisdiction where the system or service is deployed, where the users reside, or under which the deploying entity is chartered or incorporated will inform this decision. It may be wise to obtain legal counsel regarding these obligations at the outset of activities.

Identify a security architect or security architecture team

Agreement on the role of the security architect in the enterprise architecture process and in the architecture and IT governance should also be established. Security considerations can conflict with functional considerations and a security advocate is required to ensure that all issues are addressed and conflicts of interest do not prevent explicit consideration of difficult issues. Executive policy decisions should be established at this point about what security policies can be negotiable and which policies must be enforced for regulatory or statutory reasons.

Identify first-order assumptions and boundary conditions

If the business model of the organization does encompass federation with other organizations, the extent of the security federation should be established at this point in the process. Contractual federation agreements should be examined for their security implications and agreements. It may be necessary to establish joint architecture meetings with other members of a federation to establish interfaces and protocols for exchange of security information related to federated identity, authentication, and authorization.

21.5.1 Security Inputs

- Written security policy
- Relevant statutes
- List of applicable jurisdictions

21.5.2 Security Outputs

- List of applicable regulations
- List of applicable security policies
- Security team roster
- List of security assumptions and boundary conditions

21.6   Phase A: Architecture Vision

Definition of relevant stakeholders and discovery of their concerns and objectives will require development of a high-level scenario. Key business requirements will also be established through this early scenario work. The TOGAF ADM business scenario process may be useful here and at later stages.

Obtain management support for security measures

In similar fashion to obtaining management recognition and endorsement for the overall architecture project, so too endorsement of the security-related aspects of the architecture development effort should be obtained. Recognition that the project might have development and infrastructure impact that are not readily visible by looking solely at the systems in question should be made clear. Thorough consideration and mitigation of issues related to risk and security may be perceived as a waste of resources and time; the level of management support must be understood and communicated throughout the team.

Define necessary security-related management sign-off milestones of this architecture development cycle

The traceability of security-related architecture decisions should be documented and the appropriate executives and line management who need to be informed of security-related aspects of the project need to be identified and the frequency of reporting should be established. It should be recognized that the tension between delivery of new business function and enforcement of security policies does exist, and that a process for resolving such disputes that arise should be established early in the project. Such tensions often have the result of putting the security architect seemingly "in the way of completing the project". It needs to be understood by management and the other architects involved that the role of the security architect is to safeguard the assets of the enterprise.

Determine and document applicable disaster recovery or business continuity plans/requirements

Any existing disaster recovery and business continuity plans must be understood and their relationship with the planned system defined and documented.

Identify and document the anticipated physical/business/regulatory environment(s) in which the system(s) will be deployed

All architecture decisions must be made within the context of the environments within which the system will be placed and operate. Physical environments that should be documented may include battlefield environments, commercial environments, outdoor environments, mobile environments, and the like. In a similar fashion, the business environment must be defined. Potential business environments may include different assumptions regarding users and interfaces, and those users or interfaces may carry the onus of regulatory environments in which the system must operate (users under the age of thirteen in the US, for example).

Determine and document the criticality of the system: safety-critical/mission-critical/non-critical

Safety-critical systems place lives in danger in case of failure or malfunction.

Mission-critical systems place money, market share, or capital at risk in case of failure.

Non-critical systems have little or no consequence in case of failure.

21.6.1 Security Inputs

- List of applicable security policies
- List of applicable jurisdictions
- Complete disaster recovery and business continuity plans

21.6.2 Security Outputs

- Physical security environment statement
- Business security environment statement
- Regulatory environment statement
- Security policy cover letter signed by CEO or delegate
- List of architecture development checkpoints for security sign-off
- List of applicable disaster recovery and business continuity plans
- Systems criticality statement

21.7 Phase B: Business Architecture

Determine who are the legitimate actors who will interact with the product/service/process

Development of the business scenarios and subsequent high-level use-cases of the project concerned will bring to attention the people actors and system actors involved. Many subsequent decisions regarding authorization will rely upon a strong understanding of the intended users, administrators, and operators of the system, in addition to their expected capabilities and characteristics. It must be borne in mind that users may not be humans; software applications may be legitimate users. Those tending to administrative needs, such as backup operators, must also be identified, as must users outside boundaries of trust, such as Internet-based customers.

Assess and baseline current security-specific business processes (enhancement of existing objective)

The business process regarding how actors are vetted as proper users of the system should be documented. Consideration should also be made for actors from outside the organization who are proper users of the system. The outside entities will be determined from the high-level scenarios developed as part of Phase A.

Determine whom/how much it is acceptable to inconvenience in utilizing security measures

Security measures, while important, can impose burden on users and administrative personnel. Some will respond to that burden by finding ways to circumvent the measures. Examples include administrators finding ways to create "back doors" or customers choosing a competitor to avoid the perceived burden of the infrastructure. The trade-offs can require balancing security advantages against business advantages and demand informed judicious choice.

Identify and document interconnecting systems beyond project control

Every cybernetic or business system must rely upon existing systems beyond the control of the project. These systems possess advantages and disadvantages, risks and benefits. Examples include the Domain Name System (DNS) that resolves computer and service names to Internet addresses, or paper currency issued by the local treasury. The address returned by the host or service DNS may not always be trustworthy; paper currency may not always be genuine, and recourse will vary in efficacy between jurisdictions. These interfaces must be understood and documented.

Determine the assets at risk if something goes wrong — "What are we trying to protect?"

Assets are not always tangible and are not always easy to quantify. Examples include: loss of life, loss of customer good will, loss of a AAA bond rating, loss of market share.

Determine the cost (both qualitative and quantitative) of asset loss/impact in failure cases

It must be remembered that those assets most challenging to quantify can be the most valuable and must not be neglected. Even qualitative estimates will prove valuable in assessing comparative risks.

Identify and document the ownership of assets

Assets may be owned by outside entities, or by inside entities. Inside entities may be owned by individuals or by organizations. Determine:

- Where trust is assumed
- How it is established
- How it is communicated

Always trace it to the real world; i.e.:

- Assessment (credit searches, personal vouching)
- Liability (monetary damages, jail terms, sanctions)

All security decisions rely upon trust that has been established in some fashion. No trust assumptions have any value if they cannot be rooted in real-world assessment and liability. In most business environments, trust is established through contracts that define liability where the trust is breached. The onus for assessing trust is the responsibility of those choosing to enter into the contracts and their legal counsel. It is important to note that technology (e.g., digital certificates, SAML, etc.) cannot create trust, but can only convey in the electronic world the trust that already exists in the real world through business relationships, legal agreements, and security policy consistencies.

Determine and document appropriate security forensic processes

To be able to enforce security policies, breaches of security need to be properly captured so that problem determination and possible policy or legal action can be taken against the entity causing the breach. Forensic practices suitable to provide evidence where necessary need to be established and documented. Security personnel should be trained to follow the forensic procedures and training material regarding the need to collect evidence should be considered for the standard security education given to employees.

Identify the criticality of the availability and correct operation of the overall service

The risks associated with loss of availability may have already been adequately considered in the foregoing mission-critical/safety-critical assessment.

Determine and document how much security (cost) is justified by the threats and the value of the assets at risk

A risk analysis (an understanding of the value of assets at risk and the likelihood of potential threats) provides an important guideline for investments in mitigation strategies for the identified threats.

Reassess and confirm Architecture Vision decisions

Business analysis involves a number of rigorous thought exercises and may call into question the initial assumptions identified in the Architecture Vision.

Assess alignment or conflict of identified security policies with business goals

The security policies identified in the Preliminary phase may have provisions that are difficult or impossible to reconcile with the business goals in light of the identified risks. Possible responses include alteration of aspects of the business environment, modification of the intended user population, or technical mitigation of risks (addressed in Phase C).

Determine "what can go wrong?"

Perform a threat analysis that identifies the high-level threats bearing upon the system and their likelihood.

21.7.1 Security Inputs

- Initial business and regulatory security environment statements
- List of applicable disaster recovery and business continuity plans
- List of applicable security policies and regulations

21.7.2 Security Outputs

- List of forensic processes
- List of new disaster recovery and business continuity requirements
- Validated business and regulatory environment statements
- List of validated security policies and regulations
- List of target security processes
- List of baseline security processes
- List of security actors
- List of interconnecting systems
- Statement of security tolerance for each class of security actor
- Asset list with values and owners
- List of trust paths
- Availability impact statement(s)
- Threat analysis matrix

21.8 Phase C: Information Systems Architectures

Assess and baseline current security-specific architecture elements (enhancement of existing objective)

A full inventory of architecture elements that implement security services must be compiled in preparation for a gap analysis.

Identify safe default actions and failure states

Every state change in any system is precipitated by some trigger. Commonly, an enumerated set of expected values of that trigger initiates a change in state. However, there are likely other potential trigger inputs that must be accommodated in non-normative cases. Additionally, system failure may take place at any point in time. Safe default actions and failure modes must be defined for the system informed by the current state, business environment, applicable policies, and regulatory obligations. Safe default modes for an automobile at zero velocity may no longer be applicable at speed. Safe failure states for medical devices will differ markedly from safe failure states for consumer electronics.

Identify and evaluate applicable recognized guidelines and standards

Standards are justly credited for reducing cost, enhancing interoperability, and leveraging innovation. From a security standpoint, standard protocols, standard object libraries, and standard implementations that have been scrutinized by experts in their fields help to ensure that errors do not find their way into implementations. From a security standpoint, errors are security vulnerabilities.

Revisit assumptions regarding interconnecting systems beyond project control

In light of the risk assessments performed, assumptions regarding interconnecting systems may require modification.

Determine and document the sensitivity or classification level of information stored/created/used

Information stored, created, or manipulated by the system may or may not be subject to an official classification that defines its sensitivity and the obligations to which the system and its owners are subject. The absence of any official classification does not necessarily absolve the onus on maintaining the confidentiality of data. Consideration must be made for different legislative burden that may hold jurisdiction over the system and the data stored.

Identify and document custody of assets

All assets of value are kept and maintained on behalf of the owner. The specific persons or organizations charged with this responsibility must be identified.

Identify the criticality of the availability and correct operation of each function

Presumably, in the event of system failure or loss of functionality, some value is lost to stakeholders. The cost of this opportunity loss should be quantified, if possible, and documented.

Determine the relationship of the system under design with existing business disaster/continuity plans

Existing business disaster/continuity plans may accommodate the system under consideration. If not, some analysis is called for to determine the gap and the cost if that gap goes unfilled.

Identify what aspects of the system must be configurable to reflect changes in policy/business environment/access control

No environment is static and systems must evolve to accommodate change. Systems architected for ready reconfiguration will better reflect that change and result in lower cost over the life of the system. Security is enhanced when security-related changes can be implemented inexpensively and are, hence, not sidelined. Security is also enhanced when changes require no changes to code; changes to code introduce bugs and bugs introduce security vulnerabilities.

Identify lifespan of information used as defined by business needs and regulatory requirements

Information maintained beyond its useful lifespan represents wasted resources and, potentially, business decisions based upon suboptimal data. Regulation, however, sometimes mandates the timetable for maintenance of information as archival data.

Determine approaches to address identified risks:

- Mitigate

- Accept

- Transfer

- Avoid

There are several standard ways to address identified and quantified risk. The list above is not intended to be exhaustive for all approaches.

Identify actions/events that warrant logging for later review or triggering forensic processes

Anomalous actions and states will outnumber planned actions and states. These transitions will warrant logging to reconstruct chains of events, facilitate root cause analysis, and, potentially, establish evidence for civil or criminal action. It must be borne in mind that logs must be regularly reviewed to be introduced as evidence into a court of law in some jurisdictions.

Identify and document requirements for rigor in proving accuracy of logged events (non-repudiation)

Since malicious tampering of systems is commonly accompanied by tampering of logged data to thwart investigation and apprehension, the ability to protect and establish the veracity of logs through cryptographic methods will remove uncertainty from investigations and bolster cases in legal proceedings.

Identify potential/likely avenues of attack

Thinking like an adversary will prepare the architect for creation of a robust system that resists malicious tampering and, providentially, malfunction arising from random error.

Determine "what can go wrong?"

21.8.1 Security Inputs

- Threat analysis matrix

- Risk analysis

- Documented forensic processes

- Validated business policies and regulations

- List of interconnecting systems

- New disaster recovery and business continuity requirements

21.8.2 Security Outputs

- Event log-level matrix and requirements
- Risk management strategy
- Data lifecycle definitions
- List of configurable system elements
- Baseline list of security-related elements of the system
- New or augmented security-related elements of the system
- Security use-case models:
    — Normative models
    — Non-normative models
- List of applicable security standards:
    — Protocols
    — Object libraries
    — Others ...
- Validated interconnected system list
- Information classification report
- List of asset custodians
- Function criticality statement
- Revised disaster recovery and business continuity plans
- Refined threat analysis matrix

21.9 Phase D: Technology Architecture

Assess and baseline current security-specific technologies (enhancement of existing objective)

Revisit assumptions regarding interconnecting systems beyond project control

Identify and evaluate applicable recognized guidelines and standards

Identify methods to regulate consumption of resources

Every system will rely upon resources that may be depleted in cases that may or may not be anticipated at the point of system design. Examples include network bandwidth, battery power, disk space, available memory, and so on. As resources are utilized approaching depletion, functionality may be impaired or may fail altogether. Design steps that identify non-renewable resources, methods that can recognize resource depletion, and measures that can respond through limiting the causative factors, or through limiting the effects of resource depletion to non-critical functionality, can enhance the overall reliability and availability of the system.

Engineer a method by which the efficacy of security measures will be measured and communicated on an ongoing basis

As systems are deployed and operated in dynamic environments, security measures will perform to varying degrees of efficacy as unexpected threats arise and as expected threats change in the environment. A method that facilitates ongoing evaluation of the value of security measures will inform ongoing changes to the system in response to changing user needs, threat patterns, and problems found.

Identify the trust (clearance) level of:

- All users of the system
- All administrators of the system
- All interconnecting systems beyond project control

Regulatory requirements, information classification levels, and business needs of the asset owners will all influence the required level of trust that all interactive entities will be required to fulfil to qualify for access to data or services.

Identify minimal privileges required for any entity to achieve a technical or business objective

Granting sweeping capabilities to any user, application, or other entity can simplify successful transaction completion at the cost of complicating or precluding effective control and audit. Many regulatory obligations are more challenging to demonstrate compliance where privileges are sweeping and controls are loose.

Identify mitigating security measures, where justified by risk assessment

This objective is where the classic security services of identification, authentication, authorization, data confidentiality, data integrity, non-repudiation, assurance, and audit are brought into play, after their applicability is determined and the cost/value of protection has been identified.

Determine "what can go wrong?"

21.9.1 Security Inputs

- List of security-related elements of the system
- List of interconnected systems
- List of applicable security standards
- List of security actors
- Risk management strategy
- Validated security policies
- Validated regulatory requirements
- Validated business policies related to trust requirements

21.9.2 Security Outputs

- Baseline list of security technologies
- Validated interconnected systems list
- Selected security standards list
- Resource conservation plan
- Security metrics and monitoring plan
- User authorization policies
- Risk management plan
- User trust (clearance) requirements

21.10 Phase E: Opportunities & Solutions

Identify existing security services available for re-use

From the Baseline Security Architecture and the Enterprise Continuum, there will be existing security infrastructure and security building blocks that can be applied to the requirements derived from this architecture development engagement. For example, if the requirement exists for application access control external to an application being developed, and such a system already exists, it can be used again. Statutory or regulatory requirements may call for physical separation of domains which may eliminate the ability to re-use existing infrastructure. Known products, tools, building blocks, and patterns can be used, though newly implemented.

Engineer mitigation measures addressing identified risks

Having determined the risks amenable to mitigation and evaluated the appropriate investment in that mitigation as it relates to the assets at risk, those mitigation measures must be designed, implemented, deployed, and/or operated.

Evaluate tested and re-usable security software and security system resources

Since design, code, and configuration errors are the roots of many security vulnerabilities, taking advantage of any problem solutions already engineered, reviewed, tested, and field-proven will reduce security exposure and enhance reliability.

Identify new code/resources/assets that are appropriate for re-use

Having successfully engineered new solutions in the absence of existing re-usable solutions, it is appropriate to evaluate those new solutions for inclusion into any existing libraries, archives, or other repositories for future re-use.

Determine "what can go wrong?"

21.11　Phase F: Migration Planning

Assess the impact of new security measures upon other new components or existing leveraged systems

In a phased implementation the new security components are usually part of the infrastructure in which the new system is implemented. The security infrastructure needs to be in a first or early phase to properly support the project.

Implement assurance methods by which the efficacy of security measures will be measured and communicated on an ongoing basis

During the operational phases, mechanisms are utilized to monitor the performance of many aspects of the system. Its security and availability are no exception.

Identify correct secure installation parameters, initial conditions, and configurations

Security of any system depends not on design and implementation alone, but also upon installation and operational state. These conditions must be defined and monitored not just at deployment, but also throughout operation.

Implement disaster recovery and business continuity plans or modifications

Determine "what can go wrong?"

21.12　Phase G: Implementation Governance

Establish architecture artifact, design, and code reviews and define acceptance criteria for the successful implementation of the findings

Many security vulnerabilities originate as design or code errors and the simplest and least expensive method to locate and find such errors is generally an early review by experienced peers in the craft. Locating such errors, of course, is the first step and implementing corrections at an appropriate point in the development lifecycle is necessary to benefit from the investment. Follow-on inspections or formalized acceptance reviews may be warranted in high-assurance or safety-critical environments.

Implement methods and procedures to review evidence produced by the system that reflects operational stability and adherence to security policies

While planning and specification is necessary for all aspects of a successful enterprise, they are insufficient in the absence of testing and audit to ensure adherence to that planning and specification in both deployment and operation. Among the methods to be exercised are:

- Review system configurations with security impact which can be modified to ensure configuration changes have not compromised security design

- Audit the design, deployment, and operations against security policies

- Audit the design, deployment, and operations against business objectives

- Run test cases against systems to ensure the security systems have been implemented as designed
- Run disaster recovery tests
- Run business continuity tests

Implement necessary training to ensure correct deployment, configuration, and operations of security-relevant subsystems and components; ensure awareness training of all users and non-privileged operators of the system and/or its components

Training is not necessary simply to preclude vulnerabilities introduced through operations and configuration error, though this is critical to correct ongoing secure performance. In many jurisdictions, proper training must be performed and documented to demonstrate due diligence and substantiate corrective actions or sanctions in cases where exploits or error compromise business objectives or to absolve contributory responsibility for events that bring about harm or injury.

Determine "what has gone wrong?"

The very purpose of governance is the establishment of a feedback loop that determines the efficacy of plan execution and implements corrections, where required. It must be borne in mind that the imperfections in plans executed are rooted both in human processes and cybernetic processes.

21.13 Phase H: Architecture Change Management

As stated in Part II, Chapter 17 (Requirements Management), change is driven by new requirements. Changes in security requirements are often more disruptive than a simplification or incremental change. Changes in security policy can be driven by statute, regulation, or something that has gone wrong.

Changes in security standards are usually less disruptive since the trade-off for their adoption is based on the value of the change. However, standards changes can also be mandated. Similar approaches to these changes as mentioned above are good rules of thumb for security as well. However, security changes are often infrastructure changes, and can have a greater impact. A seemingly small security requirement change can easily trigger a new architecture development cycle.

Determine "what has gone wrong?"

Good security forensics practices in conjunction with a written published security policy make determination of what has gone wrong possible. Further, they make enforcement possible. As the guidance above suggests, minor changes can be made in the context of change management and major changes will require a new architecture effort.

Incorporate security-relevant changes to the environment into the requirements for future enhancement (enhancement of existing objective)

Changes that arise as a result of a security problem or new security technology will feed into the Requirements Management process.

21.14 References

- NIST 80018: Guide for Developing Security Plans for Information Technology Systems
- NIST 80027: Engineering Principles for Information Technology Security (A Baseline for Achieving Security)
- NIST 80030: Guide for Risk Management for Information Technology Systems

Chapter 22: Using TOGAF to Define & Govern SOAs

22.1 Overview

This chapter discusses:

- Service Oriented Architecture (SOA) as an architectural style
- Factors relating to the adoption and deployment of SOA within the enterprise
- Correspondences between SOA and TOGAF terminology
- The definition and structure of service contracts

Note: The Open Group SOA Working Group is currently working to develop a Practical Guide that will enable a certified TOGAF practitioner to use TOGAF to develop an SOA. More information on the SOA Working Group can be found at www.opengroup.org/projects/soa. More information on the SOA/TOGAF Practical Guide project can be found at www.opengroup.org/projects/soa-togaf.

22.2 Introduction

As the business environment becomes more sophisticated, the challenges facing large organizations are shifting away from questions of efficiency and automation towards questions of complexity management and business agility. Complex webs of existing applications and interfaces create highly complex IT landscapes where change becomes more and more difficult and the impacts of change become harder to predict and understand.

The concept of an SOA provides an architectural style that is specifically intended to simplify the business and the interoperation of different parts of that business. By structuring capability as meaningful, granular services as opposed to opaque, siloed business units, it becomes possible to quickly identify functional capabilities of an organization and to avoid duplicating similar capabilities across different areas of the organization. By standardizing the behavior and interoperation of services, it is possible to limit the impacts of change and also to understand in advance the likely chain of impacts.

From a software development perspective, SOA focuses on structuring applications in a way that facilitates system flexibility and agility — a necessity in today's complex and fast-moving business environment. SOA aims to break down traditional application silos into portfolios of more granular services that operate in open and interoperable ways, whilst extracting commodity capability into a virtualized infrastructure platform of shared re-usable utility services.

22.3   Business-Led SOA Community

In response to the business opportunities presented by SOA technology, a growing community of professionals is examining SOA as a business opportunity and looking at how business can be restructured to gain from more flexible, agile, and open IT solutions. Rather than addressing challenges of software engineering, the business-led SOA community focuses on issues such as sharing of business capability, sourcing of business capability, and exposure of business capabilities to new audiences and channels.

Fundamental to the business-led SOA approach is:

- Rich domain knowledge of both horizontal, cross-cutting concerns, such as human resources (HR), finance, and procurement alongside vertical, industry-specific concerns

- A structured, quantitative understanding of business value, costs, differentiators, and quality measures

- Broad understanding of current capability, showing both business capability and how it is supported by IT

- Broad understanding of the feasibility and viability of particular SOA technology-driven solutions

This remit is in sharp contrast to the technology-centric, "developer-led" SOA community that maintains a core focus on the similarities across industries, organizations, and products to achieve benefit.

22.4   Business- & Developer-Led SOA Communities

Although the business-led and developer-led SOA communities maintain a different focus, their activities are complementary and intersect at the concept of a "service" (see Figure 22-1).

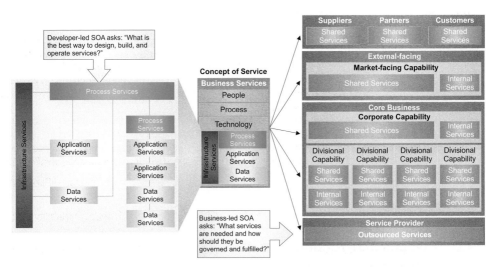

Figure 22-1 Business-Led versus Developer-Led SOA Communities

Business-led SOA considers a business service to be a unit of business capability supported by a combination of people, process, and technology. A business service may be:

- Fulfilled by manual processes, or may be fully automated

- Fulfilled within an organization, or outsourced to a partner

- Exposed to any combination of employees, customers, partners, and suppliers

- Fulfilled at the point of use, at a divisional level, or as a corporate competency center

Defining business services allows an organization to differentiate between business capability, the fulfilment of business capability, and the consumption of business capability. This differentiation allows the organization to consider sourcing, procurement, federation, centralization, and channel exposure in a much more flexible way, prioritizing investment and focus in areas that are core differentiators, whilst cost controlling and divesting areas that are considered to be context to the business.

Developer-led SOA considers an information system service to be a unit of application code providing an open interface that is abstracted from its implementation. Information system services support separation of concerns between:

- Encapsulation of business flow and application composition as **Process Services**

- Encapsulation of application function as **Application Services**

- Management of data access and persistence within **Data Services**

- Commoditization and sharing of common utility functions, such as monitoring and security within **Infrastructure Services**

Creation of this separation of concerns between information system service types supports more effective application re-use and the creation of multiple composite applications from a single service portfolio. For example, all applications can share common security services, many application functions can share the same data services, and many process-centric applications can share the same application services.

Additionally, the separation of service types supports specialization of infrastructure and tooling to optimize development, maintenance, and operational performance. For example, business process services can be developed, viewed, and maintained in a Business Process Management (BPM) environment, specifically designed for flow definition.

Finally, as all information system services operate in a consistent manner, a common SOA platform or SOA fabric can be deployed that manages hygiene factors for services in a consistent way. For example, service communication can be standardized and virtualized through the use of Enterprise Service Bus (ESB) infrastructure. Application monitoring can be abstracted from particular implementation stacks using agents and devices that monitor standards-based communications.

22.5   Complexities Arising from SOA

Alignment between business and IT within an organization is a fundamental challenge facing SOA adopters. However, even with a fully aligned organization, there are still significant differences between an SOA landscape and a traditional IT landscape that create new points of stress and focus.

In the past the "application" concept has provided the key to understanding the link between business and IT. Applications historically map closely onto organizational silos and as the number of applications is small, it is a straightforward task to govern these applications. However, within an SOA the concept of the application is augmented by the concept finer-grained application services, creating new challenges and complexity.

Whilst providing much greater business flexibility and agility, the breaking up of siloed business functions and applications into services comes at a cost, in that it creates a much more fine-grained IT landscape that needs to be managed. As a by-product or producing finer-grained capabilities, an increased volume of services must be managed (100s or 1000s of services as opposed to 10s or 100s of applications) with correspondingly increased complexity around the usage of and interaction between services:

- New stress points are created around understanding the relationships between technology portfolio and service portfolio
- New stress points are created around SLA definition, governance, and impact management
- New stress points are created around tracing business to IT
- New stress points are created around communication, alignment, and semantics
- New stress points are created around platform and interoperability
- New stress points are created around performance visibility and optimization

Technology can provide tooling to address many of these stress points, but the real issue here is that effective operation of an SOA requires a much more formalized understanding of the IT landscape with explicit linkages to the business it supports. Without this understanding, there is a very real risk that the possibilities of SOA will lead to an organically developed IT landscape, characterized by:

- Proliferation of unplanned, misaligned services at inappropriate levels of granularity, known as "service sprawl"

- Inability to carry out impact assessment and consequent overspend on infrastructure or poor quality of service

- Multiple technology stacks that are costly to support and do not interoperate, creating islands of services tied to implementation specifics that result in a brittle IT landscape and high operational costs, due to more complex service management and IT operations

- Inability for potential service consumers to identify services for re-use, resulting in duplicated capability, lack of visibility, and increased integration complexity

22.6 How Enterprise Architecture Supports SOA

Enterprise architecture is the application of architectural discipline to the end-to-end enterprise, treating the enterprise or industry value-chain as a system. What enterprise architecture provides in an SOA context is a set of tools and techniques to link top-down business-led SOA to bottom-up developer-led SOA in a robust and maintainable way that addresses many of the non-technical challenges associated with SOA adoption.

Enterprise architecture discipline provides the following tools and techniques to assist organizations with SOAs:

- Enterprise architecture defines structured traceable representations of business and technology that link IT assets to the business they support in a clear and measurable way. These models in turn support impact assessment and portfolio management against a much richer context.

- Enterprise architecture defines principles, constraints, frameworks, patterns, and standards that form the basis of design governance, ensuring aligned services, interoperability, and re-use.

- Enterprise architecture links many different perspectives to a single business problem (e.g., business, data, application, technology, abstracted, concrete, etc.) providing a consistent model to address various problem domains and extensive test for completeness.

- Enterprise architecture provides consistent abstractions of high-level strategies and project deliverables, enabling both bottom-up and top-down outputs to be collated in a shared repository to support planning and analysis.

Using these techniques, enterprise architecture becomes a foundation for service-orienting an organization, because:

- It links SOA stakeholders together, ensuring that the needs of each stakeholder community are met and that each stakeholder community is aware of appropriate context.

- It provides a link from business to IT that can be used to justify the cost of IT re-engineering against business value.

- It shows which services should be built and how they should be re-used.

- It shows how services should be designed and how platforms must interoperate.

- It provides a repository to hold and maintain design-related information on an ongoing basis.

22.7   SOA and TOGAF

A number of concepts are captured in the TOGAF content metamodel that support the modeling of SOA concepts:

- **Function**: A function is a thing that a business does. Services support functions, are functions, and have functions, but functions are not necessarily services. Services have more specific constraints than functions.

- **Business Service**: A business service is a thing that a business does that has a defined, measured interface and has contracts with consumers of the service. A business service is supported by combinations of people, process, and technology.

- **Information System Service**: An information system service is a thing that a business does that has a defined, measured interface and has contracts with consumers of the service. Information system services are directly supported by applications and have associations to SOA service interfaces.

- **Application Component**: An application component is a configured and deployed system, or independently governed piece of a configured and deployed system. Application components provide information system services. Application components can be physical applications and also logical applications that group together applications of a similar type.

- **Technology Component**: A technology component is a piece of software or hardware that can be purchased from an internal or external supplier. Technology components are configured, combined, built on, and deployed in order to produce application components.

Figure 22-2 shows how these TOGAF concepts (in blue) can be equated to common SOA terminology (in red).

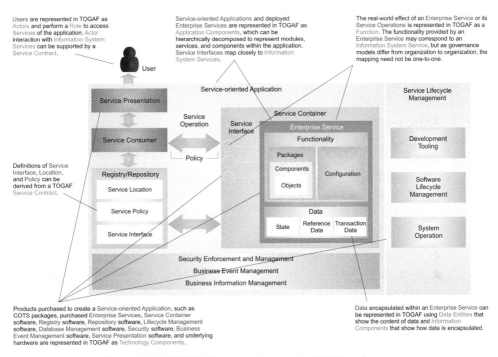

Users are represented in TOGAF as Actors and perform a Role to access Services of the application. Actor interaction with Information System Services can be supported by a Service Contract.

Service-oriented Applications and deployed Enterprise Services are represented in TOGAF as Application Components, which can be hierarchically decomposed to represent modules, services, and components within the application. Service Interfaces map closely to Information System Services.

The real-world effect of an Enterprise Service or its Service Operations is represented in TOGAF as a Function. The functionality provided by an Enterprise Service may correspond to an Information System Service, but as governance models differ from organization to organization, the mapping need not be one-to-one.

Definitions of Service Interface, Location, and Policy can be derived from a TOGAF Service Contract.

Products purchased to create a Service-oriented Application, such as COTS packages, purchased Enterprise Services, Service Container software, Registry software, Repository software, Lifecycle Management software, Database Management software, Security software, Business Event Management software, Service Presentation software, and underlying hardware are represented in TOGAF as Technology Components.

Data encapsulated within an Enterprise Service can be represented in TOGAF using Data Entities that show the content of data and Information Components that show how data is encapsulated.

Figure 22-2 TOGAF Concepts Mapped to SOA Terminology

Within the TOGAF Architecture Development Method (ADM), specific consideration is made to SOA concerns at various stages to ensure that appropriate pre-requisites are in place.

TOGAF Phase	SOA Concept	Benefits to an SOA Initiative
Preliminary	The TOGAF framework provides a metamodel and process that is capable of incorporating both business-led and developer-led SOA concepts in a holistic framework.	Using TOGAF will provide a direct linkage between business-led and developer-led communities, initiatives and benefits within an organization.

TOGAF Phase	SOA Concept	Benefits to an SOA Initiative
Architecture Vision	The TOGAF ADM includes specific steps to address SOA concerns, including: ■ Consideration of business capability — which capabilities are most valuable, volatile, and differentiating for the business? ■ Consideration of technology capability — how technically mature is the organization and how mature does it desire to be? ■ Consideration of IT governance impacts — what impacts is the Architecture Vision going to have on current IT governance models?	TOGAF Business Capability Assessments provide an opportunity to look at the business services that exist or are desired and how these business services can be realized. This Business Capability Assessment formalizes the work of business-led SOA stakeholders in a way that can be transferred to developer-led initiatives. The TOGAF Technology Capability Assessment provides an opportunity to look at technology risk and maturity, allowing the organization to make informed decisions on how fast to adopt SOA technology and also to select strategies for deployment of SOA and service technology platforms. The TOGAF IT governance assessment provides an opportunity to identify SOA-related governance impacts and to factor any new capability requirements into the overall Target Architecture.
Business Architecture	The Business Architecture phase elaborates the capabilities of the business and defines explicit portfolios of business services, accompanied by service contracts that formalize service consumption.	Business services are explicitly identified and tied to ownership, usage, and business value, forming the detail of a business-led SOA strategy in a way that can be linked into a developer-led world.
Information Systems Architectures	The Information Systems Architectures phase shows how the identified business services map to applications and data.	Information system services are explicitly identified and tied to business service, data encapsulation, and applications, elaborating a high-level framework for developer-led SOA implementation.

TOGAF Phase	SOA Concept	Benefits to an SOA Initiative
Technology Architecture	The Technology Architecture phase shows how application capabilities identified in the Information Systems Architecture are mapped onto SOA platforms and off-the-shelf SOA services, providing a blueprint for implementation.	SOA technology selection is not carried out in isolation as a pure feature comparison between products. SOA technology architectures are developed with traceable reference to: ■ Business ownership and value ■ A defined organizational position on baseline and target technology maturity ■ Service contracts that identify service consumers, SLAs, and non-functional requirements for services ■ Landscape visibility of how technologies will support delivery of applications and information system services ■ Consideration of the IT governance model, requirements, and issues
Opportunities & Solutions Migration Planning	The TOGAF ADM allows for identification of improvement opportunities and then selection, prioritization, and sequencing of those opportunities according to architectural analysis and stakeholder need.	Development of a multi-disciplinary Architecture Roadmap allows SOA capability to be incrementally developed, including proof-of-concept, pilot, and mainstream SOA enabling. Considerations — such as standards, guidelines, technology selection, design governance, operational governance, and security — can be considered holistically and charted for an organization in a way that supports incremental capability development, but avoids organic growth of "accidental architectures".

TOGAF Phase	SOA Concept	Benefits to an SOA Initiative
Implementation Governance	TOGAF provides specific processes for design governance during the implementation of an architecture.	TOGAF identifies the need for design governance, which can include SOA design governance. This approach provides a framework in which to apply an organization's standards, guidelines, and specifications to implementation projects.
Architecture Change Management	TOGAF allows for implementation issues and external factors to be incorporated into the architecture, allowing the overall approach to be refined.	Lessons learned from proof-of-concept and pilot activities can be leveraged and used to shape the strategy from a bottom-up perspective.

22.8   Guidelines for Service Contract Definition

22.8.1   Service Qualities and TOGAF

Besides the set of components making up the Technical Reference Model (TRM) — see Part VI, Chapter 43, there is a set of attributes or "qualities" that are applicable across the components.

The Detailed TRM diagram captures this concept by depicting the TRM components sitting on a backplane of **Qualities**.

Qualities are specified in detail during the development of the Target Architecture, and then used on an ongoing basis to govern and measure the success of the architecture.

Service contracts are an example of such qualities. This section defines further detail on how to create appropriate contracts for architectural services.

22.8.2   Purpose of a Service Contract

It is commonly understood that specifying the external characteristics of required IT capabilities, in a way that aligns with business objectives, supports creation of higher quality architecture.

The design and parameters around each service are analyzed more thoroughly, re-use potential is maximized, and governance parameters are aligned with business expectation and focus.

As Business Architecture is all about defining a formal corporate business model, prior to modeling service boundaries, it is this phase in an enterprise architecture engagement where "service modeling" should be considered. The approach must center around logical building blocks representing business services, and concentrate on defining the interfaces and Service Level Agreements (SLAs) between service providers and service consumers.

For services to interact, they do not need to share anything but a formal agreement that describes each service and defines the terms of the information exchange between consumer and supplier. A contract is a set of metadata that describes how parties will interact both functionally and non-functionally.

The outcome of this approach is that IT systems can respond to changes in policies and contracts without the need for more tightly coupled, inflexible programming — essentially, the policy needs to be changed and the contract adjusted, and the consumers and providers simply follow the amended contract. This is the ultimate vision of SOA.

The link between a business service and its service contracts is important — changes in an organization's business strategy and vision will trigger changes in these contracts — and their impact on the enterprise architecture needs to be understood.

22.8.3 Service Governance Considerations

An enterprise architecture includes many independent and self-contained moving parts — components which are re-used widely across the organization that become a vital part of mission-critical business processes.

If this is the case:

- What happens when a service is changed?
- Who owns the service?
- What SLAs govern the service?
- Who needs to test the service before it goes into production?
- How can you be sure the service you are consuming is of high quality?
- How can you be sure a new service is compliant with IT, business, and regulatory policies?
- How can you ensure predictable uptime of a service?

These questions illustrate the need for service governance. Service governance is about managing the quality, consistency, predictability, change, and inter-dependencies of services.

Service governance is a topic in itself. The IT Infrastructure Library (ITIL) Service Delivery Guide provides detailed guidance on the definition and management of SLAs and service governance.

A significant challenge facing IT organizations today is that while the management of service quality is paramount, simply having quality is not enough.

For the first time, quality must be proven and demonstrable to consumers to gain their trust and create an effective shared-service environment.

The cost of an ungoverned enterprise architecture is a lack of re-use, disruption and failure of business process, escalation of support costs resulting from service outages, security breaches, and non-compliance with enterprise or governmental regulations.

Service governance requires a cohesive strategy involving multiple elements that include service contracts, service policies, service lifecycle management, and service metadata.

Service Contracts

Contracts are key architectural tools for communicating and enforcing policies, as well as other requirements in a heterogeneous and distributed IT environment. Just as a business contract ensures a healthy commercial relationship, a service contract ensures a healthy provider/consumer relationship, and helps to establish an agreement and maintain trust between these parties. In other words, a service contract should provide a precise and unambiguous agreement for how the provider and consumer interact. Contracts are typically unique to a specific provider/consumer relationship, and they act as the container for both formal policies, as well as agreements that are unique to the parties.

Service Policies

The nature of SOA (highly distributed, heterogeneous, and very dynamic) means that it is critical for SOA artifacts to be governed by specific business, technical, and regulatory policies. In SOA, policies are not hard coded into a specific application, but are coupled to services.

An SOA policy defines configurable rules and conditions that affect services during both design time and run time. This means that policies must be used to validate services before they are published, and as a basis for enforcing specific standards and behaviors at run time.

Non-SOA applications also require effective definition and management of interaction policies. However, due to the coarse-grained, siloed nature of traditional systems, policy is less significant and is typically encoded into the application code and platform rather than being governed at the architectural and design level.

Service Lifecycle Management

Service artifacts need to be managed across a complete lifecycle.

Service lifecycle management is about:

- Ensuring the quality, performance, and applicability of services that are published
- Providing a means for consumers to discover and re-use services and other artifacts
- Managing versions, security, and state change of services and other artifacts
- Assessing and managing the impact of change across a network of consumers
- The lifecycle of individual services as they are designed, built, and deployed (which is primarily the concern of the service provider)
- The lifecycle of a network of services (in which services are accessed and used by changing populations of service consumers, and where the lifecycle primarily concerns those consumers)

Service Metadata

In traditional IT environments, metadata is typically defined within the code of systems and applications.

Externalizing service metadata from the native system enables the classification and governance of these independent services. Thus, metadata becomes a key artifact that needs to be managed within the overall architecture.

22.9   Content and Structure of a Service Contract

In any service consumer/provider relationship, there are two different senses of contract:

- A **Governance Contract** between two business entities which specifies what interaction is needed, inputs, outputs, SLAs, OLAs, and KPIs
- A **Operational Contract** which specifies the actual communication protocols and message formats

In TOGAF, at the architecture level, the main concern is the Governance Contract.

Just as legal contracts are documents that outline a set of enforceable rules and agreements written in a language that both parties can understand, in IT a contract should be defined that stipulates IT "rules of engagement" in a standardized manner that both the consumer and provider can understand.

It is during Business Architecture that definition of service contracts (in business terms) begins, before making decisions about how these services are to be implemented technically.

The service contract specifies the quality and integrity of the interaction between services. This specification allows the development of service-level objectives (irrespective of whether they are formalized into an SLA).

Service contracts form an important insight to developing the critical operational path, and they set the quality and security benchmarks for Application and Technology Architecture components.

If technically automated as an XML web service, a service contract can be comprised of a collection of service descriptions and documents including:

- **WSDL Definition**: An XML-based service description that describes the public interface, protocol bindings, and message formats required to interact with a web service.
- **XSD Schema**: An XSD defines a type of XML document in terms of constraints upon what elements and attributes may appear, their relationship to each other, and what types of data may be in them.
- **Policy**.

However, there a range of technical interface methods available to exchange information, not just XML web services; for example,

- IBM Websphere MQ
- CORBA
- Java Message Service (JMS)
- Database Replication or Synchronization
- Sending an ASCII file or email
- Putting a paper form in an envelope and posting it
- Simply displaying a sign on a wall for people to read

The contract is between whoever is providing the service, and whoever is consuming the service. Put it in the simplest terms, the contract provides details about the service being created by the provider. By agreeing to a contract, both parties understand exactly what will be provided, often before any decisions are made on the approach to realize a service (which may include outsourcing, purchasing a package, writing code, manual fulfilment, etc.).

This higher-level contract is crucially important, because these contracts frequently have not only technical implications but also business implications. A contract may include details of how the service will be authenticated, and so have details about authentication, encryption, and authorization. It may also include SLAs and how billing, metering, and monitoring will be done.

Contracts allow a provider company to create a single service, and then sell that service to many different customers, by simply creating a separate contract for each customer. A provider company may provide a service, but may charge more for that service if it responds more quickly to an identity, or provides a higher level of reliability. By including the information in the contract rather than the service, the service only needs to be created once. To re-use it with a different partner, only the contract needs to be changed.

Loose coupling mandates between parties should be able to conduct service fulfilment and optimize service realization as long as the terms of the agreed contract are met. Loose coupling is realized by implementing contracted interfaces on systems and making sure that those contracted relationships are enforced while allowing each party to change how they implement the contract independently.

22.10 Service Contract Template

Service contracts should be defined very carefully and clearly. The architecture performance will be based on these contract characteristics.

The contract should describe functional requirements; that is, what a provider will give to any consumer that chooses to abide by the terms of the contract. The contract should define what functionality is provided, what data it will return, or typically some combination of both.

Contracts must also specify non-functional requirements that detail not what the service does, but the way in which it goes about its business. This includes information both about the responsibility of the providers for providing their functionality and/or data as well as the expected responsibilities of the consumers of that information and what they will need to provide in return, such as availability, security, and other quality of service considerations.

A contract is an expression of the visible aspects of service behavior, and so contracts never include the data that providers and consumers actually exchange, or any specifics about how a provider or a consumer will meet the requirements of the contract. In addition, since consumers vary just as much as providers, there might be multiple contracts for a single service.

Attribute Type	Attribute	Description
General	Reference	A unique identifier within the architecture information for cross-reference, clarity, and differentiation from other similar artifacts.
General	Name	A suitable, preferably unique, short form name for the artifact.
General	Description	Name of the service. Should indicate in general terms what it does, but not be the only definition. A narrative of what the artifact is, what it does, and its relevance to the architecture.

Attribute Type	Attribute	Description
General	Source	The source of the artifact, which may be a person or a document, along with a date to support traceability of the architecture.
General	Owner	The owner of the artifact is the name (person or group) who validated the details of this artifact; the person/team in charge of the service.
General	Type	The type of the service to help distinguish it in the layer in which it resides; e.g., data, process, functionality, presentation, functional.
General	Version	The version of the service contract.
Business	RACI	**Responsible**: The role is the person/team responsible for the deliverables of this contract/service. **Accountable**: Ultimate decision-maker in terms of this contract/service. **Consulted**: Who must be consulted before action is taken on this contract/service. This is two-way communication. These people have an impact on the decision and/or the execution of that decision. **Informed**: Who must be informed that a decision or action is being taken. This is a one-way communication. These people are impacted by the decision or execution of that decision, but have no control over the action.
Business	Service name "caller"	Name of the consuming service.
Business	Service name "called"	Name of the provider service.
Business	Functional Requirements	The functionality in specific bulleted items of what exactly this service accomplishes. The language should be such that it allows test cases to prove the functionality is accomplished.
Business	Importance to the process	What happens if the service is unavailable.
Business	Quality of information required	The quality that is expected from the service consumer in terms of input, and what quality is expected from the service provider in terms of output.
Business	Contract control requirements	How the contract will be monitored and controlled.
Business	Result control requirements	How the results of the service will be monitored and controlled.
Business	Quality of service	Determines the allowable failure rate.
Business	Service Level Agreement	Determines the amount of latency the service is allowed to have to perform its actions.

Attribute Type	Attribute	Description
Non-functional Requirements	Throughput	Volume of transactions estimated; e.g., 100,000.
Non-functional Requirements	Throughput period	The period in which those transactions are expected, e.g., 100,000 per day.
Non-functional Requirements	Growth	The growth rate of transactions over time (estimated based on service take-up and business growth); e.g., 10,000.
Non-functional Requirements	Growth period	The period in which the growth is estimated to occur; e.g., 10,000 per year.
Non-functional Requirements	Service times	The available hours/days the service is needed; for example, 9 to 5 Monday to Friday (excluding Bank Holidays).
Non-functional Requirements	Peak profile short term	The profile of the short-term level of peak transactions; for example, 50% increase between hours of 10 to 12 am.
Non-functional Requirements	Peak profile long term	The profile of the long-term level of peak transactions; for example, 50% increase at month end.
Non-functional Requirements	Security requirements	Who can execute this service in terms of roles or individual partners, etc. and which invocation mechanism they can invoke.
Non-functional Requirements	Response requirements	The level and type of response required.
Technical	Invocation	The invocation means of the service. This includes the URL, interface, etc. There may be multiple invocation paths for the same service. There may be the same functionality for an internal and an external client, each with a different invocation means and interface. For example, SalesApp, events triggers, receipt of a written request form. The service end point address to which the invocation is directed should be included.
Technical	Invocation preconditions	Any pre-conditions that must be met by the consumer (authentication, additional input, etc.).
Technical	Business objects	Business objects transferred by the service.
Technical	Behavior characteristics	The criteria and conditions for successful interaction and any dependencies (on other service interactions, etc.). This should include any child services that will be invoked/spawned by this service (in addition to dependencies on other services).

Chapter 23: Architecture Principles

This chapter describes principles for use in the development of an enterprise architecture.

This chapter builds on work done by the US Air Force in establishing its Headquarters Air Force Principles for Information Management (June 29, 1998), with the addition of other input materials.

23.1   Introduction

Principles are general rules and guidelines, intended to be enduring and seldom amended, that inform and support the way in which an organization sets about fulfilling its mission.

In their turn, principles may be just one element in a structured set of ideas that collectively define and guide the organization, from values through to actions and results.

Depending on the organization, principles may be established at any or all of three levels:

- **Enterprise** principles provide a basis for decision-making throughout an enterprise, and inform how the organization sets about fulfilling its mission. Such enterprise-level principles are commonly found in governmental and not-for-profit organizations, but are encountered in commercial organizations also, as a means of harmonizing decision-making across a distributed organization. In particular, they are a key element in a successful architecture governance strategy (see Chapter 50).

- **Information Technology** (IT) principles provide guidance on the use and deployment of all IT resources and assets across the enterprise. They are developed in order to make the information environment as productive and cost-effective as possible.

- **Architecture** principles are a subset of IT principles that relate to architecture work. They reflect a level of consensus across the enterprise, and embody the spirit and thinking of the enterprise architecture. Architecture principles can be further divided into:

   — Principles that govern the architecture process, affecting the development, maintenance, and use of the enterprise architecture

   — Principles that govern the implementation of the architecture, establishing the first tenets and related guidance for designing and developing information systems

These sets of principles form a hierarchy, in that IT principles will be informed by, and elaborate on, the principles at the enterprise level; and architecture principles will likewise be informed by the principles at the two higher levels.

The remainder of this section deals exclusively with architecture principles.

23.2   Characteristics of Architecture Principles

Architecture principles define the underlying general rules and guidelines for the use and deployment of all IT resources and assets across the enterprise. They reflect a level of consensus among the various elements of the enterprise, and form the basis for making future IT decisions.

Each architecture principle should be clearly related back to the business objectives and key architecture drivers.

23.3   Components of Architecture Principles

It is useful to have a standard way of defining principles. In addition to a definition statement, each principle should have associated rationale and implications statements, both to promote understanding and acceptance of the principles themselves, and to support the use of the principles in explaining and justifying why specific decisions are made.

A recommended template is given in Table 23-1.

Name	Should both represent the essence of the rule as well as be easy to remember. Specific technology platforms should not be mentioned in the name or statement of a principle. Avoid ambiguous words in the Name and in the Statement such as: "support", "open", "consider", and for lack of good measure the word "avoid", itself, be careful with "manage(ment)", and look for unnecessary adjectives and adverbs (fluff).
Statement	Should succinctly and unambiguously communicate the fundamental rule. For the most part, the principles statements for managing information are similar from one organization to the next. It is vital that the principles statement be unambiguous.
Rationale	Should highlight the business benefits of adhering to the principle, using business terminology. Point to the similarity of information and technology principles to the principles governing business operations. Also describe the relationship to other principles, and the intentions regarding a balanced interpretation. Describe situations where one principle would be given precedence or carry more weight than another for making a decision.
Implications	Should highlight the requirements, both for the business and IT, for carrying out the principle — in terms of resources, costs, and activities/tasks. It will often be apparent that current systems, standards, or practices would be incongruent with the principle upon adoption. The impact to the business and consequences of adopting a principle should be clearly stated. The reader should readily discern the answer to: "How does this affect me?" It is important not to oversimplify, trivialize, or judge the merit of the impact. Some of the implications will be identified as potential impacts only, and may be speculative rather than fully analyzed.

Table 23-1 Recommended Format for Defining Principles

An example set of architecture principles following this template is given in Section 23.6.

23.4   Developing Architecture Principles

Architecture principles are typically developed by the lead enterprise architect, in conjunction with the enterprise CIO, Architecture Board, and other key business stakeholders.

Appropriate policies and procedures must be developed to support the implementation of the principles.

Architecture principles will be informed by overall IT principles and principles at the enterprise level, if they exist. They are chosen so as to ensure alignment of IT strategies with business strategies and visions. Specifically, the development of architecture principles is typically influenced by the following:

- **Enterprise mission and plans**: the mission, plans, and organizational infrastructure of the enterprise.

- **Enterprise strategic initiatives**: the characteristics of the enterprise — its strengths, weaknesses, opportunities, and threats — and its current enterprise-wide initiatives (such as process improvement and quality management).

- **External constraints**: market factors (time-to-market imperatives, customer expectations, etc.); existing and potential legislation.

- **Current systems and technology**: the set of information resources deployed within the enterprise, including systems documentation, equipment inventories, network configuration diagrams, policies, and procedures.

- **Computer industry trends**: predictions about the usage, availability, and cost of computer and communication technologies, referenced from credible sources along with associated best practices presently in use.

23.4.1   Qualities of Principles

Merely having a written statement that is called a principle does not mean that the principle is good, even if everyone agrees with it.

A good set of principles will be founded in the beliefs and values of the organization and expressed in language that the business understands and uses. Principles should be few in number, future-oriented, and endorsed and championed by senior management. They provide a firm foundation for making architecture and planning decisions, framing policies, procedures, and standards, and supporting resolution of contradictory situations. A poor set of principles will quickly become disused, and the resultant architectures, policies, and standards will appear arbitrary or self-serving, and thus lack credibility. Essentially, principles drive behavior.

There are five criteria that distinguish a good set of principles:

- **Understandable**: the underlying tenets can be quickly grasped and understood by individuals throughout the organization. The intention of the principle is clear and unambiguous, so that violations, whether intentional or not, are minimized.

- **Robust**: enable good quality decisions about architectures and plans to be made, and enforceable policies and standards to be created. Each principle should be sufficiently definitive and precise to support consistent decision-making in complex, potentially controversial situations.

■ **Complete**: every potentially important principle governing the management of information and technology for the organization is defined. The principles cover every situation perceived.

■ **Consistent**: strict adherence to one principle may require a loose interpretation of another principle. The set of principles must be expressed in a way that allows a balance of interpretations. Principles should not be contradictory to the point where adhering to one principle would violate the spirit of another. Every word in a principle statement should be carefully chosen to allow consistent yet flexible interpretation.

■ **Stable**: principles should be enduring, yet able to accommodate changes. An amendment process should be established for adding, removing, or altering principles after they are ratified initially.

23.5   Applying Architecture Principles

Architecture principles are used to capture the fundamental truths about how the enterprise will use and deploy IT resources and assets. The principles are used in a number of different ways:

1. To provide a framework within which the enterprise can start to make conscious decisions about IT

2. As a guide to establishing relevant evaluation criteria, thus exerting strong influence on the selection of products or product architectures in the later stages of managing compliance to the IT architecture

3. As drivers for defining the functional requirements of the architecture

4. As an input to assessing both existing IS/IT systems and the future strategic portfolio, for compliance with the defined architectures. These assessments will provide valuable insights into the transition activities needed to implement an architecture, in support of business goals and priorities

5. The Rationale statements (see below) highlight the value of the architecture to the enterprise, and therefore provide a basis for justifying architecture activities

6. The Implications statements (see below) provide an outline of the key tasks, resources, and potential costs to the enterprise of following the principle; they also provide valuable inputs to future transition initiative and planning activities

7. Support the architecture governance activities in terms of:

   — Providing a "back-stop" for the standard Architecture Compliance assessments where some interpretation is allowed or required

   — Supporting the decision to initiate a dispensation request where the implications of a particular architecture amendment cannot be resolved within local operating procedure

Principles are inter-related, and need to be applied as a set.

Principles will sometimes compete; for example, the principles of "accessibility" and "security" tend towards conflicting decisions. Each principle must be considered in the context of "all other things being equal".

At times a decision will be required as to which information principle will take precedence on a particular issue. The rationale for such decisions should always be documented.

A common reaction on first reading of a principle is "this is motherhood", but the fact that a principle seems self-evident does not mean that the principle is actually observed in an organization, even when there are verbal acknowledgements of the principle.

Although specific penalties are not prescribed in a declaration of principles, violations of principles generally cause operational problems and inhibit the ability of the organization to fulfil its mission.

23.6   Example Set of Architecture Principles

Too many principles can reduce the flexibility of the architecture. Many organizations prefer to define only high-level principles, and to limit the number to between 10 and 20.

The following example illustrates both the typical content of a set of architecture principles, and the recommended format for defining them, as explained above.

Another example of architecture principles is contained in the US Government's Federal Enterprise Architecture Framework (FEAF).

23.6.1 Business Principles

Principle 1:   **Primacy of Principles**

Statement: These principles of information management apply to all organizations within the enterprise.

Rationale: The only way we can provide a consistent and measurable level of quality information to decision-makers is if all organizations abide by the principles.

Implications: ▪ Without this principle, exclusions, favoritism, and inconsistency would rapidly undermine the management of information.

                       ▪ Information management initiatives will not begin until they are examined for compliance with the principles.

                       ▪ A conflict with a principle will be resolved by changing the framework of the initiative.

Principle 2:   **Maximize Benefit to the Enterprise**

Statement: Information management decisions are made to provide maximum benefit to the enterprise as a whole.

Rationale: This principle embodies "service above self". Decisions made from an enterprise-wide perspective have greater long-term value than decisions made from any particular organizational perspective. Maximum return on investment requires information management decisions to adhere to enterprise-wide drivers and priorities. No minority group will detract from the benefit of the whole. However, this principle will not preclude any minority group from getting its job done.

Implications:

- Achieving maximum enterprise-wide benefit will require changes in the way we plan and manage information. Technology alone will not bring about this change.

- Some organizations may have to concede their own preferences for the greater benefit of the entire enterprise.

- Application development priorities must be established by the entire enterprise for the entire enterprise.

- Applications components should be shared across organizational boundaries.

- Information management initiatives should be conducted in accordance with the enterprise plan. Individual organizations should pursue information management initiatives which conform to the blueprints and priorities established by the enterprise. We will change the plan as we need to.

- As needs arise, priorities must be adjusted. A forum with comprehensive enterprise representation should make these decisions.

Principle 3:   **Information Management is Everybody's Business**

Statement: All organizations in the enterprise participate in information management decisions needed to accomplish business objectives.

Rationale: Information users are the key stakeholders, or customers, in the application of technology to address a business need. In order to ensure information management is aligned with the business, all organizations in the enterprise must be involved in all aspects of the information environment. The business experts from across the enterprise and the technical staff responsible for developing and sustaining the information environment need to come together as a team to jointly define the goals and objectives of IT.

Implications:

- To operate as a team, every stakeholder, or customer, will need to accept responsibility for developing the information environment.

- Commitment of resources will be required to implement this principle.

Principle 4:   **Business Continuity**

Statement: Enterprise operations are maintained in spite of system interruptions.

Rationale: As system operations become more pervasive, we become more dependent on them; therefore, we must consider the reliability of such systems throughout their design and use. Business premises throughout the enterprise must be provided with the capability to continue their business functions regardless of external events. Hardware failure, natural disasters, and data corruption should not be allowed to disrupt or stop enterprise activities. The enterprise business functions must be capable of operating on alternative information delivery mechanisms.

Implications:
- Dependency on shared system applications mandates that the risks of business interruption must be established in advance and managed. Management includes but is not limited to periodic reviews, testing for vulnerability and exposure, or designing mission-critical services to ensure business function continuity through redundant or alternative capabilities.

- Recoverability, redundancy, and maintainability should be addressed at the time of design.

- Applications must be assessed for criticality and impact on the enterprise mission, in order to determine what level of continuity is required and what corresponding recovery plan is necessary.

Principle 5: **Common Use Applications**

Statement: Development of applications used across the enterprise is preferred over the development of similar or duplicative applications which are only provided to a particular organization.

Rationale: Duplicative capability is expensive and proliferates conflicting data.

Implications:
- Organizations which depend on a capability which does not serve the entire enterprise must change over to the replacement enterprise-wide capability. This will require establishment of and adherence to a policy requiring this.

- Organizations will not be allowed to develop capabilities for their own use which are similar/duplicative of enterprise-wide capabilities. In this way, expenditures of scarce resources to develop essentially the same capability in marginally different ways will be reduced.

- Data and information used to support enterprise decision-making will be standardized to a much greater extent than previously. This is because the smaller, organizational capabilities which produced different data (which was not shared among other organizations) will be replaced by enterprise-wide capabilities. The impetus for adding to the set of enterprise-wide capabilities may well come from an organization making a convincing case for the value of the data/information previously produced by its organizational capability, but the resulting capability will become part of the enterprise-wide system, and the data it produces will be shared across the enterprise.

Principle 6: **Service Orientation**

Statement: The architecture is based on a design of services which mirror real-world business activities comprising the enterprise (or inter-enterprise) business processes.

Rationale: Service orientation delivers enterprise agility and Boundaryless Information Flow.

Implications:
- Service representation utilizes business descriptions to provide context (i.e., business process, goal, rule, policy, service interface, and service component) and implements services using service orchestration.

- Service orientation places unique requirements on the infrastructure, and implementations should use open standards to realize interoperability and location transparency.

- Implementations are environment-specific; they are constrained or enabled by context and must be described within that context.

- Strong governance of service representation and implementation is required.

- A "Litmus Test", which determines a "good service", is required.

Principle 7:   **Compliance with Law**

Statement: Enterprise information management processes comply with all relevant laws, policies, and regulations.

Rationale: Enterprise policy is to abide by laws, policies, and regulations. This will not preclude business process improvements that lead to changes in policies and regulations.

Implications:
- The enterprise must be mindful to comply with laws, regulations, and external policies regarding the collection, retention, and management of data.

- Education and access to the rules. Efficiency, need, and common sense are not the only drivers. Changes in the law and changes in regulations may drive changes in our processes or applications.

Principle 8:   **IT Responsibility**

Statement: The IT organization is responsible for owning and implementing IT processes and infrastructure that enable solutions to meet user-defined requirements for functionality, service levels, cost, and delivery timing.

Rationale: Effectively align expectations with capabilities and costs so that all projects are cost-effective. Efficient and effective solutions have reasonable costs and clear benefits.

Implications:
- A process must be created to prioritize projects.

- The IT function must define processes to manage business unit expectations.

- Data, application, and technology models must be created to enable integrated quality solutions and to maximize results.

Principle 9:   **Protection of Intellectual Property**

Statement: The enterprise's Intellectual Property (IP) must be protected. This protection must be reflected in the IT architecture, implementation, and governance processes.

Rationale: A major part of an enterprise's IP is hosted in the IT domain.

Implications:
- While protection of IP assets is everybody's business, much of the actual protection is implemented in the IT domain. Even trust in non-IT processes can be managed by IT processes (email, mandatory notes, etc.).

- A security policy, governing human and IT actors, will be required that can substantially improve protection of IP. This must be capable of both avoiding compromises and reducing liabilities.

- Resources on such policies can be found at the SANS Institute (refer to www.sans.org/newlook/home.php).

23.6.2 Data Principles

Principle 10:   Data is an Asset

Statement: Data is an asset that has value to the enterprise and is managed accordingly.

Rationale: Data is a valuable corporate resource; it has real, measurable value. In simple terms, the purpose of data is to aid decision-making. Accurate, timely data is critical to accurate, timely decisions. Most corporate assets are carefully managed, and data is no exception. Data is the foundation of our decision-making, so we must also carefully manage data to ensure that we know where it is, can rely upon its accuracy, and can obtain it when and where we need it.

Implications:
- This is one of three closely-related principles regarding data: data is an asset; data is shared; and data is easily accessible. The implication is that there is an education task to ensure that all organizations within the enterprise understand the relationship between value of data, sharing of data, and accessibility to data.

- Stewards must have the authority and means to manage the data for which they are accountable.

- We must make the cultural transition from "data ownership" thinking to "data stewardship" thinking.

- The role of data steward is critical because obsolete, incorrect, or inconsistent data could be passed to enterprise personnel and adversely affect decisions across the enterprise.

- Part of the role of data steward, who manages the data, is to ensure data quality. Procedures must be developed and used to prevent and correct errors in the information and to improve those processes that produce flawed information. Data quality will need to be measured and steps taken to improve data quality — it is probable that policy and procedures will need to be developed for this as well.

- A forum with comprehensive enterprise-wide representation should decide on process changes suggested by the steward.

- Since data is an asset of value to the entire enterprise, data stewards accountable for properly managing the data must be assigned at the enterprise level.

Principle 11:   **Data is Shared**

Statement: Users have access to the data necessary to perform their duties; therefore, data is shared across enterprise functions and organizations.

Rationale: Timely access to accurate data is essential to improving the quality and efficiency of enterprise decision-making. It is less costly to maintain timely, accurate data in a single application, and then share it, than it is to maintain duplicative data in multiple applications. The enterprise holds a wealth of data, but it is stored in hundreds of incompatible stovepipe databases. The speed of data collection, creation, transfer, and assimilation is driven by the ability of the organization to efficiently share these islands of data across the organization.

Shared data will result in improved decisions since we will rely on fewer (ultimately one virtual) sources of more accurate and timely managed data for all of our decision-making. Electronically shared data will result in increased efficiency when existing data entities can be used, without re-keying, to create new entities.

Implications:
- This is one of three closely-related principles regarding data: data is an asset; data is shared; and data is easily accessible. The implication is that there is an education task to ensure that all organizations within the enterprise understand the relationship between value of data, sharing of data, and accessibility to data.

- To enable data sharing we must develop and abide by a common set of policies, procedures, and standards governing data management and access for both the short and the long term.

- For the short term, to preserve our significant investment in legacy systems, we must invest in software capable of migrating legacy system data into a shared data environment.

- We will also need to develop standard data models, data elements, and other metadata that defines this shared environment and develop a repository system for storing this metadata to make it accessible.

- For the long term, as legacy systems are replaced, we must adopt and enforce common data access policies and guidelines for new application developers to ensure that data in new applications remains available to the shared environment and that data in the shared environment can continue to be used by the new applications.

- For both the short term and the long term we must adopt common methods and tools for creating, maintaining, and accessing the data shared across the enterprise.

- Data sharing will require a significant cultural change.

- This principle of data sharing will continually "bump up against" the principle of data security. Under no circumstances will the data sharing principle cause confidential data to be compromised.

- Data made available for sharing will have to be relied upon by all users to execute their respective tasks. This will ensure that only the most accurate and timely data is relied upon for decision-making. Shared data will become the enterprise-wide "virtual single source" of data.

Principle 12:   **Data is Accessible**

Statement: Data is accessible for users to perform their functions.

Rationale: Wide access to data leads to efficiency and effectiveness in decision-making, and affords timely response to information requests and service delivery. Using information must be considered from an enterprise perspective to allow access by a wide variety of users. Staff time is saved and consistency of data is improved.

Implications:
- This is one of three closely-related principles regarding data: data is an asset; data is shared; and data is easily accessible. The implication is that there is an education task to ensure that all organizations within the enterprise understand the relationship between value of data, sharing of data, and accessibility to data.

- Accessibility involves the ease with which users obtain information.

- The way information is accessed and displayed must be sufficiently adaptable to meet a wide range of enterprise users and their corresponding methods of access.

- Access to data does not constitute understanding of the data. Personnel should take caution not to misinterpret information.

- Access to data does not necessarily grant the user access rights to modify or disclose the data. This will require an education process and a change in the organizational culture, which currently supports a belief in "ownership" of data by functional units.

Principle 13:   **Data Trustee**

Statement: Each data element has a trustee accountable for data quality.

Rationale: One of the benefits of an architected environment is the ability to share data (e.g., text, video, sound, etc.) across the enterprise. As the degree of data sharing grows and business units rely upon common information, it becomes essential that only the data trustee makes decisions about the content of data. Since data can lose its integrity when it is entered multiple times, the data trustee will have sole responsibility for data entry which eliminates redundant human effort and data storage resources.

Note: A trustee is different than a steward — a trustee is responsible for accuracy and currency of the data, while responsibilities of a steward may be broader and include data standardization and definition tasks.

Implications:
- Real trusteeship dissolves the data "ownership" issues and allows the data to be available to meet all users' needs. This implies that a cultural change from data "ownership" to data "trusteeship" may be required.

- The data trustee will be responsible for meeting quality requirements levied upon the data for which the trustee is accountable.

- It is essential that the trustee has the ability to provide user confidence in the data based upon attributes such as "data source".

- It is essential to identify the true source of the data in order that the data authority can be assigned this trustee responsibility. This does not mean that classified sources will be revealed nor does it mean the source will be the trustee.

- Information should be captured electronically once and immediately validated as close to the source as possible. Quality control measures must be implemented to ensure the integrity of the data.

- As a result of sharing data across the enterprise, the trustee is accountable and responsible for the accuracy and currency of their designated data element(s) and, subsequently, must then recognize the importance of this trusteeship responsibility.

Principle 14:   Common Vocabulary and Data Definitions

Statement: Data is defined consistently throughout the enterprise, and the definitions are understandable and available to all users.

Rationale: The data that will be used in the development of applications must have a common definition throughout the Headquarters to enable sharing of data. A common vocabulary will facilitate communications and enable dialog to be effective. In addition, it is required to interface systems and exchange data.

Implications:
- We are lulled into thinking that this issue is adequately addressed because there are people with "data administration" job titles and forums with charters implying responsibility. Significant additional energy and resources must be committed to this task. It is key to the success of efforts to improve the information environment. This is separate from but related to the issue of data element definition, which is addressed by a broad community — this is more like a common vocabulary and definition.

- The enterprise must establish the initial common vocabulary for the business. The definitions will be used uniformly throughout the enterprise.

- Whenever a new data definition is required, the definition effort will be co-ordinated and reconciled with the corporate "glossary" of data descriptions. The enterprise data administrator will provide this co-ordination.

- Ambiguities resulting from multiple parochial definitions of data must give way to accepted enterprise-wide definitions and understanding.

- Multiple data standardization initiatives need to be co-ordinated.

- Functional data administration responsibilities must be assigned.

Principle 15:   Data Security

Statement: Data is protected from unauthorized use and disclosure. In addition to the traditional aspects of national security classification, this includes, but is not limited to, protection of pre-decisional, sensitive, source selection-sensitive, and proprietary information.

Rationale: Open sharing of information and the release of information via relevant legislation must be balanced against the need to restrict the availability of classified, proprietary, and sensitive information.

Existing laws and regulations require the safeguarding of national security and the privacy of data, while permitting free and open access. Pre-decisional (work-in-progress, not yet authorized for release) information must be protected to avoid unwarranted speculation, misinterpretation, and inappropriate use.

Implications: ■ Aggregation of data, both classified and not, will create a large target requiring review and de-classification procedures to maintain appropriate control. Data owners and/or functional users must determine whether the aggregation results in an increased classification level. We will need appropriate policy and procedures to handle this review and de-classification. Access to information based on a need-to-know policy will force regular reviews of the body of information.

■ The current practice of having separate systems to contain different classifications needs to be rethought. Is there a software solution to separating classified and unclassified data? The current hardware solution is unwieldy, inefficient, and costly. It is more expensive to manage unclassified data on a classified system. Currently, the only way to combine the two is to place the unclassified data on the classified system, where it must remain.

■ In order to adequately provide access to open information while maintaining secure information, security needs must be identified and developed at the data level, not the application level.

■ Data security safeguards can be put in place to restrict access to "view only", or "never see". Sensitivity labeling for access to pre-decisional, decisional, classified, sensitive, or proprietary information must be determined.

■ Security must be designed into data elements from the beginning; it cannot be added later. Systems, data, and technologies must be protected from unauthorized access and manipulation. Headquarters information must be safeguarded against inadvertent or unauthorized alteration, sabotage, disaster, or disclosure.

■ Need new policies on managing duration of protection for pre-decisional information and other works-in-progress, in consideration of content freshness.

23.6.3   Application Principles

Principle 16:   **Technology Independence**

Statement: Applications are independent of specific technology choices and therefore can operate on a variety of technology platforms.

Rationale: Independence of applications from the underlying technology allows applications to be developed, upgraded, and operated in the most cost-effective and timely way. Otherwise technology, which is subject to continual obsolescence and vendor dependence, becomes the driver rather than the user requirements themselves.

Realizing that every decision made with respect to IT makes us dependent on that technology, the intent of this principle is to ensure that Application Software is not dependent on specific hardware and operating systems software.

Implications: ▪ This principle will require standards which support portability.

▪ For Commercial Off-The-Shelf (COTS) and Government Off-The-Shelf (GOTS) applications, there may be limited current choices, as many of these applications are technology and platform-dependent.

▪ Subsystem interfaces will need to be developed to enable legacy applications to interoperate with applications and operating environments developed under the enterprise architecture.

▪ Middleware should be used to decouple applications from specific software solutions.

▪ As an example, this principle could lead to use of Java, and future Java-like protocols, which give a high degree of priority to platform-independence.

Principle 17:   **Ease-of-Use**

Statement: Applications are easy to use. The underlying technology is transparent to users, so they can concentrate on tasks at hand.

Rationale: The more a user has to understand the underlying technology, the less productive that user is. Ease-of-use is a positive incentive for use of applications. It encourages users to work within the integrated information environment instead of developing isolated systems to accomplish the task outside of the enterprise's integrated information environment. Most of the knowledge required to operate one system will be similar to others. Training is kept to a minimum, and the risk of using a system improperly is low.

Using an application should be as intuitive as driving a different car.

Implications: ▪ Applications will be required to have a common "look-and-feel" and support ergonomic requirements. Hence, the common look-and-feel standard must be designed and usability test criteria must be developed.

▪ Guidelines for user interfaces should not be constrained by narrow assumptions about user location, language, systems training, or physical capability. Factors such as linguistics, customer physical infirmities (visual acuity, ability to use keyboard/mouse), and proficiency in the use of technology have broad ramifications in determining the ease-of-use of an application.

23.6.4 Technology Principles

Principle 18:   Requirements-Based Change

Statement: Only in response to business needs are changes to applications and technology made.

Rationale: This principle will foster an atmosphere where the information environment changes in response to the needs of the business, rather than having the business change in response to IT changes. This is to ensure that the purpose of the information support — the transaction of business — is the basis for any proposed change. Unintended effects on business due to IT changes will be minimized. A change in technology may provide an opportunity to improve the business process and, hence, change business needs.

Implications: ▪ Changes in implementation will follow full examination of the proposed changes using the enterprise architecture.

                  ▪ We don't fund a technical improvement or system development unless a documented business need exists.

                  ▪ Change management processes conforming to this principle will be developed and implemented.

                  ▪ This principle may bump up against the responsive change principle. We must ensure the requirements documentation process does not hinder responsive change to meet legitimate business needs. The purpose of this principle is to keep us focused on business, not technology needs — responsive change is also a business need.

Principle 19:   Responsive Change Management

Statement: Changes to the enterprise information environment are implemented in a timely manner.

Rationale: If people are to be expected to work within the enterprise information environment, that information environment must be responsive to their needs.

Implications: ▪ We have to develop processes for managing and implementing change that do not create delays.

                  ▪ A user who feels a need for change will need to connect with a "business expert" to facilitate explanation and implementation of that need.

                  ▪ If we are going to make changes, we must keep the architectures updated.

                  ▪ Adopting this principle might require additional resources.

                  ▪ This will conflict with other principles (e.g., maximum enterprise-wide benefit, enterprise-wide applications, etc.).

Principle 20:　　**Control Technical Diversity**

Statement:　　Technological diversity is controlled to minimize the non-trivial cost of maintaining expertise in and connectivity between multiple processing environments.

Rationale:　　There is a real, non-trivial cost of infrastructure required to support alternative technologies for processing environments. There are further infrastructure costs incurred to keep multiple processor constructs interconnected and maintained.

Limiting the number of supported components will simplify maintainability and reduce costs.

The business advantages of minimum technical diversity include: standard packaging of components; predictable implementation impact; predictable valuations and returns; redefined testing; utility status; and increased flexibility to accommodate technological advancements. Common technology across the enterprise brings the benefits of economies of scale to the enterprise. Technical administration and support costs are better controlled when limited resources can focus on this shared set of technology.

Implications:
- Policies, standards, and procedures that govern acquisition of technology must be tied directly to this principle.
- Technology choices will be constrained by the choices available within the technology blueprint. Procedures for augmenting the acceptable technology set to meet evolving requirements will have to be developed and emplaced.
- We are not freezing our technology baseline. We welcome technology advances and will change the technology blueprint when compatibility with the current infrastructure, improvement in operational efficiency, or a required capability has been demonstrated.

Principle 21:　　**Interoperability**

Statement:　　Software and hardware should conform to defined standards that promote interoperability for data, applications, and technology.

Rationale:　　Standards help ensure consistency, thus improving the ability to manage systems and improve user satisfaction, and protect existing IT investments, thus maximizing return on investment and reducing costs. Standards for interoperability additionally help ensure support from multiple vendors for their products, and facilitate supply chain integration.

Implications:
- Interoperability standards and industry standards will be followed unless there is a compelling business reason to implement a non-standard solution.
- A process for setting standards, reviewing and revising them periodically, and granting exceptions must be established.
- The existing IT platforms must be identified and documented.

Chapter 24: Stakeholder Management

24.1 Introduction

Stakeholder Management is an important discipline that successful architecture practitioners can use to win support from others. It helps them ensure that their projects succeed where others fail.

The benefits of successful Stakeholder Management are that:

- The most powerful stakeholders can be identified early and their input can then be used to shape the architecture; this ensures their support and improves the quality of the models produced.

- Support from the more powerful stakeholders will help the engagement win more resource, thus making the architecture engagement more likely to succeed.

- By communicating with stakeholders early and frequently, the architecture team can ensure that they fully understand the architecture process, and the benefits of enterprise architecture; this means they can support the architecture team more actively when necessary.

- The architecture engagement team can more effectively anticipate likely reactions to the architecture models and reports, and can build into the plan the actions that will be needed to capitalize on positive reaction whilst avoiding or addressing any negative reactions.

It is essential in any initiative to identify the individuals and groups within the organization who will contribute to the development of the architecture, identify those that will gain and those that will lose from its introduction, and then develop a strategy for dealing with them.

24.2   Approach to Stakeholder Management

Stakeholder analysis should be used during Phase A (Architecture Vision) to identify the key players in the engagement, and also be updated throughout each phase; different stakeholders may be uncovered as the engagement progresses through into Opportunities & Solutions, Migration Planning, and Architecture Change Management.

Complex architectures are extremely hard to manage, not only in terms of the architecture development process itself, but also in terms of obtaining agreement from the large numbers of stakeholders touched by it.

For example, just as a building architect will create wiring diagrams, floor plans, and elevations to describe different facets of a building to its different stakeholders (electricians, owners, planning officials), so an enterprise architect must create different views of the business, information system, and technology architecture for the stakeholders who have concerns related to these aspects.

TOGAF specifically identifies this issue throughout the ADM through the following concepts (as defined in Section 35.1):

- Stakeholders
- Concerns
- Views
- Viewpoints

24.3   Steps in the Stakeholder Management Process

The following sections detail recommended Stakeholder Management activity.

24.3.1   Identify Stakeholders

Identify the key stakeholders of the enterprise architecture.

The first task is to brainstorm who the main enterprise architecture stakeholders are. As part of this, think of all the people who are affected by it, who have influence or power over it, or have an interest in its successful or unsuccessful conclusion.

It might include senior executives, project organization roles, client organization roles, system developers, alliance partners, suppliers, IT operations, customers, etc.

When identifying stakeholders there is a danger of concentrating too heavily on the formal structure of an organization as the basis for identification. Informal stakeholder groups may be just as powerful and influential as the formal ones.

Most individuals will belong to more than one stakeholder group, and these groups tend to arise as a result of specific events.

Look at who is impacted by the enterprise architecture project:

- Who gains and who loses from this change?
- Who controls change management of processes?
- Who designs new systems?
- Who will make the decisions?
- Who procures IT systems and who decides what to buy?
- Who controls resources?
- Who has specialist skills the project needs?
- Who has influence?

In particular, influencers need to be identified. These will be well respected and moving up, participate in important meetings and committees (look at meeting minutes), know what's going on in the company, be valued by their peers and superiors, and not necessarily be in any formal position of power.

Although stakeholders may be both organizations and people, ultimately the enterprise architecture team will need to communicate with people. It is the correct individual stakeholders within a stakeholder organization that need to be formally identified.

It is possible to distinguish five broad categories of stakeholder, as shown in Figure 24-1.

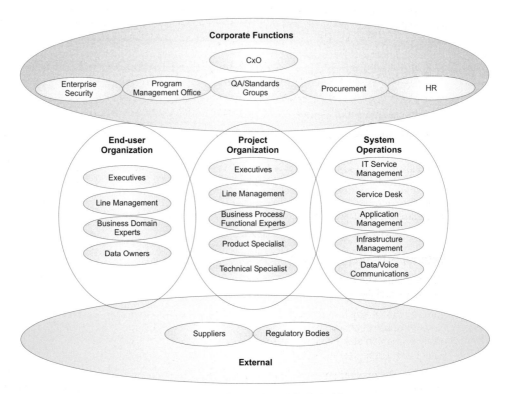

Figure 24-1 Categories of Stakeholder

Consider both the Visible team — those obviously associated with the project/change — and the Invisible team — those who must make a real contribution to the project/change for it to be successful but who are not obviously associated with it (e.g., providers of support services).

24.3.2 Classify Stakeholder Positions

Develop a good understanding of the most important stakeholders and record this analysis for reference and refresh during the project. An example stakeholder analysis is shown in Table 24-1.

Stakeholder Group	Stakeholder	Ability to Disrupt Change	Current Under-standing	Required Under-standing	Current Commit-ment	Required Commit-ment	Required Support
CIO	John Smith	H	M	H	L	M	H
CFO	Jeff Brown	M	M	M	L	M	M

Table 24-1 Example Stakeholder Analysis

It is also important to assess the readiness of each stakeholder to behave in a supportive manner (i.e., demonstrate commitment to the enterprise architecture initiative).

This can be done by asking a series of questions:

- Is that person ready to change direction and begin moving towards the Target Architecture? If so, how ready?
- Is that person capable of being a credible advocate or agent of the proposed enterprise architecture initiative? If so, how capable?
- How involved is the individual in the enterprise architecture initiative? Are they simply an interested observer, or do they need to be involved in the details?
- Has that person made a contractual commitment to the development of the enterprise architecture, and its role in the governance of the development of the organization?

Then, for each person whose commitment is critical to ensure success, make a judgment as to their current level of commitment and the desired future level of commitment.

24.3.3 Determine Stakeholder Management Approach

The previous steps identified a long list of people and organizations that are affected by the enterprise architecture project.

Some of these may have the power either to block or advance. Some may be interested in what the enterprise architecture initiative is doing; others may not care. This step enables the team to easily see which stakeholders are expected to be blockers or critics, and which stakeholders are likely to be advocates and supporters of the initiative.

Work out stakeholder power, influence, and interest, so as to focus the enterprise architecture engagement on the key individuals. These can be mapped onto a power/interest matrix, which also indicates the strategy to adopt for engaging with them. Figure 24-2 shows an example power grid matrix.

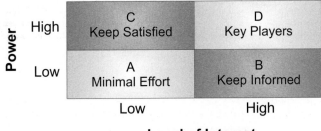

Figure 24-2 Stakeholder Power Grid

24.3.4 Tailor Engagement Deliverables

Identify viewpoints, matrices, and views that the architecture engagement needs to produce and validate with each stakeholder group to deliver an effective architecture model.

It is important to pay particular attention to stakeholder interests by defining specific viewpoints, matrices, and views of the enterprise architecture model. This enables the architecture to be communicated to, and understood by, all the stakeholders, and enables them to verify that the enterprise architecture initiative will address their concerns.

24.4 Template Stakeholder Map

The following table provides an example stakeholder map for a TOGAF architecture project.

Stakeholder	Involvement	Class	Relevant Viewpoints
CxO (Corporate Functions); e.g., CEO, CFO, CIO, COO	This stakeholder group is interested in the high-level drivers, goals, and objectives of the organization, and how these are translated into an effective process and IT architecture to advance the business.	KEEP SATISFIED	Business Footprint Goal/Objective/Service Model Organization Chart
Program Management Office (Corporate Functions); e.g., Project Portfolio Managers	This stakeholder group is interested in prioritizing, funding, and aligning change activity. An understanding of project content and technical dependencies between projects adds a further dimension of richness to portfolio management decision-making.	KEEP SATISFIED	Roadmaps Business Footprint Application Communication Functional Decomposition

Stakeholder	Involvement	Class	Relevant Viewpoints
Procurement (Corporate Functions); e.g., Acquirers	Major concerns for these stakeholders are understanding what building blocks of the architecture can be bought, and what constraints (or rules) exist that are relevant to the purchase. The acquirer will shop with multiple vendors looking for the best cost solution while adhering to the constraints (or rules) applied by the architecture, such as standards. The key concern is to make purchasing decisions that fit the architecture, and thereby to reduce the risk of added costs arising from non-compliant components.	KEY PLAYERS	Cost View Standards View
Human Resources (HR) (Corporate Functions); e.g., HR Managers, Training & Development Managers	Key features of the enterprise architecture are the roles and Actors that support the functions, applications, and technology of the organization. HR are important stakeholders in ensuring that the correct roles and actors are represented.	KEEP INFORMED	Organization Chart Organization/Actor/Location
Enterprise Security (Corporate Functions); e.g., Corporate Risk Management, Security Officers, IT Security Managers	Major concerns for this group are understanding how to ensure that the information, data, and systems of the organization are available to only those that have permission, and how to protect the information, data, and systems from unauthorized tampering.	KEY PLAYERS	Data Security View Networked Computing Hardware View Communications View

Stakeholder	Involvement	Class	Relevant Viewpoints
QA/Standards Group (Corporate Functions); e.g., Data Owners, Process Owners, Technical Standards Bodies	Major concerns for this group are ensuring the consistent governance of the organization's business, data, application, and technology assets.	KEY PLAYERS	Standards Guidelines Specifications Standards View Application Portfolio Technology Portfolio Technology Standards
Executive (End User Organization); e.g., Business Unit Directors, Business Unit CxOs, Business Unit Head of IT/Architecture	This stakeholder group is interested in the high-level drivers, goals, and objectives of the organization, and how these are translated into an effective process and IT architecture to advance the business.	KEEP SATISFIED	Business Footprint Goal/Objective/ Service Model Organization Chart
Line Management (End User Organization); e.g., Senior Business Managers, Operations Regional Managers, IT Managers	This stakeholder is interested in the top-level functions and processes of the organization, and how the key applications of the IT estate support these processes.	KEY PLAYERS	Organization/Actor/ Location Goal/Objective/ Service Model Cost View Application & User Location View
Business Domain Experts (End User Organization); e.g., Business Process Experts, Business/Process Analyst, Process Architect, Process Designer, Functional Managers, Business Analyst	This stakeholder is interested in the functional aspects of processes and systems. This can cover the human actors involved in the system, the user processes involved in the system, the functions required to support the processes, and the information required to flow in support of the processes.	KEY PLAYERS	Process Flow Use-case Service/Information Events Functional Decomposition Application — Application Communication View Data Entity/Business Function Matrix

Stakeholder	Involvement	Class	Relevant Viewpoints
IT Service Management (Systems Operations); e.g., Service Delivery Manager	Major concerns for this group are ensuring that IT services provided to the organization meet the service levels required by that organization to succeed in business.	KEEP INFORMED	Standards View Enterprise Manageability View
IT Operations — Applications (System Operations); e.g., Application Architecture, System & Software Engineers	Major concerns for these stakeholders are: Development Approach, Software Modularity and Re-use, Portability Migration, and Interoperability.	KEY PLAYERS	Process — System Realization View Application — Data View Application Migration Cost View Software Engineering View Platform Decomposition View Networked Computing — Hardware View Software Distribution View Data Entities to Application Systems View
IT Operations — Infrastructure (System Operations); e.g., Infrastructure Architect, Wintel support, Mid-range support, Operational DBA, Service Desk	Infrastructure stakeholders are typically concerned with location, modifiability, re-usability, and availability of all components of the system. In general these stakeholders are concerned with ensuring that the appropriate components are developed and deployed within the system in an optimal manner.	KEY PLAYERS	Platform Decomposition View Standards View Enterprise Manageability View Networked Computing — Hardware View Processing View Environments & Locations View

Stakeholder	Involvement	Class	Relevant Viewpoints
IT Operations — Data/Voice Communications (System Operations); e.g., Network Management	Communications engineers are typically concerned with location, modifiability, re-usability, and availability of communications and networking services. In general these stakeholders are concerned with ensuring that the appropriate communications and networking services are developed and deployed within the system in an optimal manner.	KEY PLAYERS	Communications View
Executive (Project Organization); e.g., Sponsor, Program Manager	This stakeholder group is interested in on-time, on-budget delivery of a change initiative that will realize expected benefits for the organization.	KEEP INFORMED	Architecture Requirements Architecture Principles Architecture Vision Functional Decomposition Application & User Location View
Line Management (Project Organization); e.g., Project Manager	This stakeholder group is responsible for operationally achieving on-time, on-budget delivery of a change initiative with an agreed scope.	KEEP INFORMED	Application — Application Communication View Functional Decomposition Environments & Locations View
Business Process/Functional Expert (Project Organization); e.g., Financials FICO Functional Consultant, HR Functional Consultant	This stakeholder group will elaborate the functional requirements of a change initiative based on experience and interaction with business domain experts in the end-user organization.	KEY PLAYERS	Process Flow Use-case Service/Information Events Functional Decomposition Application — Application Communication View

Stakeholder	Involvement	Class	Relevant Viewpoints
Product Specialist (Project Organization); e.g., Portal Product Specialist	This stakeholder group is responsible for specifying technology product designs in order to meet project requirements and comply with the Architecture Vision of the solution. In a packages and packaged services environment, product expertise can be used to identify product capabilities that can be readily leveraged and can provide guidance on strategies for product customization.	KEY PLAYERS	Software Engineering View Application — Data View
Technical Specialist (Project Organization); e.g., Application Architect	This stakeholder group is responsible for specifying technology product designs in order to meet project requirements and comply with the Architecture Vision of the solution.	KEY PLAYERS	Software Engineering View Platform Decomposition View Process System Realization View Application — Data View Application Migration Cost View
Regulatory Bodies (Outside Services); e.g., Financial Regulator, Industry Regulator	The main concerns of this group are that they can receive the information they need in order to regulate the client organization, and that their information requirements are being understood and properly satisfied. They are specifically interested in reporting processes, and the data and applications used to provide regulatory return information.	KEEP SATISFIED	Business Footprint Application — Application Communication View

Stakeholder	Involvement	Class	Relevant Viewpoints
Suppliers (Outside Services); e.g., Alliance Partners, Key Suppliers	The main concerns of this group are that the information exchange requirements that they have are met in order that agreed service contracts with the client organizations can be fulfilled.	KEEP SATISFIED	Business Footprint Service-Information View Application — Application Communication View

Chapter 25: Architecture Patterns

This chapter provides guidelines for using architecture patterns.

25.1 Introduction

Patterns for system architecting are very much in their infancy. They have been introduced into TOGAF essentially to draw them to the attention of the systems architecture community as an emerging important resource, and as a placeholder for hopefully more rigorous descriptions and references to more plentiful resources in future versions of TOGAF.

They have not (as yet) been integrated into TOGAF. However, in the following, we attempt to indicate the potential value to TOGAF, and to which parts of the TOGAF Architecture Development Method (ADM) they might be relevant.

25.1.1 Background

A "pattern" has been defined as: "an idea that has been useful in one practical context and will probably be useful in others" [*Analysis Patterns — Re-usable Object Models*].

In TOGAF, patterns are considered to be a way of putting building blocks into context; for example, to describe a re-usable solution to a problem. Building blocks are what you use: patterns can tell you how you use them, when, why, and what trade-offs you have to make in doing so.

Patterns offer the promise of helping the architect to identify combinations of Architecture and/or Solution Building Blocks (ABBs/SBBs) that have been proven to deliver effective solutions in the past, and may provide the basis for effective solutions in the future.

Pattern techniques are generally acknowledged to have been established as a valuable architectural design technique by Christopher Alexander, a buildings architect, who described this approach in his book *The Timeless Way of Building*, published in 1979. This book provides an introduction to the ideas behind the use of patterns, and Alexander followed it with two further books (*A Pattern Language* and *The Oregon Experiment*) in which he expanded on his description of the features and benefits of a patterns approach to architecture.

Software and buildings architects have many similar issues to address, and so it was natural for software architects to take an interest in patterns as an architectural tool. Many papers and books have been published on them since Alexander's 1979 book, perhaps the most renowned being *Design Patterns: Elements of Re-usable Object-Oriented Software*. This book describes simple and elegant solutions to specific problems in object-oriented software design.

25.1.2 Content of a Pattern

Several different formats are used in the literature for describing patterns, and no single format has achieved widespread acceptance. However, there is broad agreement on the types of things that a pattern should contain. The headings which follow are taken from *Pattern-Oriented Software Architecture: A System of Patterns*. The elements described below will be found in most patterns, even if different headings are used to describe them.

Name
: A meaningful and memorable way to refer to the pattern, typically a single word or short phrase.

Problem
: A description of the problem indicating the intent in applying the pattern — the intended goals and objectives to be reached within the context and forces described below (perhaps with some indication of their priorities).

Context
: The preconditions under which the pattern is applicable — a description of the initial state before the pattern is applied.

Forces
: A description of the relevant forces and constraints, and how they interact/conflict with each other and with the intended goals and objectives. The description should clarify the intricacies of the problem and make explicit the kinds of trade-offs that must be considered. (The need for such trade-offs is typically what makes the problem difficult, and generates the need for the pattern in the first place.) The notion of "forces" equates in many ways to the "qualities" that architects seek to optimize, and the concerns they seek to address, in designing architectures. For example:

  — Security, robustness, reliability, fault-tolerance

  — Manageability

  — Efficiency, performance, throughput, bandwidth requirements, space utilization

  — Scalability (incremental growth on-demand)

  — Extensibility, evolvability, maintainability

  — Modularity, independence, re-usability, openness, composability (plug-and-play), portability

  — Completeness and correctness

  — Ease-of-construction

  — Ease-of-use

  — etc., . . .

Solution
: A description, using text and/or graphics, of how to achieve the intended goals and objectives. The description should identify both the solution's static structure and its dynamic behavior — the people and computing actors, and their collaborations. The description may include guidelines for implementing the solution. Variants or specializations of the solution may also be described.

Resulting Context
: The post-conditions after the pattern has been applied. Implementing the solution normally requires trade-offs among competing forces. This element describes which forces have been resolved and how, and which remain unresolved. It may

also indicate other patterns that may be applicable in the new context. (A pattern may be one step in accomplishing some larger goal.) Any such other patterns will be described in detail under Related Patterns.

Examples   One or more sample applications of the pattern which illustrate each of the other elements: a specific problem, context, and set of forces; how the pattern is applied; and the resulting context.

Rationale   An explanation/justification of the pattern as a whole, or of individual components within it, indicating how the pattern actually works, and why — how it resolves the forces to achieve the desired goals and objectives, and why this is "good". The Solution element of a pattern describes the external structure and behavior of the solution: the Rationale provides insight into its internal workings.

Related Patterns

The relationships between this pattern and others. These may be predecessor patterns, whose resulting contexts correspond to the initial context of this one; or successor patterns, whose initial contexts correspond to the resulting context of this one; or alternative patterns, which describe a different solution to the same problem, but under different forces; or co-dependent patterns, which may/must be applied along with this pattern.

Known Uses   Known applications of the pattern within existing systems, verifying that the pattern does indeed describe a proven solution to a recurring problem. Known Uses can also serve as Examples.

Patterns may also begin with an Abstract providing an overview of the pattern and indicating the types of problems it addresses. The Abstract may also identify the target audience and what assumptions are made of the reader.

25.1.3 Terminology

Although design patterns have been the focus of widespread interest in the software industry for several years, particularly in the object-oriented and component-based software fields, it is only recently that there has been increasing interest in architecture patterns — extending the principles and concepts of design patterns to the architecture domain.

The technical literature relating to this field is complicated by the fact that many people in the software field use the term "architecture" to refer to software, and many patterns described as "architecture patterns" are high-level software design patterns. This simply makes it all the more important to be precise in use of terminology.

25.1.3.1 Architecture Patterns and Design Patterns

The term "design pattern" is often used to refer to any pattern which addresses issues of software architecture, design, or programming implementation. In *Pattern-Oriented Software Architecture: A System of Patterns*, the authors define these three types of patterns as follows:

- An **Architecture Pattern** expresses a fundamental structural organization or schema for software systems. It provides a set of predefined subsystems, specifies their responsibilities, and includes rules and guidelines for organizing the relationships between them.

- A **Design Pattern** provides a scheme for refining the subsystems or components of a software system, or the relationships between them. It describes a commonly recurring structure of communicating components that solves a general design problem within a particular context.

- An **Idiom** is a low-level pattern specific to a programming language. An idiom describes how to implement particular aspects of components or the relationships between them using the features of the given language.

These distinctions are useful, but it is important to note that architecture patterns in this context still refers solely to software architecture. Software architecture is certainly an important part of the focus of TOGAF, but it is not its only focus.

In this section we are concerned with patterns for enterprise system architecting. These are analogous to software architecture and design patterns, and borrow many of their concepts and terminology, but focus on providing re-usable models and methods specifically for the architecting of enterprise information systems — comprising software, hardware, networks, and people — as opposed to purely software systems.

25.1.3.2 *Patterns and the Architecture Continuum*

Although architecture patterns have not (as yet) been integrated into TOGAF, each of the first four main phases of the ADM (Phases A through D) gives an indication of the stage at which relevant re-usable architecture assets from the enterprise's Architecture Continuum should be considered for use. Architecture patterns are one such asset.

An enterprise that adopts a formal approach to use and re-use of architecture patterns will normally integrate their use into the enterprise's Architecture Continuum.

25.1.3.3 *Patterns and Views*

Architecture views are selected parts of one or more models representing a complete system architecture, focusing on those aspects that address the concerns of one or more stakeholders. Patterns can provide help in designing such models, and in composing views based on them.

25.1.3.4 *Patterns and Business Scenarios*

Relevant architecture patterns may well be identified in the work on business scenarios.

25.1.4 Architecture Patterns in Use

Two examples of architecture patterns in use are outlined in the following subsections, one from the domain of an IT customer enterprise's own architecture framework, and the other from a major system vendor who has done a lot of work in recent years in the field of architecture patterns.

- The US Treasury Architecture Development Guidance (TADG) document (see Section 25.2) provides a number of explicit architecture patterns, in addition to explaining a rationale, structure, and taxonomy for architectural patterns as they relate to the US Treasury.

■ The IBM Patterns for e-Business web site (see Section 25.3) gives a series of architecture patterns that go from the business problem to specific solutions, firstly at a generic level and then in terms of specific IBM product solutions. A supporting resource is IBM's set of *Red Books*.

The following material is intended to give the reader pointers to some of the places where architecture patterns are already being used and made available, in order to help readers make their own minds up as to the usefulness of this technique for their own environments.

25.2   US Treasury Architecture Development Guidance (TADG)

The *US Treasury Architecture Development Guidance* (TADG) document — formerly known as the *Treasury Information System Architecture Framework* (TISAF) — provides a number of explicit architecture patterns.

Section 7 of the TADG document describes a rationale, structure, and taxonomy for architecture patterns, while the patterns themselves are formally documented in Appendix D. The architecture patterns presented embrace a larger set of systems than just object-oriented systems. Some architecture patterns are focused on legacy systems, some on concurrent and distributed systems, and some on real-time systems.

25.2.1   TADG Pattern Content

The content of an architecture pattern as defined in the TADG document contains the following elements:

Name   Each architecture pattern has a unique, short descriptive name. The collection of architecture pattern names can be used as a vocabulary for describing, verifying, and validating Information Systems Architectures.

Problem   Each architecture pattern contains a description of the problem to be solved. The problem statement may describe a class of problems or a specific problem.

Rationale   The rationale describes and explains a typical specific problem that is representative of the broad class of problems to be solved by the architecture pattern. For a specific problem, it can provide additional details of the nature of the problem and the requirements for its resolution.

Assumptions   The assumptions are conditions that must be satisfied in order for the architecture pattern to be usable in solving the problem. They include constraints on the solution and optional requirements that may make the solution more easy to use.

Structure   The architecture pattern is described in diagrams and words in as much detail as is required to convey to the reader the components of the pattern and their responsibilities.

Interactions   The important relationships and interactions among the components of the pattern are described and constraints on these relationships and interactions are identified.

Consequences   The advantages and disadvantages of using this pattern are described, particularly in terms of other patterns (either required or excluded) as well as resource limitations that may arise from using it.

Implementation   Additional implementation advice that can assist designers in customizing this architectural design pattern for the best results.

25.2.2 TADG Architecture Patterns

The TADG document contains the following patterns.

Architectural Design Pattern Name	Synopsis
Client-Proxy Server	Acts as a concentrator for many low-speed links to access a server.
Customer Support	Supports complex customer contact across multiple organizations.
Reactor	Decouples an event from its processing.
Replicated Servers	Replicates servers to reduce burden on central server.
Layered Architecture	A decomposition of services such that most interactions occur only between neighboring layers.
Pipe and Filter Architecture	Transforms information in a series of incremental steps or processes.
Subsystem Interface	Manages the dependencies between cohesive groups of functions (subsystems).

25.3 IBM Patterns for e-Business

The *IBM Patterns for e-Business* web site (refer to www.ibm.com/framework/patterns) provides a group of re-usable assets aimed at speeding the process of developing e-Business applications. A supporting IBM web site is *Patterns for e-Business Resources* (refer to www.ibm.com/developerworks/patterns/library). This is also known as the "Red Books".

The rationale for IBM's provision of these patterns is to:

- Provide a simple and consistent way to translate business priorities and requirements into technical solutions

- Assist and speed up the solution development and integration process by facilitating the assembly of a solution and minimizing custom one-of-a-kind implementations

- Capture the knowledge and best practices of experts and make it available for use by less experienced personnel

- Facilitate the re-use of intellectual capital such as reference architectures, frameworks, and other architecture assets

IBM's patterns are focused specifically on solutions for e-Business; i.e., those which allow an organization to leverage web technologies in order to re-engineer business processes, enhance communications, and lower organizational boundaries with:

- Customers and shareholders (across the Internet)

- Employees and stakeholders (across a corporate Intranet)

- Vendors, suppliers, and partners (across an Extranet)

They are intended to address the following challenges encountered in this type of environment:

- High degree of integration with legacy systems within the enterprise and with systems outside the enterprise

- The solutions need to reach users faster; this does not mean sacrificing quality, but it does mean coming up with better and faster ways to develop these solutions

- Service Level Agreements (SLAs) are critical

- Need to adapt to rapidly changing technologies and dramatically reduced product cycles

- Address an acute shortage of the key skills needed to develop quality solutions

IBM defines five types of pattern:

- **Business Patterns**, which identify the primary business actors, and describe the interactions between them in terms of different archetypal business interactions such as:

    - Service (a.k.a. user-to-business) — users accessing transactions on a 24x7 basis

    - Collaboration (a.k.a. user-to-user) — users working with one another to share data and information

    - Information Aggregation (a.k.a. user-to-data) — data from multiple sources aggregated and presented across multiple channels

    - Extended Enterprise (a.k.a. business-to-business) — integrating data and processes across enterprise boundaries

- **Integration Patterns**, which provide the "glue" to combine business patterns to form solutions. They characterize the business problem, business processes/rules, and existing environment to determine whether front-end or back-end integration is required.

    - Front-end integration (a.k.a. access integration) — focused on providing seamless and consistent access to business functions. Typical functions provided include single sign-on, personalization, transcoding, etc.

    - Back-end integration (a.k.a. application integration) — focused on connecting, interfacing, or integrating databases and systems. Typical integration can be based on function, type of integration, mode of integration, and by topology.

- **Composite Patterns**, which are previously identified combinations and selections of business and integration patterns, for previously identified situations such as: electronic commerce solutions, (public) enterprise portals, enterprise intranet portal, collaboration ASP, etc.

- **Application Patterns**: Each business and integration pattern can be implemented using one or more application patterns. An application pattern characterizes the coarse-grained structure of the application — the main application components, the allocation of processing functions and the interactions between them, the degree of integration between them, and the placement of the data relative to the applications.

- **Runtime Patterns**: Application patterns can be implemented by run-time patterns, which demonstrate non-functional, service-level characteristics, such as performance, capacity, scalability, and availability. They identify key resource constraints and best practices.

The IBM web site also provides specific (IBM) product mappings for the run-time patterns, indicating specific technology choices for implementation.

25.4   Some Pattern Resources

- The Patterns Home Page (refer to hillside.net/patterns) hosted by the Hillside Group provides information about patterns, links to online patterns, papers, and books dealing with patterns, and patterns-related mailing lists.

- The Patterns-Discussion FAQ (refer to g.oswego.edu/dl/pd-FAQ/pd-FAQ.html) maintained by Doug Lea provides a very thorough and highly readable FAQ about patterns.

- *Patterns and Software: Essential Concepts and Terminology* by Brad Appleton (refer to www.cmcrossroads.com/bradapp/docs/patterns-intro.html) provides another thorough and readable account of the patterns field.

Chapter 26: Business Scenarios

This chapter describes a method for deriving business requirements for architecture and the implied technical requirements.

26.1 Introduction

A key factor in the success of an enterprise architecture is the extent to which it is linked to business requirements, and demonstrably supporting and enabling the enterprise to achieve its business objectives.

Business scenarios are an important technique that may be used at various stages of the enterprise architecture, principally the Architecture Vision and the Business Architecture, but in other architecture domains as well, if required, to derive the characteristics of the architecture directly from the high-level requirements of the business. They are used to help identify and understand business needs, and thereby to derive the business requirements that the architecture development has to address.

A business scenario describes:

- A business process, application, or set of applications that can be enabled by the architecture

- The business and technology environment

- The people and computing components (called "actors") who execute the scenario

- The desired outcome of proper execution

A good business scenario is representative of a significant business need or problem, and enables vendors to understand the value to the customer organization of a developed solution.

A good business scenario is also "SMART":

- **Specific**, by defining what needs to be done in the business

- **Measurable**, through clear metrics for success

- **Actionable**, by:
  - Clearly segmenting the problem
  - Providing the basis for determining elements and plans for the solution

- **Realistic**, in that the problem can be solved within the bounds of physical reality, time, and cost constraints

■ **Time-bound**, in that there is a clear statement of when the solution opportunity expires

Section 26.9 provides detailed examples on objectives that could be considered. Whatever objectives you use, the idea is to make those objectives SMART.

26.2   Benefits of Business Scenarios

A business scenario is essentially a complete description of a business problem, both in business and in architectural terms, which enables individual requirements to be viewed in relation to one another in the context of the overall problem. Without such a complete description to serve as context:

■ There is a danger of the architecture being based on an incomplete set of requirements that do not add up to a whole problem description, and that can therefore misguide architecture work.

■ The business value of solving the problem is unclear.

■ The relevance of potential solutions is unclear.

Also, because the technique requires the involvement of business line management and other stakeholders at an early stage in the architecture project, it also plays an important role in gaining the buy-in of these key personnel to the overall project and its end-product — the enterprise architecture.

An additional advantage of business scenarios is in communication with vendors. Most architecture nowadays is implemented by making maximum use of Commercial Off-The-Shelf (COTS) software solutions, often from multiple vendors, procured in the open market. The use of business scenarios by an IT customer can be an important aid to IT vendors in delivering appropriate solutions. Vendors need to ensure that their solution components add value to an open solution and are marketable. Business scenarios provide a language with which the vendor community can link customer problems and technical solutions. Besides making obvious what is needed, and why, they allow vendors to solve problems optimally, using open standards and leveraging each other's skills.

26.3   Creating the Business Scenario

26.3.1   Overall Process

Creating a business scenario involves the following, as illustrated in Figure 26-1:

1. Identifying, documenting, and ranking the problem driving the scenario

2. Identifying the business and technical environment of the scenario and documenting it in scenario models

3. Identifying and documenting desired objectives (the results of handling the problems successfully); get "SMART"

4. Identifying the human actors (participants) and their place in the business model

5. Identifying computer actors (computing elements) and their place in the technology model

6. Identifying and documenting roles, responsibilities, and measures of success per actor; documenting the required scripts per actor, and the results of handling the situation

7. Checking for "fitness-for-purpose" and refining only if necessary

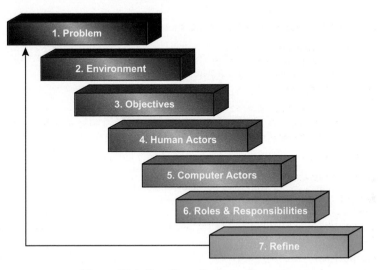

Figure 26-1 Creating a Business Scenario

A business scenario is developed over a number of iterative phases of Gathering, Analyzing, and Reviewing the information in the business scenario.

In each phase, each of the areas above is successively improved. The refinement step involves deciding whether to consider the scenario complete and go to the next phase, or whether further refinement is necessary. This is accomplished by asking whether the current state of the business scenario is fit for the purpose of carrying requirements downstream in the architecture process.

The three phases of developing a business scenario are described in detail below, and depicted in Figure 26-2.

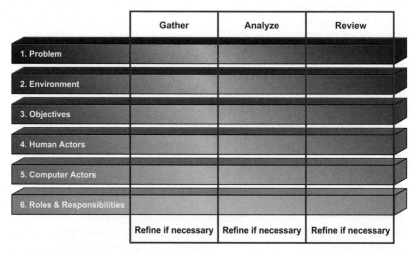

Figure 26-2 Phases of Developing Business Scenarios

26.3.2 Gathering

The Gathering phase is where information is collected on each of the areas in Figure 26-1. If information gathering procedures and practices are already in place in an organization — for example, to gather information for strategic planning — they should be used as appropriate, either during business scenario workshops or in place of business scenario workshops.

Multiple techniques may be used in this phase, such as information research, qualitative analysis, quantitative analysis, surveys, requests for information, etc. As much information as possible should be gathered and preprocessed "off-line" prior to any face-to-face workshops (described below). For example, a request for information may include a request for strategic and operational plans. Such documents typically provide great insights, but the information that they contain usually requires significant preprocessing. The information may be used to generate an initial draft of the business scenario prior to the workshop, if possible. This will increase the understanding and confidence of the architect, and the value of the workshop to its participants.

A very useful way to gather information is to hold business scenario workshops, whereby a business scenario consultant leads a select and small group of business representatives through a number of questions to elicit the information surrounding the problem being addressed by the architecture effort. The workshop attendees must be carefully selected from high levels in the business and technical sides of the organization. It is important to get people that can and will provide information openly and honestly. Where a draft of the business scenario already exists — for example, as a result of preprocessing information gathered during this phase, as described above — the workshop may also be used to review the state of the business scenario draft.

Sometimes it is necessary to have multiple workshops: in some cases, to separate the gathering of information on the business side from the gathering of information on the technical side; and in other cases simply to get more information from more people.

When gathering information, the architect can greatly strengthen the business scenario by obtaining "real-world examples"; i.e., case studies to which the reader can easily relate. When citing real-world examples, it is important to maintain a level of anonymity of the parties involved, to avoid blame.

26.3.3 Analyzing

The Analyzing phase is where a great deal of real Business Architecture work is actually done. This is where the information that is gathered is processed and documented, and where the models are created to represent that information, typically visually.

The Analyzing phase takes advantage of the knowledge and experience of the business scenario consultant using past work and experience to develop the models necessary to depict the information captured. Note that the models and documentation produced are not necessarily reproduced *verbatim* from interviews, but rather filtered and translated according to the real underlying needs.

In the Analyzing phase it is important to maintain linkages between the key elements of the business scenario. One technique that assists in maintaining such linkages is the creation of matrices that are used to relate business processes to each of:

- Constituencies

- Human Actors

- Computer Actors

- Issues

- Objectives

In this way, the business process becomes the binding focal point, which makes a great deal of sense, since in most cases it is business process improvement that is being sought.

26.3.4 Reviewing

The Reviewing phase is where the results are fed back to the sponsors of the project to ensure that there is a shared understanding of the full scope of the problem, and the potential depth of the technical impact.

Multiple business scenario workshops or "readout" meetings with the sponsors and involved parties are recommended. The meetings should be set up to be open and interactive. It is recommended to have exercises built into meeting agendas, in order to test attendees' understanding and interest levels, as well as to test the architect's own assumptions and results.

This phase is extremely important, as the absence of shared expectations is in many cases the root cause of project failures.

26.4   Contents of a Business Scenario

The documentation of a business scenario should contain all the important details about the scenario. It should capture, and sequence, the critical steps and interactions between actors that address the situation. It should also declare all the relevant information about all actors, specifically: the different responsibilities of the actors; the key pre-conditions that have to be met prior to proper system functionality; and the technical requirements for the service to be of acceptable quality.

There are two main types of content: graphics (models), and descriptive text. Both have a part to play.

- **Business Scenario Models** capture business and technology views in a graphical form, to aid comprehension. Specifically, they relate actors and interactions, and give a starting point to confirm specific requirements.

- **Business Scenario Descriptions** capture details in a textual form. A typical contents list for a business scenario is given below.

Table of Contents
PREFACE
EXECUTIVE SUMMARY
DOCUMENT ROADMAP
BUSINESS SCENARIO
BUSINESS SCENARIO OVERVIEW
BACKGROUND OF SCENARIO
PURPOSE OF SCENARIO
DEFINITIONS/DESCRIPTIONS OF TERMS USED
VIEWS OF ENVIRONMENTS AND PROCESSES
BUSINESS ENVIRONMENT
Constituencies
PROCESS DESCRIPTIONS
Process "a"
etc. . . .
TECHNICAL ENVIRONMENT
Technical environment "a"
etc. . . .
ACTORS AND THEIR ROLES AND RESPONSIBILITIES
COMPUTER ACTORS AND ROLES
RELATIONSHIP OF COMPONENTS AND PROCESSES
HUMAN ACTORS AND ROLES
RELATIONSHIP OF HUMANS AND PROCESSES
INFORMATION FLOW ANALYSIS
PRINCIPLES AND CONSTRAINTS
IT Principles
Constraints
REQUIREMENTS
BUSINESS SCENARIO ANALYSIS
PROBLEM SUMMARY
Issues
Objectives
SUMMARY
APPENDIXES
APPENDIX A: BUSINESS SCENARIOS — ADDITIONAL INFORMATION
APPENDIX B-n: BUSINESS SCENARIO WORKSHOP NOTES

26.5   Contributions to the Business Scenario

It is important to realize that the creation of a business scenario is not solely the province of the architect. As mentioned previously, business line management and other stakeholders in the enterprise are involved, to ensure that the business goals are accurately captured. In addition, depending on the relationship that an organization has with its IT vendors, the latter also may be involved, to ensure that the roles of technical solutions are also accurately captured, and to ensure communication with the vendors.

Typically, the involvement of the business management is greatest in the early stages, while the business problems are being explored and captured, while the involvement of the architect is greatest in the later stages, and when architectural solutions are being described. Similarly, if vendors are involved in the business scenario process, the involvement of the customer side (business management plus enterprise architects) is greatest in the early stages, while that of the vendors is greatest in the later stages, when the role of specific technical solutions is being explored and captured. This concept is illustrated in Figure 26-3.

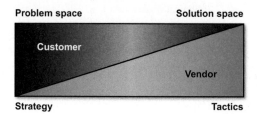

Figure 26-3 Relative Contributions to a Business Scenario

Vendor IT architects might be able to assist enterprise IT architects with integration of the vendors' products into the enterprise architecture. This assistance most probably falls in the middle of the timeline in Figure 26-3.

26.6   Business Scenarios and the TOGAF ADM

Business scenarios figure most prominently in the initial phase of the Architecture Development Method (ADM), Architecture Vision, when they are used to define relevant business requirements, and to build consensus with business management and other stakeholders.

However, the business requirements are referred to throughout all phases of the ADM cycle, as illustrated in Figure 26-4.

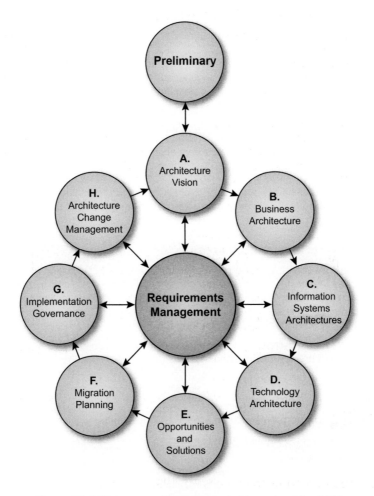

Figure 26-4 Relevance of Requirements Throughout the ADM

Because business requirements are important throughout all phases of the ADM cycle, the business scenario technique has an important role to play in the TOGAF ADM, by ensuring that the business requirements themselves are complete and correct.

26.7   Guidelines on Developing Business Scenarios

26.7.1   General Guidelines

The stakeholders (e.g., business managers, end users) will tell you what they want, but as an architect you must still gain an understanding of the business, so you must know the most important actors in the system. If the stakeholders do not know what they want:

- Take time, observe, and record how they are working today
- Structure information in such a way that it can be used later
- Uncover critical business rules from domain experts
- Stay focused on what needs to be accomplished, and how it is to be accomplished

This effort provides the anchor for a chain of reason from business requirements through to technical solutions. It will pay off later to be diligent and critical at the start.

26.7.2   Questions to Ask for Each Area

The business scenario workshops mentioned above in the Gathering phase are really structured interviews. While there is no single set of appropriate questions to ask in all situations, the following provides some guidance to help business scenario consultants in asking questions.

Identifying, Documenting, and Ranking the Problem

Is the problem described as a statement of *what* needs to be accomplished, like steps in a process, and not *how* (with technology "push")?

If the problem is too specific or a "how":

- Raise a red flag
- Ask "Why do you need to do it that way?" questions

If the problem is too vague or unactionable:

- Raise a red flag
- Ask "What is it you need to do, or will be able to do if this problem is solved?" questions

Ask questions that help to identify where and when the problem exists:

- Where are you experiencing this particular problem? In what business process?
- When do you encounter these issues? During the beginning of the process, the middle, the end?

Ask questions that help to identify the costs of the problem:

- Do you account for the costs associated with this problem? If so, what are they?
- Are there hidden costs? If so, what are they?
- Is the cost of this problem covered in the cost of something else? If so, what and how much?

- Is the problem manifested in terms of poor quality or a perception of an ineffective organization?

Identifying the Business & Technical Environment, and Documenting in Models

Questions to ask about the business environment:

- What key process suffers from the issues? What are the major steps that need to be processed?
- Location/scale of internal business departments?
- Location/scale of external business partners?
- Any specific business rules and regulations related to the situation?

Questions to ask about the current technology environment:

- What technology components are already presupposed to be related to this problem?
- Are there any technology constraints?
- Are there any technology principles that apply?

Identifying and Documenting Objectives

Is the "what" sufficiently backed up with the rationale for "why"? If not, ask for measurable rationale in the following areas:

- Return on investment
- Scalability
- Performance needs
- Compliance to standards
- Ease-of-use measures

Identifying Human Actors and their Place in the Business Model

An actor represents anything that interacts with or within the system. This can be a human, or a machine, or a computer program. Actors initiate activity with the system, for example:

- Computer user with the computer
- Phone user with the telephone
- Payroll clerk with the payroll system
- Internet subscriber with the web browser

An actor represents a role that a user plays; i.e., a user is someone playing a role while using the system (e.g., John (user) is a dispatcher (actor)). Each actor uses the system in different ways (otherwise they should be the same actor). Ask about the humans that will be involved, from different viewpoints, such as:

- Developer
- Maintainer

- Operator
- Administrator
- User

Identifying Computer Actors and their Place in the Technology Model

Ask about the computer components likely to be involved, again from different points of view. What must they do?

Documenting Roles, Responsibilities, Measures of Success, Required Scripts

When defining roles, ask questions like:

- What are the main tasks of the actor?
- Will the actor have to read/write/change any information?
- Will the actor have to inform the system about outside changes?
- Does the actor wish to be informed about unexpected changes?

Checking for Fitness-for-Purpose, and refining if necessary

Is there enough information to identify who/what could fulfil the requirement? If not, probe more deeply.

Is there a description of when, and how often, the requirement needs to be addressed? If not, ask about timing.

26.8   Guidelines on Business Scenario Documentation

26.8.1 Textual Documentation

Effective business scenario documentation requires a balance between ensuring that the detail is accessible, and preventing it from overshadowing the results and overwhelming the reader. To this end, the business scenario document should have the main findings in the body of the document and the details in appendices.

In the appendices:

- Capture all the important details about a business scenario:
  - Situation description and rationale
  - All measurements
  - All actor roles and sub-measurements
  - All services required
- Capture the critical steps between actors that address the situation, and sequence the interactions
- Declare relevant information about all actors:

— Partition the responsibility of the actors

— List pre-conditions that have to be met prior to proper system functionality

— Provide technical requirements for the service to be of acceptable quality

In the main body of the business scenario:

- Generalize all the relevant data from the detail in the appendices

26.8.2 Business Scenario Models

- Remember the purpose of using models:

  — Capture business and technology views in a graphical form

  — Help comprehension

  — Give a starting point to confirm requirements

  — Relate actors and interactions

- Keep drawings clear and neat:

  — Do not put too much into one diagram

  — Simpler diagrams are easier to understand

- Number diagrams for easy reference:

  — Maintain a catalog of the numbers to avoid duplicates

26.9 Guidelines on Goals and Objectives

26.9.1 Importance of Goals

One of the first steps in the development of an architecture is to define the overall goals and objectives for the development. The objectives should be derived from the business goals of the organization, and the way in which IT is seen to contribute to meeting those goals.

Every organization behaves differently in this respect, some seeing IT as the driving force for the enterprise and others seeing IT in a supporting role, simply automating the business processes which already exist. The essential thing is that the architectural objectives should be very closely aligned with the business goals and objectives of the organization.

26.9.2 Importance of SMART Objectives

Not only must goals be stated in general terms, but also specific measures need to be attached to them to make them SMART, as described above.

The amount of effort spent in doing this will lead to greater clarity for the sponsors of the architecture evolution cycle. It will pay back by driving proposed solutions much more closely toward the goals at each step of the cycle. It is extremely helpful for the different stakeholders inside the organization, as well as for suppliers and consultants, to have a clear yardstick for measuring fitness-for-purpose. If done well, the ADM can be used to trace specific decisions back to criteria, and thus yield their justification.

The goals below have been adapted from those given in previous versions of TOGAF. These are categories of goals, each with a list of possible objectives. Each of these objectives should be made SMART with specific measures and metrics for the task. However, since the actual work to be done will be specific to the architecture project concerned, it is not possible to provide a list of generic SMART objectives that will relate to any project.

Instead, we provide here some example SMART objectives.

Example of Making Objectives SMART

Under the general goal heading "Improve User Productivity" below, there is an objective to provide a "Consistent User Interface" and it is described as follows:

> "A consistent user interface will ensure that all user-accessible functions and services will appear and behave in a similar, predictable fashion regardless of application or site. This will lead to better efficiency and fewer user errors, which in turn may result in lower recovery costs."

To make this objective SMART, we ask whether the objective is specific, measurable, actionable, realistic, and time-bound, and then augment the objective appropriately.

The following captures an analysis of these criteria for the stated objective:

- **Specific**: The objective of providing "a consistent user interface that will ensure all user accessible functions and services will appear and behave in a similar, predictable fashion regardless of application or site". is pretty specific. However, the measures listed in the second sentence could be more specific . . .

- **Measurable**: As stated above, the objective is measurable, but could be more specific. The second sentence could be amended to read (for example): "This will lead to 10% greater user efficiency and 20% fewer order entry user errors, which in turn may result in 5% lower order entry costs".

- **Actionable**: The objective does appear to be actionable. It seems clear that consistency of the user interface must be provided, and that could be handled by whoever is responsible for providing the user interface to the user device.

- **Realistic**: The objective of providing "a consistent user interface that will ensure all user accessible functions and services will appear and behave in a similar, predictable fashion regardless of application or site" might not be realistic. Considering the use today of PDAs at the user end might lead us to augment this objective to ensure that the downstream developers don't unduly create designs that hinder the use of new technologies. The objective could be re-stated as "a consistent user interface, across user interface devices that provide similar functionality, that will ensure . . ." etc.

- **Time-bound**: The objective as stated is not time-bound. To be time-bound the objective could be re-stated as "By the end of Q3, provide a consistent . . .".

The above results in a SMART objective that looks more like this (again remember this is an example):

"By the end of Q3, provide a consistent user interface across user interface devices that provide similar functionality to ensure all user accessible functions and services appear and behave in a similar way when using those devices in a predictable fashion regardless of application or site. This will lead to 10% greater user efficiency and 20% fewer order entry user errors, which in turn may result in 5% lower order entry costs."

26.9.3 Categories of Goals and Objectives

Although every organization will have its own set of goals, some examples may help in the development of an organization-specific list. The goals given below are categories of goals, each with a list of possible objectives, which have been adapted from the goals given in previous versions of TOGAF.

Each of the objectives given below should be made SMART with specific measures and metrics for the task involved, as illustrated in the example above. However, the actual work to be done will be specific to the architecture project concerned, and it is not possible to provide a list of generic SMART objectives that will relate to any project.

Goal: Improve Business Process Performance

Business process improvements can be realized through the following objectives:

- Increased process throughput
- Consistent output quality
- Predictable process costs
- Increased re-use of existing processes
- Reduced time of sending business information from one process to another process

Goal: Decrease Costs

Cost improvements can be realized through the following objectives:

- Lower levels of redundancy and duplication in assets throughout the enterprise
- Decreased reliance on external IT service providers for integration and customization
- Lower costs of maintenance

Goal: Improve Business Operations

Business operations improvements can be realized through the following objectives:

- Increased budget available to new business features
- Decreased costs of running the business
- Decreased time-to-market for products or services
- Increased quality of services to customers
- Improved quality of business information

Goal: Improve Management Efficacy

Management efficacy improvements can be realized through the following objectives:

- Increased flexibility of business
- Shorter time to make decisions
- Higher quality decisions

Goal: Reduce Risk

Risk improvements can be realized through the following objectives:

- Ease of implementing new processes
- Decreased errors introduced into business processes through complex and faulty systems
- Decreased real-world safety hazards (including hazards that cause loss of life)

Goal: Improve Effectiveness of IT Organization

IT organization effectiveness can be realized through the following objectives:

- Increased rollout of new projects
- Decreased time to rollout new projects
- Lower cost in rolling out new projects
- Decreased loss of service continuity when rolling out new projects
- Common development: applications that are common to multiple business areas will be developed or acquired once and re-used rather than separately developed by each business area.
- Open systems environment: a standards-based common operating environment, which accommodates the injection of new standards, technologies, and applications on an organization-wide basis, will be established. This standards-based environment will provide the basis for development of common applications and facilitate software re-use.
- Use of products: as far as possible, hardware-independent, off-the-shelf items should be used to satisfy requirements in order to reduce dependence on custom developments and to reduce development and maintenance costs.
- Software re-use: for those applications that must be custom developed, development of portable applications will reduce the amount of software developed and add to the inventory of software suitable for re-use by other systems.
- Resource sharing: data processing resources (hardware, software, and data) will be shared by all users requiring the services of those resources. Resource sharing will be accomplished in the context of security and operational considerations.

Goal: Improve User Productivity

User productivity improvements can be realized through the following objectives:

- Consistent user interface: a consistent user interface will ensure that all user-accessible functions and services will appear and behave in a similar, predictable fashion regardless of application or site. This will lead to better efficiency and fewer user errors, which in turn may result in lower recovery costs.

- Integrated applications: applications available to the user will behave in a logically consistent manner across user environments, which will lead to the same benefits as a consistent user interface.

- Data sharing: databases will be shared across the organization in the context of security and operational considerations, leading to increased ease-of-access to required data.

Goal: Improve Portability and Scalability

The portability and scalability of applications will be through the following objectives:

- Portability: applications that adhere to open systems standards will be portable, leading to increased ease-of-movement across heterogeneous computing platforms. Portable applications can allow sites to upgrade their platforms as technological improvements occur, with minimal impact on operations.

- Scalability: applications that conform to the model will be configurable, allowing operation on the full spectrum of platforms required.

Goal: Improve Interoperability

Interoperability improvements across applications and business areas can be realized through the following objectives:

- Common infrastructure: the architecture should promote a communications and computing infrastructure based on open systems and systems transparency including, but not limited to, operating systems, database management, data interchange, network services, network management, and user interfaces.

- Standardization: by implementing standards-based platforms, applications will be provided with and will be able to use a common set of services that improve the opportunities for interoperability.

Goal: Increase Vendor Independence

Vendor independence will be increased through the following objectives:

- Interchangeable components: only hardware and software that have standards-based interfaces will be selected, so that upgrades or the insertion of new products will result in minimal disruption to the user's environment.

- Non-proprietary specifications: capabilities will be defined in terms of non-proprietary specifications that support full and open competition and are available to any vendor for use in developing commercial products.

Goal: Reduce Lifecycle Costs

Lifecycle costs can be reduced through most of the objectives discussed above. In addition, the following objectives directly address reduction of lifecycle costs:

- Reduced duplication: replacement of isolated systems and islands of automation with interconnected open systems will lead to reductions in overlapping functionality, data duplication, and unneeded redundancy because open systems can share data and other resources.

- Reduced software maintenance costs: reductions in the quantity and variety of software used in the organization will lead to reductions in the amount and cost of software maintenance. Use of standard off-the-shelf software will lead to further reductions in costs since vendors of such software distribute their product maintenance costs across a much larger user base.

- Incremental replacement: common interfaces to shared infrastructure components allow for phased replacement or upgrade with minimal operational disturbance.

- Reduced training costs: common systems and consistent Human Computer Interfaces (HCIs) will lead to reduced training costs.

Goal: Improve Security

Security can be improved in the organization's information through the following objectives:

- Consistent security interfaces for applications: consistent security interfaces and procedures will lead to fewer errors when developing applications and increased application portability. Not all applications will need the same suite of security features, but any features used will be consistent across applications.

- Consistent security interfaces for users: a common user interface to security features will lead to reduced learning time when moving from system to system.

- Security independence: application deployment can use the security policy and mechanisms appropriate to the particular environment if there is good layering in the architecture.

- A 25% reduction in calls to the help desk relating to security issues.

- A 20% reduction in "false positives" detected in the network (a false positive is an event that appears to be an actionable security event, but in fact is a false alarm).

Goal: Improve Manageability

Management improvement can be realized through the following objectives:

- Consistent management interface: consistent management practices and procedures will facilitate management across all applications and their underlying support structures. A consistent interface can simplify the management burden, leading to increased user efficiency.

- Reduced operation, administration, and maintenance costs: operation, administration, and maintenance costs may be reduced through the availability of improved management products and increased standardization of the objects being managed.

26.10 Summary

Business scenarios help address one of the most common issues facing IT executives: aligning IT with the business.

The success of any major IT project is measured by the extent to which it is linked to business requirements, and demonstrably supports and enables the enterprise to achieve its business objectives. Business scenarios are an important technique that may be used at various stages of defining enterprise architecture, or any other major IT project, to derive the characteristics of the architecture directly from the high-level requirements of the business. Business scenarios are used to help identify and understand business needs, and thereby to derive the business requirements that the architecture development, and ultimately the IT, has to address.

However, it is important to remember that business scenarios are just a tool, not the objective. They are a part of, and enable, the larger process of architecture development. The architect should use them, but not get lost in them. The key is to stay focused — watch out for "feature creep", and address the most important issues that tend to return the greatest value.

Chapter 27: Gap Analysis

The technique known as gap analysis is widely used in the TOGAF Architecture Development Method (ADM) to validate an architecture that is being developed. The basic premise is to highlight a shortfall between the Baseline Architecture and the Target Architecture; that is, items that have been deliberately omitted, accidentally left out, or not yet defined.

27.1   Introduction

A key step in validating an architecture is to consider what may have been forgotten. The architecture must support all of the essential information processing needs of the organization. The most critical source of gaps that should be considered is stakeholder concerns that have not been addressed in prior architectural work.

Potential sources of gaps include:

- Business domain gaps:
    - People gaps (e.g., cross-training requirements)
    - Process gaps (e.g., process inefficiencies)
    - Tools gaps (e.g., duplicate or missing tool functionality)
    - Information gaps
    - Measurement gaps
    - Financial gaps
    - Facilities gaps (buildings, office space, etc.)
- Data domain gaps:
    - Data not of sufficient currency
    - Data not located where it is needed
    - Not the data that is needed
    - Data not available when needed
    - Data not created
    - Data not consumed
    - Data relationship gaps
- Applications impacted, eliminated, or created

- Technologies impacted, eliminated, or created

27.2 Suggested Steps

The suggested steps are as follows:

- Draw up a matrix with all the Architecture Building Blocks (ABBs) of the Baseline Architecture on the vertical axis, and all the ABBs of the Target Architecture on the horizontal axis.

- Add to the Baseline Architecture axis a final row labeled "New", and to the Target Architecture axis a final column labeled "Eliminated".

- Where an ABB is available in both the Baseline and Target Architectures, record this with "Included" at the intersecting cell.

- Where an ABB from the Baseline Architecture is missing in the Target Architecture, each must be reviewed. If it was correctly eliminated, mark it as such in the appropriate "Eliminated" cell. If it was not, an accidental omission in the Target Architecture has been uncovered that must be addressed by reinstating the ABB in the next iteration of the architecture design — mark it as such in the appropriate "Eliminated" cell.

- Where an ABB from the Target Architecture cannot be found in the Baseline Architecture, mark it at the intersection with the "New" row as a gap that needs to filled, either by developing or procuring the building block.

When the exercise is complete, anything under "Eliminated" or "New" is a gap, which should either be explained as correctly eliminated, or marked as to be addressed by reinstating or developing/procuring the function.

27.3 Example

Figure 27-1 shows an example analysis for ABBs that are services from the Network Services category of the Technical Reference Model (TRM), and shows a number of services from the Baseline Architecture missing from the Target Architecture.

Target → Architecture Baseline Architecture ↓	Video Conferencing Services	Enhanced Telephony Services	Mailing List Services	Eliminated Services ↓
Broadcast Services				Intentionally eliminated
Video Conferencing Services	Included			
Enhanced Telephony Services		Potential match		
Shared Screen Services				Unintentionally excluded - a gap in Target Architecture
New →		Gap: Enhanced services to be developed or produced	Gap: To be developed or produced	

Figure 27-1 Gap Analysis Example

Chapter 28: Migration Planning Techniques

This chapter contains a number of techniques used to support migration planning in Phases E and F.

28.1 Implementation Factor Assessment and Deduction Matrix

The technique of creating an Implementation Factor Assessment and Deduction matrix can be used to document factors impacting the architecture Implementation and Migration Plan.

The matrix should include a list of the factors to be considered, their descriptions, and the deductions that indicate the actions or constraints that have to be taken into consideration when formulating the plans.

An example matrix is shown in Figure 28-1.

Implementation Factor Assessment and Deduction Matrix		
Factor	**Description**	**Deduction**
<Name of Factor>	<Description of Factor>	<Impact on Migration Plan>
Change in Technology	Shut down the message centers, saving 700 personnel, and have them replaced by email.	• Need for personnel training, re-assignment • Email has major personnel savings and should be given priority
Consolidation of Services		
Introduction of New Customer Service		

Figure 28-1 Implementation Factor Assessment and Deduction Matrix

28.2 Consolidated Gaps, Solutions, and Dependencies Matrix

The technique of creating a Consolidated Gaps, Solutions, and Dependencies matrix allows the architect to group the gaps identified in the domain architecture gap analysis results and assess potential solutions and dependencies to one or more gaps.

This matrix can be used as a planning tool when creating work packages. The identified dependencies will drive the creation of projects and migration planning in Phases E and F.

An example matrix is shown in Figure 28-2.

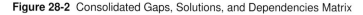

Consolidated Gaps, Solutions, and Dependencies Matrix				
No.	Architecture	Gap	Potential Solutions	Dependencies
1	Business	New Order Processing Process	Use COTS software tool process Implement custom solution	Drives applications (2)
2	Application	New Order Processing Application	COTS software tool X Develop in-house	
3	Information	Consolidated Customer Information Base	Use COTS customer base Develop customer data mart	

Figure 28-2 Consolidated Gaps, Solutions, and Dependencies Matrix

28.3 Architecture Definition Increments Table

The technique of creating an Architecture Definition Increments table allows the architect to plan a series of Transition Architectures outlining the status of the enterprise architecture at specified times.

A table should be drawn up, as shown in Figure 28-3, listing the projects and then assigning their incremental deliverables across the Transition Architectures.

Architecture Definition - Project Objectives by Increment (Example Only)				
Project	April 2007/2008 Transition Architecture 1: Preparation	April 2008/2009 Transition Architecture 2: Initial Operational Capability	April 2009/2010 Transition Architecture 3: Benefits	Comments
Enterprise e-Services Capability	Training and Business Process	e-Licensing Capability	e-Employment Benefits	
IT e-Forms	Design and Build			
IT e-Information Environment	Design and Build Information Environment	Client Common Data Web Content Design and Build	Enterprise Common Data Component Management Design and Build	
. . .	. . .	. . .	. . .	. . .

Figure 28-3 Architecture Definition Increments Table

28.4   Enterprise Architecture State Evolution Table

The technique of creating the Enterprise Architecture State Evolution table allows the architect to show the proposed state of the architectures at various levels using the Technical Reference Model (TRM).

A table should be drawn, listing the services from the TRM used in the enterprise, the Transition Architectures, and proposed transformations, as shown in Figure 28-4.

All Solution Building Blocks (SBBs) should be described with respect to their delivery and impact on these services. They should also be marked to show the progression of the enterprise architecture. In the example, where target capability has been reached, this is shown as "new" or "retain"; where capability is transitioned to a new solution, this is marked as "transition"; and where a capability is to be replaced, this is marked as "replace".

Architectural State using the Technical Reference Model				
Sub-Domain	Service	Transition Architecture 1	Transition Architecture 2	Transition Architecture 3
Infrastructure Applications	Information Exchange Services	Solution System A (replace)	Solution System B-1 (transition)	Solution System B-2 (new)
	Data Management Services	Solution System D (retain)	Solution System D (retain)	Solution System D (retain)
. . .	. . .	. . .	. . .	. . .

Figure 28-4 Enterprise Architecture State Evolution Table

Another technique (not shown here) is to use color coding in the matrix; for example:

- Green: Service SBB in place (either new or retained).
- Yellow: Service being transitioned into a new solution.
- Red: Service to be replaced.

28.5 Business Value Assessment Technique

A technique to assess business value is to draw up a matrix based on a value index dimension and a risk index dimension. An example is shown in Figure 28-5. The value index should include criteria such as compliance to principles, financial contribution, strategic alignment, and competitive position. The risk index should include criteria such as size and complexity, technology, organizational capacity, and impact of a failure. Each criterion should be assigned an individual weight.

The index and its criteria and weighting should be developed and approved by senior management. It is important to establish the decision-making criteria before the options are known.

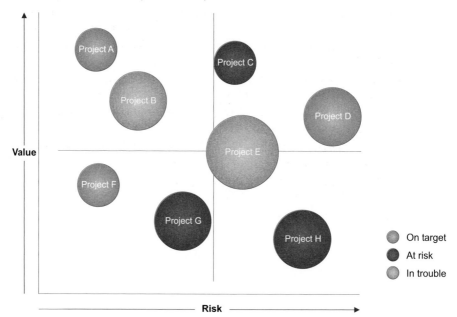

(Project size indicated by size of circle.)

Figure 28-5 Sample Project Assessment with Respect to Business Value and Risk

Chapter 29: Interoperability Requirements

This chapter provides guidelines for defining and establishing interoperability requirements.

29.1 Overview

A definition of interoperability is "the ability to share information and services". Defining the degree to which the information and services are to be shared is a very useful architectural requirement, especially in a complex organization and/or extended enterprise.

The determination of interoperability is present throughout the Architecture Development Method (ADM) as follows:

- In the Architecture Vision (Phase A), the nature and security considerations of the information and service exchanges are first revealed within the business scenarios.

- In the Business Architecture (Phase B), the information and service exchanges are further defined in business terms.

- In the Data Architecture (Phase C), the content of the information exchanges are detailed using the corporate data and/or information exchange model.

- In the Application Architecture (Phase C), the way that the various applications are to share the information and services is specified.

- In the Technology Architecture (Phase D), the appropriate technical mechanisms to permit the information and service exchanges are specified.

- In Opportunities & Solutions (Phase E), the actual solutions (e.g., Commercial Off-The-Shelf (COTS) packages) are selected.

- In Migration Planning (Phase F), the interoperability is logically implemented.

29.2   Defining Interoperability

There are many ways to define interoperability and the aim is to define one that is consistently applied within the enterprise and extended enterprise. It is best that both the enterprise and the extended enterprise use the same definitions.

Many organizations find it useful to categorize interoperability as follows:

- **Operational or Business Interoperability** defines how business processes are to be shared.

- **Information Interoperability** defines how information is to be shared.

- **Technical Interoperability** defines how technical services are to be shared or at least connect to one another.

From an IT perspective, it is also useful to consider interoperability in a similar vein to Enterprise Application Integration (EAI); specifically:

- **Presentation Integration/Interoperability** is where a common look-and-feel approach through a common portal-like solution guides the user to the underlying functionality of the set of systems.

- **Information Integration/Interoperability** is where the corporate information is seamlessly shared between the various corporate applications to achieve, for example, a common set of client information. Normally this is based upon a commonly accepted corporate ontology and shared services for the structure, quality, access, and security/privacy for the information.

- **Application Integration/Interoperability** is where the corporate functionality is integrated and shareable so that the applications are not duplicated (e.g., one change of address service/component; not one for every application) and are seamlessly linked together through functionality such as workflow. This impacts the business and infrastructure applications and is very closely linked to corporate business process unification/interoperability.

- **Technical Integration/Interoperability** includes common methods and shared services for the communication, storage, processing, and access to data primarily in the application platform and communications infrastructure domains. This interoperability is premised upon the degree of rationalization of the corporate IT infrastructure, based upon standards and/or common IT platforms. For example, multiple applications sharing one infrastructure or 10,000 corporate web sites using one centralized content management/web server (rather than thousands of servers and webmasters spread throughout the country/globe).

Many organizations create their own interoperability models, such as illustrated in the example below from the Canadian Government. They have a high-level definition of the three classes of interoperability and identify the nature of the information and services that they wish to share. Interoperability is coined in terms of e-enablers for e-Government. Their interoperability breakdown is as follows:

- Information Interoperability:

    — Knowledge management

    — Business intelligence

- — Information management
- — Trusted identity
- ■ Business Interoperability:
    - — Delivery networks
    - — e-Democracy
    - — e-Business
    - — Enterprise resource management
    - — Relationship and case management
- ■ Technical Interoperability:
    - — IT infrastructure

In certain architectural approaches, such as system of systems or a federated model, interoperability is a strongly recommended best practice that will determine how the systems interact with each other. A key consideration will be the enterprise's business operating model.

29.3   Enterprise Operating Model

Key to establishing interoperability is the determination of the corporate operating model, where the operating model is "the necessary level of business process integration and standardization for delivering goods and services to customers. An operating model describes how a company wants to thrive and grow. By providing a more stable and actionable view of the company than strategy, the operating model drives the design of the foundation for execution."[5]

For example, if lines of business or business units only need to share documents, then the Architecture and Solution Building Blocks (ABBs and SBBs) may be simpler than if there is a need to share structured transaction data. Similarly, if the Architecture Vision includes a shared services environment, then it is useful to define the level the services are to be shared.

The corporate operating model will normally indicate what type of interoperability approach will be appropriate. This model should be determined in Phase A (Architecture Vision) if not in Phase B (Business Architecture), and definitely by Phase E (Opportunities & Solutions).

Complex enterprises and/or extended enterprises (e.g., supply chain) may have more than one type of operating model. For example, it is common for the internal operating model (and supporting interoperability model) to differ from the one used for the extended enterprise.

---

5.   Enterprise Architecture as Strategy provides potential models.

29.4   Refining Interoperability

Implementing interoperability requires the creation, management, acceptance, and enforcement of realistic standards that are SMART (Specific, Measurable, Actionable, Realistic, and Time-bound). Clear measures of interoperability are key to success.

Architecture is the key for identifying standards and facilitated sessions (brainstorming) will examine potential pragmatic ways (that fit within the current or emerging business culture) to achieve the requisite degree of interoperability.

Interoperability should be refined so that it meets the needs of the enterprise and/or extended enterprise in an unambiguous way. The refined interoperability measures (degrees, types, and high-level targets) should be part of or referred to the enterprise architecture strategic direction.

These measures are instantiated within a transformation strategy that should be embedded within the Target Architecture definition and pragmatically implemented in the Transition Architectures. Upon completion, also update the consolidated gap analysis results and dependencies to ensure that all of the brainstorming nuggets are captured.

An example of specifying interoperability is the Degrees of Interoperability (used within the Canadian Department of National Defense and NATO). These organizations were focused on the sharing of information and came up with four degrees of interoperability as follows:

- **Degree 1: Unstructured Data Exchange** involves the exchange of human-interpretable unstructured data, such as the free text found in operational estimates, analysis, and papers.

- **Degree 2: Structured Data Exchange** involves the exchange of human-interpretable structured data intended for manual and/or automated handling, but requires manual compilation, receipt, and/or message dispatch.

- **Degree 3: Seamless Sharing of Data** involves the automated sharing of data amongst systems based on a common exchange model.

- **Degree 4: Seamless Sharing of Information** is an extension of Degree 3 to the universal interpretation of information through data processing based on co-operating applications.

These degrees should be further refined and made technically meaningful for each of the degrees. An example refinement of degree 3 with four subclassifications follows:

- 3A: Formal Message Exchange
- 3B: Common Data Exchange
- 3C: Complete Data Exchange
- 3D: Real-time Data Exchange

The intent is to specify the detailed degrees of interoperability to the requisite level of detail so that they are technically meaningful.

These degrees are very useful for specifying the way that information has to be exchanged between the various systems and provide critical direction to the projects implementing the systems.

Similar measures should be established to determine service/business and technical interoperability.

29.5   Determining Interoperability Requirements

Co-existence between emerging and existing systems, especially during transformation, will be a major challenge and brainstorming should attempt to figure out what has to be done to reduce the pain. It is imperative to involve the operations management staff and architects in this step as they will be responsible for operating the portfolio deliverables.

For example, there might be a need for a "wrapper" application (an application that acts as the interface [a.k.a. interpreter] between the legacy application and the emerging infrastructure). Indeed, pragmatically, in the "if it works do not fix it" world, the "wrapper" might become a permanent solution.

Regardless, using the gap analysis results and business scenarios as a foundation, brainstorm the IT issues and work them through to ensure that all of the gaps are clearly identified and addressed and verify that the organization-specific requirements will be met.

It is important to note that the ensuing development process must include recognition of dependencies and boundaries for functions and should take account of what products are available in the marketplace. An example of how this might be expressed can be seen in the building blocks example (see Part III, Chapter 37).

If a mechanism such as the Degrees of Interoperability is used, then a matrix showing the interoperability requirements is a useful tool, as illustrated in Figure 29-1 and Figure 29-2, noting that the degree of information sharing is not necessarily symmetrical or bi-directional between systems and/or stakeholders.

The matrix below can be used within the enterprise and/or within the extended enterprise as a way of detailing that information and/or services can be shared. The matrix should start in the Business Architecture (Phase B) to capture the nature of the sharing of information between stakeholders, and evolve to determine the what systems share what information in Phase C.

Phase B: Inter-stakeholder Information Interoperability Requirements (Using degrees of information interoperability)							
Stakeholders	A	B	C	D	E	F	G
A		2	3	2	3	3	3
B	2		3	2	3	2	2
C	3	3		2	2	2	3
D	2	2	2		3	3	3
E	4	4	2	3		3	3
F	4	4	2	3	3		2
G	2	2	3	3	3	3	

Figure 29-1 Business Information Interoperability Matrix

Figure 29-1 shows that Stakeholder A requires unstructured data exchange (degree 2) with Stakeholders/Systems B and D, and seamless sharing of data (degree 3) with Stakeholders/Systems C, E, F, and G.

The business information interoperability matrix should be refined within the Information Systems Architecture using refined measures and specifying the actual systems used by the stakeholders. A sample is shown in Figure 29-2.

Phase C: Inter-system Interoperability Requirements							
	System A	System B	System C	System D	System E	System F	System G
System A		2A	3D	2B	3A	3A	3B
System B	2E		3F	2C	3A	2B	2C
System C	3E	3F		2B	2A	2A	3B
System D	2B	2B	2B		3A	3A	3B
System E	4A	4B	2B	3A		3B	3B
System F	4A	4A	2B	3B	3A		2D
System G	2B	2B	3A	3A	3B	3B	

Figure 29-2 Information Systems Interoperability Matrix

In Figure 29-2, both the nature of the exchange is more detailed (e.g., Degree 3A *versus* only Degree 3) and the sharing is between specific systems rather than stakeholders. For example, System A shares information with the other systems in accordance with enterprise technical standards.

In many organizations the Business Architectures describe the nature of the information shared between stakeholders and/or organizations (e.g., in defense the term is "operational node"), and the Data Architecture specifies the information shared between systems.

Update the defined target data and Application Architecture (Version 1.0) with the interoperability issues that were raised.

29.6 Reconciling Interoperability Requirements with Potential Solutions

The enterprise architect will have to ensure that there are no interoperability conflicts, especially if there is an intention to re-use existing SBBs and/or COTS.

The most significant issue to be addressed is in fact business interoperability. Most SBBs or COTS will have their own business processes and most likely information architecture embedded. Changes to the information architecture will be technically challenging, but achievable; however, changing the embedded business processes will often require so much work, that the advantages of re-using solutions will be lost. There are numerous examples of this in the past.

Furthermore, there is the workflow aspect between the various systems that has to be taken into account. The enterprise architect will have to ensure that any change to the business interoperability requirements is signed off by the business architects and architecture sponsors in a revised Statement of Architecture Work.

Assess the Architecture Vision and Target Architectures as well as Implementation Factor Assessment and Deduction matrix and Consolidated Gaps, Solutions, and Dependencies matrix to look for any constraints on interoperability required by the potential set of solutions.

29.7 Summary

Defining interoperability in a clear unambiguous manner at several levels (business/service, information, and technical) is a useful architecture planning tool. The notions of interoperability will become ever more important in the Service Oriented Architecture (SOA) environment where services will be shared internally and externally in ever more inter-dependent extended enterprises.

Chapter 30: Business Transformation Readiness Assessment

This chapter describes a technique known as Business Transformation Readiness Assessment, used for evaluating and quantifying an organization's readiness to undergo change.

This chapter builds on work by the Canadian Government and its Business Transformation Enablement Program (BTEP).[6]

30.1   Introduction

Enterprise architecture is a major endeavor within an organization and most often an innovative Architecture Vision (Phase A) and supporting Architecture Definition (Phases B to D) will entail considerable change. There are many dimensions to change, but by far the most important is the human element. For example, if the enterprise envisages a consolidation of information holdings and a move to a new paradigm such as service orientation for integrated service delivery, then the human resource implications are major. Potentially coupled with a change-averse culture and a narrowly skilled workforce, the most sound and innovative architecture could go nowhere.

Understanding the readiness of the organization to accept change, identifying the issues, and then dealing with them in the Implementation and Migration Plans is key to successful architecture transformation in Phases E and F. This will be a joint effort between corporate (especially human resources) staff, lines of business, and IT planners.

The recommended activities in an assessment of an organization's readiness to address business transformation are:

- Determine the readiness factors that will impact the organization
- Present the readiness factors using maturity models
- Assess the readiness factors, including determination of readiness factor ratings
- Assess the risks for each readiness factor and identify improvement actions to mitigate the risk
- Work these actions into Phase E and F Implementation and Migration Plan

---

6.   Refer to www.tbs-sct.gc.ca/btep-pto/index_e.asp.

30.1.1 Business Transformation Enablement Program (BTEP)

The Canadian Government Business Transformation Enablement Program (BTEP) provides guidance on how to identify the business transformation-related issues.

The BTEP recommends that all projects conduct a transformation readiness assessment to at least uncover the business transformation issues. This assessment is based upon the determination and analysis/rating of a series of readiness factors. The outcome is a deeper understanding of the challenges and opportunities that could be presented in the course of the endeavor. Many of the challenges translate directly into risks that have to be addressed, monitored, and, if possible, mitigated.

The following sections describe Business Transformation Readiness Assessment using the BTEP method, including some lessons learned. Readers should keep in mind that most organizations will have their own unique set of factors and criteria, but most are similar.

30.2 Determine Readiness Factors

The first step is to determine what factors will impact on the business transformation associated with the migration from the Baseline to Target Architectures.

This can be best achieved through the conduct of a facilitated workshop with individuals from different parts of the organization. It is important that all perspectives are sought as the issues will be varied. In this workshop it is very useful to start off with a tentative list of factors that participants can re-use, reject, augment, or replace.

An example set of factors drawn from the BTEP follows:

- **Vision** is the ability to clearly define and communicate what is to be achieved. This is where management is able to clearly define the objectives, in both strategic and specific terms. Leadership in defining vision and needs comes from the business side with IT input. Predictable and proven processes exist for moving from vision to statement of requirements. The primary drivers for the initiative are clear. The scope and approach of the transformation initiative have been clearly defined throughout the organization.

- **Desire, Willingness, and Resolve** is the presence of a desire to achieve the results, willingness to accept the impact of doing the work, and the resolve to follow through and complete the endeavor. There is active discussion regarding the impact that executing the project may have on the organization, with clear indication of the intent to accept the impacts. Key resources (e.g., financial, human, etc.) are allocated for the endeavor and top executives project the clear message that the organization will follow through; a message that identifies the effort as well as the benefits. Organizationally there is a history of finishing what is started and of coming to closure on issues in the timeframes needed and there is agreement throughout the organization that the transformation initiative is the "right" thing to do.

- **Need**, in that there is a compelling need to execute the endeavor. There are clear statements regarding what the organization will not be able to do if the project does not proceed, and equally clear statements of what the project will enable the organization to do. There are visible and broadly understood consequences of endeavor failure and success criteria have been clearly identified and communicated.

- **Business Case** exists that creates a strong focus for the project, identifying benefits that must be achieved and thereby creating an imperative to succeed. The business case document identifies concrete benefits (revenues or savings) that the organization is committed to deliver and clearly and unquestionably points to goals that the organization is committed to achieving.

- **Funding**, in the form of a clear source of fiscal resources, exists that meets the endeavor's potential expenditures.

- **Sponsorship and Leadership** exists and is broadly shared, but not so broad as to diffuse accountability. Leadership keeps everyone "on board" and keeps all focused on the strategic goals. The endeavor is sponsored by an executive who is appropriately aligned to provide the leadership the endeavor needs and able to articulate and defend the needs of the endeavor at the senior management level. These executive sponsors are and will remain engaged throughout.

- **Governance** is the ability to engage the involvement and support of all parties with an interest in or responsibility to the endeavor with the objective of ensuring that the corporate interests are served and the objectives achieved. There are clearly identified stakeholders and a clear sense of their interest in and responsibility to the project; a culture that encourages participation towards corporate rather than local objectives; a history of being able to successfully manage activities that cross interest areas; a culture that fosters meaningful, as opposed to symbolic, participation in management processes; and a commitment to ongoing project review and challenge and openness to outside advice.

- **Accountability** is the assignment of specific and appropriate responsibility, recognition of measurable expectations by all concerned parties, and alignment of decision-making with areas of responsibility and with where the impact of the decisions will be felt. Accountability is aligned with the area where the benefits of success or consequences of failure of the endeavor will be felt as well as with the responsibility areas.

- **Workable Approach and Execution Model** is an approach that makes sense relative to the task, with a supporting environment, modeled after a proven approach. There are clear notions of the client and the client's role relative to the builder or prime contractor and the organization is experienced with endeavors of this type so that the processes, disciplines, expertise, and governance are already in place, proven, and available to apply to the transformation endeavor. All the players know their roles because they have played them before with success. In particular, the roles of "client" and "systems builder" are mature and stable. There is a communication plan covering all levels of the organization and meeting the needs ranging from awareness to availability of technical detail. There is a reward and recognition plan in place to recognize teams and individuals who use good change management practices, planning and prevention of crisis behaviors, and who reinforce behaviors appropriate to the new way of doing business. It is clear to everyone how implementation will occur, how it will be monitored, and how realignment actions will be made and there are adequate resources dedicated for the life of the transformation.

- **IT Capacity to Execute** is the ability to perform all the IT tasks required by the project, including the skills, tools, processes, and management capability. There has been a recent successful execution of a similar endeavor of similar size and complexity and there exist appropriate processes, discipline, skills, and a rationale model for deciding what skills and activities to source externally.

- **Enterprise Capacity to Execute** is the ability of the enterprise to perform all the tasks required by the endeavor, in areas outside of IT, including the ability to make decisions within the tight time constraints typical to project environments based upon the recent successful execution of a similar endeavor of at least half the size and complexity. There exist non-IT-specific processes, discipline, and skills to deal with this type of endeavor. The enterprise has a demonstrated ability to deal with the type of ongoing portfolio/project management issues and requirements. There is a recognition of the need for knowledge and skill-building for the new way of working as well as the value of a formal gap analysis for skills and behavior.

- **Enterprise Ability to Implement and Operate** the transformation elements and their related business processes, absorb the changes arising from implementation, and ongoing ability to operate in the new environment. The enterprise has a recent proven ability to deal with the change management issues arising from new processes and systems and has in place a solid disciplined and process-driven service management program that provides operations, maintenance, and support for existing systems.

Once the factors have been identified and defined, it is useful to call a follow-on workshop where the factors shall be assessed in some detail in terms of their impact/risk. The next section will deal with preparing for an effective assessment of these factors.

30.3 Present Readiness Factors

Once the factors are determined, it is necessary to present them in such a way that the assessment is clear and the maximum value is derived from the participants.

One such presentation is through the use of maturity models. If each factor is converted into a maturity model (a re-usable governance asset as well) accompanied by a standard worksheet template containing all of the information and deductions that have to be gathered, it can be a very useful tool.

The maturity model should enable participants to:

- Assess their current (Baseline Architecture) maturity level

- Determine the target maturity level that would have to be achieved to realize the Target Architecture

- Determine an intermediate target that would be achievable in a lesser timeframe

The care spent preparing the models (which is not insignificant) will be recouped by a focused workshop that will rapidly go through a significant number of factors.

It is important that each factor be well-defined and that the scope of the enterprise architecture endeavor (preliminary planning) be reflected in the models to keep the workshop participants focused and productive.

Circulating the models before the workshop for comments would be useful, if only to ensure that they are complete as well as allowing the participants to prepare for the workshop. Note that the model shown below also has a recommended target state put in by the enterprise architect; this again acts as governance.

An example of a maturity model is shown in Figure 30-1 for one of the BTEP factors:

Business Transformation Readiness Assessment - Maturity Model					
Factor 2: Need for Enterprise Information Architecture		**Class**	Organizational Context		
		BTEP Readiness Factor	YES		
Definition	There is recognition by the organization that information is a strategic corporate asset requiring stewardship. There is also recognition that the data is not universally understandable, of requisite quality, and accessible.				
Maturity Model Levels					
0 **Not defined**	**1** **Ad Hoc**	**2** **Repeatable**	**3** **Defined**	**4** **Managed**	**5** **Optimized**
Information is not recognized as an asset. There is no clear stewardship of data.	Data Management (DM) concepts are intuitively understood and practiced on an *ad hoc* basis. Stewardship of the data is informal. Data is recognized by certain internal experts and senior management as being of strategic importance to the organization. Focus is primarily on technically managing redundant data at the applications level.	Many parts of the organization value information/data as a strategic asset. Internal DM experts maintain clear lines of responsibility and stewardship of the data, organized along lines of business and at all senior levels. Staff put into practice DM principles and standards in their daily activities.	Data is recognized as a strategic asset in most parts of the organization, and throughout most levels from operations to senior management. Resources are committed to ensuring strong stewardship of data at the lower management and information expert levels.	Data is recognized as a strategic asset in all parts of the organization, and throughout most levels from operations to senior management. Resources are committed to ensuring strong stewardship of data at the senior management and information expert levels.	Data is treated in all levels throughout the organization as a strategic asset to be exploited and re-used. Data products and services are strongly integrated with the management practice of the organization. All staff are empowered and equipped to take stewardship of information, and are seen as "knowledge workers".
				Recommended Target State	

Figure 30-1 Business Transformation Readiness Assessment — Maturity Model

30.4 Assess Readiness Factors

Ideally, the factors should be assessed in a multi-disciplinary workshop. Using a mechanism such as maturity models, enterprise architects will normally have to cover a great deal of ground in little time.

The use of a series of templates for each factor would expedite the assessment, and ensure consistency across the wide range of factors.

The assessment should address three things, namely:

- Readiness Factor Vision
- Readiness Factor Rating
- Readiness Factor Risks & Actions

30.4.1 Readiness Factor Vision

The vision for a readiness factor is the determination of where the enterprise has to evolve to address the factor. First, the factor should be assessed with respect to its base state and then its target state.

For example, if the "IT capacity to execute" factor is rated as low, the factor should ideally be at "high" to realize the Target Architecture Vision. An intermediate target might be useful to direct the implementation. Maturity models are excellent vehicles to guide this determination.

30.4.2 Readiness Factor Rating

Once the factor visions are established, then it is useful to determine how important each factor is to the achievement of the Target Architecture as well as how challenging it will be to migrate the factor into an acceptable visionary state.

The BTEP uses a Readiness Rating Scheme that can be used as a start point for any organization in any vertical. Each one of the readiness factors are rated with respect to:

- **Urgency**, whereby if a readiness factor is urgent, it means that action is needed before a transformation initiative can begin.

- **Readiness Status**, which is rated as either Low (needs substantial work before proceeding), Fair (needs some work before proceeding), Acceptable (some readiness issues exist; no showstoppers), Good (relatively minor issues exist), or High (no readiness issues).

- **Degree of Difficulty to Fix** rates the effort required to overcome any issues identified as either No Action Needed, Easy, Moderate, or Difficult.

Although a more extensive template can be used in the workshop, it is useful to create a summary table of the findings to consolidate the factors and provide a management overview. A like summary is shown in Figure 30-2.

Business Factor Assessment Summary				
Ser	Readiness Factor	Urgency	Readiness Status	Degree of Difficulty to Fix
1	Vision			
2	Desire/willingness/resolve			
3	Need			
4	Business case			
5	Funding			
6	Sponsorship and leadership			
7	Governance			
8	Accountability			
9	Workable approach and execution model			
10	IT capacity to execute			
11	Departmental capacity to execute			
12	Ability to implement and operate			

Figure 30-2 Summary Table of Business Transformation Readiness Assessment

30.4.3 Readiness Factor Risks & Actions

Once the factors have been rated and assessed, derive a series of actions that will enable the factors to change to a favorable state.

Each factor should be assessed with respect to risk using the process highlighted in Part III, Chapter 31, including an estimate of impact and frequency.

Each factor should be discretely assessed and a series of improvement actions outlined. Before starting anew, existing actions outlined in the architectures should be checked first before creating new ones.

These newly identified actions should then be formally incorporated into the emerging Implementation and Migration Plan.

From a risk perspective, these actions are designed to mitigate the risks and produce an acceptable residual risk. As risks, they should be part of the risk management process and closely monitored as the enterprise architecture is being implemented.

30.5   Readiness and Migration Planning

The assessment exercise will provide a realistic assessment of the organization and will be a key input into the strategic migration planning that will be initiated in Phase E and completed in Phase F. It is important to note whether the business transformation actions will be on the vision's critical path and, if so, determine how they will impact implementation. There is no point deploying new IT capability without employees trained to use it and support staff ready to sustain it.

The readiness factors, as part of an overall Implementation and Migration Plan, will have to be continuously monitored (Phase G) and rapid corrective actions taken through the IT governance framework to ensure that the defined architectures can be implemented.

The readiness factors assessment will be a living document and during the migration planning and execution of the Transition Architectures, the business transformation activities will play a key role.

30.6   Marketing the Implementation Plan

The Architecture Definition should not be widely circulated until the business transformation issues are identified and mitigated, and the associated actions part of an overall "marketing" plan for the vision and the Implementation and Migration Plan.

For example, the consolidation of information holdings could result in hundreds of lost jobs and this vision should not be announced before a supporting business transformation/human resources plan is formulated to retrain or support the workers' quest for new employment.

The business transformation workshops are a critical part of the Communications Plan whereby key individuals from within the organization gather to assess the implications of transforming the enterprise. To do this they will become aware of the Architecture Vision and architecture definition (if they were not already involved through the business scenarios and Business Architecture). This group will feel ownership of the enterprise architecture, recognizing the enterprise architect as a valuable steward.

Their determination of the factors will again create a culture of understanding across the enterprise and provide useful insights for the Implementation and Migration Plan.

The latter plan should include a Communications Plan, especially to keep the affected personnel informed. In many cases collaborating with the unions and shop stewards will further assist a humane (and peaceful) transition to the target state.

30.7 Conclusion

In short, enterprise architecture implementation will require a deep knowledge and awareness of all of the business transformation factors that impact transitioning to the visionary state. With the evolution of IT, the actual technology is not the real issue any more in enterprise architecture, but the critical factors are most often the cultural ones. Any Implementation and Migration Plan has to take both into consideration. Neglecting these and focusing on the technical aspects will invariably result in a lackluster implementation that falls short of realizing the real promise of a visionary enterprise architecture.

Chapter 31: Risk Management

This chapter describes risk management, which is a technique used to mitigate risk when implementing an architecture project.

31.1 Introduction

There will always be risk with any architecture/business transformation effort. It is important to identify, classify, and mitigate these risks before starting so that they can be tracked throughout the transformation effort.

Mitigation is an ongoing effort and often the risk triggers may be outside the scope of the transformation planners (e.g., merger, acquisition) so planners must monitor the transformation context constantly.

It is also important to note that the enterprise architect may identify the risks and mitigate certain ones, but it is within the governance framework that risks have to be first accepted and then managed.

There are two levels of risk that should be considered, namely:

1. **Initial Level of Risk**: Risk categorization prior to determining and implementing mitigating actions.

2. **Residual Level of Risk**: Risk categorization after implementation of mitigating actions (if any).

The process for risk management is described in the following sections and consists of the following activities:

- Risk classification
- Risk identification
- Initial risk assessment
- Risk mitigation and residual risk assessment
- Risk monitoring

31.2   Risk Classification

Risk is pervasive in any enterprise architecture activity and is present in all phases within the Architecture Development Method (ADM). From a management perspective, it is useful to classify the risks so that the mitigation of the risks can be executed as expeditiously as possible.

One common way for risks to be classified is with respect to impact on the organization (as discussed in Section 31.4), whereby risks with certain impacts have to be addressed by certain levels of governance.

Risks are normally classified as time (schedule), cost (budget), and scope but they could also include client transformation relationship risks, contractual risks, technological risks, scope and complexity risks, environmental (corporate) risks, personnel risks, and client acceptance risks.

Other ways of delegating risk management is to further classify risks by architecture domains. Implementation risk is often quoted, but that is almost always the case. Classifying risks as business, information, applications, and technology is useful but there may be organizationally-specific ways of expressing risk that the corporate enterprise architecture directorate should adopt or extend rather than modify.

Ultimately, enterprise architecture risks are corporate risks and should be classified and as appropriate managed in the same or extended way.

31.3   Risk Identification

The maturity and transformation readiness assessments will generate a great many risks. Identify the risks and then determine the strategy to address them throughout the transformation.

The use of Capability Maturity Models (CMMs) is suitable for specific factors associated with architecture delivery to first identify baseline and target states and then identify the actions required to move to the target state. The implications of *not* achieving the target state can result in the discovery of risks. Refer to Chapter 30 for specific details.

Risk documentation is completed in the context of a Risk Management Plan, for which templates exist in standard project management methodologies (e.g., Project Management Book of Knowledge and PRINCE2) as well as with the various government methodologies.

Normally these methodologies involve procedures for contingency planning, tracking and evaluating levels of risk; reacting to changing risk level factors, as well as processes for documenting, reporting, and communicating risks to stakeholders.

31.4   Initial Risk Assessment

The next step is to classify risks with respect to effect and frequency in accordance with scales used within the organization. Combine effect and frequency to come up with a preliminary risk assessment.

There are no hard and fast rules with respect to measuring effect and frequency. The following guidelines are based upon existing risk management best practices. Effect could be assessed using the following example criteria:

- **Catastrophic** infers critical financial loss that could result in bankruptcy of the organization.

- **Critical** infers serious financial loss in more than one line of business leading to a loss in productivity and no return on investment on the IT investment.

- **Marginal** infers a minor financial loss in a line of business and a reduced return on investment on the IT investment.

- **Negligible** infers a minimal impact on a line of business' ability to deliver services and/or products.

Frequency could be indicated as follows:

- **Frequent**: Likely to occur very often and/or continuously.

- **Likely**: Occurs several times over the course of a transformation cycle (possibly once every 36 months).

- **Occasional**: Occur sporadically (not more than once per year).

- **Seldom**: Remotely possible and would probably occur not more than once in the course of the entire transformation.

- **Unlikely**: Will probably not occur during the transformation effort.

Combining the two factors to infer impact would be conducted using a heuristically-based but consistent classification scheme for the risks. A potential scheme to assess corporate impact could be as follows:

- **Extremely High Risk (E)**: The transformation effort will most likely fail with severe consequences.

- **High Risk (H)**: Significant failure of parts of the transformation effort resulting in certain goals not being achieved.

- **Moderate Risk (M)**: Noticeable failure of parts of the transformation effort threatening the success of certain goals.

- **Low Risk (L)**: Certain goals will not be wholly successful.

These impacts can be derived using a classification scheme, as shown in Figure 31-1.

Corporate Risk Impact Assessment					
	Frequency				
Effect	Frequent	Likely	Occasional	Seldom	Unlikely
Catastrophic	E	E	H	H	M
Critical	E	H	H	M	L
Marginal	H	M	M	L	L
Negligible	M	L	L	L	L

Figure 31-1 Risk Classification Scheme

31.5   Risk Mitigation and Residual Risk Assessment

Risk mitigation refers to the identification, planning, and conduct of actions that will reduce the risk to an acceptable level.

The mitigation effort could be a simple monitoring and/or acceptance of the risk to a full-blown contingency plan calling for complete redundancy in a Business Continuity Plan (with all of the associated scope, cost, and time implications).

Due to the implications of this risk assessment, it has to be conducted in a pragmatic but systematic manner. With priority going to frequent high impact risks, each risk has to be mitigated in turn.

31.6   Conduct Residual Risk Assessment

Once the mitigation effort has been identified for each one of the risks, re-assess the effect and frequency and then recalculate the impacts and see whether the mitigation effort has really made an acceptable difference. The mitigation efforts will often be resource-intensive and a major outlay for little or no residual risk should be challenged.

Once the initial risk is mitigated, then the risk that remains is called the "residual risk". The key consideration is that the mitigating effort actually reduces the corporate impact and does not just move the risk to another similarly high quadrant. For example, changing the risk from frequent/catastrophic to frequent/critical still delivers an Extremely high risk. If this occurs, then the mitigation effort has to be re-considered.

The final deliverable should be a transformation risk assessment that could be structured as a worksheet, as shown in Figure 31-2.

Risk ID	Risk	Preliminary Risk			Mitigation	Residual Risk		
		Effect	Frequency	Impact		Effect	Frequency	Impact

Figure 31-2 Sample Risk Identification and Mitigation Assessment Worksheet

31.7   Risk Monitoring and Governance (Phase G)

The residual risks have to be approved by the IT governance framework and potentially in corporate governance where business acceptance of the residual risks is required.

Once the residual risks have been accepted, then the execution of the mitigating actions has to be carefully monitored to ensure that the enterprise is dealing with residual rather than initial risk.

The risk identification and mitigation assessment worksheets are maintained as governance artifacts and are kept up-to-date in Phase G (Implementation Governance) where risk monitoring is conducted.

Implementation governance can identify critical risks that are not being mitigated and might require another full or partial ADM cycle.

31.8   Summary

Risk Management is an integral part of enterprise architecture. Practitioners are encouraged to use their corporate risk management methodology or extend it using the guidance in this chapter. In the absence of a formal corporate methodology, architects can use the guidance in this chapter as a best practice.

Chapter 32: Capability-Based Planning

This chapter provides an overview of capability-based planning, a business planning technique that focuses on business outcomes. It also copes well with the friction of co-ordinating projects across corporate functional domains that together enable the enterprise to achieve that capability (for example, electronic service delivery).

32.1 Overview

Capability-based planning focuses on the planning, engineering, and delivery of strategic business capabilities to the enterprise. It is business-driven and business-led and combines the requisite efforts of all lines of business to achieve the desired capability. Capability-based planning accommodates most, if not all, of the corporate business models and is especially useful in organizations where a latent capability to respond (e.g., an emergency preparedness unit) is required and the same resources are involved in multiple capabilities. Often the need for these capabilities are discovered and refined using business scenarios (see Part III, Chapter 26).

From an IT perspective, capability-based planning is particularly relevant. For example, setting up a data center is really about consolidating corporate data and providing the related services. Lead enterprise architects for this capability will find themselves involved in managing construction, personnel training, and other change management tasks as well as IT architecture tasks. In the past, many IT projects were less than successful even though the actual IT implementation was brilliant, but the associated other tasks (business process re-engineering, client training, support training, infrastructure, and so on) were not controlled by the enterprise architects and planners and often were not satisfactorily completed.

On the other hand, IT projects were often described in terms of technical deliverables not as business outcomes, making it difficult for business to appreciate what was being delivered and often the IT architects lost sight of the ultimate business goal. Capability-based planning frames all phases of the architecture development in the context of business outcomes, clearly linking the IT vision, architectures (ABBs and SBBs), and the Implementation and Migration Plans with the corporate strategic, business, and line of business plans.

In many governments, horizontal interoperability and shared services are emerging as cornerstones of their e-Government implementations and capability-based management is also prominent although under many guises. In the private sector, the concepts of supply chain management and Service Oriented Architecture (SOA) are increasingly forcing planners/managers to govern horizontally as well as vertically.

32.2   Capability-Based Planning Paradigm

Capability-based planning has long been entrenched in the Defense realm in the US, UK, Australia, and Canada. The associated governance mechanisms, as well as rigorous capability derivation (capability engineering), are emerging primarily in the systems engineering domain. These concepts are readily transferable into other domains, such as IT.

32.3   Concept of Capability-Based Planning

From an enterprise architecture and IT perspective, capability-based planning is a powerful mechanism to ensure that the strategic business plan drives the enterprise from a top-down approach. It is also adaptable with capability engineering to leverage emerging bottom-up innovations.

No matter how the corporation structures itself, it will have to cope with the delivery of business capabilities whose delivery will require co-ordination and alignment across business verticals.

Capabilities are business-driven and ideally business-led. One of the main challenges is that the benefits are often reaped at the enterprise and not the line of business level. Consequently, projects within line of business-led portfolios tend to take a line of business rather than corporate perspective. Managing the delivery of a capability is challenging, but the entrenchment of a capability-based perspective within an organization is a powerful mechanism to deliver synergistically derived business value that will resonate in profitability and stock value.

Capabilities should be specified using the same discipline in the specification of objectives as in business scenarios; specifically, they should follow the SMART guidelines to avoid ambiguity.

As shown in Figure 32-1, many capabilities are "horizontal" and go against the grain of normal vertical corporate governance. Most often, management direction as well as the corporate management accountability framework are based upon line of business metrics, not enterprise metrics. Enterprise architecture is also a horizontal function that looks at enterprise-level (as well as line of business-level) optimization and service delivery. Not surprisingly, capability-based planning and enterprise architecture are mutually supportive. Both often operate against the corporate grain and both have to cope with challenging business environments. Business support of enterprise architecture is crucial for its success and it is logical that it aligns with the corporate capability planners as well as provide support for those within the vertical lines of business.

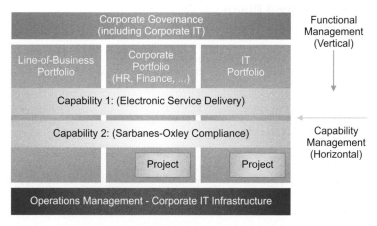

Figure 32-1 Capability-Based Planning Concept

Capabilities can also be vertical and handled in the context of the business organizational structure. In fact, capability requirements often drive organizational design, but within an organization in the process of business transformation, the organization may be trailing the capability needs.

Vertical capabilities are easier to handle and support by the enterprise architecture function, but still challenging when services are rationalized at the enterprise level and lines of business receive shared services that they do not directly control (they provide indirect control through IT governance in the Architecture Board as created in preliminary planning and used in Phase G (Implementation Governance).

For capability-based planning to succeed, it has to be managed with respect to dimensions and increments, as explained in the following two sections.

32.3.1 Capability Dimensions

Capabilities are engineered/generated taking into consideration various dimensions that straddle the corporate functional portfolios.

Every organization has a different but similar set of dimensions. An example set (based upon the Canadian Department of National Defense) could include personnel, research & development, infrastructure/facilities, concepts/processes, information management, and material. Whatever dimensions are selected, they should be well explained and understood.

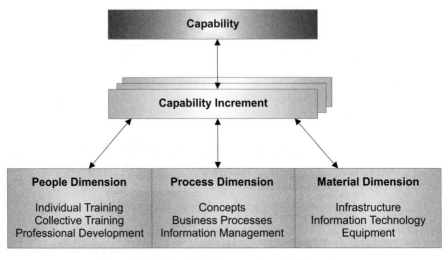

Figure 32-2 Capability Increments and Dimensions

32.3.2 Capability Increments

A capability will take an extended time to deliver (specifics will be a function of the organization and industry vertical) and will normally involve many projects delivering numerous increments. In addition, the capability needs to provide real business value to stakeholders as soon as possible and maintain momentum to achieve the Target Architecture as well as the associated executive support and corporate funding. Therefore, it is useful to break the capability into capability increments that deliver discrete, visible, and quantifiable outcomes as well as providing the focus for Transition Architectures and the deliverables from numerous inter-dependent projects. These outcomes are the Critical Success Factors (CSFs) for continued capability support.

Communicating the potentially complex incremental evolution of a capability to the stakeholder community is essential to establish buy-in at the start and to maintain their buy-in during the transition. The Capability Increment "Radar" diagram (see Figure 32-3) is a proven approach to describing how a capability will evolve over time. The architect selects the aspects of capability that are important to the stakeholder community as lines radiating from the center. Against each line, the architect draws points that represent significant "capability points" ("lower" capability points nearest the center; "higher" capability points farthest from the center). With these "markers" in place the architect can, by joining up the capability points into a closed loop, demonstrate in a simple form how each "capability increment" will extend on the previous increment. This, of course, requires that each capability point is formally defined and "labeled" in a way that is meaningful to the stakeholders. In the diagram below, we have depicted Capability Increment 0 as the starting capability.

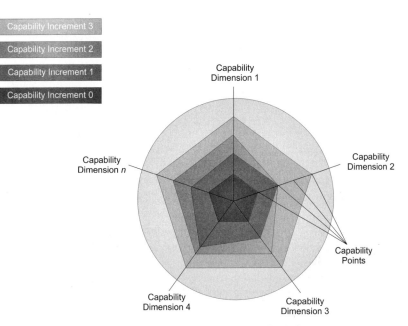

Figure 32-3 Capability Increment "Radar"

32.4 Capabilities in an Enterprise Architecture Context

The capabilities are directly derived from the corporate strategic plan by the corporate strategic planners that are and/or include the enterprise architects and satisfy the enterprise goals, objectives, and strategies. Most organizations will also have an annual business plan that describes how the organization intends to proceed over the next fiscal period in order to meet the enterprise strategic goals.

Figure 32-4 illustrates the crucial relationships between capability-based planning, enterprise architecture, and portfolio/project management. On the left hand side, capability management is aligned with enterprise architecture. The key is that all of the architectures will be expressed in terms of business outcomes and value rather than in IT terms (e.g., establishment of a server farm), thereby ensuring IT alignment with the business.

The intent is that the corporate strategic direction drives the Architecture Vision in Phase A, as well as the corporate organization which will be the basis for the creation of portfolios.

Specific capabilities targeted for completion will be the focus of the Architecture Definition (Phases B, C, and D) and, based upon the identified work packages, Phase E projects will be conceived.

The capability increments will be the drivers for the Transition Architectures (Phase E) that will structure the project increments. The actual delivery will be co-ordinated through the

Implementation and Migration Plans (Phase F).

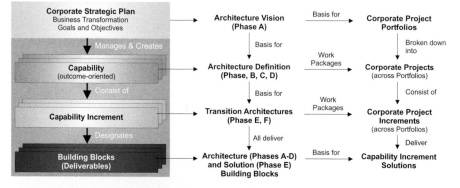

Figure 32-4 Relationship Between Capabilities, Enterprise Architecture, and Projects

Capability managers will perform similar tasks to that of the portfolio managers, but across the portfolios aligning the projects and project increments to deliver continuous business value. Whereas the portfolio managers will be concerned with the co-ordination of their projects to optimally design, build, and deliver the Solution Building Blocks (SBBs). Ideally, capability managers will also manage funding that can use the Transition Architectures as gates. Co-ordination between the portfolio and capability managers will have to be provided at the corporate level.

32.5 Summary

Capability-based planning is a versatile business planning paradigm that is very useful from an enterprise architecture perspective. It assists in aligning IT with the business and helps focus IT architects on the continuous creation of business value.

The Open Group Architecture Framework (TOGAF)

Part IV:

Architecture Content Framework

The Open Group

Chapter 33: Introduction

33.1 Overview

Architects executing the Architecture Development Method (ADM) will produce a number of outputs as a result of their efforts, such as process flows, architectural requirements, project plans, project compliance assessments, etc. The content framework provides a structural model for architectural content that allows the major work products that an architect creates to be consistently defined, structured, and presented.

The content framework provided here is intended to allow TOGAF to be used as a stand-alone framework for architecture within an enterprise. However, other content frameworks exist (such as the Zachman Framework) and it is anticipated that some enterprises may opt to use an external framework in conjunction with TOGAF. In these cases, the content framework provides a useful reference and starting point for TOGAF content to be mapped to other frameworks.

The Architecture Content Framework uses the following three categories to describe the type of architectural work product within the context of use:

- A **deliverable** is a work product that is contractually specified and in turn formally reviewed, agreed, and signed off by the stakeholders. Deliverables represent the output of projects and those deliverables that are in documentation form will typically be archived at completion of a project, or transitioned into an Architecture Repository as a reference model, standard, or snapshot of the Architecture Landscape at a point in time.

- An **artifact** is a more granular architectural work product that describes an architecture from a specific viewpoint. Examples include a network diagram, a server specification, a use-case specification, a list of architectural requirements, and a business interaction matrix. Artifacts are generally classified as catalogs (lists of things), matrices (showing relationships between things), and diagrams (pictures of things). An architectural deliverable may contain many artifacts and artifacts will form the content of the Architecture Repository.

- A **building block** represents a (potentially re-usable) component of business, IT, or architectural capability that can be combined with other building blocks to deliver architectures and solutions.

  Building blocks can be defined at various levels of detail, depending on what stage of architecture development has been reached. For instance, at an early stage, a building block can simply consist of a name or an outline description. Later on, a building block may be decomposed into multiple supporting building blocks and may be accompanied by a full specification. Building blocks can relate to "architectures" or "solutions".

— Architecture Building Blocks (ABBs) typically describe required capability and shape the specification of Solution Building Blocks (SBBs). For example, a customer services capability may be required within an enterprise, supported by many SBBs, such as processes, data, and application software.

— Solution Building Blocks (SBBs) represent components that will be used to implement the required capability. For example, a network is a building block that can be described through complementary artifacts and then put to use to realize solutions for the enterprise.

The relationships between deliverables, artifacts, and building blocks are shown in Figure 33-1.

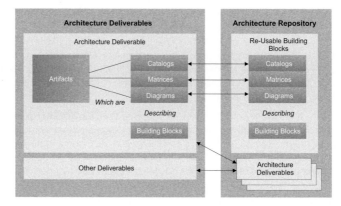

Figure 33-1 Relationships between Deliverables, Artifacts, and Building Blocks

For example, an Architecture Definition Document is a deliverable that documents an architecture description. This document will contain a number of complementary artifacts that are views of the building blocks relevant to the architecture. For example, a process flow diagram (an artifact) may be created to describe the target call handling process (a building block). This artifact may also describe other building blocks, such as the actors involved in the process (e.g., a Customer Services Representative). An example of the relationships between deliverables, artifacts, and building blocks is illustrated in Figure 33-2.

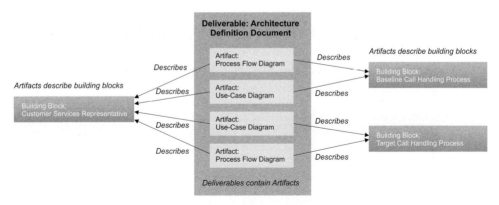

Figure 33-2 Example — Architecture Definition Document

33.2   Content Metamodel

The content metamodel provides a definition of all the types of building blocks that may exist within an architecture, showing how these building blocks can be described and related to one another. For example, when creating an architecture, an architect will identify applications, "data entities" held within applications, and technologies that implement those applications. These applications will in turn support particular groups of business user or actor, and will be used to fulfil "business services".

The content metamodel identifies all of these concerns (i.e., application, data entity, technology, actor, and business service), shows the relationships that are possible between them (e.g., actors consume business services), and finally identifies artifacts that can be used to represent them.

Figure 33-3 shows an overview of the content metamodel.

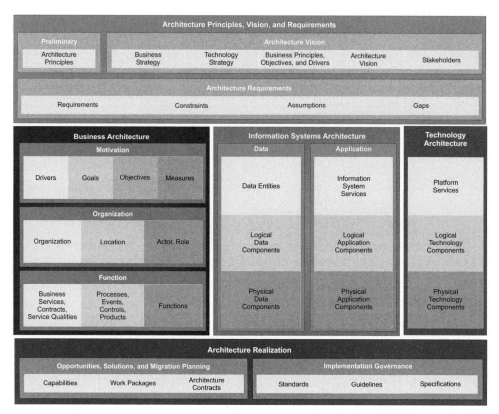

Figure 33-3 Content Metamodel Overview

33.3 Content Framework and the TOGAF ADM

The TOGAF ADM describes the process of moving from a baseline state of the enterprise to a target state of the enterprise. The ADM will address a business need through a process of visioning, architecture definition, transformation planning, and architecture governance. At each stage in this process, the ADM requires information as inputs and will create outputs as a result of executing a number of steps. The content framework provides an underlying structure for the ADM that defines inputs and outputs in more detail and puts each deliverable into the context of the holistic architecture view of the enterprise.

The content framework should therefore be used as a companion to the ADM. The ADM describes what needs to be done to create an architecture and the content framework describes what the architecture should look like once it is done.

33.4   Structure of Part IV

Part IV: Architecture Content Framework is structured as follows:

- Introduction (this chapter)
- Content Metamodel (see Chapter 34)
- Architectural Artifacts (see Chapter 35)
- Architecture Deliverables (see Chapter 36)
- Building Blocks (see Chapter 37)

Chapter 34: Content Metamodel

34.1 Overview

The TOGAF Architecture Development Method (ADM) provides a process lifecycle to create and manage architectures within an enterprise. At each phase within the ADM, a discussion of inputs, outputs, and steps describes a number of architectural work products or artifacts, such as process and application. The content metamodel provided here defines a formal structure for these terms to ensure consistency within the ADM and also to provide guidance for organizations that wish to implement their architecture within an architecture tool.

34.2 Content Metamodel Vision and Concepts

This section provides an overview of the objectives of the content metamodel, the concepts that support the metamodel, and an overview of the metamodel itself. Subsequent sections then go on to discuss each area of the metamodel in more detail. Contents of this section are as follows:

- Core content metamodel concepts (see Section 34.2.1) identifies the key concepts within the core content metamodel, including:
  - Core and extension content
  - Formal and informal modeling
  - Core metamodel entities
  - Catalog, matrix, and diagram concept
- Overview of the TOGAF content metamodel (see Section 34.2.2) provides a high-level overview of the content of the metamodel.

34.2.1 Core Content Metamodel Concepts

A TOGAF architecture is based on defining a number of architectural building blocks within architecture catalogs, specifying the relationships between those building blocks in architecture matrices, and then presenting communication diagrams that show in a precise and concise way what the architecture is.

This section introduces the core concepts that make up the TOGAF content metamodel, through the following subsections:

■ **Core and Extension Content** provides an introduction to the way in which TOGAF employs a basic core metamodel and then applies a number of extension modules to address specific architectural issues in more detail.

■ **Core Metamodel Entities** introduces the core TOGAF metamodel entities, showing the purpose of each entity and the key relationships that support architectural traceability.

■ **Catalog, Matrix, and Diagram Concept** describes the concept of catalogs, matrices, and diagrams.

Core and Extension Content

The role of TOGAF is to provide an open standard for architecture that is applicable in many scenarios and situations. In order to meet this vision, it is necessary to provide a fully featured enterprise architecture metamodel for content and also to provide the ability to avoid carrying out unnecessary activities by supporting tailoring.

The metamodel must provide a basic model with the minimum feature set and then support the inclusion of optional extensions during engagement tailoring.

The core TOGAF content metamodel and its extensions are illustrated in Figure 34-1.

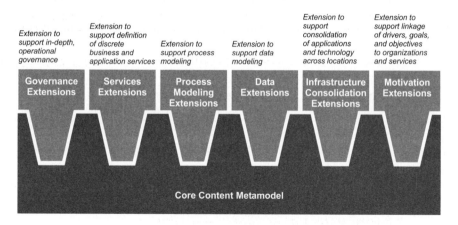

Figure 34-1 TOGAF Content Metamodel and its Extensions

The core metamodel provides a minimum set of architectural content to support traceability across artifacts. Additional metamodel concepts to support more specific or more in-depth modeling are contained within a group of extensions that logically cluster extension catalogs, matrices, and diagrams, allowing focus in areas of specific interest and focus.

All extension modules are optional and should be selected during the Preliminary phase of the architecture development to meet the needs of the organization. Additionally, the extension groupings described by the content metamodel are only a suggestion and further tailoring may be carried out to suit the specific needs at the discretion of the architects.

This core and extension concept is intended as a move towards supporting formal method extension approaches within TOGAF, such as the method plug-in concept found within the Software Process Engineering Metamodel (SPEM) developed by the Object Management Group

(OMG).[7]

Core Metamodel Entities

The content metamodel uses the terminology discussed within the TOGAF ADM as the basis for a formal metamodel. The following core terms are used:

- **Actor**: A person, organization, or system that is outside the consideration of the architecture model, but interacts with it.

- **Application Component**: An encapsulation of application functionality that is aligned to implementation structuring.

- **Business Service**: Supports business capabilities through an explicitly defined interface and is explicitly governed by an organization.

- **Data Entity**: An encapsulation of data that is recognized by a business domain expert as a discrete concept. Data entities can be tied to applications, repositories, and services and may be structured according to implementation considerations.

- **Function**: Delivers business capabilities closely aligned to an organization, but not explicitly governed by the organization.

- **Organization**: A self-contained unit of resources with line management responsibility, goals, objectives, and measures. Organizations may include external parties and business partner organizations.

- **Platform Service**: A technical capability required to provide enabling infrastructure that supports the delivery of applications.

- **Role**: An actor assumes a role to perform a task.

- **Technology Component**: An encapsulation of technology infrastructure that represents a class of technology product or specific technology product.

A more in-depth definition of terms used within the content metamodel can be found in Part I, Chapter 3.

Some of the key relationship concepts related to the core metamodel entities are described below:

- **Process should normally be used to describe flow**

  A process is a flow of interactions between functions and services and cannot be physically deployed. All processes should describe the flow of execution for a function and therefore the deployment of a process is through the function it supports; i.e., an application implements a function that has a process, not an application implements a process.

- **Function describes units of business capability at all levels of granularity**

  The term "function" is used to describe a unit of business capability at all levels of granularity, encapsulating terms such as value chain, process area, capability, business function, etc. Any bounded unit of business function should be described as a function.

---

7.   Refer to www.omg.org/technology/documents/formal/spem.htm.

- **Business services support organizational objectives and are defined at a level of granularity consistent with the level of governance needed**

  A business service operates as a boundary for one or more functions. The granularity of business services is dependent on the focus and emphasis of the business (as reflected by its drivers, goals, and objectives). A service in Service Oriented Architecture (SOA) terminology (i.e., a deployable unit of application functionality) is actually much closer to an application service, application component, or technology component, which may implement or support a business service.

- **Business services are deployed onto application components**

  Business services may be realized by business activity that does not relate to IT, or may be supported by IT. Business services that are supported by IT are deployed onto application components. Application components can be hierarchically decomposed and may support one or more business services. It is possible for a business service to be supported by multiple application components, but this is problematic from a governance standpoint and is symptomatic of business services that are too coarse-grained, or application components that are too fine-grained.

- **Application components are deployed onto technology components**

  An application component is implemented by a suite of technology components. For example, an application, such as "HR System" would typically be implemented on several technology components, including hardware, application server software, and application services.

Figure 34-2 illustrates the core entities and their relationships.

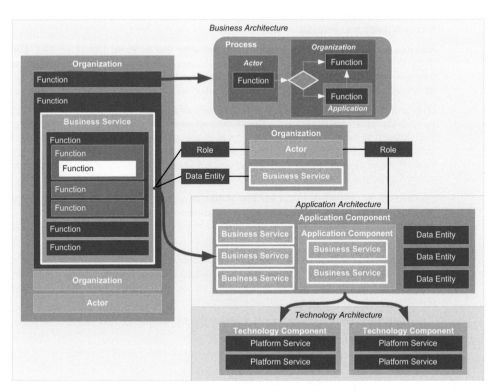

Figure 34-2 Core Entities and their Relationships

Catalog, Matrix, and Diagram Concept

The content metamodel is used as a technique to structure architectural information in an ordered way so that it can be processed to meet the stakeholder needs. The majority of architecture stakeholders do not actually need to know what the architecture metamodel is and are only concerned with specific issues, such as "what functionality does this application support?", "which processes will be impacted by this project?", etc. In order to meet the needs of these stakeholders, the TOGAF concepts of building blocks, catalogs, matrices, and diagrams are used.

Building blocks are objects of a particular type within the metamodel (for example, a business service called "Purchase Order"). Building blocks carry metadata according to the metamodel, which supports query and analysis. For example, business services have a metadata attribute for owner, which allows a stakeholder to query all business services owned by a particular organization. Building blocks may also include dependent or contained objects as appropriate to the context of the architecture (for example, a business service called "Purchase Order" may implicitly include a number of processes, data entities, application components, etc).

Catalogs are lists of building blocks of a specific type, or of related types, that are used for governance or reference purposes (for example, an organization chart, showing locations and actors). As with building blocks, catalogs carry metadata according to the metamodel, which supports query and analysis.

Matrices are grids that show relationships between two or more model entities. Matrices are used to represent relationships that are list-based rather than graphical in their usage (for example, a CRUD matrix showing which applications Create, Read, Update, and Delete a particular type of data is difficult to represent visually).

Diagrams are renderings of architectural content in a graphical format to allow stakeholders to retrieve the required information. Diagrams can also be used as a technique for graphically populating architecture content or for checking the completeness of information that has been collected. TOGAF defines a set of architecture diagrams to be created (e.g., organization chart). Each of these diagrams may be created several times for an architecture with different style or content coverage to suit stakeholder concerns.

Building blocks, catalogs, matrices, and diagrams are all concepts that are well supported by leading enterprise architecture tools. In environments where tools are used to model the architecture, such tools typically support mechanisms to search, filter, and query the Architecture Repository.

On-demand querying of the Architecture Repository (such as the business service ownership example mentioned above) can be used to generate *ad hoc* catalogs, matrices, and diagrams of the architecture. As this type of query is by nature required to be flexible, it is therefore not restricted or defined within the content metamodel.

The interactions between metamodel, building blocks, diagrams, and stakeholders are shown in Figure 34-3.

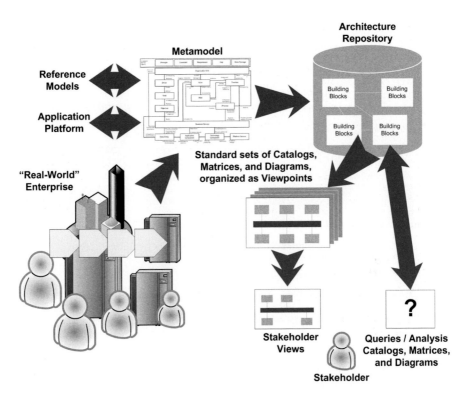

Figure 34-3 Interactions between Metamodel, Building Blocks, Diagrams, and Stakeholders

34.2.2 Overview of the Content Metamodel

The content metamodel defines a set of entities that allow architectural concepts to be captured, stored, filtered, queried, and represented in a way that supports consistency, completeness, and traceability.

At the highest level, the content framework is divided up in line with the TOGAF ADM phases, as shown in Figure 34-4.

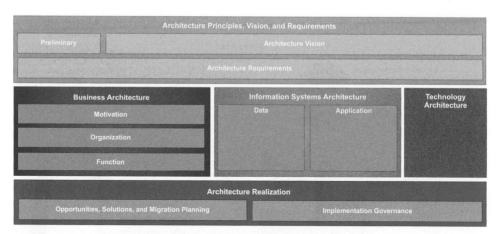

Figure 34-4 Content Framework by ADM Phases

- **Architecture Principles, Vision, and Requirements** artifacts are intended to capture the surrounding context of formal architecture models, including general architecture principles, strategic context that forms input for architecture modeling, and requirements generated from the architecture. The architecture context is typically collected in the Preliminary and Architecture Vision phases.

- **Business Architecture** artifacts capture architectural models of business operation, looking specifically at factors that motivate the enterprise, how the enterprise is organizationally structured, and also what functional capabilities the enterprise has.

- **Information Systems Architecture** artifacts capture architecture models of IT systems, looking at applications and data in line with the TOGAF ADM phases.

- **Technology Architecture** artifacts capture procured technology assets that are used to implement and realize information system solutions.

- **Architecture Realization** artifacts capture change roadmaps showing transition between architecture states and binding statements that are used to steer and govern an implementation of the architecture.

A more detailed representation of the content metamodel is shown in Figure 34-5.

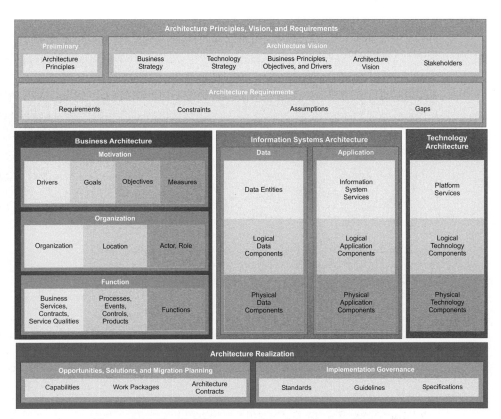

Figure 34-5 Detailed Representation of the Content Metamodel

34.3   Content Metamodel in Detail

This section contains the following subsections:

- Core Content Metamodel (see Section 34.3.1) describes the metamodel entities that form the core content metamodel.

- Core Architecture Artifacts (see Section 34.3.2) lists the set of artifacts intended to accompany the core content metamodel.

- Full Content Metamodel (see Section 34.3.3) describes the metamodel entities that form extensions to the content metamodel.

34.3.1 Core Content Metamodel

Figure 34-6 shows the metamodel entities and relationships that are present within the core content metamodel.

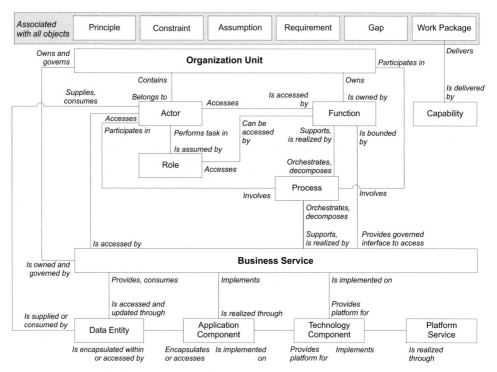

Figure 34-6 Entities and Relationships Present within the Core Content Metamodel

34.3.2 Core Architecture Artifacts

Chapter 35 discusses in detail the way in which the underlying content metamodel can be used to present a set of catalogs, matrices, and diagrams to address stakeholder concerns.

The following set of artifacts are intended to accompany the core content metamodel:

ADM Phase	Artifacts
Preliminary	Principles Catalog
Architecture Vision	Stakeholder Map Matrix Value Chain Diagram Solution Concept Diagram
Business Architecture	Organization/Actor Catalog

ADM Phase	Artifacts
	Role Catalog Business Service/Function Catalog Business Interaction Matrix Actor/Role Matrix Business Footprint Diagram Business Service/Information Diagram Functional Decomposition Diagram Product Lifecycle Diagram
Information Systems (Data Architecture)	Data Entity/Data Component Catalog Data Entity/Business Function Matrix System/Data Matrix Class Diagram Data Dissemination Diagram
Information Systems (Application Architecture)	Application Portfolio Catalog Interface Catalog System/Organization Matrix Role/System Matrix System/Function Matrix Application Interaction Matrix Application Communication Diagram Application and User Location Diagram System Use-Case Diagram
Technology Architecture	Technology Standards Catalog Technology Portfolio Catalog System/Technology Matrix Environments and Locations Diagram Platform Decomposition Diagram
Opportunities and Solutions	Project Context Diagram Benefits Diagram
Requirements Management	Requirements Catalog

34.3.3 Full Content Metamodel

When all extensions are applied to the core content metamodel, a number of new metamodel entities are introduced. Figure 34-7 shows which entities are contained in the core content metamodel and which new entities are introduced by which extension.

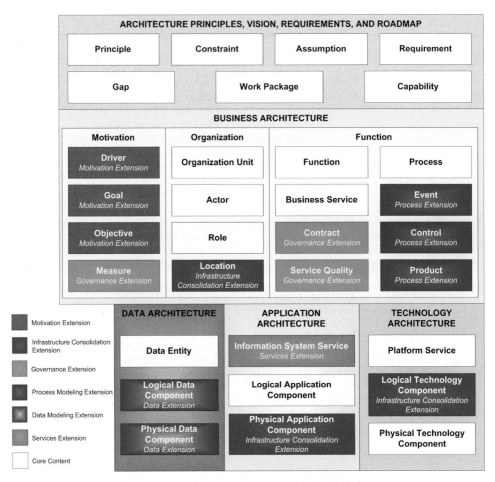

Figure 34-7 Content Metamodel with Extensions

The relationships between entities in the full metamodel are shown in Figure 34-8.

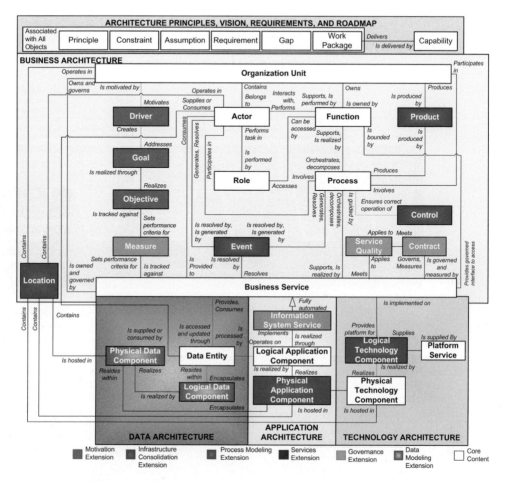

Figure 34-8 Relationships between Entities in the Full Metamodel

34.4   Content Metamodel Extensions

As discussed earlier, the TOGAF content metamodel supports a number of extension modules that allow more in-depth consideration for particular architecture concerns. Figure 34-9 shows the core content metamodel and predefined extension modules.

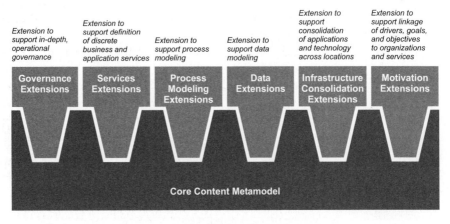

Figure 34-9 Core Content Metamodel and Predefined Extension Modules

During the Architecture Vision phase of a particular engagement, the scope of the engagement will be used to make a determination on appropriate extensions to be employed in order to adequately address the architecture requirements. For example, the scope of an engagement could be defined as core content, plus the governance extensions, as shown in Figure 34-10.

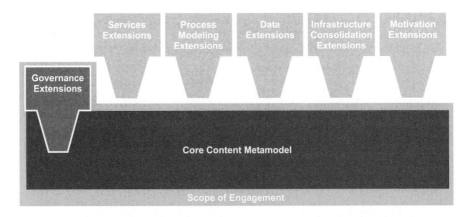

Figure 34-10 Core Content with Governance Extensions

The following sections provide a more detailed description of the purpose and content of each of the extension modules.

34.4.1 Governance Extensions

Purpose

The governance extension is intended to allow additional structured data to be held against objectives and business services, supporting operational governance of the landscape.

The scope of this extension is as follows:

- The ability to apply measures to objectives and then link those measures to services
- The ability to apply contracts to service communication or service interactions with external users and systems
- The ability to define re-usable service qualities defining a service-level profile that can be used in contracts
- Creation of additional diagrams to show ownership and management of systems

This extension should be used in the following situations:

- When an organization is considering IT change that will result in a significant impact to existing operational governance models
- When an organization has granular requirements for service levels that differ from service to service
- When an organization is looking to transform its operational governance practice
- When an organization has very strong focus on business drivers, goals, and objectives and how these trace to service levels

The benefits of using this extension are as follows:

- Service levels are defined in a more structured way, with:
  — More detail
  — The ability to re-use service profiles across contracts
  — Stronger tracing to business objectives
- Impacts to operations and operational governance models are considered in a more structured way, with:
  — Additional diagrams of system and data ownership
  — Additional diagrams of system operation and dependencies on operations processes

In addition to the extensions described here, organizations wishing to focus on architecture governance should also consult:

- The COBIT framework for IT governance provided by the Information Systems Audit and Control Association (ISACA); refer to www.isaca.org
- The IT Portfolio Management Facility (ITPMF) from the OMG; refer to http://www.omg.org/docs/bei/04-06-07.pdf

Required Changes to the Metamodel

Changes to the metamodel entities and relationships are shown in Figure 34-11.

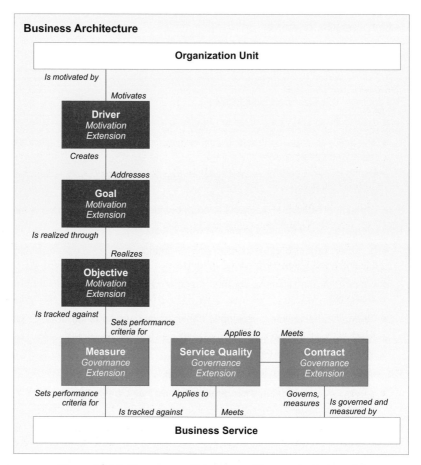

Figure 34-11 Governance Extensions: Changes to Metamodel

Changes to the metamodel entities and relationships are as follows:

- Measure is added as a new entity that links objective and business service.

- Service Quality is added as a new entity that provides a generic service profile template to be applied to business services or contracts.

- Contract is added as a new entity that formalizes the functional and non-functional characteristics of a service interaction with other services, external applications, or users.

Changes to the metamodel attributes are as follows:

■ Attributes are added for the new metamodel entities of Measure, Service Quality, and Service Contract

Additional diagrams to be created are as follows:

■ Enterprise Manageability diagram

34.4.2 Services Extensions

Purpose

The services extension is intended to allow more sophisticated modeling of the service portfolio by creating a concept of IS services in addition to the core concept of business services. IS services are directly supported by applications and creating the layer of abstraction relaxes the constraints on business services whilst simultaneously allowing technical stakeholders to put more formality into an IS service catalog.

The scope of this extension is as follows:

■ Creation of IS services as an extension of business service

This extension should be used in the following situations:

■ When the business has a preset definition of its services that does not align well to technical and architectural needs

■ When business and IT use different language to describe similar capabilities

■ Where IT service is misaligned with business need, particularly around the areas of quality of service, visibility of performance, and management granularity

■ Where IT is taking initial steps to engage business in discussions about IT architecture

The benefits of using this extension are as follows:

■ Business services can be defined outside of the constraints that exist in the core metamodel. This allows for a more natural engagement with business stakeholders.

■ IS services can be defined according to a model that maps closely to implementation, providing a more realistic solution abstraction to support IT decision-making.

■ Business and IS service relationships show where the business view aligns with the IS view and where there are misalignments.

In addition to the extensions described here, organizations wishing to focus on services-centric architectures should also consult:

■ The Service Component Architecture (SCA) specification developed by the Open Service Oriented Architecture (OSOA) collaboration; refer to www.osoa.org/display/Main/Service+Component+Architecture+Home

■ The Service Data Objects (SDO) specification developed by the Open Service Oriented Architecture (OSOA) collaboration; refer to www.osoa.org/display/Main/Service+Data+Objects+Home

■ The IT Infrastructure Library (ITIL); refer to www.itil-officialsite.com/home/home.asp

Required Changes to the Metamodel

Changes to the metamodel entities and relationships are shown in Figure 34-12.

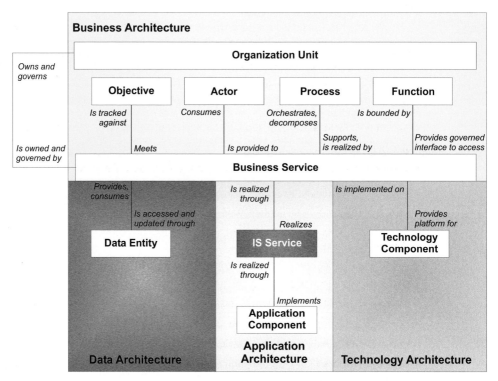

Figure 34-12 Services Extension: Changes to Metamodel

Changes to the metamodel entities and relationships are as follows:

■ IS Service is added as a new metamodel entity, extending business service.

■ IS Service inherits all the relationships of a business service.

■ A new relationship is created linking an IS service to a business service.

Changes to the metamodel attributes are as follows:

■ IS Service is added as a new type of business service.

Additional diagrams to be created are as follows:

■ Business Use-Case Diagram

- Organization Decomposition Diagram

34.4.3 Process Modeling Extensions

Purpose

The process modeling extension is intended to allow detailed modeling of process flows by adding events, products, and controls to the metamodel. Typically, enterprise architecture does not drill into process flow, but in certain process-centric or event-centric organizations it may be necessary to elaborate process in a much more formal manner using this extension module.

The scope of this extension is as follows:

- Creation of events as triggers for processes
- Creation of controls that business logic and governance gates for process execution
- Creation of products to represent the output of a process
- Creation of event diagrams to track triggers and state changes across the organization

This extension should be used in the following situations:

- Where the architecture must pay specific attention to state and events
- Where the architecture is required to explicitly identify and store process control steps; for example, to support regulatory compliance
- Where the architecture features critical or elaborate process flows

The benefits of using this extension are as follows:

- This extension allows detailed process modeling and the cataloging of process artifacts.
- May be used to support regulatory compliance activities.
- May be used to re-purpose legacy or non-architectural process decomposition analysis.

In addition to the extensions described here, organizations wishing to focus on process-centric architectures should also consult:

- The Business Process Modeling Notation (BPMN) specification, provided by the OMG; refer to www.bpmn.org
- The Software Process Engineering Metamodel (SPEM) specification, provided by the OMG; refer to www.omg.org/technology/documents/formal/spem.htm

Required Changes to the Metamodel

Changes to the metamodel entities and relationships are shown in Figure 34-13.

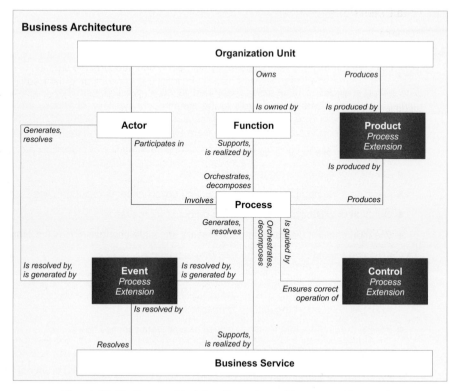

Figure 34-13 Process Modeling Extensions: Changes to Metamodel

Changes to the metamodel entities and relationships are as follows:

- Event is added as a metamodel entity, sitting between Actor, Process, and Service
- Control is added as a metamodel entity, relating to a Process.
- Product is added as a metamodel entity, linking Organization and Processes.

Changes to the metamodel attributes are as follows:

- Attributes are added for the new metamodel entities of Event, Control, and Product.

Additional diagrams to be created are as follows:

- Process Flow diagrams, showing the way in which business functions, events, controls, and products are linked to support a particular business scenario
- Event diagrams, showing events, were they are received from, and what processes they trigger

34.4.4 Data Extensions

Purpose

The data extension is intended to allow more sophisticated modeling and the encapsulation of data. The core model provides a data entity concept which supports the creation of data models, which is then extended by this extension to include the concept of a data component. Data components form a logical or physical encapsulation of abstract data entities into units that can be governed and deployed into applications.

The scope of this extension is as follows:

- Creation of logical data components that group data entities into encapsulated modules for governance, security, and deployment purposes
- Creation of physical data components that implement logical data components and are analogous to databases, registries, repositories, schemas, and other techniques of segmenting data
- Creation of data lifecycle, data security, and data migration diagrams of the architecture to show data concerns in more detail

This extension should be used in the following situations:

- Where the architecture features significant complexity and risk around the location, encapsulation, and management of or access to data

The benefits of using this extension are as follows:

- The structure of data is modeled independently from its location, allowing data models to be developed that span multiple systems without being tied to physical concerns.
- Logical groupings of data can be used to set governance, security, or deployment boundaries around data, providing a much more holistic appreciation of data issues surrounding the architecture.

Required Changes to the Metamodel

Changes to the metamodel entities and relationships are shown in Figure 34-14.

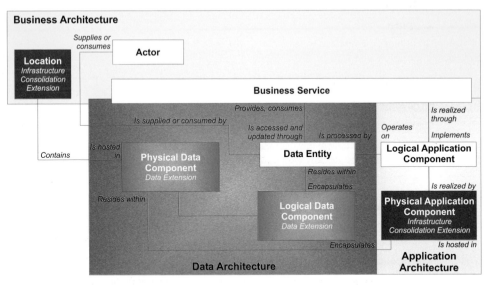

Figure 34-14 Data Extensions: Changes to Metamodel

Changes to the metamodel entities and relationships are as follows:

- Logical Data Component is added as a new metamodel entity, encapsulating data entities.
- Physical Data Component is added as a new metamodel entity, extending Logical Data Component.
- A relationship is created between Physical Data Component and Application Component. If the infrastructure consolidation extension is applied, this should be to Physical Application Component.
- If the infrastructure consolidation extension is applied, Physical Data Components will have a relationship with Location.

Changes to the metamodel attributes are as follows:

- Attributes are added for the new metamodel entities of Logical Data Component and Physical Data Component.

Additional diagrams to be created are as follows:

- Data Security diagram
- Class Hierarchy diagram
- Data Migration diagram
- Data Lifecycle diagram

34.4.5 Infrastructure Consolidation Extensions

Purpose

The infrastructure consolidation extension is intended to be used in landscapes where the application and technology portfolios have become fragmented and the architecture seeks to consolidate the business as usual capability into a smaller number of locations, applications, or technology components.

The scope of this extension is as follows:

- Creation of a location entity to hold the location of IT assets and external consumers of service

- Creation of logical and physical application components to abstract the capability of an application away from the actual applications in existence

- Creation of logical and physical application components to abstract product type from the actual technology products in existence

- Creation of additional diagrams focusing on the location of assets, compliance with standards, structure of applications, application migration, and infrastructure configuration

This extension should be used in the following situations:

- Where many technology products are in place with duplicate or overlapping capability

- Where many applications are in place with duplicate or overlapping functionality

- Where applications are geographically dispersed and the decision logic for determining the location of an application is not well understood

- When applications are going to be migrated into a consolidated platform

- When application features are going to be migrated into a consolidated application

The benefits of using this extension are as follows:

- Allows visibility and analysis of redundant duplication of capability in the application and technology domains

- Supports analysis of standards compliance

- Supports analysis of migration impact of application or technology consolidation

- Supports detailed architectural definition of application structure

In addition to the extensions described here, organizations wishing to focus on infrastructure consolidation should also consult:

- The Unified Modeling Language (UML), provided by the OMG; refer to www.uml.org

- The Systems Modeling Language (SysML) — www.sysml.org — which reduces the complexity and software engineering focus of UML for the purposes of systems modeling

- The IT Portfolio Management Facility (ITPMF) from the OMG; refer to www.omg.org/docs/bei/04-06-07.pdf

Required Changes to the Metamodel

Changes to the metamodel entities and relationships are shown in Figure 34-15.

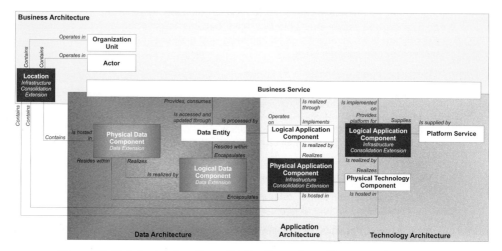

Figure 34-15 Infrastructure Consolidation Extensions: Changes to Metamodel

Changes to the metamodel entities and relationships are as follows:

- Location attributes on Organization, Actor, Application Component, Data Component, and Technology Component are enhanced to create a location entity within the metamodel.
- Application Components are extended to include Logical Application Components (a class of application) and Physical Application Components (an actual application).
- Technology Components are extended to include Logical Technology Components (a class of technology product) and Physical Technology Components (an actual technology product).

Changes to the metamodel attributes are as follows:

- Creation of attributes for the new Metamodel entities of Logical Application Component, Physical Application Component, Logical Technology Component, Physical Technology Component, and Location
- Removal of Location as an attribute of entities that have a location and replacement with a relationship with the Location entity

Additional diagrams to be created are as follows:

- Process/System Realization diagram
- Software Engineering diagram
- Application Migration diagram

- Software Distribution diagram
- Processing diagram
- Networked Computing/Hardware diagram
- Communications Engineering diagram

34.4.6 Motivation Extensions

Purpose

The motivation extension is intended to allow additional structured modeling of the drivers, goals, and objectives that influence an organization to provide business services to its customers. This in turn allows more effective definition of service contracts and better measurement of business performance.

The scope of this extension is as follows:

- Creation of a new metamodel entity for Driver that shows factors generally motivating or constraining an organization
- Creation of a new metamodel entity for Goal that shows the strategic purpose and mission of an organization
- Creation of a new metamodel entity for Objective that shows near to mid-term achievements that an organization would like to attain
- Creation of a Goal/Objective/Service diagram showing the traceability from drivers, goals, and objectives through to services

This extension should be used in the following situations:

- When the architecture needs to understand the motivation of organizations in more detail than the standard business or engagement principles and objectives that are informally modeled within the core content metamodel
- When organizations have conflicting drivers and objectives and that conflict needs to be understood and addressed in a structured form
- When service levels are unknown or unclear

The benefits of using this extension are as follows:

- Highlights misalignment of priorities across the enterprise and how these intersect with shared services (e.g., some organizations may be attempting to reduce costs, while others are attempting to increase capability)
- Shows competing demands for business services in a more structured fashion, allowing compromise service levels to be defined

In addition to the extensions described here, organizations wishing to focus on architecture modeling of business motivation should also consult:

- The Business Motivation Model (BMM) specification, provided by the OMG; refer to www.omg.org/technology/documents/bms_spec_catalog.htm

Required Changes to the Metamodel

Changes to the metamodel entities and relationships are shown in Figure 34-16.

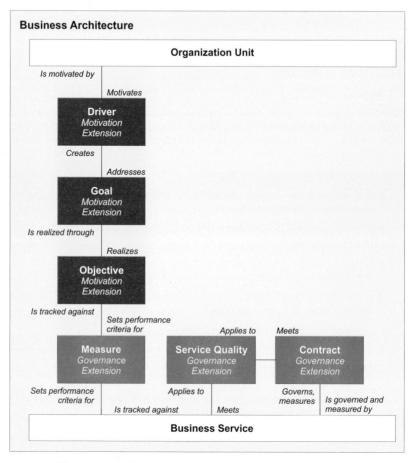

Figure 34-16 Motivation Extensions: Changes to Metamodel

Changes to the metamodel entities and relationships are as follows:

- Driver, Goal, and Objective are added as new entities that link Organization Unit to Business Service.

Changes to the metamodel attributes are as follows:

- Attributes are added for the new metamodel entities of Driver, Goal, and Objective.

Additional diagrams to be created are as follows:

- Goal/Objective/Service diagram

34.5   Content Metamodel Objects

The following table lists and describes the objects within the content metamodel.

Metamodel Object	Description
Actor	A person, organization, or system that has a role that initiates or interacts with activities; for example, a sales representative who travels to visit customers. Actors may be internal or external to an organization. In the automotive industry, an original equipment manufacturer would be considered an actor by an automotive dealership that interacts with its supply chain activities.
Application Component	An encapsulation of application functionality aligned to implementation structure. For example, a purchase request processing application. See also *Logical Application Component* and *Physical Application Component.*
Assumption	A statement of probable fact that has not been fully validated at this stage, due to external constraints. For example, it may be assumed that an existing application will support a certain set of functional requirements, although those requirements may not yet have been individually validated.
Business Service	Supports business capabilities through an explicitly defined interface and is explicitly governed by an organization.
Capability	A business-focused outcome that is delivered by the completion of one or more work packages. Using a capability-based planning approach, change activities can be sequenced and grouped in order to provide continuous and incremental business value.
Constraint	An external factor that prevents an organization from pursuing particular approaches to meet its goals. For example, customer data is not harmonized within the organization, regionally or nationally, constraining the organization's ability to offer effective customer service.
Contract	An agreement between a service consumer and a service provider that establishes functional and non-functional parameters for interaction.
Control	A decision-making step with accompanying decision logic used to determine execution approach for a process or to ensure that a process complies with governance criteria. For example, a sign-off control on the purchase request processing process that checks whether the total value of the request is within the sign-off limits of the requester, or whether it needs escalating to higher authority.

Metamodel Object	Description
Data Entity	An encapsulation of data that is recognized by a business domain expert as a thing. Logical data entities can be tied to applications, repositories, and services and may be structured according to implementation considerations.
Driver	An external or internal condition that motivates the organization to define its goals. An example of an external driver is a change in regulation or compliance rules which, for example, require changes to the way an organization operates; i.e., Sarbanes-Oxley in the US.
Event	An organizational state change that triggers processing events; may originate from inside or outside the organization and may be resolved inside or outside the organization.
Function	Delivers business capabilities closely aligned to an organization, but not necessarily explicitly governed by the organization. Also referred to as "business function".
Gap	A statement of difference between two states. Used in the context of gap analysis, where the difference between the Baseline and Target Architecture is identified. **Note:** Gap analysis is described in Part III, Chapter 27.
Goal	A high-level statement of intent or direction for an organization. Typically used to measure success of an organization.
Information System Service	The automated elements of a business service. An information system service may deliver or support part or all of one or more business services.
Location	A place where business activity takes place and can be hierarchically decomposed.
Logical Application Component	An encapsulation of application functionality that is independent of a particular implementation. For example, the classification of all purchase request processing applications implemented in an enterprise.
Logical Data Component	A boundary zone that encapsulates related data entities to form a logical location to be held; for example, external procurement information.
Logical Technology Component	An encapsulation of technology infrastructure that is independent of a particular product. A class of technology product; for example, supply chain management software as part of an Enterprise Resource Planning (ERP) suite, or a Commercial Off-The-Shelf (COTS) purchase request processing enterprise service.
Measure	An indicator or factor that can be tracked, usually on an ongoing basis, to determine success or alignment with objectives and goals.
Objective	A time-bounded milestone for an organization used to demonstrate progress towards a goal; for example, "Increase capacity utilization by 30% by the end of 2009 to support the planned increase in market share".

Metamodel Object	Description
Organization Unit	A self-contained unit of resources with line management responsibility, goals, objectives, and measures. Organizations may include external parties and business partner organizations.
Physical Application Component	An application, application module, application service, or other deployable component of functionality. For example, a configured and deployed instance of a Commercial Off-The-Shelf (COTS) Enterprise Resource Planning (ERP) supply chain management application.
Physical Data Component	A boundary zone that encapsulates related data entities to form a physical location to be held. For example, a purchase order business object, comprising purchase order header and item business object nodes.
Physical Technology Component	A specific technology infrastructure product or technology infrastructure product instance. For example, a particular product version of a Commercial Off-The-Shelf (COTS) solution, or a specific brand and version of server.
Platform Service	A technical capability required to provide enabling infrastructure that supports the delivery of applications.
Principle	A qualitative statement of intent that should be met by the architecture. Has at least a supporting rationale and a measure of importance. **Note:** A sample set of architecture principles is defined in Part III, Chapter 23.
Process	A process represents flow of control between or within functions and/or services (depends on the granularity of definition). Processes represent a sequence of activities that together achieve a specified outcome, can be decomposed into sub-processes, and can show operation of a function or service (at next level of detail). Processes may also be used to link or compose organizations, functions, services, and processes.
Product	Output generated by the business. The business product of the execution of a process.
Requirement	A quantitative statement of business need that must be met by a particular architecture or work package.
Role	The usual or expected function of an actor, or the part somebody or something plays in a particular action or event. An actor may have a number of roles. See also *Actor*.
Service	An element of behavior that provides specific functionality in response to requests from actors or other services. A service delivers or supports business capabilities, has an explicitly defined interface, and is explicitly governed. Services are defined for business, information systems, and platforms.

Metamodel Object	Description
Service Quality	A preset configuration of non-functional attributes that may be assigned to a service or service contract.
Technology Component	An encapsulation of technology infrastructure that represents a class of technology product or specific technology product.
Work Package	A set of actions identified to achieve one or more objectives for the business. A work package can be a part of a project, a complete project, or a program.

34.6 Content Metamodel Attributes

The following table shows typical attributes for each of the metamodel objects described previously.

Metamodel Object	Metamodel Attribute	Description
All Metamodel Objects	ID	Unique identifier for the architecture object.
	Name	Brief name of the architecture object.
	Description	Textual description of the architecture object.
	Category	User-definable categorization taxonomy for each metamodel object.
	Source	Location from where the information was collected.
	Owner	Owner of the architecture object.
Capability	Business value	Describes how this capability provides value to the enterprise.
	Increments	Lists possible maturity/quality levels for the capability.
Constraint	No additional attributes	This metamodel object has only basic attributes.
Gap	No additional attributes	This metamodel object has only basic attributes.

Metamodel Object	Metamodel Attribute	Description
Location	Category	The following categories of Location apply: Region (applies to a grouping of countries or territory; e.g., South East Asia, UK, and Ireland), Country (applies to a single country; e.g., US), and Building (applies to a site of operation; where several offices are collected in a single city, this category may represent a city), Specific Location (applies to any specific location within a building, such as a server room).
Principle	Category	The following categories of principle apply: Guiding Principle, Business Principle, Data Principle, Application Principle, Integration Principle, Technology Principle.
	Priority	Priority of this principle relative to other principles.
	Statement of principle	Statement of what the principle is.
	Rationale	Statement of why the principle is required and the outcome to be reached.
	Implication	Statement of what the principle means in practical terms.
	Metric	Identifies mechanisms that will be used to measure whether the principle has been met or not.
Requirement	Statement of requirement	Statement of what the requirement is, including a definition of whether the requirement shall be met, should be met, or may be met.
	Rationale	Statement of why the requirement exists.
	Acceptance criteria	Statement of what tests will be carried out to ensure that the requirement will be met.
Actor	# FTEs	Estimated number of FTEs that operate as this Actor.
	Actor goal	Objectives that this actor has, in general terms.
	Actor tasks	Tasks that this actor performs, in general terms.

Metamodel Object	Metamodel Attribute	Description
Business Service	Standards class	Non-Standard, Proposed Standard, Provisional Standard, Standard, Phasing-Out Standard, Retired Standard.
	Standard creation date	If the product is a standard, when the standard was created.
	Last standard review date	Last date that the standard was reviewed.
	Next standard review date	Next date for the standard to be reviewed.
	Retire date	Date when the standard was/will be retired.
Contract	Behavior characteristics	Functional behavior to be supported within the scope of the contract.
	Service name "caller"	Consuming service.
	Service name "called"	Providing service.
	Service quality characteristics	Non-functional behavior to be supported within the scope of the contract
	Availability characteristics	Degree to which something is available for use.
	Service times	Hours during which the service must be available.
	Manageability characteristics	Ability to gather information about the state of something and control it.
	Serviceability characteristics	Ability to identify problems and take corrective action, such as to repair or upgrade a component in a running system.
	Performance characteristics	Ability of a component to perform its tasks in an appropriate time.
	Response requirements	Response times that the service provider must meet for particular operations.
	Reliability characteristics	Resistance to failure.
	Quality of information required	Contracted requirements on accuracy and completeness of information.
	Contract control requirements	Level of governance and enforcement applied to the contractual parameters for overall service.
	Result control requirements	Measures in place to ensure that each service request meets contracted criteria.

Metamodel Object	Metamodel Attribute	Description
	Recoverability characteristics	Ability to restore a system to a working state after an interruption.
	Locatability characteristics	Ability of a system to be found when needed.
	Security characteristics	Ability of a system to prevent unauthorized access to functions and data.
	Privacy characteristics	Protection of data from unauthorized access.
	Integrity characteristics	Ability of a system to ensure that data has not been corrupted.
	Credibility characteristics	Ability of a system to ensure that the service request originates from an authorized source.
	Localization characteristics	Ability of a service to support localized variants for different consumer groups.
	Internationalization characteristics	Ability of a service to support international variations in business logic and data representation (such as character set).
	Interoperability characteristics	Ability of the service to interoperate with different technical environments, inside and outside of the organization.
	Scalability characteristics	Ability of the service to grow or shrink its performance or capacity appropriately to the demands of the environment in which it operates.
	Portability characteristics	Of data, people, applications, and components.
	Extensibility characteristics	Ability to accept new functionality.
	Capacity characteristics	Contracted capacity of the service provider to meet requests.
	Throughput	Required throughput capacity.
	Throughput period	Time period needed to deliver throughput capacity.
	Growth	Expected future growth rate of service request.
	Growth period	Time period needed to reach the expected growth rate.

Metamodel Object	Metamodel Attribute	Description
	Peak profile short term	Short-term profile of peak service traffic.
	Peak profile long term	Long-term profile of peak service traffic.
Control	No additional attributes	This metamodel object has only basic attributes.
Driver	No additional attributes	This metamodel object has only basic attributes.
Event	No additional attributes	This metamodel object has only basic attributes.
Function	Standards class	Non-Standard, Proposed Standard, Provisional Standard, Standard, Phasing-Out Standard, Retired Standard.
	Standard creation date	If the product is a standard, when the standard was created.
	Last standard review date	Last date that the standard was reviewed.
	Next standard review date	Next date for the standard to be reviewed.
	Retire date	Date when the standard was/will be retired.
Goal	No additional attributes	This metamodel object has only basic attributes.
Measure	No additional attributes	This metamodel object has only basic attributes.
Objective	No additional attributes	This metamodel object has only basic attributes.
Organization Unit	Headcount	Number of FTEs working within the organization.
Process	Standards class	Non-Standard, Proposed Standard, Provisional Standard, Standard, Phasing-Out Standard, Retired Standard.
	Standard creation date	If the product is a standard, when the standard was created.
	Last standard review date	Last date that the standard was reviewed.
	Next standard review date	Next date for the standard to be reviewed.
	Retire date	Date when the standard was/will be retired.
	Process criticality	Criticality of this process to business operations.
	Manual or automated	Whether this process is supported by IT or is a manual process.

Metamodel Object	Metamodel Attribute	Description
	Process volumetrics	Data on frequency of process execution.
Product	No additional attributes	This metamodel object has only basic attributes.
Role	Estimated number of FTEs that operate in this Role	This metamodel object has only basic attributes.
Service Quality	No additional attributes	This metamodel object has only basic attributes.
Service	Standards class	Non-Standard, Proposed Standard, Provisional Standard, Standard, Phasing-Out Standard, Retired Standard.
	Standard creation date	If the product is a standard, when the standard was created.
	Last standard review date	Last date that the standard was reviewed.
	Next standard review date	Next date for the standard to be reviewed.
	Retire date	Date when the standard was/will be retired.
Application Component	Standards class	Non-Standard, Proposed Standard, Provisional Standard, Standard, Phasing-Out Standard, Retired Standard.
	Standard creation date	If the product is a standard, when the standard was created.
	Last standard review date	Last date that the standard was reviewed.
	Next standard review date	Next date for the standard to be reviewed.
	Retire date	Date when the standard was/will be retired.
Information System Service	Standards class	Non-Standard, Proposed Standard, Provisional Standard, Standard, Phasing-Out Standard, Retired Standard.
	Standard creation date	If the product is a standard, when the standard was created.
	Last standard review date	Last date that the standard was reviewed.
	Next standard review date	Next date for the standard to be reviewed.
	Retire date	Date when the standard was/will be retired.

Metamodel Object	Metamodel Attribute	Description
Logical Application Component	Standards class	Non-Standard, Proposed Standard, Provisional Standard, Standard, Phasing-Out Standard, Retired Standard.
	Standard creation date	If the product is a standard, when the standard was created.
	Last standard review date	Last date that the standard was reviewed.
	Next standard review date	Next date for the standard to be reviewed.
	Retire date	Date when the standard was/will be retired.
Physical Application Component	Lifecycle status	Proposed, In Development, Live, Phasing Out, Retired.
	Standards class	Non-Standard, Proposed Standard, Provisional Standard, Standard, Phasing-Out Standard, Retired Standard.
	Standard creation date	If the product is a standard, when the standard was created.
	Last standard review date	Last date that the standard was reviewed.
	Next standard review date	Next date for the standard to be reviewed.
	Retire date	Date when the standard was/will be retired.
	Initial live date	Date when the first release of the application was/will be released into production.
	Date of last release	Date when the last release of the application was released into production.
	Date of next release	Date when the next release of the application will be released into production.
	Retirement date	Date when the application was/will be retired.
	Availability characteristics	Degree to which something is available for use.
	Service times	Hours during which the application must be available.
	Manageability characteristics	Ability to gather information about the state of something and control it.
	Serviceability characteristics	Ability to identify problems and take corrective action, such as to repair or upgrade a component in a running system.

Metamodel Object	Metamodel Attribute	Description
	Performance characteristics	Ability of a component to perform its tasks in an appropriate time.
	Reliability characteristics	Resistance to failure.
	Recoverability characteristics	Ability to restore a system to a working state after an interruption.
	Locatability characteristics	Ability of a system to be found when needed.
	Security characteristics	Ability of a system to prevent unauthorized access to functions and data.
	Privacy characteristics	Protection of data from unauthorized access.
	Integrity characteristics	Ability of a system to ensure that data has not been corrupted.
	Credibility characteristics	Ability of a system to ensure that the service request originates from an authorized source.
	Localization characteristics	Ability of a service to support localized variants for different consumer groups.
	Internationalization characteristics	Ability of a service to support international variations in business logic and data representation (such as character set).
	Interoperability characteristics	Ability of the service to interoperate with different technical environments, inside and outside of the organization.
	Scalability characteristics	Ability of the service to grow or shrink its performance or capacity appropriately to the demands of the environment in which it operates.
	Portability characteristics	Of data, people, applications, and components.
	Extensibility characteristics	Ability to accept new functionality.
	Capacity characteristics	Contracted capacity of the service provider to meet requests.
	Throughput	Required throughput capacity.
	Throughput period	Time period needed to deliver throughput capacity.

Metamodel Object	Metamodel Attribute	Description
	Growth	Expected future growth rate of service request.
	Growth period	Time period needed to reach the expected growth rate.
	Peak profile short term	Short-term profile of peak service traffic.
	Peak profile long term	Long-term profile of peak service traffic.
Data Entity	Category	The following categories of data entity apply: Message, Internally Stored Entity.
	Privacy classification	Level of restriction placed on access to the data.
	Retention classification	Level of retention to be placed on the data.
Logical Data Component	Standards class	Non-Standard, Proposed Standard, Provisional Standard, Standard, Phasing-Out Standard, Retired Standard.
	Standard creation date	If the product is a standard, when the standard was created.
	Last standard review date	Last date that the standard was reviewed.
	Next standard review date	Next date for the standard to be reviewed.
	Retire date	Date when the standard was/will be retired.
Physical Data Component	Standards class	Non-Standard, Proposed Standard, Provisional Standard, Standard, Phasing-Out Standard, Retired Standard.
	Standard creation date	If the product is a standard, when the standard was created.
	Last standard review date	Last date that the standard was reviewed.
	Next standard review date	Next date for the standard to be reviewed.
	Retire date	Date when the standard was/will be retired.
Logical Technology Component	Standards class	Non-Standard, Proposed Standard, Provisional Standard, Standard, Phasing-Out Standard, Retired Standard.
	Standard creation date	If the product is a standard, when the standard was created.
	Last standard review date	Last date that the standard was reviewed.

Metamodel Object	Metamodel Attribute	Description
	Next standard review date	Next date for the standard to be reviewed.
	Retire date	Date when the standard was/will be retired.
	Category	Logical Technology Components are categorized according to the TOGAF TRM, which may be extended to meet the needs of an individual organization.
Physical Technology Component	Standards class	Non-Standard, Proposed Standard, Provisional Standard, Standard, Phasing-Out Standard, Retired Standard.
	Standard creation date	If the product is a standard, when the standard was created.
	Last standard review date	Last date that the standard was reviewed.
	Next standard review date	Next date for the standard to be reviewed.
	Retire date	Date when the standard was/will be retired.
	Category	Physical Technology Components are categorized according to the TOGAF TRM, which may be extended to meet the needs of an individual organization.
	Product name	Name of the product making up the technology component.
	Module name	Module, or other sub-product, name making up the technology component.
	Vendor	Vendor providing the technology component.
	Version	Version of the product making up the technology component.
Platform Service	Standards class	Non-Standard, Proposed Standard, Provisional Standard, Standard, Phasing-Out Standard, Retired Standard.
	Category	Platform Services are categorized according to the TOGAF TRM, which may be extended to meet the needs of an individual organization.

Metamodel Object	Metamodel Attribute	Description
Technology Component	Standards class	Non-Standard, Proposed Standard, Provisional Standard, Standard, Phasing-Out Standard, Retired Standard.
Work Package	Category	The following categories of work package apply: Work Package, Work Stream, Project, Program, Portfolio.
	Capability delivered	Describes the contribution this work package makes to capability delivery.

34.7 Metamodel Relationships

Source Object	Target Object	Name	Extension Module
Actor	Event	Generates	Process
Actor	Event	Resolves	Process
Actor	Function	Interacts with	Core
Actor	Function	Performs	Core
Actor	Location	Operates in	Infrastructure Consolidation
Actor	Organization Unit	Belongs to	Core
Actor	Process	Participates in	Core
Actor	Role	Performs task in	Core
Actor	Service	Consumes	Core
Actor	Actor	Decomposes	Core
Actor	Data Entity	Supplies/Consumes	Core
Capability	Work Package	Is delivered by	Core
Contract	Service	Governs and Measures	Governance
Contract	Service Quality	Meets	Governance
Control	Process	Ensures correct operation of	Process
Data Entity	Logical Application Component	Is processed by	Core
Data Entity	Logical Data Component	Resides within	Data
Data Entity	Service	Is accessed and updated through	Core
Data Entity	Data Entity	Decomposes	Core
Data Entity	Data Entity	Relates to	Core
Driver	Goal	Creates	Motivation
Driver	Organization Unit	Motivates	Motivation
Driver	Driver	Decomposes	Motivation

Source Object	Target Object	Name	Extension Module
Event	Actor	Is resolved by	Process
Event	Actor	Is generated by	Process
Event	Process	Is resolved by	Process
Event	Process	Is generated by	Process
Event	Service	Is resolved by	Process
Function	Actor	Supports	Core
Function	Actor	Is performed by	Core
Function	Organization Unit	Is owned by	Core
Function	Process	Supports	Core
Function	Process	Is realized by	Core
Function	Role	Can be accessed by	Core
Function	Service	Is bounded by	Core
Function	Function	Decomposes	Core
Function	Function	Communicates with	Core
Goal	Driver	Addresses	Motivation
Goal	Objective	Is realized through	Motivation
Goal	Goal	Decomposes	Motivation
Location	Actor	Contains	Infrastructure Consolidation
Location	Organization Unit	Contains	Infrastructure Consolidation
Location	Physical Application Component	Contains	Infrastructure Consolidation
Location	Physical Data Component	Contains	Infrastructure Consolidation
Location	Physical Technology Component	Contains	Infrastructure Consolidation
Location	Location	Decomposes	Infrastructure Consolidation
Logical Application Component	Data Entity	Operates on	Core
Logical Application Component	Physical Application Component	Is extended by	Infrastructure Consolidation
Logical Application Component	Service	Implements	Core
Logical Application Component	Logical Application Component	Decomposes	Core
Logical Application Component	Logical Application Component	Communicates with	Core
Logical Data Component	Data Entity	Encapsulates	Data
Logical Data Component	Physical Data Component	Is extended by	Data
Logical Technology Component	Physical Technology Component	Is extended by	Infrastructure Consolidation
Logical Technology Component	Platform Service	Supplies	Core

Source Object	Target Object	Name	Extension Module
Logical Technology Component	Service	Provides platform for	Core
Logical Technology Component	Logical Technology Component	Decomposes	Core
Logical Technology Component	Logical Technology Component	Is dependent on	Core
Measure	Objective	Sets performance criteria for	Governance
Measure	Service	Sets performance criteria for	Governance
Measure	Measure	Decomposes	Governance
Objective	Goal	Realizes	Motivation
Objective	Measure	Is tracked against	Governance
Objective	Objective	Decomposes	Motivation
Organization Unit	Actor	Contains	Core
Organization Unit	Driver	Is motivated by	Core
Organization Unit	Function	Owns	Core
Organization Unit	Location	Operates in	Core
Organization Unit	Product	Produces	Core
Organization Unit	Service	Owns and Governs	Core
Organization Unit	Organization Unit	Decomposes	Core
Physical Application Component	Location	Is hosted in	Infrastructure Consolidation
Physical Application Component	Logical Application Component	Extends	Infrastructure Consolidation
Physical Application Component	Physical Data Component	Encapsulates	Data Modeling
Physical Application Component	Physical Technology Component	Is realized by	Core
Physical Application Component	Physical Application Component	Decomposes	Core
Physical Application Component	Physical Application Component	Communicates with	Core
Physical Data Component	Location	Is hosted in	Infrastructure Consolidation
Physical Data Component	Logical Data Component	Extends	Data
Physical Data Component	Physical Data Component	Decomposes	Core
Physical Data Component	Physical Application Component	Encapsulates	Data Modeling
Physical Technology Component	Location	Is hosted in	Infrastructure Consolidation
Physical Technology Component	Physical Application Component	Realizes	Core
Physical Technology Component	Logical Technology Component	Extends	Infrastructure Consolidation
Physical Technology Component	Physical Technology Component	Decomposes	Core

Source Object	Target Object	Name	Extension Module
Physical Technology Component	Physical Technology Component	Is dependent on	Core
Platform Service	Logical Technology Component	Is supplied by	Core
Process	Actor	Involves	Core
Process	Control	Is guided by	Process
Process	Event	Generates	Process
Process	Event	Resolves	Process
Process	Function	Orchestrates	Core
Process	Function	Decomposes	Core
Process	Product	Produces	Process
Process	Service	Orchestrates	Core
Process	Service	Decomposes	Core
Process	Process	Decomposes	Core
Process	Process	Precedes/Follows	Core
Product	Organization Unit	Is produced by	Process
Product	Process	Is produced by	Process
Role	Actor	Is performed by	Core
Role	Function	Accesses	Core
Role	Role	Decomposes	Core
Service	Actor	Is provided to	Core
Service	Contract	Is governed and measured by	Governance
Service	Data Entity	Provides	Core
Service	Data Entity	Consumes	Core
Service	Event	Resolves	Process
Service	Function	Provides governed interface to access	Core
Service	Logical Application Component	Is realized through	Core
Service	Logical Technology Component	Is implemented on	Core
Service	Measure	Is tracked against	Governance
Service	Organization Unit	Is owned and governed by	Core
Service	Process	Supports	Core
Service	Process	Is realized by	Core
Service	Service Quality	Meets	Governance
Service	Service	Consumes	Core
Service	Service	Decomposes	Core
Service Quality	Contract	Applies to	Governance
Service Quality	Service	Applies to	Governance
Work Package	Capability	Delivers	Core

Chapter 35: Architectural Artifacts

This chapter describes a set of atomic work products that are created when developing an architecture. An artifact represents an individual model of a system or solution, which could potentially be re-used in a variety of contexts. An artifact is distinct from a deliverable, which is a contracted output from a project. In general cases, deliverables will contain artifacts and each artifact may exist in many deliverables.

This chapter discusses the concepts surrounding architecture artifacts and then goes on to discuss the artifacts that are created at each phase within the Architecture Development Method (ADM).

35.1   Basic Concepts

Architectural artifacts are created in order to describe a system, solution, or state of the enterprise. The concepts discussed in this section have been adapted from more formal definitions contained in ISO/IEC 42010:2007 and illustrated in Figure 35-1.[8]

Note: The notation used is from the Unified Modeling Language (UML) specification.

---

8.   Figure 35-1 is reprinted, with permission, from IEEE Std 1471-2000, Systems and Software Engineering — Recommended Practice for Architectural Description of Software-intensive Systems, Copyright© 2000, by IEEE. The IEEE disclaims any responsibility or liability resulting from the placement and use in the described manner.

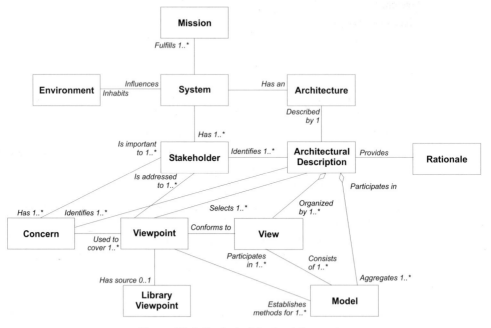

Figure 35-1 Basic Architectural Concepts

A "system" is a collection of components organized to accomplish a specific function or set of functions.

The "architecture" of a system is the system's fundamental organization, embodied in its components, their relationships to each other and to the environment, and the principles guiding its design and evolution.

An "architecture description" is a collection of artifacts that document an architecture. In TOGAF, architecture views are the key artifacts in an architecture description.

"Stakeholders" are people who have key roles in, or concerns about, the system; for example, as users, developers, or managers. Different stakeholders with different roles in the system will have different concerns. Stakeholders can be individuals, teams, or organizations (or classes thereof).

"Concerns" are the key interests that are crucially important to the stakeholders in the system, and determine the acceptability of the system. Concerns may pertain to any aspect of the system's functioning, development, or operation, including considerations such as performance, reliability, security, distribution, and evolvability.

A "view" is a representation of a whole system from the perspective of a related set of concerns.

In capturing or representing the design of a system architecture, the architect will typically create one or more architecture models, possibly using different tools. A view will comprise selected parts of one or more models, chosen so as to demonstrate to a particular stakeholder or group of stakeholders that their concerns are being adequately addressed in the design of the system architecture.

A "viewpoint" defines the perspective from which a view is taken. More specifically, a viewpoint defines: how to construct and use a view (by means of an appropriate schema or template); the information that should appear in the view; the modeling techniques for expressing and analyzing the information; and a rationale for these choices (e.g., by describing the purpose and intended audience of the view).

- A view is what you see. A viewpoint is where you are looking from — the vantage point or perspective that determines what you see.

- Viewpoints are generic, and can be stored in libraries for re-use. A view is always specific to the architecture for which it is created.

- Every view has an associated viewpoint that describes it, at least implicitly. ISO/IEC 42010:2007 encourages architects to define viewpoints explicitly. Making this distinction between the content and schema of a view may seem at first to be an unnecessary overhead, but it provides a mechanism for re-using viewpoints across different architectures.

In summary, then, architecture views are representations of the overall architecture in terms meaningful to stakeholders. They enable the architecture to be communicated to and understood by the stakeholders, so they can verify that the system will address their concerns.

Note: The terms "concern" and "requirement" are not synonymous. A concern is an area of interest. So, system reliability might be a concern/area of interest for some stakeholders. The reason why architects should identify concerns and associate them with viewpoints, is to ensure that those concerns will be addressed in some fashion by the models of the architecture. For example, if the only viewpoint selected by an architect is a structural viewpoint, then reliability concerns are almost certainly not being addressed, since they cannot be represented in a structural model. Within that concern, stakeholders may have many distinct requirements: different classes of users may have very different reliability requirements for different capabilities of the system.

Concerns are the root of the process of decomposition into requirements. Concerns are represented in the architecture by these requirements. Requirements should be SMART (e.g., specific metrics).

35.1.1 Simple Example of a Viewpoint and View

For many architectures, a useful viewpoint is that of business domains, which can be illustrated by an example from The Open Group itself.

The viewpoint is specified as follows:

Viewpoint Element	Description
Stakeholders	Management Board, Chief Executive Officer
Concerns	Show the top-level relationships between geographical sites and business functions.
Modeling technique	Nested boxes diagram. Outer boxes = locations; inner boxes = business functions. Semantics of nesting = functions performed in the locations.

The corresponding view of The Open Group (in 2008) is shown in Figure 35-2.

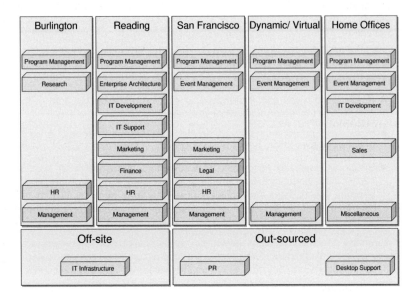

Figure 35-2 Example View — The Open Group Business Domains in 2008

35.2   Developing Views in the ADM

35.2.1   General Guidelines

The choice of which particular architecture views to develop is one of the key decisions that the architect has to make.

The architect has a responsibility for ensuring the completeness (fitness-for-purpose) of the architecture, in terms of adequately addressing all the pertinent concerns of its stakeholders; and the integrity of the architecture, in terms of connecting all the various views to each other, satisfactorily reconciling the conflicting concerns of different stakeholders, and showing the trade-offs made in so doing (as between security and performance, for example).

The choice has to be constrained by considerations of practicality, and by the principle of fitness-for-purpose (i.e., the architecture should be developed only to the point at which it is fit-for-purpose, and not reiterated *ad infinitum* as an academic exercise).

As explained in Part II: Architecture Development Method (ADM), the development of architecture views is an iterative process. The typical progression is from business to technology, using a technique such as business scenarios (see Part III, Chapter 26) to properly identify all pertinent concerns; and from high-level overview to lower-level detail, continually referring back to the concerns and requirements of the stakeholders throughout the process.

Moreover, each of these progressions has to be made for two distinct environments: the existing environment (referred to as the baseline in the ADM) and the target environment. The architect must develop pertinent architecture views of both the Baseline Architecture and the Target Architecture. This provides the context for the gap analysis at the end of Phases B, C, and D of the ADM, which establishes the elements of the Baseline Architecture to be carried forward and the elements to be added, removed, or replaced.

This whole process is explained in Part III, Chapter 27.

35.2.2 View Creation Process

As mentioned above, at the present time TOGAF encourages but does not mandate the use of ISO/IEC 42010:2007. The following description therefore covers both the situation where ISO/IEC 42010:2007 has been adopted and where it has not.

ISO/IEC 42010:2007 itself does not require any specific process for developing viewpoints or creating views from them. Where ISO/IEC 42010:2007 has been adopted and become well-established practice within an organization, it will often be possible to create the required views for a particular architecture by following these steps:

1. Refer to an existing library of viewpoints

2. Select the appropriate viewpoints (based on the stakeholders and concerns that need to be covered by views)

3. Generate views of the system by using the selected viewpoints as templates

This approach can be expected to bring the following benefits:

- Less work for the architects (because the viewpoints have already been defined and therefore the views can be created faster)

- Better comprehensibility for stakeholders (because the viewpoints are already familiar)

- Greater confidence in the validity of the views (because their viewpoints have a known track record)

However, situations can always arise in which a view is needed for which no appropriate viewpoint has been predefined. This is also the situation, of course, when an organization has not yet incorporated ISO/IEC 42010:2007 into its architecture practice and established a library of viewpoints.

In each case, the architect may choose to develop a new viewpoint that will cover the outstanding need, and then generate a view from it. (This is ISO/IEC 42010:2007 recommended practice.) Alternatively, a more pragmatic approach can be equally successful: the architect can create an *ad hoc* view for a specific system and later consider whether a generalized form of the implicit viewpoint should be defined explicitly and saved in a library, so that it can be re-used. (This is one way of establishing a library of viewpoints initially.)

Whatever the context, the architect should be aware that every view has a viewpoint, at least implicitly, and that defining the viewpoint in a systematic way (as recommended by ISO/IEC 42010:2007) will help in assessing its effectiveness; i.e., does the viewpoint cover the relevant stakeholder concerns?.

35.3   Views, Tools, and Languages

The need for architecture views, and the process of developing them following the ADM, are explained above. This section describes the relationships between architecture views, the tools used to develop and analyze them, and a standard language enabling interoperability between the tools.

35.3.1   Overview

In order to achieve the goals of completeness and integrity in an architecture, architecture views are usually developed, visualized, communicated, and managed using a tool.

In the current state of the market, different tools normally have to be used to develop and analyze different views of the architecture. It is highly desirable that an architecture description be encoded in a standard language, to enable a standard approach to the description of architecture semantics and their re-use among different tools.

A viewpoint is also normally developed, visualized, communicated, and managed using a tool, and it is also highly desirable that standard viewpoints (i.e., templates or schemas) be developed, so that different tools that deal in the same views can interoperate, the fundamental elements of an architecture can be re-used, and the architecture description can be shared among tools.

Issues relating to the evaluation of tools for architecture work are discussed in detail in Part V, Chapter 42.

35.4   Views and Viewpoints

35.4.1   Example of Views and Viewpoints

To illustrate the concepts of views and viewpoints, consider the example of a very simple airport system with two different stakeholders: the pilot and the air traffic controller.

One view can be developed from the viewpoint of the pilot, which addresses the pilot's concerns. Equally, another view can be developed from the viewpoint of the air traffic controller. Neither view completely describes the system in its entirety, because the viewpoint of each stakeholder constrains (and reduces) how each sees the overall system.

The viewpoint of the pilot comprises some concerns that are not relevant to the controller, such as passengers and fuel, while the viewpoint of the controller comprises some concerns not relevant to the pilot, such as other planes. There are also elements shared between the two viewpoints, such as the communication model between the pilot and the controller, and the vital information about the plane itself.

A viewpoint is a model (or description) of the information contained in a view. In our example, one viewpoint is the description of how the pilot sees the system, and the other viewpoint is how the controller sees the system.

Pilots describe the system from their perspective, using a model of their position and vector toward or away from the runway. All pilots use this model, and the model has a specific language that is used to capture information and populate the model.

Controllers describe the system differently, using a model of the airspace and the locations and vectors of aircraft within the airspace. Again, all controllers use a common language derived from the common model in order to capture and communicate information pertinent to their viewpoint.

Fortunately, when controllers talk with pilots, they use a common communication language. (In other words, the models representing their individual viewpoints partially intersect.) Part of this common language is about location and vectors of aircraft, and is essential to safety.

So in essence each viewpoint is an abstract model of how all the stakeholders of a particular type — all pilots, or all controllers — view the airport system.

Tools exist to assist stakeholders, especially when they are interacting with complex models such as the model of an airspace, or the model of air flight.

The interface to the human user of a tool is typically close to the model and language associated with the viewpoint. The unique tools of the pilot are fuel, altitude, speed, and location indicators. The main tool of the controller is radar. The common tool is a radio.

To summarize from the above example, we can see that a view can subset the system through the perspective of the stakeholder, such as the pilot *versus* the controller. This subset can be described by an abstract model called a viewpoint, such as an air flight *versus* an air space model. This description of the view is documented in a partially specialized language, such as "pilot-speak" *versus* "controller-speak". Tools are used to assist the stakeholders, and they interface with each other in terms of the language derived from the viewpoint ("pilot-speak" *versus'* "controller-speak").

When stakeholders use common tools, such as the radio contact between pilot and controller, a common language is essential.

35.4.2 Views and Viewpoints in Enterprise Architecture

Now let us map this example to the enterprise architecture. Consider two stakeholders in a new small computing system: the users and the developers.

The users of the system have a viewpoint that reflects their concerns when interacting with the system, and the developers of the system have a different viewpoint. Views that are developed to address either of the two viewpoints are unlikely to exhaustively describe the whole system, because each perspective reduces how each sees the system.

The viewpoint of the user is comprised of all the ways in which the user interacts with the system, not seeing any details such as applications or Database Management Systems (DBMS).

The viewpoint of the developer is one of productivity and tools, and doesn't include things such as actual live data and connections with consumers.

However, there are things that are shared, such as descriptions of the processes that are enabled by the system and/or communications protocols set up for users to communicate problems directly to development.

In this example, one viewpoint is the description of how the user sees the system, and the other viewpoint is how the developer sees the system. Users describe the system from their perspective, using a model of availability, response time, and access to information. All users of the system use this model, and the model has a specific language.

Developers describe the system differently than users, using a model of software connected to hardware distributed over a network, etc. However, there are many types of developers (database, security, etc.) of the system, and they do not have a common language derived from the model.

35.4.3 Need for a Common Language and Interoperable Tools for Architecture Description

Tools exist for both users and developers. Tools such as online help are there specifically for users, and attempt to use the language of the user. Many different tools exist for different types of developers, but they suffer from the lack of a common language that is required to bring the system together. It is difficult, if not impossible, in the current state of the tools market to have one tool interoperate with another tool.

Issues relating to the evaluation of tools for architecture work are discussed in detail in Part V, Chapter 42.

35.5 Conclusions

This section attempts to deal with views in a structured manner, but this is by no means a complete treatise on views.

In general, TOGAF embraces the concepts and definitions presented in ISO/IEC 42010:2007, specifically the concepts that help guide the development of a view and make the view actionable. These concepts can be summarized as:

- Selecting a key stakeholder
- Understanding their concerns and generalizing/documenting those concerns
- Understanding how to model and deal with those concerns

In the following sections, TOGAF presents some recommended viewpoints, some or all of which may be appropriate in a particular architecture development. This is not intended as an exhaustive set of viewpoints, but simply as a starting point. Those described may be supplemented by additional viewpoints as required. These TOGAF sections on viewpoints should be considered as guides for the development and treatment of a view, not as a full definition of a viewpoint.

35.6   Taxonomy of Architecture Viewpoints

TOGAF defines a set of architecture viewpoints that may be adopted, enhanced, and combined to produce views that describe an architecture. In order to aid in re-use and consistency, a number of atomic viewpoints are outlined below that enable the development of individual views for many different purposes. In a typical enterprise, stakeholder concerns will be identified in order to develop richer and more complex viewpoints that address specific stakeholder groups.

Part III, Chapter 24 provides an outline of the major stakeholder groups that are typically encountered when developing enterprise architecture. The likely concerns of each stakeholder group are also identified.

Figure 35-3 shows the viewpoints that are associated with the core content metamodel and each of the content extensions.

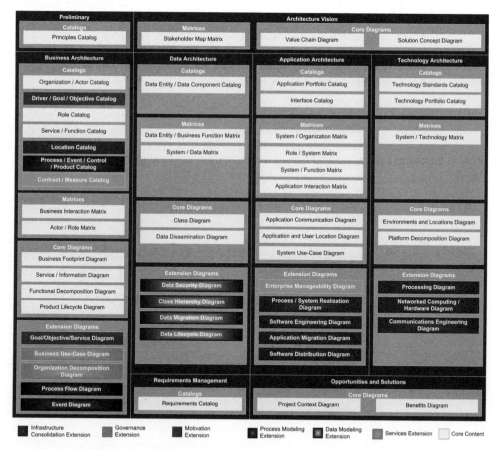

Figure 35-3 Viewpoints Associated with the Core Content Metamodel and Extensions

The specific classes of viewpoint are as follows:

- **Catalogs** are specific foundational viewpoints that represent lists of building blocks.

- **Matrices** are specific foundational viewpoints that show the relationships between building blocks of specific types.

- **Diagrams** are graphical viewpoints that present building blocks in a rich and visual way, more suited to stakeholder communication.

The TOGAF architecture domains are themselves viewpoints that can be used to group the foundational catalogs, matrices, and diagrams:

- The **Business Architecture domain** addresses the needs of users, planners, and business management.

- The **Data Architecture domain** addresses the needs of database designers, database administrators, and system engineers.

- The **Application Architecture domain** addresses the needs of system and software engineers.

- The **Technology Architecture domain** addresses the needs of acquirers, operators, administrators, and managers.

When applying TOGAF within a particular enterprise or project, it may be necessary to take each one of these stakeholder types (e.g., user, database administrator, acquirer, etc.) and create an explicit set of stakeholder concerns. These concerns can then be used to refine and enhance the basic viewpoints provided by TOGAF.

It is expected that, when applying TOGAF to a specific architectural problem, a number of tailoring steps should take place:

- The viewpoints provided should be customized to create a set of architecture views that ensure all stakeholder concerns are met. For example, selection of core and extension content identified within Business Architecture allows for a lightweight or detailed view of Business Architecture.

- New viewpoints and views should be created to address specific needs of the problem. For example, an Enterprise Security view could be created that spans Business, Data, Application, and Technology Architecture to show security from all aspects.

35.7   Viewpoints in the Preliminary Phase

The following catalogs, matrices, and diagrams may be produced in the Preliminary phase.

- Catalogs:
  - — Principles catalog
- Matrices:
  - — No matrices are defined to be created during the Preliminary phase.
- Core diagrams:

— No core diagrams are defined to be created during the Preliminary phase.

■ Extension diagrams:

— No extension diagrams are defined to be created during the Preliminary phase.

The following describes each of the catalogs, matrices, and diagrams created within the Preliminary phase.

Principles Catalog

The Principles catalog captures principles of the business and architecture principles that describe what a "good" solution or architecture should look like. Principles are used to evaluate and agree an outcome for architecture decision points. Principles are also used as a tool to assist in architectural governance of change initiatives.

The Principles catalog contains the following metamodel entities:

■ Principle

35.8 Viewpoints in Phase A

The following catalogs, matrices, and diagrams may be produced in Phase A (Architecture Vision).

■ Catalogs:

— No catalogs are defined to be created during Phase A.

■ Matrices:

— Stakeholder Map matrix

■ Core diagrams:

— Value Chain diagram

— Solution Concept diagram

■ Extension diagrams:

— No extension diagrams are defined to be created during Phase A.

The following describes each of the catalogs, matrices, and diagrams created within Phase A (Architecture Vision).

Stakeholder Map Matrix

The purpose of the Stakeholder Map matrix is to identify the stakeholders for the architecture engagement, their influence over the engagement, and their key questions, issues, or concerns that must be addressed by the architecture framework.

Understanding stakeholders and their requirements allows an architect to focus effort in areas that meet the needs of stakeholders (see Part III, Chapter 24).

Due to the potentially sensitive nature of stakeholder mapping information and the fact that the Architecture Vision phase is intended to be conducted using informal modeling techniques, no specific metamodel entities will be used to generate a stakeholder map.

Value Chain Diagram

A Value Chain diagram provides a high-level orientation view of an enterprise and how it interacts with the outside world. In contrast to the more formal Functional Decomposition diagram developed within Phase B (Business Architecture), the Value Chain diagram focuses on presentational impact.

The purpose of this diagram is to quickly on-board and align stakeholders for a particular change initiative, so that all participants understand the high-level functional and organizational context of the architecture engagement.

Solution Concept Diagram

A Solution Concept diagram provides a high-level orientation of the solution that is envisaged in order to meet the objectives of the architecture engagement. In contrast to the more formal and detailed architecture diagrams developed in the following phases, the solution concept represents a "pencil sketch" of the expected solution at the outset of the engagement.

This diagram may embody key objectives, requirements, and constraints for the engagement and also highlight work areas to be investigated in more detail with formal architecture modeling.

The purpose of this diagram is to quickly on-board and align stakeholders for a particular change initiative, so that all participants understand what the architecture engagement is seeking to achieve and how it is expected that a particular solution approach will meet the needs of the enterprise.

35.9   Viewpoints in Phase B

The following catalogs, matrices, and diagrams may be produced in Phase B (Business Architecture).

- Catalogs:
    - Organization/Actor catalog
    - Driver/Goal/Objective catalog
    - Role catalog
    - Business Service/Function catalog
    - Location catalog
    - Process/Event/Control/Product catalog
    - Contract/Measure catalog
- Matrices:
    - Business Interaction matrix
    - Actor/Role matrix
- Core diagrams:
    - Business Footprint diagram

- — Business Service/Information diagram
- — Functional Decomposition diagram
- — Product Lifecycle diagram
- ■ Extension diagrams:
  - — Goal/Objective/Service diagram
  - — Use-case diagram
  - — Organization Decomposition diagram
  - — Process Flow diagram
  - — Event diagram

The following describes each of the catalogs, matrices, and diagrams created within Phase B (Business Architecture).

Organization/Actor Catalog

The purpose of the Organization/Actor catalog is to capture a definitive listing of all participants that interact with IT, including users and owners of IT systems.

The Organization/Actor catalog can be referenced when developing requirements in order to test for completeness.

For example, requirements for an application that services customers can be tested for completeness by verifying exactly which customer types need to be supported and whether there are any particular requirements or restrictions for user types.

The Organization/Actor catalog contains the following metamodel entities:

- ■ Organization Unit
- ■ Actor
- ■ Location (may be included in this catalog if an independent Location catalog is not maintained)

Driver/Goal/Objective Catalog

The purpose of the Driver/Goal/Objective catalog is to provide a cross-organizational reference of how an organization meets its drivers in practical terms through goals, objectives, and (optionally) measures.

Publishing a definitive breakdown of drivers, goals, and objectives allows change initiatives within the enterprise to identify synergies across the organization (e.g., multiple organizations attempting to achieve similar objectives), which in turn allow stakeholders to be identified and related change initiatives to be aligned or consolidated.

The Driver/Goal/Objective catalog contains the following metamodel entities:

- ■ Organization Unit
- ■ Driver
- ■ Goal

- Objective

- Measure (may optionally be included)

Role Catalog

The purpose of the Role catalog is to provide a listing of all authorization levels or zones within an enterprise. Frequently, application security or behavior is defined against locally understood concepts of authorization that create complex and unexpected consequences when combined on the user desktop.

If roles are defined, understood, and aligned across organizations and applications, this allows for a more seamless user experience and generally more secure applications, as administrators do not need to resort to workarounds in order to enable users to carry out their jobs.

In addition to supporting security definition for the enterprise, the Role catalog also forms a key input to identifying organizational change management impacts, defining job functions, and executing end-user training.

As each role implies access to a number of business functions, if any of these business functions are impacted, then change management will be required, organizational responsibilities may need to be redefined, and retraining may be needed.

The Role catalog contains the following metamodel entities:

- Role

Business Service/Function Catalog

The purpose of the Business Service/Function catalog is to provide a functional decomposition in a form that can be filtered, reported on, and queried, as a supplement to graphical Functional Decomposition diagrams.

The Business Service/Function catalog can be used to identify capabilities of an organization and to understand the level that governance is applied to the functions of an organization. This functional decomposition can be used to identify new capabilities required to support business change or may be used to determine the scope of change initiatives, applications, or technology components.

The Business Service/Function catalog contains the following metamodel entities:

- Organization Unit

- Business Function

- Business Service

- Information System Service (may optionally be included here)

Location Catalog

The Location catalog provides a listing of all locations where an enterprise carries out business operations or houses architecturally relevant assets, such as data centers or end-user computing equipment.

Maintaining a definitive list of locations allows change initiatives to quickly define a location scope and to test for completeness when assessing current landscapes or proposed target solutions. For example, a project to upgrade desktop operating systems will need to identify all locations where desktop operating systems are deployed.

Similarly, when new systems are being implemented, a diagram of locations is essential in order to develop appropriate deployment strategies that comprehend both user and application location and identify location-related issues, such as internationalization, localization, timezone impacts on availability, distance impacts on latency, network impacts on bandwidth, and access.

The Location catalog contains the following metamodel entities:

- Location

Process/Event/Control/Product Catalog

The Process/Event/Control/Product catalog provides a hierarchy of processes, events that trigger processes, outputs from processes, and controls applied to the execution of processes. This catalog provides a supplement to any Process Flow diagrams that are created and allows an enterprise to filter, report, and query across organizations and processes to identify scope, commonality, or impact.

For example, the Process/Event/Control/Product catalog allows an enterprise to see relationships of processes to sub-processes in order to identify the full chain of impacts resulting from changing a high-level process.

The Process/Event/Control/Product catalog contains the following metamodel entities:

- Process
- Event
- Control
- Product

Contract/Measure Catalog

The Contract/Measure catalog provides a listing of all agreed service contracts and (optionally) the measures attached to those contracts. It forms the master list of service levels agreed to across the enterprise.

The Contract/Measure catalog contains the following metamodel entities:

- Business Service
- Information System Service (optionally)
- Contract
- Measure

Business Interaction Matrix

The purpose of this matrix is to depict the relationship interactions between organizations and business functions across the enterprise.

Understanding business interaction of an enterprise is important as it helps to highlight value chain and dependencies across organizations.

The Business Interaction matrix shows the following metamodel entities and relationships:

- Organization

- Business Function
- Business Service
- Business Service *communicates with* Business Service relationships
- Business Service *is dependent on* Business Service relationships

Actor/Role Matrix

The purpose of this matrix is to show which actors perform which roles, supporting definition of security and skills requirements.

Understanding Actor-to-Role relationships is a key supporting tool in definition of training needs, user security settings, and organizational change management.

The Actor/Role matrix shows the following metamodel entities and relationships:

- Actor
- Role
- Actor *performs* Role relationships

Business Footprint Diagram

A Business Footprint diagram describes the links between business goals, organizational units, business functions, and services, and maps these functions to the technical components delivering the required capability.

A Business Footprint diagram provides a clear traceability between a technical component and the business goal that it satisfies, whilst also demonstrating ownership of the services identified.

A Business Footprint diagram demonstrates only the key facts linking organization unit functions to delivery services and is utilized as a communication platform for senior-level (CxO) stakeholders.

Business Service/Information Diagram

The Business Service/Information diagram shows the information needed to support one or more business services. The Business Service/Information diagram shows what data is consumed by or produced by a business service and may also show the source of information.

The Business Service/Information diagram shows an initial representation of the information present within the architecture and therefore forms a basis for elaboration and refinement within Phase C (Data Architecture).

Functional Decomposition Diagram

The purpose of the Functional Decomposition diagram is to show on a single page the capabilities of an organization that are relevant to the consideration of an architecture. By examining the capabilities of an organization from a functional perspective, it is possible to quickly develop models of what the organization does without being dragged into extended debate on how the organization does it.

Once a basic Functional Decomposition diagram has been developed, it becomes possible to layer heat-maps on top of this diagram to show scope and decisions. For example, the capabilities to be implemented in different phases of a change program.

Product Lifecycle Diagram

The purpose of the Product Lifecycle diagram is to assist in understanding the lifecycles of key entities within the enterprise. Understanding product lifecycles is becoming increasingly important with respect to environmental concerns, legislation, and regulation where products must be tracked from manufacture to disposal. Equally, organizations that create products that involve personal or sensitive information must have a detailed understanding of the product lifecycle during the development of Business Architecture in order to ensure rigor in design of controls, processes, and procedures. Examples of this would include credit cards, debit cards, store/loyalty cards, smart cards, user identity credentials (identity cards, passports, etc.).

Goal/Objective/Service Diagram

The purpose of a Goal/Objective/Service diagram is to define the ways in which a service contributes to the achievement of a business vision or strategy.

Services are associated with the drivers, goals, objectives, and measures that they support, allowing the enterprise to understand which services contribute to similar aspects of business performance. The Goal/Objective/Service diagram also provides qualitative input on what constitutes high performance for a particular service.

Business Use-Case Diagram

A Business Use-Case diagram displays the relationships between consumers and providers of business services. Business services are consumed by actors or other business services and the Business Use-Case diagram provides added richness in describing business capability by illustrating how and when that capability is used.

The purpose of the Business Use-Case diagram is to help to describe and validate the interaction between actors and their roles to processes and functions. As the architecture progresses, the use-case can evolve from the business level to include data, application, and technology details. Architectural business use-cases can also be re-used in systems design work.

Organization Decomposition Diagram

An Organization Decomposition diagram describes the links between actor, roles, and location within an organization tree.

An organization map should provide a chain of command of owners and decision-makers in the organization. Although it is not the intent of the Organization Decomposition diagram to link goal to organization, it should be possible to intuitively link the goals to the stakeholders from the Organization Decomposition diagram.

Process Flow Diagram

The purpose of the Process Flow diagram is to depict all models and mappings related to the process metamodel entity.

Process Flow diagrams show sequential flow of control between activities and may utilize swim-lane techniques to represent ownership and realization of process steps. For example, the application that supports a process step may be shown as a swim-lane.

In addition to showing a sequence of activity, process flows can also be used to detail the controls that apply to a process, the events that trigger or result from completion of a process, and also the products that are generated from process execution.

Process Flow diagrams are useful in elaborating the architecture with subject specialists, as they allow the specialist to describe "how the job is done" for a particular function. Through this process, each process step can become a more fine-grained function and can then in turn be elaborated as a process.

Event Diagram

The purpose of the Event diagram is to depict the relationship between events and process.

Certain events — such as arrival of certain information (e.g., customer submits sales order) or a certain point in time (e.g., end of fiscal quarter) — cause work and certain actions need to be undertaken within the business. These are often referred to as "business events" or simply "events" and are considered as triggers for a process. It is important to note that the event has to trigger a process and generate a business response or result.

35.10 Viewpoints in the Phase C Data Architecture

The following catalogs, matrices, and diagrams may be produced in Phase C (Data Architecture).

- Catalogs:
    - Data Entity/Data Component catalog
- Matrices:
    - Data Entity/Business Function matrix
    - System/Data matrix
- Core diagrams:
    - Class diagram
    - Data Dissemination diagram
- Extension diagrams:
    - Data Security diagram
    - Class Hierarchy diagram
    - Data Migration diagram
    - Data Lifecycle diagram

The following describes each of the catalogs, matrices, and diagrams created within Phase C (Data Architecture).

Data Entity/Data Component Catalog

The purpose of the Data Entity/Data Component catalog is to identify and maintain a list of all the data use across the enterprise, including data entities and also the data components where data entities are stored. An agreed Data Entity/Data Component catalog supports the definition and application of information management and data governance policies and also encourages effective data sharing and re-use.

The Data Entity/Data Component catalog contains the following metamodel entities:

- Data Entity
- Logical Data Component
- Physical Data Component

Data Entity/Business Function Matrix

The purpose of the Data Entity/Business Function matrix is to depict the relationship between data entities and business functions within the enterprise. Business functions are supported by business services with explicitly defined boundaries and will be supported and realized by business processes. The mapping of the Data Entity-Business Function relationship enables the following to take place:

- Assign ownership of data entities to organizations
- Understand the data and information exchange requirements business services
- Support the gap analysis and determine whether any data entities are missing and need to be created
- Define system of origin, system of record, and system of reference for data entities
- Enable development of data governance programs across the enterprise (establish data steward, develop data standards pertinent to the business function, etc.)

The Data Entity/Business Function matrix shows the following entities and relationships:

- Data Entity
- Business Function
- Data Entity relationship to owning Organization Unit

System/Data Matrix

The purpose of the System/Data matrix is to depict the relationship between systems (i.e., application components) and the data entities that are accessed and updated by them.

Systems will create, read, update, and delete specific data entities that are associated with them. For example, a CRM application will create, read, update, and delete customer entity information.

The data entities in a package/packaged services environment can be classified as master data, reference data, transactional data, content data, and historical data. Applications that operate on the data entities include transactional applications, information management applications, and business warehouse applications.

The mapping of the Application Component-Data Entity relationship is an important step as it enables the following to take place:

- Assign access of data to specific applications in the organization
- Understand the degree of data duplication within different applications, and the scale of the data lifecycle
- Understand where the same data is updated by different applications
- Support the gap analysis and determine whether any of the applications are missing and as a result need to be created

The System/Data matrix is a two-dimensional table with Logical Application Component on one axis and Data Entity on the other axis.

Class Diagram

The key purpose of the Class diagram is to depict the relationships among the critical data entities (or classes) within the enterprise. This diagram is developed to clearly present the relationships and to help understand the lower-level data models for the enterprise.

Data Dissemination Diagram

The purpose of the Data Dissemination diagram is to show the relationship between data entity, business service, and application components. The diagram shows how the logical entities are to be physically realized by application components. This allows effective sizing to be carried out and the IT footprint to be refined. Moreover, by assigning business value to data, an indication of the business criticality of application components can be gained.

Additionally, the diagram may show data replication and system ownership of the master reference for data. In this instance, it can show two copies and the master-copy relationship between them. This diagram can include services; that is, services encapsulate data and they reside in an application, or services that reside on an application and access data encapsulated within the application.

Data Security Diagram

Data is considered as an asset to the enterprise and data security simply means ensuring that enterprise data is not compromised and that access to it is suitably controlled.

The purpose of the Data Security diagram is to depict which actor (person, organization, or system) can access which enterprise data. This relationship can be shown in a matrix form between two objects or can be shown as a mapping.

The diagram can also be used to demonstrate compliance with data privacy laws and other applicable regulations (HIPAA, SOX, etc). This diagram should also consider any trust implications where an enterprise's partners or other parties may have access to the company's systems, such as an outsourced situation where information may be managed by other people and may even be hosted in a different country.

Class Hierarchy Diagram

The purpose of the Class Hierarchy diagram is to show the technical stakeholders a perspective of the class hierarchy. The advantage of this diagram is that it allows the stakeholders a technical utilization/usage diagram of the data entity. This diagram gives the stakeholders an idea of who is using the data, how, why, and when. A possible variant can be to use this diagram in auditing.

Data Migration Diagram

Data migration is critical when implementing a package or packaged service-based solution. This is particularly true when an existing legacy application is replaced with a package or an enterprise is to be migrated to a larger packages/packaged services footprint. Packages tend to have their own data model and during data migration the legacy application data may need to be transformed prior to loading into the package.

Data migration activities will usually involve the following steps:

- Extract data from source applications (baseline systems)
- Profile source data
- Perform data transformation operations, including data quality processes:
    - Standardize, normalize, de-duplicate source data (data cleansing)
    - Match, merge, and consolidate data from different source(s)
    - Source-to-target mappings
- Load into target applications (target systems)

The purpose of the Data Migration diagram is to show the flow of data from the source to the target applications. The diagram will provide a visual representation of the spread of sources/targets and serve as a tool for data auditing and establishing traceability. This diagram can be elaborated or enhanced as detailed as necessary. For example, the diagram can contain just an overall layout of migration landscape or could go into individual application metadata element level of detail.

Data Lifecycle Diagram

The Data Lifecycle diagram is an essential part of managing business data throughout its lifecycle from conception until disposal within the constraints of the business process.

The data is considered as an entity in its own right, decoupled from business process and activity. Each change in state is represented on the diagram which may include the event or rules that trigger that change in state.

The separation of data from process allows common data requirements to be identified which enables resource sharing to be achieved more effectively.

35.11 Viewpoints in the Phase C Application Architecture

The following catalogs, matrices, and diagrams may be produced in Phase C (Application Architecture):

- Catalogs:
    - Application Portfolio catalog
    - Interface catalog
- Matrices:
    - System/Organization matrix
    - Role/System matrix
    - System/Function matrix
    - Application Interaction matrix
- Core diagrams:
    - Application Communication diagram

    — Application and User Location diagram

    — System Use-Case diagram

- Extension diagrams:

    — Enterprise Manageability diagram

    — Process/System Realization diagram

    — Software Engineering diagram

    — Application Migration diagram

    — Software Distribution diagram

The following describes each of the catalogs, matrices, and diagrams created within Phase C (Application Architecture).

Application Portfolio Catalog

The purpose of this catalog is to identify and maintain a list of all the applications in the enterprise. This list helps to define the horizontal scope of change initiatives that may impact particular kinds of applications. An agreed Application Portfolio allows a standard set of applications to be defined and governed.

The Application Portfolio catalog provides a foundation on which to base the remaining matrices and diagrams. It is typically the start point of the Application Architecture phase.

Existing application registries and repositories — such as SAP's Solution Manager and System Landscape Directory products — also provide input into this catalog from a baseline and target perspective.

The Application Portfolio catalog contains the following metamodel entities:

- Information System Service
- Logical Application Component
- Physical Application Component

Interface Catalog

The purpose of the Interface catalog is to scope and document the interfaces between applications to enable the overall dependencies between applications to be scoped as early as possible.

Systems will create, read, update, and delete data within other systems; this will be achieved by some kind of interface, whether via a batch file that is loaded periodically, a direct connection to another system's database, or via some form of API or web service.

The mapping of the Application Component-Application Component entity relationship is an important step as it enables the following to take place:

- Understand the degree of interaction between applications, identifying those that are central in terms of their dependencies on other systems
- Understand the number and types of interfaces between applications

- Understand the degree of duplication of interfaces between applications
- Identify the potential for simplification of interfaces when considering the target Application Portfolio
- Support the gap analysis and determine whether any of the applications are missing and as a result need to be created

The Interface catalog contains the following metamodel entities:

- Logical Application Component
- Physical Application Component
- Application *communicates with* application relationship

System/Organization Matrix

The purpose of this matrix is to depict the relationship between systems (i.e., application components) and organizational units within the enterprise.

Business functions are performed by organizational units. Some of the functions and services performed by those organizational units will be supported by IT systems. The mapping of the Application Component-Organization Unit relationship is an important step as it enables the following to take place:

- Assign usage of applications to the organization units that perform business functions
- Understand the application support requirements of the business services and processes carried out by an organization unit
- Support the gap analysis and determine whether any of the applications are missing and as a result need to be created
- Define the application set used by a particular organization unit

The System/Organization matrix is a two-dimensional table with Logical/Physical Application Component on one axis and Organization Unit on the other axis.

The relationship between these two entities is a composite of a number of metamodel relationships that need validating:

- Organization Units *own* Services
- Actors that *belong to* Organization Units *use* Services
- Services are *realized by* Logical/Physical Application Components

Role/System Matrix

The purpose of the Role/System matrix is to depict the relationship between systems (i.e., application components) and the business roles that use them within the enterprise.

People in an organization interact with systems. During this interaction, these people assume a specific role to perform a task; for example, product buyer.

The mapping of the Application Component-Role relationship is an important step as it enables the following to take place:

- Assign usage of applications to the specific roles in the organization
- Understand the application security requirements of the business services and processes supporting the function, and check these are in line with current policy
- Support the gap analysis and determine whether any of the applications are missing and as a result need to be created
- Define the application set used by a particular business role; essential in any move to role-based computing

The Role/System matrix is a two-dimensional table with Logical Application Component on one axis and Role on the other axis.

The relationship between these two entities is a composite of a number of metamodel relationships that need validating:

- Role *accesses* Function
- Function *is bounded by* Service
- Services are *realized by* Logical/Physical Application Components

System/Function Matrix

The purpose of the System/Function matrix is to depict the relationship between systems (i.e., application components) and business functions within the enterprise.

Business functions are performed by organizational units. Some of the business functions and services will be supported by IT systems. The mapping of the Application Component-Function relationship is an important step as it enables the following to take place:

- Assign usage of applications to the business functions that are supported by them
- Understand the application support requirements of the business services and processes carried out
- Support the gap analysis and determine whether any of the applications are missing and as a result need to be created
- Define the application set used by a particular business function

The System/Organization matrix is a two-dimensional table with Logical Application Component on one axis and Function on the other axis.

The relationship between these two entities is a composite of a number of metamodel relationships that need validating:

- Function *is bounded by* Service
- Services are *realized by* Logical/Physical Application Components

Application Interaction Matrix

The purpose of the Application Interaction matrix is to depict communications relationships between systems (i.e., application components).

The mapping of the application interactions shows in matrix form the equivalent of the Interface Catalog or an Application Communication diagram.

The Application Interaction matrix is a two-dimensional table with Application Service, Logical Application Component, and Physical Application Component on both the rows and the columns of the table.

The relationships depicted by this matrix include:

- Application Service *consumes* Application Service
- Logical Application Component *communicates with* Logical Application Component
- Physical Application Component *communicates with* Physical Application Component

Application Communication Diagram

The purpose of the Application Communication diagram is to depict all models and mappings related to communication between applications in the metamodel entity.

It shows application components and interfaces between components. Interfaces may be associated with data entities where appropriate. Applications may be associated with business services where appropriate. Communication should be logical and should only show intermediary technology where it is architecturally relevant.

Application and User Location Diagram

The Application and User Location diagram shows the geographical distribution of applications. It can be used to show where applications are used by the end user; the distribution of where the host application is executed and/or delivered in thin client scenarios; the distribution of where applications are developed, tested, and released; etc.

Analysis can reveal opportunities for rationalization, as well as duplication and/or gaps.

The purpose of this diagram is to clearly depict the business locations from which business users typically interact with the applications, but also the hosting location of the application infrastructure.

The diagram enables:

- Identification of the number of package instances needed to sufficiently support the user population that may be spread out geographically
- Estimation of the number and the type of user licenses for the package or other software
- Estimation of the level of support needed for the users and location of support center
- Selection of system management tools, structure, and management system required to support the enterprise users/customers/partners both locally and remotely
- Appropriate planning for the technological components of the business, namely server sizing and network bandwidth, etc.

- Performance considerations while implementing application and technology architecture solutions

Users typically interact with applications in a variety of ways; for example:

- To support the operations of the business day-to-day

- To participate in the execution of a business process

- To access information (look-up, read)

- To develop the application

- To administer and maintain the application

System Use-Case Diagram

A System Use-Case diagram displays the relationships between consumers and providers of application services. Application services are consumed by actors or other application services and the Application Use-Case diagram provides added richness in describing application functionality by illustrating how and when that functionality is used.

The purpose of the System Use-Case diagram is to help to describe and validate the interaction between actors and their roles with applications. As the architecture progresses, the use-case can evolve from functional information to include technical realization detail.

Architectural system use-cases can also be re-used in more detailed systems design work.

Enterprise Manageability Diagram

The Enterprise Manageability diagram shows how one or more applications interact with application and technology components that support operational management of a solution.

This diagram is really a filter on the Application Communication diagram, specifically for enterprise management class software.

Analysis can reveal duplication and gaps, and opportunities in the IT service management operation of an organization.

Process/System Realization Diagram

The purpose of the Process/System Realization diagram is to clearly depict the sequence of events when multiple applications are involved in executing a business process.

It enhances the Application Communication diagram by augmenting it with any sequencing constraints, and hand-off points between batch and real-time processing.

It would identify complex sequences that could be simplified, and identify possible rationalization points in the architecture in order to provide more timely information to business users. It may also identify process efficiency improvements that may reduce interaction traffic between applications.

Software Engineering Diagram

The Software Engineering diagram breaks applications into packages, modules, services, and operations from a development perspective.

It enables more detailed impact analysis when planning migration stages, and analyzing opportunities and solutions.

It is ideal for application development teams and application management teams when managing complex development environments.

Application Migration Diagram

The Application Migration diagram identifies application migration from baseline to target application components. It enables a more accurate estimation of migration costs by showing precisely which applications and interfaces need to be mapped between migration stages.

It would identify temporary applications, staging areas, and the infrastructure required to support migrations (for example, parallel run environments, etc).

Software Distribution Diagram

The Software Distribution diagram shows how application software is structured and distributed across the estate. It is useful in systems upgrade or application consolidation projects.

This diagram shows how physical applications are distributed across physical technology and the location of that technology.

This enables a clear view of how the software is hosted, but also enables managed operations staff to understand how that application software is maintained once installed.

35.12 Viewpoints in Phase D

The following catalogs, matrices, and diagrams may be produced in Phase D (Technology Architecture).

- Catalogs:
    - Technology Standards catalog
    - Technology Portfolio catalog
- Matrices:
    - System/Technology matrix
- Core diagrams:
    - Environments and Locations diagram
    - Platform Decomposition diagram
- Extension diagrams:
    - Processing diagram

— Networked Computing/Hardware diagram

— Communications Engineering diagram

The following section describes each of the catalogs, matrices, and diagrams created within Phase D (Technology Architecture).

Technology Standards Catalog

The Technology Standards catalog documents the agreed standards for technology across the enterprise covering technologies, and versions, the technology lifecycles, and the refresh cycles for the technology.

Depending upon the organization, this may also include location or business domain-specific standards information.

This catalog provides a snapshot of the enterprise standard technologies that are or can be deployed, and also helps identify the discrepancies across the enterprise.

If technology standards are currently in place, apply these to the Technology Portfolio catalog to gain a baseline view of compliance with technology standards.

The Technology Portfolio catalog contains the following metamodel entities:

- Platform Service
- Logical Technology Component
- Physical Technology Component

Technology Portfolio Catalog

The purpose of this catalog is to identify and maintain a list of all the technology in use across the enterprise, including hardware, infrastructure software, and application software. An agreed technology portfolio supports lifecycle management of technology products and versions and also forms the basis for definition of technology standards.

The Technology Portfolio catalog provides a foundation on which to base the remaining matrices and diagrams. It is typically the start point of the Technology Architecture phase.

Technology registries and repositories also provide input into this catalog from a baseline and target perspective.

Technologies in the catalog should be classified against the TOGAF Technology Reference Model (TRM) — see Part VI, Chapter 43 — extending the model as necessary to fit the classification of technology products in use.

The Technology Portfolio catalog contains the following metamodel entities:

- Platform Service
- Logical Technology Component
- Physical Technology Component

System/Technology Matrix

The System/Technology matrix documents the mapping of business systems to technology platform.

This matrix should be aligned with and complement one or more platform decomposition diagrams.

The System/Technology matrix shows:

- Logical/Physical Application Components
- Services, Logical Technology Components, and Physical Technology Components
- Physical Technology Component *realizes* Physical Application Component relationships

Environments and Locations Diagram

The Environments and Locations diagram depicts which locations host which applications, identifies what technologies and/or applications are used at which locations, and finally identifies the locations from which business users typically interact with the applications.

This diagram should also show the existence and location of different deployment environments, including non-production environments, such as development and pre production.

Platform Decomposition Diagram

The Platform Decomposition diagram depicts the technology platform that supports the operations of the Information Systems Architecture. The diagram covers all aspects of the infrastructure platform and provides an overview of the enterprise's technology platform. The diagram can be expanded to map the technology platform to appropriate application components within a specific functional or process area. This diagram may show details of specification, such as product versions, number of CPUs, etc. or simply could be an informal "eye-chart" providing an overview of the technical environment.

The diagram should clearly show the enterprise applications and the technology platform for each application area can further be decomposed as follows:

- Hardware:
  - Logical Technology Components (with attributes)
  - Physical Technology Components (with attributes)
- Software:
  - Logical Technology Components (with attributes)
  - Physical Technology Components (with attributes)

Depending upon the scope of the enterprise architecture work, additional technology cross-platform information (e.g., communications, telco, and video information) may be addressed.

Processing Diagram

The Processing diagram focuses on deployable units of code/configuration and how these are deployed onto the technology platform. A deployment unit represents grouping of business function, service, or application components. The Processing diagram addresses the following:

- Which set of application components need to be grouped to form a deployment unit

- How one deployment unit connects/interacts with another (LAN, WAN, and the applicable protocols)

- How application configuration and usage patterns generate load or capacity requirements for different technology components

The organization and grouping of deployment units depends on separation concerns of the presentation, business logic, and data store layers and service-level requirements of the components. For example, presentation layer deployment unit is grouped based on the following:
    Application components that provide UI or user access functions

- Application components that are differentiated by location and user roles

There are several considerations to determine how application components are grouped together. Each deployment unit is made up of sub-units, such as:

- **Installation**: Part that holds the executable code or package configuration (in case of packages).

- **Execution**: Application component with its associated state at run time.

- **Persistence**: Data that represents the persistent state of the application component.

Finally, these deployment units are deployed on either dedicated or shared technology components (workstation, web server, application server, or database server, etc.). It is important to note that technology processing can influence and have implications on the services definition and granularity.

Networked Computing/Hardware Diagram

Starting with the transformation to client-server systems from mainframes and later with the advent of e-Business and J2EE, large enterprises moved predominantly into a highly network-based distributed network computing environment with firewalls and demilitarized zones. Currently, most of the applications have a web front-end and, looking at the deployment architecture of these applications, it is very common to find three distinct layers in the network landscape; namely a web presentation layer, an business logic or application layer, and a back-end data store layer. It is a common practice for applications to be deployed and hosted in a shared and common infrastructure environment.

So it becomes highly critical to document the mapping between logical applications and the technology components (e.g., server) that supports the application both in the development and production environments. The purpose of this diagram is to show the "as deployed" logical view of logical application components in a distributed network computing environment. The diagram is useful for the following reasons:

- Enable understanding of which application is deployed where in the distributed network computing environment

- Establishing authorization, security, and access to these technology components

- Understand the Technology Architecture that support the applications during problem resolution and troubleshooting

- Isolate performance problems encountered by applications, determine whether it is application code-related or technology platform-related, and perform necessary upgrade to specific physical technology components

- Identify areas of optimization as and when newer technologies are available which will eventually reduce cost

- Enable application/technology auditing and prove compliance with enterprise technology standards

- Serve as an important tool to introduce changes to the Technology Architecture, thereby supporting effective change management

- Establish traceability and changing application end-point address while moving application either from a shared environment to a dedicated environment or *vice versa*

The scope of the diagram can be appropriately defined to cover a specific application, business function, or the entire enterprise. If chosen to be developed at the enterprise level, then the network computing landscape can be depicted in an application agnostic way as well.

Communications Engineering Diagram

The Communications Engineering diagram describes the means of communication — the method of sending and receiving information — between these assets in the Technology Architecture; insofar as the selection of package solutions in the preceding architectures put specific requirements on the communications between the applications.

The Communications Engineering diagram will take logical connections between client and server components and identify network boundaries and network infrastructure required to physically implement those connections. It does not describe the information format or content, but will address protocol and capacity issues.

35.13 Viewpoints in Phase E

The following catalogs, matrices, and diagrams may be produced in Phase E (Opportunities & Solutions).

- Catalogs:
    - No catalogs are defined to be created during Phase E.
- Matrices:
    - No matrices are defined to be created during Phase E.
- Core diagrams:
    - Project Context diagram
    - Benefits diagram

- Extension diagrams:

    — No extension diagrams are defined to be created during Phase E.

The following section describes each of the catalogs, matrices, and diagrams created within Phase E (Opportunities & Solutions).

Project Context Diagram

A Project Context diagram shows the scope of a work package to be implemented as a part of a broader transformation roadmap. The Project Context diagram links a work package to the organizations, functions, services, processes, applications, data, and technology that will be added, removed, or impacted by the project.

The Project Context diagram is also a valuable tool for project portfolio management and project mobilization.

Benefits Diagram

The Benefits diagram shows opportunities identified in an architecture definition, classified according to their relative size, benefit, and complexity. This diagram can be used by stakeholders to make selection, prioritization, and sequencing decisions on identified opportunities.

35.14 Viewpoints for Requirements Management

The following catalogs, matrices, and diagrams may be produced in the Requirements Management phase.

- Catalogs:

    — Requirements catalog

- Matrices:

    — No matrices are defined to be created during the Requirements Management phase.

- Core diagrams:

    — No core diagrams are defined to be created during the Requirements Management phase.

- Extension diagrams:

    — No extension diagrams are defined to be created during the Requirements Management phase.

The following section describes each of the catalogs, matrices, and diagrams created within the Requirements Management phase.

Requirements Catalog

The Requirements catalog captures things that the enterprise needs to do to meet its objectives. Requirements generated from architecture engagements are typically implemented through change initiatives identified and scoped during Phase E (Opportunities & Solutions). Requirements can also be used as a quality assurance tool to ensure that a particular architecture is fit-for-purpose (i.e., can the architecture meet all identified requirements).

The Requirements catalog contains the following metamodel entities:

- Requirement
- Assumption
- Constraint
- Gap

35.15 Developing a Business Architecture View

The Business Architecture view is concerned with addressing the concerns of users.

35.15.1 Stakeholders and Concerns

This view should be developed for the users. It focuses on the functional aspects of the system from the perspective of the users of the system.

Addressing the concerns of the users includes consideration of the following:

People	The human resource aspects of the system. It examines the human actors involved in the system.
Process	Deals with the user processes involved in the system.
Function	Deals with the functions required to support the processes.
Business Information	Deals with the information required to flow in support of the processes.
Usability	Considers the usability aspects of the system and its environment.
Performance	Considers the performance aspects of the system and its environment.

35.15.2 Developing the View

Business scenarios (see Part III, Chapter 26) are an important technique that may be used prior to, and as a key input to, the development of the Business Architecture view, to help identify and understand business needs, and thereby to derive the business requirements and constraints that the architecture development has to address. Business scenarios are an extremely useful way to depict what should happen when planned and unplanned events occur. It is highly recommended that business scenarios be created for planned change, and for unplanned change.

The following section describe some of the key issues that the architect might consider when constructing business scenarios.

35.15.3 Key Issues

The Business Architecture view considers the functional aspects of the system; that is, what the new system is intended to do. This can be built up from an analysis of the existing environment and of the requirements and constraints affecting the new system.

The new requirements and constraints will appear from a number of sources, possibly including:

- Existing internal specifications and lists of approved products
- Business goals and objectives
- Business process re-engineering activities
- Changes in technology

What should emerge from the Business Architecture view is a clear understanding of the functional requirements for the new architecture, with statements like: "Improvements in handling customer enquiries are required through wider use of computer/telephony integration".

The Business Architecture view considers the usability aspects of the system and its environment. It should also consider impacts on the user such as skill levels required, the need for specialized training, and migration from current practice. When considering usability the architect should take into account:

- The ease-of-use of the user interface, and how intuitive it is
- Whether or not there is transparent access to data and applications, irrespective of location
- Ease-of-management of the user environment by the user
- Application interoperability through means such as drag-and-drop
- Online help facilities
- Clarity of documentation
- Security and password aspects, such as avoiding the requirement for multiple sign-on and password dialogs
- Access to productivity applications, such as mail or a spreadsheet

Note that, although security and management are thought about here, it is from a usability and functionality point of view. The technical aspects of security and management are considered in the Enterprise Security view (see Section 35.16) and the Enterprise Manageability view (see Section 35.21).

35.16 Developing an Enterprise Security View

The Enterprise Security view is concerned with the security aspects of the system.

35.16.1 Stakeholders and Concerns

This view should be developed for security engineers of the system. It focuses on how the system is implemented from the perspective of security, and how security affects the system properties. It examines the system to establish what information is stored and processed, how valuable it is, what threats exist, and how they can be addressed.

Major concerns for this view are understanding how to ensure that the system is available to only those that have permission, and how to protect the system from unauthorized tampering.

35.16.2 Developing the View

The subjects of the general architecture of a "security system" are components that are secured, or components that provide security services. Additionally Access Control Lists (ACLs) and security schema definitions are used to model and implement security.

35.16.3 Basic Concepts

This section presents basic concepts required for an understanding of information system security.

The essence of security is the controlled use of information. The purpose of this section is to provide a brief overview of how security protection is implemented in the components of an information system. Doctrinal or procedural mechanisms, such as physical and personnel security procedures and policy, are not discussed here in any depth.

Figure 35-4 depicts an abstract view of an Information Systems Architecture, which emphasizes the fact that an information system from the security perspective is either part of a Local Subscriber Environment (LSE) or a Communications Network (CN). An LSE may be either fixed or mobile. The LSEs by definition are under the control of the using organization. In an open system distributed computing implementation, secure and non-secure LSEs will almost certainly be required to interoperate.

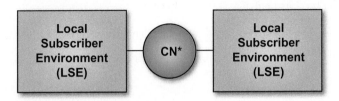

*CN = Communications Network

Figure 35-4 Abstract Security Architecture View

35.16.3.1 Information Domains

The concept of an information domain provides the basis for discussing security protection requirements. An information domain is defined as a set of users, their information objects, and a security policy. An information domain security policy is the statement of the criteria for membership in the information domain and the required protection of the information objects. Breaking an organization's information down into domains is the first step in reducing the task of security policy development to a manageable size.

The business of most organizations requires that their members operate in more than one information domain. The diversity of business activities and the variation in perception of threats to the security of information will result in the existence of different information domains within one organization security policy. A specific activity may use several information domains, each with its own distinct information domain security policy.

Information domains are not necessarily bounded by information systems or even networks of systems. The security mechanisms implemented in information system components may be evaluated for their ability to meet the information domain security policies.

35.16.3.2 Strict Isolation

Information domains can be viewed as being strictly isolated from one another. Information objects should be transferred between two information domains only in accordance with established rules, conditions, and procedures expressed in the security policy of each information domain.

35.16.3.3 Absolute Protection

The concept of "absolute protection" is used to achieve the same level of protection in all information systems supporting a particular information domain. It draws attention to the problems created by interconnecting LSEs that provide different strengths of security protection. This interconnection is likely because open systems may consist of an unknown number of heterogeneous LSEs. Analysis of minimum security requirements will ensure that the concept of absolute protection will be achieved for each information domain across LSEs.

35.16.4 Security Generic Architecture View

Figure 35-5 shows a generic architecture view which can be used to discuss the allocation of security services and the implementation of security mechanisms. This view identifies the architectural components within an LSE. The LSEs are connected by CNs. The LSEs include end systems, relay systems, and Local Communications Systems (LCSs), described below.

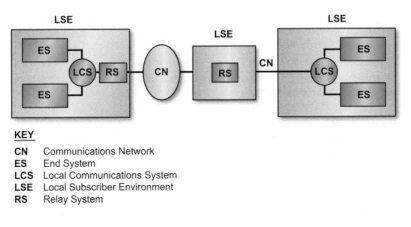

KEY

CN	Communications Network
ES	End System
LCS	Local Communications System
LSE	Local Subscriber Environment
RS	Relay System

Figure 35-5 Generic Security Architecture View

- **Relay System (RS)**: The component of an LSE, the functionality of which is limited to information transfer and is only indirectly accessible by users (e.g., router, switch, multiplexor, Message Transfer Agent (MTA)). It may have functionality similar to an end system, but an end user does not use it directly. Note that relay system functions may be provided in an end system.

- **Local Communication System (LCS)**: A network that provides communications capabilities between LSEs or within an LSE with all of the components under control of an LSE.

- **Communications Network (CN)**: A network that provides inter-LSE communications capabilities, but is not controlled by LSEs (e.g., commercial carriers).

The end system and the relay system are viewed as requiring the same types of security protection. For this reason, a discussion of security protection in an end system generally also applies to a relay system. The security protections in an end system could occur in both the hardware and software.

35.16.5 Security Services Allocation

Security protection of an information system is provided by mechanisms implemented in the hardware and software of the system and by the use of doctrinal mechanisms. The mechanisms implemented in the system hardware and software are concentrated in the end system or relay system. This focus for security protection is based on the open system, distributed computing approach for information systems. This implies use of commercial common carriers and private common-user communications systems as the CN provider between LSEs. Thus, for operation of end systems in a distributed environment, a greater degree of security protection can be ensured from implementation of mechanisms in the end system or relay system.

However, communications networks should satisfy the availability element of security in order to provide appropriate security protection for the information system. This means that CNs must provide an agreed level of responsiveness, continuity of service, and resistance to accidental and intentional threats to the communications service availability.

Implementing the necessary security protection in the end system occurs in three system service areas of TOGAF. They are operating system services, network services, and system management services.

Most of the implementation of security protection is expected to occur in software. The hardware is expected to protect the integrity of the end-system software. Hardware security mechanisms include protection against tampering, undesired emanations, and cryptography.

35.16.5.1 *Operating System Services*

A "security context" is defined as a controlled process space subject to an information domain security policy. The security context is therefore analogous to a common operating system notion of user process space. Isolation of security contexts is required. Security contexts are required for all applications (e.g., end-user and security management applications). The focus is on strict isolation of information domains, management of end-system resources, and controlled sharing and transfer of information among information domains. Where possible, security-critical functions should be isolated into relatively small modules that are related in well-defined ways.

The operating system will isolate multiple security contexts from each other using hardware protection features (e.g., processor state register, memory mapping registers) to create separate address spaces for each of them. Untrusted software will use end-system resources only by invoking security-critical functions through the separation kernel. Most of the security-critical functions are the low-level functions of traditional operating systems.

35.16.5.2 *Network Services*

Two basic classes of communications are envisioned for which distributed security contexts may need to be established. These are interactive and staged (store and forward) communications.

The concept of a "security association" forms an interactive distributed security context. A security association is defined as all the communication and security mechanisms and functions that extend the protections required by an information domain security policy within an end system to information in transfer between multiple end systems. The security association is an extension or expansion of an OSI application layer association. An application layer association is composed of appropriate application layer functions and protocols plus all of the underlying communications functions and protocols at other layers of the OSI model. Multiple security protocols may be included in a single security association to provide for a combination of security services.

For staged delivery communications (e.g., email), use will be made of an encapsulation technique (termed "wrapping process") to convey the necessary security attributes with the data being transferred as part of the network services. The wrapped security attributes are intended to permit the receiving end system to establish the necessary security context for processing the transferred data. If the wrapping process cannot provide all the necessary security protection, interactive security contexts between end systems will have to be used to ensure the secure staged transfer of information.

35.16.5.3 System Security Management Services

Security management is a particular instance of the general information system management functions discussed in earlier chapters. Information system security management services are concerned with the installation, maintenance, and enforcement of information domain and information system security policy rules in the information system intended to provide these security services. In particular, the security management function controls information needed by operating system services within the end system security architecture. In addition to these core services, security management requires event handling, auditing, and recovery. Standardization of security management functions, data structures, and protocols will enable interoperation of Security Management Application Processes (SMAPs) across many platforms in support of distributed security management.

35.17 Developing a Software Engineering View

The Software Engineering view is concerned with the development of new software systems.

35.17.1 Stakeholders and Concerns

Building a software-intensive system is both expensive and time-consuming. Because of this, it is necessary to establish guidelines to help minimize the effort required and the risks involved. This is the purpose of the Software Engineering view, which should be developed for the software engineers who are going to develop the system.

Major concerns for these stakeholders are:

- Development approach
- Software modularity and re-use
- Portability
- Migration and interoperability

35.17.1.1 Development Approach

There are many lifecycle models defined for software development (waterfall, prototyping, etc.). A consideration for the architect is how best to feed architectural decisions into the lifecycle model that is going to be used for development of the system.

35.17.1.2 Software Modularity and Re-Use

As a piece of software grows in size, so the complexity and inter-dependencies between different parts of the code increase. Reliability will fall dramatically unless this complexity can be brought under control.

Modularity is a concept by which a piece of software is grouped into a number of distinct and logically cohesive sub-units, presenting services to the outside world through a well-defined interface. Generally speaking, the components of a module will share access to common data, and the interface will provide controlled access to this data. Using modularity, it becomes possible to build a software application incrementally on a reliable base of pre-tested code.

A further benefit of a well-defined modular system is that the modules defined within it may be re-used in the same or on other projects, cutting development time dramatically by reducing both development and testing effort.

In recent years, the development of object-oriented programming languages has greatly increased programming language support for module development and code re-use. Such languages allow the developer to define "classes" (a unit of modularity) of objects that behave in a controlled and well-defined manner. Techniques such as inheritance — which enables parts of an existing interface to an object to be changed — enhance the potential for re-usability by allowing predefined classes to be tailored or extended when the services they offer do not quite meet the requirement of the developer.

If modularity and software re-use are likely to be key objectives of new software developments, consideration must be given to whether the component parts of any proposed architecture may facilitate or prohibit the desired level of modularity in the appropriate areas.

35.17.1.3 Portability

Software portability — the ability to take a piece of software written in one environment and make it run in another — is important in many projects, especially product developments. It requires that all software and hardware aspects of a chosen Technology Architecture (not just the newly developed application) be available on the new platform. It will, therefore, be necessary to ensure that the component parts of any chosen architecture are available across all the appropriate target platforms.

35.17.1.4 Migration and Interoperability

Interoperability is always required between the component parts of a new architecture. It may also, however, be required between a new architecture and parts of an existing legacy system; for example, during the staggered replacement of an old system. Interoperability between the new and old architectures may, therefore, be a factor in architectural choice.

35.17.2 Key Issues

- Data-intensive *versus* information-intensive software systems
- Achieving interoperability
- Software tiers
- Uses of a data access tier
- Distribution

35.17.2.1 Data-Intensive versus Information-Intensive Software Systems

This view considers two general categories of software systems. First, there are those systems that require only a user interface to a database, requiring little or no business logic built into the software. These systems can be called "data-intensive". Second, there are those systems that require users to manipulate information that might be distributed across multiple databases, and to do this manipulation according to a predefined business logic. These systems can be called "information-intensive"

Data-intensive systems can be built with reasonable ease through the use of 4GL tools. In these systems, the business logic is in the mind of the user; i.e., the user understands the rules for manipulating the data and uses those rules while doing his work.

Information-intensive systems are different. Information is defined as "meaningful data"; i.e., data in a context that includes business logic. Information is different from data. Data is the tokens that are stored in databases or other data stores. Information is multiple tokens of data combined to convey a message. For example, "3" is data, but "3 widgets" is information. Typically, information reflects a model. Information-intensive systems also tend to require information from other systems and, if this path of information passing is automated, usually some mediation is required to convert the format of incoming information into a format that can be locally used. Because of this, information-intensive systems tend to be more complex than others, and require the most effort to build, integrate, and maintain.

This view is concerned primarily with information-intensive systems. In addition to building systems that can manage information, though, systems should also be as flexible as possible. This has a number of benefits. It allows the system to be used in different environments; for example, the same system should be usable with different sources of data, even if the new data store is a different configuration. Similarly, it might make sense to use the same functionality but with users who need a different user interface. So information systems should be built so that they can be reconfigured with different data stores or different user interfaces. If a system is built to allow this, it enables the enterprise to re-use parts (or components) of one system in another.

35.17.2.2 Achieving Interoperability

The word "interoperate" implies that one processing system performs an operation on behalf of or at the behest of another processing system. In practice, the request is a complete sentence containing a verb (operation) and one or more nouns (identities of resources, where the resources can be information, data, physical devices, etc.). Interoperability comes from shared functionality.

Interoperability can only be achieved when information is passed, not when data is passed. Most information systems today get information both from their own data stores and other information systems. In some cases the web of connectivity between information systems is quite extensive. The US Air Force, for example, has a concept known as "A5 Interoperability". This means that the required data is available Anytime, Anywhere, by Anyone, who is Authorized, in Any way. This requires that many information systems are architecturally linked and provide information to each other.

There must be some kind of physical connectivity between the systems. This might be a Local Area Network (LAN), a Wide Area Network (WAN), or, in some cases, it might simply be the passing data storage media between systems. Assuming a network connects the systems, there must be agreement on the protocols used. This enables the transfer of bits.

When the bits are assembled at the receiving system, they must be placed in the context that the receiving system needs. In other words, both the source and destination systems must agree on an information model. The source system uses this model to convert its information into data to be passed, and the destination system uses this same model to convert the received data into information it can use.

This usually requires an agreement between the architects and designers of the two systems. In the past, this agreement was often documented in the form of an Interface Control Document (ICD). The ICD defines the exact syntax and semantics that the sending system will use so that the receiving system will know what to do when the data arrives. The biggest problem with ICDs is that they tend to be unique solutions between two systems. If a given system must share information with *n* other systems, there is the potential need for *n*2 ICDs. This extremely tight integration prohibits flexibility and the ability of a system to adapt to a changing environment. Maintaining all these ICDs is also a challenge.

New technology, such as eXtensible Markup Language (XML), has the promise of making data "self describing". Use of new technologies such as XML, once they become reliable and well documented, might eliminate the need for an ICD. Further, there would be Commercial Off-The-Shelf (COTS) products available to parse and manipulate the XML data, eliminating the need to develop these products in-house. It should also ease the pain of maintaining all the interfaces.

Another approach is to build "mediators" between the systems. Mediators would use metadata that is sent with the data to understand the syntax and semantics of the data and convert it into a format usable by the receiving system. However, mediators do require that well-formed metadata be sent, adding to the complexity of the interface.

35.17.2.3 Software Tiers

Typically, software architectures are either two-tier or three-tier.[9]

Each tier typically presents at least one capability.

Two-Tier

In a two-tier architecture, the user interface and business logic are tightly coupled while the data is kept independent. This gives the advantage of allowing the data to reside on a dedicated data server. It also allows the data to be independently maintained. The tight coupling of the user interface and business logic ensure that they will work well together, for this problem in this domain. However, the tight coupling of the user interface and business logic dramatically increases maintainability risks while reducing flexibility and opportunities for re-use.

Three-Tier

A three-tier approach adds a tier that separates the business logic from the user interface. This in principle allows the business logic to be used with different user interfaces as well as with different data stores. With respect to the use of different user interfaces, users might want the same user interface but using different COTS presentation servers; for example, Java Virtual Machine (JVM). Similarly, if the business logic is to be used with different data stores, then each data store must use the same data model[10] (data standardization), or a mediation tier must be added above the data store (data encapsulation).

---

9.   These are different from two and three-tiered system architectures in which the middle tier is usually middleware. In the approach being presented here, middleware is seen as an enabler for the software components to interact with each other. See Section 35.17.2.8 for more details.

10.   If, for example, SQL statements are to be embedded in the business logic.

Five-Tier

To achieve maximum flexibility, software should utilize a five-tier scheme for software which extends the three-tier paradigm (see Figure 35-6). The scheme is intended to provide strong separation of the three major functional areas of the architecture. Since there are client and server aspects of both the user interface and the data store, the scheme then has five tiers.[11]

The presentation tier is typically COTS-based. The presentation interface might be an X Server, Win32, etc. There should be a separate tier for the user interface client. This client establishes the look-and-feel of the interface; the server (presentation tier) actually performs the tasks by manipulating the display. The user interface client hides the presentation server from the application business logic.

The application business logic (e.g., a scheduling engine) should be a separate tier. This tier is called the "application logic" and functions as a server for the user interface client. It interfaces to the user interface typically through callbacks. The application logic tier also functions as a client to the data access tier.

If there is a user need to use an application with multiple databases with different schema, then a separate tier is needed for data access. This client would access the data stores using the appropriate COTS interface[12] and then convert the raw data into an abstract data type representing parts of the information model. The interface into this object network would then provide a generalized Data Access Interface (DAI) which would hide the storage details of the data from any application that uses that data.

Each tier in this scheme can have zero or more components. The organization of the components within a tier is flexible and can reflect a number of different architectures based on need. For example, there might be many different components in the application logic tier (scheduling, accounting, inventory control, etc.) and the relationship between them can reflect whatever architecture makes sense, but none of them should be a client to the presentation server.

This clean separation of user interface, business logic, and information will result in maximum flexibility and componentized software that lends itself to product line development practices. For example, it is conceivable that the same functionality should be built once and yet be usable by different presentation servers (e.g., on PCs or UNIX system boxes), displayed with different looks and feels depending on user needs, and usable with multiple legacy databases. Moreover, this flexibility should not require massive rewrites to the software whenever a change is needed.

---

11. Note that typical "layered" architectures require each layer to be a client of the layer below it and a server to the layer above it. The scheme presented here is not compliant with this description and therefore we have used the word "tier" instead of "layer".

12. The interface to the data store might utilize embedded SQL. A more flexible way would be to use the Distributed Relational Database Architecture (DRDA) or ODBC since either of these standards would enable an application to access different DBMSs in a location-independent manner using the same SQL statements.

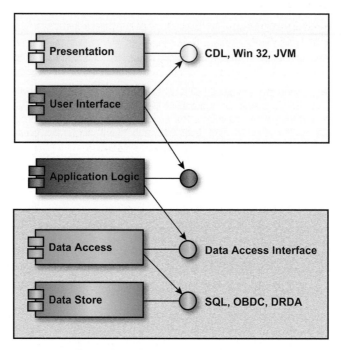

Figure 35-6 The Five-Tier Organization

35.17.2.4 Some Uses of a Data Access Tier

The data access tier provides a standardized view of certain classes of data, and as such functions as a server to one or more application logic tiers. If implemented correctly, there would be no need for application code to "know" about the implementation details of the data. The application code would only have to know about an interface that presents a level of abstraction higher than the data. This interface is called the Data Access Interface (DAI).

For example, should a scheduling engine need to know what events are scheduled between two dates, that query should not require knowledge of tables and joins in a relational database. Moreover, the DAI could provide standardized access techniques for the data. For example, the DAI could provide a Publish and Subscribe (P&S) interface whereby systems which require access to data stores could register an interest in certain types of data, perhaps under certain conditions, and the DAI would provide the required data when those conditions occur.

35.17.2.5 One Possible Instantiation of a DAI

One means to instantiate a data access component is with three layers, as shown in Figure 35-7. This is not the only means to build a DAI, but is presented as a possibility.

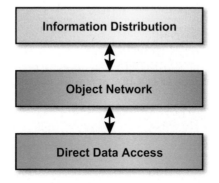

Figure 35-7 Data Access Interface (DAI)

Whereas the Direct Data Access layer contains the implementation details of one or more specific data stores, the Object Network and the Information Distribution layer require no such knowledge. Instead, the upper two layers reflect the need to standardize the interface for a particular domain. The Direct Data Access layer spans the gap between the Data Access tier and the Data Store tier, and therefore has knowledge of the implementation details of the data. SQL statements, either embedded or via a standard such as DRDA or ODBC, are located here.

The Object Network layer is the instantiation in software of the information model. As such, it is an efficient means to show the relationships that hold between pieces of data. The translation of data accesses to objects in the network would be the role of the Direct Data Access layer.

Within the Information Distribution layer lies the interface to the "outside world". This interface typically uses a data bus to distribute the data (see below).[13] It could also contain various information-related services; for example, a P&S registry and publication service or an interface to a security server for data access control.[14] The Information Distribution layer might also be used to distribute applications or applets required to process distributed information. Objects in the object network would point to the applications or applets, allowing easy access to required processing code.

---

13. Although it could use other mechanisms. For example, the DAI could be built as a shared library to be linked with the application logic at compile time.

14. The security server itself would use a five-tier architecture. The security application logic tier would interface with the DAI of other systems to provide data access control.

35.17.2.6 DAIs Enable Flexibility

The DAI enables a very flexible architecture. Multiple raw capabilities can access the same or different data stores, all through the same DAI. Each DAI might be implemented in many ways, according to the specific needs of the raw capabilities using it. Figure 35-8 illustrates a number of possibilities, including multiple different DAIs in different domains accessing the same database, a single DAI accessing multiple databases, and multiple instantiations of the same DAI access the same database.

It is not always clear that a DAI is needed, and it appears to require additional work during all phases of development. However, should a database ever be redesigned, or if an application is to be re-used and there is no control over how the new data is implemented, using a DAI saves time in the long run.

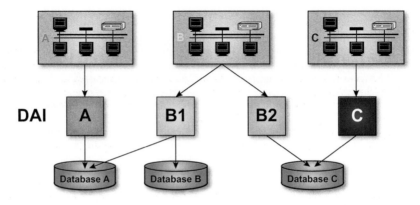

Figure 35-8 Multiple Uses of a Data Access Interface (DAI)

35.17.2.7 Distribution

The ISO Reference Model for Open Distributed Processing (RM-ODP) offers a meta-standard that is intended to allow more specific standards to emerge. The RM-ODP Reference Model defines a set of distribution transparencies that are applicable to the TOGAF Software Engineering view.

- **Access Transparency** masks differences in data representation and invocation mechanisms to enable interworking between objects. This transparency solves many of the problems of interworking between heterogeneous systems, and will generally be provided by default.

- **Failure Transparency** masks from an object the failure and possible recovery of other objects (or itself) to enable fault tolerance. When this transparency is provided, the designer can work in an idealized world in which the corresponding class of failures does not occur.

- **Location Transparency** masks the use of information about location in space when identifying and binding to interfaces. This transparency provides a logical view of naming, independent of actual physical location.

- **Migration Transparency** masks from an object the ability of a system to change the location of that object. Migration is often used to achieve load balancing and reduce latency.

- **Relocation Transparency** masks relocation of an interface from other interfaces bound to it. Relocation allows system operation to continue even when migration or replacement of some objects creates temporary inconsistencies in the view seen by their users.

- **Replication Transparency** masks the use of a group of mutually behaviorally compatible objects to support an interface. Replication is often used to enhance performance and availability.

- **Transaction Transparency** masks co-ordination of activities amongst a configuration of objects to achieve consistency.

35.17.2.8 Infrastructure Bus

The infrastructure bus represents the middleware that establishes the client/server relationship. This commercial software is like a backplane onto which capabilities can be plugged. A system should adhere to a commercial implementation of a middleware standard. This is to ensure that capabilities using different commercial implementations of the standard can interoperate. If more than one commercial standard is used (e.g., COM and CORBA), then the system should allow for interoperability between implementations of these standards via the use of commercial bridging software.[15] Wherever practical, the interfaces should be specified in the appropriate Interface Description Language (IDL). Taken this way, every interface in the five-tier scheme represents an opportunity for distribution.

Clients can interact with servers via the infrastructure bus. In this interaction, the actual network transport (TCP/IP, HTTP, etc.), the platform/vendor of the server, and the operating system of the server are all transparent.

---

15.   For example, many people believe that the user interface should be built on COM, while the data access tiers should be built on CORBA.

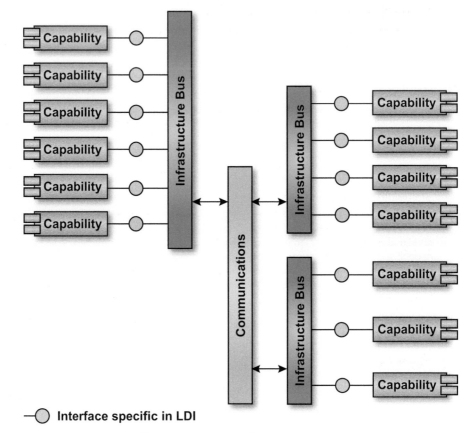

Figure 35-9 Notional Distribution Model

35.17.3 Conclusion

The Software Engineering view gives guidance on how to structure software in a very flexible manner. By following these guidelines, the resulting software will be componentized. This enables the re-use of components in different environments. Moreover, through the use of an infrastructure bus and clean interfaces, the resulting software will be location-independent, enabling its distribution across a network.

35.18 Developing a System Engineering View

The System Engineering view is concerned with assembling software and hardware components into a working system.

35.18.1 Stakeholders and Concerns

This view should be developed for the systems engineering personnel of the system, and should focus on how the system is implemented from the perspective of hardware/software and networking.

Systems engineers are typically concerned with location, modifiability, re-usability, and availability of all components of the system. The System Engineering view presents a number of different ways in which software and hardware components can be assembled into a working system. To a great extent, the choice of model determines the properties of the final system. It looks at technology which already exists in the organization, and what is available currently or in the near future. This reveals areas where new technology can contribute to the function or efficiency of the new architecture, and how different types of processing platform can support different parts of the overall system.

Major concerns for this view are understanding the system requirements. In general these stakeholders are concerned with ensuring that the appropriate components are developed and deployed within the system in an optimal manner.

Developing this view assists in the selection of the best configurations for the system.

35.18.2 Key Issues

This view of the architecture focuses on computing models that are appropriate for a distributed computing environment. To support the migration of legacy systems, this section also presents models that are appropriate for a centralized environment. The definitions of many of the computing models (e.g., host-based, master/slave, and three-tiered) historically preceded the definition of the client/server model, which attempts to be a general-purpose model. In most cases the models have not been redefined in the computing literature in terms of contrasts with the client/server model. Therefore, some of the distinctions of features are not always clean. In general, however, the models are distinguished by the allocation of functions for an information system application to various components (e.g., terminals, computer platforms). These functions that make up an information system application are presentation, application function, and data management.

35.18.2.1 Client/Server Model

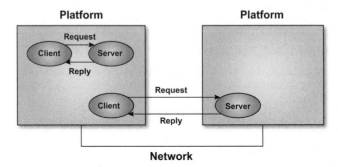

Figure 35-10 Basic Client/Server Model

Client/server processing is a special type of distributed computing termed "co-operative processing" because the clients and servers co-operate in the processing of a total application (presentation, functional processing, data management). In the model, clients are processes that request services, and servers are processes that provide services. Clients and servers can be located on the same processor, different multi-processor nodes, or on separate processors at remote locations. The client typically initiates communications with the server. The server typically does not initiate a request with a client. A server may support many clients and may act as a client to another server. Figure 35-10 depicts a basic client/server model, which emphasizes the request-reply relationships. Figure 35-11 shows the same model drawn following the TOGAF TRM, showing how the various entities and interfaces can be used to support a client/server model, whether the server is local or remote to the client. In these representations, the request-reply relationships would be defined in the API.

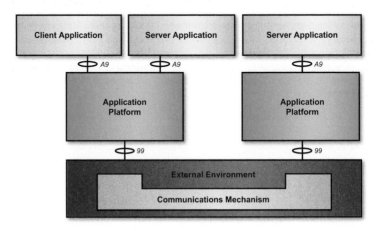

Figure 35-11 Reference Model Representation of Client/Server Model

Clients tend to be generalized and can run on one of many nodes. Servers tend to be specialized and run on a few nodes. Clients are typically implemented as a call to a routine. Servers are typically implemented as a continuous process waiting for service requests (from clients). Many client/server implementations involve remote communications across a network. However, nothing in the client/server model dictates remote communications, and the physical location of clients is usually transparent to the server. The communication between a client and a server may involve a local communication between two independent processes on the same machine.

An application program can be considered to consist of three parts:

- Data handling

- Application function

- Presentation

In general, each of these can be assigned to either a client or server application, making appropriate use of platform services. This assignment defines a specific client/server configuration.

35.18.2.2 Master/Slave and Hierarchic Models

In this model, slave computers are attached to a master computer. In terms of distribution, the master/slave model is one step up from the host-based model. Distribution is provided in one direction — from the master to the slaves. The slave computers perform application processing only when directed to by the master computer. In addition, slave processors can perform limited local processing, such as editing, function key processing, and field validation. A typical configuration might be a mainframe as the master with PCs as the slaves acting as intelligent terminals, as illustrated in Figure 35-12.

The hierarchic model is an extension of the master/slave model with more distribution capabilities. In this approach, the top layer is usually a powerful mainframe, which acts as a server to the second tier. The second layer consists of LAN servers and clients to the first layer as well as servers to the third layer. The third layer consists of PCs and workstations. This model has been described as adding true distributed processing to the master/slave model. Figure 35-12 shows an example hierarchic model in the third configuration, and below, Figure 35-13 shows the hierarchic model represented in terms of the entities and interfaces of the TRM.

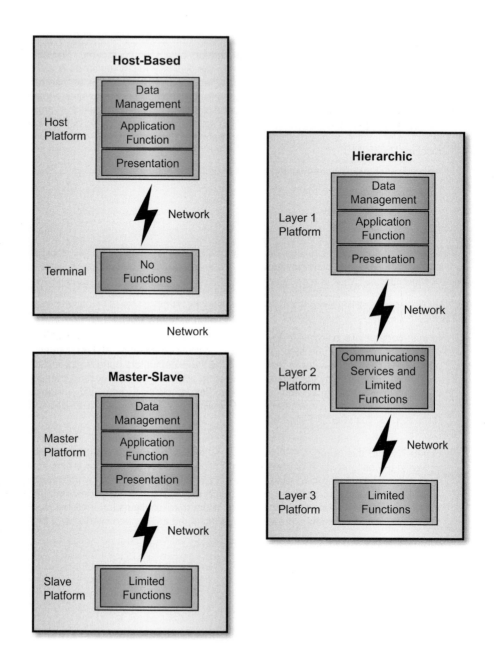

Figure 35-12 Host-Based, Master/Slave, and Hierarchic Models

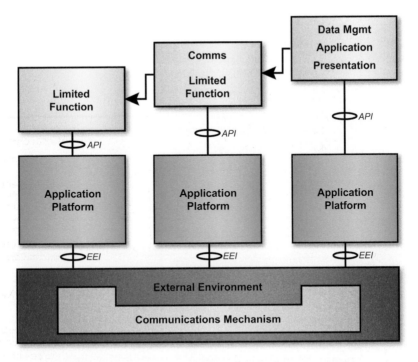

Figure 35-13 Hierarchic Model using the Reference Model

35.18.2.3 Peer-to-Peer Model

In the peer-to-peer model there are co-ordinating processes. All of the computers are servers in that they can receive requests for services and respond to them; and all of the computers are clients in that they can send requests for services to other computers. In current implementations, there are often redundant functions on the participating platforms.

Attempts have been made to implement the model for distributed heterogeneous (or federated) database systems. This model could be considered a special case of the client/server model, in which all platforms are both servers and clients. Figure 35-14 (A) shows an example peer-to-peer configuration in which all platforms have complete functions.

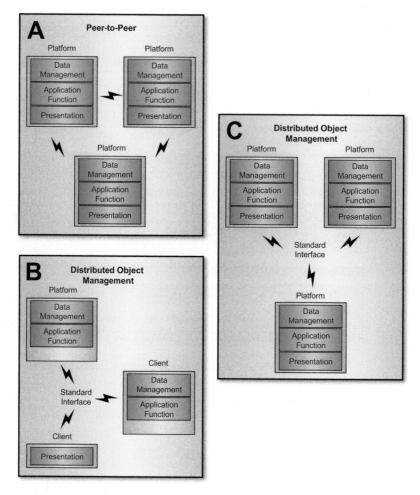

Figure 35-14 Peer-to-Peer and Distributed Object Management Models

35.18.2.4 Distributed Object Management Model

In this model the remote procedure calls typically used for communication in the client/server and other distributed processing models are replaced by messages sent to objects. The services provided by systems on a network are treated as objects. A requester need not know the details of how the object is configured. The approach requires:

- A mechanism to dispatch messages

- A mechanism to co-ordinate delivery of messages

- Applications and services that support a messaging interface

This approach does not contrast with client/server or peer-to-peer models but specifies a consistent interface for communicating between co-operating platforms. It is considered by some as an implementation approach for client/server and peer-to-peer models. Figure 35-14 presents two distributed object model examples. Example B shows how a client/server configuration would be altered to accommodate the distributed object management model. Example C shows how a peer-to-peer model would be altered to accomplish distributed object management.

The Object Management Group (OMG), a consortium of industry participants working toward object standards, has developed an architecture — the Common Object Request Broker Architecture (CORBA) — which specifies the protocol a client application must use to communicate with an Object Request Broker (ORB), which provides services. The ORB specifies how objects can transparently make requests and receive responses. In addition, Microsoft's Object Linking and Embedding (OLE) standard for Windows is an example of an implementation of distributed object management, whereby any OLE-compatible application can work with data from any other OLE-compatible application.

35.19 Developing a Communications Engineering View

The Communications Engineering view is concerned with structuring communications and networking elements to simplify network planning and design.

35.19.1 Stakeholders and Concerns

This view should be developed for the communications engineering personnel of the system, and should focus on how the system is implemented from the perspective of the communications engineer.

Communications engineers are typically concerned with location, modifiability, re-usability, and availability of communications and networking services. Major concerns for this view are understanding the network and communications requirements. In general these stakeholders are concerned with ensuring that the appropriate communications and networking services are developed and deployed within the system in an optimal manner.

Developing this view assists in the selection of the best model of communications for the system.

35.19.2 Key Issues

Communications networks are constructed of end devices (e.g., printers), processing nodes, communication nodes (switching elements), and the linking media that connect them. The communications network provides the means by which information is exchanged. Forms of information include data, imagery, voice, and video. Because automated information systems accept and process information using digital data formats rather than analog formats, the TOGAF communications concepts and guidance will focus on digital networks and digital services. Integrated multimedia services are included.

The Communications Engineering view describes the communications architecture with respect to geography, discusses the Open Systems Interconnection (OSI) reference model, and describes a general framework intended to permit effective system analysis and planning.

35.19.2.1 Communications Infrastructure

The Communications Infrastructure may contain up to three levels of transport — local, regional/metropolitan, and global — as shown in Figure 35-15. The names of the transport components are based on their respective geographic extent, but there is also a hierarchical relationship among them. The transport components correspond to a network management structure in which management and control of network resources are distributed across the different levels.

The local components relate to assets that are located relatively close together geographically. This component contains fixed communications equipment and small units of mobile communications equipment. LANs, to which the majority of end devices will be connected, are included in this component. Standard interfaces will facilitate portability, flexibility, and interoperability of LANs and end devices.

Regional and Metropolitan Area Networks (MANs) are geographically dispersed over a large area. A regional or metropolitan network could connect local components at several fixed bases or connect separate remote outposts. In most cases, regional and metropolitan networks are used to connect local networks. However, shared databases, regional processing platforms, and network management centers may connect directly or through a LAN. Standard interfaces will be provided to connect local networks and end devices.

Global or Wide Area Networks (WANs) are located throughout the world, providing connectivity for regional and metropolitan networks in the fixed and deployed environment. In addition, mobile units, shared databases, and central processing centers can connect directly to the global network as required. Standard interfaces will be provided to connect regional and metropolitan networks and end devices.

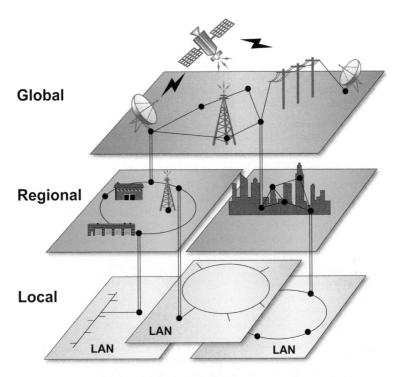

Figure 35-15 Communications Infrastructure

35.19.2.2 Communications Models

The geographically divided infrastructure described above forms the foundation for an overall communications framework. These geographic divisions permit the separate application of different management responsibilities, planning efforts, operational functions, and enabling technologies to be applied within each area. Hardware and software components and services fitted to the framework form the complete model.

The following sections describe the OSI Reference Model and a grouping of the OSI layers that facilitates discussion of interoperability issues.

The OSI Reference Model

The Open Systems Interconnection (OSI) Reference Model, portrayed in Figure 35-16, is the model used for data communications in TOGAF. Each of the seven layers in the model represents one or more services or protocols (a set of rules governing communications between systems), which define the functional operation of the communications between user and network elements. Each layer (with the exception of the top layer) provides services for the layer above it. This model aims at establishing open systems operation and implies standards-based implementation. It strives to permit different systems to accomplish complete interoperability and quality of operation throughout the network.

The seven layers of the OSI model are structured to facilitate independent development within each layer and to provide for changes independent of other layers. Stable international standard protocols in conformance with the OSI Reference Model layer definitions have been published by various standards organizations. This is not to say that the only protocols which fit into TOGAF are OSI protocols. Other protocol standards such as SNA or TCP/IP can be described using the OSI seven layer model as a reference.

Support and business area applications, as defined in TOGAF, are above the OSI Reference Model protocol stack and use its services via the applications layer.

Communications Framework

A communications system based on the OSI Reference Model includes services in all the relevant layers, the support and business area application software which sits above the application layer of the OSI Reference Model, and the physical equipment carrying the data. These elements may be grouped into architectural levels that represent major functional capabilities, such as switching and routing, data transfer, and the performance of applications.

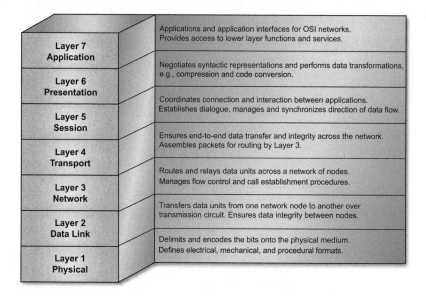

Figure 35-16 OSI Reference Model

These architectural levels are:

- The **Transmission level** (below the physical layer of the OSI Reference Model) provides all of the physical and electronic capabilities, which establish a transmission path between functional system elements (wires, leased circuits, interconnects, etc.).

- The **Network Switching level** (OSI layers 1 through 3) establishes connectivity through the network elements to support the routing and control of traffic (switches, controllers, network software, etc.).

- The **Data Exchange level** (OSI layers 4 through 7) accomplishes the transfer of information after the network has been established (end-to-end, user-to-user transfer) involving more capable processing elements (hosts, workstations, servers, etc.).

  In the TRM, OSI application layer services are considered to be part of the application platform entity, since they offer standardized interfaces to the application programming entity.

- The **Applications Program level** (above the OSI) includes the support and business area applications (non-management application programs).

The communications framework is defined to consist of the three geographical components of the Communications Infrastructure (local, regional, and global) and the four architectural levels (Transmission, Network Switching, Data Exchange, and Applications Program), and is depicted in Figure 35-17. Communications services are performed at one or more of these architectural levels within the geographical components. Figure 35-17 shows computing elements (operating at the Applications Program level) with supporting data exchange elements, linked with each other through various switching elements (operating at the Network Switching level), each located within its respective geographical component. Figure 35-17 also identifies the relationship of TOGAF to the communication architecture.

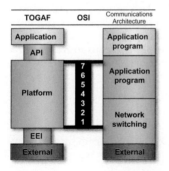

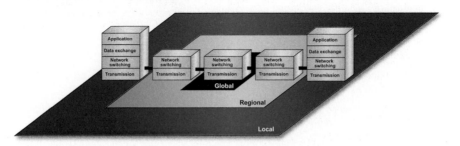

Figure 35-17 Communications Framework

Allocation of Services to Components

The Communications Infrastructure consists of the local, regional, and global transport components. The services allocated to these components are identical to the services of the Application Program, Data Exchange, Network Switching, or Transmission architectural levels that apply to a component. Data Exchange and Network Switching level services are identical to the services of the corresponding OSI Reference Model layers. Typically, only Network Switching and Transmission services are allocated to the regional and global components, which consist of communications nodes and transmission media. All services may be performed in the local component, which includes end devices, processing nodes, communications nodes, and linking media. Transmission, switching, transport, and applications are all performed in this component.

35.20 Developing a Data Flow View

The Data Flow view is concerned with storage, retrieval, processing, archiving, and security of data.

35.20.1 Stakeholders and Concerns

This view should be developed for database engineers of the system.

Major concerns for this view are understanding how to provide data to the right people and applications with the right interfaces at the right time. This view deals with the architecture of the storage, retrieval, processing, archiving, and security of data. It looks at the flow of data as it is stored and processed, and at what components will be required to support and manage both storage and processing. In general, these stakeholders are concerned with ensuring ubiquitous access to high quality data.

35.20.2 Developing the View

The subjects of the general architecture of a "database system" are database components or components that provide database services.

The modeling of a "database" is typically done with entity-relationship diagrams and schema definitions, including document type definitions.

35.20.3 Key Issues

Data management services may be provided by a wide range of implementations. Some examples are:

- Mega-centers providing functionally-oriented corporate databases supporting local and remote data requirements

- Distributed DBMSs that support the interactive use of partitioned and partially replicated databases

- File systems provided by operating systems, which may be used by both interactive and batch processing applications

Data management services include the storage, retrieval, manipulation, backup, restart/recovery, security, and associated functions for text, numeric data, and complex data such as documents, graphics, images, audio, and video. The operating system provides file management services, but they are considered here because many legacy databases exist as one or more files without the services provided by a DBMS.

Major components that provide data management services that are discussed in this section are:

- Database Management Systems (see Section 35.20.3.1)

- Data Dictionary/Directory Systems (see Section 35.20.3.2)

- Data Administration (see Section 35.20.3.3)

- Data Security (see Section 35.20.3.4)

These are critical aspects of data management for the following reasons. The DBMS is the most critical component of any data management capability, and a data dictionary/directory system is necessary in conjunction with the DBMS as a tool to aid the administration of the database. Data security is a necessary part of any overall policy for security in information processing.

35.20.3.1 Database Management Systems

A Database Management System (DBMS) provides for the systematic management of data. This data management component provides services and capabilities for defining the data, structuring the data, accessing the data, as well as security and recovery of the data. A DBMS performs the following functions:

- Structures data in a consistent way

- Provides access to the data

- Minimizes duplication

- Allows reorganization; that is, changes in data content, structure, and size

- Supports programming interfaces

- Provides security and control

A DBMS must provide:

- Persistence; the data continues to exist after the application's execution has completed

- Secondary storage management

- Concurrency

- Recovery

- Data Definition/Data Manipulation Language (DDL/DML), which may be a graphical interface

Database Models

The logical data model that underlies the database characterizes a DBMS. The common logical data models are as follows:

- **Relational Model**: A Relational Database Management System (RDBMS) structures data into tables that have certain properties:

    — Each row in the table is distinct from every other row.

    — Each row contains only atomic data; that is, there is no repeating data or such structures as arrays.

    — Each column in the relational table defines named data fields or attributes.

    A collection of related tables in the relational model makes up a database. The mathematical theory of relations underlies the relational model — both the organization of data and the languages that manipulate the data. Edgar Codd, then at IBM, developed the relational model in 1973. It has been popular, in terms of commercial use, since the early 1980s.

- **Hierarchical Model**: The hierarchical data model organizes data in a tree structure. There is a hierarchy of parent and child data segments. This structure implies that a record can have repeating information, generally in the child data segments. For example, an organization might store information about an employee, such as name, employee number, department, salary. The organization might also store information about an employee's children, such as name and date of birth. The employee and children data forms a hierarchy, where the employee data represents the parent segment and the children data represents the child segment. If an employee has three children, then there would be three child segments associated with one employee segment. In a hierarchical database the parent-child relationship is one-to-many. This restricts a child segment to having only one parent segment. Hierarchical DBMSs were popular from the late 1960s, with the introduction of IBM's Information Management System (IMS) DBMS, through the 1970s.

- **Network Model**: The popularity of the network data model coincided with the popularity of the hierarchical data model. Some data was more naturally modeled with more than one parent per child. So, the network model permitted the modeling of many-to-many relationships in data. In 1971, the Conference on Data Systems Languages (CODASYL) formally defined the network model. The basic data modeling construct in the network model is the set construct. A set consists of an owner record type, a set name, and a member record type. A member record type can have that role in more than one set, hence the multi-parent concept is supported. An owner record type can also be a member or owner in another set. The CODASYL network model is based on mathematical set theory.

- **Object-Oriented Model**: An Object-Oriented Database Management System (OODBMS) must be both a DBMS and an object-oriented system. As a DBMS it must provide the capabilities identified above. OODBMSs typically can model tabular data, complex data, hierarchical data, and networks of data. The following are important features of an object-oriented system:

    — Complex objects: e.g., objects may be composed of other objects.

    — Object identity: each object has a unique identifier external to the data.

    — Encapsulation: an object consists of data and the programs (or methods) that manipulate it.

— Types or classes: a class is a collection of similar objects.

— Inheritance: subclasses inherit data attributes and methods from classes.

— Overriding with late binding: the method particular to a subclass can override the method of a class at run time.

— Extensibility: e.g., a user may define new objects.

— Computational completeness: a general-purpose language (such as Ada, C, or C++) is computationally complete. The special-purpose language SQL is not. Most OODBMSs incorporate a general-purpose programming language.

- **Flat Files**: A flat file system is usually closely associated with a storage access method. An example is IBM's Indexed Sequential Access Method (ISAM). The models discussed earlier in this section are logical data models; flat files require the user to work with the physical layout of the data on a storage device. For example, the user must know the exact location of a data item in a record. In addition, flat files do not provide all of the services of a DBMS, such as naming of data, elimination of redundancy, and concurrency control. Further, there is no independence of the data and the application program. The application program must know the physical layout of the data.

Distributed DBMSs

A distributed DBMS manages a database that is spread over more than one platform. The database can be based on any of the data models discussed above (except the flat file). The database can be replicated, partitioned, or a combination of both. A replicated database is one in which full or partial copies of the database exist on the different platforms. A partitioned database is one in which part of the database is on one platform and parts are on other platforms. The partitioning of a database can be vertical or horizontal. A vertical partitioning puts some fields and the associated data on one platform and some fields and the associated data on another platform. For example, consider a database with the following fields: employee ID, employee name, department, number of dependents, project assigned, salary rate, tax rate. One vertical partitioning might place employee ID, number of dependents, salary rate, and tax rate on one platform and employee name, department, and project assigned on another platform. A horizontal partitioning might keep all the fields on all the platforms but distribute the records. For example, a database with 100,000 records might put the first 50,000 records on one platform and the second 50,000 records on a second platform.

Whether the distributed database is replicated or partitioned, a single DBMS manages the database. There is a single schema (description of the data in a database in terms of a data model; e.g., relational) for a distributed database. The distribution of the database is generally transparent to the user. The term "distributed DBMS" implies homogeneity.

Distributed Heterogeneous DBMSs

A distributed, heterogeneous database system is a set of independent databases, each with its own DBMS, presented to users as a single database and system. "Federated" is used synonymously with "distributed heterogeneous". The heterogeneity refers to differences in data models (e.g., network and relational), DBMSs from different suppliers, different hardware platforms, or other differences. The simplest kinds of federated database systems are commonly called "gateways". In a gateway, one vendor (e.g., Oracle) provides single-direction access through its DBMS to another database managed by a different vendor's DBMS (e.g., IBM's DB2). The two DBMSs need not share the same data model. For example, many RDBMS vendors provide gateways to hierarchical and network DBMSs.

There are federated database systems both on the market and in research that provide more general access to diverse DBMSs. These systems generally provide a schema integration component to integrate the schemas of the diverse databases and present them to the users as a single database, a query management component to distribute queries to the different DBMSs in the federation, and a transaction management component, to distribute and manage the changes to the various databases in the federation.

35.20.3.2 Data Dictionary/Directory Systems

The second component providing data management services, the Data Dictionary/Directory System (DD/DS), consists of utilities and systems necessary to catalog, document, manage, and use metadata (data about data). An example of metadata is the following definition: a six-character long alphanumeric string, for which the first character is a letter of the alphabet and each of the remaining five characters is an integer between 0 and 9; the name for the string is `"employee ID"`. The DD/DS utilities make use of special files that contain the database schema. (A schema, using metadata, defines the content and structure of a database.) This schema is represented by a set of tables resulting from the compilation of Data Definition Language (DDL) statements. The DD/DS is normally provided as part of a DBMS but is sometimes available from alternate sources. In the management of distributed data, distribution information may also be maintained in the network directory system. In this case, the interface between the DD/DS and the network directory system would be through the API of the network services component on the platform.

In current environments, data dictionaries are usually integrated with the DBMS, and directory systems are typically limited to a single platform. Network directories are used to expand the DD/DS realms. The relationship between the DD/DS and the network directory is an intricate combination of physical and logical sources of data.

35.20.3.3 Data Administration

Data administration properly addresses the Data Architecture, which is outside the scope of TOGAF. We discuss it briefly here because of areas of overlap. It is concerned with all of the data resources of an enterprise, and as such there are overlaps with data management, which addresses data in databases. Two specific areas of overlap are the repository and database administration, which are discussed briefly below.

Repository

A repository is a system that manages all of the data of an enterprise, which includes data and process models and other enterprise information. Hence, the data in a repository is much more extensive than that in a DD/DS, which generally defines only the data making up a database.

Database Administration

Data administration and database administration are complementary processes. Data administration is responsible for data, data structure, and integration of data and processes. Database administration, on the other hand, includes the physical design, development, implementation, security, and maintenance of the physical databases. Database administration is responsible for managing and enforcing the enterprise's policies related to individual databases.

35.20.3.4 Data Security

The third component providing data management services is data security. This includes procedures and technology measures implemented to prevent unauthorized access, modification, use, and dissemination of data stored or processed by a computer system. Data security also includes data integrity (i.e., preserving the accuracy and validity of the data), and protecting the system from physical harm (including preventative measures and recovery procedures).

Authorization control allows only authorized users to have access to the database at the appropriate level. Guidelines and procedures can be established for accountability, levels of control, and type of control. Authorization control for database systems differs from that in traditional file systems because, in a database system, it is not uncommon for different users to have different rights to the same data. This requirement encompasses the ability to specify subsets of data and to distinguish between groups of users. In addition, decentralized control of authorizations is of particular importance for distributed systems.

Data protection is necessary to prevent unauthorized users from understanding the content of the database. Data encryption, as one of the primary methods for protecting data, is useful for both information stored on disk and for information exchanged on a network.

35.21 Developing an Enterprise Manageability View

The Enterprise Manageability view is concerned with operations, administration, and management of the system.

35.21.1 Stakeholders and Concerns

This view should be developed for the operations, administration, and management personnel of the system.

Major concerns for these stakeholders are understanding how the system is managed as a whole, and how all components of the system are managed. The key concern is managing change in the system and predicting necessary preventative maintenance.

In general, these stakeholders are concerned with ensuring that the availability of the system does not suffer when changes occur. Managing the system includes managing components such as:

- Security components
- Data assets
- Software assets
- Hardware assets
- Networking assets

35.21.2 Developing the View

Business scenarios are an extremely useful way to depict what should happen when planned and unplanned events occur. It is highly recommended that business scenarios be created for planned change, and for unplanned change.

The following paragraphs describe some of the key issues that the architect might consider when constructing business scenarios.

35.21.3 Key Issues

The Enterprise Manageability view acts as a check and balance on the difficulties and day-to-day running costs of systems built within the new architecture. Often, system management is not considered until after all the important purchasing and development decisions have been taken, and taking a separate management view at an early stage in architecture development is one way to avoid this pitfall. It is good practice to develop the Enterprise Manageability view with close consideration of the System Engineering view since, in general, management is difficult to retrofit into an existing design.

Key elements of the Enterprise Manageability view are:

- The policies, procedures, and guidelines that drive your management requirements (such as a policy to restrict downloading software from the Internet)
- How your shop measures system availability
- The management services and utilities required
- The likely quantity, quality, and location of management and support personnel
- The ability of users to take on system management tasks, such as password maintenance
- The manageability of existing and planned components in each of the component categories
- Whether management should be centralized or distributed
- Whether security is the responsibility of system managers or a separate group, bearing in mind any legal requirements

Key technical components categories that are the subject of the Enterprise Manageability view deal with change, either planned upgrades, or unplanned outages. The following table lists specific concerns for each component category.

Component Category	Planned Change Considerations	Unplanned Change Considerations
Security Components	How is a security change propagated throughout the system? Who is responsible for making changes; end users, or security stewards?	What should happen when security is breached? What should happen if a security component fails?
Data Assets	How are new data elements added? How is data imported/exported or loaded/unloaded? How is backup managed while running continuously? How is data change propagated in a distributed environment?	What are the backup procedures and are all the system capabilities there to backup in time?
Software Assets	How is a new application introduced into the systems? What procedures are there to control software quality? How are application changes propagated in a distributed environment? How is unwanted software introduction restricted given the Internet?	What do you want to happen when an application fails? What do you want to happen when a resource of the application fails?
Hardware Assets	How do you assess the impact of new hardware on the system, especially network load?	What do you want to happen when hardware outages occur?
Networking Assets	How do you assess the impact of new networking components? How do you optimize your networking components?	

35.22 Developing an Acquirer View

The Acquirer view is concerned with acquiring Commercial Off-The-Shelf (COTS) software and hardware.

35.22.1 Stakeholders and Concerns

This view should be developed for personnel involved in the acquisition of any components of the subject architecture.

Major concerns for these stakeholders are understanding what building blocks of the architecture can be bought, and what constraints (or rules) exist that are relevant to the purchase. The acquirer will shop with multiple vendors looking for the best cost solution while adhering to the constraints (or rules) applied by the architecture, such as standards.

The key concern is to make purchasing decisions that fit the architecture, and thereby to reduce the risk of added costs arising from non-compliant components.

35.22.2 Developing the View

The Acquirer view is normally represented as an architecture of Solution Building Blocks (SBBs), supplemented by views of the standards to be adhered to by individual building blocks.

35.22.3 Key Issues

The acquirer typically executes a process similar to the one below. Within the step descriptions we can see the concerns and issues that the acquirer faces.

Procurement Process Steps	Step Description and Output
Acquisition Planning	Creates the plan for the purchase of some component. For IT systems, the following considerations are germane to building blocks.
	This step requires access to Architecture Building Blocks (ABBs) and SBBs.
	■ The procurer needs to know which ABBs apply constraints (standards) for use in assessment and for creation of RFP/RFIs.
	■ The procurer needs to know which candidate SBBs adhere to these standards.
	■ The procurer also needs to know which suppliers provide accepted SBBs and where they have been deployed.
	■ The procurer needs to know what budget this component was given relative to the overall system cost.

Procurement Process Steps	Step Description and Output
Concept Exploration	In this step the procurer looks at the viability of the concept. Building blocks give the planner a sense of the risk involved; if many ABBs or SBBs exist that match the concept, the risk is lower.
	This step requires access to ABBs and SBBs. The planner needs to know which ABBs apply constraints (standards), and needs to know which candidate SBBs adhere to these standards.
Concept Demonstration and Validation	In this step, the procurer works with development to prototype an implementation. The procurer recommends the re-usable SBBs based upon standards fit, and past experience with suppliers.
	This step requires access to re-usable SBBs.
Development	In this step the procurer works with development to manage the relationship with the vendors supplying the SBBs. Building blocks that are proven to be fit-for-purpose get marked as approved. This step requires an update of the status to "procurement approved" of an SBB.
Production	In this step, the procurer works with development to manage the relationship with the vendors supplying the SBBs. Building blocks that are put into production get marked appropriately.
	This step requires an update of the status to "in production" of SBBs, with the system identifier of where the building block is being developed.
Deployment	In this step, the procurer works with development to manage the relationship with the vendors supplying the SBBs. Building blocks that are fully deployed get marked appropriately.
	This step requires an update of the status to "deployed" of SBBs, with the system identifier of where the building block was deployed.

Chapter 36: Architecture Deliverables

This chapter provides descriptions of deliverables referenced in the Architecture Development Method (ADM).

36.1 Introduction

This chapter defines the deliverables that will typically be consumed and produced across the TOGAF ADM cycle. As deliverables are typically the contractual or formal work products of an architecture project, it is likely that these deliverables will be constrained or altered by any overarching project or process management for the enterprise (such as CMMI, PRINCE2, PMBOK, or MSP).

This chapter therefore is intended to provide a typical baseline of architecture deliverables in order to better define the activities required in the ADM and act as a starting point for tailoring within a specific organization.

The TOGAF Content Framework (see Part IV, Chapter 33) identifies deliverables that are produced as outputs from executing the ADM cycle and potentially consumed as inputs at other points in the ADM. Other deliverables may be produced elsewhere and consumed by the ADM.

Deliverables produced by executing the ADM are shown in the table below.

Deliverable	Output from...	Input to...
Architecture Building Blocks (see Section 36.2.1)	F, H	A, B, C, D
Architecture Contract (see Section 36.2.2)	F	G
Architecture Definition Document (see Section 36.2.3)	B, C, D	C, D, E, F, G, H
Architecture Principles (see Section 36.2.4)	Preliminary, A, B, C, D	Preliminary, A, B, C, D, E, F, G, H
Architecture Repository (see Section 36.2.5)	Preliminary	Preliminary, A, B, C, D, E, F, G, H, Requirements Management
Architecture Requirements Specification (see Section 36.2.6)	B, C, D, E, F, Requirements Management	C, D, Requirements Management
Architecture Roadmap (see Section 36.2.7)	B, C, D, E, F	C, D, E, F, G, H
Architecture Vision (see Section 36.2.8)	A	B, C, D, E, F, G, H, Requirements Management

Deliverable	Output from...	Input to...
Business Principles, Business Goals, and Business Drivers (see Section 36.2.9)	Preliminary, A, B	A, B
Capability Assessment (see Section 36.2.10)	A, E	B, C, D, E, F
Change Request (see Section 36.2.11)	H	—
Communications Plan (see Section 36.2.12)	A	B, C, D, E, F
Compliance Assessment (see Section 36.2.13)	G	H
Implementation and Migration Plan (see Section 36.2.14)	E, F	F
Implementation Governance Model (see Section 36.2.15)	F	G, H
Organizational Model for Enterprise Architecture (see Section 36.2.16)	Preliminary	Preliminary, A, B, C, D, E, F, G, H, Requirements Management
Request for Architecture Work (see Section 36.2.17)	Preliminary, F	A, G
Requirements Impact Assessment (see Section 36.2.18)	H, Requirements Management	Requirements Management
Solution Building Blocks (see Section 36.2.19)	G	A, B, C, D
Statement of Architecture Work (see Section 36.2.20)	A, B, C, D	B, C, D, E, F, G, H, Requirements Management
Tailored Architecture Framework (see Section 36.2.21)	Preliminary, A	Preliminary, A, B, C, D, E, F, G, H, Requirements Management
Transition Architecture (see Section 36.2.22)	E, F	G, H

36.2 Deliverable Descriptions

The following sections provide example descriptions of deliverables referenced in the ADM.

Note that not all the content described here need be contained in a particular deliverable. Rather, it is recommended that external references be used where possible; for example, the strategic plans of a business should not be copied into a Request for Architecture Work, but rather the title of the strategic plans should be referenced.

Also, it is not suggested that these descriptions should be followed to the letter. However, each element should be considered carefully; ignoring any input or output item may cause problems downstream.

36.2.1 Architecture Building Blocks

Architecture documentation and models from the enterprise's Architecture Repository; see Part IV, Chapter 37.

36.2.2 Architecture Contract

Purpose

Architecture Contracts are the joint agreements between development partners and sponsors on the deliverables, quality, and fitness-for-purpose of an architecture. Successful implementation of these agreements will be delivered through effective architecture governance (see Part VII, Chapter 50). By implementing a governed approach to the management of contracts, the following will be ensured:

- A system of continuous monitoring to check integrity, changes, decision-making, and audit of all architecture-related activities within the organization

- Adherence to the principles, standards, and requirements of the existing or developing architectures

- Identification of risks in all aspects of the development and implementation of the architecture(s) covering the internal development against accepted standards, policies, technologies, and products as well as the operational aspects of the architectures such that the organization can continue its business within a resilient environment

- A set of processes and practices that ensure accountability, responsibility, and discipline with regard to the development and usage of all architectural artifacts

- A formal understanding of the governance organization responsible for the contract, their level of authority, and scope of the architecture under the governance of this body

Content

Typical contents of an Architecture Design and Development Contract are:

- Introduction and background
- The nature of the agreement
- Scope of the architecture
- Architecture and strategic principles and requirements
- Conformance requirements
- Architecture development and management process and roles
- Target Architecture measures
- Defined phases of deliverables
- Prioritized joint workplan
- Time window(s)
- Architecture delivery and business metrics

Typical contents of a Business Users' Architecture Contract are:

- Introduction and background
- The nature of the agreement
- Scope
- Strategic requirements
- Conformance requirements
- Architecture adopters
- Time window
- Architecture business metrics
- Service architecture (includes Service Level Agreement (SLA))

For more detail on the use of Architecture Contracts, see Part VII, Chapter 49.

36.2.3 Architecture Definition Document

Purpose

The Architecture Definition Document is the deliverable container for the core architectural artifacts created during a project. The Architecture Definition Document spans all architecture domains (business, data, application, and technology) and also examines all relevant states of the architecture (baseline, interim state(s), and target).

The Architecture Definition Document is a companion to the Architecture Requirements Specification, with a complementary objective:

- The Architecture Definition Document provides a qualitative view of the solution and aims to communicate the intent of the architects.
- The Architecture Requirements Specification provides a quantitative view of the solution, stating measurable criteria that must be met during the implementation of the architecture.

Content

Typical contents of an Architecture Definition Document are:

- Scope
- Goals, objectives, and constraints
- Architecture principles
- Baseline Architecture
- Architecture models (for each state to be modeled):
  - Business Architecture models
  - Data Architecture models
  - Application Architecture models
  - Technology Architecture models

- Rationale and justification for architectural approach
- Mapping to Architecture Repository:
  - — Mapping to Architecture Landscape
  - — Mapping to reference models
  - — Mapping to standards
  - — Re-use assessment
- Gap analysis
- Impact assessment

36.2.4 Architecture Principles

Purpose

Principles are general rules and guidelines, intended to be enduring and seldom amended, that inform and support the way in which an organization sets about fulfilling its mission.

In their turn, principles may be just one element in a structured set of ideas that collectively define and guide the organization, from values through to actions and results.

Content

See Part III, Chapter 23 for guidelines and a detailed set of generic architecture principles, including:

- Business principles (see Section 23.6.1)
- Data principles (see Section 23.6.2)
- Application principles (see Section 23.6.3)
- Technology principles (see Section 23.6.4)

36.2.5 Architecture Repository

Purpose

The Architecture Repository acts as a holding area for all architecture-related projects within the enterprise. The repository allows projects to manage their deliverables, locate re-usable assets, and publish outputs to stakeholders and other interested parties.

Content

See Part V, Chapter 41 for a detailed description of the content of an Architecture Repository.

Typical contents of an Architecture Repository are:

- Architecture Framework
- Standards Information Base

- Architecture Landscape
- Reference Architectures
- Governance Log

36.2.6 Architecture Requirements Specification

Purpose

The Architecture Requirements Specification provides a set of quantitative statements that outline what an implementation project must do in order to comply with the architecture. An Architecture Requirements Specification will typically form a major component of an implementation contract or contract for more detailed Architecture Definition.

As mentioned above, the Architecture Requirements Specification is a companion to the Architecture Definition Document, with a complementary objective:

- The Architecture Definition Document provides a qualitative view of the solution and aims to communicate the intent of the architect.
- The Architecture Requirements Specification provides a quantitative view of the solution, stating measurable criteria that must be met during the implementation of the architecture.

Content

Typical contents of an Architecture Requirements Specification are:

- Success measures
- Architecture requirements
- Business service contracts
- Application service contracts
- Implementation guidelines
- Implementation specifications
- Implementation standards
- Interoperability requirements
- Constraints
- Assumptions

36.2.7 Architecture Roadmap

Purpose

The Architecture Roadmap lists individual increments of change and lays them out on a timeline to show progression from the Baseline Architecture to the Target Architecture. The Architecture Roadmap forms a key component of Transition Architectures and is incrementally developed throughout Phases B, C, D, E, and F within the ADM.

Content

Typical contents of an Architecture Roadmap are:

- Project list:
    - Name, description, and objectives of each impacted project
    - Prioritized list of impacted projects to implement the proposed architecture
- Time-oriented Migration Plan:
    - Benefits of migration, determined (including mapping to business requirements)
    - Estimated costs of migration options
- Implementation recommendations:
    - Criteria measures of effectiveness of projects
    - Risks and issues
    - Solution Building Blocks (SBBs) — description and model

36.2.8 Architecture Vision

Purpose

The Architecture Vision is created early on in the project lifecycle and provides a high-level, aspirational view of the end architecture product. The purpose of the vision is to agree at the outset what the desired outcome should be for the architecture, so that architects can then focus on the critical areas to validate feasibility. Providing an Architecture Vision also supports stakeholder communication by providing an executive summary version of the full Architecture Definition.

Content

Typical contents of an Architecture Vision are:

- Problem description:
    - Stakeholders and their concerns
    - List of issues/scenarios to be addressed
- Detailed objectives
- Environment and process models:

- — Process description
- — Process steps mapped to environment
- — Process steps mapped to people
- — Information flow
- Actors and their roles and responsibilities:
  - — Human actors and roles
  - — Computer actors and roles
  - — Requirements
- Resulting architecture model;
  - — Constraints
  - — IT principles
  - — Architecture supporting the process
  - — Requirements mapped to architecture

36.2.9 Business Principles, Business Goals, and Business Drivers

Purpose

Business principles, business goals, and business drivers provide context for architecture work, by describing the needs and ways of working employed by the enterprise. Many factors that lie outside the consideration of architecture discipline may nevertheless have significant implications for the way that architecture is developed.

Content

The content and structure of business context for architecture is likely to vary considerably from one organization to the next.

36.2.10 Capability Assessment

Purpose

Before embarking upon a detailed Architecture Definition, it is valuable to understand the baseline and target capability level of the enterprise. This Capability Assessment can be examined on several levels:

- What is the capability level of the enterprise as a whole? Where does the enterprise wish to increase or optimize capability? What are the architectural focus areas that will support the desired development of the enterprise?

- What is the capability or maturity level of the IT function within the enterprise? What are the likely implications of conducting the architecture project in terms or design governance, operational governance, skills, and organization structure? What is an appropriate style, level of formality, and amount of detail for the architecture project to fit with the culture and capability of the IT organization?

                TOGAF Version 9 (2009)

- What is the capability and maturity of the architecture function within the enterprise? What architectural assets are currently in existence? Are they maintained and accurate? What standards and reference models need to be considered? Are there likely to be opportunities to create re-usable assets during the architecture project?

- Where capability gaps exist, to what extent is the business ready to transform in order to reach the target capability? What are the risks to transformation, cultural barriers, and other considerations to be addressed beyond the basic capability gap?

Content

Typical contents of a Capability Assessment are:

- Business Capability Assessment, including:
  - Capabilities of the business
  - Baseline state assessment of the performance level of each capability
  - Future state aspiration for the performance level of each capability
  - Baseline state assessment of how each capability is realized
  - Future state aspiration for how each capability should be realized

- IT Capability Assessment, including:
  - Baseline and target maturity level of change process
  - Baseline and target maturity level of operational processes
  - Baseline capability and capacity assessment
  - Assessment of likely impacts to the IT organization resulting from execution of the architecture project

- Architecture maturity assessment, including:
  - Architecture governance processes, organization, roles, and responsibilities
  - Architecture skills assessment
  - Breadth, depth, and quality of landscape definition with the Architecture Repository
  - Breadth, depth, and quality of standards definition with the Architecture Repository
  - Breadth, depth, and quality of reference model definition with the Architecture Repository
  - Assessment of re-use potential

- Business Transformation Readiness Assessment, including:
  - Readiness factors
  - Vision for each readiness factor
  - Current and target readiness ratings
  - Readiness risks

36.2.11 Change Request

Purpose

During implementation of an architecture, as more facts become known, it is possible that the original Architecture Definition and requirements are not suitable or are not sufficient to complete the implementation of a solution. In these circumstances, it is necessary for implementation projects to either deviate from the suggested architectural approach or to request scope extensions. Additionally, external factors — such as market factors, changes in business strategy, and new technology opportunities — may open up opportunities to extend and refine the architecture.

In these circumstances, a Change Request may be submitted in order to kick-start a further cycle of architecture work.

Content

Typical contents of a Change Request are:

- Description of the proposed change
- Rationale for the proposed change
- Impact assessment of the proposed change, including:
    - Reference to specific requirements
    - Stakeholder priority of the requirements to date
    - Phases to be revisited
    - Phase to lead on requirements prioritization
    - Results of phase investigations and revised priorities
    - Recommendations on management of requirements
- Repository reference number

36.2.12 Communications Plan

Purpose

Enterprise architectures contain large volumes of complex and inter-dependent information. Effective communication of targeted information to the right stakeholders at the right time is a critical success factor for enterprise architecture. Development of a Communications Plan for architecture allows for this communication to be carried out within a planned and managed process.

Content

Typical contents of a Communications Plan are:

- Identification of stakeholders and grouping by communication requirements

- Identification of communication needs, key messages in relation to the Architecture Vision, communication risks, and Critical Success Factors (CSFs)

- Identification of mechanisms that will be used to communicate with stakeholders and allow access to architecture information, such as meetings, newsletters, repositories, etc.

- Identification of a communications timetable, showing which communications will occur with which stakeholder groups at what time and in what location

36.2.13 Compliance Assessment

Purpose

Once an architecture has been defined, it is necessary to govern that architecture through implementation to ensure that the original Architecture Vision is appropriately realized and that any implementation learnings are fed back into the architecture process. Period compliance reviews of implementation projects provide a mechanism to review project progress and ensure that the design and implementation is proceeding in-line with the strategic and architectural objectives.

Content

Typical contents of a Compliance Assessment are:

- Overview of project progress and status

- Overview of project architecture/design

- Completed architecture checklists:
    - Hardware and operating system checklist
    - Software services and middleware checklist
    - Applications checklists
    - Information management checklists
    - Security checklists
    - System management checklists
    - System engineering checklists
    - Methods and tools checklists

36.2.14 Implementation and Migration Plan

Purpose

The Implementation and Migration Plan provides a schedule for implementation of the solution described by a Transition Architecture. The Implementation and Migration Plan includes timing, cost, resources, benefits, and milestones for the implementation.

Content

Typical contents of an Implementation and Migration Plan are:

- Implementation and Migration Strategy:
    - Strategic implementation direction
    - Implementation sequencing approach
- Interactions with other management frameworks:
    - Approach to aligning architecture and business planning
    - Approach to integration of architecture efforts
    - Approach to aligning architecture and portfolio/project management
    - Approach to aligning architecture and operations management
- Project charters:
    - Capabilities delivered by projects
    - Included work packages
    - Business value
    - Risk, issues, assumptions, dependencies
- Implementation Plan:
    - Phase and workstream breakdown of implementation effort
    - Allocation of work packages to phase and workstream
    - Milestones and timing
    - Work breakdown structure
    - Resource requirements and costs

36.2.15 Implementation Governance Model

Purpose

Once an architecture has been defined, it is necessary to plan how the Transition Architecture that implements the architecture will be governed through implementation. Within organizations that have established architecture functions, there is likely to be a governance framework already in place, but specific processes, organizations, roles, responsibilities, and measures may need to be defined on a project-by-project basis.

The Implementation Governance Model ensures that a project transitioning into implementation also smoothly transitions into appropriate architecture governance.

Content

Typical contents of an Implementation Governance Model are:

- Governance processes
- Governance organization structure
- Governance roles and responsibilities
- Governance checkpoints and success/failure criteria

36.2.16 Organizational Model for Enterprise Architecture

Purpose

In order for an architecture framework to be used successfully, it must be supported by the correct organization, roles, and responsibilities within the enterprise. Of particular importance is the definition of boundaries between different enterprise architecture practitioners and the governance relationships that span across these boundaries.

Content

Typical contents of an Organizational Model for enterprise architecture are:

- Scope of organizations impacted
- Maturity assessment, gaps, and resolution approach
- Roles and responsibilities for architecture team(s)
- Constraints on architecture work
- Budget requirements
- Governance and support strategy

36.2.17 Request for Architecture Work

This is a document that is sent from the sponsoring organization to the architecture organization to trigger the start of an architecture development cycle. Requests for Architecture Work can be created as an output of the Preliminary phase, a result of approved architecture Change Requests, or terms of reference for architecture work originating from migration planning.

In general, all the information in this document should be at a high level.

Requests for Architecture Work typically include:

- Organization sponsors
- Organization's mission statement
- Business goals (and changes)
- Strategic plans of the business
- Time limits
- Changes in the business environment
- Organizational constraints
- Budget information, financial constraints
- External constraints, business constraints
- Current business system description
- Current architecture/IT system description
- Description of developing organization
- Description of resources available to developing organization

36.2.18 Requirements Impact Assessment

Purpose

Throughout the ADM, new information is collected relating to an architecture. As this information is gathered, new facts may come to light that invalidate existing aspects of the architecture. A Requirements Impact Assessment assesses the current architecture requirements and specification to identify changes that should be made and the implications of those changes.

Content

Typical contents of a Requirements Impact Assessment are:

- Reference to specific requirements
- Stakeholder priority of the requirements to date
- Phases to be revisited
- Phase to lead on requirements prioritization
- Results of phase investigations and revised priorities

- Recommendations on management of requirements
- Repository reference number

36.2.19 Solution Building Blocks

Implementation-specific building blocks from the enterprise's Architecture Repository; see Part IV, Chapter 37.

36.2.20 Statement of Architecture Work

Purpose

The Statement of Architecture Work defines the scope and approach that will be used to complete an architecture project. The Statement of Architecture Work is typically the document against which successful execution of the architecture project will be measured and may form the basis for a contractual agreement between the supplier and consumer of architecture services.

Content

Typical contents of a Statement of Architecture Work are:

- Statement of Architecture Work title
- Project request and background
- Project description and scope
- Overview or outline of Architecture Vision
- Managerial approach
- Change of scope procedures
- Roles, responsibilities, and deliverables
- Acceptance criteria and procedures
- Project plan and schedule
- Support of the Enterprise Continuum
- Signature approvals

36.2.21 Tailored Architecture Framework

Purpose

TOGAF provides an industry standard framework for architecture that may be used in a wide variety of organizations. However, before TOGAF can be effectively used within an architecture project, tailoring at two levels is necessary.

Firstly, it is necessary to tailor the TOGAF model for integration into the enterprise. This tailoring will include integration with project and process management frameworks, customization of terminology, development of presentational styles, selection, configuration, and deployment of architecture tools, etc. The formality and detail of any frameworks adopted should also align with other contextual factors for the enterprise, such as culture, stakeholders, commercial models for enterprise architecture, and the existing level of architecture capability.

Once the framework has been tailored to the enterprise, further tailoring is necessary in order to tailor the framework for the specific architecture project. Tailoring at this level will select appropriate deliverables and artifacts to meet project and stakeholder needs.

See Part II, Section 6.4.5 for further considerations when selecting and tailoring the architecture framework.

Content

Typical contents of a Tailored Architecture Framework are:

- Tailored architecture method
- Tailored architecture content (deliverables and artifacts)
- Configured and deployed tools
- Interfaces with governance models and other frameworks:
    - Enterprise Architecture Management Framework
    - Capability Management Framework
    - Portfolio Management Framework
    - Project Management Framework
    - Operations Management Framework

36.2.22 Transition Architecture

Purpose

A Transition Architecture shows the enterprise at incremental states reflecting periods of transition that sit between the Baseline and Target Architectures. Transition Architectures are used to allow for individual work packages and projects to be grouped into managed portfolios and programs, illustrating the business value at each stage.

Content

Typical contents of a Transition Architecture are:

- Opportunity portfolio:
    - Consolidated gaps, solutions, and dependency assessment
    - Opportunity description
    - Benefit assessment
    - Capabilities and capability increments
    - Interoperability and co-existence requirements
- Work package portfolio:
    - Work package description (name, description, objectives, deliverables)
    - Functional requirements
    - Dependencies
    - Relationship to opportunity
    - Relationship to Architecture Definition Document and Architecture Requirements Specification
- Milestone and milestone Transition Architectures:
    - Definition of transition states
    - Business Architecture for each transition state
    - Data Architecture for each transition state
    - Application Architecture for each transition state
    - Technology Architecture for each transition state
- Implementation Factor Assessment and Deduction matrix, including:
    - Risks
    - Issues
    - Assumptions
    - Dependencies
    - Actions

- Consolidated Gaps, Solutions, and Dependencies matrix, including:
  - Architecture domain
  - Gap
  - Potential solutions
  - Dependencies

Chapter 37: Building Blocks

This chapter explains the concept of building blocks and contains a fictional example illustrating building blocks in architecture.

37.1 Overview

This section is intended to explain and illustrate the concept of building blocks in architecture.

Following this overview, there are three main parts:

- Introduction to Building Blocks (see Section 37.2), discusses the general concepts of building blocks, and explains the differences between Architecture Building Blocks (ABBs) and Solution Building Blocks (SBBs).

- Building Blocks and the ADM (see Section 37.3), summarizes the stages at which building block design and specification occurs within the TOGAF Architecture Development Method (ADM).

- Building Blocks Example (see Section 37.4), comprises a series of separate subsections that together provide a detailed worked example showing how building block context is captured, how building blocks are identified, and how building blocks are defined when executing the major steps of the ADM.

37.2 Introduction to Building Blocks

This section is an introduction to the concept of building blocks.

37.2.1 Overview

This section describes the characteristics of building blocks. The use of building blocks in the ADM is described separately in Section 37.3.

37.2.2 Generic Characteristics

Building blocks have generic characteristics as follows:

- A building block is a package of functionality defined to meet the business needs across an organization.

- A building block has a type that corresponds to the TOGAF content metamodel (such as actor, business service, application, or data entity)

- A building block has a defined boundary and is generally recognizable as "a thing" by domain experts.

- A building block may interoperate with other, inter-dependent, building blocks.

- A good building block has the following characteristics:

  - It considers implementation and usage, and evolves to exploit technology and standards.
  - It may be assembled from other building blocks.
  - It may be a subassembly of other building blocks.
  - Ideally a building block is re-usable and replaceable, and well specified.

A building block's boundary and specification should be loosely coupled to its implementation; i.e., it should be possible to realize a building block in several different ways without impacting the boundary or specification of the building block. The way in which assets and capabilities are assembled into building blocks will vary widely between individual architectures. Every organization must decide for itself what arrangement of building blocks works best for it. A good choice of building blocks can lead to improvements in legacy system integration, interoperability, and flexibility in the creation of new systems and applications.

Systems are built up from collections of building blocks, so most building blocks have to interoperate with other building blocks. Wherever that is true, it is important that the interfaces to a building block are published and reasonably stable.

Building blocks can be defined at various levels of detail, depending on what stage of architecture development has been reached.

For instance, at an early stage, a building block can simply consist of a name or an outline description. Later on, a building block may be decomposed into multiple supporting building blocks and may be accompanied by a full specification.

The level of detail to which a building block should be specified is dependent on the objectives of the architecture and, in some cases, less detail may be of greater value (for example, when presenting the capabilities of an enterprise, a single clear and concise picture has more value than a dense 100-page specification).

The OMG have developed a standard for Re-usable Asset Specification (RAS),[16] which provides a good example of how building blocks can be formally described and managed.

---

16.   Refer to www.omg.org/technology/documents/formal/ras.htm.

37.2.3 Architecture Building Blocks

Architecture Building Blocks (ABBs) relate to the Architecture Continuum (see Part V, Section 39.4.1), and are defined or selected as a result of the application of the ADM.

37.2.3.1 Characteristics

ABBs:

- Capture architecture requirements; e.g., business, data, application, and technology requirements
- Direct and guide the development of SBBs

37.2.3.2 Specification Content

ABB specifications include the following as a minimum:

- Fundamental functionality and attributes: semantic, unambiguous, including security capability and manageability
- Interfaces: chosen set, supplied
- Interoperability and relationship with other building blocks
- Dependent building blocks with required functionality and named user interfaces
- Map to business/organizational entities and policies

37.2.4 Solution Building Blocks

Solution Building Blocks (SBBs) relate to the Solutions Continuum (see Part V, Section 39.4.2), and may be either procured or developed.

37.2.4.1 Characteristics

SBBs:

- Define what products and components will implement the functionality
- Define the implementation
- Fulfil business requirements
- Are product or vendor-aware

37.2.4.2 Specification Content

SBB specifications include the following as a minimum:

- Specific functionality and attributes
- Interfaces; the implemented set

- Required SBBs used with required functionality and names of the interfaces used
- Mapping from the SBBs to the IT topology and operational policies
- Specifications of attributes shared across the environment (not to be confused with functionality) such as security, manageability, localizability, scalability
- Performance, configurability
- Design drivers and constraints, including the physical architecture
- Relationships between SBBs and ABBs

37.3   Building Blocks and the ADM

37.3.1   Basic Principles

This section focuses on the use of building blocks in the ADM. General considerations and characteristics of building blocks are described in Section 37.2.

37.3.1.1   Building Blocks in Architecture Design

An architecture is a set of building blocks depicted in an architectural model, and a specification of how those building blocks are connected to meet the overall requirements of the business.

The various building blocks in an architecture specify the scope and approach that will be used to address a specific business problem.

There are some general principles underlying the use of building blocks in the design of specific architectures:

- An architecture need only contain building blocks that are relevant to the business problem that the architecture is attempting to address.
- Building blocks may have complex relationships to one another. One building block may support multiple building blocks or may partially support a single building block (for example, the business service of "complaint handling" would be supported by many data entities and possibly multiple application components).
- Building blocks should conform to standards relevant to their type, the principles of the enterprise, and the standards of the enterprise.

37.3.1.2   Building Block Design

The process of identifying building blocks includes looking for collections of capabilities or assets that interact with one another and then drawing them together or making them different:

- Consider three classes of building blocks:
    - Re-usable building blocks, such as legacy items
    - Building blocks to be the subject of development, such as new applications

> — Building blocks to be the subject of purchase; i.e., Commercial Off-The-Shelf (COTS) applications

- Use the desired level of integration to bind or combine functions into building blocks. For instance, legacy elements could be treated as large building blocks to avoid breaking them apart.

In the early stages and during views of the highest-level enterprise, the building blocks are often kept at a broad integration definition. It is during these exercises that the services definitions can often be best viewed. As implementation considerations are addressed, more detailed views of building blocks can often be used to address implementation decisions, focus on the critical strategic decisions, or aid in assessing the value and future impact of commonality and re-usability.

37.3.2 Building Block Specification Process in the ADM

The process of building block definition takes place gradually as the ADM is followed, mainly in Phases A, B, C, and D. It is an iterative process because as definition proceeds, detailed information about the functionality required, the constraints imposed on the architecture, and the availability of products may affect the choice and the content of building blocks.

The key parts of the ADM at which building blocks are designed and specified are summarized below.

The major work in these steps consists of identifying the ABBs required to meet the business goals and objectives. The selected set of ABBs is then refined in an iterative process to arrive at a set of SBBs which can either be bought off-the-shelf or custom developed.

The specification of building blocks using the ADM is an evolutionary and iterative process. The key phases and steps of the ADM at which building blocks are evolved and specified are summarized below, and illustrated in Figure 37-1.

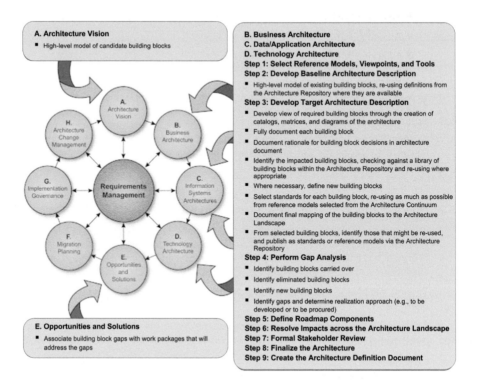

A. Architecture Vision
- High-level model of candidate building blocks

B. Business Architecture
C. Data/Application Architecture
D. Technology Architecture
Step 1: Select Reference Models, Viewpoints, and Tools
Step 2: Develop Baseline Architecture Description
- High-level model of existing building blocks, re-using definitions from the Architecture Repository where they are available

Step 3: Develop Target Architecture Description
- Develop view of required building blocks through the creation of catalogs, matrices, and diagrams of the architecture
- Fully document each building block
- Document rationale for building block decisions in architecture document
- Identify the impacted building blocks, checking against a library of building blocks within the Architecture Repository and re-using where appropriate
- Where necessary, define new building blocks
- Select standards for each building block, re-using as much as possible from reference models selected from the Architecture Continuum
- Document final mapping of the building blocks to the Architecture Landscape
- From selected building blocks, identify those that might be re-used, and publish as standards or reference models via the Architecture Repository

Step 4: Perform Gap Analysis
- Identify building blocks carried over
- Identify eliminated building blocks
- Identify new building blocks
- Identify gaps and determine realization approach (e.g., to be developed or to be procured)

Step 5: Define Roadmap Components
Step 6: Resolve Impacts across the Architecture Landscape
Step 7: Formal Stakeholder Review
Step 8: Finalize the Architecture
Step 9: Create the Architecture Definition Document

E. Opportunities and Solutions
- Associate building block gaps with work packages that will address the gaps

Figure 37-1 Key ADM Phases/Steps at which Building Blocks are Evolved/Specified

37.4 Building Blocks Example

37.4.1 Introduction

This section provides a detailed worked example showing how building block context is captured, how building blocks are identified, and how building blocks are defined when executing the major steps of the ADM.

37.4.2 Structure

The levels of modeling within the ADM are explained in Section 37.3, and the example follows the structure of modeling explained there:

- Background to the Example (see Section 37.4.3)
- Identifying Building Block Scope (see Section 37.4.4)

- Identifying Building Block Requirements and Constraints (see Section 37.4.5)
- Architecture Modeling (see Section 37.4.6)
- Opportunity Identification (see Section 37.4.7)
- Building Block Re-Use Level (see Section 37.4.8)

37.4.3 Background to the Example

In this example, a fictional company called XYZ Manufacturing has decided to improve the efficiency of its mobile sales force by replacing paper-based configuration and ordering systems with an IT solution.

The XYZ team have already done the preliminary stages of describing their existing system and reviewing it from a number of different viewpoints, and as a result have established a number of goals and objectives for the new system.

The principal goal is to give the sales force in the field direct access to the sales process back at base. This will allow sales staff to create and verify the product configuration, to check the price and availability of the goods, and to place the order while actually with the customer.

Other stages of the sales process — such as initiating the sale and determining the customer requirements — are considered to be outside the scope of this example.

37.4.4 Identifying Building Block Scope

As a preliminary to Phase B (Business Architecture), it is necessary to define the scope of activity, including what is in scope, what is out of scope, what the limits are, and what the financial envelope is. Within this step fall defining the business process, recording the assumptions made, and developing any new requirements. The information collected is used to gauge the baseline system and to determine the return on investment of potential changes. Use-cases are a useful tool in this step to describe the business processes and they can be used to do a sanity check against the resulting architecture.

In the example in this section, the business goals driving improvements in the sales process were:

- Improve the quality of the sales process
- Reduce the number of errors in the sales process
- Speed up the sales process

In this example, financial and time constraints and business return have not been dealt with in detail, but normally these constraints would be used to guide the process along the entire way to avoid over-engineering or "creeping elegance". The architect should especially look at these constraints whenever iterating between steps. Also not shown in this example are the use-case scenarios. However, the process described below does include participants, or actors, of the use-case with brief descriptions of their roles in Table 37-1.

For the sake of brevity in this example, it is assumed that the scope of the architectural work would not extend beyond the sales arena, and that the proposed solutions fit within the financial and time constraints imposed by XYZ.

The assumptions made by the XYZ architect during Phase B are:

- To support the mission of the business, it is desired to have the sales person and the customer meet and interact face-to-face at the customer location.
- The model for such a customer visit should be two persons interacting using a shared PC.
- The sales person needs to be able to close the deal on-site, and then synchronize with information held at the sales base.
- There is a clearly-defined product set subject of the sales process; e.g., there is a car to buy.

The relevant business process in scope of this example in the XYZ company is the customer-facing portion of the sales process and the supporting systems. This sales process consists of the following steps:

1. Initiate the sales process with the customer:
   a. Sales Person
   b. Customer

2. Discuss the customer requirements:
   a. Customer
   b. Sales Person

3. Work with the customer to create a product configuration:
   a. Sales Person
   b. Sales Person's Laptop
   c. Sales Person's Local (LIPR) and Central (CIPR) Information Process Resources
   d. Product Configurator
   e. Customer

4. Verify that the desired configuration can be delivered:
   a. Sales Person
   b. Sales Person's Laptop
   c. Inventory Control System
   d. Scheduling System
   e. Customer Accepts or Rejects

5. Determine the price of the requested configuration:
   a. Sales Person
   b. Sales Person's Laptop
   c. Pricing System

6. Confirm the desire to purchase with the customer:
   a. Sales Person

        b. Customer

  7. Place an order:

        a. Sales Person

        b. Sales Person's Laptop with Printer (for Fax)

        c. Order System

        d. Customer

  8. Customer acceptance:

        a. Sales Person

        b. Customer

The following use-case table represents participants (sometimes referred to as "actors" in use-cases) in the rows, steps of the business process in the columns, and roles in the cells. Note that this is an example, and it is not intended to be accurate, but rather demonstrative. Constructing a use-case table is a comparatively small effort that will ultimately enhance the speed and quality of the resulting architecture.

The meanings of the various acronyms used in the table, and in subsequent figures, are listed below:

CIPR	Central Information Processing Resource
ICSys	Inventory Control System
LIPR	Local Information Processing Resource
OrdSys	Order Processing/Information System
ProdConfig	Product Configurator System
ProdSys	Product Information System
SchSys	Scheduling System
$Sys	Pricing Information System

	1:Initiate	2:Discuss Reqmts	3:Create Config	4:Verify Config	5:Price	6:Confirm	7:Order	8:Accept
Sales Person	Greets customer	Listens	Represents options with different capabilities	Accesses ICSys and SchSys and presents availability to customer	Accesses price system and presents price to customer	Presents offer	Accesses order system	Presents contract
Customer	Accepts sales person	Discusses problems/ desires	Listens and decides on options based on capabilities	Accepts or rejects		Accepts or rejects		Signs or rejects
Sales Person's Laptop			Interacts with configurator	Interacts with ICSys and SchSys	Interacts with price system		Interacts with order system and receives fax response	
Sales Person's CIPR			Provides central information processing					
Sales Person's LIPR			Provides local information processing					
ProdConfig			Presents configs to sales person per needs, providing capabilities					
ICSys				Provides availability				
SchSys				Provides delivery date				
$Sys					Provides price information on a config			
OrderSys							Processes order and sends fax of order to sales person's laptop	

Table 37-1 Use-Case Table of Sales Process

Steps 1, 2, 6, and 8 are not within scope of the architecture work since the only participants involved are humans. The other steps are considered within scope since there are computing components involved in supporting the sales process. Note the computing participants are the first set of identified candidate building blocks — Business Process-Driven List.

During Phase A, the business goals were developed into more detailed business requirements, and these were:

- To improve on the current turnaround time of 48 hours for order processing
- To reduce the number of errors in orders by a factor of three

A very simplified view of the candidate building blocks required to support the business process with an idea of location is provided below. This model was built from elements of the above table.

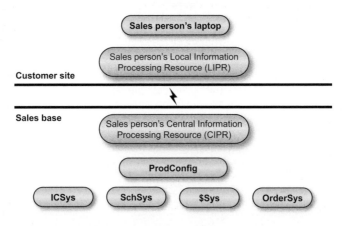

Figure 37-2 Candidate Building Blocks: Business Process-Driven List

37.4.5 Identifying Building Block Requirements and Constraints

The objective of the first step in Phases B, C, and D of the ADM is to build a high-level description of the characteristics of the current system, re-usable building blocks from the current system, the technical functionality needed to address the business problem, and to identify additional constraints. This is necessary as the description documents the starting point for architectural development and lists the interoperability issues that the final architecture will have to take into account. Potential re-usable building blocks may be contained in the existing environment. They are identified in this step.

The best approach is to describe the system in terms already used within the organization. A reliable picture can be built up of the business functions served and the platforms which support those functions. Gather and analyze only that information that allows informed decisions to be made regarding the Target Architecture.

The inputs to this step are:

- Descriptions of the current system
- Information on the Baseline Architecture
- Model of candidate building blocks

The essential outputs from this activity are:

- A clear description of the current system and its functions
- A statement of the constraints imposed by the internal organization
- A statement of the constraints imposed by the business or external environments
- Architecture principles embodied in the current system
- Assumptions of required technical functionality
- Candidate building blocks — Baseline-Driven List
- Model of candidate building blocks (see Figure 37-5)

The key input to this step is the Baseline Architecture. In this example, a depiction of a Baseline Architecture is shown in Figure 37-3. Additionally depicted in this architecture model are pointers to existing problems with the Baseline Architecture. These pointers are used by the architect to determine where existing components are failing, and where existing systems can be re-used.

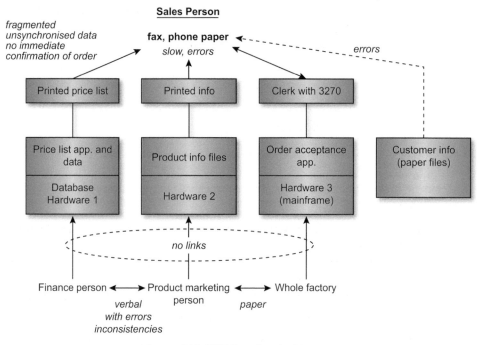

Figure 37-3 XYZ Baseline Architecture

It is necessary to record strategic decisions about the existing architectural and technological issues such as:

- The Baseline Architecture is founded on the mainframe.

- Databases are tied to application logic.

- Security is embedded in the application.

The next step consists of restating the business process, considering what functionality will be required, and deciding what constraints apply. Decisions at this stage are not definitive, but act as input for the following steps and iterations.

The architects of XYZ identified the following pieces of technical functionality as necessary to support the business processes. This list was produced using standard brainstorming techniques.

37.4.5.1 *Assumptions of Required Technical Functionality*

- Access to central functions

- Application support for simultaneous access by multiple sales persons through multiple connections

- Execution of local functions at the point-of-sale

- Access to product information

- Entering and checking the required product configuration

- Access to customer information

- Access to price information

- Order entry

- Order acceptance

- Delivery of confirmation of order to the customer

- The process must be secured

Also in the brainstorming session, some assumptions were made and therefore must be documented as they should be used throughout the process:

- Initiation of the sales process and determination/agreement of the customer requirements were outside the scope of the current work.

- Functionality could be distributed between the point-of-sale and a central base.

- Closure of the order should take place at the central location.

- The price list and product information could be made available electronically.

- Access could be provided to the acceptance and confirmation of order systems.

- The ordering, product information, and price information systems could be linked together.

One constraint was put on the development because XYZ already had systems in place to support the sales process:

- Existing systems should be used to support product information, order placement, and customer information.

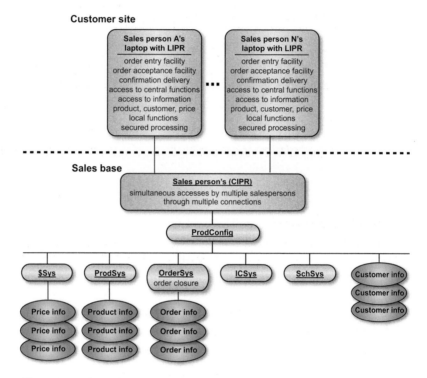

Figure 37-4 Candidate Building Blocks Augmented with Technical Functionality

The above model is scrutinized and questions are asked about the functionality that could be provided by the existing system. Figure 37-5 depicts the set of candidate building blocks from the existing system, resulting from this question.

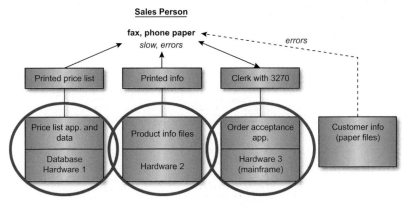

Figure 37-5 Candidate Building Blocks from the Baseline-Driven List

37.4.6 Architecture Modeling

In Phases B, C, and D a number of different architecture views are considered and used to build up a model of the new architecture. At XYZ, the architectural model level was developed in the following steps:

1. A Baseline Description in the TOGAF format

2. Consider different architecture views

3. Create an architectural model of building blocks

4. Select the services portfolio required per building block

5. Confirm that the business goals and objectives are met

6. Determine criteria for specification selection

7. Complete the Architecture Definition

8. Conduct a gap analysis

In executing Step 1, the Baseline Architecture was assessed:

- To describe the baseline features principles of the Baseline Architecture

- To describe the Baseline Architecture in TOGAF terms

- To identify new requirements, inhibitors, and opportunities

Baseline Features

- The existing architecture model is founded on the mainframe.
- Databases are tied to application logic.
- Security is embedded in the application.

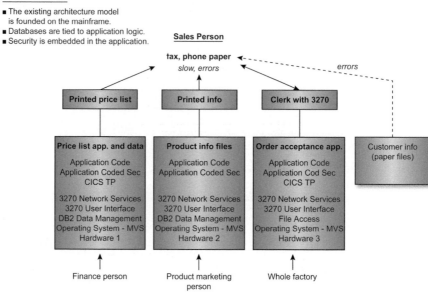

Figure 37-6 Baseline Architecture in TOGAF Terms

Notice how in Figure 37-6 and Figure 37-7 the legacy systems supporting the price list, product information, and order acceptance applications are easy to handle as monolithic building blocks. Figure 37-8, Figure 37-9, and Figure 37-10 show they can be connected to new building blocks using adapters.

In Step 2, the function view was examined based upon what the system was intended to do, and how it should behave. The function view is depicted in Figure 37-7. Note that the inventory control and scheduling system are not covered.

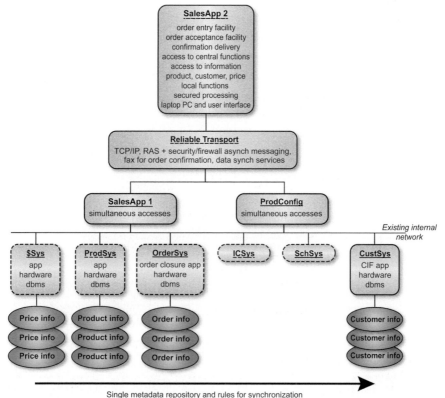

Figure 37-7 Target Architecture of Functions

In executing Step 2, a view of the Target Architecture was created by processing the technical functionality that must be provided by:

- Identifying obvious additions
- Identifying what would be carried forward from the old system
- Determining the return on investment for various options, allowing them to be ranked
- Assessing the risk of the various changes
- Checking the coverage of the technical functionality
- Adding technical functionality required for completeness, checking against the TOGAF Technical Reference Model (TRM)
- Updating and clarifying the business requirements and technical functionality

- Iteratively adding precision and detail to the Target Architecture

- For each architectural decision, completely following through the impact of it

- Noting the rationale for each decision whether the answer was yes or no, so as to avoid reopening old issues later

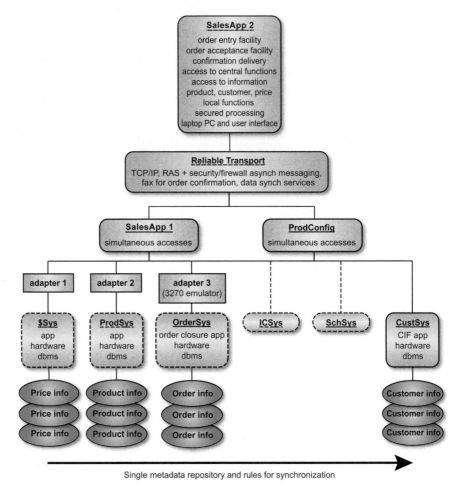

Figure 37-8 Augmented Target Architecture of Functions

Figure 37-8 shows how the constraints identified in the earlier technical functionality and constraints work have been incorporated. It was necessary to retain the existing systems for order handling and product information. The initial constraint list also included retaining the existing system for customer information, but this was overridden by the need to improve the quality of the sales process and a new system is proposed to deal with this. Return on investment is the driving force behind the decision to retain the existing system for price data.

Quality problems with the price system highlighted in Figure 37-3 will be resolved through a single metadata definition and rules for synchronization as shown in Figure 37-7. These legacy systems are integrated into the new SalesApp (Sales Order Application) by developing adapter software. The following describes the SalesApp application.

- SalesApp consists of two parts. SalesApp1 runs at the central site, and SalesApp2 on a portable system carried by the sales person. Communication between the two is carried by a reliable transport (TCP/IP and RAS), and includes security provided by a firewall. Asynchronous messaging is also provided. Fax services are required at the central site so as to provide the customer with written confirmation of acceptance of the order. Data synchronization services are needed to keep the sales person's portable systems and the central systems up-to-date with each other. Iteration of the architecture development process to validate the results against the business requirements is helped by considering detailed "use-cases". For instance, consider the activity of verifying an entered configuration.

- Entry is handled by SalesApp2, running on the sales person's portable system. SalesApp2 must deal with:
  - Establishment of the link to SalesApp1:
    - Physical link
    - Protocols
  - Security check
  - Direct information request to the proper database

- Then, at the central site:
  - SalesApp1 contacts the configurator.
  - The configurator:
    - Reacts to the named request
    - Gets information from the price, product information, customer information, and production systems
    - Determines the yes or no result
    - Returns to SalesApp1
  - SalesApp1 returns the result to SalesApp2.

- All of the separate elements in the use-case must be supplied by the Solution Architecture. Another way of refining the developing architectural model is to use the architecture views:
  - The Computing view is often the default.
  - The Data Management view is often useful.
  - The Security and Management views are of growing importance.
  - Performance is an important consideration both on the Baseline Architecture to discover the underlying assumptions and on the Target Architecture to document the assumptions and provide a basis for change in performance limits. Performance should be addressed in a number of views, including the Computing, Communications, and Builder's views.

To ensure that building blocks are as re-usable as possible, detailed information is needed about the building block. For this reason it is helpful to take views of individual building blocks and not just of the complete system. For the maximum benefit, it may be necessary to take views of both ABBs and SBBs.

It is the responsibility of the architect to foresee the integration of any application with the rest of the enterprise regardless of the isolated position of the application today. This future integration is facilitated by complete definition of building blocks. It is the responsibility of the business unit to implement in accordance with the rules of the architecture.

Step 3 consists of creating an architecture model of building blocks. Figure 37-8 depicts a Target Architecture model of functions, but does not express the relationships and interfaces between the elements in the architecture model. As the architectural development process continues, it becomes important to define a manageable granularity for building blocks and to fully define their linkages. Without this work there is no guarantee of interoperability between the various building blocks chosen.

We have identified two lists of candidate building blocks in the above steps. Prior to building a model of building blocks, these lists are processed and some candidates become recommended building blocks.

Candidate Building Blocks: Business Process-Driven List	Candidate Building Blocks: Baseline-Driven List
Sales person's laptop	Price list application, data, and platform
Sales person's CIPR	Product information and platform
Sales person's LIPR	Order acceptance application, data, and platform
ProdConfig	
ICSys	
SchSys	
$Sys	
OrderSys	

Table 37-2 Candidate Building Blocks — Lists

The process of identifying building blocks includes looking for collections of functions which require integration to draw them together or make them different.

First, it is recommended that the candidate building blocks from list B be selected as building blocks because they are re-usable legacy items. With these, a building block containing all the adapters is identified given the affinity of similar logic; e.g., providing the network adapter functionality on behalf of all the legacy applications.

Next a network building block appears to be required as it is a new network that must be built or purchased and is independent of the applications implemented. It itself can be a re-usable building block for other applications.

The laptop with the SalesApp2 application is identified as a building block because it is a modular pack of functionality specially built with applications and data tightly integrated for the mobile sales force. However, a RAS-capable firewall was also identified as a separable building block.

The new customer information system is also identified as a re-usable building block given its applicability across applications past, new, and future. The SalesApp1 and configuration systems were identified as two additional building blocks.

We depict the ABBs at a high level in Figure 37-9.

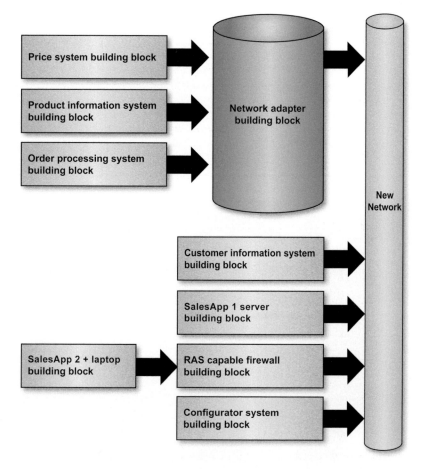

Figure 37-9 Representation of XYZ SalesApp System

Figure 37-9 presents a relationship view of the system. Compare this with Figure 37-8, a functional view, to see how different diagrammatic views of the same system can be used to show different things.

In executing Step 3, the Target Architecture was created by processing the technical functionality that must be provided and:

- Diagrams of larger systems drawn with this notation quickly show what interfaces are needed between building blocks and which ones need to be identical to realize interoperability benefits.

- Figure 37-9 clearly shows where and how glue software is required to bind the legacy systems to the new network.

Step 4 is to select the services portfolio required per building block. Figure 37-10 depicts the services mapped to components in the architecture model.

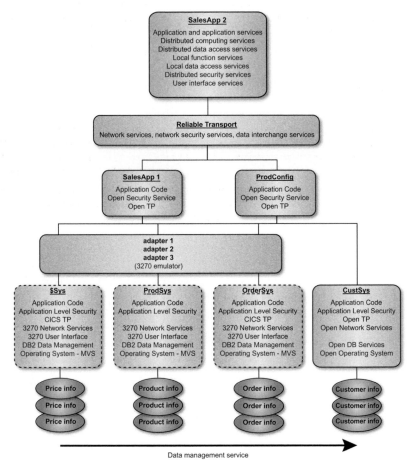

Figure 37-10 Services Map

Step 5 in the process is to confirm that the architecture supports the business goals and objectives. This is a relatively subjective task of answering the questions developed in Step 1. In this example, we did not establish a set of questions that would be used to test the architecture, but such questions (and how to pose them in light of the architecture) could easily be envisioned. For example, one question could be: "Does the architecture prohibit the immediate processing of an order by a customer?" which would be answered "no" in our case above.

The use-cases developed earlier are a handy tool to test the completeness and applicability of the architecture and its building blocks.

Building block specifications should be recorded in detail. An example of a building block specification document is given in Section 37.4.6.1.

Where an enterprise architecture exists or is being developed, it may be valuable at this point to review the new set of building blocks. Anything of benefit to the wider enterprise should be abstracted back to an architectural level and then fed back into the enterprise architecture development process.

Step 8 is to conduct a gap analysis, and is not covered in this example.

37.4.6.1   *Customer Information System Building Block Specification*

Description

This system is put in place of the existing paper-based customer information system to support the goal of improving the speed and quality of order closure. It shields the database from the complexity of the many applications looking at it, but it contains an architectural break-point which could be used later on to make the database itself accessible to other applications.

The interfaces selected must go through an internal approval process modeled on the interface adoption criteria of The Open Group. This means that all specifications must be or become part of the corporate Standards Information Base (SIB).

Functionality Category	Functionality	Interfaces (APIs, Formats, & Protocols)	Product or Project
CIF Application Code	Respects metadata repository spec	User-defined	User-defined
	Implements business rules	User-defined	User-defined
	Has remote access by SalesApp and configurator	DCE RPC	See SIB
	Uses SQL	ANSI SQL CLI	
	Uses UNIX	UNIX 03	
Open DB Services	Relational	Codd	
	Supports concurrent access	Codd	
	Offers SQL	ANSI SQL	
Open Security Services	Single sign-on		
	Authorization	DCE	
	Authentication	DCE	
	Integrity		
	Audit	DCE	
	Non-repudiation		
Open Operating System	UNIX	UNIX 03	
Network Services	Existing internal network	User-defined	User-defined
Open TP	Multiple concurrent access	The Open Group XA	
	Load leveling		
+Performance	50 enquiries per second		
+Manageability	Online software update		
	Service-level data provision	DMTF Spec	
	Integration into enterprise management system	TBD	
+Availability	24 by 7 by 52		

Mandated Building Blocks

Building Block Name	Owner	Required Functionality	Named Used Interfaces
Enterprise Management System	Corporate IT	Service-level data handling Integration — TBD	
Enterprise Network	Corporate IT		
CIF System	Marketing		

Map to Business Organization Entities and Policies

Policy	Entity	Comments
Security	Corporate admin	
Audit	Corporate admin	
Development and deployment	Corporate IT	
Metadata definition	Corporate IT	
Data quality	Corporate IT	
IT architecture	Corporate IT	
Corporate SIB	Corporate IT	This is linked to The Open Group SIB.

37.4.7 Opportunity Identification

This is the step where projects are identified, ranked, and selected.

The steps illustrated above have laid the foundation for this analysis. Figure 37-8, for instance, shows the SalesApp applications, the reliable transport, the adapters, and the new customer information system as potential projects.

37.4.8 Building Block Re-Use Level

In ADM Phases F to G, the choice of building blocks may be affected by outside events, such as a change in the availability of products. They can also affect and be affected by issues such as the cost of retraining users during migration from one product to another. Perhaps the most important impact though is the effect that building block choice can have on other work in progress within an organization. This section shows how a diagrammatic representation of the building blocks in a system can be used to identify or prioritize future projects.

An important benefit of defining the building blocks and their linkages is that it becomes possible to pick out re-usable components in the architecture. The best way to do this is to draw up a matrix of the building blocks used in an architecture and the applications that use them. Such a matrix for a simple subset of the XYZ case is shown in Figure 37-11.

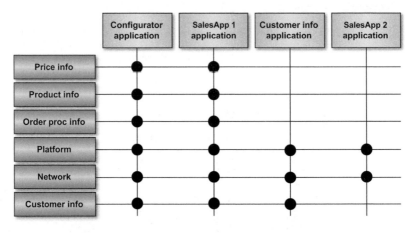

Figure 37-11 Simple Component/Application Matrix

Careful ordering of the building blocks in the left-hand column allows the architect to identify subsets of functionality common to a number of applications. Figure 37-12 shows such a subset. In this case, the subset of platform, network, and customer information database gives a strong indication that the configurator, SalesApp1, and customer information applications should be hosted on the same platform.

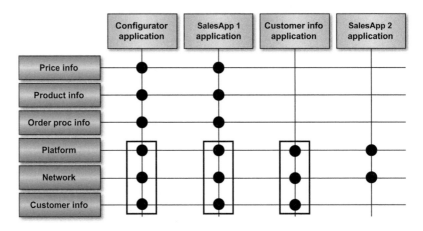

Figure 37-12 Identifying Common Functionality

Such identifiable subsets of building blocks also serve another purpose, which is that they can draw attention to opportunities for component re-use. If, in the future, XYZ decides to implement a customer care system, adding that into the matrix reveals that there would be significant advantages to building the customer care system on the same building blocks used for the configurator, SalesApp1, and customer information applications.

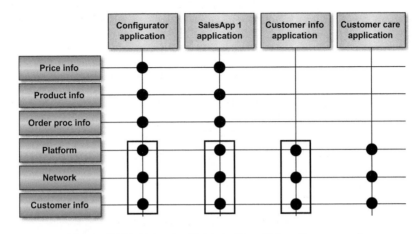

Figure 37-13 Using the Matrix to Steer Future Procurement

The key to success in working with building blocks is to establish a useful level of granularity. Too much detail in the chosen set of building blocks will make the architecture unworkable, while too coarse a level of detail will make the work valueless.

The Open Group Architecture Framework (TOGAF)

Part V:

Enterprise Continuum and Tools

The Open Group

Chapter 38: Introduction

This chapter provides an introduction to and an overview of the contents of Part V: Enterprise Continuum & Tools.

38.1 Introduction

It is usually impossible to create a single unified architecture that meets all requirements of all stakeholders for all time. Therefore, the enterprise architect will need to deal not just with a single enterprise architecture, but with many related enterprise architectures.

Each architecture will have a different purpose and architectures will relate to one another. Effectively bounding the scope of an architecture is therefore a critical success factor in allowing architects to break down a complex problem space into manageable components that can be individually addressed.

The Enterprise Continuum provides a view of the Architecture Repository that shows the evolution of these related architectures from generic to specific, from abstract to concrete, and from logical to physical.

This part of TOGAF discusses the Enterprise Continuum; including the Architecture Continuum and the Solutions Continuum. It describes how architectures can be partitioned and organized within a repository. It also describes tools for architecture development.

38.2 Structure of Part V

Part V: Enterprise Continuum & Tools is structured as follows:

- Introduction (this chapter)
- The Enterprise Continuum (see Chapter 39) describes a view of the Architecture Repository that provides methods for classifying architecture and solution artifacts, showing how the different types of artifact evolve, and how they can be leveraged and re-used.
- Architecture Partitioning (see Chapter 40) describes the various characteristics that can be applied to classify and then partition architectures.
- The Architecture Repository (see Chapter 41) shows how the abstract classifications of architecture can be applied to a repository structure so that architectures can be organized and easily accessed.

- Tools for Architecture Development (see Chapter 42) provides guidelines on selecting a toolset to create and manage architectural artifacts.

Chapter 39: Enterprise Continuum

39.1   Overview

The Enterprise Continuum is a view of the Architecture Repository that provides methods for classifying architecture and solution artifacts, both internal and external to the Architecture Repository, as they evolve from generic Foundation Architectures to Organization-Specific Architectures.

The Enterprise Continuum is an important aid to communication and understanding, both within individual enterprises, and between customer enterprises and vendor organizations. Without an understanding of "where in the continuum you are", people discussing architecture can often talk at cross-purposes because they are referencing different points in the continuum at the same time, without realizing it.

Any architecture is context-specific; for example, there are architectures that are specific to individual customers, industries, subsystems, products, and services. Architects, on both the buy side and supply side, must have at their disposal a consistent language to effectively communicate the differences between architectures. Such a language will enable engineering efficiency and the effective leveraging of Commercial Off-The-Shelf (COTS) product functionality. The Enterprise Continuum provides that consistent language.

Not only does the Enterprise Continuum represent an aid to communication, it represents an aid to organizing re-usable architecture and solution assets. This is explained further in the following sections.

39.2   Enterprise Continuum and Architecture Re-Use

The simplest way of thinking of the Enterprise Continuum is as a view of the repository of all the architecture assets. It can contain architecture descriptions, models, building blocks, patterns, viewpoints, and other artifacts — that exist both within the enterprise and in the IT industry at large, which the enterprise considers to have available for the development of architectures for the enterprise.

Examples of internal architecture and solution artifacts are the deliverables of previous architecture work, which are available for re-use. Examples of external architecture and solution artifacts are the wide variety of industry reference models and architecture patterns that exist, and are continually emerging, including those that are highly generic (such as TOGAF's own Technical Reference Model (TRM)); those specific to certain aspects of IT (such as a web services architecture, or a generic manageability architecture); those specific to certain types of information processing, such as e-Commerce, supply chain management, etc.; and those specific to certain vertical industries, such as the models generated by vertical consortia like TMF (in the Telecommunications sector), ARTS (Retail), Energistics (Petrotechnical), etc.

The enterprise architecture determines which architecture and solution artifacts an organization includes in its Architecture Repository. Re-use is a major consideration in this decision.

39.3   Constituents of the Enterprise Continuum

An overview of the context and constituents of the Enterprise Continuum is shown in Figure 39-1.

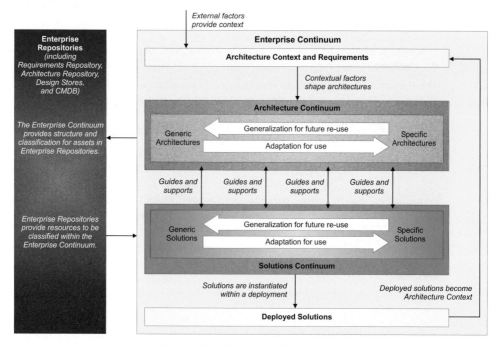

Figure 39-1 Enterprise Continuum

The Enterprise Continuum is partitioned into three distinct continua as follows:

- The **Enterprise Continuum** (see Section 39.4) is the outermost continuum and classifies assets related to the context of the overall enterprise architecture. The Enterprise Continuum classes of assets may influence architectures, but are not directly used during the ADM architecture development. The Enterprise Continuum classifies contextual assets used to develop architectures, such as policies, standards, strategic initiatives, organizational structures, and enterprise-level capabilities. The Enterprise Continuum can also classify solutions (as opposed to descriptions or specifications of solutions). Finally, the Enterprise Continuum contains two specializations, namely the Architecture and

Solutions Continua.

- The **Architecture Continuum** (see Section 39.4.1) offers a consistent way to define and understand the generic rules, representations, and relationships in an architecture, including traceability and derivation relationships (e.g., to show that an Organization-Specific Architecture is based on an industry or generic standard). The Architecture Continuum represents a structuring of Architecture Building Blocks (ABBs) which are re-usable architecture assets. ABBs evolve through their development lifecycle from abstract and generic entities to fully expressed Organization-Specific Architecture assets. The Architecture Continuum assets will be used to guide and select the elements in the Solutions Continuum (see below). The Architecture Continuum shows the relationships among foundational frameworks (such as TOGAF), common system architectures (such as the III-RM), industry architectures, and enterprise architectures. The Architecture Continuum is a useful tool to discover commonality and eliminate unnecessary redundancy.

- The **Solutions Continuum** (see Section 39.4.2) provides a consistent way to describe and understand the implementation of the assets defined in the Architecture Continuum. The Solutions Continuum defines what is available in the organizational environment as re-usable Solution Building Blocks (SBBs). The solutions are the results of agreements between customers and business partners that implement the rules and relationships defined in the architecture space. The Solutions Continuum addresses the commonalities and differences among the products, systems, and services of implemented systems.

The Enterprise Continuum classifies architecture assets that are applicable across the entire scope of the enterprise architecture. These assets, which may be referred to as building blocks, can represent a variety of elements that collectively define and constrain the enterprise architecture. They can take the form of business goals and objectives, strategic initiatives, capabilities, policies, standards, and principles.

The Enterprise Continuum also contains the Architecture Continuum and the Solutions Continuum. Each of these continua is described in greater detail in the following sections.

39.4   Enterprise Continuum in Detail

The Enterprise Continuum is intended to represent the classification of all assets that are available to an enterprise. It classifies assets that exist within the enterprise along with other assets in the wider environment that are relevant to the enterprise, such as products, research, market factors, commercial factors, business strategies, and legislation.

TOGAF is intended to be a framework for conducting enterprise architecture and as a result many of the assets that reside within the Enterprise Continuum are beyond the specific consideration of the TOGAF framework. However, architectures are fundamentally shaped by concerns outside the practice of architecture and it is therefore of paramount importance that any architecture must accurately reflect external context.

The specific contextual factors to be identified and incorporated in an architecture will vary from architecture to architecture. However, typical contextual factors for architecture development are likely to include:

- External influencing factors, such as regulatory change, technological advances, and competitor activity

- Business strategy and context, including mergers, acquisitions, and other business transformation requirements

- Current business operations, reflecting deployed architectures and solutions

By observing the context for architecture, it can be seen that architecture development activity exists within a wider enterprise lifecycle of continuous change.

ABBs are defined in relation to a set of contextual factors and then realized through SBBs. SBBs are deployed as live solutions and become a part of the baseline operating model of the enterprise. The operating model of the enterprise and empiric information on the performance of the enterprise shapes the context and requirements for future change. Finally, these new requirements for change create a feedback-loop to influence the creation of new Target Architectures.

39.4.1 Architecture Continuum

The Architecture Continuum illustrates how architectures are developed and evolved across a continuum ranging from Foundation Architectures, such as the one provided by TOGAF, through Common Systems Architectures, and Industry Architectures, and to an enterprise's own Organization-Specific Architectures.

The arrows in the Architecture Continuum represent the relationship that exists between the different architectures in the Architecture Continuum. The leftwards direction focuses on meeting enterprise needs and business requirements, while the rightwards direction focuses on leveraging architectural components and building blocks.

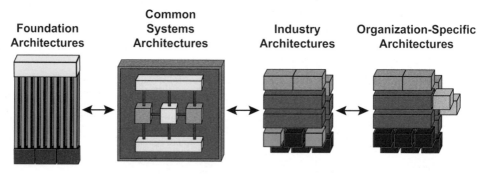

Figure 39-2 Architecture Continuum

The enterprise needs and business requirements are addressed in increasing detail from left to right. The architect will typically look to find re-usable architectural elements toward the left of the continuum. When elements are not found, the requirements for the missing elements are passed to the left of the continuum for incorporation. Those implementing architectures within their own organizations can use the same continuum models specialized for their business.

The four particular architecture types illustrated in Figure 39-2 are intended to indicate the range of different types of architecture that may be developed at different points in the continuum; they are not fixed stages in a process.

Many different types of architecture may occur at points in between those illustrated in Figure 39-2. Although the evolutionary transformation continuum illustrated does not represent a formal process, it does represent a progression, which occurs at several levels:

- Logical to physical
- Horizontal (IT-focused) to vertical (business-focused)
- Generalization to specialization
- Taxonomy to complete and specific architecture specification

At each point in the continuum, an architecture is designed in terms of the design concepts and building blocks available and relevant to that point.

The four architectures illustrated in Figure 39-2 represent main classifications of potential architectures, and will be relevant and familiar to many architects. They are analyzed in detail below.

Foundation Architecture

A Foundation Architecture is an architecture of building blocks and corresponding standards that supports all the Common Systems Architectures and, therefore, the complete enterprise operating environment. The Open Group provides a TRM Foundation Architecture. The TOGAF Architecture Development Method (ADM) is a process that would support specialization of such Foundation Architectures in order to create organization-specific models.

The TOGAF TRM describes a fundamental architecture upon which other, more specific architectures can be based. See Chapter 43 for more details.

Common Systems Architectures

Common Systems Architectures guide the selection and integration of specific services from the Foundation Architecture to create an architecture useful for building common (i.e., highly re-usable) solutions across a wide number of relevant domains.

Examples of Common Systems Architectures include: a security architecture, a management architecture, a network architecture, an operations architecture, etc. Each is incomplete in terms of overall system functionality, but is complete in terms of a particular problem domain (security, manageability, networking, operations, etc.), so that solutions implementing the architecture constitute re-usable building blocks for the creation of functionally complete operating states of the enterprise.

Other characteristics of Common Systems Architectures include:

- Reflects requirements specific to a generic problem domain
- Defines building blocks specific to a generic problem domain
- Defines business, data, application, or technology standards for implementing these building blocks
- Provides building blocks for easy re-use and lower costs

The TOGAF Integrated Information Infrastructure Reference Model (III-RM) — see Part VI, Chapter 44 — is a Common Systems Architecture that focuses on the requirements, building blocks, and standards relating to the vision of Boundaryless Information Flow.

Industry Architectures

Industry Architectures guide the integration of common systems components with industry-specific components, and guide the creation of industry solutions for targeted customer problems within a particular industry.

A typical example of an industry-specific component is a data model representing the business functions and processes specific to a particular vertical industry, such as the Retail industry's "Active Store" architecture, or an Industry Architecture that incorporates the Energistics Data Model (refer to www.energistics.org).

Other characteristics of Industry Architectures include:

- Reflects requirements and standards specific to a vertical industry
- Defines building blocks specific to a generic problem domain
- Contains industry-specific logical data and process models
- Contains industry-specific applications and process models, as well as industry-specific business rules
- Provides guidelines for testing collections of systems
- Encourages levels of interoperability throughout the industry

Organization-Specific Architectures

Organization-Specific Architectures are the most relevant to the IT customer community, since they describe and guide the final deployment of solution components for a particular enterprise or extended network of connected enterprises.

There may be a variety of Organization-Specific Architectures that are needed to effectively cover the organization's requirements by defining the architectures in increasing levels of detail. Alternatively, this might result in several more detailed Organization-Specific Architectures for specific entities within the global enterprise. Breaking down Organization-Specific Architectures into constituent pieces is addressed in Chapter 40.

The Organization-Specific Architecture guides the final customization of the solution, and has the following characteristics:

- Provides a means to communicate and manage business operations across all four architectural domains
- Reflects requirements specific to a particular enterprise
- Defines building blocks specific to a particular enterprise
- Contains organization-specific business models, data, applications, and technologies
- Provides a means to encourage implementation of appropriate solutions to meet business needs
- Provides the criteria to measure and select appropriate products, solutions, and services
- Provides an evolutionary path to support growth and new business needs

39.4.2 Solutions Continuum

The Solutions Continuum represents the detailed specification and construction of the architectures at the corresponding levels of the Architecture Continuum. At each level, the Solutions Continuum is a population of the architecture with reference building blocks — either purchased products or built components — that represent a solution to the enterprise's business need expressed at that level. A populated repository based on the Solutions Continuum can be regarded as a solutions inventory or re-use library, which can add significant value to the task of managing and implementing improvements to the enterprise.

The Solutions Continuum is illustrated in Figure 39-3.

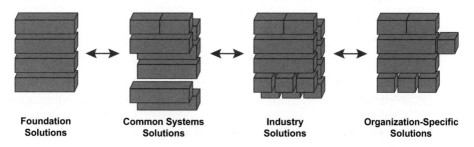

| Foundation
Solutions | Common Systems
Solutions | Industry
Solutions | Organization-Specific
Solutions |

Figure 39-3 Solutions Continuum

"Moving to the right" on the Solutions Continuum is focused on providing solutions value (i.e., foundation solutions provide value in creating common systems solutions; common systems solutions are used to create industry solutions; and industry solutions are used to create organization-specific solutions). "Moving to the left" on the Solutions Continuum is focused on addressing enterprise needs.

These two viewpoints are significant for a company attempting to focus on its needs while maximizing the use of available resources through leverage.

The following subsections describe each of the solution types within the Solutions Continuum.

Foundation Solutions

Foundation Solutions are highly generic concepts, tools, products, services, and solution components that are the fundamental providers of capabilities. Services include professional services — such as training and consulting services — that ensure the maximum investment value from solutions in the shortest possible time; and support services — such as Help Desk — that ensure the maximum possible value from solutions (services that ensure timely updates and upgrades to the products and systems).

Example Foundation Solutions would include programming languages, operating systems, foundational data structures (such as EDIFACT), generic approaches to organization structuring, foundational structures for organizing IT operations (such as ITIL), etc.

Common Systems Solutions

A Common Systems Solution is an implementation of a Common Systems Architecture comprised of a set of products and services, which may be certified or branded. It represents the highest common denominator for one or more solutions in the industry segments that the Common Systems Solution supports.

Common Systems Solutions represent collections of common requirements and capabilities, rather than those specific to a particular customer or industry. Common Systems Solutions provide organizations with operating environments specific to operational and informational needs, such as high availability transaction processing and scalable data warehousing systems. Examples of Common Systems Solutions include: an enterprise management system product or a security system product.

Computer systems vendors are the typical providers of technology-centric Common Systems Solutions. "Software as a service" vendors are typical providers of common application solutions. Business process outsourcing vendors are typical provides of business capability-centric Common Systems Solutions.

Industry Solutions

An Industry Solution is an implementation of an Industry Architecture, which provides re-usable packages of common components and services specific to an industry.

Fundamental components are provided by Common Systems Solutions and/or Foundation Solutions, and are augmented with industry-specific components. Examples include: a physical database schema or an industry-specific point-of-service device.

Industry Solutions are industry-specific, aggregate procurements that are ready to be tailored to an individual organization's requirements.

In some cases an industry solution may include not only an implementation of the Industry Architecture, but also other solution elements, such as specific products, services, and systems solutions that are appropriate to that industry.

Organization-Specific Solutions

An Organization-Specific Solution is an implementation of the Organization-Specific Architecture that provides the required business functions. Because solutions are designed for specific business operations, they contain the highest amount of unique content in order to accommodate the varying people and processes of specific organizations.

Building Organization-Specific Solutions on Industry Solutions, Common Systems Solutions, and Foundation Solutions is the primary purpose of connecting the Architecture Continuum to the Solutions Continuum, as guided by the architects within an enterprise.

An Organization-Specific Solution will be structured in order to support specific Service Level Agreements (SLAs) to ensure support of the operational systems at desired service levels. For example, a third-party application hosting provider may offer different levels of support for operational systems. These agreements would define the terms and conditions of that support.

Other key factors to be defined within an Organization-Specific Solution are the key operating parameters and quality metrics that can be used to monitor and manage the environment.

The Enterprise Continuum can provide a key link between architecture, development, and operations personnel by allowing them to communicate and reach agreement on anticipated operational support requirements. Operations personnel can in turn access the Enterprise

Continuum to obtain information regarding the operation concepts and service support requirements of the deployed system.

39.5 Relationship between the Enterprise Continuum and TOGAF ADM

The TOGAF ADM describes the process of developing an enterprise-specific architecture and an enterprise-specific solution(s) which conform to that architecture by adopting and adapting (where appropriate) generic architectures and solutions (left to right in the continuum classification). In a similar fashion, specific architectures and solutions that prove to be credible and effective will be generalized for re-use (right to left in the continuum classification).

At relevant places throughout the TOGAF ADM, there are pointers to useful architecture assets at the relevant level of generality in the continuum classification. In some cases — for example, in the development of a Technology Architecture — this may be TOGAF's own TRM Foundation Architecture (see below). In other cases — for example, in the development of a Business Architecture — it may be a reference model for e-Commerce taken from the industry at large.

TOGAF itself provides two reference models for consideration for use in developing an organization's architecture:

1. The **TOGAF Foundation Architecture**, which comprises a TRM of generic services and functions that provides a firm foundation on which more specific architectures and architectural components can be built.

2. The **Integrated Information Infrastructure Reference Model** (III-RM), which is based on the TOGAF Foundation Architecture, and is specifically designed to help the realization of architectures that enable and support the vision of Boundaryless Information Flow.

However, in developing architectures in the various domains within an overall enterprise architecture, the architect will need to consider the use and re-use of a wide variety of different architecture assets, and the Enterprise Continuum provides an approach for categorizing and communicating these different assets.

39.6 Enterprise Continuum and Your Organization

The preceding sections have described the Enterprise Continuum, the Architecture Continuum, and the Solutions Continuum. The following sections describe the relationships between each of the three continua and how these relationships should be applied within your organization.

39.6.1 Relationships

Each of the three continua contains information about the evolution of the architectures during their lifecycle:

- The Enterprise Continuum provides an overall context for architectures and solutions and classifies assets that apply across the entire scope of the enterprise.

- The Architecture Continuum provides a classification mechanism for assets that collectively define the architecture at different levels of evolution from generic to specific.

- The Solutions Continuum provides the classification for assets to describe specific solutions for the organization that can be implemented to achieve the intent of the architecture.

The relationships between the Architecture Continuum and Solutions Continuum are shown in Figure 39-4.

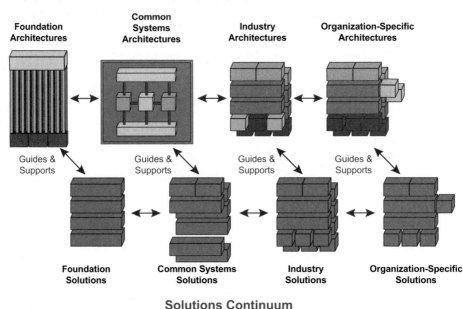

Figure 39-4 Relationships between Architecture and Solutions Continua

The relationship between the Architecture Continuum and the Solutions Continuum is one of guidance, direction, and support. For example, Foundation Architectures guide the creation or selection of Foundation Solutions. Foundation Solutions support the Foundation Architecture by helping to realize the architecture defined in the Architecture Continuum. The Foundation Architecture also guides development of Foundation Solutions, by providing architectural direction, requirements and principles that guide selection, and realization of appropriate solutions. A similar relationship exists between the other elements of the Enterprise Continuum.

The Enterprise Continuum presents mechanisms to help improve productivity through leverage. The Architecture Continuum offers a consistent way to understand the different architectures and their components. The Solutions Continuum offers a consistent way to understand the different products, systems, services, and solutions required.

The Enterprise Continuum should not be interpreted as representing strictly chained relationships. Organization-Specific Architectures could have components from a Common Systems Architecture, and Organization-Specific Solutions could contain Foundation Solutions. The relationships depicted in Figure 39-1 are an illustration showing opportunities for leveraging architecture and solution components.

39.6.2 Your Enterprise

TOGAF provides a method for you to "architect" the systems in your enterprise. Your architecture organization will have to deal with each type of architecture described above. For example, it is recommended that you have your own Foundation Architecture that governs all of your systems. You should also have your own Common Systems Architectures that govern major shared systems — such as the networking system or management system. You may have your own industry-specific architectures that govern the way your systems must behave within your industry. Finally, any given department or organization within your business may need its own individual Organization-Specific Architecture to govern the systems within that department.

Your architecture organization will either adopt or adapt existing architectures, or will develop its own architectures from the ground up. In either case, TOGAF is a tool to help. It provides a method to assist you in generating/maintaining any type of architecture within the Architecture Continuum while leveraging architecture assets already defined, internal or external to your organization. The TOGAF ADM helps you to re-use architecture assets, making your architecture organization more efficient and effective.

Chapter 40: Architecture Partitioning

40.1 Overview

In a typical enterprise, many architectures will be in existence at any point in time. Some architectures will address very specific needs; others will be more general. Some will address detail; some will provide a big picture. Likewise, there will also be many solutions in use, or being considered for use, to meet the needs of the enterprise.

Each of these solutions and architectures does not exist in a vacuum and the Enterprise Continuum, discussed in Chapter 39, provides a classification model for all related architectures and solutions. Within the Enterprise Continuum, boundaries, relationships, and ordering can be established for both solutions and architectures in order to simplify the development and management of the enterprise.

For example, any particular characteristic of architectures (e.g., time) can be used to create a "sliding scale" for this characteristic (e.g., a timeline), which can then be applied to individual architectures to create an ordered listing (e.g., architectures in chronological order, or an Architecture Roadmap). Finally, the ordered listing can then be used to drive policy and process within the enterprise (e.g., five-year architectures are developed by a particular team).

Both solutions and architectures have a set of characteristics that can be used to define what they are and how they are managed. When specifically considering architectures, there are some characteristics that relate to the architecture and others that are inherited from the solutions that the architecture is describing.

These characteristics can be used to create a partitioning model for the enterprise, showing the boundaries of individual architectures and also groupings of related architectures.

We need to partition architectures because:

- Addressing all problems within a single architecture is too complex.

- Different architectures conflict with one another (e.g., the state of the enterprise changes over time and an architecture from one time period will conflict with an architecture for a different time period).

- Different people need to work on different elements of architecture at the same time and partitions allow for specific groups of architects to own and develop specific segments of the architecture.

- Effective architecture re-use requires modular architecture segments that can be taken and incorporated into broader architectures and solutions.

However, it is difficult to present a definitive partitioning model for architecture, as each enterprise is likely to adopt a partitioning model that reflects its own operating model. An example approach to partitioning architectures into segments within the US Federal Government can be found within the Federal Enterprise Architecture Practice Guidance.[17]

This chapter discusses the classification criteria that are generally applied to architectures or solutions and how these can be leveraged to partition the enterprise into a set of architectures with manageable complexity.

40.2 Characteristics of Solutions

When attempting to describe a solution, it is possible to use a number of different approaches. The following three characteristics can be used to derive a good characterization of the majority of solutions:

- **Subject Matter**: The most obvious way to describe a solution is to examine its content, structure, and function (i.e., its subject matter). Additionally, the solution may be described by examining the boundary of the solution and all the external factors that interact with the solution at the solution boundary (e.g., pre-conditions, post-conditions, consumers, suppliers, ownership, operation, influencing factors).

- **Time**: All solutions exist for a period of time. The subject matter and environment of a solution are likely to fundamentally change over time, so identifying the time period of a solution is a key contextual factor to consider. Additionally, when future solutions are being described, often the time period of the solution represents a target realization date and is used to plan and organize change activity.

- **Maturity/Volatility**: The extent to which the subject matter and environment of a solution are likely to change over time. Highly volatile or immature solutions are likely to be managed and valued very differently to very stable or mature solutions (e.g., flexible solutions are more valuable in volatile environments).

40.3 Characteristics of Architectures

Architectures are representations of particular solutions. As representations rather than actual solutions, architectures possess specific characteristics in addition to those described for solutions:

- **Subject Matter**: Architectures describe specific solutions and consequently inherit the objective characteristics of the solution that they represent (i.e., the subject matter, environment, time, and volatility).

- **Viewpoint**: The architectural domains considered and specific artifacts produced will provide a partial representation of the solution based on the needs of stakeholders. This viewpoint may be general, or specific to a particular architecture domain (i.e., business, data, application, and technology) or other consideration (i.e., Security, Operational Management, Integration, Construction, etc.).

---

17. Refer to www.whitehouse.gov/omb/egov/documents/FEA_Practice_Guidance_Nov_2007.pdf

- **Level of Detail**: The level of detail used to represent a solution has a strong influence on how an architecture can be used. Generally, less detailed architectures are more effective in communicating an overall solution approach, but less effective in supporting its realization.

- **Level of Abstraction**: A consideration for architecture characterization is how abstracted the architecture is from the solutions that it represents. For example, some architectures provide a direct description of a solution and others may describe an approach or pattern that is used across many solutions.

- **Accuracy**: Any architecture is a representation of reality and is not necessarily a completely accurate description of the intended solution. Typically, the level and quality of resource invested in the creation of an architecture will determine the accuracy of the result.

40.4   Applying Classification to Create Partitioned Architectures

The characteristics outlined in the previous section provide a comprehensive mechanism to describe and classify both architectures and solutions. Once these characteristics have been defined, they can then be used to partition and organize the Enterprise Continuum into a set of related solutions and architectures with:

- Manageable complexity for each individual architecture or solution

- Defined groupings

- Defined hierarchies and navigation structures

- Appropriate processes, roles, and responsibilities attached to each grouping

The following table shows how each classification criteria can be used to support partitioning of solutions:

Characteristic	Usage to Support Partitioning
Subject Matter	Solutions are naturally organized into groups to support operational management and control. Examples of solution partitions according to subject matter would include applications, departments, divisions, products, services, service centers, sites, etc. Solution decomposition by subject matter is typically the fundamental technique for structuring both solutions and the architectures that represent them.
Time	Solution lifecycles are typically organized around a timeline, which allows the impact of solution development, introduction, operation, and retirement to be managed against other business activity occurring in similar time periods.
Maturity/Volatility	The maturity and volatility of a solution will typically impact the speed of execution required for the solution lifecycle. Additionally, volatility and maturity will shape investment priorities. Solutions existing in highly volatile environments may be better suited to rapid, agile development techniques.

The following table shows how each classification criteria can be used to support partitioning of architectures:

Characteristic	Usage to Support Partitioning
Subject Matter	Architectures are usually grouped by subject matter along similar lines to the solutions that they represent.
Viewpoint	Stakeholders with an operational management remit typically view the enterprise according to a "vertical" functional subject matter breakdown. However, many other stakeholders with a domain or discipline remit will view the enterprise "horizontally"; for example, looking at the use of information across the entire landscape. The combination of "horizontal" and "vertical" classes of viewpoint provides a number of alternative approaches to organizing architecture artifacts that complement the general subject matter-centric approach. In particular, "horizontal" views of the Architecture Continuum support the definition and enforcement of architectural standards.

Characteristic	Usage to Support Partitioning
Level of Detail	The level of detail within an architecture has a strong correlation to the stakeholder groups that will be interested in the architecture.
	Typically less detailed architectures will be of interest to executive stakeholders. As architectures increase in detail, their relevance to implementation and operational personnel will also increase.
	Level of detail is commonly used as an organizing characteristic for architectures; for example, the Contextual, Conceptual, Logical, Physical scheme used within the Zachman Framework can be equated to level of detail.
Level of Abstraction	The level of abstraction within an architecture has a strong bearing on how that architecture will be used.
	Architectures that provide a very direct representation of solutions will typically be used to understand current and future states of the enterprise.
	More abstract architectures are used to communicate concepts or reference models which can then be applied to specific problems in further architectures.
Accuracy	The accuracy of an architecture generally increases as it is developed. Appropriate architecture development and project management methods are used to guide architectures in development through successive iterations of development, verification, and validation which in turn increase quality.
	Once an architecture is developed, approach governance and change management processes are used to ensure that the architecture remains accurate against a changing enterprise reality.
	Configuration management systems and processes are typically used to control successive versions of architectural artifacts (V0.1, 0.2, 0.3, etc.).

In practical terms, architecture discipline is used to support a number of different types of architecture that are used for different objectives. The classification criteria described above can be used in different ways to support the achievement of each objective.

40.4.1 Partitioning the Architecture Landscape to Understand the State of the Enterprise

Typically architectures are used to provide summary views of the Architecture Landscape (i.e., the state of the enterprise) at particular points in time. The following characteristics are typically used to partition the Architecture Landscape:

- **Subject Matter**: The subject matter area is generally the primary organizing characteristic for describing an Architecture Landscape. Architectures are functionally decomposed into a hierarchy of specific subject areas or segments.

- **Level of Detail**: With broader subject areas, less detail is needed to ensure that the architecture has a manageable size and complexity. More specific subject matter areas will generally permit (and require) more detailed architectures.

- **Time Period**: For a specific subject matter and level of detail an enterprise can create a Baseline Architecture and a set of Target Architectures that stretch into the future. Broader and less detailed architectures will generally be valid for longer periods of time and can provide a vision for the enterprise that stretches further into the future.

- **Viewpoint**: For a particular subject area, level of detail, and time period the stakeholders for architecture will have requirements to see architectures that address particular issues or viewpoints.

- **Accuracy**: Finally, each architecture view will progress through a development cycle where it increases in accuracy until finally approved. After approval, an architecture will begin to decrease in accuracy if not actively maintained. In some cases recency may be used as an organizing factor for historic architectures.

The following characteristics are generally not used to partition an Architecture Landscape:

- Architectures used to describe the Architecture Landscape are generally not abstract.

- Solution volatility generally prevents architectures from being defined that are far in the future. Volatility also reduces the accuracy of historic architectures over time, as the organization changes and adapts to new circumstances.

Using the criteria above, architectures can be grouped into Strategic, Segment, and Capability Architecture tiers, as described in Section 41.2.

Figure 40-1 shows a summary of the classification model for Architecture Landscapes.

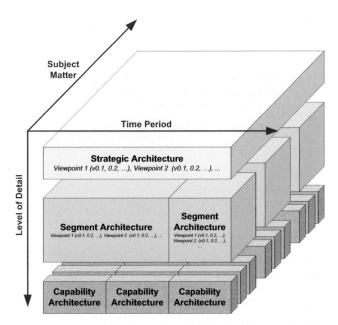

Figure 40-1 Summary Classification Model for Architecture Landscapes

In the same way that this classification model can be applied to the Architecture Landscape, it is also possible to apply a similar classification model to the Solutions Continuum (which is a collection of all the solutions that are represented by architectures) as shown in Figure 40-2.

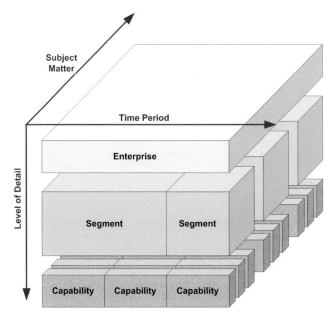

Figure 40-2 Summary Classification Model for Solutions

40.4.2 Partitioning Reference Models to Encourage Good Practice and Re-Use

Architectures that describe particular solution approaches, best practices, or patterns can be developed (or acquired) and shared across the enterprise as reference models. The following characteristics are typically used to partition architecture reference models:

- **Level of Abstraction**: Because reference models aim to be abstract, re-usable solution approaches that can be adopted in many circumstances, the level of abstraction is generally a good starting place for organizing reference models. Highly abstracted models may be applicable to all enterprises. As these models become more specific they may only be relevant to certain types of system, certain industries, or even be specific to a single enterprise or line of business.

- **Subject Matter**: Within a particular level of abstraction several related models may address a particular theme or topic and therefore partitioning according to subject matter allows for ease-of-reference.

- **Viewpoint**: For any given subject, a number of reference models may address that subject from different complementary viewpoints. Related viewpoints can be grouped together to provide a richer understanding of the desired approach.

The following characteristics are generally not used to partition architecture reference models:

- Reference models are typically quite specific to a particular problem, with detail levels that are appropriate to show the desired approach. Reference models generally do not provide a graded breakdown into subsequent levels of detail.

- Accuracy, maturity, and stability are generally pre-requisites for an architecture to be considered a reference model.

- Because reference models are generally abstract and are not explicitly tied to deployed solutions, their time period is not relevant or difficult to manage in a structured form.

Using the criteria above, reference models can be grouped into four categories:

1. **Foundation Architectures** are very abstract reference models that could be applied to all enterprise architectures or solutions.

2. **Common Systems Architectures** show patterns and approaches for common systems that occur across many enterprises and industries, such as Enterprise Resource Planning (ERP) systems.

3. **Industry Architectures** provide shared blueprints that can apply to many partners or competitors within a single industry.

4. **Organization-Specific Architectures** provide common reference models that are specific to the enterprise, but still can apply across several business areas.

A summary of the classification model for architecture reference models is shown in Figure 40-3.

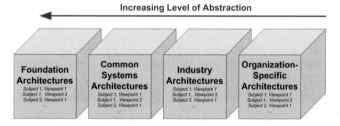

Figure 40-3 Summary Classification Model for Architecture Reference Models

40.4.3 Enforce Corporate Policy though Compliance with Standards

Organizations will generally attempt to encourage desired approaches and behaviors by defining and mandating a set of standards. The following characteristics are typically used to partition architectural standards:

- **Viewpoint**: As the intent of standards is to encourage consistent and desirable behaviors across the enterprise, it is typical to use "horizontal" viewpoints as a primary basis for partitioning standards. The architecture domains of business, data, application, and technology are common starting points, although other specific viewpoints, such as security, may exist in their own right.

- **Subject Matter**: Within a particular viewpoint, related standards can be grouped by subject matter.

- **Maturity/Volatility**: The maturity of a standard can be used to dictate its lifecycle stage. Immature standards can be marked as such and would typically carry a lower level of endorsement from the enterprise. As standards become mature, compliance with the standard is expected. As standards approach obsolescence, their usage is deprecated.

The following characteristics are typically not used to partition architectural standards:

- Standards are applied according to their maturity and generally not for specific time periods.

- Standards need to be detailed enough to assess compliance and are therefore not typically partitioned according to level of detail.

- Standards need to be concrete and specific enough to assess compliance and are therefore not typically partitioned according to level of abstraction.

- Standards are assumed to be accurate.

Using the criteria above, architecture standards can be grouped into four categories:

1. **Business Standards** relate to standard practice in the Business Architecture domain, including standard processes, roles, responsibilities, organization models, etc.

2. **Data Standards** relate to standard practice in the Data Architecture domain, including standard data models, data governance models, etc.

3. **Application Standards** relate to standard practice in the Application Architecture domain, including standard applications, application types, and application functionality.

4. **Technology Standards** relate to standard practice in the Technology Architecture domain, including standard products, product types, and proper usage constraints for technologies.

A summary of the classification model for architecture standards is shown in Figure 40-4.

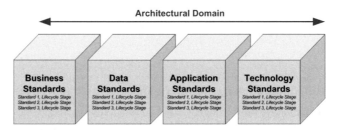

Figure 40-4 Summary Classification Model for Architecture Standards

The ADM provides a process that is well suited to the application of a partitioned architecture approach:

- The Preliminary phase supports the identification of appropriate architecture partitions and establishment of governance relationships between related architecture partitions.

- ADM Phases A to F allow definition of the architecture within a specific partition.

- ADM Phases G and H allow the implementation of an architecture to be governed. This governance may apply to the direct realization of a solution, or may address the governance of architectures being developed in other partitions.

The following subsections provide more detailed guidance on how a partitioned architecture approach can be applied within the ADM.

40.4.4 Activities within the Preliminary Phase

One of the key objectives of the Preliminary phase is to establish the "architecture footprint" for the enterprise. In practical terms this activity will require the establishment of a number of architecture partitions, with defined boundaries and ownership.

Generally speaking, each team carrying out architecture activity within the enterprise will own a number of partitioned architectures and will execute the ADM to define, govern, and realize their architectures.

If more than one team is expected to work on a single architecture, this can become problematic, as the precise responsibilities of each team are difficult to establish. For this reason, it is preferable to apply partitioning to the architecture until each architecture has one owning team.

Finally, it is worth considering the distinction between standing capabilities of the enterprise and temporary teams mobilized to support a particular change initiative. Although the remit of standing teams within the enterprise can be precisely defined, it is more difficult to anticipate and specify the responsibilities of (possibly unknown) temporary architecture teams. In the cases of these temporary teams, each team should come under the governance of a standing architecture team and there should be a process within the ADM cycle of these teams to establish appropriate architecture partitioning.

Steps within the Preliminary phase to support architecture partitioning are as follows:

- **Determine the organization structure for architecture within the enterprise**: The various teams that will create the architecture should be identified. For each of these teams, appropriate boundaries should be established, including:

  — Governance bodies that are applicable to the team

  — Team membership

  — Team reporting lines

  — Whether the team is a standing capability or a temporary change team

- **Determine the responsibilities for each architecture team**: For each architecture team, the responsibilities should be identified. This step applies partitioning logic to the enterprise architecture in order to firstly identify the scope of each team and secondly to partition the architecture under the remit of a single team. Once complete, this step should have partitioned the entire scope of the enterprise and should have assigned responsibility for each partitioned architecture to a single team. Partitioning should create a definition of each architecture that includes:

  — Subject matter areas being covered

— Level of detail that the team will work at

— Time periods to be covered

— Stakeholders

- **Determine the relationships between architectures**: Once a set of partitioned architectures has been created, the relationships between architectures should be developed. This step allows governance relationships to be formalized and also shows where artifacts from one architecture are expected to be re-used within other architectures. Areas of consideration include:

  — Where do different architectures overlap/dovetail/drill-down?

  — What are the compliance requirements between architectures?

  — Start each team running their own instance of the ADM

Once the Preliminary phase is complete, the teams conducting the architecture should be understood. Each team should have a defined scope and the relationships between teams and architecture should be understood. Allocation of teams to architecture scope is illustrated in Figure 40-5.

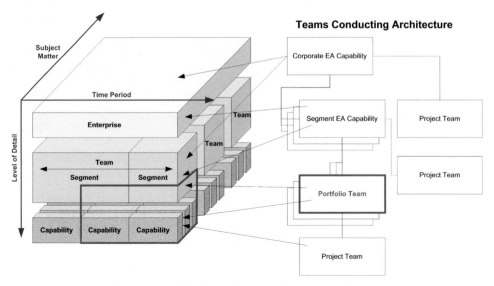

Figure 40-5 Allocation of Teams to Architecture Scope

40.4.5 Activities within Phases A to F

Within ADM Phases A to F an architecture team will create an architecture that addresses a specific scope of work. The focus within these phases is on content creation, and occurs at three levels:

- **Architecture Vision**: The Architecture Vision is developed within Phase A of the ADM. The Architecture Vision provides a high-level, informal view of the Target Architecture. Depending on the scope and requirements of the architecture, the Architecture Vision may provide a target for implementation, or may represent a view of the future that is well beyond current implementation plans, but serves as a directional guideline to assist in architectural planning and decision-making. For example, a ten-year vision for customer services capability would allow architects to see likely future developments and the long-term goal, but would not be directly implemented within a single project.

- **Architecture Definition**: The Architecture Definition is developed within Phases B, C, and D of the ADM. The Architecture Definition provides a formal model of the Baseline Architecture, Target Architecture, and gaps between the two states. The Architecture Definition may address the entirety of the Architecture Vision, or may select a tactical subset for consideration. As with the Architecture Vision, not all of the Architecture Definition needs to be immediately implemented. The Architecture Definition may, for example, outline a multi-phase roadmap to reach a long-term Target Architecture.

- **Transition Architecture**: Transition Architectures are developed within Phases E and F of the ADM. A Transition Architecture considers a range of activities that will be directly realized within a single change initiative. The Transition Architecture takes a Baseline and Target Architecture definition as the start and end points and considers the practical steps required to transition from one state to the next.

Considering architectures at the three levels of abstraction described above has a number of advantages, not least of which is the ability to carry out continuous architecture development, or "just in time" architecture.

Under this model, a long-term vision is established. A set of milestones are defined to achieve the vision, with architectures defined for the first key steps. The initial wave of implementation is then specified in detail through a Transition Architecture. As implementation of the initial Transition Architecture progresses, it can be governed against the Architecture Vision and Architecture Definition. Subsequent transitions can be defined in parallel with the implementation of the initial transition. As implementation progresses, the Architecture Vision and Architecture Definition can be refined using new information.

Using the "just in time" technique, architecture is only developed when it is needed, but implementation activity is still guided by a strategic vision and change roadmap.

Steps within the Architecture Vision phase to support architecture partitioning are as follows:

- Use the relationships between architectures defined in the Preliminary phase as a starting point; collect inputs from feeding architectures.

- Using the architecture boundaries defined in the Preliminary phase as a starting point, establish the scope of this ADM cycle:
  - Level of detail, subject matter, and time period for the Architecture Vision

— Initial expectations for detail, subject matter, and time period to be covered in the Architecture Definition, including segmentation to be used (e.g., Are there different domain architectures? Are there different architecture states or milestones to be considered?); generally, the Architecture Definition should address a subset of the coverage of the Architecture Vision

— Initial expectations for subject matter and time period to be covered for the first wave of implementation

- Establish the relationships between the architecture and the operational impact of the architecture. Use this to determine appropriate stakeholders.

- Define an Architecture Vision, including appropriate reference models from other architectures.

- Identify follow-on architectures that will be needed and define the hand-off points.

- For each follow-on architecture, determine whether this team will create the architecture in a subsequent ADM cycle, or whether a different team will take on the development work.

- Extract appropriate re-usable content for integration or use as reference models elsewhere.

Steps within the Business Architecture, Information Systems Architecture, and Technology Architecture phases to support architecture partitioning are as follows:

- Use the scope of the Architecture Vision as a starting point and select which areas of the vision will be elaborated in more detail.

- Develop (more) formal models of the solution, including appropriate reference models from other architectures. This could be for the entire scope of the vision, or for a subset of the vision.

- For each state/milestone to be addressed, define the Baseline Architecture, Target Architecture, and gaps.

- Extract appropriate re-usable content for integration or use as reference models elsewhere.

Steps within the Opportunities & Solutions and Migration Planning phases to support architecture partitioning are as follows:

- Define appropriate Transition Architectures, including appropriate reference models from other architectures.

- Re-visit the states and milestones of change identified in the Architecture Vision and Architecture Definition, based on an understanding of feasibility, viability, priority, and dependency. Circle back if needed to create a new Architecture Vision or set of Architecture Definitions.

- Define scope and terms of reference for out-of-context, detailed work. This work may involve doing architecture, or may be restricted to directly delivering a change solution that complies with the architectures that were developed.

- Extract appropriate re-usable content for integration or use as reference models elsewhere.

- Start up out-of-context, detailed work.

Development of an Architecture Vision, Architecture Definitions, and Transition Architectures is illustrated in Figure 40-6.

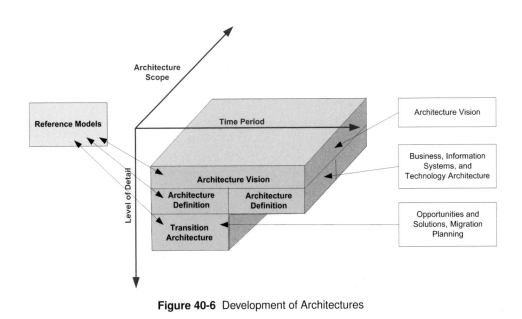

Figure 40-6 Development of Architectures

40.4.6 Activities within Phases G and H

Within Phases G and H the architecture team will oversee the realization of the architecture. Oversight of the architecture realization is through Implementation Governance (assessing compliance of realization efforts against the architecture) and Architecture Change Management (reacting to situations where the realization efforts do not and cannot comply with the architecture). Ultimately the architecture will be transitioned into operations and will become part of the new baseline of the enterprise.

Where architecture realization occurs through the definition of further, more detailed (i.e., out-of-context) architectures developed by other teams, these architectures should reside within separate partitions and the governance relationships between the architectures should be captured within the partitioning model.

40.4.7 Content Aggregation and Integration

Creation of a number of partitioned architectures within an enterprise runs the risk of producing a fragmented and disjointed collection of architectures that cannot be integrated to form an overall big picture.

In order to mitigate against this risk, standards for content integration should be defined and architecture governance should address content integration as a condition of architectural compliance. Content frameworks, such as the TOGAF content framework (refer to Part IV: Architecture Content Framework) can be used to specify standard building blocks and artifacts that are the subject of content integration standards.

For example, a standard catalog of business processes can be agreed for an enterprise. Subsequent architectures can then ease integration by using the same process list and cross-referencing other aspects of the architecture to those standard processes.

Content aggregation and integration can be addressed from a number of dimensions:

- Integration across the architectural domains provides a cross-domain view of the state of a segment of the enterprise for a point in time.

- Integration across the organizational scope of the business provides a cross-segment view of the enterprise.

- The Architecture Vision provides an integrated summary of Architecture Definitions, which provide an integrated summary of Transition Architectures.

Figure 40-7 shows how architectural content can be aggregated using a variety of techniques.

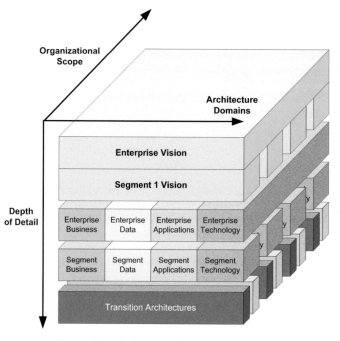

Figure 40-7 Architecture Content Aggregation

Chapter 41: Architecture Repository

41.1 Overview

Operating a mature architecture capability within a large enterprise creates a huge volume of architectural output. Effective management and leverage of these architectural work products require a formal taxonomy for different types of architectural asset alongside dedicated processes and tools for architectural content storage.

This section of TOGAF provides a structural framework for an Architecture Repository that allows an enterprise to distinguish between different types of architectural assets that exist at different levels of abstraction in the organization. This Architecture Repository is one part of the wider Enterprise IT Repository, which provides the capability to link architectural assets to components of the Detailed Design, Deployment, and Service Management Repositories.

At a high level, six classes of architectural information are expected to be held within an Architecture Repository:

- The **Architecture Metamodel** describes the organizationally tailored application of an architecture framework, including a method for architecture development and a metamodel for architecture content.

- The **Architecture Capability** defines the parameters, structures, and processes that support governance of the Architecture Repository.

- The **Architecture Landscape** shows an architectural view of the building blocks that are in use within the organization today (e.g., a list of the live applications). The landscape is likely to exist at multiple levels of granularity to suit different architecture objectives.

- The **Standards Information Base** captures the standards with which new architectures must comply, which may include industry standards, selected products and services from suppliers, or shared services already deployed within the organization.

- The **Reference Library** provides guidelines, templates, patterns, and other forms of reference material that can be leveraged in order to accelerate the creation of new architectures for the enterprise.

- The **Governance Log** provides a record of governance activity across the enterprise.

The relationships between these areas of the Architecture Repository are shown in Figure 41-1.

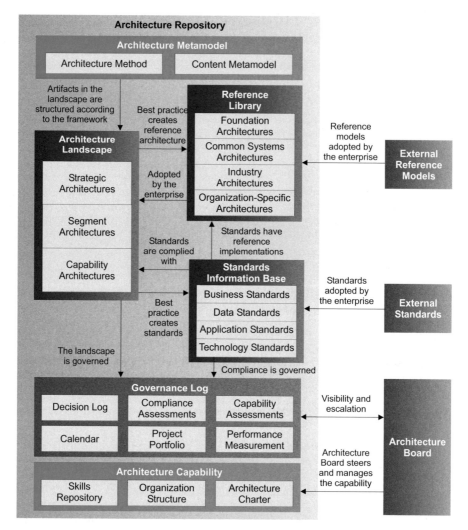

Figure 41-1 Overview of Architecture Repository

This section of TOGAF describes the structure and content of the repository areas that hold the output of projects, namely the Architecture Landscape, the Reference Library, the Standards Information Base, and the Governance Log.

This section also discusses requirements to be considered when selecting tools to manage an Architecture Repository.

41.2   Architecture Landscape

The Architecture Landscape holds architectural views of the state of the enterprise at particular points in time. Due to the sheer volume and the diverse stakeholder needs throughout an entire enterprise, the Architecture Landscape is divided into three levels of granularity:

1. **Strategic Architectures** (see Part I, Section 3.82) show a long-term summary view of the entire enterprise. Strategic Architectures provide an organizing framework for operational and change activity and allow for direction setting at an executive level.

2. **Segment Architectures** (see Part I, Section 3.72) provide more detailed operating models for areas within an enterprise. Segment Architectures can be used at the program or portfolio level to organize and operationally align more detailed change activity.

3. **Capability Architectures** (see Part I, Section 3.31) show in a more detailed fashion how the enterprise can support a particular unit of capability. Capability Architectures are used to provide an overview of current capability, target capability, and capability increments and allow for individual work packages and projects to be grouped within managed portfolios and programs.

41.3   Reference Library

41.3.1   Overview

The Reference Library provides a repository area to hold best practice or template materials that can be used to construct architectures within an enterprise. Reference materials held in the Reference Library may be obtained from a variety of sources, including:

- Standards bodies
- Product and service vendors
- Industry communities or forums
- Corporately defined templates
- Best practice resulting from project implementation

Generally speaking, the source of a reference architecture is likely to have significant bearing on the way that architecture is used to support the execution of projects.

Reference models that originate from within the enterprise and have been tried and tested are likely to have a much better fit to the needs of the organization, because they will already be adapted to meet constraints of the enterprise. Reference models that originate from outside the enterprise are likely to have been tested by many enterprises and will therefore allow the adopting organization to adopt best practice and converge with peer organizations.

In order to segregate different classes of architecture reference model, the Reference Library can use the Architecture Continuum as a method for classification, as shown in Figure 41-2.

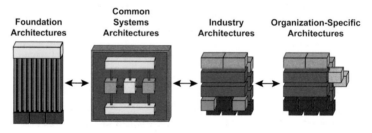

Figure 41-2 Architecture Continuum

The Reference Library classification scheme illustrates how reference architectures are organized across a range — from Foundation Architectures such as TOGAF's, through Common Systems Architectures, and Industry-Specific Architectures, to an enterprise's own individual architectures.

The enterprise needs and business requirements are addressed in increasing detail from left to right. The architect will typically look to find re-usable architectural elements toward the left of the range. When elements are not found, the requirements for the missing elements are passed to the left of the range for incorporation.

41.4 Standards Information Base

41.4.1 Overview

The Standards Information Base provides a repository area to hold a set of specifications, to which architectures must conform. Establishment of a Standards Information Base provides an unambiguous basis for architectural governance because:

- The standards are easily accessible to projects and therefore the obligations of the project can be understood and planned for

- Standards are stated in a clear and unambiguous manner, so that compliance can be objectively assessed

41.4.2 Types of Standard

Standards typically fall into three classes:

- **Legal and Regulatory Obligations**: These standards are mandated by law and therefore an enterprise must comply or face serious consequences.

- **Industry Standards**: These standards are established by industry bodies, such as The Open Group, and are then selected by the enterprise for adoption. Industry Standards offer potential for interoperation and sharing across enterprises, but also fall outside of the control of the enterprise and therefore must be actively monitored.

- **Organizational Standards**: These standards are set within the organization and are based on business aspiration (e.g., selection of standard applications to support portfolio consolidation). Organizational Standards require processes to allow for exemptions and standards evolution.

41.4.3 Standards Lifecycle

Standards do not generally exist for all time. New standards are identified and managed through a lifecycle process. Typically standards pass through the following stages:

- **Trial Standard**: A Trial Standard has been identified as a potential standard for the organization, but has not been tried and tested to a level where its value is fully understood. Projects wishing to adopt Trial Standards may do so, but under specific pilot conditions, so that the viability of the standard can be examined in more detail.

- **Active Standard**: An Active Standard defines a mainstream solution that should generally be used as the approach of choice.

- **Deprecated Standard**: A Deprecated Standard is approaching the end of its useful lifecycle. Projects that are re-using existing components can generally continue to make use of Deprecated Standards. Deployment of new instances of the Deprecated Standard are generally discouraged.

- **Obsolete Standard**: An Obsolete Standard is no longer accepted as valid within the landscape. In most cases, remedial action should be taken to remove the Obsolete Standard from the landscape. Change activity on an Obsolete Standard should only be accepted as a part of an overall decommissioning plan.

All standards should be periodically reviewed to ensure that they sit within the right stage of the standards lifecycle. As a part of standards lifecycle management, the impact of changing the lifecycle status should be addressed to understand the landscape impact of a standards change and plan for appropriate action to address it.

41.4.4 Standards Classification within the Standards Information Base

Standards within the Standards Information Base are categorized according to the building blocks within the TOGAF content metamodel. Each metamodel entity can potentially have standards associated with it (e.g., Business Service, Technology Component).

Standards may relate to "approved" building blocks (e.g., a list of standard Technology Components) or may specify appropriate use of a building block (e.g., scenarios where messaging infrastructure is appropriate, application communication standards are defined).

At the top level, standards are classified in line with the TOGAF architecture domains, including the following areas:

- **Business Standards**:

  — Standard shared business functions

  — Standard role and actor definitions

  — Security and governance standards for business activity

- **Data Standards**:
  - — Standard coding and values for data
  - — Standard structures and formats for data
  - — Standards for origin and ownership of data
  - — Restrictions on replication and access
- **Applications Standards**:
  - — Standard/shared applications supporting specific business functions
  - — Standards for application communication and interoperation
  - — Standards for access, presentation, and style
- **Technology Standards**;
  - — Standard hardware products
  - — Standard software products
  - — Standards for software development

41.5   Governance Log

41.5.1 Overview

The Governance Log provides a repository area to hold shared information relating to the ongoing governance of projects. Maintaining a shared repository of governance information is important, because:

- Decisions made during projects (such as standards deviations or the rationale for a particular architectural approach) are important to retain and access on an ongoing basis. For example, if a system is to be replaced, having sight of the key architectural decisions that shaped the initial implementation is highly valuable, as it will highlight constraints that may otherwise be obscured.

- Many stakeholders are interested in the outcome of project governance (e.g., other projects, customers of the project, the Architecture Board, etc.).

41.5.2 Contents of the Governance Log

The Governance Log should contain the following items:

- **Decision Log**: A log of all architecturally significant decisions that have been made in the organization. This would typically include:
  - — Product selections
  - — Justification for major architectural features of projects
  - — Standards deviations

— Standards lifecycle changes

— Change request evaluations and approvals

— Re-use assessments

- **Compliance Assessments**: At key checkpoint milestones in the progress of a project, a formal architecture review will be carried out. This review will measure the compliance of the project to the defined architecture standards. For each project, this log should include:

  — Project overview

  — Progress overview (timeline, status, issues, risks, dependencies, etc.)

  — Completed architecture checklists

  — Standards compliance assessment

  — Recommended actions

- **Capability Assessments**: Depending on their objectives, some projects will carry out assessments of business, IT, or architecture capability. These assessments should be periodically carried out and tracked to ensure that appropriate progress is being made. This log should include:

  — Templates and reference models for executing Capability Assessments

  — Business Capability Assessments

  — IT capability, maturity, and impact assessments

  — Architecture maturity assessments

- **Calendar**: The Calendar should show a schedule of in-flight projects and formal review sessions to be held against these projects.

- **Project Portfolio**: The Project Portfolio should hold summary information about all in-flight projects that fall under architectural governance, including:

  — The name and description of the project

  — Architectural scope of the project

  — Architectural roles and responsibilities associated with the project

- **Performance Measurement**: Based on a charter for the architecture function, a number of performance criteria will typically be defined. The Performance Measurement log should capture metrics relating to project governance and any other performance metrics relating to the architecture charter so that performance can be measured and evaluated on an ongoing basis.

Chapter 42: Tools for Architecture Development

This section discusses tools and techniques helpful in using TOGAF.

42.1 Overview

As an enterprise architecture framework, TOGAF provides a basis for developing architectures in a uniform and consistent manner. Its purpose in this respect is to ensure that the various architecture descriptions developed within an enterprise, perhaps by different architects or architecture teams, support the comparison and integration of architectures within and across architecture domains (business, data, application, technology), and relating to different business area scopes within the enterprise.

To support this goal, TOGAF defines numerous deliverables in the form of architectures, represented as architecture models, architecture views of those models, and other artifacts. Over time, these artifacts become a resource that needs to be managed and controlled, particularly with a view to re-use. This concept is referred to in TOGAF as the "Enterprise Continuum".

Architecture models and views are discussed in detail separately in Part IV, Chapter 35. This section discusses considerations in choosing automated tools in order to generate such architecture models and views, and to maintain them over time.

42.2 Issues in Tool Standardization

In the current state of the tools market, many enterprises developing enterprise architectures struggle with the issue of standardizing on tools, whether they seek a single "one size fits all" tool or a multi-tool suite for modeling architectures and generating the different architecture views required.

There are ostensible advantages associated with selecting a single tool. Organizations following such a policy can hope to realize benefits such as reduced training, shared licenses, quantity discounts, maintenance, and easier data interchange.

However, there are also reasons for refusing to identify a single mandated tool, including reasons of principle (endorsing a single architecture tool would not encourage competitive commercial innovation or the development of advanced tool capability); and the fact that a single tool would not accommodate a variety of architecture development "maturity levels" and specific needs across an enterprise. Successful enterprise architecture teams are often those that harmonize their architecture tools with their architecture maturity level, team/organizational capabilities, and objectives or focus. If different organizations within an enterprise are at different architecture maturity levels and have different objectives or focus (e.g., Enterprise *versus*

Business *versus* Technology Architecture), it becomes very difficult for one tool to satisfy all organizations' needs.

42.3   Evaluation Criteria and Guidelines

TOGAF does not require or recommend any specific tool. However, in recognition of the problems that enterprise architects currently face in this area, this section provides a set of proposed evaluation criteria for selecting architecture tools to develop the various architecture models and views that are required.

Individual enterprises may wish to adapt these generic evaluation criteria to their particular circumstances and requirements. In particular, such an exercise would typically produce weightings of the various criteria that can be used to produce a "score" for the specific tools evaluated.

42.3.1   Tool Criteria

42.3.1.1   Functionality

Key Features and Functions

- Does it support the framework that your organization has chosen to use?
    - Does it support production of the deliverables required?
    - If not, does it support some of the known frameworks; e.g., TOGAF or Zachman Framework out-of-the-box?
- Glossary:
    - Glossary extendible to become a taxonomy?
    - Active Glossary to enforce a taxonomy?
- Ability to represent architecture models and views in a way meaningful to non-Technology Architecture stakeholders
- Does it support metamodels; e.g., ability to configure and tailor models?
- Does it support enterprise use; e.g., multi-user collaboration support?
- Does it allow drill down; e.g., conceptual, logical, physical, etc.?
- Does it provide a mechanism for linking requirements to the resulting enterprise architecture; i.e., requirements traceability?
- Security features:
    - Does it facilitate access control; e.g., different permissions for different roles?
    - Does its security design support corporate security policies?
- Does it natively support report generation?
- Does it support a common language and notation?

Intuitiveness/Ease-of-Use Factors

- An easy to follow "process map" guiding use of the tool
- Online help
- Relevant out-of-the-box architecture constructs, be it business, data, application, or technology
- Relevant out-of-the-box templates or patterns for constructs, which can be used to help organizations "jump start"
- Support for visualization modeling; e.g., drag-and-drop and lines that equate to links
- Can it be extended or customized and does it provide utilities to do that?
- Does it track and audit changes?
- Does it provide a way for consistently naming and organizing those artifacts?
- Can those artifacts/components be easily viewed, used, and re-used?
- What requirements are there for use of programmatic languages?

Organizational Compatibility Factors

- Internationalization/localization capability:
    - Can the tool be used in all the geographic locations and/or language domains in which architecture work is done?

Tool Capacity/Scalability Constraints

- Does the tool have capacity constraints?
    - Size of data
    - Number of files
    - Number of data entries/records?
- What are the tool's design "sweet spots" (i.e., optimal design configuration parameters), and how scalable is it around those optima?
    - Is there an upgrade path beyond the capacity constraints of the tool?

42.3.1.2 Architecture of the Tool

- Repository distributed or central?
- Dynamic repository?
- Does the tool function with multiple industry standard data stores (e.g., Oracle, Sybase) or is storage proprietary?
- Backwards-compatibility with prior releases of the tool?
- Does it allow integration and consolidation of data into a central repository?
- Does it include version control?

- Is it accessible through a web client?
- What platforms (hardware, OS, DBMS, network) does it run on?

42.3.1.3 Full Lifecycle Support

- Does it provide full lifecycle support?
- Does it support various relevant views out-of-the-box; e.g., Business Process, Data, Application, Technology?
- Does it support the creation of custom views?
- Does it use modeling methods and techniques relevant to this enterprise's architecture practice?
- Does is support simulation?
- Is the model that it produces executable?

42.3.1.4 Interoperability Factors

- Import/Export:
  - Can it create an artifact inside the tool and export it to other commonly used tools, and have the users of those tools use the artifact intact?
  - Can it import an artifact created in another tool, and use the artifact intact?
- Does it integrate with other tools?
- Does it provide and support industry standard APIs?
- Does it use relevant industry standards; e.g., XML, HTML, produce hypertext, UML, other industry standard?

42.3.1.5 Financial Considerations

- What is the acquisition cost?
- What is the total cost of ownership?
  - Maintenance
  - Equipment costs
  - Support costs
  - Number of resources required to keep it up-to-date
  - Administration responsibilities/time constraints
  - Will there be any impacts of introducing the tool into your environment; e.g., does it require some unique infrastructure?
  - Training
  - Licensing models

42.3.1.6 Vendor Factors

- Will vendor remain viable?
- How long has vendor existed in this arena?
- Do they have large customers?
- Do they have professional services?
- Third-party support?
- Does the tool have history at the organization and, if so, what is its reputation?
- Has the vendor certified the tool within The Open Group's TOGAF certification program?
- Training factors:
  - Availability
  - Costs
  - Amount required to become productive
  - Style of learning (CBT, classroom)

42.3.2 General Pointers

- Value of the tool is dependent upon the architecture maturity of the organization.
- Need to match the tool to the capability of your organization; i.e., where it is architecturally?
- Trade-off between tactical considerations (competency, familiarity, etc.) and strategical considerations (overall organization's standards and directions).
- Teaming can positively or negatively affect a tool's success.

The Open Group Architecture Framework (TOGAF)

Part VI:

TOGAF Reference Models

The Open Group

Chapter 43: Foundation Architecture: Technical Reference Model

This chapter describes the Technical Reference Model (TRM), including core taxonomy, graphical representation, and the detailed platform taxonomy.

The detailed platform taxonomy is described in Section 43.5.

43.1   Concepts

This section describes the role of the TRM, the components of the TRM, and using other TRMs.

43.1.1   Role of the TRM in the Foundation Architecture

The TOGAF Foundation Architecture is an architecture of generic services and functions that provides a foundation on which more specific architectures and architectural components can be built. This Foundation Architecture is embodied within the Technical Reference Model (TRM), which provides a model and taxonomy of generic platform services.

The TRM is universally applicable and, therefore, can be used to build any system architecture.

43.1.2   TRM Components

Any TRM has two main components:

1. A **taxonomy**, which defines terminology, and provides a coherent description of the components and conceptual structure of an information system

2. An associated **TRM graphic**, which provides a visual representation of the taxonomy, as an aid to understanding

The objective of the TOGAF TRM is to provide a widely accepted core taxonomy, and an appropriate visual representation of that taxonomy. The TRM graphic is illustrated in Section 43.3, and the taxonomy is explained in Section 43.4.

43.1.3 Other TRMs

One of the great difficulties in developing an architecture framework is in choosing a TRM that works for everyone.

The TOGAF TRM was originally derived from the Technical Architecture Framework for Information Management (TAFIM) TRM (which in turn was derived from the IEEE 1003.0 model). This TRM is "platform-centric": it focuses on the services and structure of the underlying platform necessary to support the use and re-use of applications (i.e., on application portability). In particular, it centers on the interfaces between that platform and the supported applications, and between the platform and the external environment.

The current TOGAF TRM is an amended version of the TAFIM TRM, which aims to emphasize the aspect of interoperability as well as that of portability.

The objective of the TRM is to enable structured definition of the standardized application platform and its associated interfaces. The other entities, which are needed in any specific architecture, are only addressed in the TRM insofar as they influence the application platform. The underlying aim in this approach is to ensure that the higher-level building blocks which make up business solutions have a complete, robust platform on which to run.

Other architectural models — taxonomies and/or graphics — not only are possible, but may be preferable for some enterprises. For example, such an enterprise-specific model could be derived by extension or adaptation of the TOGAF TRM. Alternatively, a different taxonomy may be embodied in the legacy of previous architectural work by an enterprise, and the enterprise may prefer to perpetuate use of that taxonomy. Similarly, an enterprise may prefer to represent the TOGAF taxonomy (or its own taxonomy) using a different form of graphic, which better captures legacy concepts and proves easier for internal communication purposes.

In addition to its use as a reference model for the development of technology architecture, the TRM can be used as a taxonomy to develop a Standards Information Base (SIB) within a specific organization. The core of TOGAF is its ADM: the TRM is a tool used in applying the ADM in the development of specific architectures. Provided consistency between TRM and SIB are maintained, the TOGAF ADM is valid whatever the choice of specific taxonomy, TRM graphic, or SIB toolset.

43.2 High-Level Breakdown

This section describes the major elements of the TRM.

43.2.1 Overview

The coarsest breakdown of the TRM is shown in Figure 43-1, which shows three major entities (Application Software, Application Platform, and Communications Infrastructure) connected by two interfaces (Application Platform Interface and Communications Infrastructure Interface).

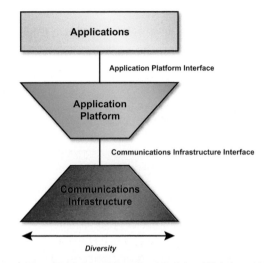

Figure 43-1 Technical Reference Model — High-Level View

The diagram says nothing about the detailed relationships between the entities; only that they exist.

Each of the elements in this diagram is discussed in detail in Section 43.3.

43.2.2　Portability and Interoperability

The high-level TRM seeks to emphasize two major common architectural objectives:

1. **Application Portability**, via the Application Platform Interface — identifying the set of services that are to be made available in a standard way to applications via the platform

2. **Interoperability**, via the Communications Infrastructure Interface — identifying the set of Communications Infrastructure services that are to be leveraged in a standard way by the platform

Both of these goals are essential to enable integration within the enterprise and trusted interoperability on a global scale between enterprises.

In particular, the high-level model seeks to reflect the increasingly important role of the Internet as the basis for inter- and intra-enterprise interoperability.

The horizontal dimension of the model in Figure 43-1 represents diversity, and the shape of the model is intended to emphasize the importance of minimum diversity at the interface between the Application Platform and the Communications Infrastructure.

This in turn means focusing on the core set of services that can be guaranteed to be supported by every IP-based network, as the foundation on which to build today's interoperable enterprise computing environments.

43.3   TRM in Detail

This section describes the TRM in detail, including platform service categories and external environment sub-entities.

43.3.1   Introduction

Figure 43-2 expands on Figure 43-1 to present the service categories of the Application Platform and the two categories of Application Software.

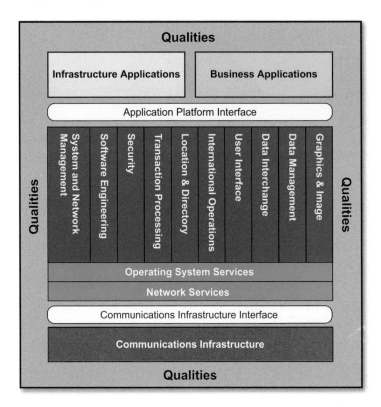

Figure 43-2 Detailed Technical Reference Model (Showing Service Categories)

Figure 43-2 is only a depiction of the TRM entities: it neither implies nor inhibits inter-relationships among them.

IT architectures derived from TOGAF may differ greatly depending on the requirements of the information system. In practice, many architectures will not include all of the services discussed here, and many will include additional services to support Application Software that is specific to the organization or to its vertical industry.

In building an architecture, users of TOGAF should assess their own requirements and select the services, interfaces, and standards that satisfy their own business needs.

43.3.2 TRM Entities and Interfaces

The following sections discuss in detail each element of the TRM illustrated in Figure 43-2. They are dealt with in the following order:

- The three entities:
    - Application Software (see Section 43.3.3)
    - Application Platform (see Section 43.3.4)
    - Communications Infrastructure (see Section 43.3.5)
- The two interfaces:
    - Application Platform Interface (see Section 43.3.6)
    - Communications Infrastructure Interface (see Section 43.3.7)

43.3.3 Application Software

The detailed TRM recognizes two categories of Application Software:

1. **Business Applications**, which implement business processes for a particular enterprise or vertical industry. The internal structure of business applications relates closely to the specific application software configuration selected by an organization.
2. **Infrastructure Applications**, which provide general-purpose business functionality, based on infrastructure services.

During development of the Technology Architecture, business applications and infrastructure applications are important sources of requirements for Technology Architecture services, and the selection of standards for the Application Platform will be influenced strongly by the Application Software configuration to be supported.

43.3.3.1 Business Applications

Business applications are applications that are specific to a particular enterprise or vertical industry. Such applications typically model elements of an enterprise's domain of activity or business processes. Examples of business applications might include:

- Patient record management services used in the Medical industry
- Inventory management services used in the Retail industry
- Geological data modeling services used in the Petroleum industry

Over time, particular business applications may become infrastructure applications, if they become sufficiently ubiquitous, interoperable, and general-purpose to be potentially useful to a broad range of enterprise IT users.

43.3.3.2 Infrastructure Applications

Infrastructure applications are applications that have all, or nearly all, of the following characteristics:

- Widespread availability as Commercial Off-The-Shelf (COTS) software means that it is uneconomic to consider custom implementation.
- User interaction is an important part of the application's function.
- Implementations are based on infrastructure services.
- Implementations may include significant extensions beyond that needed to use the underlying infrastructure services.
- Interoperability is a strong requirement.

Examples of applications in this category include:

- Electronic payment and funds transfer services
- Electronic mail client services
- Publish and subscribe
- Intelligent agents
- Calendaring and scheduling services
- Groupware services
- Workflow services
- Spreadsheets
- Presentation software
- Document editing and presentation
- Management applications, performing general-purpose system and network management functions for the system administrator
- Software engineering tools, providing software development functions for systems development staff

Infrastructure applications have strong dependencies on lower-level services in the architecture. For example, a workflow application may use platform services such as messaging or transaction processing to implement the flow of work among tasks. Similarly, a groupware application is likely to make extensive use of both data and communication services for the structure of documents, as well as the mechanics of storing and accessing them.

Infrastructure applications by definition are applications that are considered sufficiently ubiquitous, interoperable, and general-purpose within the enterprise to be effectively considered as part of the IT infrastructure. Just as business applications may over time come to be regarded as infrastructure applications, so infrastructure applications are normally candidates for inclusion as infrastructure services in future versions of an IT architecture.

43.3.4 Application Platform

43.3.4.1 Platform Concept

The term "platform" is used in many different ways within the IT industry today. Because of the different usages, the term is often qualified; for example, "application platform", "standardized" and "proprietary platforms", "client" and "server platforms", "distributed computing platform", "portability platform". Common to all these usages is the idea that someone needs a set of services provided by a particular kind of platform, and will implement a "higher-level" function that makes use of those services.

The TOGAF TRM focuses on the Application Platform, and the "higher-level function" is the set of Application Software, running on top of the Application Platform, that is needed to address the enterprise's business requirements.

It is important to recognize that the Application Platform in the TOGAF TRM is a single, generic, conceptual entity. From the viewpoint of the TOGAF TRM, the Application Platform contains all possible services. In a specific Target Architecture, the Application Platform will contain only those services needed to support the required functions.

Moreover, the Application Platform for a specific Target Architecture will typically not be a single entity, but rather a combination of different entities for different, commonly required functions, such as desktop client, file server, print server, application server, Internet server, database server, etc., each of which will comprise a specific, defined set of services necessary to support the specific function concerned.

It is also important to recognize that many of the real-world IT systems that are procured and used today to implement a Technology Architecture come fully equipped with many advanced services, which are often taken for granted by the purchaser. For example, a typical desktop computer system today comes with software that implements services from most if not all of the service categories of the TOGAF TRM. Since the purchaser of such a system often does not consider anything "smaller" than the total bundle of services that comes with the system, that service bundle can very easily become the "platform". Indeed, in the absence of a Technology Architecture to guide the procurement process, this is invariably what happens. As this process is repeated across an enterprise, different systems purchased for similar functions (such as desktop client, print server, etc.) can contain markedly different bundles of services.

Service bundles are represented in a Technology Architecture in the form of "building blocks". One of the key tasks of the IT architect in going from the conceptual Application Platform of the TRM to an enterprise-specific Technology Architecture is to look beyond the set of real-world platforms already in existence in the enterprise. The IT architect must analyze the services actually needed in order to implement an IT infrastructure that meets the enterprise's business requirements in the optimal manner, and to define the set of optimal Solution Building Blocks (SBBs) — real-world "platforms" — to implement that architecture.

43.3.4.2 Extending the TRM

The TOGAF TRM identifies a generic set of platform services, and provides a taxonomy in which these platform services are divided into categories of like functionality. A particular organization may need to augment this set with additional services or service categories which are considered to be generic in its own vertical market segment.

The set of services identified and defined for the Application Platform will change over time. New services will be required as new technology appears and as application needs change.

43.3.4.3 Interfaces Between Services

In addition to supporting Application Software through the Application Platform Interface (API), services in the Application Platform may support each other, either by openly specified interfaces which may or may not be the same as the API, or by private, unexposed interfaces. A key goal of architecture development is for service modules to be capable of replacement by other modules providing the same service functionality via the same service API. Use of private, unexposed interfaces among service modules may compromise this ability to substitute. Private interfaces represent a risk that should be highlighted to facilitate future transition.

43.3.4.4 Future Developments

The TRM deals with future developments in the Application Platform in two ways. Firstly, as interfaces to services become standardized, functionality which previously formed part of the Application Software entity migrates to become part of the Application Platform. Secondly, the TRM may be extended with new service categories as new technology appears.

Examples of functional areas which may fall into Application Platform service categories in the future include:

- Spreadsheet functions, including the capability to create, manipulate, and present information in tables or charts; this capability should include fourth generation language-like capabilities that enable the use of programming logic within spreadsheets

- Decision support functions, including tools that support the planning, administration, and management of projects

- Calculation functions, including the capability to perform routine and complex arithmetic calculations

- Calendar functions, including the capability to manage projects and co-ordinate schedules via an automated calendar

A detailed taxonomy of the Application Platform is given in Section 43.4.

43.3.5 Communications Infrastructure

The Communications Infrastructure provides the basic services to interconnect systems and provide the basic mechanisms for opaque transfer of data. It contains the hardware and software elements which make up the networking and physical communications links used by a system, and of course all the other systems connected to the network. It deals with the complex world of networks and the physical Communications Infrastructure, including switches, service providers, and the physical transmission media.

A primary driver in enterprise-wide Technology Architecture in recent years has been the growing awareness of the utility and cost-effectiveness of the Internet as the basis of a Communications Infrastructure for enterprise integration. This is causing a rapid increase in Internet usage and a steady increase in the range of applications linking to the network for distributed operation.

This is considered further in Section 43.3.7.

43.3.6 Application Platform Interface

The Application Platform Interface (API) specifies a complete interface between the Application Software and the underlying Application Platform across which all services are provided. A rigorous definition of the interface results in application portability, provided that both platform and application conform to it. For this to work, the API definition must include the syntax and semantics of not just the programmatic interface, but also all necessary protocol and data structure definitions.

Portability depends on the symmetry of conformance of both applications and the platform to the architected API. That is, the platform must support the API as specified, and the application must use no more than the specified API.

The API specifies a complete interface between an application and one or more services offered by the underlying Application Platform. An application may use several APIs, and may even use different APIs for different implementations of the same service.

43.3.7 Communications Infrastructure Interface

The Communications Infrastructure Interface is the interface between the Application Platform and the Communications Infrastructure.

Figure 43-1 seeks to reflect the increasingly important role of the Internet as the basis for inter- and intra-enterprise interoperability. The horizontal dimension of the model in Figure 43-1 represents diversity, and the shape of the model is specifically intended to emphasize minimum diversity at the interface between the Application Platform and the Communications Infrastructure.

In particular, the model emphasizes the importance of focusing on the core set of services that can be guaranteed to be supported by every IP-based network, as the foundation on which to build today's interoperable enterprise computing environments.

43.3.8 Qualities

Besides the set of components making up the TRM, there is a set of attributes or qualities that are applicable across the components. For example, for the management service to be effective, manageability must be a pervasive quality of all platform services, applications, and Communications Infrastructure services.

Figure 43-2 captures this concept by depicting the TRM components sitting on a backplane of qualities.

Another example of a service quality is security. The proper system-wide implementation of security requires not only a set of Security services, corresponding to the security services category shown in the platform, but also the support (i.e., the "security awareness") of software in other parts of the TRM. Thus, an application might use a security service to mark a file as read-only, but it is the correct implementation of the security quality in the operating system services which prevents write operations on the file. Security and operating system services must co-operate in making the file secure.

Qualities are specified in detail during the development of a Target Architecture. Some qualities are easier than others to describe in terms of standards. For instance, support of a set of locales can be defined to be part of the specification for the international operation quality. Other qualities can better be specified in terms of measures rather than standards. An example would be performance, for which standard APIs or protocols are of limited use.

43.4   Application Platform — Taxonomy

This section describes the Application Platform taxonomy, including basic principles and a summary of services and qualities. A detailed taxonomy of platform services and qualities can be found in Section 43.5.

43.4.1   Basic Principles

The TOGAF TRM has two main components:

1. A **taxonomy**, which defines terminology, and provides a coherent description of the components and conceptual structure of an information system

2. An associated **TRM graphic**, which provides a visual representation of the taxonomy, as an aid to understanding

This section describes in detail the taxonomy of the TOGAF TRM. The aim is to provide a core taxonomy that provides a useful, consistent, structured definition of the Application Platform entity and is widely acceptable.

No claims are made that the chosen categorization is the only one possible, or that it represents the optimal choice.

Indeed, it is important to emphasize that the use of TOGAF, and in particular the TOGAF ADM, is in no way dependent on use of the TOGAF TRM taxonomy. Other taxonomies are perfectly possible, and may be preferable for some organizations.

For example, a different taxonomy may be embodied in the legacy of previous architectural work by an organization, and the organization may prefer to perpetuate use of that taxonomy. Alternatively, an organization may decide that it can derive a more suitable, organization-specific taxonomy by extending or adapting the TOGAF TRM taxonomy.

In the same way, an organization may prefer to depict the TOGAF taxonomy (or its own taxonomy) using a different form of TRM graphic, which better captures legacy concepts and proves easier for internal communication purposes.

43.4.2   Application Platform Service Categories

The major categories of services defined for the Application Platform are listed below.

Note that "Object Services" does not appear as a category in the TRM taxonomy. This is because all the individual object services are incorporated into the relevant main service categories. However, the various descriptions are also collected into a single subsection (see Section 43.4.2.1) in order to provide a single point of reference which shows how object services relate to the main service categories.

- Data Interchange Services (see Section 43.5.1):

  — Document generic data typing and conversion services

  — Graphics data interchange services

  — Specialized data interchange services

  — Electronic data interchange services

  — Fax services

  — Raw graphics interface functions

  — Text processing functions

  — Document processing functions

  — Publishing functions

  — Video processing functions

  — Audio processing functions

  — Multimedia processing functions

  — Media synchronization functions

  — Information presentation and distribution functions

  — Hypertext functions

- Data Management Services (see Section 43.5.2):

  — Data dictionary/repository services

  — Database Management System (DBMS) services

  — Object-Oriented Database Management System (OODBMS) services

  — File management services

  — Query processing functions

  — Screen generation functions

  — Report generation functions

  — Networking/concurrent access functions

  — Warehousing functions

- Graphics and Imaging Services (see Section 43.5.3):

  — Graphical object management services

  — Drawing services

  — Imaging functions

- International Operation Services (see Section 43.5.4):

  — Character sets and data representation services

  — Cultural convention services

  — Local language support services

- Location and Directory Services (see Section 43.5.5):
  - Directory services
  - Special-purpose naming services
  - Service location services
  - Registration services
  - Filtering services
  - Accounting services
- Network Services (see Section 43.5.6):
  - Data communications services
  - Electronic mail services
  - Distributed data services
  - Distributed file services
  - Distributed name services
  - Distributed time services
  - Remote process (access) services
  - Remote print spooling and output distribution services
  - Enhanced telephony functions
  - Shared screen functions
  - Video conferencing functions
  - Broadcast functions
  - Mailing list functions
- Operating System Services (see Section 43.5.7):
  - Kernel operations services
  - Command interpreter and utility services
  - Batch processing services
  - File and directory synchronization services
- Software Engineering Services (see Section 43.5.8):
  - Programming language services
  - Object code linking services
  - Computer-aided software engineering (CASE) environment and tools services
  - Graphical user interface (GUI) building services
  - Scripting language services
  - Language binding services

  - Run-time environment services
  - Application binary interface services
- Transaction Processing Services (see Section 43.5.9):
  - Transaction manager services
- User Interface Services (see Section 43.5.10):
  - Graphical client/server services
  - Display objects services
  - Window management services
  - Dialog support services
  - Printing services
  - Computer-based training and online help services
  - Character-based services
- Security Services (see Section 43.5.11):
  - Identification and authentication services
  - System entry control services
  - Audit services
  - Access control services
  - Non-repudiation services
  - Security management services
  - Trusted recovery services
  - Encryption services
  - Trusted communication services
- System and Network Management Services (see Section 43.5.12):
  - User management services
  - Configuration management (CM) services
  - Performance management services
  - Availability and fault management services
  - Accounting management services
  - Security management services
  - Print management services
  - Network management services
  - Backup and restore services
  - Online disk management services

— License management services

— Capacity management services

— Software installation services

— Trouble ticketing services

43.4.2.1 Object-Oriented Provision of Services

A detailed description of each of these service categories is given in Section 43.5.13.

- Object Request Broker (ORB) Services:

  — Implementation repository services

  — Installation and activation services

  — Interface repository services

  — Replication services

- Common Object Services:

  — Change management services

  — Collections services

  — Concurrency control services

  — Data interchange services

  — Event management services

  — Externalization services

  — Licensing services

  — Lifecycle services

  — Naming services

  — Persistent object services

  — Properties services

  — Query services

  — Relationship services

  — Security services

  — Start-up services

  — Time services

  — Trading services

  — Transaction services

43.4.3 Application Platform Service Qualities

43.4.3.1 Principles

Besides the platform service categories delineated by functional category, service qualities affect Information Systems Architectures. A service quality describes a behavior such as adaptability or manageability. Service qualities have a pervasive effect on the operation of most or all of the functional service categories.

In general a requirement for a given level of a particular service quality requires one or more functional service categories to co-operate in achieving the objective. Usually this means that the software building blocks that implement the functional services contain software which contributes to the implementation of the quality.

For the quality to be provided properly, all relevant functional services must have been designed to support it. Service qualities may also require support from software in the Application Software entity and the External Environment as well as the Application Platform.

In some cases, a service quality affects each of the service categories in a similar fashion, while in other cases, the service quality has a unique influence on one particular service category. For instance, international operation depends on most of the service categories in the same way, both providing facilities and needing their co-operation for localization of messages, fonts, and other features of a locale, but it may have a more profound effect on the software engineering services, where facilities for producing internationalized software may be required.

During the process of architecture development, the architect must be aware of the existence of qualities and the extent of their influence on the choice of software building blocks used in implementing the architecture. The best way of making sure that qualities are not forgotten is to create a quality matrix, describing the relationships between each functional service and the qualities that influence it.

43.4.3.2 Taxonomy of Service Qualities

The service qualities presently identified in the TRM taxonomy are:

- **Availability** (the degree to which something is available for use), including:
  - **Manageability**, the ability to gather information about the state of something and to control it
  - **Serviceability**, the ability to identify problems and take corrective action, such as to repair or upgrade a component in a running system
  - **Performance**, the ability of a component to perform its tasks in an appropriate time
  - **Reliability**, or resistance to failure
  - **Recoverability**, or the ability to restore a system to a working state after an interruption
  - **Locatability**, the ability of a system to be found when needed
- **Assurance**, including:
  - **Security**, or the protection of information from unauthorized access

   — **Integrity**, or the assurance that data has not been corrupted

   — **Credibility**, or the level of trust in the integrity of the system and its data

- **Usability**, or ease-of-operation by users, including:

   — **International Operation**, including multi-lingual and multi-cultural abilities

- **Adaptability**, including:

   — **Interoperability**, whether within or outside the organization (for instance, interoperability of calendaring or scheduling functions may be key to the usefulness of a system)

   — **Scalability**, the ability of a component to grow or shrink its performance or capacity appropriately to the demands of the environment in which it operates

   — **Portability**, of data, people, applications, and components

   — **Extensibility**, or the ability to accept new functionality

   — The ability to offer access to services in new paradigms such as object-orientation

43.5   Detailed Platform Taxonomy

This section provides a detailed taxonomy of platform services and qualities.

43.5.1   Data Interchange Services

Data interchange services provide specialized support for the exchange of information between applications and the external environment. These services are designed to handle data interchange between applications on the same platform and applications on different (heterogeneous) platforms. An analogous set of services exists for object-oriented data interchange, which can be found under Data Interchange services and Externalization services in Section 43.5.13.

- **Document Generic Data Typing and Conversion** services are supported by specifications for encoding the data (e.g., text, picture, numeric, special character) and both the logical and visual structures of electronic documents, including compound documents.

- **Graphics Data Interchange** services are supported by device-independent descriptions of picture elements for vector-based graphics and descriptions for raster-based graphics.

- **Specialized Data Interchange** services are supported by specifications that describe data used by specific vertical markets. Markets where such specifications exist include the Medical, Library, Dental, Assurance, and Oil industries.

- **Electronic Data Interchange** services are used to create an electronic (paperless) environment for conducting commerce and achieving significant gains in quality, responsiveness, and savings afforded by such an environment. Examples of applications that use electronic commerce services include: vendor search and selection; contract award; product data; shipping, forwarding, and receiving; customs; payment information; inventory control; maintenance; tax-related data; and insurance-related data.

- **Fax** services are used to create, examine, transmit, and/or receive fax images.

The following functional areas are currently supported mainly by Application Software, but are progressing towards migration into the Application Platform:

- **Raw Graphics Interface** functions support graphics data file formats such as TIFF, JPEG, GIF, and CGM.

- **Text Processing** functions, including the capability to create, edit, merge, and format text.

- **Document Processing** functions, including the capability to create, edit, merge, and format documents. These functions enable the composition of documents that incorporate graphics, images, and even voice annotation, along with stylized text. Included are advanced formatting and editing functions such as style guides, spell checking, use of multiple columns, table of contents generation, headers and footers, outlining tools, and support for scanning images into bit-mapped formats. Other capabilities include compression and decompression of images or whole documents.

- **Publishing** functions, including incorporation of photographic quality images and color graphics, and advanced formatting and style features such as wrapping text around graphic objects or pictures and kerning (i.e., changing the spacing between text characters). These functions also interface with sophisticated printing and production equipment. Other capabilities include color rendering and compression and decompression of images or whole documents.

- **Video Processing** functions, including the capability to capture, compose, edit, compress, and decompress video information using formats such as MPEG. Still graphics and title generation functions are also provided.

- **Audio Processing** functions, including the capability to capture, compose, edit, compress, and decompress audio information.

- **Multimedia Processing** functions, including the capability to store, retrieve, modify, sort, search, and print all or any combination of the above-mentioned media. This includes support for microfilm media, optical storage technology that allows for storage of scanned or computer produced documents using digital storage techniques, a scanning capability, and data compression and decompression.

- **Media Synchronization** functions allow the synchronization of streams of data such as audio and video for presentation purposes.

- **Information Presentation and Distribution** functions are used to manage the distribution and presentation of information from batch and interactive applications. These functions are used to shield business area applications from how information is used. They allow business area applications to create generic pools of information without embedding controls that dictate the use of that information. Information distribution and presentation functions include the selection of the appropriate formatting functions required to accomplish the distribution and presentation of information to a variety of business area applications and users. Information presentation and distribution functions also include the capability to store, archive, prioritize, restrict, and recreate information.

- **Hypertext** functions support the generation, distribution, location, search, and display of text and images either locally or globally. These functions include searching and browsing, hypertext linking, and the presentation of multimedia information.

43.5.2 Data Management Services

Central to most systems is the management of data that can be defined independently of the processes that create or use it, maintained indefinitely, and shared among many processes. Data management services include:

- **Data Dictionary/Repository** services allow data administrators and information engineers to access and modify data about data (i.e., metadata). Such data may include internal and external formats, integrity and security rules, and location within a distributed system. Data dictionary and repository services also allow end users and applications to define and obtain data that is available in the database. Data administration defines the standardization and registration of individual data element types to meet the requirements for data sharing and interoperability among information systems throughout the enterprise. Data administration functions include procedures, guidelines, and methods for effective data planning, analysis, standards, modeling, configuration management, storage, retrieval, protection, validation, and documentation. Data dictionaries are sometimes tied to a single Database Management System (DBMS), but heterogeneous data dictionaries will support access to different DBMSs. Repositories can contain a wide variety of information including Management Information Bases (MIB) or CASE-related information. Object-oriented systems may provide repositories for objects and interfaces, described under Implementation Repository services and Interface Repository services in Section 43.5.13.

- **Database Management System (DBMS)** services provide controlled access to structured data. To manage the data, the DBMS provides concurrency control and facilities to combine data from different schemas. Different types of DBMS support different data models, including relational, hierarchical, network, object-oriented, and flat-file models. Some DBMSs are designed for special functions such as the storage of large objects or multimedia data. DBMS services are accessible through a programming language interface, an interactive data manipulation language interface (such as SQL), or an interactive/fourth-generation language interface. Look-up and retrieval services for objects are described separately under Query services in Section 43.5.13. For efficiency, DBMSs often provide specific services to create, populate, move, backup, restore, recover, and archive databases, although some of these services could be provided by the general file management capabilities described in Section 43.5.7 or a specific backup service. Some DBMSs support distribution of the database, including facilities for remotely updating records, data replication, locating and caching data, and remote management.

- **Object-Oriented Database Management System** (OODBMS) services provide storage for objects and interfaces to those objects. These services may support the Implementation Repository, Interface Repository, and Persistent Object services in Section 43.5.13.

- **File Management** services provide data management through file access methods including indexed sequential (ISAM) and hashed random access. Flat file and directory services are described in Section 43.5.7.

The following functional areas are currently supported mainly by Application Software, but are progressing towards migration into the Application Platform:

- **Query Processing** functions that provide for interactive selection, extraction, and formatting of stored information from files and databases. Query processing functions are invoked via user-oriented languages and tools (often referred to as fourth generation languages), which simplify the definition of searching criteria and aid in creating effective presentation of the retrieved information (including use of graphics).

■ **Screen Generation** functions that provide the capability to define and generate screens that support the retrieval, presentation, and update of data.

■ **Report Generation** functions that provide the capability to define and generate hardcopy reports composed of data extracted from a database.

■ **Networking/Concurrent Access** functions that manage concurrent user access to Database Management System (DBMS) functions.

■ **Warehousing** functions that provide the capability to store very large amounts of data — usually captured from other database systems — and to perform online analytical processing on it in support of *ad hoc* queries.

43.5.3 Graphics and Imaging Services

Graphics services provide functions required for creating, storing, retrieving, and manipulating images. These services include:

■ **Graphical Object Management** services, including defining multi-dimensional graphic objects in a form that is independent of output devices, and managing hierarchical structures containing graphics data. Graphical data formats include two- and three-dimensional geometric drawings as well as images.

■ **Drawing** services support the creation and manipulation of images with software such as GKS, PEX, PHIGS, or OpenGL.

The following functional areas are currently supported mainly by Application Software, but are progressing towards migration into the Application Platform:

■ **Imaging** functions providing for the scan, creation, edit, compression, and decompression of images in accordance with recognized image formatting standards; for example, PIKS/IPI, OpenXIL, or XIE.

43.5.4 International Operation Services

As a practice, information system developers have generally designed and developed systems to meet the requirements of a specific geographic or linguistic market segment, which may be a nation or a particular cultural market. To make that information system viable, or marketable, to a different segment of the market, a full re-engineering process was usually required. Users or organizations that needed to operate in a multi-national or multi-cultural environment typically did so with multiple, generally incompatible information processing systems.

International operation provides a set of services and interfaces that allow a user to define, select, and change between different culturally-related application environments supported by the particular implementation. In general, these services should be provided in such a way that internationalization issues are transparent to the application logic.

■ **Character Sets and Data Representation** services include the capability to input, store, manipulate, retrieve, communicate, and present data independently of the coding scheme used. This includes the capability to maintain and access a central character set repository of all coded character sets used throughout the platform. Character sets will be uniquely identified so that the end user or application can select the coded character set to be used. This system-independent representation supports the transfer (or sharing) of the values and syntax, but not the semantics, of data records between communicating systems. The specifications are independent of the internal record and field representations of the communicating systems. Also included is the capability to recognize the coded character set of data entities and subsequently to input, communicate, and present that data.

- **Cultural Convention** services provide the capability to store and access rules and conventions for cultural entities maintained in a cultural convention repository called a "locale". Locales should be available to all applications. Locales typically include date and currency formats, collation sequences, and number formats. Standardized locale formats and APIs allow software entities to use locale information developed by others.

- **Local Language Support** services provide the capability to support more than one language concurrently on a system. Messages, menus, forms, and online documentation can be displayed in the language selected by the user. Input from keyboards that have been modified locally to support the local character sets can be correctly interpreted.

The proper working of international operation services depends on all the software entities involved having the capability to:

- Use locales

- Switch between locales as required

- Maintain multiple active locales

- Access suitable fonts

This requires software entities to be written to a particular style and to be designed from the outset with internationalization in mind.

43.5.5 Location and Directory Services

Location and directory services provide specialized support for locating required resources and for mediation between service consumers and service providers.

The World Wide Web, based on the Internet, has created a need for locating information resources, which currently is mainly satisfied through the use of search engines. Advancements in the global Internet, and in heterogeneous distributed systems, demand active mediation through broker services that include automatic and dynamic registration, directory access, directory communication, filtration, and accounting services for access to resources.

- **Directory** services provide services for clients to establish where resources are, and by extension how they can be reached. "Clients" may be humans or computer programs, and "resources" may be a wide variety of things, such as names, email addresses, security certificates, printers, web pages, etc.

- **Special-Purpose Naming** services provide services that refer names (ordered strings of printable characters) to objects within a given context (namespaces). Objects are typically hierarchically organized within namespaces. Examples are:
  - File systems
  - Security databases
  - Process queues

- **Service Location** services provide access to "Yellow Pages" services in response to queries based on constraints.

- **Registration** services provide services to register identity, descriptions of the services a resource is providing, and descriptions of the means to access them.

- **Filtering** services provide services to select useful information from data using defined criteria.

- **Accounting** services provide services such as account open, account update, account balance, account detail, account close, account discounts, account bill/usage tally, account payment settlement based on message traffic, and/or connection time, and/or resource utilization, and/or broker-specific (e.g., value-based).

43.5.6 Network Services

Network services are provided to support distributed applications requiring data access and applications interoperability in heterogeneous or homogeneous networked environments.

A network service consists of both an interface and an underlying protocol.

- **Data Communications**, which include interfaces and protocols for reliable, transparent, end-to-end data transmission across communications networks. Data communications services include both high-level functions (such as file transfer, remote login, remote process execution, or PC integration services) and low-level functions (such as a sockets API) giving direct access to communications protocols.

- **Electronic Mail** services include the capability to send, receive, forward, store, display, retrieve, prioritize, authenticate, and manage messages. This includes the capability to append files and documents to messages. Messages may include any combination of data, text, audio, graphics, and images and should be capable of being formatted into standard data interchange formats. This service includes the use of directories and distribution lists for routing information, the ability to assign priorities, the use of pre-formatted electronic forms, and the capability to trace the status of messages. Associated services include a summarized listing of incoming messages, a log of messages received and read, the ability to file or print messages, and the ability to reply to or forward messages.

- **Distributed Data** services provide access to, and modification of, data/metadata in remote or local databases. In a distributed environment, data not available on the local database is fetched from a remote data server at the request of the local client.

- **Distributed File** services provide for transparent remote file access. Applications have equivalent access to data regardless of the data's physical location. Ancillary services for this function can include transparent addressing, cached data, data replication, file locking, and file logging.

- **Distributed Name** services provide a means for unique identification of resources within a distributed computing system. These services are available to applications within the network and provide information that can include resource name, associated attributes, physical location, and resource functionality. Note that all system resources should be identifiable, in all information systems, by the distributed name. This permits physical location to change, not only to accommodate movement, but also load balancing, system utilization, scaling (adding processors and moving resources to accommodate the increased resources), distributed processing, and all aspects of open systems. Distributed name services include directory services such as X.500 and network navigation services. Distributed name services include ways to locate data objects both by name and by function. Section 43.5.13 describes equivalent services under Naming services and Trading services, respectively.

- **Distributed Time** services provide synchronized time co-ordination as required among distributed processes in different timezones. An equivalent service is described under Time services in Section 43.5.13.

- **Remote Process (Access)** services provide the means for dispersed applications to communicate across a computer network. These services facilitate program-to-program communications regardless of their distributed nature or operation on heterogeneous platforms. Remote process services including remote procedure call (RPC) and asynchronous messaging mechanisms underpin client/server applications.

- **Remote Print Spooling and Output Distribution** services provide the means for printing output remotely. The services include management of remote printing including printer and media selection, use of forms, security, and print queue management.

The following functional areas are currently supported mainly by Application Software, but are progressing towards migration into the Application Platform:

- **Enhanced Telephony** functions, including call set-up, call co-ordination, call forwarding, call waiting, programmed directories, teleconferencing, automatic call distribution (useful for busy customer service categories), and call detail recording.

- **Shared Screen** functions that provide audio teleconferencing with common workstation windows between two or more users. This includes the capability to refresh windows whenever someone displays new material or changes an existing display. Every user is provided with the capability to graphically annotate or modify the shared conference window.

- **Video-Conferencing** functions that provide two-way video transmission between different sites. These functions include call set-up, call co-ordination, full motion display of events and participants in a bi-directional manner, support for the management of directing the cameras, ranging from fixed position, to sender directed, to receiver directed, to automated sound pickup.

- **Broadcast** functions that provide one-way audio or audio/video communications functions between a sending location and multiple receiving locations or between multiple sending and receiving locations.

- **Mailing List** functions that allow groups to participate in conferences. These conferences may or may not occur in real time. Conferees or invited guests can drop in or out of conferences or subconferences at will. The ability to trace the exchanges is provided. Functions include exchange of documents, conference management, recording facilities, and search and retrieval capabilities.

43.5.7 Operating System Services

Operating system services are responsible for the management of platform resources, including the processor, memory, files, and input and output. They generally shield applications from the implementation details of the machine. Operating system services include:

- **Kernel Operations** provide low-level services necessary to:
  - Create and manage processes and threads of execution
  - Execute programs
  - Define and communicate asynchronous events
  - Define and process system clock operations
  - Implement security features
  - Manage files and directories
  - Control input/output processing to and from peripheral devices

  Some kernel services have analogues described in Section 43.5.13, such as concurrency control services.

- **Command Interpreter and Utility** services include mechanisms for services at the operator level, such as:
  - Comparing, printing, and displaying file contents
  - Editing files
  - Searching patterns
  - Evaluating expressions
  - Logging messages
  - Moving files between directories
  - Sorting data
  - Executing command scripts
  - Local print spooling
  - Scheduling signal execution processes
  - Accessing environment information

- **Batch Processing** services support the capability to queue work (jobs) and manage the sequencing of processing based on job control commands and lists of data. These services also include support for the management of the output of batch processing, which frequently includes updated files or databases and information products such as printed reports or electronic documents. Batch processing is performed asynchronously from the user requesting the job.

- **File and Directory Synchronization** services allow local and remote copies of files and directories to be made identical. Synchronization services are usually used to update files after periods of offline working on a portable system.

43.5.8   Software Engineering Services

The functional aspect of an application is embodied in the programming languages used to code it. Additionally, professional system developers require tools appropriate to the development and maintenance of applications. These capabilities are provided by software engineering services, which includo:

- **Programming Language** services provide the basic syntax and semantic definition for use by a software developer to describe the desired Application Software function. Shell and executive script language services enable the use of operating system commands or utilities rather than a programming language. Shells and executive scripts are typically interpreted rather than compiled, but some operating systems support compilers for executive scripts. In contrast, some compilers produce code to be interpreted at run time. Other tools in this group include source code formatters and compiler compilers.

- **Object Code Linking** services provide the ability for programs to access the underlying application and operating system platform through APIs that have been defined independently of the computer language. It is used by programmers to gain access to these services using methods consistent with the operating system and specific language used. Linking is operating system-dependent, but language-independent.

- **Computer-Aided Software Engineering (CASE) Environment and Tools** services include systems and programs that assist in the automated development and maintenance of software. These include, but are not limited to, tools for requirements specification and analysis, for design work and analysis, for creating, editing, testing, and debugging program code, for documenting, for prototyping, and for group communication. The interfaces among these tools include services for storing and retrieving information about systems and exchanging this information among the various components of the system development environment. An adjunct to these capabilities is the ability to manage and control the configuration of software components, test data, and libraries to record changes to source code or to access CASE repositories. Other language tools include code generators and translators, artificial intelligence tools, and tools like the UNIX system command *make*, which uses knowledge of the inter-dependencies between modules to recompile and link only those parts of a program which have changed.

- **Graphical User Interface (GUI) Building** services assist in the development of the Human Computer Interface (HCI) elements of applications. Tools include services for generating and capturing screen layouts, and for defining the appearance, function, behavior, and position of graphical objects.

- **Scripting Language** services provide interpreted languages which allow the user to carry out some complicated function in a simple way. Application areas served by special-purpose scripting languages include calculation, graphical user interface development, and development of prototype applications.

- **Language Binding** services provide mappings from interfaces provided by programming languages onto the services provided by the Application Platform. In many cases the mapping is straightforward since the platform supplies analogous services to those expected by the application. In other cases the language binding service must use a combination of Application Platform services to provide a fully functional mapping.

- **Run-Time Environment** services provide support for Application Software at run time. This support includes locating and connecting dynamically linked libraries, or even emulation of an operating environment other than the one which actually exists.

- **Application Binary Interface** services provide services that make the Application Platform comply with defined application binary interface standards.

43.5.9 Transaction Processing Services

Transaction Processing (TP) services provide support for the online processing of information in discrete units called "transactions", with assurance of the state of the information at the end of the transaction. This typically involves predetermined sequences of data entry, validation, display, and update or inquiry against a file or database. It also includes services to prioritize and track transactions. TP services may include support for distribution of transactions to a combination of local and remote processors.

A transaction is a complete unit of work. It may comprise many computational tasks, which may include user interface, data retrieval, and communications. A typical transaction modifies shared resources. Transactions must also be able to be rolled back (that is, undone) if necessary, at any stage. When a transaction is completed without failure, it is committed. Completion of a transaction means either commitment or rollback.

Typically a TP service will contain a transaction manager, which links data entry and display software with processing, database, and other resources to form the complete service.

The sum of all the work done anywhere in the system in the course of a single transaction is called a "global transaction". Transactions are not limited to a single Application Platform.

- **Transaction Manager** services, which allow an application to demarcate transactions, and direct their completion. Transaction manager services include:

  - Starting a transaction

  - Co-ordination of recoverable resources involved in a transaction

  - Committing or rolling back transactions

  - Controlling timeouts on transactions

  - Chaining transactions together

  - Monitoring transaction status

  Some transaction manager services have equivalents described in Section 43.5.13, under Transaction services.

43.5.10 User Interface Services

User interface services define how users may interact with an application. Depending on the capabilities required by users and the applications, these interfaces may include the following:

- **Graphical Client/Server** services that define the relationships between client and server processes operating graphical user interface displays, usually within a network. In this case, the program that controls each display unit is a server process, while independent user programs are client processes that request display services from the server.

- **Display Objects** services that define characteristics of display elements such as color, shape, size, movement, graphics context, user preferences, font management, and interactions among display elements.

- **Window Management** services that define how windows are created, moved, stored, retrieved, removed, and related to each other.

- **Dialog Support** services translate the data entered for display to that which is actually displayed on the screen (e.g., cursor movements, keyboard data entry, and external data entry devices).

- **Printing** services support output of text and/or graphical data, including any filtering or format conversion necessary. Printing services may include the ability to print all or part of a document, to print and collate more than one copy, to select the size and orientation of output, to choose print resolution, colors, and graphical behavior, and to specify fonts and other characteristics.

- **Computer-Based Training and Online Help** services provide an integrated training environment on user workstations. Training is available on an as-needed basis for any application available in the environment. Electronic messages are provided at the stroke of a key from anywhere within the application. This includes tutorial training on the application in use and the availability of offline, on-site interactive training.

- **Character-Based** services, which deal with support for non-graphical terminals. Character-based services include support for terminal type-independent control of display attributes, cursor motions, programmable keys, audible signals, and other functions.

The services associated with a window system include the visual display of information on a screen that contains one or more windows or panels, support for pointing to an object on the screen using a pointing device such as a mouse or touch-screen, and the manipulation of a set of objects on the screen through the pointing device or through keyboard entry. Other user interfaces included are industrial controls and virtual reality devices.

43.5.11 Security Services

Security services are necessary to protect sensitive information in the information system. The appropriate level of protection is determined based upon the value of the information to the business area end users and the perception of threats to it.

To be effective, security needs to be made strong, must never be taken for granted, and must be designed into an architecture and not bolted on afterwards. Whether a system is stand-alone or distributed, security must be applied to the whole system. It must not be forgotten that the requirement for security extends not only across the range of entities in a system but also through time.

In establishing a security architecture, the best approach is to consider what is being defended, what value it has, and what the threats to it are. The principal threats to be countered are:

- Loss of confidentiality of data

- Unavailability of data or services

- Loss of integrity of data

- Unauthorized use of resources

Counters to these threats are provided by the following services:

- **Identification and Authentication** services provide:

  — Identification, accountability, and audit of users and their actions

  — Authentication and account data

  — Protection of authentication data

  — Active user status information

  — Password authentication mechanisms

- **System Entry Control** services provide:

  — Warning to unauthorized users that the system is security-aware

  — Authentication of users

  — Information, displayed on entry, about previous successful and unsuccessful login attempts

  — User-initiated locking of a session preventing further access until the user has been re-authenticated

- **Audit** services provide authorized control and protection of the audit trail, recording of detailed information security-relevant events, and audit trail control, management, and inspection.

- **Access Control** services provide:

  — Access control attributes for subjects (such as processes) and objects (such as files)

  — Enforcement of rules for assignment and modification of access control attributes

  — Enforcement of access controls

  — Control of object creation and deletion, including ensuring that re-use of objects does not allow subjects to accidentally gain access to information previously held in the object

  Access control services also appear under Security services in Section 43.5.13.

- **Non-Repudiation** services provide proof that a user carried out an action, or sent or received some information, at a particular time. Non-repudiation services also appear under Security services in Section 43.5.13.

- **Security Management** services provide secure system set-up and initialization, control of security policy parameters, management of user registration data, and system resources and restrictions on the use of administrative functions.

- **Trusted Recovery** services provide recovery facilities such as restoring from backups in ways that do not compromise security protection.

- **Encryption** services provide ways of encoding data such that it can only be read by someone who possesses an appropriate key, or some other piece of secret information. As well as providing data confidentiality for trusted communication, encryption services are used to underpin many other services including identification and authentication, system entry control, and access control services.

- **Trusted Communication** services provide:

— A secure way for communicating parties to authenticate themselves to each other without the risk of an eavesdropper subsequently masquerading as one of the parties

— A secure way of generating and verifying check values for data integrity

— Data encipherment and decipherment for confidentiality and other purposes

— A way to produce an irreversible hash of data for support of digital signature and non-repudiation functions

— Generation, derivation, distribution, storage, retrieval, and deletion of cryptographic keys

Security services require other software entities to co-operate in:

- Access control for resources managed by the entity

- Accounting and audit of security-relevant events

- The import and export of data

- Potentially all other security services depending on the particular implementation approach

Security services are one category where a wide view is particularly important, as a chain is only as strong as its weakest link. This is one category of services where the external environment has critical implications on the Application Platform. For instance, the presence of a firewall may provide a single point of access onto a network from the outside world, making it possible to concentrate access control in one place and relax requirements behind the firewall.

43.5.12 System and Network Management Services

Information systems are composed of a wide variety of diverse resources that must be managed effectively to achieve the goals of an open system environment. While the individual resources (such as printers, software, users, processors) may differ widely, the abstraction of these resources as managed objects allows for treatment in a uniform manner. The basic concepts of management — including operation, administration, and maintenance — may then be applied to the full suite of information system components along with their attendant services.

System and network management functionality may be divided in several different ways; one way is to make a division according to the management elements that generically apply to all functional resources. This division reduces as follows:

- **User Management** services provide the ability to maintain a user's preferences and privileges.

- **Configuration Management (CM)** services address four basic functions:

  — Identification and specification of all component resources

  — Control, or the ability to freeze configuration items, changing them only through agreed processes

  — Status accounting of each configuration item

  — Verification through a series of reviews to ensure conformity between the actual configuration item and the information recorded about it

  These services include: Processor CM, Network CM, Distributed System CM, Topology CM, and Application CM. Processor CM takes a platform-centric approach. Network CM and Distributed System CM services allow remote systems to be managed and monitored including the interchange of network status. Topology CM is used to control the topology of physical or logical entities that are distributed. Application CM focuses on applications. Configuration management also appears as Change Management services in Section 43.5.13.

- **Performance Management** services monitor performance aspects of hardware, platform and application software, and network components and provide ways to tune the system to meet performance targets.

- **Availability and Fault Management** services allow a system to react to the loss or incorrect operation of system components including hardware, platform software, and application software.

- **Accounting Management** services provide the ability to cost services for charging and reimbursement.

- **Security Management** services control the security services in accordance with applicable security policies.

- **Print Management** services provide the ability to manage both local and remote print spooling services.

- **Network Management** services comprise elements of all the services described above, but are often treated as a separate service.

- **Backup and Restore** services provide a multi-level storage facility to ensure continued data security in case of component or subsystem failure.

- **Online Disk Management** services manage the utilization of disk storage against threshold values and invoke corrective action.

- **License Management** services support the effective enforcement of software license agreements. Licensing services for objects are described under Licensing services in Section 43.5.13.

- **Capacity Management** services address three basic functions:

  - Capacity management analyzing current and historic performance and capacity

  - Workload management to identify and understand applications that use the system

  - Capacity planning to plan required hardware resources for the future

- **Software Installation** services support distribution, installation, removal, relocation, activation, and automatic update of software or data packages from transportable media or over networks. Similar services for objects are described under Installation and Activation services in Section 43.5.13.

The following functional areas are currently supported mainly by Application Software, but are progressing towards migration into the Application Platform:

- **Trouble Ticketing** services support the generation, processing, and tracking of problem reports. Trouble ticketing is a term originating in the telecommunications world, referring to the ability to pass fault reports both within and between telecommunications service providers. In this environment, faults are often found by a customer of one provider, while the cause of the problem lies within the administrative domain of another provider. Trouble ticketing is a common service that may be useful to an increasing range of applications if the necessary work is done to extend it from telecommunications into wider areas of distributed applications such as email.

This breakout of system and network management services parallels the breakout of emerging OSI network management, thereby presenting an overall coherent framework that applies equally to whole networks and the individual nodes of the networks.

One important consideration of the standards supporting the services in this category is that they should not enforce specific management policies, but rather enable a wide variety of different management policies to be implemented, selected according to the particular needs of the end-user installations.

System and network management services require the co-operation of other software entities in:

- Providing status information
- Notifying events
- Responding to management instructions

43.5.13 Object-Oriented Provision of Services

This section shows how services are provided in an object-oriented manner. "Object Services" does not appear as a category in the Technical Reference Model (TRM) since all the individual object services are incorporated as appropriate in the given service categories.

An object is an identifiable, encapsulated entity that provides one or more services that can be requested by a client. Clients request a service by invoking the appropriate method associated with the object, and the object carries out the service on the client's behalf. Objects provide a programming paradigm that can lead to important benefits, including:

- Increased modularity
- A reduction in errors
- Ease of debugging

Object management services provide ways of creating, locating, and naming objects, and allowing them to communicate in a distributed environment. The complete set of object services identified so far is listed below for the sake of completeness. Where a particular object service is part of a more generally applicable service category, a pointer to the other service category is given. Object services include:

- **Object Request Broker (ORB)** services, which enable objects to transparently make and receive requests and responses in a distributed environment. ORB services include:
  - **Implementation Repository** services support the location and management of object implementations. The services resemble those provided by the Data Dictionary/Repository services in Section 43.5.2.
  - **Installation and Activation** services provide ways to distribute, install, activate, and relocate objects. This corresponds to the Software Installation services in Section 43.5.12.
  - **Interface Repository** services support the storage and management of information about interfaces to objects. The services resemble those provided by the Data Dictionary/Repository services in Section 43.5.2.

- **Replication** services support replication of objects in distributed systems, including management of consistency between the copies.

- **Common Object** services, which provide basic functions for using and implementing objects. These are the services necessary to construct any distributed application. Common object services include:

  - **Change Management** services provide for version identification and configuration management of object interfaces, implementations, and instances. This corresponds to the Configuration Management services described in Section 43.5.12.

  - **Collections** services provide operations on collections of objects, such as lists, trees, stacks, or queues. Services include establishing, adding objects to, or removing them from collections, testing set membership, forming unions and intersections of sets, and so on.

  - **Concurrency Control** services enable multiple clients to co-ordinate their access to shared resources. Synchronization like this is normally provided using the Kernel services provided in Section 43.5.7.

  - **Data Interchange** services support the exchange of visible state information between objects. Depending on the kind of object involved, this corresponds to one or more of the services provided in Section 43.5.1.

  - **Event Management** services provide basic capabilities for the management of events, including asynchronous events, event "fan-in", notification "fan-out", and reliable event delivery.

  - **Externalization** services define protocols and conventions for externalizing and internalizing objects. Externalizing means recording the object state in a stream of data, and internalizing means recreating an object state from a data stream. This is one example of the Information Presentation and Distribution functions in Section 43.5.1.

  - **Licensing** services support policies for object licensing, and measurement and charging for object use. This corresponds to the License Management services in Section 43.5.12.

  - **Lifecycle** services define conventions for creating, deleting, copying, and moving objects. The creation of objects is defined in terms of factory objects, which are objects that create other objects.

  - **Naming** services provide the ability to bind a name to an object, and to locate an object by its name. This is analogous to the Distributed Name service described in Section 43.5.6.

  - **Persistent Object** services provide common interfaces for retaining and managing the persistent state of objects. Objects are often stored in an OODBMS, described as one of the services in Section 43.5.2.

  - **Properties** services support the creation, deletion, assignment, and protection of dynamic properties associated with objects.

  - **Query** services support indexing and query operations on collections of objects that return a subset of the collection. This is similar to database look-up, a part of the DBMS functions in Section 43.5.2.

— **Relationship** services allow relationships between objects (such as ownership or containment) to be explicitly represented as objects.

— **Security** services support access control on objects and non-repudiation of operations on objects. Access control is defined as a security service (see Section 43.5.11). Non-repudiation, which is also a Security service, provides proof that an action was carried out by a particular user at a particular time.

— **Start-Up** services support automatic start-up and termination of object services at ORB start-up or termination.

— **Time** services support synchronization of clocks in a distributed system. This is the same as the Distributed Time service in Section 43.5.6.

— **Trading** services allow clients to locate objects by the services the objects provide, rather than by name. This is similar to the Distributed Name service in Section 43.5.6.

— **Transaction** services provide facilities for grouping operations into atomic units, called "transactions", with the certainty that a transaction will be carried out in its entirety or not at all. This corresponds to some of the Transaction Manager services in Section 43.5.9.

Chapter 44: Integrated Information Infrastructure Reference Model

This chapter describes the Integrated Information Infrastructure Reference Model (III-RM), in terms of its concepts, an overview, and taxonomy.

44.1 Basic Concepts

This section looks at the basic concepts of the III-RM, including background, components, and drivers.

44.1.1 Background

With the emergence of Internet-based technologies in recent years, for many organizations the main focus of attention, and the main return on investment in architecture effort, has shifted from the Application Platform space to the Application Software space. (Indeed, this has been one of the drivers behind the migration of TOGAF itself from a framework and method for Technology Architecture to one for overall enterprise architecture.)

The TOGAF Technical Reference Model (TRM) described in Chapter 43 focuses on the Application Platform space.

This section describes a reference model that focuses on the Application Software space, and "Common Systems Architecture" in Enterprise Continuum terms. This is the Integrated Information Infrastructure Reference Model (III-RM).

The III-RM is a subset of the TOGAF TRM in terms of its overall scope, but it also expands certain parts of the TRM — in particular, the business applications and infrastructure applications parts — in order to provide help in addressing one of the key challenges facing the enterprise architect today: the need to design an integrated information infrastructure to enable Boundaryless Information Flow. These concepts are explained in detail below.

This introductory section examines the concept of Boundaryless Information Flow; why an integrated information infrastructure is necessary to enable it; and how the III-RM can help the architect in designing an integrated information infrastructure for their enterprise.

44.1.2 Components of the Model

Like the TOGAF TRM, the III-RM has two main components:

1. A **taxonomy**, which defines terminology, and provides a coherent description of the components and conceptual structure of an integrated information infrastructure

2. An associated **III-RM graphic**, which provides a visual representation of the taxonomy, and the inter-relationship of the components, as an aid to understanding

The model assumes the underlying existence of a computing and network platform, as described in the TRM; these are not depicted in the model.

44.1.3 Relationship to Other parts of TOGAF

The relationship of the III-RM to the TRM is explained above.

Although the III-RM is intended as a useful tool in the execution of the TOGAF Architecture Development Method (ADM), it is important to emphasize that the ADM is in no way dependent on use of the III-RM (any more than it is dependent on use of the TRM). Other taxonomies and reference models exist in this space that can be used in conjunction with the ADM, and indeed may be preferable for some organizations.

44.1.4 Key Business and Technical Drivers

44.1.4.1 Problem Space: The Need for Boundaryless Information Flow

The Boundaryless Information Flow problem space is one that is shared by many customer members of The Open Group, and by many similar organizations worldwide. It is essentially the problem of getting information to the right people at the right time in a secure, reliable manner, in order to support the operations that are core to the extended enterprise.

In General Electric, Jack Welch invented the term "the Boundaryless Organization", not to imply that there are no boundaries, but that they should be made permeable.

Creating organizational structures that enabled each individual department to operate at maximum efficiency was for a long time accepted as the best approach to managing a large enterprise. Among other benefits, this approach fostered the development of specialist skills in staff, who could apply those skills to specific aspects of an overall activity (such as a manufacturing process), in order to accomplish the tasks involved better, faster, and cheaper.

As each overall activity progressed through the organization, passing from department to department (for example, from Design to Production to Sales), each department would take inputs from the previous department in the process, apply its own business processes to the activity, and send its output to the next department in line.

In today's world where speed, flexibility, and responsiveness to changing markets make all the difference between success and failure, this method of working is no longer appropriate. Organizations have been trying for some time to overcome the limitations imposed by traditional organization structures. Many business process re-engineering efforts have been undertaken and abandoned because they were too ambitious, while others cost far more in both time and money than originally intended.

However, organizations today recognize that they need not abandon functional or departmental organization altogether. They can enable the right people to come together in cross-functional teams so that all the skills, knowledge, and expertise can be brought to bear on any specific problem or business opportunity.

But this in turn poses its own challenges. CIOs are under enormous pressure to provide access to information to each cross-functional team on an as-required basis, and yet the sources of this data can be numerous and the volumes huge.

Even worse, the IT systems, which have been built over a period of 20 or 30 years at a cost of many billions of dollars, and are not about to be thrown out or replaced wholesale, were built for each functional department. So although it may be possible to get people to work together effectively (no minor achievement in itself), the IT systems they use are designed to support the old-style thinking. The IT systems in place today do not allow for information to flow in support of the boundaryless organization. When they do, then we will have Boundaryless Information Flow.

44.1.4.2 *Solution Space: The Need for Integrated Information Infrastructure*

The Open Group's Interoperable Enterprise Business Scenario[18] originally published in 2001, crystallizes this need for Boundaryless Information Flow and describes the way in which this need drives IT customers' deployment of their information infrastructure.

In this scenario, the customer's problem statement says that I (as the customer enterprise) could gain significant operational efficiencies and improve the many different business processes of the enterprise — both internal processes, and those spanning the key interactions with suppliers, customers, and partners — if only I could provide my staff with:

- **Integrated information** so that different and potentially conflicting pieces of information are not distributed throughout different systems

- **Integrated access to that information** so that staff can access all the information they need and have a right to, through one convenient interface

The infrastructure that enables this vision is termed the "integrated information infrastructure".

As an example, one current approach to integrated information infrastructure is to provide "enterprise portals" that allow integrated access to information from different applications systems enterprise-wide, via a convenient, web-enabled interface (one of the colored segments in the ends of the cylinder in Figure 44-1).

18.　　Available at www.opengroup.org/bookstore/catalog/k022.htm.

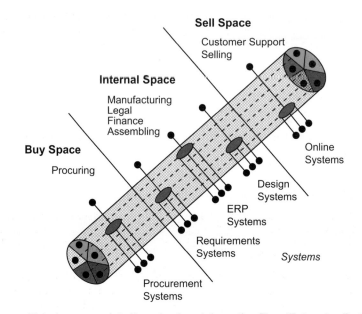

Figure 44-1 An approach to Boundaryless Information Flow (Enterprise Portals)

One of the key challenges for the architect in today's enterprise is to work out, and then communicate to senior management, how far technologies such as web services, application integration services, etc., can go toward achieving an integrated information infrastructure, and realizing the vision of Boundaryless Information Flow, in the enterprise concerned.

The Open Group's follow-up analysis of the Interoperable Enterprise Business Scenario has resulted in the development of an integrated information infrastructure model (the III-RM), which depicts the major components required to address the Boundaryless Information Flow problem space, and can help the architect in this task.

The III-RM thus provides insights related to customer needs for Boundaryless Information Flow in enterprise environments. The model also points to rules and standards to assist in leveraging solutions and products within the value chain.

The following subsections discuss the model in detail.

44.1.5 Status of the III-RM

The III-RM is documented as it stands today, and is by no means considered a finished article. However, it is a model that has been developed and approved by the members of The Open Group as a whole, in response to the Interoperable Enterprise Business Scenario, which itself was developed in response to an urgent need articulated by the customer members of The Open Group for assistance in this field.

The Business Scenario and the Reference Model thus represent a problem and a solution approach that The Open Group membership as a whole fully endorses.

It is hoped that publication of the model as part of TOGAF will encourage its widespread adoption and use, and provide a channel of communication whereby experience with use of the model can be fed back, improvement points assimilated, and the model refined and republished as necessary.

44.2 High-Level View

This section provides a high-level view of the III-RM, including derivation of the model, high-level graphic, and components.

44.2.1 Derivation of the III-RM from the TRM

The III-RM is a model of the major component categories for developing, managing, and operating an integrated information infrastructure. It is a model of a set of applications that sits on top of an Application Platform. This model is a subset of the TOGAF TRM, and it uses a slightly different orientation.

Consider Figure 44-2 where two views of the TOGAF TRM are presented. The left side is the familiar view of the TOGAF TRM; it is a side view, where we look at the model as if looking at a house from the side, revealing the contents of the "floors". The top-down view on the right-hand side depicts what one might see if looking at a house from the "roof" down.

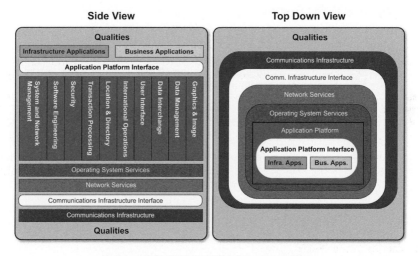

Figure 44-2 TOGAF TRM Orientation Views

The subset of the TRM that comprises the III-RM is depicted in Figure 44-3, in which those parts of the TRM not relevant to the III-RM are "greyed out".

Figure 44-3 illustrates that the focus is on the Application Software, Application Platform, and qualities subset of the TOGAF TRM.

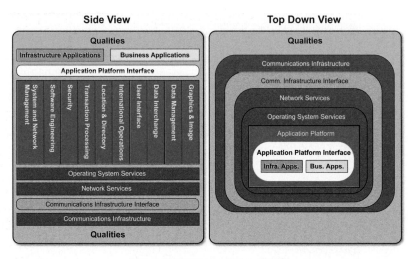

Figure 44-3 Focus of the III-RM

44.2.2 High-Level III-RM Graphic

The resulting III-RM itself is depicted in Figure 44-4. It is fundamentally an Application Architecture reference model — a model of the application components and application services software essential for an integrated information infrastructure. (There are more business applications and infrastructure applications than these in the environment, of course, but these are the subsets relevant to the Boundaryless Information Flow problem space.)

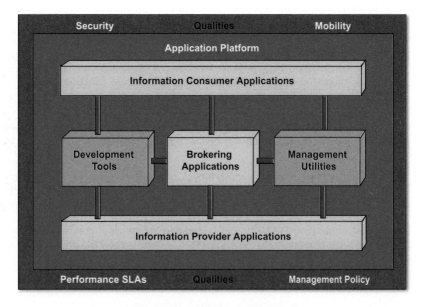

Figure 44-4 III-RM — High-Level

As explained above, the model assumes the underlying existence of a computing and network platform, and does not depict them explicitly.

Although the computing and network platform are not depicted, there may be requirements on them that must be met, in addition to requirements on the components of the III-RM, in order to fully address the Boundaryless Information Flow problem space.

44.2.3 Components of the High-Level III-RM

The III-RM has the following core components:

- **Business Applications**, denoted by the yellow boxes in the high-level model (corresponding to the "Business Applications" box in the TRM graphic). There are three types of Business Application in the model:

    - **Brokering Applications**, which manage the requests from any number of clients to and across any number of Information Provider Applications

    - **Information Provider Applications**, which provide responses to client requests and rudimentary access to data managed by a particular server

    - **Information Consumer Applications**, which deliver content to the user of the system, and provide services to request access to information in the system on the user's behalf

- **Infrastructure Applications**, denoted by the orange boxes in the high-level model (corresponding to the "Infrastructure Applications" box in the TRM graphic). There are two types of Infrastructure Application in the model:

  - **Development Tools**, which provide all the necessary modeling, design, and construction capabilities to develop and deploy applications that require access to the integrated information infrastructure, in a manner consistent with the standards of the environment

  - **Management Utilities**, which provide all the necessary utilities to understand, operate, tune, and manage the run-time system in order to meet the demands of an ever-changing business, in a manner consistent with the standards of the environment

- An **Application Platform**, which provides supporting services to all the above applications — in areas such as location, directory, workflow, data management, data interchange, etc. — and thereby provides the ability to locate, access, and move information within the environment. This set of services constitutes a subset of the total set of services of the TRM Application Platform, and is denoted by the dark green underlay in the high-level model (corresponding to the Application Platform in the TRM graphic).

- The **Interfaces** used between the components. Interfaces include formats and protocols, application programming interfaces, switches, data values, etc. Interfaces among components at the application level are colored red. Interfaces between any application-level components and their supporting services in the Application Platform are colored white (corresponding to the API box in the TRM graphic).

- The **Qualities** backplane, denoted by the brown underlay in the high-level model (corresponding to the Qualities backplane in the TRM graphic). The Application Software and Application Platform must adhere to the policies and requirements depicted by the qualities backplane.

44.3   Detailed Taxonomy

This section provides a detailed taxonomy of the III-RM, including detailed graphic, platform service categories, and external environment sub-entities.

44.3.1   Detailed III-RM Graphic

The detailed III-RM is depicted in Figure 44-5.

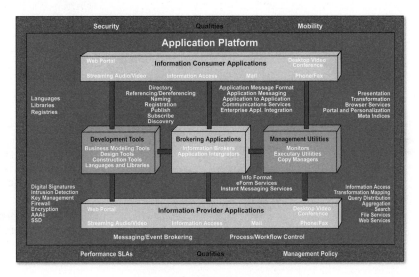

Figure 44-5 III-RM — Detailed

The remaining subsections expand on the taxonomy/component detail shown in Figure 44-5.

44.3.2   Business Applications

There are three types of business application in the model:

- **Information Provider Applications**, which provide responses to client requests and rudimentary access to data managed by a particular server

- **Brokering Applications**, which manage the requests from any number of clients to and across any number of service providers

- **Information Consumer Applications**, which deliver content to the user of the system, and provide services to request access to information in the system on the user's behalf

The overall set of Information Provider, Information Consumer, and Brokerage Applications collectively creates an environment that provides a rich set of end-user services for transparently accessing heterogeneous systems, databases, and file systems.

44.3.2.1 Information Provider Applications

To the extent that information today can be regarded as being "held hostage", as depicted in Figure 44-6, Information Provider Applications are those applications that "liberate" data from their silos.

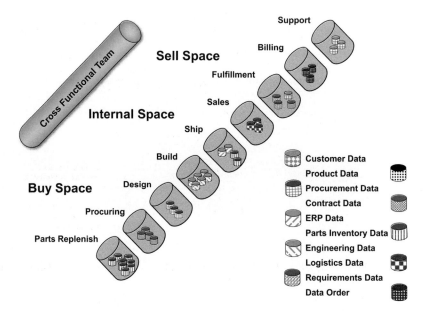

Figure 44-6 Liberate Data Silos to Meet Information Needs of Cross-Functional Enterprise Teams

Information Provider Applications achieve this by providing an open interface to a potentially proprietary silo interface, as illustrated in Figure 44-7, where the interfaces on the left of the Information Provider Applications are open interfaces and the interfaces between the Information Provider Applications and silo data are proprietary interfaces.

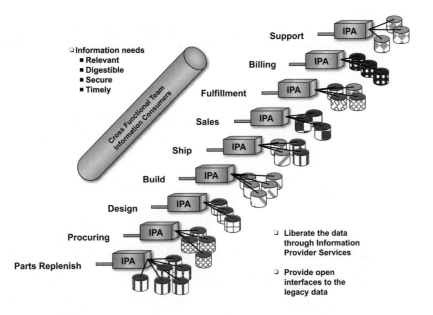

Figure 44-7 Information Provider Applications Liberate Data by Providing Open Interfaces to Data Silos

44.3.2.2 Brokerage Applications

Brokerage Applications serve up single requests that require access to multiple information sources. A Brokerage Application breaks down such a request, distributes the request to multiple information sources, collects the responses, and sends a single response back to the requesting client.

Brokerage Applications access Information Provider Applications using the open interfaces provided by the Information Provider Applications (as described above); they integrate information from multiple Information Provider Applications and pass the integrated information to Information Consumer Applications using open interfaces.

Brokerage Applications also enable access to information within the enterprise by strategic partners.

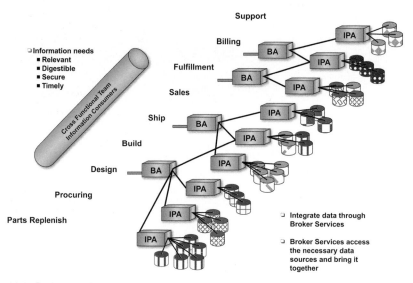

Figure 44-8 Brokerage Applications Integrate Information from Information Provider Applications

44.3.2.3 *Information Consumer Applications*

Information Consumer Applications provide information to end users in the form in which they need it, when they need it, and in a secured manner. This includes providing the information in text, video, audio, English, German, etc.

Information Consumer Applications communicate with Brokerage Applications or Information Provider Applications using the open interfaces that the Brokerage and Information Provider Applications provide. Security is provided through the firewalls and/or security services.

Figure 44-9 depicts the Information Consumer Applications with the security services depicted as the brick pattern.

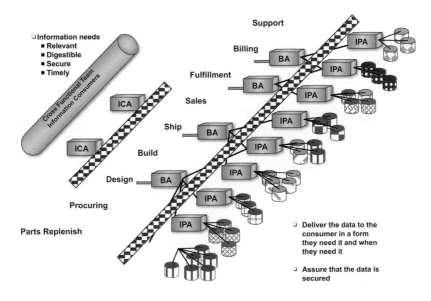

Figure 44-9 Information Consumer Applications Communicate using Open Interfaces

44.3.3 Infrastructure Applications

There are two types of Infrastructure Application in the model:

- **Development Tools**, which provide all the necessary modeling, design, and construction capabilities to develop and deploy applications that require access to the integrated information infrastructure, in a manner consistent with the standards of the environment

- **Management Utilities**, which provide all the necessary utilities to understand, operate, tune, and manage the run-time system in order to meet the demands of an ever-changing business, in a manner consistent with the standards of the environment

44.3.3.1 Development Tools

The Development Tools component of the model comprises applications that take the form of tools for modeling, designing, and constructing the integrated information infrastructure. Specifically, it includes tools for business, process, and data modeling, as well as the traditional application construction tools that transform the business model into software that automates the business processes revolving around information.

Note that each set of tools will be logically connected through a directory, allowing one tool to be driven by data from another. The following sections describe the requirements for components of Development Tools. The tool set also includes a repository.

Business Modeling Tools

This category covers tools for the modeling of business rules and business process rules.

Business modeling describes and documents the business in a comprehensive knowledge base. It establishes a consensus among general management of the business direction, organization, processes, information requirements, and the current environment of the business. Perhaps most importantly, this understanding is documented in a common, business-oriented format to be utilized for subsequent enhancement.

Design Modeling Tools

This category covers tools for designing, defining, and documenting the most pertinent IT elements of the business based upon the business and business process rules. Examples of elements to be designed include: connections between people, organizations, workflows and computers; data and object models; physical data translation and translation rules; and constraints.

Implementation and Construction Tools

Implementation tools enable timely development of re-usable processes, applications, and application services. Such tools include intelligent browsers, data manipulation language compilers and optimizers, distributed application compilers and debuggers, heterogeneous client and server development tools, policy definition tools, and workflow script generation tools.

Data Modeling Tools

Deployment Tools

Deployment tools are necessary to move implemented software from the development environment into the operational environment.

Libraries

This component includes re-usable libraries of software that use the standards of the operational environment.

44.3.3.2 *Management Utilities*

This category covers applications that take the form of utilities for operations, administration, and systems management, and for the management of data based on availability and cost requirements. Such utilities may execute in an attended or an unattended environment.

Operations, Administration, and Management (OA&M) Utilities

The OA&M component covers traditional systems management and administration utilities that manage business rules and information objects. Examples include: utilities for installation, copyright and license management; and miscellaneous administration, configuration, and registration functions. Additionally there are utilities for the control of service billing, service triggering, and account management.

Quality of Service Manager Utilities

These include health monitoring and management utilities.

Copy Management Utilities

Copy Management utilities are those that manage data movement from any given operational system to necessary distribution points in the enterprise, in order to ensure the maximum leverage of operational systems data. They also include tools that detect and flag poor quality data.

Storage Management Utilities

These are utilities that provide least-cost data storage management. Storage management utilities support the wide variety of storage mechanisms and are connected to file, object, and database systems.

44.3.4 Application Platform

All the different types of application described above are built on top of the services provided by the Application Platform.

The Application Platform component of the III-RM comprises a subset of all the services defined in the TOGAF TRM, the subset that pertains to integrated information infrastructure. Specifically, it comprises all those services in the TRM Application Platform that allow applications to focus on understanding and processing the information required, rather than understanding the form, format, and/or location of the information.

The services of the Application Platform component can be used to support conventional applications as well as Brokerage, Information Consumer, and Information Provider applications. When used as part of an overall Application Architecture in this way, such an approach enables maximum leverage of a single operational environment that is designed to ensure effective and consistent transfer of data between processes, and to support fast and efficient development, deployment, and management of applications.

The Application Platform component comprises the following categories of service.

44.3.4.1 Software Engineering Services

- Languages
- Libraries
- Registries

44.3.4.2 Security Services

- Authentication, authorization, and access control
- Single sign-on
- Digital signature
- Firewall
- Encryption
- Intrusion detection
- Identity management
- Key management

44.3.4.3 Location and Directory Services

Location and directory services provide access facilities for name, location, description, and relationship data that describes the integrated information infrastructure.

Directory services support the deployment and enterprise-wide availability of an integrated information infrastructure directory. The data in the directory is made available to all other components in the architecture model.

Figure 44-10 depicts the juxtaposition of location and directory services to the other components.

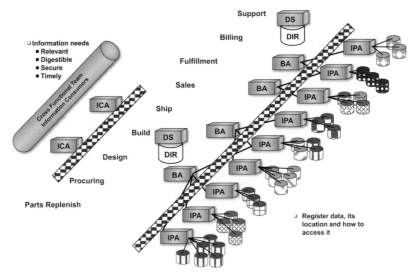

Figure 44-10 Juxtaposition of Location and Directory Services to Other Components

Specific services include:

- Directory
- Registration
- Publish/subscribe
- Discovery
- Naming
- Referencing/dereferencing

44.3.4.4 *Human Interaction Services*

Human Interaction services provide the means to consistently present data to the end user in the appropriate format. They comprise services that assist in the formulation of customer data requests and enable visualization and presentation of the data accessed.

Specific services include:

- Presentation
- Transformation
- Browser
- Meta indices

- Portal and personalization

44.3.4.5 Data Interchange Services

Specific services include:

- Information format
- eForm
- Instant messaging
- Application messaging
- Application-to-application communications
- Enterprise application integration

44.3.4.6 Data Management Services

Specific services include:

- Information and data access
- Transformation mapping
- Query distribution
- Aggregation
- Search
- File

Information access services provide the ability for an application to access an integrated view of data, regardless of whether the data exists in a mainframe system or in a distributed system. The information access services ensure that data integrity is maintained among multiple databases, and also provide online data cleansing (whereby data is checked against data rules for each access).

Data access services provide open interfaces to legacy data, provide new applications standard database access services to vast amounts of existing data, and provide standard access services to new data types.

44.3.4.7 Additional Operating System Services

Specific services include:

- Event brokering
- Workflow

These additional services enable the flow of information, as depicted in Figure 44-11.

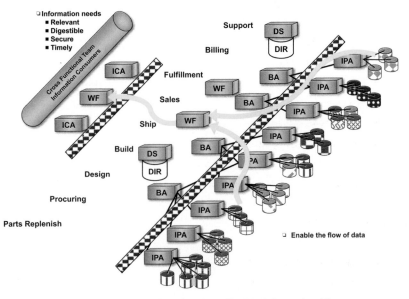

Figure 44-11 Workflow Services Enable Information Flow

Workflow denotes the concept of automating processes by facilitating user interactions and executing applications according to a process map. Workflow services enable integration of enterprise applications, resulting in applications of extended value.

Workflow services also address the needs of managing an environment where legacy systems are prevalent.

Workflow services also provide a means to encapsulate existing applications, thereby supporting customer needs for leverage of existing assets.

44.3.5 Qualities

The qualities component of the model is supported by quality of service services, including the various services required to maintain the quality of the system as specified in Service Level Agreements (SLAs).

Included in this are the services to post conditions to, and react to requests from, the Quality of Service Manager.

The Open Group Architecture Framework (TOGAF)

Part VII:

Architecture Capability Framework

The Open Group

Chapter 45: Introduction

This chapter provides an introduction to and an overview of the contents of Part VII: Architecture Capability Framework.

45.1   Overview

In order to successfully operate an architecture function within an enterprise, it is necessary to put in place appropriate organization structures, processes, roles, responsibilities, and skills to realize the architecture capability.

Part VII: Architecture Capability Framework provides a set of reference materials for how to establish such an architecture function. Readers should note that although this part contains a number of guidelines to support key activities, in its current form, the Architecture Capability Framework is not intended to be a comprehensive template for operating an enterprise architecture capability.

An overall structure for the Architecture Capability Framework is shown in Figure 45-1.

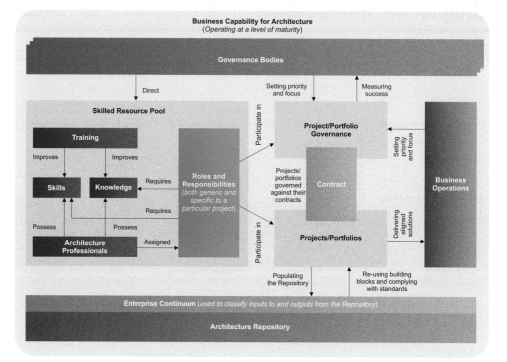

Figure 45-1 Mature Architecture Capability

45.2   Structure of Part VII

Part VII: Architecture Capability Framework is structured as follows:

- Introduction (this chapter)
- Establishing an Architecture Capability (see Chapter 46)
- Architecture Board (see Chapter 47)
- Architecture Compliance (see Chapter 48)
- Architecture Contracts (see Chapter 49)
- Architecture Governance (see Chapter 50)
- Architecture Maturity Models (see Chapter 51)
- Architecture Skills Framework (see Chapter 52)

Chapter 46: Establishing an Architecture Capability

This chapter provides guidelines on how to use the ADM to establish an architecture capability.

46.1 Overview

As with any business capability, the establishment of an enterprise architecture capability can be supported by the TOGAF Architecture Development Method (ADM). Successful use of the ADM will provide a customer-focused, value-adding, and sustainable architecture practice that enables the business, helps maximize the value of investments, and pro-actively identifies opportunities to gain business benefits and manage risk.

Establishing a sustainable architecture practice within an organization can be achieved by adhering to the same approach that is used to establish any other capability — such as a business process management capability — within an organization. The ADM is an ideal method to be used to architect and govern the implementation of such a capability. Applying the ADM with the specific Architecture Vision to establish an architecture practice within the organization would achieve this objective.

This shouldn't be seen as a phase of an architecture project, or a one-off project, but rather as an ongoing practice that provides the context, environment, and resources to govern and enable architecture delivery to the organization. As an architecture project is executed within this environment it might request a change to the architecture practice that would trigger another cycle of the ADM to extend the architecture practice.

Implementing any capability within an organization would require the design of the four domain architectures: Business, Data, Application, and Technology. Establishing the architecture practice within an organization would therefore require the design of:

- The **Business Architecture** of the architecture practice that will highlight the architecture governance, architecture processes, architecture organizational structure, architecture information requirements, architecture products, etc.

- The **Data Architecture** that would define the structure of the organization's Enterprise Continuum and Architecture Repository

- The **Application Architecture** specifying the functionality and/or applications services required to enable the architecture practice

- The **Technology Architecture** that depicts the architecture practice's infrastructure requirements and deployment in support of the architecture applications and Enterprise Continuum

The steps in establishing an architecture practice are explained below, against the context of the ADM phases. The reader should therefore refer to the relevant ADM phase in Part II: Architecture Development Method (ADM), to understand the complete scope of each step. In this section, key aspects will be highlighted for each ADM phase that should be considered and are specific to establishing an architecture practice. The intent is therefore not to repeat each ADM phase description, but to guide the reader to apply each ADM phase within the context of establishing an architecture practice.

46.2   Phase A: Architecture Vision

The purpose of this phase within the context of establishing an architecture practice is to define or review the vision, stakeholders, and principles of the architecture practice. The focus in this phase would be on the architecture practice as a whole and not on a particular architecture project.

The following should be considered in terms of understanding the steps in the context of establishing an architecture practice:

- **Establish the Project**: This step should focus on defining the stakeholders in the architecture practice. The stakeholders would include the roles and organization units participating in the architecture practice, as well as those that will benefit from the deliverables generated by the architecture practice that can therefore be defined as customers of the architecture practice.

- **Identify Stakeholders and Concerns, Business Requirements, and Architecture Vision**: This step generates the first, very high-level definitions of the baseline and target environments, from a business information systems and technology perspective for the architecture practice.

- **Identify Business Goals and Business Drivers**: This would be more relevant for the architecture practice than for a particular architecture project. An understanding of the business goals and drivers is essential to align the architecture practice to the business.

- **Define Scope**: Defining the scope of the architecture practice would be a high-level project plan of what should be addressed in terms of architecture for the next period.

- **Define Constraints**: The focus in this step should be on the enterprise-wide constraints that would impact on all architecture projects.

- **Review Architecture Principles, including Business Principles**: The intent in this step should be to define the principles that would govern and guide the running of the architecture practice. Where architecture principles usually govern the architecture deliverables, the architecture practice principles would address the architecture practice organization, content, tools, and process.

- **Develop Statement of Architecture Work and Secure Approval**: This step should generate the architecture practice vision and scope.

Another step that can be considered during this phase is to conduct an architecture maturity assessment. Refer to Chapter 51 for guidance on this topic.

46.3   Phase B: Business Architecture

Key areas of focus during this phase of establishing or refining the Business Architecture of the architecture practice are:

- An **Architecture Ontology** defining the architectural terms and definitions that will be used in the organization in order to establish a common understanding of these terms.

- The **Architecture Process** where the ADM would form the base of the process and need to be customized to meet the organization's requirements and architecture practice vision. Refer to Section 5.3 for guidance on developing this process. The required architecture governance processes should be included in the overall architecture process.

- The **Architecture Viewpoints and Views** that lists all the viewpoints and views that should be addressed by the architecture practice. The identified architecture practice stakeholders would guide the development of this definition. One of the viewpoints to be included is the architecture governance viewpoint; refer to Part IV, Chapter 35 for guidance on this output.

- The **Architecture Framework** describing the various architecture deliverables that will be generated by the architecture practice, the inter-relationships and dependencies between the architecture deliverables, as well as the rules and guidelines governing the design of these deliverables. The defined architecture viewpoints and views should be used to guide the definition of the architecture framework. Part II: Architecture Development Method (ADM) and Chapter 36 are useful references that will assist in describing the architecture framework.

- The **Architecture Accountability Matrix** defining the roles in the architecture practice and allocating accountability of the roles to architecture deliverables and processes. This matrix would include the required architecture governance structures and roles. Part II: Architecture Development Method (ADM) as well as Chapter 47, Chapter 50, and Chapter 52 would provide guidance on this output.

- The **Architecture Performance Metrics** identifying and describing the metrics that will be used to monitor the performance of the architecture practice against its stated architecture practice vision and objectives.

- The **Architecture Governance Framework** which is a specific view of the defined architecture process and Architecture Accountability Matrix.

46.4   Phase C: Information Systems Architecture — Data

The Data Architecture of the architecture practice would specify and govern the structure of the organization's Enterprise Continuum and Architecture Repository. The Data Architecture should be defined based on the architecture framework. The Data Architecture is sometimes referred to as the metamodel of the architecture practice.

46.5   Phase C: Information Systems Architecture — Application

The Application Architecture of the architecture practice defines the functionality required to generate, maintain, publish, distribute, and govern the architecture deliverables as defined in the architecture framework. A key focus should be on the modeling toolsets required for modeling, but it should not be the only focus. Refer to Chapter 42 for guidance on selecting a toolset. Publishing the architecture deliverables to address specific views in the architecture framework would sometimes require specialized or customized functionality and should not be neglected.

46.6   Phase D: Technology Architecture

The Technology Architecture of the architecture practice should define technology infrastructure supporting the architecture practice.

46.7   Phase E: Opportunities & Solutions

A critical factor to consider during this phase of planning the establishment of the architecture practice is the organizational change that is required and how this will be achieved.

46.8   Phase F: Migration Planning

The focus should not only be on the Information Systems Architecture components in this phase, but include the Business Architecture. The adoption of the architecture process and framework will have a major impact on the overall establishment of the architecture practice in the organization.

46.9   Phase G: Implementation Governance

The implementation of the Business Architecture of the architecture practice should be the focus of this phase. Changing practices within the organization to adopt a more structured and disciplined approach will be a challenge and should be addressed by the appropriate organizational change techniques.

46.10   Phase H: Architecture Change Management

Changes to the architecture of the architecture practice should be managed by this phase. These changes are usually triggered during the execution of architecture projects. A typical change would be the requirement for a new architecture deliverable. This would impact on all the architecture domains of the architecture practice.

46.11   Requirements Management

Understanding and managing the requirements for the architecture practice is crucial. Requirements should be clearly articulated and align to the architecture practice vision.

Chapter 47: Architecture Board

This chapter provides guidelines for establishing and operating an Enterprise Architecture Board.

47.1 Role

A key element in a successful architecture governance strategy (see Chapter 50) is a cross-organization Architecture Board to oversee the implementation of the strategy. This body should be representative of all the key stakeholders in the architecture, and will typically comprise a group of executives responsible for the review and maintenance of the overall architecture.

The costs of establishing and operating an Architecture Board are more than offset by the savings that accrue as a result of preventing one-off solutions and unconstrained developments across the enterprise, which invariably lead to:

- High costs of development
- High costs of operation and support:
    - Numerous run-time environments
    - Numerous implementation languages
    - Numerous interfaces and protocols ...
- Lower quality
- Higher risk
- Difficulty in replicating and re-using solutions

Architecture Boards may have global, regional, or business line scope. Particularly in larger enterprises, Architecture Boards typically comprise representatives from the organization at a minimum of two levels:

- Local (domain experts, line responsibility)
- Global (organization-wide responsibility)

In such cases, each board will be established with identifiable and articulated:

- Responsibilities and decision-making capabilities
- Remit and authority limits

47.2 Responsibilities

The Architecture Board is typically made responsible, and accountable, for achieving some or all of the following goals:

- Consistency between sub-architectures
- Identifying re-usable components
- Flexibility of enterprise architecture:
    - To meet changing business needs
    - To leverage new technologies
- Enforcement of Architecture Compliance
- Improving the maturity level of architecture discipline within the organization
- Ensuring that the discipline of architecture-based development is adopted
- Providing the basis for all decision-making with regard to changes to the architectures
- Supporting a visible escalation capability for out-of-bounds decisions

Further responsibilities from an operational perspective should include:

- All aspects of monitoring and control of the Architecture Contract
- Meeting on a regular basis
- Ensuring the effective and consistent management and implementation of the architectures
- Resolving ambiguities, issues, or conflicts that have been escalated
- Providing advice, guidance, and information
- Ensuring compliance with the architectures, and granting dispensations that are in keeping with the technology strategy and objectives
- Considering policy (schedule, Service Level Agreements (SLAs), etc.) changes where similar dispensations are requested and granted; e.g., new form of service requirement
- Ensuring that all information relevant to the implementation of the Architecture Contract is published under controlled conditions and made available to authorized parties
- Validation of reported service levels, cost savings, etc.

From a governance perspective, the Architecture Board is also responsible for:

- The production of usable governance material and activities
- Providing a mechanism for the formal acceptance and approval of architecture through consensus and authorized publication
- Providing a fundamental control mechanism for ensuring the effective implementation of the architecture
- Establishing and maintaining the link between the implementation of the architecture, the architectural strategy and objectives embodied in the enterprise architecture, and the strategic objectives of the business

■ Identifying divergence from the architecture and planning activities for realignment through dispensations or policy updates

47.3   Setting Up the Architecture Board

47.3.1   Triggers

One or more of the following occurrences typically triggers the establishment of an Architecture Board:

■ New CIO

■ Merger or acquisition

■ Consideration of a move to newer forms of computing

■ Recognition that IT is poorly aligned to business

■ Desire to achieve competitive advantage via technology

■ Creation of an enterprise architecture program

■ Significant business change or rapid growth

■ Requirement for complex, cross-functional solutions

In many companies, the executive sponsor of the initial architecture effort is the CIO (or other senior executive). However, to gain broad corporate support, a sponsoring body has more influence. This sponsoring body is here called an Architecture Board, but the title is not important. Whatever the name, it is the executive-level group responsible for the review and maintenance of the strategic architecture and all of its sub-architectures.

The Architecture Board is the sponsor of the architecture within the enterprise, but the Architecture Board itself needs an executive sponsor from the highest level of the corporation. This commitment must span the planning process and continue into the maintenance phase of the architecture project. In many companies that fail in an architecture planning effort, there is a notable lack of executive participation and encouragement for the project.

A frequently overlooked source of Architecture Board members is the company's Board of Directors. These individuals invariably have diverse knowledge about the business and its competition. Because they have a significant impact on the business vision and objectives, they may be successful in validating the alignment of IT strategies to business objectives.

47.3.2   Size of the Board

The recommended size for an Architecture Board is four or five (and no more than ten) permanent members.

In order to keep the Architecture Board to a reasonable size, while ensuring enterprise-wide representation on it over time, membership of the Architecture Board may be rotated, giving decision-making privileges and responsibilities to various senior managers. This may be required in any case, due to some Architecture Board members finding that time constraints prevent long-term active participation.

However, some continuity must exist on the Architecture Board, to prevent the corporate architecture from varying from one set of ideas to another. One technique for ensuring rotation with continuity is to have set terms for the members, and to have the terms expire at different times.

In the ongoing architecture process following the initial architecture effort, the Architecture Board may be re-chartered. The executive sponsor will normally review the work of the Architecture Board and evaluate its effectiveness; if necessary, the Architecture Compliance review process is updated or changed.

47.3.3 Board Structure

The TOGAF Architecture Governance Framework (see Section 50.2) provides a generic organizational framework that positions the Architecture Board in the context of the broader governance structures of the enterprise. This structure identifies the major organizational groups and responsibilities, as well as the relationship between each group. This is a best practice structure, and may be subject to change depending on the organization's form and existing structures.

Consideration must be given to the size of the organization, its form, and how the IT functions are implemented. This will provide the basis for designing the Architecture Board structure within the context of the overall governance environment. In particular, consideration should be given to the concept of global ownership and local implementation, and the integration of new concepts and technologies from all areas implementing against architectures.

The structure of the Architecture Board should reflect the form of the organization. The architecture governance structure required may well go beyond the generic structures outlined in the TOGAF Architecture Governance Framework (see Section 50.2). The organization may need to define a combination of the IT governance process in place and the existing organizational structures and capabilities, which typically include the following types of body:

- Global governance board
- Local governance board
- Design authorities
- Working parties

47.4 Operation of the Architecture Board

This section describes the operation of the Architecture Board particularly from the governance perspective.

47.4.1 General

Architecture Board meetings should be conducted within clearly identified agendas with explicit objectives, content coverage, and defined actions. In general, board meetings will be aligned with best practice, such as given in the COBIT framework (see Section 50.1.4.1).

These meetings will provide key direction in:

- Supporting the production of quality governance material and activities
- Providing a mechanism for formal acceptance through consensus and authorized publication
- Providing a fundamental control mechanism for ensuring the effective implementation of the architectures
- Establishing and maintaining the link between the implementation of the architectures and the stated strategy and objectives of the organization (business and IT)
- Identifying divergence from the contract and planning activities to realign with the contract through dispensations or policy updates

47.4.2 Preparation

Each participant will receive an agenda and any supporting documentation — e.g., dispensation requests, performance management reports, etc. — and will be expected to be familiar with the contents of each.

Where actions have been allocated to an individual, it is that person's responsibility to report on progress against these.

Each participant must confirm their availability and attendance at the Architecture Board meeting.

47.4.3 Agenda

This section outlines the contents of a Architecture Board meeting agenda. Each agenda item is described in terms of its content only.

Minutes of Previous Meeting

Minutes contain the details of previous Architecture Board meeting as per standard organizational protocol.

Requests for Change

Items under this heading are normally change requests for amendments to architectures, principles, etc., but may also include business control with regard to Architecture Contracts; e.g., ensure that voice traffic to premium numbers, such as weather reports, are barred and data traffic to certain web sites is controlled.

Any request for change is made within agreed authority levels and parameters defined by the Architecture Contract.

Dispensations

A dispensation is used as the mechanism to request a change to the existing architectures, contracts, principles, etc. outside of normal operating parameters; e.g., exclude provision of service to a subsidiary, request for unusual service levels for specific business reasons, deploy non-standard technology or products to support specific business initiatives.

Dispensations are granted for a given time period and set of identified services and operational criteria that must be enforced during the lifespan of the dispensation. Dispensations are not granted indefinitely, but are used as a mechanism to ensure that service levels and operational levels, etc. are met while providing a level flexibility in their implementation and timing. The time-bound nature of dispensations ensures that they are a trigger to the Architecture Compliance activity.

Compliance Assessments

Compliance is assessed against SLAs, Operational Level Agreements (OLAs), cost targets, and required architecture refreshes. These assessments will be reviewed and either accepted or rejected depending on the criteria defined within the Architecture Governance Framework. The Architecture Compliance assessment report will include details as described.

Dispute Resolution

Disputes that have not been resolved through the Architecture Compliance and dispensation processes are identified here for further action and are documented through the Architecture Compliance assessments and dispensation documentation.

Architecture Strategy and Direction Documentation

This describes the architecture strategies, direction, and priorities and will only be formulated by the global Architecture Board. It should take the form of standard architecture documentation.

Actions Assigned

This is a report on the actions assigned at previous Architecture Board meetings. An action tracker is used to document and keep the status of all actions assigned during the Architecture Board meetings and should consist of at least the following information:

- Reference
- Priority
- Action description
- Action owner
- Action details
- Date raised
- Due date
- Status
- Type
- Resolution date

Contract Documentation Management

This is a formal acceptance of updates and changes to architecture documentation for onward publication.

Any Other Business (AOB)

Description of issues not directly covered under any of the above. These may not be described in the agenda but should be raised at the beginning of the meeting. Any supporting documentation must be managed as per all architecture governance documentation.

Schedule of Meetings

All meeting dates detail should be detailed and published.

Chapter 48: Architecture Compliance

This chapter provides guidelines for ensuring project compliance to the architecture.

48.1 Introduction

Ensuring the compliance of individual projects with the enterprise architecture is an essential aspect of architecture governance (see Chapter 50). To this end, the IT governance function within an enterprise will normally define two complementary processes:

- The **Architecture** function will be required to prepare a series of Project Architectures; i.e., project-specific views of the enterprise architecture that illustrate how the enterprise architecture impacts on the major projects within the organization. (See ADM Phases A to F.)

- The **IT Governance** function will define a formal Architecture Compliance review process (see Section 48.3) for reviewing the compliance of projects to the enterprise architecture.

Apart from defining formal processes, the architecture governance (see Chapter 50) function may also stipulate that the architecture function should extend beyond the role of architecture definition and standards selection, and participate also in the technology selection process, and even in the commercial relationships involved in external service provision and product purchases. This may help to minimize the opportunity for misinterpretation of the enterprise architecture, and maximize the value of centralized commercial negotiation.

48.2 Terminology: The Meaning of Architecture Compliance

A key relationship between the architecture and the implementation lies in the definitions of the terms "conformant", "compliant", etc. While terminology usage may differ between organizations, the concepts of levels of conformance illustrated in Figure 48-1 should prove useful in formulating an IT compliance strategy.

Irrelevant:
The implementation has no features in common with the architecture specification (so the question of conformance does not arise).

Consistent:
The implementation has some features in common with the architecture specification, and those common features are implemented in accordance with the specification. However, some features in the architecture specification are not implemented, and the implementation has other features that are not covered by the specification.

Compliant:
Some features in the architecture specification are not implemented, but all features implemented are covered by the specification, and in accordance with it.

Conformant:
All the features in the architecture specification are implemented in accordance with the specification, but some more features are implemented that are not in accordance with it.

Fully Conformant:
There is full correspondence between architecture specification and implementation. All specified features are implemented in accordance with the specification, and there are no features implemented that are not covered by the specification.

Non-conformant:
Any of the above in which some features in the architecture specification are implemented not in accordance with the specification.

Figure 48-1 Levels of Architecture Conformance

The phrase "In accordance with" in Figure 48-1 means:

- Supports the stated strategy and future directions
- Adheres to the stated standards (including syntax and semantic rules specified)
- Provides the stated functionality
- Adheres to the stated principles; for example:
  — Open wherever possible and appropriate
  — Re-use of component building blocks wherever possible and appropriate

48.3   Architecture Compliance Reviews

An Architecture Compliance review is a scrutiny of the compliance of a specific project against established architectural criteria, spirit, and business objectives. A formal process for such reviews normally forms the core of an enterprise Architecture Compliance strategy.

48.3.1   Purpose

The goals of an Architecture Compliance review include some or all of the following:

- First and foremost, catch errors in the project architecture early, and thereby reduce the cost and risk of changes required later in the lifecycle. This in turn means that the overall project time is shortened, and that the business gets the bottom-line benefit of the architecture development faster.

- Ensure the application of best practices to architecture work.

- Provide an overview of the compliance of an architecture to mandated enterprise standards.

- Identify where the standards themselves may require modification.

- Identify services that are currently application-specific but might be provided as part of the enterprise infrastructure.

- Document strategies for collaboration, resource sharing, and other synergies across multiple architecture teams.

- Take advantage of advances in technology.

- Communicate to management the status of technical readiness of the project.

- Identify key criteria for procurement activities (e.g., for inclusion in Commercial Off-The-Shelf (COTS) product RFI/RFP documents).

- Identify and communicate significant architectural gaps to product and service providers.

Apart from the generic goals related to quality assurance outlined above, there are additional, more politically-oriented motivations for conducting Architecture Compliance reviews, which may be relevant in particular cases:

- The Architecture Compliance review can be a good way of deciding between architectural alternatives, since the business decision-makers typically involved in the review can guide decisions in terms of what is best for the business, as opposed to what is technically more pleasing or elegant.

- The output of the Architecture Compliance review is one of the few measurable deliverables to the CIO to assist in decision-making.

- Architecture reviews can serve as a way for the architecture organization to engage with development projects that might otherwise proceed without involvement of the architecture function.

- Architecture reviews can demonstrate rapid and positive support to the enterprise business community:

— The enterprise architecture and Architecture Compliance helps ensure the alignment of IT projects with business objectives.

— Architects can sometimes be regarded as being deep into technical infrastructure and far removed from the core business.

— Since an Architecture Compliance review tends to look primarily at the critical risk areas of a system, it often highlights the main risks for system owners.

While compliance to architecture is required for development and implementation, non-compliance also provides a mechanism for highlighting:

- Areas to be addressed for realignment

- Areas for consideration for integration into the architectures as they are uncovered by the compliance processes

The latter point identifies the ongoing change and adaptability of the architectures to requirements that may be driven by indiscipline, but also allows for changes to be registered by faster moving changes in the operational environment. Typically dispensations (see Section 50.1.4) will be used to highlight these changes and set in motion a process for registering, monitoring, and assessing the suitability of any changes required.

48.3.2 Timing

Timing of compliance activities should be considered with regard to the development of the architectures themselves.

Compliance reviews are held at appropriate project milestones or checkpoints in the project's lifecycle. Specific checkpoints should be included as follows:

- Development of the architecture itself (ADM compliance)

- Implementation of the architecture(s) (architecture compliance)

Architecture project timings for assessments should include:

- Project initiation

- Initial design

- Major design changes

- *Ad hoc*

The Architecture Compliance review is typically targeted for a point in time when business requirements and the enterprise architecture are reasonably firm, and the project architecture is taking shape, well before its completion.

The aim is to hold the review as soon as practical, at a stage when there is still time to correct any major errors or shortcomings, with the obvious proviso that there needs to have been some significant development of the project architecture in order for there to be something to review.

Inputs to the Architecture Compliance review may come from other parts of the standard project lifecycle, which may have an impact on timing.

48.3.3　Governance and Personnel Scenarios

In terms of the governance and conduct of the Architecture Compliance review, and the personnel involved, there are various possible scenarios:

- For smaller-scale projects, the review process could simply take the form of a series of questions that the project architects or project leaders pose to themselves, using the checklists provided below, perhaps collating the answers into some form of project report to management. The need to conduct such a process is normally included in overall enterprise-wide IT governance policies.

- Where the project under review has not involved a practicing or full-time architect to date (for example, in an application-level project), the purpose of the review is typically to bring to bear the architectural expertise of an enterprise architecture function. In such a case, the enterprise architecture function would be organizing, leading, and conducting the review, with the involvement of business domain experts. In such a scenario, the review is not a substitute for the involvement of architects in a project, but it can be a supplement or a guide to their involvement. It is probable that a database will be necessary to manage the volume of data that would be produced in the analysis of a large system or set of systems.

- In most cases, particularly in larger-scale projects, the architecture function will have been deeply involved in, and perhaps leading, the development project under review. (This is the typical TOGAF scenario.) In such cases, the review will be co-ordinated by the lead enterprise architect, who will assemble a team of business and technical domain experts for the review, and compile the answers to the questions posed during the review into some form of report. The questions will typically be posed during the review by the business and technical domain experts. Alternatively, the review might be led by a representative of an Architecture Board or some similar body with enterprise-wide responsibilities.

In all cases, the Architecture Compliance review process needs the backing of senior management, and will typically be mandated as part of corporate architecture governance policies (see Chapter 50). Normally, the enterprise CIO or enterprise Architecture Board (see Chapter 47) will mandate architecture reviews for all major projects, with subsequent annual reviews.

48.4　Architecture Compliance Review Process

48.4.1　Overview

The Architecture Compliance review process is illustrated in Figure 48-2.

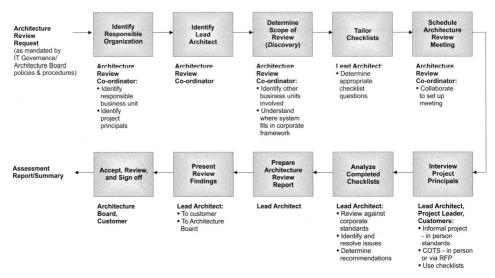

Figure 48-2 Architecture Compliance Review Process

48.4.2 Roles

The main roles in the process are tabulated below.

No.	Role	Responsibilities	Notes
1	Architecture Board	To ensure that IT architectures are consistent and support overall business needs.	Sponsor and monitor architecture activities.
2	Project Leader (or Project Board)	Responsible for the whole project.	
3	Architecture Review Co-ordinator	To administer the whole architecture development and review process.	More likely to be business-oriented than technology-oriented.
4	Lead Enterprise Architect	To ensure that the architecture is technically coherent and future-proof.	An IT architecture specialist.
5	Architect	One of the Lead Enterprise Architect's technical assistants.	
6	Customer	To ensure that business requirements are clearly expressed and understood.	Manages that part of the organization that will depend on the success of the IT described in the architecture.
7	Business Domain Expert	To ensure that the processes to satisfy the business requirements are justified and understood.	Knows how the business domain operates; may also be the customer.
8	Project Principals	To ensure that the architects have a sufficiently detailed understanding of the customer department's processes. They can provide input to the business domain expert or to the architects.	Members of the customer's organization who have input to the business requirements that the architecture is to address.

48.4.3 Steps

The main steps in the process are tabulated below.

No.	Action	Notes	Who
1	Request architecture review	As mandated by IT governance policies and procedures.	Anyone, whether IT or business oriented, with an interest in or responsibility for the business area affected.
2	Identify responsible part of organization and relevant project principals.		Architecture Review Co-ordinator
3	Identify Lead Enterprise Architect and other architects.		Architecture Review Co-ordinator
4	Determine scope of review	Identify which other business units/departments are involved. Understand where the system fits in the corporate architecture framework.	Architecture Review Co-ordinator
5	Tailor checklists.	To address the business requirements.	Lead Enterprise Architect
6	Schedule Architecture Review Meeting		Architecture Review Co-ordinator with collaboration of Lead Enterprise Architect.
7	Interview project principals	To get background and technical information: ■ For internal project: in person ■ For COTS: in person or via RFP Use checklists.	Lead Enterprise Architect and/or Architect, Project Leader, and Customers
8	Analyze completed checklists	Review against corporate standards. Identify and resolve issues. Determine recommendations.	Lead Enterprise Architect
9	Prepare Architecture Compliance review report	May involve supporting staff.	Lead Enterprise Architect
10	Present review findings	To Customer To Architecture Board	Lead Enterprise Architect
11	Accept review and sign off		Architecture Board and Customer
12	Send assessment report/summary to Architecture Review Co-ordinator		Lead Enterprise Architect

48.5   Architecture Compliance Review Checklists

The following review checklists provide a wide range of typical questions that may be used in conducting Architecture Compliance reviews, relating to various aspects of the architecture. The organization of the questions includes the basic disciplines of system engineering, information management, security, and systems management. The checklists are based on material provided by a member of The Open Group, and are specific to that organization. Other organizations could use the following checklists with other questions tailored to their own particular needs.

The checklists provided contain too many questions for any single review: they are intended to be tailored selectively to the project concerned (see Section 48.6). The checklists actually used will typically be developed/selected by subject matter experts. They are intended to be updated annually by interest groups in those areas.

Some of the checklists include a brief description of the architectural principle that provokes the question, and a brief description of what to look for in the answer. These extensions to the checklist are intended to allow the intelligent re-phrasing of the questions, and to give the user of the checklist a feel for why the question is being asked.

Occasionally the questions will be written, as in RFPs, or in working with a senior project architect. More typically they are expressed orally, as part of an interview or working session with the project.

The checklists provided here are designed for use in individual architecture projects, not for business domain architecture or for architecture across multiple projects. (Doing an architecture review for a larger sphere of activity, across multiple business processes and system projects, would involve a similar process, but the checklist categories and their contents would be different.)

48.5.1   Hardware and Operating System Checklist

1. What is the project's lifecycle approach?

2. At what stage is the project in its lifecycle?

3. What key issues have been identified or analyzed that the project believes will drive evaluations of hardware and operating systems for networks, servers, and end-user devices?

4. What system capabilities will involve high-volume and/or high-frequency data transfers?

5. How does the system design impact or involve end-user devices?

6. What is the quantity and distribution (regional and global) of usage, data storage, and processing?

7. What applications are affinitized with your project by similarities in data, application services, etc.? To what degree is data affinitized with your project?

8. What hardware and operating system choices have been made before functional design of key elements of the system?

9. If hardware and operating system decisions were made outside of the project's control:

— What awareness does the project have of the rationale for those decisions?

— How can the project influence those decisions as system design takes shape?

10. If some non-standards have been chosen:

    — What are the essential business and technical requirements for not using corporate standards?

    — Is this supported by a business case?

    — Have the assumptions in the business case been subject to scrutiny?

11. What is your process for evaluating full lifecycle costs of hardware and operating systems?

12. How has corporate financial management been engaged in evaluation of lifecycle costs?

13. Have you performed a financial analysis of the supplier?

14. Have you made commitments to any supplier?

15. Do you believe your requirements can be met by only one supplier?

48.5.2 Software Services and Middleware Checklist

1. Describe how error conditions are defined, raised, and propagated between application components.

2. Describe the general pattern of how methods are defined and arranged in various application modules.

3. Describe the general pattern for how method parameters are defined and organized in various application modules. Are [in], [in/out], [out] parameters always specified in the same order? Do Boolean values returned by modules have a consistent outcome?

4. Describe the approach that is used to minimize the number of round-trips between client and server calls, particularly for out-of-process calls, and when complex data structures are involved.

5. Describe the major data structures that are passed between major system components.

6. Describe the major communication protocols that are used between major system components.

7. Describe the marshaling techniques that are used between various system components. Describe any specialized marshaling arrangements that are used.

8. Describe to what extent the system is designed with stateful and stateless components.

9. Describe how and when state is saved for both stateful and stateless components.

10. Describe the extent to which objects are created, used, and destroyed *versus* re-used through object pooling.

11. Describe the extent to which the system relies on threading or critical section coding.

12. Describe the approach and the internal documentation that is used internally in the system to document the methods, methods arguments, and method functionality.

13. Describe the code review process that was used to build the system.

14. Describe the unit testing that has been used to test the system components.

15. Describe the pre- and post-condition testing that is included in various system modules.

16. Describe the assertion testing that is included with the system.

17. Do components support all the interface types they need to support or are certain assumptions made about what types of components will call other components either in terms of language bindings or other forms of marshaling?

18. Describe the extent to which big-endian or little-endian data format problems need to be handled across different platforms.

19. Describe if numbers or strings need to be handled differently across different platforms.

20. Describe whether the software needs to check for floating-point round-off errors.

21. Describe how time and data functions are Year 2000-compliant.

22. Describe what tools or processes have been used to test the system for memory leaks, reachability, or general robustness.

23. Describe the layering of the systems services software. Describe the general number of links between major system components. Is the system composed of a lot of point-to-point interfaces or are major messaging backbones used instead?

24. Describe to what extent the system components are either loosely coupled or tightly coupled.

25. What requirements does the system need from the infrastructure in terms of shared libraries, support for communication protocols, load balancing, transaction processing, system monitoring, naming services, or other infrastructure services?

26. Describe how the system and system components are designed for refactoring.

27. Describe how the system or system components rely on common messaging infrastructure *versus* a unique point-to-point communication structure.

48.5.3 Applications Checklists

48.5.3.1 Infrastructure (Enterprise Productivity) Applications

1. Is there need for capabilities that are not provided through the enterprise's standard infrastructure application products? For example:

   ▪ Collaboration

     — Application sharing

     — Video conferencing

     — Calendaring

     — Email

   ▪ Workflow management

- Publishing/word processing applications
  - HTML
  - SGML and XML
  - Portable document format
  - Document processing (proprietary format)
  - Desktop publishing
- Spreadsheet applications
- Presentation applications
  - Business presentations
  - Image
  - Animation
  - Video
  - Sound
  - CBT
  - Web browsers
- Data management applications
  - Database interface
  - Document management
  - Product data management
  - Data warehouses/mart
- Program management applications
  - Project management
  - Program visibility

2. Describe the business requirements for enterprise infrastructure application capabilities that are not met by the standard products.

48.5.3.2 Business Applications

1. Are any of the capabilities required provided by standard products supporting one or more line-of-business applications? For example:
   - Business acquisition applications
     - Sales and marketing
   - Engineering applications
     - Computer-aided design

- — Computer-aided engineering
- — Mathematical and statistics analysis
- Supplier management applications
  - — Supply chain management
  - — Customer relationship management
- Manufacturing applications
  - — Enterprise Resource Planning (ERP) applications
  - — Manufacturing execution systems
  - — Manufacturing quality
  - — Manufacturing process engineering
  - — Machine and adaptive control
- Customer support applications
  - — Airline logistics support
  - — Maintenance engineering
- Finance applications
- People applications
- Facilities applications
- Information systems applications
  - — Systems engineering
  - — Software engineering
  - — Web developer tools
  - — Integrated development environments
  - — Lifecycle categories
  - — Functional categories
  - — Specialty categories
- Computer-aided manufacturing
- e-Business enablement
- Business process engineering
  - — Statistical quality control

2. Describe the process requirements for business application capabilities that are not met by the standard products.

48.5.3.3　Application Integration Approach

1. What integration points (business process/activity, application, data, computing environment) are targeted by this architecture?

2. What application integration techniques will be applied (common business objects [ORBs], standard data definitions [STEP, XML, etc.], common user interface presentation/desktop)?

48.5.4　Information Management Checklists

48.5.4.1　Data Values

1. What are the processes that standardize the management and use of the data?

2. What business process supports the entry and validation of the data? Use of the data?

3. What business actions correspond to the creation and modification of the data?

4. What business actions correspond to the deletion of the data and is it considered part of a business record?

5. What are the data quality requirements required by the business user?

6. What processes are in place to support data referential integrity and/or normalization?

48.5.4.2　Data Definition

1. What are the data model, data definitions, structure, and hosting options of purchased applications (COTS)?

2. What are the rules for defining and maintaining the data requirements and designs for all components of the information system?

3. What shareable repository is used to capture the model content and the supporting information for data?

4. What is the physical data model definition (derived from logical data models) used to design the database?

5. What software development and data management tools have been selected?

6. What data owners have been identified to be responsible for common data definitions, eliminating unplanned redundancy, providing consistently reliable, timely, and accurate information, and protecting data from misuse and destruction?

48.5.4.3　Security/Protection

1. What are the data entity and attribute access rules which protect the data from unintentional and unauthorized alterations, disclosure, and distribution?

2. What are the data protection mechanisms to protect data from unauthorized external access?

3. What are the data protection mechanisms to control access to data from external sources that temporarily have internal residence within the enterprise?

48.5.4.4 Hosting, Data Types, and Sharing

1. What is the discipline for managing sole-authority data as one logical source with defined updating rules for physical data residing on different platforms?

2. What is the discipline for managing replicated data, which is derived from operational sole-authority data?

3. What tier data server has been identified for the storage of high or medium-critical operational data?

4. What tier data server has been identified for the storage of type C operational data?

5. What tier data server has been identified for the storage of decision support data contained in a data warehouse?

6. What Database Management Systems (DBMSs) have been implemented?

48.5.4.5 Common Services

1. What are the standardized distributed data management services (e.g., validation, consistency checks, data edits, encryption, and transaction management) and where do they reside?

48.5.4.6 Access Method

1. What are the data access requirements for standard file, message, and data management?

2. What are the access requirements for decision support data?

3. What are the data storage and the application logic locations?

4. What query language is being used?

48.5.5 Security Checklist

1. **Security Awareness**: Have you ensured that the corporate security policies and guidelines to which you are designing are the latest versions? Have you read them? Are you aware of all relevant computing security compliance and risk acceptance processes? (Interviewer should list all relevant policies and guidelines.)

2. **Identification/Authentication**: Diagram the process flow of how a user is identified to the application and how the application authenticates that the user is who they claim to be. Provide supporting documentation to the diagram explaining the flow from the user interface to the application/database server(s) and back to the user. Are you compliant with corporate policies on accounts, passwords, etc.?

3. **Authorization**: Provide a process flow from beginning to end showing how a user requests access to the application, indicating the associated security controls and separation of duties. This should include how the request is approved by the appropriate data owner, how the user is placed into the appropriate access-level classification profile, how the user ID, password, and access is created and provided to the user. Also include how the user is informed of their responsibilities associated with using the application, given a copy of the access agreement, how to change password, who to call for help, etc.

4. **Access Controls**: Document how the user IDs, passwords, and access profiles are added, changed, removed, and documented. The documentation should include who is responsible for these processes.

5. **Sensitive Information Protection**: Provide documentation that identifies sensitive data requiring additional protection. Identify the data owners responsible for this data and the process to be used to protect storage, transmission, printing, and distribution of this data. Include how the password file/field is protected. How will users be prevented from viewing someone else's sensitive information? Are there agreements with outside parties (partners, suppliers, contractors, etc.) concerning the safeguarding of information? If so, what are the obligations?

6. **Audit Trails and Audit Logs**: Identify and document group accounts required by the users or application support, including operating system group accounts. Identify and document individual accounts and/or roles that have superuser type privileges, what these privileges are, who has access to these accounts, how access to these accounts is controlled, tracked, and logged, and how password change and distribution are handled, including operating system accounts. Also identify audit logs, who can read the audit logs, who can modify the audit logs, who can delete the audit logs, and how the audit logs are protected and stored. Is the user ID obscured in the audit trails?

7. **External Access Considerations**: Will the application be used internally only? If not, are you compliant with corporate external access requirements?

48.5.6 System Management Checklist

1. What is the frequency of software changes that must be distributed?
2. What tools are used for software distribution?
3. Are multiple software and/or data versions allowed in production?
4. What is the user data backup frequency and expected restore time?
5. How are user accounts created and managed?
6. What is the system license management strategy?
7. What general system administration tools are required?
8. What specific application administration tools are required?
9. What specific service administration tools are required?
10. How are service calls received and dispatched?
11. Describe how the system is uninstalled.
12. Describe the process or tools available for checking that the system is properly installed.
13. Describe tools or instrumentation that are available that monitor the health and performance of the system.
14. Describe the tools or process in place that can be used to determine where the system has been installed.

15. Describe what form of audit logs are in place to capture system history, particularly after a mishap.

16. Describe the capabilities of the system to dispatch its own error messages to service personnel.

48.5.7 System Engineering/Overall Architecture Checklists

48.5.7.1 General

1. What other applications and/or systems require integration with yours?

2. Describe the integration level and strategy with each.

3. How geographically distributed is the user base?

4. What is the strategic importance of this system to other user communities inside or outside the enterprise?

5. What computing resources are needed to provide system service to users inside the enterprise? Outside the enterprise and using enterprise computing assets? Outside the enterprise and using their own assets?

6. How can users outside the native delivery environment access your applications and data?

7. What is the life expectancy of this application?

8. Describe the design that accommodates changes in the user base, stored data, and delivery system technology.

9. What is the size of the user base and their expected performance level?

10. What performance and stress test techniques do you use?

11. What is the overall organization of the software and data components?

12. What is the overall service and system configuration?

13. How are software and data configured and mapped to the service and system configuration?

14. What proprietary technology (hardware and software) is needed for this system?

15. Describe how each and every version of the software can be reproduced and re-deployed over time.

16. Describe the current user base and how that base is expected to change over the next three to five years.

17. Describe the current geographic distribution of the user base and how that base is expected to change over the next three to five years.

18. Describe how many current or future users need to use the application in a mobile capacity or who need to work off-line.

19. Describe what the application generally does, the major components of the application, and the major data flows.

20. Describe the instrumentation included in the application that allows for the health and performance of the application to be monitored.

21. Describe the business justification for the system.

22. Describe the rationale for picking the system development language over other options in terms of initial development cost *versus* long-term maintenance cost.

23. Describe the systems analysis process that was used to come up with the system architecture and product selection phase of the system architecture.

24. Who besides the original customer might have a use for or benefit from using this system?

25. What percentage of the users use the system in browse mode *versus* update mode?

26. What is the typical length of requests that are transactional?

27. Do you need guaranteed data delivery or update, or does the system tolerate failure?

28. What are the up-time requirements of the system?

29. Describe where the system architecture adheres or does not adhere to standards.

30. Describe the project planning and analysis approach used on the project.

48.5.7.2   Processors/Servers/Clients

1. Describe the client/server Application Architecture.

2. Annotate the pictorial to illustrate where application functionality is executed.

48.5.7.3   Client

1. Are functions other than presentation performed on the user device?

2. Describe the data and process help facility being provided.

3. Describe the screen-to-screen navigation technique.

4. Describe how the user navigates between this and other applications.

5. How is this and other applications launched from the user device?

6. Are there any inter-application data and process sharing capabilities? If so, describe what is being shared and by what technique/technology.

7. Describe data volumes being transferred to the client.

8. What are the additional requirements for local data storage to support the application?

9. What are the additional requirements for local software storage/memory to support the application?

10. Are there any known hardware/software conflicts or capacity limitations caused by other application requirements or situations which would affect the application users?

11. Describe how the look-and-feel of your presentation layer compares to the look-and-feel of the other existing applications.

12. Describe to what extent the client needs to support asynchronous and/or synchronous communication.

13. Describe how the presentation layer of the system is separated from other computational or data transfer layers of the system.

48.5.7.4 Application Server

1. Can/do the presentation layer and application layers run on separate processors?

2. Can/do the application layer and data access layer run on separate processors?

3. Can this application be placed on an application server independent of all other applications? If not, explain the dependencies.

4. Can additional parallel application servers be easily added? If so, what is the load balancing mechanism?

5. Has the resource demand generated by the application been measured and what is the value? If so, has the capacity of the planned server been confirmed at the application and aggregate levels?

48.5.7.5 Data Server

1. Are there other applications which must share the data server? If so, identify them and describe the data and data access requirements.

2. Has the resource demand generated by the application been measured and what is the value? If so, has the capacity of the planned server been confirmed at the application and aggregate levels?

48.5.7.6 COTS (where applicable)

1. Is the vendor substantial and stable?

2. Will the enterprise receive source code upon demise of the vendor?

3. Is this software configured for the enterprise's usage?

4. Is there any peculiar A&D data or processes that would impede the use of this software?

   — Is this software currently available?

5. Has it been used/demonstrated for volume/availability/service-level requirements similar to those of the enterprise?

   — Describe the past financial and market share history of the vendor.

48.5.8 System Engineering/Methods & Tools Checklist

1. Do metrics exist for the current way of doing business?

2. Has the system owner created evaluation criteria that will be used to guide the project? Describe how the evaluation criteria will be used.

3. Has research of existing architectures been done to leverage existing work? Describe the method used to discover and understand. Will the architectures be integrated? If so, explain the method that will be used.

4. Describe the methods that will be used on the project:

   — For defining business strategies

   — For defining areas in need of improvement

   — For defining baseline and target business processes

   — For defining transition processes

   — For managing the project

   — For team communication

   — For knowledge management, change management, and configuration management

   — For software development

   — For referencing standards and statements of direction

   — For quality assurance of deliverables

   — For design reviews and deliverable acceptance

   — For capturing metrics

5. Are the methods documented and distributed to each team member?

6. To what extent are team members familiar with these methods?

7. What processes are in place to ensure compliance with the methods?

8. Describe the infrastructure that is in place to support the use of the methods through the end of the project and anticipated releases.

   — How is consultation and trouble-shooting provided?

   — How is training co-ordinated?

   — How are changes and enhancements incorporated and cascaded?

   — How are lessons learned captured and communicated?

9. What tools are being used on the project? (Specify versions and platforms). To what extent are team members familiar with these tools?

10. Describe the infrastructure that is in place to support the use of the tools through the end of the project and anticipated releases?

    — How is consultation and trouble-shooting provided?

- — How is training co-ordinated?

- — How are changes and enhancements incorporated and cascaded?

- — How are lessons learned captured and communicated?

11. Describe how the project will promote the re-use of its deliverables and deliverable content.

12. Will the architecture designs "live" after the project has been implemented? Describe the method that will be used to incorporate changes back into the architecture designs.

13. Were the current processes defined?

14. Were issues documented, rated, and associated to current processes? If not, how do you know you are fixing something that is broken?

15. Were existing/planned process improvement activities identified and associated to current processes? If not, how do you know this activity is not in conflict with or redundant to other Statements of Work?

16. Do you have current metrics? Do you have forecasted metrics? If not, how do you know you are improving something?

17. What processes will you put in place to gather, evaluate, and report metrics?

18. What impacts will the new design have on existing business processes, organizations, and information systems? Have they been documented and shared with the owners?

48.6 Architecture Compliance Review Guidelines

48.6.1 Tailoring the Checklists

- ▪ Focus on:
  - — High risk areas
  - — Expected (and emergent) differentiators
- ▪ For each question in the checklist, understand:
  - — The question itself
  - — The principle behind it
  - — What to look for in the responses
- ▪ Ask subject experts for their views
- ▪ Fix the checklist questions for your use
- ▪ Bear in mind the need for feedback to the Architecture Board

48.6.2 Conducting Architecture Compliance Reviews

- Understand clearly the objectives of those soliciting the review; and stay on track and deliver what was asked for. For example, they typically want to know what is right or wrong with the system being architected; not what is right or wrong with the development methodology used, their own management structure, etc. It is easy to get off-track and discuss subjects that are interesting and perhaps worthwhile, but not what was solicited. If you can shed light and insight on technical approaches, but the discussion is not necessary for the review, volunteer to provide it after the review.

- If it becomes obvious during the discussion that there are other issues that need to be addressed, which are outside the scope of the requested review, bring it up with the meeting chair afterwards. A plan for addressing the issues can then be developed in accordance with their degree of seriousness.

- Stay "scientific". Rather than: "We like to see large databases hosted on *ABC* rather than *XYZ*.", say things like: "The downtime associated with *XYZ* database environments is much greater than on *ABC* database environments. Therefore we don't recommend hosting type *M* and *N* systems in an *XYZ* environment."

- Ask "open" questions; i.e., questions that do not presume a particular answer.

- There are often "hidden agendas" or controversial issues among those soliciting a review, which you probably won't know up-front. A depersonalized approach to the discussions may help bridge the gaps of opinion rather than exacerbate them.

- Treat those being interviewed with respect. They may not have built the system "the way it should be", but they probably did the best they could under the circumstances they were placed in.

- Help the exercise become a learning experience for you and the presenters.

- Reviews should include detailed assessment activities against the architectures and should ensure that the results are stored in the Enterprise Continuum.

Chapter 49: Architecture Contracts

This chapter provides guidelines for defining and using Architecture Contracts.

49.1 Role

Architecture Contracts are the joint agreements between development partners and sponsors on the deliverables, quality, and fitness-for-purpose of an architecture. Successful implementation of these agreements will be delivered through effective architecture governance (see Chapter 50). By implementing a governed approach to the management of contracts, the following will be ensured:

- A system of continuous monitoring to check integrity, changes, decision-making, and audit of all architecture-related activities within the organization

- Adherence to the principles, standards, and requirements of the existing or developing architectures

- Identification of risks in all aspects of the development and implementation of the architecture(s) covering the internal development against accepted standards, policies, technologies, and products as well as the operational aspects of the architectures such that the organization can continue its business within a resilient environment

- A set of processes and practices that ensure accountability, responsibility, and discipline with regard to the development and usage of all architectural artifacts

- A formal understanding of the governance organization responsible for the contract, their level of authority, and scope of the architecture under the governance of this body

The traditional Architecture Contract is an agreement between the sponsor and the architecture function or IS department. However, increasingly more services are being provided by systems integrators, applications providers, and service providers, co-ordinated through the architecture function or IS department. There is therefore a need for an Architecture Contract to establish joint agreements between all parties involved in the architecture development and delivery.

Architecture Contracts may occur at various stages of the Architecture Development Method (ADM); for example:

- The Statement of Architecture Work created in Phase A of Part II: Architecture Development Method (ADM) is effectively an Architecture Contract between the architecting organization and the sponsor of the enterprise architecture (or the IT governance function).

- The development of one or more architecture domains (business, data, application, technology), and in some cases the oversight of the overall enterprise architecture, may be contracted out to systems integrators, applications providers, and/or service providers.

Each of these arrangements will normally be governed by an Architecture Contract that defines the deliverables, quality, and fitness-for-purpose of the developed architecture, and the processes by which the partners in the architecture development will work together.

- At the beginning of Phase G (Implementation Governance), between the architecture function and the function responsible for implementing the enterprise architecture defined in the preceding ADM phases. Typically, this will be either the in-house systems development function, or a major contractor to whom the work is outsourced.

  — What is being "implemented" in Phase G of the ADM is the overall enterprise architecture. This will typically include the technology infrastructure (from Phase D), and also those enterprise applications and data management capabilities that have been defined in the Application Architecture and Data Architecture (from Phase C), either because they are enterprise-wide in scope, or because they are strategic in business terms, and therefore of enterprise-wide importance and visibility. However, it will typically not include non-strategic business applications, which business units will subsequently deploy on top of the technology infrastructure that is implemented as part of the enterprise architecture.

  — In larger-scale implementations, there may well be one Architecture Contract per implementation team in a program of implementation projects.

- When the enterprise architecture has been implemented (at the end of Phase G), the ADM defines an Architecture Contract between the architecting function (or the IT governance function, subsuming the architecting function) and the business users who will subsequently build and deploy business unit-specific application systems in conformance with the architected environment.

It is important to bear in mind in all these cases that the ultimate goal is not just an enterprise architecture, but a dynamic enterprise architecture; i.e., one that allows for flexible evolution in response to changing technology and business drivers, without unnecessary constraints. The Architecture Contract is crucial to enabling a dynamic enterprise architecture and is key to governing the implementation.

Typical contents of these three kinds of Architecture Contract are explained below.

49.2 Contents

49.2.1 Statement of Architecture Work

The Statement of Architecture Work is created as a deliverable of Phase A, and is effectively an Architecture Contract between the architecting organization and the sponsor of the enterprise architecture (or the IT governance function, on behalf of the enterprise).

The typical contents of a Statement of Architecture Work are as defined in Part IV, Section 36.2.20.

49.2.2 Contract between Architecture Design and Development Partners

This is a signed statement of intent on designing and developing the enterprise architecture, or significant parts of it, from partner organizations, including systems integrators, applications providers, and service providers.

Increasingly the development of one or more architecture domains (business, data, application, technology) may be contracted out, with the enterprise's architecture function providing oversight of the overall enterprise architecture, and co-ordination and control of the overall effort. In some cases even this oversight role may be contracted out, although most enterprises prefer to retain that core responsibility in-house.

Whatever the specifics of the contracting-out arrangements, the arrangements themselves will normally be governed by an Architecture Contract that defines the deliverables, quality, and fitness-for-purpose of the developed architecture, and the processes by which the partners in the architecture development will work together.

Typical contents of an Architecture Design and Development Contract are:

- Introduction and background
- The nature of the agreement
- Scope of the architecture
- Architecture and strategic principles and requirements
- Conformance requirements
- Architecture development and management process and roles
- Target architecture measures
- Defined phases of deliverables
- Prioritized joint workplan
- Time window(s)
- Architecture delivery and business metrics

The template for this contract will normally be defined as part of the Preliminary phase of the ADM, if not existing already, and the specific contract will be defined at the appropriate stage of the ADM, depending on the particular work that is being contracted out.

49.2.3 Contract between Architecting Function and Business Users

This is a signed statement of intent to conform with the enterprise architecture, issued by enterprise business users. When the enterprise architecture has been implemented (at the end of Phase F), an Architecture Contract will normally be drawn up between the architecting function (or the IT governance function, subsuming the architecting function) and the business users who will subsequently be building and deploying application systems in the architected environment.

Typical contents of a Business Users' Architecture Contract are:

- Introduction and background

- The nature of the agreement
- Scope
- Strategic requirements
- Architecture deliverables that meet the business requirements
- Conformance requirements
- Architecture adopters
- Time window
- Architecture business metrics
- Service architecture (includes Service Level Agreement (SLA))

This contract is also used to manage changes to the enterprise architecture in Phase H.

49.3 Relationship to Architecture Governance

The Architecture Contract document produced in Phase G of the ADM figures prominently in the area of architecture governance, as explained in Part VII, Chapter 50.

In the context of architecture governance, the Architecture Contract is often used as a means of driving architecture change.

In order to ensure that the Architecture Contract is effective and efficient, the following aspects of the governance framework may need to be introduced into Phase G:

- Simple processes
- People-centered authority
- Strong communication
- Timely responses and an effective escalation process
- Supporting organizational structures
- Status tracking of architecture implementation

Chapter 50: Architecture Governance

This chapter provides a framework and guidelines for architecture governance.

50.1 Introduction

This section describes the nature of governance, and the levels of governance.

50.1.1 Levels of Governance within the Enterprise

Architecture governance is the practice and orientation by which enterprise architectures and other architectures are managed and controlled at an enterprise-wide level.

Architecture governance typically does not operate in isolation, but within a hierarchy of governance structures, which, particularly in the larger enterprise, can include all of the following as distinct domains with their own disciplines and processes:

- Corporate governance
- Technology governance
- IT governance
- Architecture governance

Each of these domains of governance may exist at multiple geographic levels — global, regional, and local — within the overall enterprise.

Corporate governance is thus a broad topic, beyond the scope of an enterprise architecture framework such as TOGAF.

This and related subsections are focused on architecture governance; but they describe it in the context of enterprise-wide governance, because of the hierarchy of governance structures within which it typically operates, as explained above.

In particular, this and following sections aim to:

- Provide an overview of the nature of governance as a discipline in its own right
- Describe the governance context in which architecture governance typically functions within the enterprise
- Describe an Architecture Governance Framework that can be adapted and applied in practice, both for enterprise architecture and for other forms of IT architecture

50.1.2 Nature of Governance

50.1.2.1 *Governance: A Generic Perspective*

Governance is essentially about ensuring that business is conducted properly. It is less about overt control and strict adherence to rules, and more about guidance and effective and equitable usage of resources to ensure sustainability of an organization's strategic objectives.

The following outlines the basic principles of corporate governance, as identified by the Organization for Economic Co-operation and Development (OECD):

- Focuses on the rights, roles, and equitable treatment of shareholders
- Disclosure and transparency and the responsibilities of the board
- Ensures:
  - Sound strategic guidance of the organization
  - Effective monitoring of management by the board
  - Board accountability for the company and to the shareholders
- Board's responsibilities:
  - Reviewing and guiding corporate strategy
  - Setting and monitoring achievement of management's performance objectives

Supporting this, the OECD considers a traditional view of governance as: "... the system by which business corporations are directed and controlled. The corporate governance structure specifies the distribution of rights and responsibilities among different participants in the corporation — such as the board, managers, shareholders, and other stakeholders — and spells out the rules and procedures for making decisions on corporate affairs. By doing this, it also provides the structure through which the company objectives are set, and the means of attaining those objectives and monitoring performance" [OECD (1999)].

50.1.2.2 *Characteristics of Governance*

The following characteristics have been adapted from *Corporate Governance* (Naidoo, 2002) and are positioned here to highlight both the value and necessity for governance as an approach to be adopted within organizations and their dealings with all involved parties:

Discipline   All involved parties will have a commitment to adhere to procedures, processes, and authority structures established by the organization.

Transparency   All actions implemented and their decision support will be available for inspection by authorized organization and provider parties.

Independence   All processes, decision-making, and mechanisms used will be established so as to minimize or avoid potential conflicts of interest.

Accountability Identifiable groups within the organization — e.g., governance boards who take actions or make decisions — are authorized and accountable for their actions.

Responsibility Each contracted party is required to act responsibly to the organization and its stakeholders.

Fairness   All decisions taken, processes used, and their implementation will not be allowed to create unfair advantage to any one particular party.

50.1.3 Technology Governance

Technology governance controls how an organization utilizes technology in the research, development, and production of its goods and services. Although it may include IT governance activities, it often has broader scope.

Technology governance is a key capability, requirement, and resource for most organizations because of the pervasiveness of technology across the organizational spectrum.

Recent studies have shown that many organizations have a balance in favor of intangibles rather than tangibles that require management. Given that most of these intangibles are informational and digital assets, it is evident that businesses are becoming more reliant on IT: and the governance of IT — IT governance — is therefore becoming an even more important part of technology governance.

These trends also highlight the dependencies of businesses on not only the information itself but also the processes, systems, and structures that create, deliver, and consume it. As the shift to increasing value through intangibles increases in many industry sectors, so risk management must be considered as key to understanding and moderating new challenges, threats, and opportunities.

Not only are organizations increasingly dependent on IT for their operations and profitability, but also their reputation, brand, and ultimately their values are also dependent on that same information and the supporting technology.

50.1.4 IT Governance

IT governance provides the framework and structure that links IT resources and information to enterprise goals and strategies. Furthermore, IT governance institutionalizes best practices for planning, acquiring, implementing, and monitoring IT performance, to ensure that the enterprise's IT assets support its business objectives.

In recent years, IT governance has become integral to the effective governance of the modern enterprise. Businesses are increasingly dependent on IT to support critical business functions and processes; and to successfully gain competitive advantage, businesses need to manage effectively the complex technology that is pervasive throughout the organization, in order to respond quickly and safely to business needs.

In addition, regulatory environments around the world are increasingly mandating stricter enterprise control over information, driven by increasing reports of information system disasters and electronic fraud. The management of IT-related risk is now widely accepted as a key part of enterprise governance.

It follows that an IT governance strategy, and an appropriate organization for implementing the strategy, must be established with the backing of top management, clarifying who owns the enterprise's IT resources, and, in particular, who has ultimate responsibility for their enterprise-wide integration.

50.1.4.1   An IT Controls Framework — COBIT

As with corporate governance, IT governance is a broad topic, beyond the scope of an enterprise architecture framework such as TOGAF. A good source of detailed information on IT governance is the COBIT framework (Control OBjectives for Information and related Technology). This is an open standard for control over IT, developed and promoted by the IT Governance Institute, and published by the Information Systems Audit and Control Foundation (ISACF). COBIT controls may provide useful aides to running a compliance strategy. A comprehensive mapping between TOGAF and COBIT is available that guides the practitioner in implementing architecture governance aligned to IT governance: Mapping of TOGAF 8.1 With COBIT 4.0, by the IT Governance Institute (ITGI).[19]

50.1.5   Architecture Governance: Overview

50.1.5.1   Architecture Governance Characteristics

Architecture governance is the practice and orientation by which enterprise architectures and other architectures are managed and controlled at an enterprise-wide level. It includes the following:

- Implementing a system of controls over the creation and monitoring of all architectural components and activities, to ensure the effective introduction, implementation, and evolution of architectures within the organization

- Implementing a system to ensure compliance with internal and external standards and regulatory obligations

- Establishing processes that support effective management of the above processes within agreed parameters

- Developing practices that ensure accountability to a clearly identified stakeholder community, both inside and outside the organization

50.1.5.2   Architecture Governance as a Board-Level Responsibility

As mentioned above, IT governance has recently become a board responsibility as part of overall business governance. The governance of an organization's architectures is a key factor in effective IT/business linkage, and is therefore increasingly becoming a key board-level responsibility in its own right.

This section aims to provide the impetus for opening up IT and architecture governance so that the business responsibilities associated with architecture activities and artifacts can be elucidated and managed.

50.1.5.3   TOGAF and Architecture Governance

Phase G of the TOGAF ADM (see Part II, Chapter 15) is dedicated to implementation governance, which concerns itself with the realization of the architecture through change projects. Implementation governance is just one aspect of architecture governance, which covers the management and control of all aspects of the development and evolution of enterprise architectures and other architectures within the enterprise.

---

19.   Available at: www.opengroup.org/bookstore/catalog/w072.htm.

Architecture governance needs to be supported by an Architecture Governance Framework (described in Section 50.2) which assists in identifying effective processes so that the business responsibilities associated with architecture governance can be elucidated, communicated, and managed effectively.

50.2   Architecture Governance Framework

This section describes a conceptual and organizational framework for architecture governance.

As previously explained, Phase G of the TOGAF ADM (see Part II, Chapter 15) is dedicated to implementation governance, which concerns itself with the realization of the architecture through change projects.

Implementation governance is just one aspect of architecture governance, which covers the management and control of all aspects of the development and evolution of enterprise architectures and other architectures within the enterprise.

Architecture governance needs to be supported by an Architecture Governance Framework, described below. The governance framework described is a generic framework that can be adapted to the existing governance environment of an enterprise. It is intended to assist in identifying effective processes and organizational structures, so that the business responsibilities associated with architecture governance can be elucidated, communicated, and managed effectively.

50.2.1   Architecture Governance Framework — Conceptual Structure

50.2.1.1   Key Concepts

Conceptually, architecture governance is an approach, a series of processes, a cultural orientation, and set of owned responsibilities that ensure the integrity and effectiveness of the organization's architectures.

The key concepts are illustrated in Figure 50-1.

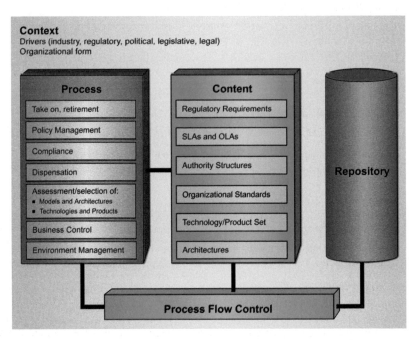

Figure 50-1 Architecture Governance Framework — Conceptual Structure

The split of process, content, and context are key to the support of the architecture governance initiative, by allowing the introduction of new governance material (legal, regulatory, standards-based, or legislative) without unduly impacting the processes. This content-agnostic approach ensures that the framework is flexible. The processes are typically independent of the content and implement a proven best practice approach to active governance.

The Architecture Governance Framework is integral to the Enterprise Continuum, and manages all content relevant both to the architecture itself and to architecture governance processes.

50.2.1.2 Key Architecture Governance Processes

Governance processes are required to identify, manage, audit, and disseminate all information related to architecture management, contracts, and implementation. These governance processes will be used to ensure that all architecture artifacts and contracts, principles, and operational-level agreements are monitored on an ongoing basis with clear auditability of all decisions made.

Policy Management and Take-On

All architecture amendments, contracts, and supporting information must come under governance through a formal process in order to register, validate, ratify, manage, and publish new or updated content. These processes will ensure the orderly integration with existing governance content such that all relevant parties, documents, contracts, and supporting information are managed and audited.

Compliance

Compliance assessments against Service Level Agreements (SLAs), Operational Level Agreements (OLAs), standards, and regulatory requirements will be implemented on an ongoing basis to ensure stability, conformance, and performance monitoring. These assessments will be reviewed and either accepted or rejected depending on the criteria defined within the governance framework.

Dispensation

A Compliance Assessment can be rejected where the subject area (design, operational, service level, or technology) are not compliant. In this case the subject area can:

1. Be adjusted or realigned in order to meet the compliance requirements
2. Request a dispensation

Where a Compliance Assessment is rejected, an alternate route to meeting interim conformance is provided through dispensations. These are granted for a given time period and set of identified service and operational criteria that must be enforced during the lifespan of the dispensation. Dispensations are not granted indefinitely, but are used as a mechanism to ensure that service levels and operational levels are met while providing a level of flexibility in their implementation and timing. The time-bound nature of dispensations ensures that they are a major trigger in the compliance cycle.

Monitoring and Reporting

Performance management is required to ensure that both the operational and service elements are managed against an agreed set of criteria. This will include monitoring against service and operational-level agreements, feedback for adjustment, and reporting.

Internal management information will be considered in Environment Management.

Business Control

Business Control relates to the processes invoked to ensure compliance with the organization's business policies.

Environment Management

This identifies all the services required to ensure that the repository-based environment underpinning the governance framework is effective and efficient. This includes the physical and logical repository management, access, communication, training, and accreditation of all users.

All architecture artifacts, service agreements, contracts, and supporting information must come under governance through a formal process in order to register, validate, ratify, manage, and publish new or updated content. These processes will ensure the orderly integration with existing governance content such that all relevant parties, documents, contracts, and supporting information are managed and audited.

The governance environment will have a number of administrative processes defined in order to effect a managed service and process environment. These processes will include user management, internal SLAs (defined in order to control its own processes), and management information reporting.

50.2.2 Architecture Governance Framework — Organizational Structure

50.2.2.1 Overview

Architecture governance is the practice and orientation by which enterprise architectures and other architectures are managed and controlled. In order to ensure that this control is effective within the organization, it is necessary to have the correct organizational structures established to support all governance activities.

An architecture governance structure for effectively implementing the approach described in this section will typically include the following levels, which may in practice involve a combination of existing IT governance processes, organizational structures, and capabilities. They will typically include the following:

- Global governance board
- Local governance board
- Design authorities
- Working parties

The architecture organization illustrated in Figure 50-2 highlights the major structural elements required for an architecture governance initiative. While each enterprise will have differing requirements, it is expected that the basics of the organizational design shown in Figure 50-2 will be applicable and implementable in a wide variety of organizational types.

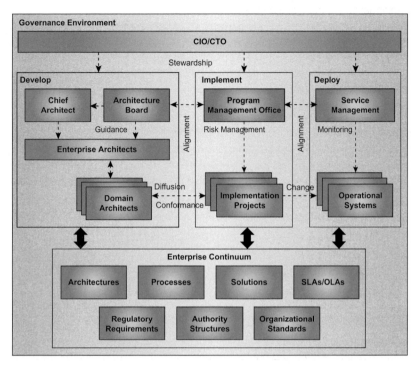

Figure 50-2 Architecture Governance Framework — Organizational Structure

50.2.2.2 Key Areas

Figure 50-2 identifies three key areas of architecture management: Develop, Implement, and Deploy. Each of these is the responsibility of one or more groups within the organization, while the Enterprise Continuum is shown to support all activities and artifacts associated with the governance of the architectures throughout their lifecycle.

The Develop responsibilities, processes, and structures are usually linked to the TOGAF ADM and its usage, while the Implement responsibilities, processes, and structures are typically linked to Phase G (see Part II, Chapter 15).

As mentioned above, the Architecture Governance Framework is integral to the Enterprise Continuum, and manages all content relevant both to the architectures themselves and to architecture governance processes.

50.2.2.3 Operational Benefits

As illustrated in Figure 50-2, the governance of the organization's architectures provides not only direct control and guidance of their development and implementation, but also extends into the operations of the implemented architectures.

The following benefits have been found to be derived through the continuing governance of architectures:

- Links IT processes, resources, and information to organizational strategies and objectives

- Integrates and institutionalizes IT best practices

- Aligns with industry frameworks such as COBIT (planning and organizing, acquiring and implementing, delivering and supporting, and monitoring IT performance)

- Enables the organization to take full advantage of its information, infrastructure, and hardware and software assets

- Protects the underlying digital assets of the organization

- Supports regulatory and best practice requirements such as auditability, security, responsibility, and accountability

- Promotes visible risk management

These benefits position the TOGAF Architecture Governance Framework as an approach, a series of processes, a cultural orientation, and a set of owned responsibilities, that together ensure the integrity and effectiveness of the organization's architectures.

50.3 Architecture Governance in Practice

This section provides practical guidelines for the effective implementation of architecture governance.

50.3.1 Architecture Governance — Key Success Factors

It is important to consider the following to ensure a successful approach to architecture governance, and to the effective management of the Architecture Contract:

- Best practices for the submission, adoption, re-use, reporting, and retirement of architecture policies, procedures, roles, skills, organizational structures, and support services

- Organizational responsibilities and structures to support the architecture governance processes and reporting requirements

- Integration of tools and processes to facilitate the take-up of the processes, both procedurally and culturally

- Criteria for the control of the architecture governance processes, dispensations, compliance assessments, SLAs, and OLAs

- Internal and external requirements for the effectiveness, efficiency, confidentiality, integrity, availability, compliance, and reliability of all architecture governance-related information, services, and processes

50.3.2 Elements of an Effective Architecture Governance Strategy

50.3.2.1 Architecture Governance and Corporate Politics

An enterprise architecture imposed without appropriate political backing is bound to fail. In order to succeed, the enterprise architecture must reflect the needs of the organization. Enterprise architects, if they are not involved in the development of business strategy, must at least have a fundamental understanding of it and of the prevailing business issues facing the organization. It may even be necessary for them to be involved in the system deployment process and to ultimately own the investment and product selection decisions arising from the implementation of the Technology Architecture.

There are three important elements of architecture governance strategy that relate particularly to the acceptance and success of architecture within the enterprise. While relevant and applicable in their own right apart from their role in governance, and therefore described separately, they also from an integral part of any effective architecture governance strategy.

- A cross-organizational Architecture Board (see Chapter 47) must be established with the backing of top management to oversee the implementation of the IT governance strategy.

- A comprehensive set of architecture principles (see Chapter 23) should be established, to guide, inform, and support the way in which an organization sets about fulfilling its mission through the use of IT.

- An Architecture Compliance (see Chapter 48) strategy should be adopted — specific measures (more than just a statement of policy) to ensure compliance with the architecture, including Project Impact Assessments, a formal Architecture Compliance review process, and possibly including the involvement of the architecture team in product procurement.

Chapter 51: Architecture Maturity Models

This chapter provides techniques for evaluating and quantifying an organization's maturity in enterprise architecture.

51.1 Overview

Organizations that can manage change effectively are generally more successful than those that cannot. Many organizations know that they need to improve their IT-related development processes in order to successfully manage change, but don't know how. Such organizations typically either spend very little on process improvement, because they are unsure how best to proceed; or spend a lot, on a number of parallel and unfocused efforts, to little or no avail.

Capability Maturity Models (CMMs) address this problem by providing an effective and proven method for an organization to gradually gain control over and improve its IT-related development processes. Such models provide the following benefits:

- They describe the practices that any organization must perform in order to improve its processes.

- They provide a yardstick against which to periodically measure improvement.

- They constitute a proven framework within which to manage the improvement efforts.

The various practices are typically organized into five levels, each level representing an increased ability to control and manage the development environment.

An evaluation of the organization's practices against the model — called an "assessment" — determines the level at which the organization currently stands. It indicates the organization's maturity in the area concerned, and the practices on which the organization needs to focus in order to see the greatest improvement and the highest return on investment.

The benefits of CMMs are well documented for software and systems engineering. Their application to enterprise architecture has been a recent development, stimulated by the increasing interest in enterprise architecture in recent years, combined with the lack of maturity in this discipline.

This section introduces into TOGAF the topic of CMMs and their associated methods and techniques, as a widely used industry standard that is mature enough to consider for use in relation to enterprise architecture.

51.2 Background

The Software Engineering Institute (SEI) — www.sei.cmu.edu — a federally funded research and development center sponsored by the US Department of Defense and operated by Carnegie Mellon University, developed the original CMM — Capability Maturity Model for Software (SW-CMM) — in the early 1990s, which is still widely used today.

CMMs have gained wide-scale acceptance over the last decade. These models and their associated methods were originally applied to IT solutions, particularly software solutions, but a number of IT-related disciplines have developed CMMs to support process improvement in areas such as:

- People — the P-CMM (People Capability Maturity Model), and the IDEAL Life Cycle Model for Improvement

- Systems Engineering — the SE-CMM (Systems Engineering Capability Maturity Model)

- Software Acquisition — the SA-CMM (Software Acquisition Capability Maturity Model)

- CMMI (Capability Maturity Model Integration)

The models have been adopted by large organizations, including the US Department of Commerce, the US DoD, the UK Government, and a number of large services organizations, to assess competencies.

The increasing interest in applying these techniques to the IT architecture and enterprise architecture fields has resulted in a series of template tools which assess:

- The state of the IT architecture process

- The IT architecture

- The organization's buy-in to both

The main issues addressed by US and UK Government use of these models include:

- e-Commerce maturity

- Process implementation and audit

- Quality measurements

- People competencies

- Investment management

They involve use of a multiplicity of models, and focus in particular on measuring business benefits and return on investment.

Another key driver is the increasing use of outsourcing. Recent analyst projections indicate that around 75% of IS organizations are refocusing their role on brokering resources and facilitating business-driven demands, rather than on being direct providers of IT services. The CMM is increasingly the standard by which outsourcers are being evaluated.

This section reviews the state of development in such techniques.

A closely related topic is that of the Architecture Skills Framework (see Chapter 52), which can be used to plan the target skills and capabilities required by an organization to successfully deliver an enterprise architecture, and to determine the training and development needs of individuals.

51.3   US DoC ACMM Framework

51.3.1 Overview

As an example of the trend towards increased interest in applying CMM techniques to enterprise architecture, all US federal agencies are now expected to provide maturity models and ratings as part of their IT investment management and audit requirements.

In particular, the US Department of Commerce (DoC) has developed an enterprise Architecture Capability Maturity Model (ACMM)[20] to aid in conducting internal assessments. ACMM Version 1.2 was published in December 2007. The ACMM provides a framework that represents the key components of a productive enterprise architecture process. The goal is to enhance the overall odds for success of enterprise architecture by identifying weak areas and providing a defined evolutionary path to improving the overall architecture process.

The ACMM comprises three sections:

1. The enterprise architecture maturity model

2. Enterprise architecture characteristics of operating units' processes at different maturity levels

3. The enterprise architecture CMM scorecard

The first two sections explain the architecture capability maturity levels and the corresponding enterprise architecture element and characteristics for each maturity level to be used as measures in the assessment process. The third section is used to derive the architecture capability maturity level that is to be reported to the DoC Chief Information Officer (CIO).

51.3.2 Elements of the ACMM

The DoC ACMM consists of six maturity levels and nine architecture elements. The six levels are:

0   None

1   Initial

2   Under development

3   Defined

4   Managed

5   Measured

The nine enterprise architecture elements are:

-   Architecture process

-   Architecture development

-   Business linkage

---

20.   Refer to ocio.os.doc.gov/ITPolicyandPrograms/Enterprise_Architecture/DEV01_003735.

- Senior management involvement
- Operating unit participation
- Architecture communication
- IT security
- Architecture governance
- IT investment and acquisition strategy

Two complementary methods are used in the ACMM to calculate a maturity rating. The first method obtains a weighted mean enterprise architecture maturity level. The second method shows the percentage achieved at each maturity level for the nine architecture elements.

51.3.3 Example: Enterprise Architecture Process Maturity Levels

The following example shows the detailed characteristics of the enterprise architecture maturity levels as applied to the first of the nine elements: architecture process.

Level 0: None

No enterprise architecture program. No enterprise architecture to speak of.

Level 1: Initial

Informal enterprise architecture process underway.

1. Processes are *ad hoc* and localized. Some enterprise architecture processes are defined. There is no unified architecture process across technologies or business processes. Success depends on individual efforts.

2. Enterprise architecture processes, documentation, and standards are established by a variety of *ad hoc* means and are localized or informal.

3. Minimal, or implicit linkage to business strategies or business drivers.

4. Limited management team awareness or involvement in the architecture process.

5. Limited operating unit acceptance of the enterprise architecture process.

6. The latest version of the operating unit's enterprise architecture documentation is on the web. Little communication exists about the enterprise architecture process and possible process improvements.

7. IT security considerations are *ad hoc* and localized.

8. No explicit governance of architectural standards.

9. Little or no involvement of strategic planning and acquisition personnel in the enterprise architecture process. Little or no adherence to existing standards.

Level 2: Under Development

Enterprise architecture process is under development.

1. Basic enterprise architecture process is documented based on OMB Circular A-130 and Department of Commerce Enterprise Architecture Guidance. The architecture process has developed clear roles and responsibilities.

2. IT vision, principles, business linkages, Baseline, and Target Architecture are identified. Architecture standards exist, but not necessarily linked to Target Architecture. Technical Reference Model (TRM) and Standards Profile framework established.

3. Explicit linkage to business strategies.

4. Management awareness of architecture effort.

5. Responsibilities are assigned and work is underway.

6. The DoC and operating unit enterprise architecture web pages are updated periodically and are used to document architecture deliverables.

7. IT security architecture has defined clear roles and responsibilities.

8. Governance of a few architectural standards and some adherence to existing Standards Profile.

9. Little or no formal governance of IT investment and acquisition strategy. Operating unit demonstrates some adherence to existing Standards Profile.

Level 3: Defined

Defined enterprise architecture including detailed written procedures and TRM.

1. The architecture is well defined and communicated to IT staff and business management with operating unit IT responsibilities. The process is largely followed.

2. Gap analysis and Migration Plan are completed. Fully developed TRM and Standards Profile. IT goals and methods are identified.

3. Enterprise architecture is integrated with capital planning and investment control.

4. Senior management team aware of and supportive of the enterprise-wide architecture process. Management actively supports architectural standards.

5. Most elements of operating unit show acceptance of or are actively participating in the enterprise architecture process.

6. Architecture documents updated regularly on DoC enterprise architecture web page.

7. IT security architecture Standards Profile is fully developed and is integrated with enterprise architecture.

8. Explicit documented governance of majority of IT investments.

9. IT acquisition strategy exists and includes compliance measures to IT enterprise architecture. Cost benefits are considered in identifying projects.

Level 4: Managed

Managed and measured enterprise architecture process.

1. Enterprise architecture process is part of the culture. Quality metrics associated with the architecture process are captured.

2. Enterprise architecture documentation is updated on a regular cycle to reflect the updated enterprise architecture. Business, Data, Application, and Technology Architectures defined by appropriate *de jure* and *de facto* standards.

3. Capital planning and investment control are adjusted based on the feedback received and lessons learned from updated enterprise architecture. Periodic re-examination of business drivers.

4. Senior management team directly involved in the architecture review process.

5. The entire operating unit accepts and actively participates in the enterprise architecture process.

6. Architecture documents are updated regularly, and frequently reviewed for latest architecture developments/standards.

7. Performance metrics associated with IT security architecture are captured.

8. Explicit governance of all IT investments. Formal processes for managing variances feed back into enterprise architecture.

9. All planned IT acquisitions and purchases are guided and governed by the enterprise architecture.

Level 5: Optimizing

Continuous improvement of enterprise architecture process.

1. Concerted efforts to optimize and continuously improve architecture process.

2. A standards and waivers process is used to improve architecture development process.

3. Architecture process metrics are used to optimize and drive business linkages. Business involved in the continuous process improvements of enterprise architecture.

4. Senior management involvement in optimizing process improvements in architecture development and governance.

5. Feedback on architecture process from all operating unit elements is used to drive architecture process improvements.

6. Architecture documents are used by every decision-maker in the organization for every IT-related business decision.

7. Feedback from IT security architecture metrics are used to drive architecture process improvements.

8. Explicit governance of all IT investments. A standards and waivers process is used to make governance-process improvements.

9. No unplanned IT investment or acquisition activity.

51.4   Capability Maturity Models Integration (CMMI)

51.4.1   Introduction

The capability models that the SEI is currently involved in developing, expanding, or maintaining include the following:

- CMMI (Capability Maturity Model Integration)
- IPD-CMM (Integrated Product Development Capability Maturity Model)
- P-CMM (People Capability Maturity Model)
- SA-CMM (Software Acquisition Capability Maturity Model)
- SE-CMM (Systems Engineering Capability Maturity Model)
- SW-CMM (Capability Maturity Model for Software)

As explained in this chapter, in recent years the industry has witnessed significant growth in the area of maturity models. The multiplicity of models available has led to problems of its own, in terms of how to integrate all the different models to produce a meaningful metric for overall process maturity.

In response to this need, the SEI has developed a Framework called Capability Maturity Model Integration (CMMI), to provide a means of managing the complexity.

According to the SEI, the use of the CMMI models improves on the best practices of previous models in many important ways, in particular enabling organizations to:

- More explicitly link management and engineering activities to business objectives
- Expand the scope of and visibility into the product lifecycle and engineering activities to ensure that the product or service meets customer expectations
- Incorporate lessons learned from additional areas of best practice (e.g., measurement, risk management, and supplier management)
- Implement more robust high-maturity practices
- Address additional organizational functions critical to its products and services
- More fully comply with relevant ISO standards

CMMI is being adopted worldwide.

51.4.2   SCAMPI Method

The Standard CMMI Appraisal Method for Process Improvement (SCAMPI) is the appraisal method associated with CMMI. The SCAMPI appraisal method is used to identify strengths, weaknesses, and ratings relative to CMMI reference models. It incorporates best practices found successful in the appraisal community, and is based on the features of several legacy appraisal methods. It is applicable to a wide range of appraisal usage modes, including both internal process improvement and external capability determinations.

The SCAMPI method definition document[21] describes the requirements, activities, and practices associated with each of the processes that compose the SCAMPI method.

51.5   Conclusions

This section has sought to introduce into TOGAF the topic of capability maturity model-based methods and techniques, as a widely used industry standard that is mature enough to consider for use in relation to enterprise architecture.

The benefits of CMMs are well documented for software and systems engineering. Their application to enterprise architecture has been a more recent development, stimulated by the increasing interest in enterprise architecture, combined with the lack of maturity in the discipline of enterprise architecture.

Future versions of TOGAF will seek to build on this base, as more experience is gained on the use of these methods and techniques specifically relating to enterprise architecture.

---

21.   Available at www.sei.cmu.edu/publications/documents/01.reports/01hb001.html.

Chapter 52: Architecture Skills Framework

This chapter provides a set of role, skill, and experience norms for staff undertaking enterprise architecture work.

52.1 Introduction

Skills frameworks provide a view of the competency levels required for specific roles. They define:

- The roles within a work area
- The skills required by each role
- The depth of knowledge required to fulfil the role successfully

They are relatively common for defining the skills required for a consultancy and/or project management assignment, to deliver a specific project or work package. They are also widely used by recruitment and search agencies to match candidates and roles.

Their value derives from their ability to provide a means of rapidly identifying skill matches and gaps. Successfully applied, they can ensure that candidates are fit for the jobs assigned to them.

Their value in the context of enterprise architecture arises from the immaturity of the enterprise architecture discipline, and the problems that arise from this.

52.2 Need for an Enterprise Architecture Skills Framework

52.2.1 Definitional Rigor

"Enterprise Architecture" and "Enterprise Architect" are widely used but poorly defined terms in industry today. They are used to denote a variety of practices and skills applied in a wide variety of architecture domains. There is a need for better classification to enable more implicit understanding of what type of architecture/architect is being described.

This lack of uniformity leads to difficulties for organizations seeking to recruit or assign/promote staff to fill positions in the architecture field. Because of the different usages of terms, there is often misunderstanding and miscommunication between those seeking to recruit for, and those seeking to fill, the various roles of the architect.

52.2.2 Basis of an Internal Architecture Practice

Despite the lack of uniform terminology, architecture skills are in increasing demand, as the discipline of architecture gains increasing attention within industry.

Many enterprises have set up, or are considering setting up, an enterprise architecture practice, as a means of fostering development of the necessary skills and experience among in-house staff to undertake the various architecting tasks required by the enterprise.

An enterprise architecture practice is a formal program of development and certification, by which an enterprise formally recognizes the skills of its practicing architects, as demonstrated by their work. Such a program is essential in order to ensure the alignment of staff skills and experience with the architecture tasks that the enterprise wishes to be performed.

The role and skill definitions on which such a program needs to be based are also required, by both recruiting and supplying organizations, in cases where external personnel are to be engaged to perform architecture work (for example, as part of a consultancy engagement).

An enterprise architecture practice is both difficult and costly to set up. It is normally built around a process of peer review, and involves the time and talent of the strategic technical leadership of an enterprise. Typically it involves establishment of a peer review board, and documentation of the process, and of the requirements for internal certification. Time is also required of candidates to prepare for peer review, by creating a portfolio of their work to demonstrate their skills, experiences, and contributions to the profession.

The TOGAF Architecture Skills Framework attempts to address this need by providing definitions of the architecting skills and proficiency levels required of personnel, internal or external, who are to perform the various architecting roles defined within the TOGAF Framework.

Because of the complexity, time, and cost involved, many enterprises do not have an internal enterprise architect certification program, preferring instead to simply interview and recruit architecture staff on an *ad hoc* basis. There are serious risks associated with this approach:

- Communication between recruiting organizations, consultancies, and employment agencies is very difficult.

- Time is wasted interviewing staff who may have applied in all good faith, but still lack the skills and/or experience required by the employer.

- Staff that are capable of filling architecture roles may be overlooked, or may not identify themselves with advertised positions and hence not even apply.

- There is increased risk of unsuitable personnel being employed or engaged, through no-one's fault, and despite everyone involved acting in good faith. This in turn can:
  - Increase personnel costs, through the need to rehire or reassign staff
  - Adversely impact the time, cost, and quality of operational IT systems, and the projects that deliver them

52.3   Goals/Rationale

52.3.1   Certification of Enterprise Architects

The main purpose behind an enterprise setting up an internal enterprise architect certification program is two-fold:

1. To formally recognize the skill of its practicing architects, as part of the task of establishing and maintaining a professional architecting organization

2. To ensure the alignment of necessary staff skills and experience with the architecture tasks that the enterprise wishes to be performed, whether these are to be performed internally to the enterprise or externally; for example, as part of a consultancy engagement

52.3.2   Specific Benefits

Specific benefits anticipated from use of the TOGAF Architecture Skills Framework include:

- Reduced time, cost, and risk in training, hiring, and managing architecture professionals, both internal and external:

  — Simplifies communication between recruiting organizations, consultancies, and employment agencies

  — Avoids wasting time interviewing staff who may have applied in all good faith, but still lack the skills and/or experience required by the employer

  — Avoids staff who are capable of filling architecture roles being overlooked, or not identifying themselves with advertised positions and hence not even applying

- Reduced time and cost to set up an internal architecture practice:

  — Many enterprises do not have an internal architecture practice due to the complexity involved in setting one up, preferring instead to simply interview and recruit architecture staff on an *ad hoc* basis.

  — By providing definitions of the architecting skills and proficiency levels required of personnel who are to perform the various architecting roles defined within TOGAF, the Architecture Skills Framework greatly reduces the time, cost, and risk of setting up a practice for the first time, and avoids "re-inventing wheels".

  — Enterprises that already have an internal architecture practice are able to set enterprise-wide norms, but still experience difficulties as outlined above in recruiting staff, or engaging consultants, from external sources, due to the lack of uniformity between different enterprises. By aligning its existing skills framework with the industry-accepted definitions provided by The Open Group, an enterprise can greatly simplify these problems.

- Reduced time and cost to implement an architecture practice helps reduce the time, cost, and risk of overall solution development:

  — Enterprises that do not have an internal architecture practice run the risk of unsuitable personnel being employed or engaged, through no-one's fault, and despite everyone involved acting in good faith. The resultant time and cost penalties far outweigh the time and cost of having an internal architecture practice:

— Personnel costs are increased, through the occasional need to rehire or reassign staff.

— Even more important is the adverse impact on the time, cost, and quality of operational IT systems, and the projects to deliver them, resulting from poor staff assignments.

52.4   Enterprise Architecture Role and Skill Categories

52.4.1   Overview

This section describes the role of an enterprise architect, the fundamental skills required, and some possible disciplines in which an enterprise architect might specialize.

TOGAF delivers an enterprise architecture, and therefore requires both business and IT-trained professionals to develop the enterprise architecture.

The TOGAF Architecture Skills Framework provides a view of the competency levels for specific roles within the enterprise architecture team. The Framework defines:

- The roles within an enterprise architecture work area
- The skills required by those roles
- The depth of knowledge required to fulfil each role successfully

The value is in providing a rapid means of identifying skills and gaps. Successfully applied, the Framework can be used as a measure for:

- Staff development
- Ensuring that the right person does the right job

52.4.2   TOGAF Roles

A typical architecture team undertaking the development of an enterprise architecture as described in TOGAF would comprise the following roles:

- Architecture Board Members
- Architecture Sponsor
- Architecture Manager
- Architects for:
    — Enterprise Architecture (which for the purpose of the tables shown below can be considered as a superset of Business, Data, Application, and Technology Architecture)
    — Business Architecture
    — Data Architecture
    — Application Architecture

> — Technology Architecture

- Program and/or Project Managers

- IT Designer

- And many others . . .

The tables that follow show, for each of these roles, the skills required and the desirable level of proficiency in each skill.

Of all the roles listed above, the one that needs particularly detailed analysis and definition is of course the central role of enterprise architect. As explained above, "Enterprise Architecture" and "Enterprise Architect" are terms that are very widely used but very poorly defined in industry today, denoting a wide variety of practices and skills applied in a wide variety of architecture domains. There is often confusion between the role of an architect and that of a designer or builder. Many of the skills required by an enterprise architect are also required by the designer, who delivers the solutions. While their skills are complementary, those of the designer are primarily technology focused and translate the architecture into deliverable components.

The final subsection below therefore explores in some detail the generic characteristics of the role of enterprise architect, and the key skill requirements, whatever the particular architecture domain (Enterprise Architecture, Business Architecture, Data Architecture, Application Architecture, Technology Architecture, etc.).

52.4.3 Categories of Skills

The TOGAF team skill set will need to include the following main categories of skills:

- **Generic Skills**: — typically comprising leadership, teamworking, inter-personal skills, etc.

- **Business Skills & Methods**: — typically comprising business cases, business process, strategic planning, etc.

- **Enterprise Architecture Skills**: — typically comprising modeling, building block design, applications and role design, systems integration, etc.

- **Program or Project Management Skills**: — typically comprising managing business change, project management methods and tools, etc.

- **IT General Knowledge Skills**: — typically comprising brokering applications, asset management, migration planning, SLAs, etc.

- **Technical IT Skills**: — typically comprising software engineering, security, data interchange, data management, etc.

- **Legal Environment**: — typically comprising data protection laws, contract law, procurement law, fraud, etc.

The tables that follow illustrate each of these categories of skills.

The tables that follow show, for each of these skills, the roles to which they are relevant and the desirable level of proficiency in each skill.

52.4.4 Proficiency Levels

The TOGAF Architecture Skills Framework identifies four levels of knowledge or proficiency in any area:

Level	Achievement	Description
1	Background	Not a required skill, though should be able to define and manage skill if required.
2	Awareness	Understands the background, issues, and implications sufficiently to be able to understand how to proceed further and advise client accordingly.
3	Knowledge	Detailed knowledge of subject area and capable of providing professional advice and guidance. Ability to integrate capability into architecture design.
4	Expert	Extensive and substantial practical experience and applied knowledge on the subject.

52.5   Enterprise Architecture Role and Skill Definitions

52.5.1 Generic Skills

Roles	Architecture Board Member	Architecture Sponsor	Enterprise Architecture Manager	Enterprise Architecture Technology	Enterprise Architecture Data	Enterprise Architecture Applications	Enterprise Architecture Business	Program/ Project Manager	IT Designer
Generic Skills									
Leadership	4	4	4	3	3	3	3	4	1
Teamwork	3	3	4	4	4	4	4	4	2
Inter-personal	4	4	4	4	4	4	4	4	2
Oral Communications	3	3	4	4	4	4	4	4	2
Written Communications	3	3	4	4	4	4	4	3	3
Logical Analysis	2	2	4	4	4	4	4	3	3
Stakeholder Management	4	3	4	3	3	3	3	4	2
Risk Management	3	3	4	3	3	3	3	4	1

52.5.2 Business Skills & Methods

Roles	Architecture Board Member	Architecture Sponsor	Enterprise Architecture Manager	Enterprise Architecture Technology	Enterprise Architecture Data	Enterprise Architecture Applications	Enterprise Architecture Business	Program/Project Manager	IT Designer
Business Skills & Methods									
Business Case	3	4	4	4	4	4	4	4	2
Business Scenario	2	3	4	4	4	4	4	3	2
Organization	3	3	4	3	3	3	4	3	2
Business Process	3	3	4	4	4	4	4	3	2
Strategic Planning	2	3	3	3	3	3	4	3	1
Budget Management	3	3	3	3	3	3	3	4	3
Visioning	3	3	4	3	3	3	4	3	2
Business Metrics	3	4	4	4	4	4	4	4	3
Business Culture	4	4	4	3	3	3	3	3	1
Legacy Investments	4	4	3	2	2	2	2	3	2
Business Functions	3	3	3	3	4	4	4	3	2

52.5.3 Enterprise Architecture Skills

Roles	Architecture Board Member	Architecture Sponsor	Enterprise Architecture Manager	Enterprise Architecture Technology	Enterprise Architecture Data	Enterprise Architecture Applications	Enterprise Architecture Business	Program/Project Manager	IT Designer
Enterprise Architecture Skills									
Business Modeling	2	2	4	3	3	4	4	2	2
Business Process Design	1	1	4	3	3	4	4	2	2
Role Design	2	2	4	3	3	4	4	2	2
Organization Design	2	2	4	3	3	4	4	2	2
Data Design	1	1	3	3	4	3	3	2	3
Application Design	1	1	3	3	3	4	3	2	3
Systems Integration	1	1	4	4	3	3	3	2	2
IT Industry Standards	1	1	4	4	4	4	3	2	3
Services Design	2	2	4	4	3	4	3	2	2
Architecture Principles Design	2	2	4	4	4	4	4	2	2
Architecture Views & Viewpoints Design	2	2	4	4	4	4	4	2	2
Building Block Design	1	1	4	4	4	4	4	2	3
Solutions Modeling	1	1	4	4	4	4	4	2	3
Benefits Analysis	2	2	4	4	4	4	4	4	2
Business Interworking	3	3	4	3	3	4	4	3	1
Systems Behavior	1	1	4	4	4	4	3	3	2
Project Management	1	1	3	3	3	3	3	4	2

52.5.4 Program or Project Management Skills

Roles	Architecture Board Member	Architecture Sponsor	Enterprise Architecture Manager	Enterprise Architecture Technology	Enterprise Architecture Data	Enterprise Architecture Applications	Enterprise Architecture Business	Program/Project Manager	IT Designer
Program or Project Management Skills									
Program Management	1	2	3	3	3	3	3	4	2
Project Management	1	2	3	3	3	3	3	4	2
Managing Business Change	3	3	4	3	3	3	4	4	2
Change Management	3	3	4	3	3	3	4	3	2
Value Management	4	4	4	3	3	3	4	3	2

52.5.5 IT General Knowledge Skills

Roles	Architecture Board Member	Architecture Sponsor	Enterprise Architecture Manager	Enterprise Architecture Technology	Enterprise Architecture Data	Enterprise Architecture Applications	Enterprise Architecture Business	Program/Project Manager	IT Designer
IT General Knowledge Skills									
IT Application Development Methodologies & Tools	2	2	3	4	4	4	2	3	3
Programming Languages	1	1	3	4	4	4	3	2	3
Brokering Applications	1	1	3	3	4	4	3	2	3
Information Consumer Applications	1	1	3	3	4	4	3	2	3
Information Provider Applications	1	1	3	3	4	4	3	2	3
Storage Management	1	1	3	4	4	2	2	2	3
Networks	1	1	3	4	3	2	2	2	3
Web-based Services	1	1	3	3	4	4	2	2	3
IT Infrastructure	1	1	3	4	3	2	2	2	3
Asset Management	1	1	4	4	3	3	3	2	3
Service Level Agreements	1	1	4	4	3	4	3	2	3
Systems	1	1	3	4	3	3	2	2	3
COTS	1	1	3	4	3	4	2	2	3
Enterprise Continuums	1	1	4	4	4	4	4	2	3
Migration Planning	1	1	4	3	4	3	3	2	3
Management Utilities	1	1	3	2	4	4	2	2	3
Infrastructure	1	1	3	4	3	4	2	2	3

52.5.6 Technical IT Skills

Roles	Architecture Board Member	Architecture Sponsor	Enterprise Architecture Manager	Enterprise Architecture Technology	Enterprise Architecture Data	Enterprise Architecture Applications	Enterprise Architecture Business	Program/ Project Manager	IT Designer
Technical IT Skills									
Software Engineering	1	1	3	3	4	4	3	2	3
Security	1	1	3	4	3	4	3	2	3
Systems & Network Management	1	1	3	4	3	3	3	2	3
Transaction Processing	1	1	3	4	3	4	3	2	3
Location & Directory	1	1	3	4	4	3	3	2	3
User Interface	1	1	3	4	4	4	3	2	3
International Operations	1	1	3	4	3	3	2	2	2
Data Interchange	1	1	3	4	4	3	2	2	3
Data Management	1	1	3	4	4	3	2	2	3
Graphics & Image	1	1	3	4	3	3	2	2	3
Operating System Services	1	1	3	4	3	3	2	2	3
Network Services	1	1	3	4	3	3	2	2	3
Communications Infrastructure	1	1	3	4	3	3	2	2	3

52.5.7 Legal Environment

Roles	Architecture Board Member	Architecture Sponsor	Enterprise Architecture Manager	Enterprise Architecture Technology	Enterprise Architecture Data	Enterprise Architecture Applications	Enterprise Architecture Business	Program/ Project Manager	IT Designer
Legal Environment									
Contract Law	2	2	2	2	2	2	2	3	1
Data Protection Law	3	3	4	3	3	3	3	2	2
Procurement Law	3	2	2	2	2	2	2	4	1
Fraud	3	3	3	3	3	3	3	3	1
Commercial Law	3	3	2	2	2	2	3	3	1

52.6   Generic Role and Skills of the Enterprise Architect

Of all the roles listed above, the one that needs particularly detailed analysis and definition is, of course, the central role of enterprise architect. As explained above, "Enterprise Architecture" and "Enterprise Architect" are terms that are very widely used but very poorly defined in industry today, denoting a wide variety of practices and skills applied in a wide variety of architecture domains.

This section therefore explores in some detail the generic characteristics of the role of enterprise architect, and some key skill requirements, whatever the particular architecture domain (Enterprise Architecture, Business Architecture, Data Architecture, Application Architecture, Technology Architecture, etc.).

52.6.1   Generic Role

Enterprise architects are visionaries, coaches, team leaders, business-to-technical liaisons, computer scientists, and industry experts.

The following is effectively a job description for an enterprise architect:

> "The architect has a responsibility for ensuring the completeness (fitness-for-purpose) of the architecture, in terms of adequately addressing all the pertinent concerns of its stakeholders; and the integrity of the architecture, in terms of connecting all the various views to each other, satisfactorily reconciling the conflicting concerns of different stakeholders, and showing the trade-offs made in so doing (as between security and performance, for example).
>
> The choice of which particular architecture views to develop is one of the key decisions that the enterprise architect has to make. The choice has to be constrained by considerations of practicality, and by the principle of fitness-for-purpose (i.e., the architecture should be developed only to the point at which it is fit-for-purpose, and not reiterated *ad infinitum* as an academic exercise)."

The role of the enterprise architect is more like that of a city planner than that of a building architect, and the product of the enterprise architect is more aptly characterized as a planned community (as opposed to an unconstrained urban sprawl), rather than as a well-designed building or set of buildings.

An enterprise architect does not create the technical vision of the enterprise, but has professional relationships with executives of the enterprise to gather and articulate the technical vision, and to produce the strategic plan for realizing it. This plan is always tied to the business plans of the enterprise, and design decisions are traceable to the business plan.

The strategic plan of the enterprise architect is tied to the architecture governance process (see Chapter 50) for the enterprise, so design decisions are not circumvented for tactical convenience.

The enterprise architect produces documentation of design decisions for application development teams or product implementation teams to execute.

An architect is involved in the entire process; beginning with working with the customer to understand real needs, as opposed to wants, and then throughout the process to translate those needs into capabilities verified to meet the needs. Additionally, the architect may present different models to the customer that communicate how those needs may be met, and is therefore an essential participant in the consultative selling process.

However, the architect is not the builder, and must remain at a level of abstraction necessary to ensure that they do not get in the way of practical implementation.

The following excerpt from *The Art of Systems Architecting* depicts this notion:

> "It is the responsibility of the architect to know and concentrate on the critical few details and interfaces that really matter, and not to become overloaded with the rest."

The architect's focus is on understanding what it takes to satisfy the client, where qualitative worth is used more than quantitative measures. The architect uses more inductive skills than the deductive skills of the builder. The architect deals more with guidelines, rather than rules that builders use as a necessity.

It also must be clear that the role of an architect may be performed by an engineer. A goal of this document is to describe the role — what should be done, regardless of who is performing it.

Thus, the role of the architect can be summarized as to:

- **Understand and interpret requirements**: probe for information, listen to information, influence people, facilitate consensus building, synthesize and translate ideas into actionable requirements, articulate those ideas to others. Identify use or purpose, constraints, risks, etc. The architect participates in the discovery and documentation of the customer's business scenarios that are driving the solution. The architect is responsible for requirements understanding and embodies that requirements understanding in the architecture specification.

- **Create a useful model**: take the requirements and develop well-formulated models of the components of the solution, augmenting the models as necessary to fit all of the circumstances. Show multiple views through models to communicate the ideas effectively. The architect is responsible for the overall architecture integrity and maintaining the vision of the offering from an architectural perspective. The architect also ensures leverage opportunities are identified, using building blocks, and is a liaison between the functional groups (especially development and marketing) to ensure that the leverage opportunities are realized. The architect provides and maintains these models as a framework for understanding the domain(s) of development work, guiding what should be done within the organization, or outside the organization. The architect must represent the organization view of the architecture by understanding all the necessary business components.

- **Validate, refine, and expand the model**: verify assumptions, bring in subject matter experts, etc. in order to improve the model and to further define it, adding as necessary new ideas to make the result more flexible and more tightly linked to current and expected requirements. The architect additionally should assess the value of solution-enhancing developments emanating from field work and incorporate these into the architecture models as appropriate.

- **Manage the architecture**: continuously monitor the models and update them as necessary to show changes, additions, and alterations. Represent architecture and issues during development and decision points of the program. The architect is an "agent of change", representing that need for the implementation of the architecture. Through this development cycle, the architect continuously fosters the sharing of customer, architecture, and technical information between organizations.

52.6.2 Characterization in Terms of the Enterprise Continuum

Under certain circumstances, the complexity of a solution may require additional architects to support the architecture effort. The different categories of architects are described below, but as they are architects, they all perform the tasks described above. Any combination of enterprise, enterprise solution, and solution architects may be utilized, as a team. In such cases each member may have a specific focus, if not specific roles and responsibilities, within the phases of the development process. In cases where a team of architects is deemed necessary, a lead enterprise architect should be assigned to manage and lead the team members.

- The **Enterprise Architect** has the responsibility for architectural design and documentation at a landscape and technical reference model level. The Enterprise Architect often leads a group of the Segment Architects and/or Solution Architects related to a given program. The focus of the Enterprise Architect is on enterprise-level business functions required.

- The **Segment Architect** has the responsibility for architectural design and documentation of specific business problems or organizations. A Segment Architect re-uses the output from all other architects, joining detailed technical solutions to the overall architectural landscape. The focus of the Segment Architect is on enterprise-level business solutions in a given domain, such as finance, human resources, sales, etc.

- The **Solution Architect** has the responsibility for architectural design and documentation at a system or subsystem level, such as management or security. A Solution Architect may shield the Enterprise/Segment Architect from the unnecessary details of the systems, products, and/or technologies. The focus of the Solution Architect is on system technology solutions; for example, a component of a solution such as enterprise data warehousing.

52.6.3 Key Characteristics of an Enterprise Architect

52.6.3.1 Skills and Experience in Producing Designs

An enterprise architect must be proficient in the techniques that go into producing designs of complex systems, including requirements discovery and analysis, formulation of solution context, identification of solution alternatives and their assessment, technology selection, and design configuration.

52.6.3.2 Extensive Technical Breadth, with Technical Depth in One or a Few Disciplines

An enterprise architect should possess an extensive technical breadth through experience in the IT industry. This breadth should be in areas of application development and deployment, and in the areas of creation and maintenance of the infrastructure to support the complex application environment. Current IT environments are heterogeneous by nature, and the experienced enterprise architect will have skills across multiple platforms, including distributed systems and traditional mainframe environments. Enterprise architects will have, as a result of their careers, skills in at least one discipline that is considered to be at the level of a subject matter expert.

52.6.3.3 Method-Driven Approach to Execution

Enterprise architects approach their job through the consistent use of recognized design methods such as the TOGAF Architecture Development Method (ADM). Enterprise architects should have working knowledge of more than one design method and be comfortable deploying parts of methods appropriate to the situation in which they are working working. This should be seen in the body of design work the enterprise architect has produced through repeated successful use of more than one design method. Proficiency in methodology use is in knowing what parts of methods to use in a given situation, and what methods not to use.

52.6.3.4 Full Project Scope Experience

While enterprise architects are responsible for design and hand-off of the project to implementors, it is vital that they have experience with all aspects of a project from design through development, testing, implementation, and production. This scope of experience will serve to keep enterprise architects grounded in the notion of fitness-for-purpose and the practical nature of system implementation. The impact of full project scope experience should lead the enterprise architect to make better design decisions, and better inform the trade-offs made in those decisions.

52.6.3.5 Leadership

Communication and team building are key to the successful role of the enterprise architect. The mix of good technical skill and the ability to lead are crucial to the job. The enterprise architect should be viewed as a leader in the enterprise by the IT organization, the clients they serve, and management.

52.6.3.6 Personal and Professional Skills

The enterprise architect must have strong communications and relationship skills. A major task of the enterprise architect is to communicate complex technical information to all stakeholders of the project, including those who do not have a technical background. Strong negotiation and problem-solving skills are also required. The enterprise architect must work with the project management team to make decisions in a timely manner to keep projects on track.

52.6.3.7 Skills and Experience in One or More Industries

Industry skill and experience will make the task of gathering requirements and deciding priorities easier and more effective for the enterprise architect. Enterprise architects must understand the business processes of the enterprise in which they work, and how those processes work with other peer enterprises in the industry. They should also be able to spot key trends and correct flawed processes, giving the IT organization the capability to lead the enterprise, not just respond to requests. The mission of the enterprise architect is strategic technical leadership.

52.7 Conclusions

The TOGAF Architecture Skills Framework provides an assessment of the skills required to deliver a successful enterprise architecture.

It is hoped that the provision of this Architecture Skills Framework will help reduce the time, cost, and risk involved in training, recruiting, and managing IT architecture professionals, and at the same time enable and encourage more organizations to institute an internal IT architecture practice, hopefully based on (or at least leveraging) the role and skill definitions provided.

The Open Group Architecture Framework (TOGAF)

Part VIII:

Appendices

The Open Group

Appendix A: Glossary of Supplementary Definitions

This appendix contains additional definitions to supplement the definitions contained in Chapter 3.

A.1   Access Control (AC)

A security service that ensures only those users with the correct rights can access a specific device, application, or data.

A.2   Ada

A high-level computer programming language developed by the US Department of Defense (DoD) and widely used within the DoD and NATO countries. It is used for real-time processing, is modular in nature, and includes object-oriented features.

A.3   Application Component

An encapsulation of application functionality aligned to implementation structure. For example, a purchase request processing application.

See also Section A.50 and Section A.64.

A.4   Application Software

Software entities which have a specific business purpose.

A.5   Availability

In the context of IT systems, the probability that system functional capabilities are ready for use by a user at any time, where all time is considered, including operations, repair, administration, and logistic time. Availability is further defined by system category for both routine and priority operations.

A.6   Batch Processing

Processing data or the accomplishment of jobs accumulated in advance in such a manner that each accumulation thus formed is processed or accomplished in the same computer run.

A.7   Business System

Hardware, software, policy statements, processes, activities, standards, and people which together implement a business function.

A.8   Catalog

A structured list of architectural outputs of a similar kind, used for reference. For example, a technology standards catalog or an application portfolio.

A.9   Client

An application component which requests services from a server.

A.10   COBIT

An acronym for Control OBjectives for Information and related Technology, created by the Information Systems Audit and Control Association (ISACA) and the IT Governance Institute (ITGI), which provides a set of recommended best practices for the governance/management of information systems and technology.

A.11   Communications Network

A set of products, concepts, and services that enable the connection of computer systems for the purpose of transmitting data and other forms (e.g., voice and video) between the systems.

A.12   Communications Node

A node that is either internal to the communications network (e.g., routers, bridges, or repeaters) or located between the end device and the communications network to operate as a gateway.

A.13 Communications System

A set of assets (transmission media, switching nodes, interfaces, and control devices) that will establish linkage between users and devices.

A.14 Composite Application

An application component that is created by composing other atomic or composite applications.

A.15 Configuration Management

A discipline applying technical and administrative direction and surveillance to:

- Identify and document the functional and physical characteristics of a configuration item
- Control changes to those characteristics
- Record and report changes to processing and implementation status

Also, the management of the configuration of enterprise architecture practice (intellectual property) assets and baselines and the control of change over of those assets.

A.16 Connectivity Service

A service area of the external environment entity of the Technical Reference Model (TRM) that provides end-to-end connectivity for communications through three transport levels (global, regional, and local). It provides general and application-specific services to platform end devices.

A.17 Contract

An agreement between a service consumer and a service provider that establishes functional and non-functional parameters for interaction.

A.18 Control

A decision-making step with accompanying decision logic used to determine execution approach for a process or to ensure that a process complies with governance criteria. For example, a sign-off control on the purchase request processing process that checks whether the total value of the request is within the sign-off limits of the requester, or whether it needs escalating to higher authority.

A.19 CxO

The chief officer within a particular function of the business; e.g., Chief Executive Officer, Chief Financial Officer, Chief Information Officer, Chief Technology Officer.

A.20 Data Dictionary

A specialized type of database containing metadata; a repository of information describing the characteristics of data used to design, monitor, document, protect, and control data in information systems and databases; an application system supporting the definition and management of database metadata.

A.21 Data Element

A basic unit of information having a meaning and that may have subcategories (data items) of distinct units and values.

A.22 Data Entity

An encapsulation of data that is recognized by a business domain expert as a thing. Logical data entities can be tied to applications, repositories, and services and may be structured according to implementation considerations.

A.23 Data Interchange Service

A service of the platform entity of the Technical Reference Model (TRM) that provides specialized support for the interchange of data between applications on the same or different platforms.

A.24 Data Management Service

A service of the platform entity of the Technical Reference Model (TRM) that provides support for the management, storage, access, and manipulation of data in a database.

A.25 Database

A structured or organized collection of data entities, which is be accessed by a computer.

A.26 Database Management System

A computer application program that accesses or manipulates the database.

A.27 Directory Service

A technology component that provides locator services that find the location of a service, or the location of data, or translation of a common name into a network-specific address. It is analogous to telephone books and may be implemented in centralized or distributed schemes.

A.28 Distributed Database

1. A database that is not stored in a central location but is dispersed over a network of interconnected computers.

2. A database under the overall control of a central Database Management System (DBMS) but whose storage devices are not all attached to the same processor.

3. A database that is physically located in two or more distinct locations.

A.29 Driver

An external or internal condition that motivates the organization to define its goals. An example of an external driver is a change in regulation or compliance rules which, for example, require changes to the way an organization operates; i.e., Sarbanes-Oxley in the US.

A.30 End User

Person who ultimately uses the computer application or output.

A.31 Enterprise Resource Planning (ERP) System

A complete suite of integrated applications that support the major business support functions of an organization; e.g., Financial (AP/AR/GL), HR, Payroll, Stock, Order Processing and Invoicing, Purchasing, Logistics, Manufacturing, etc.

A.32 Event

An organizational state change that triggers processing events may originate from inside or outside the organization and may be resolved inside or outside the organization.

A.33 External Environment Interface (EEI)

The interface that supports information transfer between the application platform and the external environment.

A.34 FORTRAN

An acronym for FORmula TRANslator, which is a high-level computer language used extensively in scientific and engineering applications.

A.35 Functional Decomposition

A hierarchy of the functions of an enterprise or organization.

A.36 Goal

A high-level statement of intent or direction for an organization. Typically used to measure success of an organization.

A.37 Guideline

An architectural document that provides guidance on the optimal ways to carry out design or implementation activities.

A.38 Hardware

The physical infrastructure needed to run software; e.g., servers, workstations, network equipment, etc.

A.39 Human Computer Interface (HCI)

Hardware and software allowing information exchange between the user and the computer.

A.40 Information Domain

Grouping of information (or data entities) by a set of criteria such as security classification, ownership, location, etc. In the context of security, information domains are defined as a set of users, their information objects, and a security policy.

A.41　Information System (IS)

The computer (or IT)-based portion of a business system.

A.42　Information System Service

The automated elements of a business service. An information system service may deliver or support part or all of one or more business services.

A.43　Interaction

A relationship between architectural building blocks (i.e., services or components) that embodies communication or usage.

A.44　Interaction Model

An architectural view, catalog, or matrix that shows a particular type of interaction. For example, a diagram showing application integration.

A.45　Interface

Interconnection and inter-relationships between, for example, people, systems, devices, applications, or the user and an application or device.

A.46　ITIL

An acronym for Information Technology Infrastructure Library, which provides a set of recommended best practices for the governance/management of information systems and technology.

A.47　Key Performance Indicator (KPI)

A way of quantifying the performance of the business or project.

A.48   Lifecycle

The period of time that begins when a system is conceived and ends when the system is no longer available for use.

A.49   Location

A place where business activity takes place and can be hierarchically decomposed.

A.50   Logical Application Component

An encapsulation of application functionality that is independent of a particular implementation. For example, the classification of all purchase request processing applications implemented in an enterprise.

A.51   Logical Data Component

A boundary zone that encapsulates related data entities to form a logical location to be held. For example, external procurement information.

A.52   Logical Technology Component

An encapsulation of technology infrastructure that is independent of a particular product. A class of technology product. For example, supply chain management software as part of an Enterprise Resource Planning (ERP) suite or a Commercial Off-The-Shelf (COTS) purchase request processing enterprise service.

A.53   Managing Successful Programs (MSP)

A best practice methodology for program management, developed by the UK Office of Government Commerce (OGC).

A.54   Matrix

A format for showing the relationship between two (or more) architectural elements in a grid format.

A.55 Measure

An indicator or factor that can be tracked, usually on an ongoing basis, to determine success or alignment with objectives and goals.

A.56 Metaview

A metaview acts as a pattern or template of the view, from which to develop individual views. A metaview establishes the purposes and audience for a view, the ways in which the view is documented (e.g., for visual modeling), and the ways in which it is used (e.g., for analysis).

See also Section 3.89 in Chapter 3.

A.57 Multimedia Service

A service of the Technical Reference Model (TRM) that provides the capability to manipulate and manage information products consisting of text, graphics, images, video, and audio.

A.58 Open Specifications

Public specifications that are maintained by an open, public consensus process to accommodate new technologies over time and that are consistent with international standards.

A.59 Open System

A system that implements sufficient open specifications for interfaces, services, and supporting formats to enable properly engineered application software:

- To be ported with minimal changes across a wide range of systems
- To interoperate with other applications on local and remote systems
- To interact with users in a style that facilitates user portability

A.60   Operational Governance

Operational governance looks at the operational performance of systems against contracted performance levels, the definition of operational performance levels, and the implementation of systems that ensure effective operation of systems.

See also Section 3.45 in Chapter 3.

A.61   Operating System Service

A core service of the application platform entity of the Technical Reference Model (TRM) that is needed to operate and administer the application platform and provide an interface between the application software and the platform (for example, file management, input/output, print spoolers).

A.62   Organization Unit

See Section 3.58 in Chapter 3.

A.63   Packaged Services

Services that are acquired from the market from a Commercial Off-The-Shelf (COTS) vendor, rather than being constructed via code build.

A.64   Physical Application Component

An application, application module, application service, or other deployable component of functionality. For example, a configured and deployed instance of a Commercial Off-The-Shelf (COTS) Enterprise Resource Planning (ERP) supply chain management application.

A.65   Physical Data Component

A boundary zone that encapsulates related data entities to form a physical location to be held. For example, a purchase order business object, comprising purchase order header and item business object nodes.

A.66   Physical Technology Component

A specific technology infrastructure product or technology infrastructure product instance. For example, a particular product version of a Commercial Off-The-Shelf (COTS) solution, or a specific brand and version of server.

A.67 Portability

1. The ease with which a system or component can be transferred from one hardware or software environment to another.

2. A quality metric that can be used to measure the relative effort to transport the software for use in another environment or to convert software for use in another operating environment, hardware configuration, or software system environment.

3. The ease with which a system, component, data, or user can be transferred from one hardware or software environment to another.

A.68 Portfolio

The complete set of change activities or systems that exist within the organization or part of the organization. For example, application portfolio and project portfolio.

A.69 PRINCE2

An acronym for PRojects IN Controlled Environments, which is a standard project management method.

A.70 Process

A process represents a sequence of activities that together achieve a specified outcome, can be decomposed into sub-processes, and can show operation of a function or service (at next level of detail). Processes may also be used to link or compose organizations, functions, services, and processes.

A.71 Product

Output generated by the business. The business product of the execution of a process.

A.72 Profile

A set of one or more base standards and, where applicable, the identification of those classes, subsets, options, and parameters of those base standards, necessary for accomplishing a particular function.

A.73 Profiling

Identifying standards and characteristics of a particular system.

A.74 Program

A co-ordinated set of change projects that deliver business benefit to the organization.

A.75 Project

A single change project which delivers business benefit to the organization.

A.76 Risk Management

The management of risks and issues that may threaten the success of the enterprise architecture practice and its ability to meet is vision, goals, and objectives, and, importantly, its service provision.

Note: Risk management is described in Part III, Chapter 31.

A.77 Scalability

The ability to use the same application software on many different classes of hardware/software platforms from PCs to super-computers (extends the portability concept). The capability to grow to accommodate increased work loads.

A.78 Security

Services which protect data, ensuring its confidentiality, availability, and integrity.

A.79 Server

An application component which responds to requests from a client.

A.80 Service

A logical representation of a repeatable business activity that has a specified outcome. A service is self-contained, may be composed of other services, and is a "black box" to its consumers. Examples are "check customer credit", "provide weather data", and "consolidate drilling reports".

A.81 Service Quality

A preset configuration of non-functional attributes that may be assigned to a service or service contract.

A.82 SMART

An acronym for Specific, Measurable, Attainable, Realistic, and Time-bound, which is an approach to ensure that targets and objectives are set in a way that can be achieved and measured.

A.83 Supplier Management

The management of suppliers of products and services to the enterprise architecture practice in concert with larger corporate procurement activities.

A.84 System

A collection of components organized to accomplish a specific function or set of functions (source: ISO/IEC 42010:2007).

A.85 System and Network Management Service

A cross-category service of the application platform entity of the Technical Reference Model (TRM) that provides for the administration of the overall information system. These services include the management of information, processors, networks, configurations, accounting, and performance.

A.86 System Stakeholder

An individual, team, or organization (or classes thereof) with interests in, or concerns relative to, a system (source: ISO/IEC 42010:2007).

A.87 Technology Component

An encapsulation of technology infrastructure that represents a class of technology product or specific technology product.

A.88 Time Period

The timeframe over which the potential impact is to be measured.

A.89 Transaction

Interaction between a user and a computer in which the user inputs a command to receive a specific result from the computer.

A.90 Transaction Sequence

Order of transactions required to accomplish the desired results.

A.91 Use-Case

A view of organization, application, or product functionality that illustrates capabilities in context with the user of that capability.

A.92 User

1. Any person, organization, or functional unit that uses the services of an information processing system.

2. In a conceptual schema language, any person or any thing that may issue or receive commands and messages to or from the information system.

A.93 User Interface Service

A service of the application platform entity of the Technical Reference Model (TRM) that supports direct human-machine interaction by controlling the environment in which users interact with applications.

Appendix B: Abbreviations

ABB	Architecture Building Block
AC	Access Control
ACL	Access Control List
ACMM	Architecture Capability Maturity Model
ACSE	Association Control Service Element
ADM	Architecture Development Method
ANSI	American National Standards Institute
API	Application Platform Interface
ARTS	Association for Retail Technology Standards
BMM	Business Motivation Model
BPM	Business Process Management
BPMN	Business Process Modeling Notation
BTEP	The Canadian Government Business Transformation Enablement Program
CAB	Change Advisory Board
CCITT	Consultative Committee on International Telegraph and Telephone, now known as the International Telecommunication Union (ITU)
CI	Configuration Item
CIPR	Central Information Process
CM	Configuration Management
CMIP	Common Management Information Protocol
CMIS	Common Management Information Service
CMM	Capability Maturity Models
CMMI	Capability Maturity Model Integration
CN	Communications Network
COBIT	Control OBjectives for Information and related Technology
CODASYL	Conference on Data Systems Languages
CORBA	Common Object Request Broker Architecture
COTS	Commercial Off-The-Shelf applications

CRM	Customer Relationship Management
CRUD	Create/Read/Update/Delete
CSF	Critical Success Factor
DAI	Data Access Interface
DBA	Database Administrator
DBMS	Database Management System
DCE	Distributed Computing Environment
DDL	Data Definition Language
DISA	US Department of Defense Information Systems Agency
DMF	Data Management Facility
DML	Data Manipulation Language
DMTF	Distributed Management Task Force
DNS	Domain Name System
DoC	US Department of Commerce
DoD	US Department of Defense
DoDAF	Department of Defense Architecture Framework
DRDA	Distributed Relational Database Architecture
EA	Enterprise Architecture
EAI	Enterprise Application Integration
EDI	Electronic Data Interchange
EEI	External Environment Interface
ERP	Enterprise Resource Planning
ES	End System
ESB	Enterprise Service Bus
ETL	Extract, Transform, Load
FEAF	Federal Enterprise Architecture Framework
FICO	Fair Isaac Corporation
FORTRAN	FORmula TRANslator
FTE	Full-Time Equivalent
GOTS	Government Off-The-Shelf applications
GUI	Graphical User Interface
HIPAA	Health Insurance Portability and Accountability Act
ICAM	Integrated Computer Aided Manufacturing

Abbreviations

ICD	Interface Control Document
ICOM	Inputs, Controls, Outputs, and Mechanisms/Resources
IDEF	Integrated Computer Aided Manufacturing (ICAM) DEFinition
IDL	Interface Description Language
IEC	International Electrotechnical Commission
IEEE	Institute of Electrical and Electronic Engineers
III	Integrated Information Infrastructure
III-RM	Integrated Information Infrastructure Reference Model
IMS	Information Management System
ISA	Information Systems Architecture
ISACA	Information Systems Audit and Control Association
ISACF	Information Systems Audit and Control Foundation
ISAM	Indexed Sequential Access Method
ISO	International Standards Organization
IT	Information Technology
ITGI	IT Governance Institute
ITIL	Information Technology Infrastructure Library
ITPMF	IT Portfolio Management Facility
ITU	International Telecommunication Union
JMS	Java Message Service
JVM	Java Virtual Machine
KPI	Key Performance Indicator
LAN	Local Area Network
LCS	Local Communications System
LIPR	Local Information Process
LSE	Local Subscriber Network
MAN	Metropolitan Area Network
MDA	Model Driven Architecture
MIB	Management Information Bases
MIS	Management Information Systems
MLS	Multi-Level Security
MTA	Message Transfer Agent
NASCIO	National Association of State Chief Information Officers

NIST	National Institute of Standards and Technology
OAG	Open Applications Group
OAGIS	Open Applications Group Integration Specification
ODBC	Open Database Connectivity
OECD	Organization for Economic Co-operation and Development
OGC	UK Office of Government Commerce
OLA	Operational Level Agreement
OMB	Office of Management and Budget
OMG	Object Management Group
OODBMS	Object-Oriented Database Management System
ORB	Object Request Broker
OS	Operating System
OSE	Open System Environment
OSI	Open Systems Interconnection
OSOA	Open Service Oriented Architecture
P-CMM	People Capability Maturity Model
PDA	Personal Digital Assistant
PDF	Portable Document Format
PEX	PHIGS Extension to the X Window system
PHIGS	Programmer's Hierarchical Interactive Graphics System
PMI	Project Management Initiative
PMBOK	Project Management Body of Knowledge
PRINCE	PRojects in Controlled Environments
QoS	Quality of Service
RACI	Responsible, Accountable, Consulted, Informed
RAS	Remote Access Services
RDA	Remote Database Access
RDBMS	Relational Database Management System
REA	Resource-Event-Agent
RFC	Request For Change
RFI	Request for Information
RFP	Request for Proposal
RFQ	Request for Quotation

Abbreviations

RM	Reference Model
RM-ODP	ISO Reference Model for Open Distributed Processing
RPC	Remote Procedure Call
RS	Relay System
SA-CMM	Software Acquisition Capability Maturity Model
SBB	Solution Building Block
SCAMPI	Standard CMMI Appraisal Method for Process Improvement
SDO	Service Data Objects
SEI	Software Engineering Institute
SGML	Standard Generalized Markup Language
SIB	Standards Information Base
SCA	Service Component Architecture
SCAMPI	CMMI Appraisal Method for Process Improvement
SLA	Service Level Agreement
SMAP	Security Management Application Process
SMART	Specific, Measurable, Attainable, Realistic, and Time-bound
SMTP	Simple Mail Transfer Protocol
SNA	System Network Architecture
SNMP	Simple Network Management Protocol
SOA	Service Oriented Architecture
SPEM	Software Processing Engineering Metamodel
SQL	Structured Query Language
STEP	STandard for the Exchange of Product model data
SWG	Special Working Group
SysML	Systems Modeling Language
TADG	Treasury Architecture Development Guidance
TAFIM	Technical Architecture Framework for Information Management
TCP/IP	Transmission Control Protocol/Internet Protocol
TISAF	Treasury Information System Architecture Framework
TRM	Technical Reference Model
TFA	Transparent File Access
TLSP	Transport Layer Security Protocol
TMF	TeleManagement Forum

TP	Transaction Processing
UML	Unified Modeling Language
UN/CEFACT	United Nations Centre for Trade Facilitation and Electronic Business
UN/EDIFACT	United Nations/Electronic Data Interchange For Administration, Commerce, and Transport
WAN	Wide Area Network
WSDL	Web Services Description Language
XML	Extensible Markup Language
XSD	XML Schema Definition

Index